PROVENCE
& THE CÔTE D'AZUR

NICOLA WILLIAMS,
ALEXIS AVERBUCK, EMILIE FILOU, FRAN PARNELL

PROVENCE & THE CÔTE D'AZUR

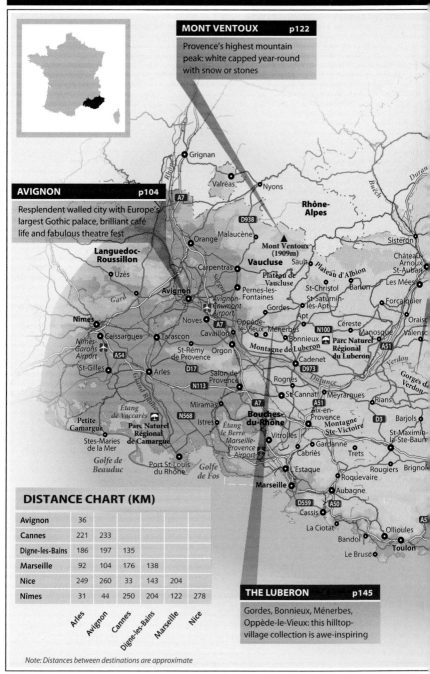

MONT VENTOUX p122

Provence's highest mountain peak: white capped year-round with snow or stones

AVIGNON p104

Resplendent walled city with Europe's largest Gothic palace, brilliant café life and fabulous theatre fest

DISTANCE CHART (KM)

	Arles	Avignon	Cannes	Digne-les-Bains	Marseille	Nice
Avignon	36					
Cannes	221	233				
Digne-les-Bains	186	197	135			
Marseille	92	104	176	138		
Nice	249	260	33	143	204	
Nîmes	31	44	250	204	122	278

THE LUBERON p145

Gordes, Bonnieux, Ménerbes, Oppède-le-Vieux: this hilltop-village collection is awe-inspiring

Note: Distances between destinations are approximate

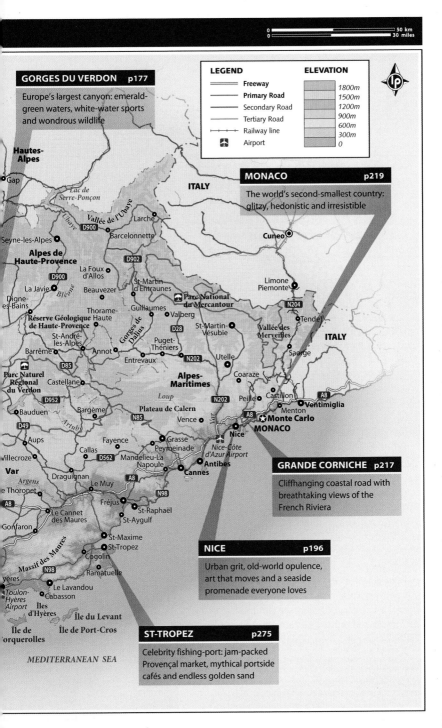

0 | **50 km**
0 | **30 miles**

GORGES DU VERDON p177

Europe's largest canyon: emerald-green waters, white-water sports and wondrous wildlife

LEGEND

Freeway
Primary Road
Secondary Road
Tertiary Road
Railway line
Airport

ELEVATION

1800m
1500m
1200m
900m
600m
300m
0

Hautes-Alpes

Gap

Lac de Serre-Ponçon

ITALY

MONACO p219

The world's second-smallest country: glitzy, hedonistic and irresistible

Ubaye *Vallée de l'Ubaye* Larche

D900

Barcelonnette

Seyne-les-Alpes

Cuneo

Alpes de Haute-Provence

D902

La Foux d'Allos

D900

La Javie

Digne-les-Bains

Bléone

Beauvezer

St-Martin-d'Entraunes

Limone Piemonte

N204

Parc National du Mercantour

Tende

Thorame-Haute

Réserve Géologique de Haute-Provence

Guillaumes

Valberg

St-André-les-Alpes

Gorges de Daluis

St-Martin-Vésubie

Vallée des Merveilles

Barrême

Annot

Puget-Théniers

Entrevaux

N202

Utelle

Saorge

ITALY

D85

Coaraze

Parc Naturel Régional du Verdon

Castellane

Loup

Alpes-Maritimes

Peille

Castillon

Ventimiglia

D952

Bargème

N85

Plateau de Calern

N202

Menton

★Monte Carlo

MONACO

Bauduen

Artuby

Vence

D49

Aups

Fayence

Grasse

Nice

Villecroze

Callas

Peymeinade

D562

Mandelieu-La Napoule

Nice-Côte d'Azur Airport

Var

Argens

Draguignan

Le Muy

A8

Antibes

Cannes

GRANDE CORNICHE p217

Cliffhanging coastal road with breathtaking views of the French Riviera

Le Thoronet

A8

Fréjus

N98

St-Raphaël

Le Cannet des Maures

Gonfaron

St-Aygulf

St-Maxime

NICE p196

Urban grit, old-world opulence, art that moves and a seaside promenade everyone loves

St-Tropez

Massif des Maures

N98

Cogolin

Ramatuelle

yères

Le Lavandou

Toulon-Hyères Airport

Cabasson

Îles d'Hyères

Île du Levant

Île de Porquerolles

Île de Port-Cros

ST-TROPEZ p275

Celebrity fishing-port: jam-packed Provençal market, mythical portside cafés and endless golden sand

MEDITERRANEAN SEA

4

INTRODUCING PROVENCE & THE CÔTE D'AZUR

NO PART OF SOUTHERN FRANCE HAS MORE ALLURE THAN THIS WEDGE OF COAST WITH ITS MOUNTAIN RETREATS AND GASTRONOMIC ART DE VIVRE.

So prepare for heart-and-soul seduction. Travelling à la Provençal means sensual sauntering past scented lavender fields and chestnut forests; through fresh apple-green vineyards and silvery olive groves; around markets, Matisse-designed chapels and medieval hilltop villages impossibly perched on rocky crags. Travelled with two wheels or four, on the back of a bicycle or with the roof rolled back in a vintage Citroën 2CV, no region better begs lazy days out, interrupted only by copious alfresco lunches.

Yet Provence and the Côte d'Azur is not all Zen-paced rural chic. Wedged between rough-cut Marseille with its urban art scene, and megalomaniacal Monte Carlo with its skyscraper skyline, this hot spot on the Med also screams action, glamour and just a hint of the ridiculous. Where else do cowboys herd cattle while Roma blaze flamenco beneath flamingo-filled skies? Where else do people flock to watch film stars strut the red carpet into a concrete bunker? Where else can you canyon white water in the morning, crack open sea urchins for lunch, see fabulous art in the afternoon, and bunk down in a tree house, old Celtic hamlet or winemaking château come dusk?

TOP A view from Vaison-la-Romaine to Mont Ventoux **BOTTOM LEFT** A hilltop village in the Luberon **BOTTOM RIGHT** A fruit and vegetable market in Nice's old town.

THE LUBERON

NICE

GORGES DU VERDON

MONACO

MONACO

TOP LEFT Gorges du Verdon, Haute-Provence TOP
RIGHT A view of Monaco from the Grande Corniche
BOTTOM LEFT La Condamine at dusk, Monaco
BOTTOM CENTRE Pont St-Bénézet (Pont d'Avignon)
spans the Rhône, with the Palais des Papes and the
walled city behind, Avignon BOTTOM RIGHT Art on
sale portside, St-Tropez

AVIGNON

ST-TROPEZ

GETTING STARTED

BETHUNE CARMICHAEL

WHAT'S NEW?

- ★ Innovative tram art in Nice, with 14 exciting works to discover (p203)

- ★ Europe's last-remaining ochre quarry (p154)

- ★ An artisan ice creamery hidden in Pays d'Aigues back country (p165)

- ★ Learning how to cook with flowers – for kids and adults alike (p259)

- ★ Jean Cocteau 'tattoos' on the glittering millionaire cape of Cap Ferrat (p214)

CLIMATE: NICE

Average Max/Min

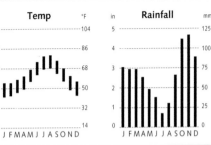

PRICE GUIDE

	BUDGET	MIDRANGE	TOP END
SLEEPING	up to €80	€80-175	over €175
MEALS	up to €20	€20-40	over €40

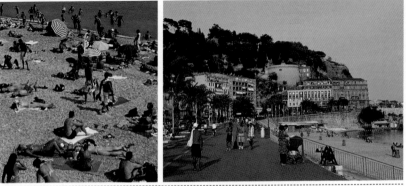

RICHARD I'ANSON

RICHARD I'ANSON

TOP A time-worn facade in Vieux Nice BOTTOM LEFT Sunbathers enjoy the beach, Nice BOTTOM RIGHT Promenade des Anglais, Nice FAR RIGHT Medieval Èze with views of Cap Ferrat

ACCOMMODATION

From age-old Provençal *mas* (farmhouses) with sun-bleached shutters, gold-stone walls and vine-shaded pergolas to wine-producing châteaux, accommodation in this essentially rural part of southern France is dreamy. *Chambres d'hôtes* (B&Bs) provide a golden opportunity to experience a taste of local life from the inside (not to mention fabulous homemade breakfasts); many serve *tables d'hôtes* (evening meals) too. But for those who prefer traditional hotel accommodation, boutique hotels and quintessential village *auberges* (inns) abound. For more on accommodation see p376.

MAIN POINTS OF ENTRY

MARSEILLE-PROVENCE AIRPORT (MRS; ☎ 04 42 14 14 14; www.marseille.aeroport.fr) Provence's main airport, 28km northwest of Marseille, has international flights including easyJet and Ryanair to and from the UK.

NICE-CÔTE D'AZUR AIRPORT (NCE; ☎ 08 20 42 33 33; www.nice-aeroport.fr) The airport for the French Riviera, 10 minutes from Nice centre, is an easyJet hub.

TOULON-HYÈRES AIRPORT (TLN; ☎ 08 25 01 83 87; www.toulon-hyeres.aeroport.fr) This airport, 3km south of Hyères and 23km from Toulon, has a few European flights.

THINGS TO TAKE

BETHUNE CARMICHAEL

★ Sunglasses, suncream, hat and mosquito repellent for the outdoors

----

★ A pocket knife, refillable water bottle and corkscrew for stylish picnics

----

★ Sturdy shoes to stroll cobble-stoned hilltop villages

★ A French phrasebook

★ An insatiable appetite, a pleasure-seeking palate and a thirst for good wine

WEBLINKS

PROVENCE & BEYOND (www.beyond.fr) Comprehensive tourist guide.

PROVENCE-ALPES-CÔTE D'AZUR (www.decouverte-paca.fr) Indispensable regional tourist board website.

PROVENCE-HIDEAWAYS (www.provence-hideaway.com) Travel guide covering inland western Provence.

RIVIERA CÔTE D'AZUR (www.guideriviera.com) Riviera tourist board site.

FESTIVALS & EVENTS

DAVID TOMLINSON

FEBRUARY

CARNAVAL DE NICE

NICE
Both the decorated floats and the crowds are gigantic at this flamboyant Mardi Gras street parade, celebrated since 1293. Don't miss the legendary flower battles. (www.nicecarnaval.com)

FÊTE DU CITRON

MENTON
Monumental sculptures and floats crafted from a zillion and one lemons make this two-week event the French Riviera's most exotic fest. (www.feteducitron.com)

MAY

CANNES FILM FESTIVAL

CANNES
The world's premier film event sees cinematic luminaries star on La Croisette. (p245; www.festival-cannes.org)

FÊTE DES GARDIANS

ARLES
The traditional Camargue cowboy and his bullish and equestrian skills are the focus of this vibrant festival on 1 May. (p90)

PÈLERINAGE DES GITANS

STES-MARIES DE LA MER
Roma from Europe pour into this remote seaside outpost to honour their patron saint for three days starting 24 May (and again in October). (p95)

MONACO GRAND PRIX

MONACO
It's fitting that the most glamorous race of the Formula One season should tear around one of the world's most glam countries. (p227; www.acm.mc)

JUNE

FÊTE DE LA TRANSHUMANCE

ST-RÉMY DE PROVENCE
Sheep fill the streets of this small Alpilles town as shepherds walk their flocks up to lush summer pastures; their return in September is equally festive.

FÉRIA DE PENTECÔTE

NÎMES
The city's bull-fighting season opens at Pentecost with five days of *novilladas* and *corridas* inside the town's monumental Roman amphitheatre and sangria-fuelled flamenco outside.

TOP Costumed celebration at the Fête du Citron, Menton **BOTTOM RIGHT** A colourful float at the Carnaval de Nice street parade

JULY/AUGUST

FESTIVAL D'AIX-EN-PROVENCE

AIX-EN-PROVENCE

Stunning music, theatre and song form the program of this prestigious July festival born in 1948. (www.festival-aix.com)

FESTIVAL D'AVIGNON & FESTIVAL OFF

AVIGNON

Theatre in every guise takes to the stage at this renowned theatre festival; fringe Off parallels the official fest. (www.festival-avignon.com)

CHORALIES

VAISON-LA-ROMAINE

There is no finer stage for Europe's largest choral festival than Vaison's Roman Théâtre Antique; the next is in 2010. (www.choralies.fr)

FESTIVAL DE LACOSTE

LACOSTE

Spooky castle ruins are the backdrop for this two-week arts festival of dance, music, theatre and opera. (www.festival delacoste.com)

MUSIQUES DANS LES VIGNES

VAUCLUSE

This month-long musicfest features classical music and jazz performed between vines tended by some of the region's loveliest wine-producing châteaux. (www .musiquesdanslesvignes.com)

DECEMBER

CHRISTMAS

Villages celebrate with midnight Mass, Provençal chants and a ceremony in which shepherds offer a newborn lamb. In Séguret the Nativity scene has a living baby – an age-old tradition. (p120)

CULTURE

BOOKS

PROVENCE: A CULTURAL HISTORY (Martin Garrett) Evocative portrait of culture through the ages, inspired by Provence's varied landscapes.

FRENCH RIVIERA: LIVING WELL WAS THE BEST REVENGE (Xavier Girard) A brilliant look at the fervent artistic creativity of 1920s and '30s Côte d'Azur.

ONE WAY (Didier van Cauweleart) A French orphan in Marseille is rescued by Roma and given false ID papers making him Moroccan.

PROVENÇAL ESCAPES (Caroline Clifton-Mogg) Image-driven snoop around 22 beautiful homes in Provence.

PROVENCE (Lawrence Durrell) British novelist who has dedicated the last 30 years of his career to penning Provençal life.

ARTIST PORTFOLIO

With its designer chapels, cutting-edge architecture and avant-garde art, the region is a living art museum. It has masterpieces to savour and an artist portfolio bursting with 20th-century greats. Local lad Paul Cézanne and Dutchman Van Gogh were among the first to paint Provence's extraordinary intensity of light, not that anyone appreciated their efforts at the time. Pointillist Paul Signac famously sailed into St-Tropez in 1890 and made the fishing port home two years later. In Nice, meanwhile, Matisse revelled in a warmth and depth of light absolutely unknown elsewhere in Europe, paving the way for Renoir, Picasso et al. It was these artists, bohemian and impoverished, who paid their way with art, hence the world-unique collections strung on the walls of a couple of Riviera restaurants. See p331 for more on 20th-century art and p36 for visual highlights.

TOP Performers at the Palais des Papes, Avignon **BOTTOM** Garden, Villa Ephrussi de Rothschild **RIGHT** Market stall, Aix-en-Provence **FAR RIGHT** An art deco star on La Croisette, Cannes

TOP CELEBRITY HAUNTS

MONACO GRAND PRIX Formula One meets high society (p227).

LA CROISETTE Trail world stars of cinema along Cannes' fabled seaside prom; lunch on the sand at the art deco Martinez (p243).

LA COLOMBE D'OR Dine with the rich and famous amid priceless art or beneath fig trees in St-Paul de Vence (p258).

LE CLUB 55 Guzzle Champagne, spot celebrities and swoon when the bill comes at St-Tropez's mythical beach restaurant (p283).

DIANA MAYFIELD

VERONICA GARBUTT

DON'T MISS EXPERIENCES

- ★ Provence markets – Aix-en-Provence (p75), Carpentras (p125) and St-Tropez (p275) are particularly vibrant

- ★ Cours Mirabeau café life – Be chic between *hôtels particuliers* (private mansions) in bourgeois Aix-en-Provence (p69)

- ★ Theatre alfresco – Catch starlit performances at the Festival d'Avignon (p107), Les Chorégies d'Orange (p115), Domaine du Rayol (p298) or Villa Ephrussi (p213)

- ★ Riviera high life – Strut amid millionaire mansions and chanting cicadas on Cap d'Antibes (p251) and Cap Ferrat (p212)

- ★ Place des Lices *pétanque* – Play *boules* beneath plane trees on this St-Tropezian square (p275)

- ★ La Friche la Belle de Mai – Cutting-edge culture next to train tracks in Marseille (p55)

BLOGS

FRENCH LANDSCAPES
(http://french-landscapes.blogspot.com)
Photo blog with stunning images of the St-Tropez area.

FRENCH WORD-A-DAY
(http://french-word-a-day.typepad.com)
French words inspire a tale of life in Provence.

PROVENCE & BEYOND
(www.provenceblog.typepad.com)
Cultural, historical and practical on-the-ground nuggets Provence-wide.

FROM FAYENCE OUTWARDS (www.go-provence.com)
Fayence-generated blog loaded with current news, chat, celebrity scoops and links.

CULTURE

GLENN BEANLAND

CURIOSITIES

ABBAYE DE ST-ROMAN
France's only troglodytic monastery, carved into a limestone outcrop (p137).

CHAPELLE DE LA GAROUPE
A shrine of local worship in Cap d'Antibes; pilgrims walk from the beach to the lighthouse (p252).

PROVENÇAL SANTONS
'Little Saints': Thumbelina-sized terracotta figures made in Marseille (p54).

CABANON LE CORBUSIER
A visit to this iconic beach hut is an architect-buff must (p215).

WORLD SOUNDS

A diverse playlist of local artists from Radio Grenouille's Stéphane Galland.

DAVID WALTERS (www.davidwalters.fr) Acoustic folk-electronic beats mix by world-electro, Marseille-based artist.

KABBALAH (www.kabbalah-music.net) Five-person Jewish band blending jazz, contemporary Mediterranean folk and klezmer (traditional eastern European music).

MASSILIA SOUND SYSTEM (www.massilia-sound system.com) Legendary reggae group combining a Marseille accent with Provençal and Marseillais slang.

RAPHAËL IMBERT Saxophonist and composer of classic jazz and sacred music; plays solo and with the Newtopia Quintet.

PROVENCE: WHAT'S IN A NAME?

Gloriously intact Roman amphitheatres, triumphal arches and other public buildings evoke that very period in its rich history that gave Provence – a Roman *provincia* – its name. Throw the region's festive spirit into the ancient arena and Roman Provence becomes rather fun: take the Pont du Gard, an aqueduct whose three tiers can be paddled beneath; the archaeological site of Glanum, aka a walk from the 3rd century BC to the 3rd century AD; or the resplendent Les Arènes and Maison Carré in Nîmes, where bullfights, concerts and films enthral spellbound audiences (see p315 for more on Roman Provence).

TOP Canoeing beneath the Pont du Gard, a Roman aqueduct west of Avignon **RIGHT** Les Arènes, a spectacular Roman amphitheatre in Nîmes

THE MUD-EATING MISTRAL

Folklore says it drives people crazy. Its namesake, Provençal poet Frédéric Mistral, cursed it. And peasants in their dried-out fields dubbed it 'mud eater'.

Inspiration for a thousand and one Provençal stories, the legendary mistral is a cold, dry northwesterly wind that whips across Provence for several days at a time. Its gusts destroy crops, rip off roofs and drive tempers round the bend. It chills the bones for 100 days a year and is fiercest in winter and spring. Its intensity is caused by high atmospheric pressure over central France, blown southwards through the Rhône Valley.

On the upside, skies are cornflower blue and clear when the mistral is in town. And the vines love it.

DOS & DON'TS

★ Cover your shoulders when visiting places of worship

★ Dress smart in Monaco, where the casino, many bars, restaurants and theatre venues demand men don a jacket and tie

---

★ Two *bises* (kisses), a fleeting peck each side, is the usual way to greet irrespective of gender

---

★ Smoking in public places, including inside restaurants, is illegal

---

★ Shop like a local: buy fresh produce from farms, roadside stalls and the weekly morning market; market days are listed in regional chapters

RUSSELL MOUNTFORD

FOOD & DRINK

COOKING COURSES

JEAN-JACQUES PRÉVOT
(www.restaurantprevot.com) Seasonal workshops (including melon, mushroom, truffle, game and asparagus) with Cavaillon's melon chef (p148).

L'ATELIER
(www.rabanel.com) Two-hour cooking sessions under the watchful eye of highly contemporary two-star chef Jean-Luc Rabanel (p91).

LES PETITS FARCIS
(www.petitsfarcis.com) Niçois cooking sessions with market and producer visits, run by Nice resident Rosa Jackson (p197).

ATELIER DE LA CUISINE DES FLEURS
(www.la-cuisine-des-fleurs.com) Crystallise violets and make rose preserve with these cooking classes (p259).

LA RECETTE MAGIQUE
Cook in Nice with Michelin-starred chefs (p204).

LE LIBERTY
Fish-fuelled cooking on the beach in St-Tropez (p278).

A SEASONAL CUISINE

Thinking, dreaming, living food is the norm in Provence, where days are geared around satisfying a passionate appetite for dining well.

Some culinary traditions are upheld everywhere: oodles of olive oil, garlic and tomatoes find their way into dozens of dishes. Yet there are regional differences, which see fishermen return with the catch of the day in seafaring Marseille; grazing bulls and paddy fields in the Camargue; lambs in the Alpilles; truffles in the Vaucluse; cheese made from cows' milk in alpine pastures; and an Italianate accent to Niçois cooking.

Ultimately, the secret of Provençal cuisine lies not in elaborate preparation techniques or sophisticated presentation, but in the use of fresh local ingredients. In Provence it is the humble rhythm and natural cycle of the land that drives what you eat and when. See p364 for more.

TOP Garlic is a staple in Provençal cooking **BOTTOM** Jars of aromatic herbs **RIGHT** Fresh seafood at a market in Nice **FAR RIGHT** Decorated squash

TOP FOODIE FESTIVALS

Food itself is a reason to celebrate.

MESSE DE LA TRUFFE Richerenches' solemn truffle Mass in January (p121)

FÊTE DU CITRON Menton's February Lemon Festival is fabulous (p233)

FÊTE DU MELON July melon madness in Cavaillon (p150)

FÉRIA DU RIZ Arles celebrates rice harvest mid-September (p90)

FÊTE DE LA CHÂTAIGNE Go nuts at Collobrières' October chestnut festival (p295)

KEVIN LEVESQUE

GREG ELM

DON'T MISS EXPERIENCES

- ★ *Bouillabaisse* – Sample this pungent yellow fish stew at least once in Marseille, preferably waterside (p59)

- ★ A *socca* aperitif – Feast on Niçois nibbles over drinks alfresco in Nice's old town (p207)

- ★ Wine tasting – Enjoy a range of respected reds in Bandol, where the surrounding sea-facing terraced hills are the heart-throb (p312)

- ★ Truffle hunting – Try your hand at snouting out these 'black diamonds' yourself near Carpentras (p102)

- ★ Mountain-cheese road trip – Motor from farm to farm around Banon sampling goat's-milk cheese wrapped in chestnut leaves (p174)

- ★ Thirteen desserts – Bite into one of each at Christmas to avoid bad luck for the coming year (p373)

MARKET MUSTS

FARMERS MARKET On Tuesdays from April to December in Apt

FRESH FISH MARKET Takes place every morning year-round on quai des Belges, Marseille

GARLIC MARKET Daily late June and July on cours Belsunce, Marseille

MELON MARKET In Cavaillon every morning from May to September

TRUFFLE MARKET On Saturdays, November to March, in Richerenches

FOOD & DRINK

BOOKS

THE PROVENCE COOKBOOK (Patricia Wells) The cookbook bible from this French-food expert and Provence resident.

A CHEF IN PROVENCE (Édouard Loubet) Learn to cook wildflowers with this esteemed creative chef.

THE OLIVE FARM (Carol Drinkwater) An olive-farm memoir and love story, the first in a trilogy.

ROSÉ EN MARCHÉ (James Ivey) A travel memoir flavoured with rosé wine and Provençal markets.

APERITIFS

Lounging over an *apéro* is one of Provence's great delights.

CÔTE DE PROVENCE ROSÉ Crisp, chilled and classic (p359).

PASTIS Aniseed-flavour drink; amber-coloured in the bottle, but milky-white when mixed with water (p55).

BEAUMES DE VENISE A sweet muscat wine to round off dessert (p359).

LIQUEUR DE CHÂTAIGNES Sweet chestnut liqueur from the Massif des Maures; mix with white wine (p296).

RINQUINQUIN DE PÊCHE, AMANDINE & LA FARIGOULE Peach, almond and thyme liqueurs from Haute-Provence (p169).

THE TRUFFLE MASS

As sacred as the cuisine into which it goes, the Messe de la Truffe honours St-Antoine, the patron saint of truffle growers. An unadulterated veneration of Provençal cuisine's most luxurious product, the Mass is celebrated on the third Sunday in January in Richerenches (p121). The faithful – local truffle growers in the main – offer knobbly pig-ugly 'black diamonds', weighed and auctioned after Mass by black-caped, black-hatted members of the local Confrérie du Diamant Noir et de la Gastronomie (Black Diamond and Gastronomy Brotherhood). Then it is aperitif time followed by a truffle lunch (see p364 for more on truffles).

TOP One of many wine cellars in a region made for wine tasting **RIGHT** The fish market at Vieux Port, Marseille

À TABLE

Cardinal sins in the Provençal book of etiquette include skipping lunch, declining a *dégustation* (wine tasting) session or disliking a delicacy such as *testicules de mouton* (sheep testicles). In restaurants, forget balancing your bread on your main-course plate (side plates are only provided in multistarred temples); crumbs on the table is fine – as is using the same knife and fork for your starter and main in many a down-to-earth bistro and *ferme auberge* (farmhouse restaurant). Irrespective of price, order *une carafe d'eau* (a jug of tap water) rather than pricy bottled water. *Santé* is the toast for alcoholic drinks and *bon appétit* is what you say before tucking in. End your meal with a short, sharp espresso; ordering anything else, tea and cappuccino included, is just not done.

STAPLES

Bite into the fresh flavours of the Provençal culinary dream.

* Olives, marinated or spiced in oil and garlic as *tapenade*

* Vegetables, particularly tomatoes and courgettes

* Fruit, melons, peaches and Apt cherries

* Aromatic herbs and fiery garlic, impossible to avoid

* Fish and other seafood on the coast

OUTDOORS

HUGH WATTS

NATURE PARKS

PARC NATIONAL DU MERCANTOUR (www.mercan tour.eu) Walking, biking, skiing and white-water sports beneath 3000m-high peaks (p183).

ÎLE DE PORT-CROS (www .portcrosparcnational.fr) Snorkelling, swimming and ambling on a bird-busy island (p304).

PARC NATUREL RÉGIONAL DU VERDON (www.parcduverdon .fr) White-water sports, walking, cycling and trekking around five green lakes and Europe's most spectacular canyon (p177).

PARC NATUREL RÉGIONAL DU LUBERON (www.parcduluberon .fr) Walking and cycling hilltop villages and limestone gorges; spot eagles and vultures (p159).

PARC NATUREL RÉGIONAL DE CAMARGUE (www.parc-camargue.fr) Horse rid-ing, birdwatching and cycling between salt pans and paddy fields (p84).

WONDERFUL WALKS

Be it a stiff mountain hike or gentle amble through lavender fields with a donkey, walking in Provence is a sensory delight. Landscapes are astonishingly varied and the diversity creates an endless panorama of contrasting hues (see p342). Coastal paths lace the coastline: walking through *garrigue* (scented scrub) in the rocky Les Ca-lanques near Marseille; or along Nice's Grande Corniche, offering gobsmacking coastal views, is dramatic. Inland, trails wind through red in the Massif de l'Estérel; through chestnut and cork oak forest in the Massif des Maures; across Al-pine foothills into the Mercantour national park; and around the foot of stone-capped Mont Ven-toux (1912m). Olive groves, cherry orchards and Cézanne canvases pave the way in lower walking pastures like the Alpilles, Montagne Ste-Victoire and Vaucluse hills. For more see p357.

ANDREW BAIN

TOP The peaks of Parc National du Mercantour **BOTTOM** Cycling near Mont Ventoux **RIGHT** Ochre-coloured cliffs, Rustrel **FAR RIGHT** Gorges worth exploring, Parc Naturel Régional du Verdon

TOP COASTAL PATHS

PRESQU'ÎLE DE ST-TROPEZ St-Tropez to gloriously sandy beach after beach (p283)

CAP LARDIER Windy seaside scrub-walking around a cape (p288)

CÔTE BLEUE Dramatic walking with Marseille city views (p65)

SENTIER DU LITTORAL RIVIERA Menton to Cap d'Ail without seeing a car; dip in the sea to cool down (p216)

CAP FERRAT Cicadas sing amid millionaire mansions along this glittering 6km cape walk (p214)

DON'T MISS EXPERIENCES

★ Ochre trails – Walk through wind-sculpted, fire-red scapes in Roussillon Gargas and Rustrel (p154)

★ Massif de l'Estérel – Climbing red-spired Mont Roux (435m) is among our top five scenic walks in the Cannes area (p262)

★ Cycling through vines – An essential Provence experience; pedal and sup around Châteauneuf du Pape (p113), Bandol (p312), La Londe (p308) or Île de Porquerolles (p303)

★ Be a gorge explorer – Revel in Provence's grand canyon by white-water raft, kayak, canoe, on foot or by car (p178)

★ Paddling – Drift beneath Pont du Gard (p144) or by moonlight around Les Calanques (p46)

★ Mountain vistas – Take in Haute-Provence's heart-stirring views (p176)

ACTIVITIES

The outdoors is great indeed in Provence, where there is an action station to suit every mood, moment and energy level.

★ White-water sports – In the Gorges du Verdon (p178)

★ Canoeing and sea kayaking – In the Camargue and Marseille (p353)

★ Cycling – Seaside, through vines or across mountain passes (p353)

★ Walking and rambling – Alone, or with a donkey in the Gorges de la Nesque or Vallée de la Durance (p355)

BETHUNE CARMICHAEL

OUTDOORS

BEACH STARS

PLAGE MALA, CAP D'AIL
Idyllic pebble-covered cove
with a trendy air (p216).

**PLAGE DU POURROUSSET,
AGAY** Small but perfect, with
fine sand and even finer views
(p270).

PLAGE DE NOTRE DAME
Beautiful beach with pure
white sand on Île de Porquerolles (p303).

CALANQUE D'EN-VAU
Pleasant pebbly beach lapped
by emerald water slipped in a
rocky cove (p63).

EXCITING GARDENS

Horticultural design is not only about the Riviera's belle époque creations (p215).

AUX FLEURS DE L'EAU (http://auxfleursdeleau.fr)
Water garden near St-Rémy de Provence.

CHÂTEAU DE BRANTES (www.jardinez.com/
jardindebrantes) Nineteenth-century-styled garden
around an 18th-century château, 12km north of
Avignon.

DOMAINE DU RAYOL (www.domainedurayol.org)
Mediterranean gardens by the sea.

JARDIN ROMAIN (www.jardin-romain.fr) Roman
garden, 15km southeast of Avignon in
Caumont-sur-Durance.

PRIEURÉ DE SALAGON (www.musee-de-salagon
.com) Medieval herb garden awash with mints,
mugworts and lavenders.

RENDEZ-VOUS AUX JARDINS

For three days in June dozens of private gardens open – among them the mosaic garden of La Chèvre d'Or (www.lachevredor.com), created with the help of English bot-
anist Basil Leng in 1950. Find a complete list at www.rendezvousauxjardins.culture.fr.

Nice-based Société Centrale d'Agriculture et d'Horticulture de Nice et des Alpes-
Maritimes (www.scah-nice.fr) organises visits to superb, lesser-known gardens, including Dirk Bogarde's former garden–olive grove in Châteauneuf du Grasse, and
a garden designed by Jean Mus (www.jeanmus.com). In Fréjus half-day gardening
workshops bloom at La Pomme d'Ambre (www.gardeninprovence.com).

TOP Fields of lavender colour the Luberon and Haute-Provence **RIGHT** Beautiful beaches abound on the
Côte d'Azur – this one in Nice

BEACHES

Cats on leads, dogs in handbags and prima donnas dusting sand from their toes with shaving brushes are madcap sights to savour on the glorious beach-riddled Côte d'Azur, where anything goes. But it pays to know your *plage*. Beaches in and east of Nice are piled with porcelain-smooth pebbles (bum-numbing? *never*); beaches west of Nice are sumptuously sandy, soft and gold. Around Marseille – a *bouillabaisse* mix of both.

Larger beaches have a *poste de secours* (safety post) staffed by lifeguards during the summer season. In water-sport areas, an area of the sea is always sectioned off for swimmers. Note the colour of the flag flying before diving in: green means safe to swim; yellow means risky; red means forbidden; and purple means the water is polluted.

WILDLIFE WATCH

* ★ Cycling or horse riding in the Camargue also means birdwatching (p79)
* ★ Spot the griffon vulture on a Gorges du Verdon trek (p178)
* ★ Watch grey wolves roam in the Mercantour (p188)
* ★ Track cicadas and other insects, mushrooms, fire-resilient forest plants and orchids with a thematic nature walk in the Massif des Maures (p297)
* ★ Observe river wildlife afloat a canoe on the Sorgue (p127 and p129)
* ★ Watch underwater marine flora through a snorkeller's mask along trails in le Rayol and Île de Port-Cros (p304)

RUSSELL MOUNTFORD

FAMILY TRAVEL

TOP SIGHTS

MUSÉE OCÉANO-GRAPHIQUE Watch the changing of the guard before visiting Monaco's renowned aquarium (p223).

ASTRORAMA Intriguing space observations and rocket launches on the Grande Corniche (p218).

PALAIS DES PAPES & CHÂTEAU D'IF Nothing like a palace (p104) or a castle on an island (p51) to fire young imaginations.

MARINELAND Leaping killer whales enthral at this Disney-style theme park (p251).

DON'T MISS EXPERIENCES

★ Walking with a farmer – Educational thematic tours across the land and around local farms, often with a chance to taste produce (p357)

★ Snorkelling – Underwater trails on Port-Cros (p304) and Domaine du Rayol (p298), and guided trips in St-Raphaël (p268)

★ Guided nature walks – Nature trails abound but those with a cork harvester in the Massif des Maures are particularly fascinating (p297)

★ Horse riding – Spend a few hours or a whole day on a trek through the flamingo-studded wetlands of the Camargue (p92)

★ Roman Provence – Pont du Gard, in particular, with its interactive museum and tiers to skip across is heaps of fun (p143)

TRAVEL WITH CHILDREN

That stretch of coastline alone makes this a family-friendly region: sandy beaches and buckets and spades are part and parcel of coastal travels, with a plethora of boats ploughing the Med between major cities and towns. Marseille and Avignon can be hard work with toddlers; plump for Nice with its relaxed air and outdoor entertainment. Most restaurants welcome pint-sized gourmets with a fixed *menu enfant* (children's menu) but highchairs are rare; pack a screw-on canvas seat. Less formal *fermes auberges* and *chambres d'hôtes* (B&Bs) serving evening meals are attractive options for those with children.

TOP *Gardians* (horsemen) gather in the wetlands of the Camargue

CONTENTS

THE AUTHORS

NICOLA WILLIAMS

**Coordinating Author, Marseille Area,
The Camargue, St-Tropez to Toulon**

For Nicola, a writer living and working in France for over a decade, it's an easy getaway to France's south, where she has spent many years eating her way around the region and revelling in its art heritage and landscapes. Nicola wrote the 1st edition of *Provence & the Côte d'Azur* and has worked on every edition since, in between several other Lonely Planet titles. She blogs at tripalong.wordpress.com and tweets @Tripalong.

ALEXIS AVERBUCK

The Luberon, Haute-Provence, History

Alexis Averbuck first visited Provence when she was four and now makes any excuse she can to visit from her home in Hydra, Greece. A California native and a travel writer for two decades, Alexis has lived in Antarctica for a year, crossed the Pacific by sailboat and written books on her journeys through Asia and the Americas. She is also a painter and each trip inspires new work, both written and visual – see her paintings at www.alexisaverbuck.com.

LONELY PLANET AUTHORS

Why is our travel information the best in the world? It's simple: our authors are passionate, dedicated travellers. They don't take freebies in exchange for positive coverage so you can be sure the advice you're given is impartial. They travel widely to all the popular spots, and off the beaten track. They don't research using just the internet or phone. They discover new places not included in any other guidebook. They personally visit thousands of hotels, restaurants, palaces, trails, galleries, temples and more. They speak with dozens of locals every day to make sure you get the kind of insider knowledge only a local could tell you. They take pride in getting all the details right, and in telling it how it is. Think you can do it? Find out how at lonelyplanet.com.

EMILIE FILOU

Cannes Area; Nice, Monaco & Menton
Emilie was born in Paris but spent many happy holidays roaming the south of France. She left France at 18 to go travelling, taking a grand total of three gap years (to balance her three-year geography degree from Oxford). Her travels have taken her to Africa, Nepal, Southeast Asia, Australia and New Zealand, but the Côte d'Azur remains one of her favourite places on earth. She now works as a business and travel journalist in London.

FRAN PARNELL

Avignon Area, Transport
Fran's love of France arose while studying Medieval French at Cambridge University. She contributed to an earlier incarnation of *Provence & the Côte d'Azur,* and was particularly delighted on this research trip to visit the 15th-century Château de Tarascon, straight from the pages of a medieval romance, to drift round the Roman city of Glanum with its haunting *'Ubi sunt?'* atmosphere, and to spend a sun-speckled afternoon canoeing on the River Sorgue.

ITINERARIES

ROMAN PROVENCE

ONE WEEK // NÎMES TO VAISON-LA-ROMAINE // 200KM

Gloriously intact amphitheatres, triumphal arches, baths and other public buildings transport travellers to the monumental period in history that gave Provence – a Roman

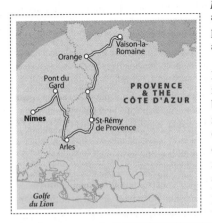

provincia – its name. Start with Roman giant **Nîmes** (p138) and its resplendent **amphitheatre** (p140), fun-fuelled **férias** (p141) and **Square House** (p140).

Next, the world's highest aqueduct **Pont du Gard** (p143) is particularly awe-inspiring when skipped atop or paddled beneath. Drive south to **Arles** (p84) to see its twinset of Roman theatres and north to **Glanum** (p133), a Gallo-Roman city on the outskirts of St-Rémy de Provence. Further north be star-struck at Orange's **Roman amphitheatre** (p115) during the magical Les Chorégies d'Orange, or at the theatre at Puymin, **Vaison-la-Romaine** (p117).

ITINERARIES

ONLY THE BEST

TWO WEEKS // NICE TO AVIGNON // 550KM

Start with belle of the Riviera ball **Nice** (p196) then explore **Monaco** (p219): revel in stupendous views from the **Grande Corniche** (p217).

Head west, stopping in Picasso's **Antibes** (p250) or fragrant **Grasse** (p260), en route to **Aix-en-Provence** (p69) with its markets and café life: to get here, coast via **St-Tropez** (p275) and its **peninsula** (p287) or dive inland past the **Gorges du Verdon** (p177), prime white-water sports terrain.

Week two, enter the Luberon near **Abbaye de Silvacane** (p164). Explore **Gordes** (p152) and other hilltop villages by bicycle. See red in **Roussillon** (p153), lavender in **Lagarde d'Apt** (p155), then whizz up/down **Mont Ventoux** (p122) en route to **Carpentras market** (p124). Finish in papal **Avignon** (p104).

COAST CUISINE

ONE WEEK // STES-MARIES DE LA MER TO MONACO // 300KM

Toast your trip with oysters in **Stes-Maries de la Mer** (p94) and clams and fish in **Méjanes** (p93). But don't think exclusively seafood: red rice and bull meat are **Arles** staples

(p90). Cruising east, sample sea urchins in **Carry-le-Rouet** (p66), *bouillabaisse* in **Marseille** (p59) – with potatoes on **Cap de Carqueiranne** (p310) – and try *tarte tropézienne* in **St-Tropez** (p284). Devote two days to **Nice** (p204) and its Italianate specialities: *socca* (chickpea-flour pancake) at the cours Saleya market; tripe and stockfish at La Merenda, *petits farcis* (stuffed vegetables) at La Petite Maison, *bagna cauda* (raw mixed vegetables dipped in anchovy paste) at La Taca d'Oli, beefy *daube* (stew) or sheep testicles at L'Escalinada. Finally munch *barbajuan* (chard- or spinach-stuffed pasty) in **Monaco** (p227).

GARDENS OF EDEN

10 DAYS // MENTON TO EYGALIÈRES // 450KM

Stroll the horticultural collection in **Menton** (p232) and understand why Provence is paradise. Equally irresistible is the designer collection in **Monaco** (p224) and the hill-top *jardins* with gobsmacking views in **Èze** (p216) and **Ste-Agnès** (p235).

Scoot southwest along the coast to go wild over ancient-Greek-inspired gardens planted in 1902 in **Beaulieu-sur-Mer** (p216), Villa Ephrussi de Rothschild in **St-Jean-Cap Ferrat** (p213) and eclectic seaside château gardens in **Mandelieu-La Napoule** (p270). Further west **Domaine du Rayol** (p298) is the epitome of paradise in the seaside hamlet of Le Rayol.

Drive two hours inland to learn about plants and dyes in **Lauris** (p163) and Provençal herbs near Lourmarin at **Ferme de Gerbaud** (p344). Then west to a garden with an unusual twist in **Eygalières** (p138).

SEVEN PERFECT LUNCHES

ONE WEEK // AVIGNON TO AGAY // 280KM

It is not taste buds alone that drive this tour: allow all afternoon for each address, where exquisite outdoor space, dreamy views and copious amounts of seasonal cuisine ensure

a deliciously lazed affair. Start in Papal Avignon with the palace and lunch at **Restaurant Brunel** (p110). Day two browse antique shops and feast on farm produce at riverside **Le Vivier** (p128) in L'Isle-sur-la-Sorgue. **Les Remparts** (p131) in Venasque, for Provençal cuisine best savoured with freshly squeezed cherry juice, is day three's address. Day four mooch gold-stone hilltop villages in the Luberon: **Véranda** (p161) in Ménerbes, gourmet **Bonnieux** (p159) and **Ferme Auberge Le Castelas** (p163) near Buoux make three perfect days. Wind up with a tummy-rumbling 'gold coast' drive to **Villa Matuzia** (p270) in Agay.

NATURALLY WONDERFUL

TWO WEEKS // NICE TO GORGES DU VERDON // 650KM

Riding the mountain railway from **Nice** to **Puget-Théniers** (p183) is the scenic way to arrive in the **Parc National du Mercantour** (p183). Otherwise, drive to Puget and along

the **Gorges de Dalius** (p186) to **Guillaumes** (p186), east to ski resort **Valberg** (p186) for a *raclette* lunch, and back south along the Bordeaux-red **Gorges du Cians** (p187). In the park's heart see Europe's highest alpine lake, **Lac d'Allos** (p185) and then head north to Europe's highest mountain pass, **Col de Restefond la Bonette** (p186). Break in Mexican **Barcelonnette** (p184) on your westward journey to the white waters of the **Vallée de l'Ubaye** (p184) and south to the spectacular fossil deposits around **Barles** (p182). End with a two-day game of gorge explorer (p177) in Europe's largest canyon, **Gorges du Verdon** (p177).

HILLTOP HAPPY

TWO WEEKS // NICE TO GORDES // 575KM

Dip into Provence's vertigo-inducing *villages perchés* (hilltop villages). **Èze** (p216) and **Roquebrune** (p217) are great excuses to drive the corniches from **Nice** (p211). A footpath

links Europe's highest seaside village, **Ste-Agnès** (p235), with **Gorbio** (p235), where you can lunch at **Beau Séjour** (p235).

Wiggle around **Arrière-Pays Niçois** (p209), then west to gallery-filled **St-Paul de Vence** (p257). Check out sky-high villages **Grimaud** (p290), **Gassin** and **Rama-tuelle** (p287) around St-Tropez. Lose the crowds afterwards in **Haut-Var** (p293).

Second week explore **Ansouis** and **Cucuron** (p165); boutique-shop in **Lourmarin** (p164); and dine in the Petit Luberon villages **Bonnieux** (p158) and **Lacoste** (p159). Finish with **Ménerbes** (p160) and a great view of **Gordes** (p152).

THE BEST OF
PROVENCE &
THE CÔTE D'AZUR

This seductive part of southern France was made for gorging: be it hilltop villages glinting gold and amber in the blistering sun, the best of 20th-century art, vineyards and almond blossoms, blazing-blue lavender fields or to-die-for black truffles, the orgy of hues, scents and tastes to devour is, quite simply, electrifying.

ABOVE Colourful wares in a shopfront in Les Baux de Provence

THE MOST FABULOUS 20TH-CENTURY ART

1 CÉZANNE // AIX-EN-PROVENCE
In chic Aix (p71) drink where Cézanne drank, visit his *atelier* (workshop) and country manor where he painted, and stride red-ochre quarries he immortalised many times on canvas. Out of town, marvel at mountains that inspired this post-Impressionist painter (p75).

2 MATISSE // NICE
Matisse was a Nice man: he slept at Hô-tel de Beau Rivage in Nice, later lived in Queen Victoria's wintering palace in the French Riviera town, painted works strung in the Musée Matisse (p201), and designed a masterpiece of a chapel in Vence (p256). He is buried in Nice.

③ PICASSO // ANTIBES & VALLAURIS

Antibes (p248), where Picasso had a studio in a 14th-century château, and Vallauris (p250), where the artist painted war and peace inside a chapel, are key stops. Complete the tour with his final resting place, Montagne Ste-Victoire (p75).

④ RENOIR // CAGNES-SUR-MER

He was 66 and arthritis-crippled when he arrived on the Riviera, but Renoir still painted, as a stroll around his studio and home proves (p254). As alluring as the house-museum are the olive and citrus groves in which it sits; bring easel and paint to create your own masterpiece.

⑤ VAN GOGH // ARLES & ST-RÉMY DE PROVENCE

Arles (p89) is a one-stop shop for fans of one of the 20th-century's most eccentric artists, whose actual work is displayed anywhere *but* the town where he painted 200-odd canvases and remodelled his ear. St-Rémy de Provence (p132) is the other place in Provence he painted excessively.

TOP The Musée Picasso, Antibes BOTTOM LEFT The Musée Matisse, Nice BOTTOM RIGHT Arles bridge, as seen by Van Gogh

THE MOST STUNNING HILLTOP VILLAGES

1 ÈZE // MOYENNE CORNICHE
Clinging to an impossible peak on the middle coastal road east of Nice, this medieval village (p216) is the Riviera crown jewel. For ultimate wow effect, hike to the château ruins, flop on a sun-lounger in the cactus garden and gorge on phenomenal views of Cap Ferrat and the Med.

2 SEILLANS // HAUT-VAR
Cobbled lanes coil to the crown of this gloriously quiet and quaint village in little-explored back-country Var. Lunch around an old stone fountain and admire the panoramic view at the 17th-century *bastide* (country house) of Scipion, knight of the Flotte d'Agout (p295).

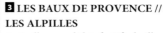

3 LES BAUX DE PROVENCE // LES ALPILLES

A stroll around this fortified village (p135), starring dramatic château ruins atop a limestone *baou* (rocky spur) and a clutch of gourmet addresses, is part of the Provence experience. Combine it with a trip around nearby olive groves (p137).

4 STE-AGNÈS & GORBIO // AROUND MENTON

A one-hour walking trail links these two *villages perchés* (hilltop villages). From Ste-Agnès, Europe's highest seaside village, climb down to pretty Gorbio for a stroll around the old stone houses, followed by lunch in a village inn (p234).

5 BONNIEUX, MÉNERBES & GORDES // THE LUBERON

This classic trio just doesn't lose its edge: Bonnieux (p158) boasts a bread-making museum and cedar forest; Ménerbes (p160) a truffle house and corkscrew museum. For a view of Gordes (p152) tumbling down the hillside, approach it from the south.

TOP Beautiful Bonnieux **BOTTOM LEFT** Èze rooftops **BOTTOM RIGHT** Les Baux de Provence

THE MOST DRAMATIC DRIVES

**1 GRANDE CORNICHE //
NICE TO ROQUEBRUNE**
One of three parallel coastal cliff-hangers,
this legendary road where Grace Kelly
cruised is a celebrity in its own right.
Crown the sensory feast with a picnic
(p219) or lunch in Roquebrune (p218).
Return via the Moyenne Corniche (p216).

**2 ROUTE DES CRÊTES & CORNICHE
SUBLIME // GORGES DU VERDON**
The emerald-green water swirling along
Europe's biggest canyon, the Gorges du
Verdon, is dizzying – keep your eyes on
the road and pack nerves of steel for this
sheer-drop drive (p177). Circling vultures
add a touch of cinema.

DAVID TOMLINSON

3 COL DU CANADEL //
MASSIF DES MAURES
This mountain pass plunges from forest to
a beautiful wedge of St-Tropez-area coast:
it's 12km of low-gear driving on a single-
lane road with too few places to pull over
and too many blind hairpins, but stunning
views (p298). Consider lunch on Bormes-
les-Mimosas' Route des Crêtes (p299).

4 ROUTE DES CRÊTES //
CASSIS TO LA CIOTAT
East of Marseille a mind-blowing panorama of coast and vines unfurls along cliff
tops between Cassis and La Ciotat. Pack
a seafood hamper in the port of Cassis
and indulge in a gourmet lunch along this
often windswept 'Road of Crests' (p64).

5 COL DE RESTEFOND–LA
BONNETTE // VALLÉE DE LA TINÉE
Europe's highest mountain pass, in the
Mercantour national park (p183), was
once a mule path. It can only be motored
in summer: snow blankets the dazzling
rock formations in winter.

TOP Views of the *calanques*, Cassis area **BOTTOM LEFT** The Gorges du Verdon provide the views along the Route des Crêtes **BOTTOM RIGHT** A valley en route to La Bonnette

TOP Lavender field at Abbaye Notre-Dame de Sénanque **RIGHT** Lavender blossoms attract more than just the cameras

THE BEST LAVENDER

1 CHÂTEAU DU BOIS // LAGARDE D'APT

Frolic along footpaths through fields of lavender at this idyllic lavender farm, one of the few producing pure lavender, in the Luberon. Late June to mid-July, when the flower is harvested, is the sweetest-smelling time to laze away an afternoon here (p155).

2 PLATEAU DE VALENSOLE // HAUTE-PROVENCE

Driving or cycling across this vast che-quered plateau (p168) is magnificent: one of the region's greatest concentrations of lavender farms, it swoops in soft contours from corn-yellow wheat fields to squares of pale purple. Plateau de Claparèdes is the other lavender-strewn plateau (p162).

3 PRIEURÉ DE SALAGON // MANE

Shop at Forcalquier market for a gourmet picnic then cycle or drive to Mane for a romantic ramble around the lavender-laden gardens framing a beautiful medi-eval priory in Provence's rural heart; its lavender museum tells a tale or two about the early-summer lilac bloom (p174).

4 ABBAYE NOTRE-DAME DE SÉNANQUE // NEAR GORDES

Get camera ready: this 12th-century Cistercian abbey is framed with a classic Provence picture-postcard surround of lavender fields. July is the month when it is at its blooming best and smells the most heavenly. Lunch afterwards at a divinely delicious Luberon address (p153).

MARSEILLE AREA

3 PERFECT DAYS

🏵 DAY 1 // SENSORY MARSEILLE

Engage in Marseille's frenzy of sights, sounds, smells and flavours: follow the sound of African drums, clinking masts and fishwives to the Vieux Port fish market. Grab a coffee at La Caravelle (p50) and sail to Château d'If (p51). Later get lost in Le Panier (p50) and take a seaside stroll to fairy-tale Vallon des Auffes for *bouillabaisse* (p59).

🏵 DAY 2 // GORGE ON GREEN

Immerse yourself in natural grandeur: hike into Les Calanques, booking a table in advance at one of the Morgiou or Sormiou restaurants (p63). Post-lunch, revel in a flurry of clifftop vistas (p64) with a slow scenic drive around Cassis. Wine taste in the afternoon and at dusk feast on sea urchins and enjoy a glass of crisp white wine at Cassis port.

🏵 DAY 3 // CÉZANNE CHIC

Be chic with local bourgeoisie in Aix-en-Provence (p69). Admire its elegant *hôtels particuliers* (private mansions; p69) and fine art (p71), and follow in the footsteps of Cézanne (p71); perhaps book a guided tour of the burnt-orange ochre quarries he loved to paint. Explore Montagne Ste-Victoire (p75), wine taste (p76), and end with a starlit dinner in best-kept secret Ventabren (p77).

MARSEILLE AREA

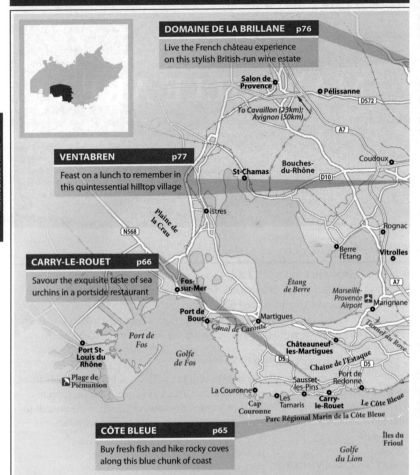

DOMAINE DE LA BRILLANE   p76

Live the French château experience
on this stylish British-run wine estate

VENTABREN   p77

Feast on a lunch to remember in
this quintessential hilltop village

CARRY-LE-ROUET   p66

Savour the exquisite taste of sea
urchins in a portside restaurant

CÔTE BLEUE   p65

Buy fresh fish and hike rocky coves
along this blue chunk of coast

Salon de Provence
Pélissanne
D572
To Cavaillon (23km);
Avignon (50km)
A7
Coudoux
St-Chamas
Bouches-du-Rhône
D10
Istres
Plaine de la Crau
N568
Rognac
Vitrolles
Berre l'Étang
A7
Étang de Berre
Marseille-Provence Airport
Marignane
Fos-sur-Mer
Port de Bouc
Canal de Caronte
Martigues
Tunnel du Rove
Port de Fos
Golfe de Fos
Châteauneuf-les-Martigues
D5
Chaîne de l'Estaque
D5
Port St-Louis du Rhône
Plage de Piémanson
La Couronne
Cap Couronne
Les Tamaris
Sausset-les-Pins
Carry-le-Rouet
Port de Redonne
Le Côte Bleue
Parc Régional Marin de la Côte Bleue
Îles du Frioul
Golfe du Lion

GETTING AROUND

Urban Marseille means torturous traffic-clogged streets
and too few places to park; best dump the car and get
around on foot, metro and bus. West of Provence's largest
city, around the airport, the coast is built-up and industrial.
Looking north, the A51 motorway links Marseille with Aix-
en-Provence, another devil of a place to park. Eastwards,
the scenic D559 climbs across the Col de la Gineste to
Cassis, from where the area's most dramatic road can be
picked up – the Route des Crêtes.

MEDITERRANEAN SEA

**CALANQUE DE SORMIOU &
CALANQUE DE MORGIOU**   p63

Dip into these rocky coves with a
scrub walk and lunch with sea view

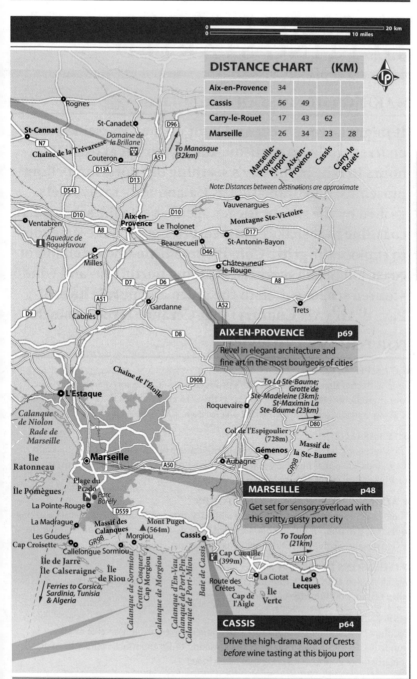

DISTANCE CHART   (KM)

	Marseille-Provence Airport	Aix-en-Provence	Cassis	Carry-le-Rouet-
Aix-en-Provence	34			
Cassis	56	49		
Carry-le-Rouet	17	43	62	
Marseille	26	34	23	28

Note: Distances between destinations are approximate

AIX-EN-PROVENCE   p69

Revel in elegant architecture and fine art in the most bourgeois of cities

MARSEILLE   p48

Get set for sensory overload with this gritty, gusty port city

CASSIS   p64

Drive the high-drama Road of Crests *before* wine tasting at this bijou port

MARSEILLE AREA GETTING STARTED

MAKING THE MOST OF YOUR TIME

It might be rough-cut and built up, but Marseille oozes an irresistible magnetism. Allow yourself at least 48 hours to take in the city's seething old port, compelling museums, and dramatic Les Calanques – rocky inlets gashed by the seas of the ice age to create the spectacular coastline that snakes southeast to Cassis. Take time too to explore the gritty Côte Bleue, a little-known chunk of coast full of fish markets. Heading north, sea- and wind-scoured scapes soften to the green and purple hues of Pays d'Aix (Aix Country) that Cézanne loved so much.

TOP TOURS & COURSES

❦ L'AMPHITYRON
Shop with chef Bruno Ungaro at Aix's produce market, grab *un café*, then cook up your ingredients over a cooking course at this Aix-en-Provence restaurant. (☎ 04 42 26 54 10; www.restaurant-amphitryon.fr, in French; 2-4 rue Paul-Doumer, Aix-en-Provence)

❦ LE PASSAGE
The short cooking sessions – fast food (€14), dinner for two (€49 to €85), cocktails (€49), kids' cake-making (€27) – at this Aix-en-Provence concept restaurant, smart in a 19th-century sweet factory, are refreshingly accessible. (p74)

❦ AIX-EN-PROVENCE WALKING TOURS
The Aix-en-Provence tourist office runs literary, art, architectural and history walking tours (€8, two hours): Émile Zola, Cézanne, Renaissance *hôtels particuliers,* Libertines & Courtesans, Secret Aix, Old-Town Aix, and so on. (p69)

❦ CALISSONS DU ROY RENÉ
Watch Aix-en-Provence's traditional sweet being made at this *calisson* (marzipan-like sweet) factory on the edge of town. (p76)

❦ SEA KAYAKING
Paddling by moonlight around rocky *calanques* (coves) from Marseille or Cassis is wondrous. Raskas Kayak organises sea-kayaking tours and tourist offices have details of many more guides. (www.raskas-kayak.com, in French)

GETTING AWAY FROM IT ALL

In such an urban part of Provence, fleeing people and/or industrial development is not always easy. Try the following to momentarily get lost in the region's natural heritage:

★ **Les Calanques** Hike along Marseille's rocky coastline (p62); the coastal path along the *calanques* of the Côte Bleue is not as busy (p66)

★ **Ventabren** Few are familiar with this hilltop village, home to a very tasty lunch address indeed (p77)

★ **Domaine de la Brillane** This successful British-run wine estate has stylish rooms with staggering vineyard views (p76)

ADVANCE PLANNING

Tips and tricks to ensure happy holidays:

★ **Marseille accommodation** Plan in advance where to stay in this urban sprawl – the best rooms get snapped up fast (p378)

★ **Festive Aix-en-Provence** The same goes for Aix-en-Provence during its summertime fiesta of festivals (p72)

★ **Sormiou & Morgiou calanques** To revel in the natural beauty of Marseille's best-known *calanques* at sunset, or minus a stiff walk in the searing heat, reserve a table at a Sormiou or Morgiou restaurant (p62), which grants you the right to drive right down to the water's edge

TOP RESTAURANTS

☙ LA PART DES ANGES
Wine-dine with urban trendies in this retro wine bar (p58)

☙ AU BORD DE L'EAU
Fresh fish on Cap Croisette (p58)

☙ LA PASSARELLE
Organic cuisine in an urban walled garden (p58)

☙ LE POIVRE D'ANE
Creative dining on Aix's prettiest square (p74)

☙ LE SCOOP
Succulent seafood and seasonal sea urchins in Carry-le-Rouet (p66)

☙ LA TABLE DE VENTABREN
Contemporary Michelin-starred dining in a hilltop village west of Aix (p77)

RESOURCES

★ **In English** (http://in-english.blogsthema .marseille-provence2013.fr) Marseille arts, culture and city events

★ **Marseille.fr** (www.marseille.fr) City website

★ **Marseille Tourisme** (www.marseille -tourisme.com) Tourist office online

★ **Visit Provence** (www.visitprovence.fr) Comprehensive info on the Bouches du Rhône *département*; lots of great itineraries

MARSEILLE AREA

MARSEILLE

· · · · · ·

pop 1.6 million

Marseille is a rich, pulsating port city bubbling over with history, cutting-edge creative spaces and hip multicultural urbanites. Since Greek settlers came ashore around 600 BC, waves of immigrants have made Marseille their home.

With buildings in hues of ripened apricot, cracked wheat and blanched almond, Marseille is infused with an irrepressible energy. With a sultry southern European tempo, France's oldest city beats to the drum of neighbouring North Africa. Its maritime heritage thrives at the vibrant Vieux Port, where fresh-off-the-boat catches are sold each morning. Along the coast, blue-rimmed coastal roads and parallel cycling tracks veer around sun-scorched coves and sandy beaches.

A feast of world cuisines, shops, music and cultural celebrations ensure the pace never slows in this busy city, where the mistral wind blows up a storm from time to time. Locals are unified by their high-spirited sing-song accent and their cherished football team, Olympique de Marseille (OM), during whose matches myriad nationalities sing as one: 'Nous sommes les Marseillais!' (We are the Marseillais!).

ESSENTIAL INFORMATION

EMERGENCIES // Hôpital de la Timone
(☎ 04 91 49 91 91, 04 91 38 60 00; www.ap-hm.fr, in French; 264 rue St-Pierre, 5e; Ⓜ La Timone) is 1km southeast of place Jean Jaurès. **Police** (Map p52; ☎ 04 88 77 58 00; 66-68 La Canebière, 1er; ⊗ 24hr; Ⓜ Estrangin-Préfecture).

TOURIST OFFICES // City Centre (Map p52; ☎ 04 91 13 89 00; www.marseille-tourisme.com; 4 La Canebière, 1er; ⊗ 9am-7pm Mon-Sat, 10am-5pm Sun; Ⓜ Vieux Port) Theatre box office; guided city walking tours (€6.50).

ORIENTATION

Greater Marseille is divided into 16 arrondissements (districts), which are indicated in addresses (eg 1er for the first arrondissement and so on). The city's main thoroughfare, La Canebière (from the Provençal word *canebe,* meaning 'hemp', after the city's traditional rope industry), in the 1st arrondissement, stretches eastwards from the Vieux Port towards the train station, a 10-minute walk or two metro stops from the water. North is Le Panier, Marseille's oldest quarter; south is the bohemian concourse of cours Julien; and southwest is the start of the coastal road.

EXPLORING MARSEILLE

Buy a cent-saving Marseille City Pass (one-/two-day €20/27) at the tourist office. It covers admission fees to 15 museums, a city tour, unlimited public-transport travel, boat trips and so on.

♥ VIEUX PORT // JOSTLE FOR FRESH FISH, STROLL, BE A CULTURE VULTURE

Ships have docked for more than 26 centuries at the city's birthplace, the colourful **Old Port** (Map p52; Ⓜ Vieux Port). The main commercial docks were transferred to the Joliette area on the coast north of here in the 1840s, but the old port remains a thriving harbour for fishing boats, pleasure yachts and tourists.

Guarding the harbour are **Bas Fort St-Nicolas** (Map p52) on the south side and, across the water, **Fort St-Jean** (Map

MARSEILLE AREA

MARSEILLE

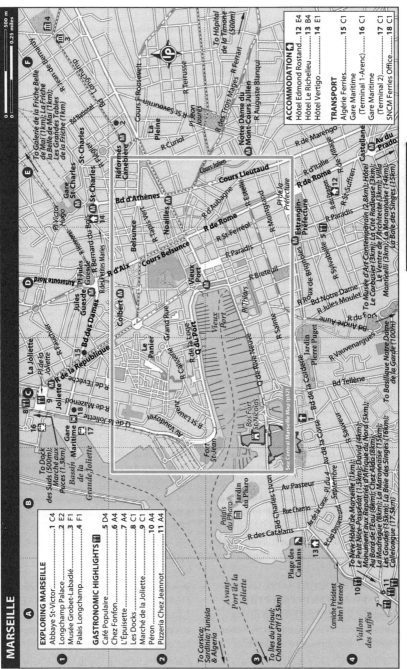

EXPLORING MARSEILLE
Abbaye St-Victor	1	C4
Longchamp Palace	2	E2
Musée Grobet-Labadié	3	F1
Palais Longchamp	4	F1

GASTRONOMIC HIGHLIGHTS
Café Populaire	5	D4
Chez Fonfon	6	A4
L'Épuisette	7	A4
Les Docks	8	C1
Marché de la Joliette	9	C1
Péron	10	A4
Pizzeria Chez Jeannot	11	A4

ACCOMMODATION
Hôtel Edmond Rostand	12	E4
Hôtel Le Richelieu	13	B4
Hôtel Vertigo	14	E1

TRANSPORT
Algérie Ferries	15	C1
Gare Maritime (Terminal 1-Arenc)	16	C1
Gare Maritime (Terminal 2)	17	C1
SNCM Ferries Office	18	C1

p52), founded in the 13th century by the Knights Hospitaller of St John of Jerusalem. Inside its square Roy Renée tower are exhibitions hosted by the national **Musée des Civilisations de l'Europe et de la Méditerranée** (Museum of European & Mediterranean Civilisations; Map p52; ☎ 04 96 13 80 90; www.musee-europemediterranee .org; Tour Carrée du Roy René, quai du Port, 2e; admission free; ☺ 1pm-7pm Wed, Thu & Sat).

The port's southern quay oozes culture: the curtain goes up on mainstream dramas in Marseille's old fish-auction house (1909), now the **Théâtre National de Marseille** (Map p52; www.theatre-lacriee.com, in French) at No 30; alternative theatre and stuff for kids goes down in a trio of small venues on **Passage des Arts** (Map p52) at No 16; the hip and cool play *pétanque* at night inside legendary nightclub **Le Trolleybus** (Map p52) at No 24; and restaurants and cafés buzz until the wee hours a block east on **place Thiars** and **cours Honoré d'Estienne d'Orves**.

Don't leave the Vieux Port without tasting the local firewater at **La Maison du Pastis** (see p55) and relaxing over a coffee or cocktail at the best seat in the house – the balcony at **La Caravelle** (Map p52; ☎ 04 96 17 05 40; 34 quai du Port, 2e; ☺ 7am-2am). If it's full, board the public-transport **Cross-Port Ferry** in front of the town hall and sail across the water to **Bar de la Marine** (Map p52; ☎ 04 91 54 95 42; 15 quai de Rive Neuve, 1er; ☺ 7am-1am), the 1930s bar where Marcel Pagnol filmed the card-party scenes in the first of his early-20th-century cult-classic trilogy, *Marius*.

♥ LE PANIER // GET LOST IN MARSEILLE'S MONTMARTRE

From the Vieux Port, hike up to this fantastic history-woven quarter, dubbed Marseille's Montmartre as much for its sloping streets as its artsy ambience. In Greek Massilia it was the site of the *agora* (marketplace), hence its name, which means 'the basket'. During WWII the quarter was dynamited and afterwards rebuilt. Today it's a mishmash of lanes hiding artisan shops, *ateliers* (workshops) and terraced houses strung with drying washing.

Create your own tour by scouring out recommended addresses such as **Compagnie de Provence** (Map p52; 1 rue Caisserie) for *savon de Marseille* (soap) and **Les Navettes des Accoules** (Map p52; 68 rue Caisserie) for traditional biscuits made from orange flour and shaped like torpedos; **Place aux Huiles** (Map p52; 2 place Daviel) for olive-oil products and bottles of local retro beer La Cagole de Marseille; and **72% Pétanque** (Map p52; 10 rue du Petit Puits) for olive-oil soap in a rainbow of flavours including tomato leaf and chocolate. Marseille architect and sculptor Pierre Puget (1620–94) was born in the house opposite. He designed the arcaded courtyard of the **Centre de la Vieille Charité** (Map p52; ☎ 04 91 14 58 80; www .vieille-charite-marseille.org, in French; 2 rue de la Charité, 2e; temporary/permanent exhibition €2/4; ☺ 11am-6pm Tue-Sat summer, 10am-5pm Tue-Sat winter) around Provence's most imposing baroque church. The centre houses the Musée d'Archéologie Méditerranéenne and the Musée des Arts Africains, Océaniens & Amérindiens today.

Creative art exhibitions for kids are held at **Préau des Accoules** (Map p52; ☎ 04 91 91 52 06; 20 montée des Accoules; admission free; ☺ 1.30-5.30pm Wed & Sat), inside an 18th-century Jesuit college.

♥ BASILIQUE NOTRE DAME DE LA GARDE // STIR YOUR SOUL WITH A CELESTIAL CITY VIEW

Everywhere you go in Marseille, you see the golden statue of the Romano-Byzantine basilica rising up from the city's highest hill, La Garde (162m). Built between 1853 and 1864, this domed **Basilica Lady of the Guard** (off Map p49; ☎ 04 91 13 40 80; www.notredamedelagarde.com; admission free; ⏰ 7am-7pm, longer hrs summer) is ornamented with coloured marble, murals and superbly restored mosaics; it gives you a 360-degree panorama of the city's sea of terracotta roofs below. Its bell tower is crowned by a 9.7m-tall gilded statue of the Virgin Mary on a 12m-high pedestal. Bus 60 links the Vieux Port with the basilica. Otherwise, it's a 1km walk or tourist-train trip (p53).

♣ CHÂTEAU D'IF & ÎLES DU FRIOUL // SAIL TO A TRIO OF WILDLIFE-RICH ISLANDS

Immortalised in Alexandre Dumas' classic 1840s novel *Le Comte de Monte Cristo* (The Count of Monte Cristo), 16th-century fortress-turned-prison **Château d'If** (☎ 04 91 59 02 30; adult/under 18yr €5/free; ⏰ 9.30am-5.30pm, to 6.30pm Jun-Aug) sits on the 30-sq-km island, **Île d'If**, 3.5km west of the Vieux Port. Political prisoners were incarcerated here, along with hundreds of Protestants, the Revolutionary hero Mirabeau, and the Communards of 1871.

MARSEILLE AREA

48 HOURS IN MARSEILLE

MUSEUM BUFF
Start at the **Vieux Port** (p48) with breakfast at **La Caravelle** (opposite) and a waterside stroll to the **Musée des Civilisations de l'Europe et de la Méditerranée** (opposite), located inside an old stone tower. Or catch at boat to revel in Monte Cristo intrigues at **Château d'If** (above). Lunch at La Passarelle (p58) then hike up to the **Basilique Notre Dame de la Garde** (opposite) or explore **Le Panier** (opposite), not missing the **Centre de la Vieille Charité** (opposite). Make art and architecture (p54) the theme of day two.

BEACH BUM
Sail to the **Îles du Frioul** (above) to lounge in a natural paradise of birdlife and pebble beach; take your own picnic or sail back to the Vieux Port and hop on a bus or walk to the postcard-pretty **Vallon des Auffes** (p56) for a rooftop pizza at **Pizzeria Chez Jeannot** (p60). Post-lunch, head along the coast on foot or by bike, ending with drinks, dinner and dancing at a **Cap Croisette** address (p56). Devote day two to the magnificent turquoise waters and bijou rocky coves of **Les Calanques** (p62); dine at dusk at **Morgiou** (p63) or **Sormiou** (p63).

GOURMET TRAVELLER
Watch eels flip in buckets at the Vieux Port **fish market** (p48). Afterwards, taste and shop for the **local firewater** (p55) in anticipation of a **bouillabaisse feast** (p59) lasting several hours for lunch. Come late afternoon, watch fishermen unload their catch in the tiny harbour of **Port de la Madrague Montredon**, before eating the catch at neighbouring **Au Bord de l'Eau** (p58). Second day, shop for olive oil and *navettes* (orange-blossom-flavoured biscuits) in **Le Panier** (opposite).

IF IT'S SUNDAY
Don't miss Marseille's Moroccan-style **Marché aux Puces** (p60).

CENTRAL MARSEILLE

MARSEILLE AREA

A few hundred metres west are the **Îles du Frioul**, the barren dyke-linked white-limestone islands of Ratonneau and Pomègues. From the 17th to the 19th century, people suspected of carrying plague or cholera were quarantined here. Sea birds and rare plants thrive on these tiny islands (each about 2.5km long, totalling 200 hectares). Ratonneau has three beaches.

From the **Gare Maritime des Navettes Frioul et If** (Map p52; 1 quai des Belges) boats depart every 45 to 60 minutes between 9am and 6.30pm daily; in July and August the last departure from Marseille/Frioul is 11.30pm/midnight. Buy tickets here at the **ticket office** (☎ 04 91 46 54 65; www.frioul-if-express.com; ☼ 9am-6.30pm): a return ticket to If or Frioul costs €10, to both €15; children under four travel for free.

**♥ BUS, TRAIN OR BOAT TOUR //
GRAB A SEAT AND SEE THE CITY
IN STYLE**
Feel the wind in your hair as you travel between key sights and museums aboard open-topped bus **Le Grand Tour** (Map p52; ☎ 04 91 91 05 82; adult one-/two-day pass €18/20).

Tickets for this hop-on-hop-off tour, sold at the tourist office or by bus drivers, include a five-language audio guide.

A calf-friendly way to see steeper parts of the city is aboard Marseille's **electric tourist trains** (Map p52; ☎ 04 91 25 24 69; www .petit-train-marseille.com; adult/child €6/3; ☼ 10am-12.30pm & 1.30-6pm; Ⓜ Vieux Port), which follow one of two circular routes. From the Vieux Port one chugs up to the basilica and the other tootles around Le Panier; tours last 65 minutes and trains depart every 20 or 30 minutes.

Croisières Calanques Marseille (☎ 08 25 13 68 80; www.croisieres-marseille-calanques.com; 74 quai du Port, 1e; Ⓜ Vieux Port) runs three-hour-return boat trips (family/adult/4 to 12 years €75/25/18) from the Vieux Port, past the clear turquoise coves of Les Calanques (p62), to Cassis. It also runs shorter two-hour trips taking in six rather than 12 *calanques* (€58/19/14); 1½-hour trips around the Baie de Marseille (€44/15/10); and evening jazz–dinner cruises (€48).

Marseille Côte Mer (☎ 04 91 33 03 29; www.marseille-cote-mer.com; 1 quai Marcel Pagnol, 1e; Ⓜ Vieux Port) sails west along the Côte Bleue (p65).

♥ AN ART & ARCHITECTURE DAY // VIEW THE CITY'S ARTISTIC PORTFOLIO

There is an art museum to suit every taste: for Provençal classics like Raoul Dufy's *Paysage de l'Estaque* (1908) or André Derain's *Pinède, Cassis* (1907) dip into the local landscapes and 17th- and 18th-century Provençal ceramics at the **Musée Cantini** (Map p52; ☎ 04 91 54 77 75; 19 rue Grignan, 6e; Ⓜ Estrangin-Préfecture; adult/10-16yr €2/1; ⏲ 10am-5pm Tue-Sun Oct-May, 11am-6pm Tue-Sun Jun-Sep).

Of more interest than the natural history museum inside is the architecture of **Palais Longchamp** (Map p49; bd Philippon, 4e; Ⓜ Cinq Avenues-Longchamp), an imposing colonnaded palace designed in the 1860s in part to disguise a water tower built at the terminus of an aqueduct from the River Durance. Four growling lions guard its terraced water gardens, and there is a picnic-perfect green park out back. Nearby, the intimate **Musée Grobet-Labadié** (Map p49; ☎ 04 91 62 21 82; 140 bd Longchamp, 1e; adult/child €2/1; ⏲ 11am-6pm Tue-Sun Jun-Sep, 10am-5pm Tue-Sun Oct-May; Ⓜ Cinq Avenues-Longchamp) paints an appealing portrait of elegant 19th-century Marseille with its collections of 13th- to 19th-century paintings, antiques, sculptures, ornate polished wooden floors, card games, fans and ceramics.

Grab a coffee, bistro lunch or *apéro* afterwards at the earthy, artsy **Longchamp Palace** (Map p49; ☎ 04 91 50 76 13; 22 bd Longchamp, 1e; mains €12-14; ⏲ 8am-midnight Mon & Tue, 8am-1.30am Wed-Fri Sep-Jul; Ⓜ Cinq Avenues-Longchamp).

Finish the art tour with the off-the-wall creations of Marseille-born sculptor César (César Baldaccini; 1921–98), who jostles for white space with Christo, Nice new realists Ben and Klein, and pop artist Andy Warhol at the **Musée d'Art Contemporain** (Museum of Contemporary Art, MAC; ☎ 04 91 25 01 07; 69 bd de Haïfa, 8e; adult/child €2/1; ⏲ 11am-6pm Tue-Sun Jun-Sep, 10am-5pm Tue-Sun Oct-May). Take bus 44 from the Prado metro stop to place Bonnefons, from where it is a short walk along av de Hambourg to rond-point Pierre Guerre: look for the giant metal thumb (a César).

♥ ATELIER ET MUSÉE DU SANTON // IMMERSE YOURSELF IN A MAGICAL MINIATURE WORLD

The Provençal custom of creating a nativity scene with figurines dates from the Avignon papacy of John XII (1319–34). But it was only after the 1789 Revolution and consequent Reign of Terror that

---

ACCOMMODATION

The best rooms in Marseille and Aix get snagged fast. Read the detailed listings in our dedicated accommodation chapter. Here are some of the best picks:

★ The breezy, beach-house vibe at Marseille's **Hôtel Le Richelieu** (p379) is contagious; we love it!

★ Marseille's **Hôtel Vertigo** (p379) is one of Europe's new-generation boutique hostels

★ Breakfast at **L'Épicerie** (p380), a creative *chambre d'hôte* decked like a 1950s grocery store, and you can easily skip lunch

★ Breakfast alfresco in a vaulted cloister, **Le Manoir** (p380), Aix-en-Provence's fabulous choice with free parking to boot

★ **Domaine de la Brillane** (p76) is a place like nowhere else to wine taste, sleep and breakfast between Coteaux d'Aix vines

THE MILK OF PROVENCE

When in Provence, do as the Provençaux do: drink pastis. The aniseed-flavoured alcoholic drink is a classic aperitif, although it is drunk any time of day.

Amber-coloured in the bottle, it turns milky white when mixed with water. Bars and cafés serve it straight, allowing you to add the water (five parts water to one part pastis). It's best drunk before lunch or as the sun sets – and never on the rocks.

A dash of *sirop de menthe* (mint syrup diluted with water) transforms a regular pastis into a *perroquet* (literally 'parrot'). A *tomate* (tomato) is tarted up with one part grenadine, and the sweet Mauresque is dressed with *orgeat* (a sweet orange and almond syrup).

Pastis, a 45% alcohol drink, was invented in 1932 in Marseille by industrialist Paul Ricard (1909–97). Leading pastis brands are Pastis 51 and Ricard, both owned by the Ricard empire.

Taste these and others at Marseille's **La Maison du Pastis** (Map p52; ☎ 04 91 90 86 77; www.lamaisondupastis.com; 108 quai du Port; Ⓜ Vieux Port). Tasting tips: (a) never order 'a pastis' at the bar – ask for it by brand such as Ricard, Janot or Casanis; (b) if you find it too strong, add sugar; and (c) bars in Marseille serve pastis in four glass sizes – a *momie* or *mominette* (a dinky shot glass), a *bock* (double-height shot glass), a *tube* (tall thin juice glass) and a *ballon* (like a brandy balloon).

these figures were cut down in size, as the people of Provence handcrafted tiny kiln-fired figures in the secrecy of their homes – hence, the birth of the *santon* (from *santoùn* in Provençal, meaning 'little saint').

Watch the enchanting terracotta figures, just 2.5cm to 5cm tall, being hand-painted at *santonnier* Marcel Carbonnel's workshop, **Atelier du Santon** (Map p52; ☎ 04 91 54 26 58; www.santonsmarcelcarbonel.com, in French; 47 rue Neuve Ste-Catherine, 7e; admission free; ⏰ 8am-1pm & 2-5pm Tue-Thu), and admire the entire collection at the neighbouring **Musée du Santon** (Map p52; ☎ 04 91 13 61 36; 49 rue Neuve Ste-Catherine, 7e; admission free; ⏰ 10am-12.30pm & 2-6.30pm Tue-Sat). A traditional Provençal crib stars 55 *santons* including the tambourine man, chestnut seller, fishwife and woman with aïoli, tinsmith, scissor grinder, trumpet-blowing angel and the patron saint of *santonniers*, St Francis of Assisi.

🎔 LA FRICHE LA BELLE DE MAI // 21ST-CENTURY MARSEILLE IN A TOBACCO FACTORY

The site of a former sugar-refining plant and subsequent tobacco factory, the theatre and artists' workshops, cinema studios, radio stations, multimedia displays, alfresco installation art, skateboard camps and electro-/world-music parties at **La Friche la Belle de Mai** (off Map p49; ☎ 04 95 04 95 04; www.lafriche.org, in French; 41 rue Jobin, 3e) are the 'voice' of contemporary Marseille. Fringe and alternative, yes, but the creative energy exuded by this modish site, half-ruined and covered in graffiti, is contagious.

Check its program online, view art in the **Galerie de la Friche Belle de Mai** (admission free; ⏰ 3-7pm Tue-Sat) or simply lunch on homemade tarts, salads and other *cuisine du quotidien et de l'extraordinaire* (everyday and extraordinary cooking) in its cavernous, stylishly industrial restaurant **Les Grandes Tables de la Friche** (off Map p49; ☎ 04 95 04 95 28; 12 rue François Simon, 3e; mains €10), inside what was the old cigarette-rolling factory. Take bus 49 from La Canabière to rue Jobin.

❧ ALONG THE COAST // WALK, RUN OR CYCLE ALONG THE MED TO THE BEACH

Mesmerising views of another Marseille unveil along **corniche Président John F Kennedy**, the coastal road that cruises south to small, sandy, beach-volleyball-busy **Plage des Catalans** (Map p49; 3 rue des Catalans; ☾ 8.30am-6.30pm Jun-Sep) and the picture-postcard fishing cove of **Vallon des Auffes** (Map p49). Walk down the staircase behind the 'Vallon des Auffes' bus stop to reach the toylike harbour crammed with colourful fishing boats. Across the road, sun-seekers bask like lizards on wooden decks built over the rocks, sliding down short ladders to dip in the sea.

Sculpted in bronze by César, the enormous propeller of the 1971 **Monument aux Repatriés d'Afrique du Nord** (off Map p49) honours those who returned from North Africa. Further south, in front of the vast **Prado beaches**, Marseille's Italian connection is demonstrated by Jules Cantini's 1903 marble replica of Michelangelo's masterpiece, **David** (off Map p49). Nearby lies green **Parc Borély** (av du Parc Borély). The beaches themselves, all gold sand, were created from backfill from the excavations for Marseille's metro.

Promenade Georges Pompidou continues south to **Cap Croisette**, from where the beautiful *calanques* (p62) can be reached on foot. Hipster beach-club addresses: **La Baie des Singes** (off Map p49; The Bay of Monkeys; ☎ 04 91 73 68 87; mains €12-25; ☾ lunch & dinner Apr-Sep), with comfy deckchairs overlooking Île Maïre and

accessible by boat or on foot along a 500m path between rocks from the Cap Croisette car park; and **La Maronnaise** (off Map p49; ☎ 04 91 73 98 58; rte de la Maronnaise, 8e, Les Goudes; ☾ Wed-Sat May-early Sep), where 30- and 40-somethings lunch, flop in the sun, dine come dusk and later dance beneath stars. To get here, take bus 83 from the Vieux Port to av du Prado, then bus 19.

❧ L'UNITÉ D'HABITATION // LUNCH IN LE CORBUSIER'S 'RADIANT CITY'

Visionary international-style architect Le Corbusier (p335) redefined urban living in 1952 with the completion of his vertical 337-apartment 'garden city', elevated on tapering pylons like a titanic dry-docked ship, known as **La Cité Radieuse** (off Map p49; The Radiant City; ☎ 04 91 16 78 00; 280 bd Michelet, 8e). Along its darkened hallways, primary-coloured downlights create a glowing tunnel leading to a minisupermarket, an architectural bookshop, **Hôtel Le Corbusier** (p378), and a rooftop terrace with avocado-tiled paddling pool and cylindrical concrete tower (camouflaging the building's utilities) to top off the steamship effect.

Anyone can walk in and stroll around or lunch at **Le Ventre de l'Architecte** (off Map p49; ☎ 04 91 16 78 23; www.myspace .com/leventredelarchitecte; mains €30, lunch menu €24; ☾ lunch & dinner Tue-Sat). Brilliantly named, the Architect's Tummy takes a contemporary cut on cuisine and proffers sweeping views of Marseille and the Med from its balcony dining area. True architecture buffs can book a **guided tour** of one of the many private apartments in the block at the tourist office (p48). Take bus 83 or 21 to the Le Corbusier stop.

LITERARY MARSEILLE & AIX

★ *The Marseilles Trilogy* (Jean-Claude Izzo) – by the Marseille-raised son of Spanish and Italian immigrants, this trilogy evokes multicultural Marseille

★ *Villa Air-Bel: WWII, Escape & A House in Marseille* (Rosemary Sullivan) and *Crossroads Marseilles: 1940* (Mary-Jayne Gold) – two compelling books based on the true story of American heiress Varian Fry, who turned a villa in Marseille into a refuge for Nazi-persecuted artists and intellectuals

★ *The Arrow of Gold* (Joseph Conrad) – 'Certain streets have an atmosphere of their own, a sort of universal fame… One such street is the Canebière'. So begins Conrad's tale (1919) of swash-buckling love and adventure, opening in Marseille.

★ *The Count of Monte Cristo* and *The Three Musketeers* (Alexandre Dumas); *The Mysteries of Marseille* (Émile Zola) – realist portraits of 19th-century Marseille by two classic French novelists

★ *Cézanne's Quarry* (Barbara Pope; http://cezannes-quarry.blogspot.com) – a body, the spurned lover of Cézanne no less, is found in a quarry near Aix-en-Provence

MARSEILLE AREA

♥ COURS JULIEN // HANG OUT IN MULTICULTURAL MARSEILLE

No address is more telling of the city's extravagant cultural diversity than **cours Julien** (Map p49; 6e; Ⓜ Notre Dame du Mont-Cours Julien), an elongated square with a fountain that has long dried up and an exotic forest of palm trees, beneath which neighbourhood kids play football. Various **morning markets** fill the pedestrian-only space with life – fresh flowers on Wednesday and Saturday, antique books alternate Saturdays, and stamps or antique books on Sunday – and a line-up of café terraces on its western side cook up world cuisine. On its eastern side square, a couple of fringe theatres and the alternative **Espace Julien** (Map p49; ☎ 04 91 24 34 10; www.espace-julien.com, in French; 39 cours Julien, 6e; Ⓜ Notre Dame du Mont-Cours Julien) entertain after dark. Everything from rock, *opérock*, alternative theatre and reggae to hip hop, Afro-groove and other cutting-edge entertainment is staged at the latter; its website lists upcoming gigs and cover charges.

FESTIVALS & EVENTS

Pèlerinage de la Chandeleur (Candlemas Pilgrimage) Each year the statue of the Black Virgin inside **Abbaye St-Victor** (Map p49; 3 rue de l'Abbaye, 7e; Ⓜ Vieux Port) is carried through the streets in this candlelit procession; 2 February.

Carnaval de Marseille Mad street carnival with decorated floats; March.

Beach Volleyball World Championships Hosted by Plage du Prado; July.

Festival de Marseille (www.festivaldemarseille .com, in French) Three weeks of contemporary international dance, theatre, music and art; July.

Five Continents Jazz Festival (www.festival -jazz-cinq-continents.com, in French) Acid jazz, funk and folk music fest; July.

Fête de l'Assomption Honours the city's traditional protector with Mass in the Nouvelle Cathédrale de la Major (p52) and a procession through Le Panier; 15 August.

Fiesta des Suds (www.dock-des-suds.org) Celebration of world music held at Dock des Suds; October.

Foire aux Santonniers Since 1803 traditional *santon* makers (see p54) have flocked to Marseille for this annual *santon* fair; December.

GASTRONOMIC HIGHLIGHTS

The Vieux Port and surrounding pedestrian streets teem with restaurant and café terraces. For world cuisine, try cours Julien and nearby rue des Trois Mages, **Le Souk** (Map p52; ☎ 04 91 91 29 29; www.restaurantlesouk.com; 98 quai du Port, 2e; Ⓜ Vieux Port) for Moroccan, and **Le Femina** (Map p52; ☎ 04 91 54 03 56; 1 rue du Musée, 1er; Ⓜ Noailles; menus €15; ⓨ lunch & dinner Tue-Sat) for Algerian.

Le Panier's western fringe flows into the commercial port area, where dining options fill the London-docks-like complex **Les Docks** (Map p49; 10 place de la Joliette, 2e; Ⓜ Joliette).

❦ AU BORD DE L'EAU €€
Off Map p49; ☎ 04 91 72 68 04; 15 rue des Arapèdes, Port de la Madrague Montredon, 8e; mains €20; ⓨ lunch & dinner Thu-Mon, lunch Tue

Promise you won't tell *too* many people about this little harbourside haven literally 'at the water's edge'. Chances are, you can thank the fishing boats moored below the sun-drenched terrace for catching the fish on your plate just hours before. Catch bus 83 to Prado, then bus 19 south to get to this sunflower-yellow seaside *cabanon* (traditional fishing cabin).

❦ CAFÉ POPULAIRE €€
Map p49; ☎ 04 91 02 53 96; 10 rue Paradis, 6e; mains €20; ⓨ lunch & dinner Wed-Sat; Ⓜ Estrangin-Préfecture

Vintage tables and chairs, old books on the shelf and a fine collection of glass soda bottles all add to the retro air of this 1950s-styled jazz *comptoir* (counter). Plump for a button stool at the zinc bar or lounge at a table with a view of the fabulous open kitchen, where simple dishes like *gambas à la plancha* (fried prawns served on a hot plate) or beetroot and coriander salad are cooked up for a hip chic crowd.

❦ CHEZ ALDO €€
Off Map p49; ☎ 04 91 73 31 55; www.chezaldo.com, in French; 27 rue Audemar-Tibido, Port de la Madrague Montredon, 8e; pizza €10-15, mains €20; ⓨ lunch & dinner Tue-Sat, lunch Sun

Sitting behind glass watching the sun set over the Med is a romantic proposition, hence the local crowd that teems into this fish restaurant down the coast. To blend in with the Marseillais families dining here, share a thin-crust *pizza au feu de bois* (wood-fired pizza) between the entire table to start, followed by fish as a main. The *bouillabaisse* (€45 per person) must be ordered in advance and the *friture mixte* (mixed plate of battered, deep-fried tiny fish – yes, eat the heads and all of the tiniest) is out of this world. Catch bus 83 to Prado, then bus 19 south.

❦ LA PART DES ANGES €
Map p52; ☎ 04 91 33 55 70; 33 rue Sainte; mains €15; ⓨ 9am-2am Mon-Sat, 9am-1pm & 6pm-2am Sun; Ⓜ Vieux Port

No address buzzes with Marseille's hip, buoyant crowd more than this fabulous all-rounder wine bistro, named after the amount of alcohol that evaporates through a barrel during wine or whisky fermentation – the angels' share *(La part des anges)*. Tables can't be reserved: head straight to the long bar, let the bar tenders know you want to eat and take your pick of dozens of wines to try by the glass. The French bistro fare is cooked to perfection.

❦ LA PASSARELLE €
Map p52; ☎ 06 68 62 77 87, 06 10 96 58 10; 52 rue du Plan Fourmiguier, 7e; mains €15; ⓨ lunch & dinner Tue-Sat; Ⓜ Vieux Port

BOUILLABAISSE

No fish dish stands out more than the city's signature *bouillabaisse*. Originally cooked by humble fishermen from the scraps of their catch, Marseille's most sought-after culinary creation stars on the menus of most of its pedigreed chefs today.

Less noble, touristy restaurants trap unsuspecting diners with *bouillabaisse* chalked up on the board for €15 – not the real McCoy. A true *bouillabaisse* is served in two parts, as a soup and then fish course; it costs around €50 per person; must be ordered up to 48 hours in advance; and is often for a minimum of two diners. See p365 for more detail.

Refined addresses of honour, signatories to the quality charter *Charte de la Bouillabaisse Marseille* no less, include **Le Miramar** (Map p52; ☎ 04 91 90 10 40; www.bouilla baisse.com, in French; 12 quai du Port, 2e; mains €25-50; ⊗ lunch & dinner Tue-Sat; Ⓜ Vieux Port), with a quayside terrace at the busy Vieux Port; twin-Michelin-starred **Le Petit Nice-Passédat** (off Map p49; ☎ 04 91 59 25 92; www.petitnice-passedat.com; Anse de Maldormé, corniche Président John F Kennedy, 7e; mains from €50; ⊗ lunch & dinner Tue-Sat), on the coast road; creative **L'Épuisette** (Map p49; ☎ 04 91 52 17 82; www.l-epuisette.com; rue du Vallon des Auffes, 7e; mains €40; ⊗ lunch & dinner Tue-Sat Sep-Jul) in a glass box by the sea; and third-generation-run **Chez Fonfon** (Map p49; ☎ 04 91 52 14 38; www.chez-fonfon.com; 140 rue du Vallon des Auffes; mains €35; ⊗ lunch & dinner Tue-Sat, dinner Mon), with an apricot-hued dining room overlooking the quaint fishing cove of Vallon des Auffes.

It is just one block back from the Vieux Port but for the moment it seems the city's journalists and savvy crowd have this inventive 'secret garden' restaurant, created around a veggie patch and herb garden, to themselves. Retro vintage tables and chairs sit beneath lime-green parasols on a terrace between foliage and strawberry beds. Everything growing in the pretty walled garden goes into something on Philippe and Patricia's predominantly organic menu, and other products are strictly local.

✿ LA VIRGULE €
Map p52; ☎ 04 91 90 91 11; http://lavirgule .marseille.free.fr, in French; 27 rue de la Loge, 2e; mains €17; ⊗ lunch & dinner; Ⓜ Vieux Port
The bistro venture of Michelin-starred chef Lionel Lévy (see also p60), The Comma appeals on several fronts: its tables are one step back from the Vieux Port hustle and bustle; its bistro fare is simple market produce cooked for a price that won't break the bank; it peppers the end product with a generous dose of contemporary design. If courgette flowers stuffed with local goats' cheese and tomato *tapanade* (olive-based dip) are on the menu, order them!

✿ LES ARCENAULX €€
Map p52; ☎ 04 91 54 85 38; 27 cours Honoré d'Estienne d'Orves, 1er; mains €17.50, menus €27 & €57; ⊗ lunch & dinner Mon-Sat; Ⓜ Vieux Port
Whet appetites with a meander around this cavernous former Louis XIV warehouse with antiquarian and contemporary bookshop, and publishing house with a bent towards gastronomy. Afterwards dine in grandiose style on sensational dishes evoking old Marseille, such as whole pigeon with caramelised quinces and contemporary classics like perfectly stuffed Provençal vegetables. The neighbouring *salon de thé* (tearoom),

particularly cosy in wet or cold weather, serves light lunchtime savoury tarts, cakes and ice cream named after literary classics.

❦ PÉRON €€€

Map p49; ☎ 04 91 52 15 22; 56 corniche Président John F Kennedy, 7e; mains €34; ☺ lunch & dinner

This designer, pistachio-coloured place set out over the sea is one of the premier addresses in Marseille for a no-holds-barred gastronomic extravaganza. Stunning views unfold over the Med – and on your plate, with highlights including lobster risotto and lots of fresh fish either à la plancha or baked. A high wall around the place ensures no peeking onto the smart wood-decking terrace (except from guests in top-floor rooms of the hotel opposite!).

❦ PIZZERIA CHEZ JEANNOT €

Map p49; ☎ 04 91 52 11 28; 129 rue du Vallon des Auffes, 7e; pizza €8-10.50, salads €12-17, mains €28; ☺ lunch & dinner Tue-Sat, lunch Sun

With a magical setting overlooking the storybook Vallon des Auffes, this affable, affordable joint has fresh-as-it-gets salads, pasta and shellfish, plus piping-hot pizzas. Meats are grilled *au feu de bois*

(over a wood-stoked fire) and mains, despite the fishy setting, veer more towards beef and duck than the catch of the day.

❦ PIZZERIA ÉTIENNE €

Map p52; 43 rue de Lorette, 2e; mains €10-15; ☺ lunch & dinner Mon-Sat; Ⓜ Colbert

This old Marseillais haunt has the best pizza in town as well as succulent *pavé de boeuf* (beef steak) and scrumptious *supions frits* (pan-fried squid with garlic and parsley), but it's not just the food that packs the place out. Because Pizzeria Étienne is a convivial meeting-point for the entire neighbourhood, you'll need to pop in beforehand to reserve in person (there's no phone), though you will get a free aperitif while you wait for a table. Credit cards aren't accepted. From rue de la République, cut down passage de Lorette and walk up the staircase.

❦ UNE TABLE AU SUD €€€

Map p52; ☎ 04 91 90 63 53; www.unetableausud .com; 2 quai du Port, 2e; lunch/dinner menu €37/49 & €74; ☺ lunch & dinner Tue-Sat; Ⓜ Vieux Port

It was the *milkshake de bouille-abaisse* that clinched it for us. And indeed, from the second you step foot inside this discreet portside address, its entrance

---

TOP FIVE

AROMATIC MARKETS

Fresh Fish Market (Map p52; quai des Belges, 1er; ☺ 8am-noon; Ⓜ Vieux Port) At the old port, circled by hungry seagulls.

Garlic Market (Map p52; cours Belsunce, 1er; ☺ late Jun-late Jul; Ⓜ Vieux Port)

Marché aux Puces (off Map p49; av du Cap Pinède, 15e; ☺ 9am-7pm Sun) Chickens killed to order and African carved animals are among the many colourful sights at this Moroccan-style market. Take bus 35 or 70 from in front of Espace Infos RTM.

Marché des Capucins (Map p52; place des Capucins, 1er; ☺ 8am-7pm; Ⓜ Noailles) Fruit, veg, fish and dried goods.

Marché de la Joliette (Map p49; place de la Joliette, 2e; ☺ 8am-2pm Mon-Fri; Ⓜ Joliette) As above, plus flowers Monday.

inconspicuous bar the eight giant plant pots flagging the way, you know you're going to eat well. Chef Lionel Lévy continues to break the Modern Mediterranean mould, utilising local ingredients in ever-inventive ways.

♥ VINONEO BISTRO €

Map p52; ☎ 04 91 90 40 26; 6 place Daviel, 2e; lunch menu €14; ☺ lunch & dinner Thu-Sat, lunch Mon-Wed; Ⓜ Vieux Port

Next-door neighbour to the Église des Accoulès, this unassuming bistro has rapidly made a name for itself as a highly recommended lunch address. Wine is its speciality and every dish on the menu is married with a recommended wine that can be savoured by the glass. Should you want no more than an *assiette* (plate) of mixed cheese or cold meats in the company of a fine wine, this contemporary space is the perfect match for you.

TRANSPORT

TO/FROM THE AIRPORT

BUS // **Shuttle buses** (www.navettemarseille aeroport.com; airport ☎ 04 42 14 31 27; train station ☎ 04 91 50 59 34) link. **Marseille-Provence airport** (☎ 04 42 14 14 14; www.marseille.aeroport .fr, www.mp2.aeroport.fr), 28km northwest of Marseille in Marignane, with Marseille's central train station every 20 minutes. A single adult/6 to 12 years fare is €8.50/4.

GETTING AROUND

BIKE // With city-sponsored scheme **Le Vélo** (☎ 0800 801 225; www.levelo-mpm.fr, in French; seven-day subscription €1, first half-hour free, then per hr €1; ☺ 24hrs), pick up free wheels at one station, drop off at another.

BOAT // The **Cross-Port Ferry** (admission free; ☺ 10.30am-12.30pm & 1.30-6.30 or 7.30pm) yo-yos between the town hall on quai du Port and place aux Huiles on quai de Rive Neuve, taking about three minutes.

For ferry services to/from Corsica, Sardinia, Tunisia and Algeria from Marseille's **Gare Maritime** (Map p49; ☎ 04 91 39 45 66; 23 place de la Joliette, 2e; Ⓜ Joliette) run by **SNCM** (Map p49; ☎ 08 91 70 18 01; www. sncm.fr; 61 bd des Dames, 2e; Ⓜ Joliette) and **Algérie Ferries** (Map p49; ☎ 04 91 90 89 28; 29 bd des Dames, 2e; Ⓜ Joliette) see p418. Ferries to Corsica, Sardinia and Tunisia usually leave from Gare Maritime's Terminal 1.

BUS, TRAM & METRO // Marseille's buses, trams and two-line metro run from around 5am to 9pm. From 9.25pm to 12.30am, metro and tram routes are covered every 15 minutes by buses M1 and M2. Most night buses begin in front of the **Espace Infos RTM** (Map p52; ☎ 04 91 91 92 10; www.rtm.fr, in French; 6 rue des Fabres, 1er; ☺ 8.30am-6pm Mon-Fri, 9am-12.30pm & 2-5.30pm Sat), where you can pick up transport maps and tickets (€1.70). A one-/three-day pass costs €4.50/10.

PARKING // Central underground car parks include **Parking Bourse** (Map p52; rue Reine Elisabeth, 1er; Ⓜ Vieux Port) and **Parking de Gaulle** (Map p52; 22 place du Général de Gaulle, 1er; Ⓜ Vieux Port), off La Canebière. Expect to pay about €2/15 per hour/day.

TRAIN // From **Gare St-Charles** (Map p52; Ⓜ Gare St-Charles, 1er), trains run to/from Aix-en-Provence centre (€6.70, 40 minutes), Avignon (€17.60, one hour), Nîmes (€18.40, 1¼ hours), Arles (€13, 45 minutes), Orange (€20.10, 1½ hours) and other destinations. More than 20 trains go east daily on the Marseille-Vintimille line linking Marseille with Toulon (€10.70, around 45 minutes) and beyond. Marseille–Hyères trains stop at Cassis, Bandol, Ollioules, Sanary-sur-Mer and Toulon.

TAXI // Call **Marseille Taxi** (☎ 04 91 02 20 20) or **Taxis France** (☎ 04 91 49 91 00).

AROUND MARSEILLE

· · · · · ·

Butting up against Marseille's built-up environs are spectacular stretches of coast hiding crystalline coves, charming towns and celebrated vineyards.

The threat of forest fire to the semi-arid flora skirting Marseille's limestone coastline prompts the Office National des Forêts (ONF; National Forests Office) to close Les Calanques each year from 1 July until the second Saturday in September – and at any other time when conditions are too dry. April to June, they're closed on Saturday and Sunday. At other times walkers can usually access footpaths between 6am and 11am only (reduced hours in high-risk conditions) – check with tourist offices for updates. On-the-spot fines are issued for breaching the strictly enforced rules.

LES CALANQUES

Skirting 20km of pristine turquoise coves, Les Calanques (including the 500 sq km of the rugged inland Massif des Calanques) have been protected since 1975. They are most spectacular viewed from a boat and myriad boat excursions leave from Marseille and Cassis to the east, the two gateways into the rocky inlets.

Despite its barren landscape, the massif shelters an extraordinary wealth of flora and fauna – 900 plant species including the protected dwarf red behen, Marseille astragalus and tartonraire sparrow wort. The Bonelli's eagle is a frequent visitor here, as is Europe's largest lizard (the 60cm eyed lizard) and longest snake (the 2m Montpellier snake).

Although largely inaccessible by car, Les Calanques offer ample walking opportunities of varying degrees of difficulty. The coastal GR98 leads south from the Marseille suburb of La Madrague to Callelongue on Cap Croisette, and then east along the coast to Cassis. Count on 11 to 12 hours at least to walk the full 28km stretch across the cliffs. Lonely Planet's *Walking in France* includes step-

---

∽ WORTH A TRIP ∽

From Gémenos, a couple of kilometres east of Aubagne, take the eastbound D2 towards 'Vallée St-Pons & La Ste-Baume'. The going soon gets green and dramatic, the smooth tarmac road snaking uphill through the dry scrubby terrain of the **Parc Départemental de St-Pons**. After 8km, as the sea pops on the horizon, the road narrows. A kilometre and several hairpins later, road markings return for the final 2km climb to the **Col de l'Espigoulier** (728m), a mountain pass with dramatic coastline views.

The winding descent is dominated by the **Massif de la Ste-Baume**, a hulk of a mountain topped by a 12km-long shelf. At the D45a/D2 junction, continue on the D2 to **La Ste-Baume** (8km), from where a 40-minute forest trail leads to the **Grotte de Ste-Madeleine** (950m), a mountain cave where Mary Magdalene is said to have spent the last years of her life. Daily Mass is celebrated at 10.30am. Its entrance offers a breathtaking panorama of Montagne Ste-Victoire, Mont Ventoux and the Alps.

To finish take the D80 northeast via Nans-les-Pins then turn right on the N560 (about 20km all up) to reach the pastel-hued town of **St-Maximin La Ste-Baume**. Its fabulous Gothic **Ste-Madeleine Basilica** (place Jean Salusse) was built in 1295 as the home of what are claimed to be the relics of Mary Magdalene, discovered in a crypt on the site around 1279. Afterwards lunch in the adjacent convent, now the sumptuous **Hôtel Le Couvent Royal** (☎ 04 94 86 55 66; www.hotelfp-saintmaximin.com; place Jean Salusse; d low/high season from €89/96; mains €20; ☉ lunch & dinner daily).

by-step coverage along Les Calanques west from Cassis to Morgiou.

Marseille's tourist office (p48) runs guided walks in the *calanques*. Participants must be aged over eight years and sturdy shoes are a must.

❦ CALANQUE DE SORMIOU //
HIKE HARD FOR LUNCH WITH A
FABULOUS VIEW

The largest rocky inlet hit the headlines in October 1991 when Henri Cosquer, a diver from Cassis, swam through a narrow, 150m-long passage 36m underwater into an underwater cave to find its interior adorned with prehistoric wall-paintings from around 20,000 BC. Now named the **Grotte Cosquer**, the cave is a protected historical monument and closed to the public. Many more are believed to exist.

Two seasonal restaurants in the cove cook up lunch with fabulous views. Perched up above the water, **Le Château** (☎ 04 91 25 08 69; ☽ lunch & dinner Apr–mid-Oct) – nothing at all to do with a château – has all the typical fishy fare, fish soup, mussels, grilled fish and so on, as does **Le Lunch** (☎ 04 91 25 05 39; ☽ Apr–mid-Oct), right by the water. Atmospheric dining, lunch or come dusk, is guaranteed.

To get here by car, follow the southbound av de Hambourg past César's thumb on rond-point Pierre Guerre and follow the Sormiou signs. From the end of chemin de Sormiou, a forest track (a 45-minute walk) leads to Sormiou's small, isolated fishing port and beach. Diners with a table reservation are allowed to drive through; otherwise, it's open to cars weekdays from September to June. By bus take the 23 from the rond-point du Prado metro stop to La Cayolle stop, from where it is a 3km walk.

❦ CALANQUE DE MORGIOU //
A SCENTED WALK TO A DREAMY
LITTLE COVE

The scrubby windswept Cap Morgiou separates Sormiou from Morgiou. Nestled on the eastern side of the cape, this *calanque* has a pretty little port bobbing with a handful of fishing boats, and plenty of sheer rock-faces from which climbers dangle. An evening spent at its one restaurant, the delightful **Nautic Bar** (☎ 04 91 40 06 37; mains €20.25; ☽ lunch & dinner Apr-Oct), is dreamy. Its covered terrace overlooks the boats and a fish-strewn menu comprises various fish *à la provençale* and *supions* (pan-fried squid in garlic) to die for. Look for the pretty peach cottage with a green canopy. No credit cards.

From av de Hambourg, follow the Morgiou road signs past Marseille's sinister prison in Les Beaumettes. Morgiou beach is a good one hour's walk from the car park; the hair-raisingly steep and narrow hairpin-laced road (3.5km) that plunges right down to the rocky inlet is open to motorists Monday to Friday from September to June (daily year-round if you have a table reservation at Nautic Bar).

❦ EN-VAU, PORT-PIN & PORT-
MIOU // EMERALD WATERS
ENCASED BY CLIFFS

Continuing east along the stone-sculptured coast brings you to **Calanque d'En-Vau**, with emerald waters encased by cliffs, where climbers sometimes dangle precariously, and a pebbly beach. Its entrance is guarded by the **Doigt de Dieu** (God's Finger), a giant rock pinnacle. The car park on the Col de la Gardiole (south off the D559), 5km west along a dirt road from Cassis, is closed from July to the second Saturday of September, or when the fire risk is too great.

Accessible when the car park is open, a *steep* three-hour marked trail leads from here to En-Vau. The slippery limestone surface and sheer descents into En-Vau are for the truly hardcore only, and definitely not for those prone to vertigo. Approaching from the east, it is a solid 1½-hour walk on the GR98 from **Calanque de Port-Miou**, immediately west of Cassis. En route you pass the neighbouring **Calanque de Port-Pin**, a 30-minute walk from Port-Miou. Cassis' tourist office distributes free maps of the walking trails leading to these three *calanques*.

CASSIS

pop 7900

Nestled at the foot of a dramatic rocky outcrop crowned by a 14th-century château (now a hotel and only visitable by guests of its five rarefied suites), this St-Tropez–like little fishing port is all charm – hence the crowds that pile into its waterside old town to frolic on the waterfront, play on shingle beaches, visit terraced vineyards and sip fabled white Cassis wine.

CLIFFHANGERS

Europe's highest maritime cliff, the hollow limestone **Cap Canaille** (399m) towers above the southwestern side of **Baie de Cassis** (Cassis Bay). From the top, captivating views unfold across Cassis and **Mont Puget** (564m), the highest peak in the Massif des Calanques.

Offering equally heart-stopping panoramic views, D141 unfurls along the **Route des Crêtes** (Road of Crests; closed during high winds), wiggling 16km along the clifftops from Cassis to La Ciotat.

The town's name has nothing to do with the blackcurrant liqueur (pronounced 'ca-sees') used to create a kir aperitif. Rather it comes from the Roman *Carsicis Portus,* meaning 'crowned port', so christened for the imperial rock Couronne de Charlemagne (Crown of Charlemagne), which is visible from far out to sea.

ESSENTIAL INFORMATION

TOURIST OFFICES // Tourist Office (☎ 08 92 25 98 92; www.ot-cassis.com; quai des Moulins; ⏰ 9am-7pm Mon-Fri, 9.30am-12.30pm & 3-6pm Sat & Sun Jul & Aug, shorter hrs rest of yr)

EXPLORING CASSIS

✿ A SEAFOOD PORTSIDE LUNCH // DINE IN THE COMPANY OF CRISP WHITE CASSIS

It might heave with holidaymakers in summer but there is no disputing the appeal of the **Vieux Port** or, more specifically, sitting down to lunch at one of its dozens of waterside terraces, glass of white in hand. The catch of the day is at its freshest at **La Poissonerie** (☎ 04 42 01 71 56; 5 quai JJ Barthélemy; menu du pêcheur €19.90; ⏰ closed Mon, lunch Thu & Jan), a locals' favourite run by two brothers – one who fishes, one who cooks. Pick from a humble plate of sardines with a glass of white (€13.90), grilled fish (per 100g €7) or a more royal *bouillabaisse* (€38.90). Before leaving, peek in its adjoining fish shop with striped blue-and-white canopy and lovely old tiled interior. No credit cards.

Or buy a shellfish platter to savour on the sand from **La Canaille** (☎ 04 42 01 72 36; 22 quai des Baux; mains €25; ⏰ lunch & dinner), a sleek contemporary restaurant with plane tree-shaded tables and a menu built solely from seafood. September to April, it has *oursins de Cassis* (local sea urchins) chalked on the board for €16 a dozen.

Portside picnics can be built from the pick of Provence's rich, heavenly scented fruit harvest at **Au Paysan de Cassis** (☎ 04 42 01 89 59; 5 rue Séverin), an upmarket greengrocers with an astonishing choice of fresh herbs, courgette flowers, lettuce and other salad leaves, rare tomatoes and so on. Cassis' twice-weekly **market** (place Baragnon; ⊙ Wed & Fri) is an equally tasty affair.

☙ EXPLORING LES CALANQUES // SAIL OR STROLL AROUND SPECTACULAR ROCKY INLETS

Few visit busy Cassis without taking a boat trip to Les Calanques, the drop-dead gorgeous, turquoise coves propped up by dramatic rock formations along its coastline west. Boats sails year-round from Quai St-Pierre at the old port; buy tickets here at the portside **kiosk** (☎ 04 42 01 90 83; www.cassis-calanques.com; sq Gilbert Savon). A 45-minute trip to three *calanques* (Port-Miou, Port-Pin and En-Vau) costs €13/7 per adult/2 to 10 years; a 65-minute trip covering these plus Oule and Devenson *calanques* is €15/10; and a 1½-hour trip covering eight *calanques* (including Morgiou) costs €19/13. In July and August spectacular evening cruises (€13, one hour) depart daily at 10.30pm. No credit cards.

The tourist office has information on **walking itineraries**, including a one-hour trail from the village to Port-Pin, which has a small sandy beach. Not for the faint-hearted is the spectacular, two-hour trail to En-Vau, which climaxes with a very steep descent to the tiny cove's small shingle beach. Before setting out, stock up on drinking water and always check at the tourist office about the risk of forest fire (p403).

Adventurers can **rock climb** up or **deep-sea dive** around Les Calanques. For less ambitious sorts, paddling around the rocks in a **sea kayak** is an equally soul-stirring option. The tourist office has information on all these activities.

☙ WINE TASTING // SWILL, SNIFF, SIP OR SPIT CRISP WHITE WINE

Twelve estates producing the Cassis appellation wines (Appellation d'Origine Contrôlée; AOC) ribbon the hillsides surrounding Cassis; the tourist office has a list of suggested itineraries and estates you can visit to taste and buy – most require advance reservation.

In town, bottle-lined wine bar **Le Chai Cassidain** (☎ 04 42 01 99 80; 7 rue Séverin Icard; ⊙ 11am-1pm & 4-10pm Apr-Oct, 11am-1pm & 4-8pm Tue-Sun Nov-Mar) sells locals wines by the glass and often has free tastings.

On the first Sunday in September, the **Ban des Vendanges** celebrates the grape harvest with a Mass, blessing of the vines, traditional dancing, a joyous street procession and lots of *dégustation* (tasting) alfresco.

TRANSPORT

BUS // Cassis is on the Bandol–Marseille (five daily) and La Ciotat–Aix-en-Provence (three to 12 daily) bus routes; find schedules at www.lepilote.com, in French. Buses stop at rond-point du Pressoir, a five-minute walk along av du Professeur René Leriche and rue de l'Arène to the port.

TRAIN // Cassis train station (av de la Gare), 3.5km east of the centre, is on the Marseille–Hyères rail line with regular daily trains in both directions. Buses 2, 3 and 4 link Cassis train station with the town centre.

CÔTE BLEUE

The contrast between the Côte d'Azur and the Côte Bleue is summed up by their very names. Infinitely more down-to-earth than its romanticised counterpart,

MARSEILLE AREA

the rocky Blue Coast clambers from Marseille's western edge, past gritty fishing villages, to Cap Couronne. Marine-life-rich waters around the sandy cape are protected by the **Parc Régional Marin de la Côte Bleue**.

Inland, the uninhabitable massif **Chaîne de l'Estaque** forms a natural barrier between the Mediterranean and the petrol-producing oil refineries dominating the industralised **Étang de Berre**, a large brine lake.

A weekend favourite with Marseillais, **L'Estaque** (www.estaque.com), abutting the city's northern suburbs, lured artists from the Impressionist, fauvist and cubist movements. A trail follows in the footsteps of Renoir, Cézanne, Dufy and Braque around its port and shabby old town. On the water's edge buy *chichi frégi* (sugar-coated doughnuts) and *panisses* (chickpea-flour cakes) to munch.

♥ LES CALANQUES // REVEL IN A DIZZYING CLUSTER OF ROCKY INLETS

The Côte Bleue has its own precious trove of *calanques*, which competes with the best of those everyone knows between Marseille and Cassis. Spend a day discovering them by car and on foot. First up is **Calanque de Niolon**, 12km west of L'Estaque. Rocky spurs and hillocks ensnare the perilously perched village of Niolon, which has a handful of cafés and the lovely **Auberge du Mérou** (☎ 04 91 46 98 69; www.aubergedumerou.fr, in French; menus €28 & €34), with a terrace peering down on rocks and water. Its upside-down onion-tart topped with local *brousses du Rove* (goat's-milk cheese from Rove, 5km north) alone is worth the trip. You can also find the cheese at the village *épicerie,* should you fancy some to take away.

Further west is the clustered trio of **La Redonne, Les Figuières** and **Méjean.** From the tiny waterside Port du Redonne, a single-track road controlled by a traffic light climbs up and over to Les Figuières (1km), the Petit Méjean (1.7km) and the Grand Méjean (1.8km). On foot count 50 gorgeous scenic minutes from Port du Redonne to the latter, or two hours from Redonne to Niolon. In Grand Méjean you can pick up a stunning 2.1km-long coastal trail to **Calanque de l'Érevine**; even if you don't have time for the full monty it's worth hiking up the rock-embedded steps at the start of the trail to inhale breathtaking Marseille city and coastal views.

♥ CARRY-LE-ROUET // GET HIGH ON SEA URCHINS

There is one exquisite reason to visit this harbour town 17km west of L'Estaque: prickly *oursins* (sea urchins) can only be caught off the coast of Carry-le-Route between September and April; fishing for them in summer, when they reproduce, is forbidden. Several restaurants on its old-port quays serve *châtaignes de mer* (sea chestnuts), particularly exquisite in the company of chilled Cassis white wine. At **Le Scoop** (☎ 04 42 06 17 22; www.brasserielescoop.fr; quai Professeur Émile Vayssière; mains €18; ☺ lunch & dinner), a contemporary bistro with wood-decking terrace, locals begin with a starter of a dozen sea urchins (€11), followed by a *dégustation de coquillages* platter piled high with oysters, mussels, *palourdes* (clams), king prawns and so on as a main.

Each year, on the first three Sundays of February, Carry-le-Rouet's sea-urchin festival, **L'Oursinade**, sees a giant open-air picnic spill across the old-port quays, allowing everyone to taste the delicacy around shared tables. For more details contact Carry **tourist office** (☎ 04 42 13 20 36; www.carry-lerouet.com, in French; av Aristide Briand; ☺ 10am-noon & 2-5pm Tue-Sat).

☙ SAUSSET-LES-PINS // SHOP FOR FRESH FISH AND NAIL-SIZED TELLINES

Don't expect to find any manicuring at this gritty fishing port with rocky coastline, immediately west of Carry-le-Rouet. Fishing boats pull into the harbour each day to offload their catch at the early-morning fish market (look for the sign *'Ventes de Poissons frais'*), and a block in from the water a trio of mouth-watering *poissonneries* (fishmongers) sell a heady choice of fish. **Poissonnerie du Port** (☎ 04 42 45 62 20; 22 av Siméon Gouin) sells magnificent *plateaux de coquillages* (shellfish platters) ready to go, as well as fresh mackerel, red mullet and everything you need for *bouillabaisse.* A few doors down, **Poissonnerie du Golfe** (☎ 04 42 45 05 50; 1 av Clement Monnier) is the place for *tellines:* buy a kilo (€14.20) or so of the delicate-pink nail-sized clams, soak in salty water (use gros sel, 'coarse salt') for several hours to get rid of the sand, drain, and pan-fry with finely-chopped garlic and baby onions in cream and a little white wine.

☙ MARTIGUES // LUNCH IN VENICE

Dip deep and a chink of picture-postcard quaintness can still be found in this large and sprawling fishing port on the shore of the Étang de Berre. Indeed, indulge in lunch or dinner at **Le Miroir aux Oiseaux** (☎ 04 42 80 50 45; quai Brescon; mains €23, menus €17.50, €24.50 & €35.50; ☺ closed Wed evening & Sat lunch), perched on the edge of a canal on a little island criss-crossed with bridges, and the town's nickname – the 'Venice of Provence' – is suddenly believable. Inside an old fisherman's house with pale-grey shutters and a leafy veranda out front, the old-town restaurant cooks up a bounty of seafood: *poutargue* (the 'caviar of the Provence', made with mullet eggs, which are salted, dried and pressed into lumps, costing a hefty €150 per kilo), *mêlets* (anchovies prepared with fennel) and other catch of the day. Book ahead to reserve a table on its gorgeous terrace, which is inches from colourful old rowing boats, paint peeling, bobbing on the canal in front.

SALON DE PROVENCE

pop 40,850

Oil from the olive groves shrouding this small medieval-walled town go into its best-known product, *savon de Marseille* (Marseille soap). A former residence of the Arles bishops, Salon de Provence was where philosopher Nostradamus (1503–66) wrote his prophecies. Its many art deco facades are a legacy of an earthquake that struck in 1909, forcing a rebuild.

Should eight jets suddenly roar above your head in a puff of tricolour smoke, do not fear: it's just the École de l'Air – France's Red Arrows, stationed here since 1937 – out on a jaunt. The military school can't be visited but its pilots take to the skies to practise most afternoons when at home.

The **tourist office** (☎ 04 90 56 27 60; www.visitsalondeprovence.com, in French; 56 cours Gimon; ☺ 9.30am-6.30pm Mon-Sat & to 12.30pm Sun Jul & Aug, 9.30am-12.30pm & 2-6pm Mon-Sat Sep-Jun) runs various guided tours, including visits to a nearby olive farm.

EXPLORING SALON DE PROVENCE

☙ VIEILLE VILLE // PHILOSOPHERS, BISHOPS AND A SMOKED BLACK VIRGIN

Delve into the old town, fortified in the 12th century, from place Crousillat,

Salon's prettiest square, which has a couple of tree-shaded café terraces overlooking the giant mushroom-shaped, moss-covered **Fontaine Moussue**. From 1547 until his death in 1566, the philosopher Nostradamus lived in a small house within the walls of the city, the **Maison de Nostradamus** (☎ 04 90 56 64 31; 11 rue Nostradamus; adult/7-18yr €3.05/2.30; 9am-noon & 2-6pm Mon-Fri, 2-6pm Sat & Sun). His remains lie behind a plaque inside the Gothic 14th-century **Collégiale St-Laurent** (place St-Laurent). After visiting here, hike up to **Château de l'Empéri** (☎ 04 90 56 22 36; place du Château; adult/7-18yr €3.05/2.30; 10am-noon & 2-6pm Wed-Mon), home to the archbishops of Arles from the 9th to the 18th centuries. Only go inside the castle if pre-WWI French military history is your thing. A combined ticket for both museums is €5.35/3.05.

Within the old walls, **La Table du Roy** (☎ 04 90 56 53 42; 35 rue Moulin d'Isnard; menus €18-28, mains €20; lunch & dinner Wed-Sun), with its lovely old facade, and the more contemporary **L'Atelier de Michel Medhi** (☎ 04 90 55 67 39; place des Centuries; lunch menus €9.60 & €12.30; lunch & dinner Tue-Sat), beneath the château, are recommended lunch addresses.

Leave the old town through the **Tour du Bourg Neuf**, a city gate graced by a statue of the Black Virgin, whose ebony colour supposedly comes from the smoke of candles held by women who venerated it in the 13th century hoping to conceive.

🍴 SAVONNERIES // LEARN HOW SOAP IS MADE

From the turn of the 20th century until the 1950s, soap was a buoyant business thanks to Salon's abundance of olive oil and the exotic palm and copra oils that arrived in nearby Marseille from the French colonies. Run by three generations of the same family, the **Savonnerie Marius Fabre** (☎ 04 90 53 24 77; www.marius -fabre.fr; 148 av Paul Borret; admission with/without guided tour €3.85/3; 9.30am-noon & 2-5pm Mon-Thu, to 4pm Fri, guided tours 10.30am Mon & Thu), dating from 1900, paints a vivid portrait of the industry with its small museum.

The inner workings of the **Savonnerie Rampal-Latour** (☎ 04 90 56 07 28; www .rampal-latour.com; 71 rue Félix Pyat; admission free; 8am-noon & 2-6pm Mon-Fri, guided tours 10.30am Tue & Fri) are also revealed to visitors; buy soap at cheaper factory prices in its beautiful 1907 boutique.

🍴 LA SALLE À MANGER // DINE FINE IN A SECRET GARDEN

With its elegant creamy facade interspersed with delicate aqua-blue wooden shutters and ornate wrought-iron balconies, this 19th-century *hôtel particulier* (private mansion) promises great things. And indeed, dining at the **Dining Room** (☎ 04 90 56 28 01; 6 rue du Maréchal Joffre; menu €27; lunch & dinner Tue-Sat) is a truly Provençal experience. Aperitifs are served in the company of a lavender dip, several mains fuse French with world tastes, and a choice of 40 desserts – including thyme, lavender and rosemary sorbet – is the icing on the cake. For less feisty and/or fast appetites the lunchtime *express du midi* (€15) is perfect.

TRANSPORT

BUS // From the **bus station** (☎ 04 90 56 50 98; cnr bd Maréchal Foch & bd Victor Joly) there are regular daily services to/from Aix-en-Provence (€5.20, 35 minutes) and Arles (€5.20, 1¼ hours).

TRAIN // From the **train station** (av Émile Zola), a 1km-walk from town, trains run to/from Marseille (€9, one hour) and Avignon (€8.80, one hour).

PAYS D'AIX

· · · · · ·

It's hard to believe picturesque Pays d'Aix (Aix Country), within which oh-so-elegant Aix-en-Provence is ensconced, is just 25km or so from chaotic Marseille.

AIX-EN-PROVENCE

pop 145,700

A pocket of left-bank Parisian chic deep in Provence, Aix (pronounced like the letter X) is all class: its leafy boulevards and public squares are lined with 17th- and 18th-century mansions, punctuated by gurgling moss-covered fountains. Haughty stone lions guard its grandest avenue, café-laced cours Mirabeau, where fashionable Aixois pose on polished pavement terraces sipping overpriced espresso.

Aix marks the spot where Roman forces enslaved the inhabitants of the Ligurian Celtic stronghold of Entremont, 3km north. In 123 BC the military camp was named Aquae Sextiae (Waters of Sextius) for the thermal springs that still flow today. In the 12th century the counts of Provence proclaimed Aix their capital, which it remained until the Revolution when it was supplanted by Marseille. The city became a centre of culture under arts patron King René (1409–80): painter Paul Cézanne and novelist Émile Zola are its most famous sons.

Like Paris' left bank, Aix is a prestigious student hub (its university dates from 1409) and is pricier than other Provençal towns.

ESSENTIAL INFORMATION

EMERGENCIES // Centre Hospitalier du Pays d'Aix (☎ 04 42 33 50 00; www.ch-aix.fr, in French; av des Tamaris) Hospital. **Police Station**

(☎ 04 42 93 97 00; 10 av de l'Europe). **SOS Médecins** (☎ 04 42 26 24 00) Emergency medical care (phone only).

TOURIST INFORMATION // Tourist Office (☎ 04 42 16 11 61; www.aixenprovencetourism.com; 2 place du Général de Gaulle; ☾ 8.30am-7pm Mon-Sat, 10am-1pm & 2-6pm Sun) Extended hours in summer. In the basement, the **billetterie** (☾ 9.30am-6pm Mon-Sat) sells festival, concert and event tickets.

EXPLORING AIX-EN-PROVENCE

Exploring this fountain-blessed city is all art, architecture and elegance. First up, buy the appropriate pass at the tourist office: the **Aix City Pass** (€15), valid five days, includes a guided walking tour and admission to the Atelier Paul Cézanne, Jas de Bouffan and Musée Granet; the **Pass Trio** (€15) covers three museums; and the **Visa** (€2) yields a stash of discounts on admission fees in and around Aix.

❦ COURS MIRABEAU // DON YOUR SHADES AND HIT THE CATWALK

No avenue better epitomises Provence's most graceful city than mythical **cours Mirabeau**, sprinkled with elegant Renaissance *hôtels particuliers* and crowned with a summertime roof of leafy green plane trees. Named after the revolutionary hero Comte de Mirabeau, it was laid out in the 1640s and has been the city's literal and spiritual heart ever since. Cézanne and Zola famously hung out at **Les Deux Garçons** (☎ 04 42 26 00 51; 53 cours Mirabeau), one of a clutch of pavement cafés on the street's southern side. Riding high on its lavish history (the café dates from 1792), Les Deux Garçons buzzes with people-watchers and poseurs beneath its racing-green canopy despite its elevated prices and mediocre food.

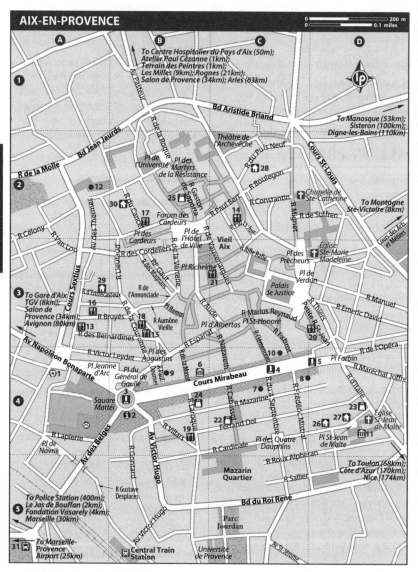

AIX-EN-PROVENCE

Fountains stud the cours' length. The eclectic **Fontaine de la Rotonde** (1860) bookends it at the west with a trio of lion-guarded sculptures representing Justice, the Arts and Agriculture; and at its eastern end King René clasps a bunch of muscat grapes atop the statue-adorned **Fontaine du Roi René** (1819). Midway along, the mossy mound of **Fontaine d'Eau Chaude** (1734) spouts 34°C water.

Its collection of *hôtels particuliers* is equally gawp-worthy: among the most impressive is **Hôtel d'Espargnet** (1647) at No 38, now home to the university's economics department. The Marquis of Entrecasteaux murdered his wife in their family home, **Hôtel d'Isoard de Vauvenarges** (1710) at No 10; and photography and contemporary art gets an airing inside **Hôtel de Castillon**, now the **Galérie d'Art du Conseil Général des Bouches du Rhône** (☎ 04 42 93 03 67; 21bis cours Mirabeau; admission free; 🕑 10.15am-12.45pm & 1.30-6.30pm Mon-Sat).

🌱 MUSÉE GRANET // WORLD-CLASS ART IN THE CHIC MAZARIN QUARTIER

South of cours Mirabeau lies the 17th-century street-grid of the stylish Mazarin Quartier, peppered with some splendid Renaissance buildings – the city's priciest real estate. **Place des Quatre Dauphins**, with its elegant frame of *hôtels particuliers* and fish-spouting fountain (1667) at its heart, is particularly enchanting.

The Mazarin Quartier's crown jewel is the **Musée Granet** (☎ 04 42 52 88 32; www.museegranet-aixenprovence.fr; place St-Jean de Malte; adult/under 18yr €4/free, first Sun of month free; 🕑 11am-7pm Tue-Sun Jun-Sep, noon-6pm Tue-Sun Oct-May), an exceptional art museum at home in a 17th-century priory of the Knights of Malta and named after the Provençal painter François Marius Granet (1775–1849), who donated a large number of works. Its collections include

16th- to 20th-century Italian, Flemish and French paintings, including the museum's pride and joy – nine Cézanne works. Admission fees differ during temporary exhibitions.

🌱 CÉZANNE SIGHTS // SEE WHERE THIS LOCAL LAD ATE, DRANK, PAINTED, DIED

His star may not have reached its giddiest heights until after his death, but the life of local lad Paul Cézanne (1839–1906) is treasured in Aix. To see where he ate, drank, studied and painted, pick up the **Sur Les Pas de Cézanne** (In the Footsteps of Cézanne) brochure at the tourist office and follow the mapped walking itinerary around town, from the house where he was born at 28 rue de l'Opéra to cafés he frequented, his apartments at 14 rue de la Glacière and 14 rue Matheron, and so on.

In 1859 Cézanne's father bought **Le Jas de Bouffan** (☎ 04 42 16 10 91; adult/13-25yr €5.50/2; 🕑 guided tours 10.30am-5.30pm daily Jun-Sep, 10.30am-5.30pm Tue, Thu & Sat Apr, May & Oct, 10am Wed & Sat Jan-Feb), a country manor west of Aix centre where Cézanne painted furiously – 36 oils and 17 watercolours in the decades that followed depicting the house, farm, chestnut alley, green park and so forth. Visits are by guided tour only and must be reserved in advance at the tourist office. To get to Le Jas de Bouffan, take bus 6 from La Rotonde (av Victor Hugo) to the Corsy stop; by foot it is a 20-minute walk from town.

In 1895 the Aixois artist rented a *cabanon* (cabin) at **Les Carrières de Bibemus** (☎ 04 42 16 10 91; adult/13-25yr €6.60/3.10; ☉ guided tours 9.45am daily Jun-Sep, 10.30am-5pm Mon, Wed, Fri & Sun Apr, May & Oct, 3pm Wed & Sat Jan-Mar) on the edge of town where he painted prolifically. Atmospheric one-hour tours of the ochre quarry take visitors on foot through the dramatic burnt-orange rocks Cézanne captured so vividly on canvas. Book tours in advance at the tourist office, wear sturdy shoes and avoid wearing white.

Cezanne's final stop was the studio he had built on a piece of land he bought in 1901. Ironically the most visited but the least inspirational of all the Cézanne sights, the **Atelier Paul Cézanne** (☎ 04 42 21 06 53; www.atelier-cezanne.com; 9 av Paul Cézanne; adult/13-25yr €5.50/2; ☉ 10am-noon & 2-5pm, to 6pm Apr-Jun & Sep, 10am-6pm Jul & Aug) doesn't hold any works by Cézanne but rather recreates his studio. Not all the tools and still-life models (recognise that green glass bottle?!) strewn around the single room were his; many were added by the scholar who bought the studio after Cézanne's death. The tall wooden frame in one corner is not an easel but rather a cherry-picking ladder Cézanne used to paint the studio walls grey. Take bus 1 from La Rotonde (av des Belges) to the Cézanne stop and walk five minutes downhill to the mustard house, or walk the 1.5km from town.

A 10-minute walk uphill from the bus stop is the **Terrain des Peintres** (opp 62 av Paul Cézanne), a wonderful terraced garden perfect for a picnic, from where Cézanne, among others, painted the Montagne Ste-Victoire (p75). The view of the jagged mountain is inspirational.

❧ FONDATION VASARELY // THINK ABSTRACT WITH THE FATHER OF OP ART

Abstract geometric shapes create bold 3D illusions inside this **temple to optical art** (☎ 04 42 20 01 09; www.fondation vasarely.fr; 1 av Marcel Pagnol; adult/7-18yr €7/4; ☉ 10am-1pm & 2-6pm Tue-Sat), 4km west of town in Jas de Bouffan. The Bauhaus-style construction linking 16 hexagonal spaces was built in 1976 to house the works of Hungarian artist Victor Vasarely (1906–97), who lived and worked in Paris from the 1930s – it was he who designed the museum. Take bus 4 from La Rotonde (av Napoleon Bonaparte) to the Vasarely stop.

❧ THERMES SEXTIUS // BLISS OUT ROMAN STYLE

When in Aix, do as the Romans did back in the 1st century BC with some old-fashioned pampering at these modern **thermal spas** (☎ 04 42 23 81 82; www.thermes-sextius.com; 55 cours Sextius). Built on the site of Roman Aquae Sextiae's thermal springs, the excavated remains of the Roman spa are displayed beneath glass in the lobby. Decadent hydrotherapy treatments include a 'Zen spray massage' beneath warm thermal water mixed with essential oils (€69); a simple day's access to the fitness centre costs €42, and all-day pampering packages start at €89. Fancy a body scrub with Camargue *fleur de sel* (salt crystals)?

FESTIVALS & EVENTS

Festival du Tambourin (Tambourine Festival) Two-day festival; mid-April.

Festival d'Aix-en-Provence (www.festival -aix.com) Aix's sumptuous cultural calendar is capped by this month-long festival of classical music, opera and ballet; July.

GASTRONOMIC HIGHLIGHTS

Aix excels at Provençal cuisine and terraces spill across backstreet squares (see below). On cours Mirabeau adopt the local savvy approach of 'look but don't touch' or rather look but don't sit down: you can sample substantially more startling and better value cuisine elsewhere in the city.

☙ CHARLOTTE €

☎ 04 42 26 77 56; 32 rue des Bernardines; menus €15 & €18.50; ⟡ lunch & dinner Tue-Sat

It's all very cosy at Charlotte, a real family affair where everyone knows everyone, based on the amount of *bisous* (kissing) going on. The owner spends most of his time sitting down at tables chatting, and the cuisine is equally homely. French classics like veal escalope and beef steak fill the handwritten menu – interwoven with family pics in a fuchsia-pink photo album – and there are always a couple of imaginative *plats du jour* (daily specials), which regulars always plump for. In summer everything moves into the garden.

☙ CHEZ FÉRAUD €€

☎ 04 42 63 07 27; 8 rue Puits Juif; lunch menu Tue-Fri €22; ⟡ lunch & dinner Tue-Sat Sep-Jul

Conjure up a quintessential image of Provence and that's Chez Féraud. From the olive tree growing out front to the pale grey wooden shutters and vine-covered facade, this family-run restaurant tucked down a side street is as pretty as a picture. Cuisine is equally Provençal, with all the classics – *soupe au pistou, aubergine en gratin,* red peppers stuffed with *brandade de morue,* sheep tripe et al – chalked on the board. Unsurprisingly, the wine list is almost exclusively AOC Coteaux d'Aix-en-Provence.

☙ CHEZ GRAND MÈRE €€

☎ 04 42 53 33 47; 1 rue des Bernardines; mains €20, menus €21.50 & €28.50; ⟡ lunch & dinner Tue-Sat, lunch Sun

Staunchly Provençal cuisine bubbling up in grandma's cooking pot aside, the main draw of this traditional address is its old-town location on pretty place des Corses. Get here early to snag one of the two tables teetering beneath striped awning on the square, then tuck into classics like frogs' legs, homemade *pieds et paquets* (sheep tripe), *alouettes sans tête* (stuffed parcels of finely sliced beef) or a simple plate of *pistou*-doused tagliatelles.

TOP FIVE

ALFRESCO APERÓS

Vieil Aix is saturated with old-town stone squares overflowing with cafés made for people-watching over coffee, *citron pressé* (freshly squeezed lemon juice) or dusk-time *apéros* (aperitifs). Particularly adorable:

★ **Place de l'Hôtel de Ville** – a square one step off the tourist track

★ **Place des Cardeurs & Forum des Cardeurs** – with dozens of tables astride beautiful old cobblestones, this is Aix's loveliest evening venue

★ **Place Ramus** – buskers often strike up on this restaurant-filled square off pedestrian rue Annonciade

★ **Place d'Albertas** – musicians often play on midsummer nights on this pretty fountain-clad square just west of place St-Honoré

★ **Place des Augustins** – another fountain-pierced cutie

♥ LA CHIMIÈRE CAFÉ €€

☎ 04 42 38 30 00; www.lachimerecafe.com, in French; 1 rue Bruyès; menus €28 & €32; ☽ lunch & dinner Tue-Sun

Well hidden down a dusty deserted lane where no one much goes bar those who live there, this small, select address stacks up theatrical baroque on three floors. Tables are tightly packed Parisian style, glass chandeliers light up the blue room, birds flit across the sky in the bar and to say the *salle rouge* is red is an understatement. It's trendy year-round, but particularly hot in winter. Food is classic French.

♥ LA TOMATE VERTE €€

☎ 04 42 60 04 58; www.latomateverte.com, in French; 15 rue des Tanneurs; menus €26 & €29; ☽ lunch & dinner Tue-Sat

Start with a green tomato *tarte tatin* at this strikingly contemporary, apple-green bistro much appreciated by local Aixois who love their food. The interior is crisp, smart and forms a marvellous stage for the deliciously modern but staunchly Provençal fare.

♥ LE PASSAGE €

☎ 04 42 37 09 00; www.le-passage.fr, in French; 10 rue Villars; mains €15, menus €13-35; ☽ 10am-midnight; ♿

This bustling concept restaurant is modern, cavernous and ideal for getting lost in the Aixois lunchtime crowd. In a rejuvenated 19th-century *calisson* factory, operational until the 1950s, it oozes industrial panache: metal walkways strung with tables criss-cross four floors, a glass roof tops the space and B&W photos of the factory hang on the walls in the loos. Fare is bistro (seafood platters, steak tartare etc) and the place is constantly innovating: jazz on Monday, Sunday brunch, Thai on the second floor, cooking courses and so on.

♥ LE POIVRE D'ANE €€

☎ 04 42 21 32 66; 40 place des Cardeurs; menus €27, €33 & €45; ☽ lunch & dinner

Fancy a haddock milkshake, duck sushi or thyme and cinnamon apple tart with Baileys whipped cream? This young kid on the gastronomic block is the talk of the town: its contemporary cuisine is creative and stylish, its chefs (whose 'whites' are bold red) mixing plenty of bright-eyed quirks in with traditional Provençal ingredients. Decor is bold chic – one wall is orange – and in summer its designer tables spill across one of Aix's loveliest pedestrian squares (see boxed text, p73).

♥ L'OFFICE €€

☎ 04 42 54 14 25; http://loffice-sfw.com, in French; Petite Rue St-Jean; menus €24 & €31.50; ☽ lunch & dinner Tue-Sat

A great big creativity stamp marks this modern glass-fronted space, tucked down a quiet lane near the Palais de Justice. 'Slow food & wine' is its strapline, which translates as authentic market cuisine cooked up in a designer setting: think 1950s-style lighting, raw concrete bar, transparent bar stools and a lovely wine list that calls rosés 'pinkies' and dessert wines 'sweeties'. Suited crowds flock to the Office for its good-value weekday *formule* (€16.80 for a main course, glass of wine and coffee).

♥ PRODUCE MARKET

place Richelme

No spot in Aix revs up your tastebuds more than the city's premier food market, where trestle tables groan each morning under the weight of marinated olives, goats' cheese, garlic, lavender, honey, peaches, melons, cherries and a bounty of other buxom sun-kissed fruit, veg and seasonal foods. Plane trees provide ample shade on the atmospheric T-shaped square, endowed with a couple of corner cafés where Aixois catch up on the gossip over *un café* post–market shop.

RECOMMENDED SHOPS

Shopping is at its most chic along pedestrian rue Marius Reynaud, which winds behind the Palais de Justice on place de Verdun (host to a flea market Tuesday, Thursday and Saturday mornings). Elegant fashion boutiques also grace cours Mirabeau.

Rainbows of flowers fill place des Prêcheurs (Sunday morning) and place de l'Hôtel de Ville (Tuesday, Thursday and Saturday mornings) during the colourful weekly flower markets.

Book in Bar (☎ 04 42 26 60 07; www.bookin bar.com; 4 rue Cabassol) is a fabulous English bookshop with café.

TRANSPORT

BIKE // Pick up a pair of wheels at one of 16 street stations embraced by the city-bike scheme **V'Hello** (www.vhello.fr, in French; 1st hr free, next half-hr €1, subsequent hr per hr €2); machines only accept chip-and-pin credit cards.

BUS // From Aix **bus station** (☎ 04 42 91 26 80, 08 91 02 40 25; av de l'Europe) there are regular daily buses to/from Marseille (€4.50, 35 minutes), Arles (€10, 1¾ hours), Avignon (€14, one hour) and Toulon (€10, one hour). Half-hourly **shuttles** (☎ 04 42 93 59 13) link the bus station with Gare d'Aix TGV train station (€3.70) and Marseille-Provence airport (€7.80), 25km south. Intercity buses run by **Aix en Bus** (☎ 04 42 26 37 28; www.aixenbus.com, in French; 2 place du Général de Gaulle; single/carnet of 10 tickets €1.10/7.70; ☙ 8.30am-7pm Mon-Sat), with a desk inside the tourist office, stop at La Rotonde.

CAR // Navigating the one-way, three-lane orbital system encircling the old town can be nightmarish in heavy traffic. Find major car-hire companies next to the Gare d'Aix TGV train station.

PARKING // Street parking spaces are like hen's teeth, but pricier covered parking is plentiful.

TRAIN // Non-TGV trains chug between Aix **central train station** and Marseille (€7.80, 35 minutes, at least 18 daily). TGV services to/from Marseille (€7.90, 15 minutes), Avignon (€24.50, 20 minutes) and Nice (€35.60, 3¾ hours) use Gare d'Aix TGV train station, 8km west.

TAXI // Call ☎ 04 42 27 71 11 or ☎ 04 42 21 61 61.

AROUND AIX

Mountains immortalised in oil and watercolour by Cézanne, a grisly WWII concentration camp (p77) and some fabulous lunch addresses are just a short drive from Aix. North slumbers Rognes (pop 4191), a small village known for its big Grand Marché Truffes et Gastronomie (Truffle & Gastronomy Market), celebrated the Sunday before Christmas: 75% of Provence black truffles are unearthed here (for more on truffles, see also p364).

🌱 MONTAGNE STE-VICTOIRE // GO GREEN IN AIX'S MAGNIFICENT MOUNTAIN RIDGE

Heading east from Aix along the D17, you pass artists at their easels recreating Cézanne's favourite haunt, the magnificent silvery mountain ridge of Montagne Ste-Victoire, with its dry slopes carpeted in *garrigue* (scented scrub), lower lush pine forests, burnt-orange soil and pea-green Coteaux d'Aix-en-Provence vineyards.

Le Relais de Cézanne (☎ 04 42 66 91 91; place du Village; salads/pizza €13/10, menus €24.50 & €30.50) in Le Tholonet, 9km east, is a handy roadside lunch spot. Nearby, the **Sentier Au Fil d'Eau** encourages amblers to discover local flora and fauna along a 7km-long walking trail (two hours). Mountains more info on walking

SWEET TREAT

Aix's sweetest treat since one of King René's wedding banquets (he married twice and sources differ as to which it was) is the *calisson,* a diamond-shaped marzipan-like sweet, 12g to 14g in weight, cut out on a sheet of communion wafer and topped with royal white icing. When plague came into town in 1630, *calissons* supposedly staved off the disease – each year on the first Sunday in September *calissons* are still brought to church and blessed to honour the city's patron saint, Virgo of the Seds.

By the start of the 20th century some 20 *calissonniers* had set up shop in Aix; nine traditional *calissonniers* remain today including **Maison Bechard** (12 cours Mirabeau), **Brémond** (16 rue d'Italie) and **Roy René** (www.calisson.com; rue Gaston de Saporta), which also makes creamy *glace calissons d'Aix* (*calisson* ice cream) and fruity fig, lemon and other colourful variations of the traditional recipe. Roy René runs *calisson*-making workshops for four or five people (€100) and has a tiny museum in its basement showing how *calissons* are made.

To watch the process first-hand, visit its factory **Calissons du Roy René** (☎ 04 42 39 29 90; admission €1; ☷ 10am Tue & Thu), wedged between Botanic and Picard on the Pôle Commercial de la Pioline on the fringe of the city in Aix-les-Milles. Just 1% of the obligatory ground almonds, sugar and candied melon that go into a *calisson d'Aix* can be varied, hence the smidgen of candied orange that Roy René adds to its *calissons.*

Eight plainly wrapped *calissons* (100g) cost €4.

and mountain biking in this scenic scape can be picked up at the **Maison de Ste-Victoire** (☎ 04 42 66 84 40; www .grandsitesaintevictoire.com, in French; ☷ 10am-6.30pm Mon-Fri, 10.15am-7pm Sat & Sun Jul & Aug, 9.30am-6pm Mon-Fri, 10.15am-7pm Sat & Sun Apr, Jun, Sep & Oct, 9.30am-6pm Nov-Mar), 5km further east along the D17 in St-Antonin-sur-Bayon. Save the roads that cross it, the entire mountain is closed between 1 July and 1 September due to the threat of forest fire.

Returning to Aix via the westbound D10, you pass Vauvenargues, home to 14th-century **Château de Vauvenargues**, where Picasso is buried. The red-brick castle, bought by the artist in 1958 and his home between 1959 and 1961, still belongs to the Picassos and, despite exceptionally opening its doors to visitors for a few special months in 2009, it remains firmly closed for the moment.

☙ DOMAINE DE LA BRILLANE // TASTE, SLEEP, DREAM FINE ORGANIC WINE

A superb experience, this organic wine-making estate just 7km north of Aix-en-Provence is the stuff of dreams. In 2001 English investment banker Rupert Birch traded in a high-flying career in the finance world for **Domaine de la Brillane** (☎ 04 42 54 21 44, 06 80 93 55 63; www .labrillane.com; rte de Couteron; ☷ wine tasting 9am-1pm Sat & by appointment), a brilliant ochre-coloured château surrounded by a sea of vineyards. Rupert tirelessly restored the château and worked with partner Mary to build the sterling reputation their estate has today. For the ultimate experience, stay in one of their gorgeous *chambres d'hôtes* (p380). Domaine de la Brillane is signposted 1km off the northbound D13 from Aix to St-Canadet; an unpaved road twists through vineyards for the last 500m until, suddenly, you're round the bend and wow – the vivid rust-coloured château sitting like an elegant ship among the vines stops you in your tracks.

☙ VENTABREN // THE CLASSIC PROVENÇAL LUNCH OUT
Something of a secret, this delightful hilltop village (population 5000, altitude 238m), 16km west of Aix-en-Provence, provides the perfect lazy day out. Meander its narrow cobbled lanes and take in the *maisons de village* of golden stone, faded wooden shutters and pretty green-leaf camouflage; peep inside its 17th-century church; and hike uphill to enjoy panoramic views of Ste-Victoire, Étang de Berre and northern Luberon from the ruins of **Château de la Reine Jeanne**. The **tourist office** (☎ 04 42 28 76 47; www.ventabren.fr, in French; 4 bd de Provence) has information on more challenging walks and horse treks.

Reason itself to visit Ventabren is **La Table de Ventabren** (☎ 04 42 28 79 33; www .latabledeventabren.com; 1 rue Cézanne, Ventabran; menus €30, €39 & €40; ☽ lunch & dinner Tue & Thu-Sat, dinner Wed, lunch Sun), a one-star Michelin restaurant with a canvas-canopied terrace looking out to mountains on the horizon – magical on starry summer evenings. Inside, exposed stone walls, smart Alessi crockery, coffee with green sugar and pink nougat are design-led details that make this stylish address so very special. Chef Dan Bessoudo creates inventive, wholly modern French dishes and his desserts – a menagerie of themed tastes – are out of this world.

☙ 2CV EXPERIENCE.COM // CRUISE AROUND PROVENCE IN A MYTHICAL 2CV
Grab the picnic basket, upload some Mamas & Papas onto the MP3 player

MARSEILLE AREA

∼ WORTH A TRIP ∼

Drive 6km west of Aix along the D9 to **Camp des Milles** (☎ 04 42 24 33 02; chemin de la Badesse, Les Milles; ☽ 9am-noon & 12.45-5pm Mon-Fri), a red-brick tile factory that manufactured 30,000 tonnes of bricks and tiles a year from 1882 until 31 August 1939, when it became a WWII concentration camp. By June 1940 some 3500 artists and intellectuals – predominantly Germans living around Marseille, including surrealist painters Max Ernst (1891–1976) and Hans Bellmer (1902–75) – were interned here. Frescoes painted by the prisoners on the refectory walls remain untouched, as does a railway carriage used to transport prisoners from Les Milles to Drancy and onto Auschwitz; chemin des Deportées opposite the factory entrance leads to the **Wagon Souvenir de la Deportation** (☎ 04 42 16 11 61, 04 42 24 20 30; ☽ by appointment only).

Search out light relief with a stroll beneath **Aqueduc de Roquefavour**, the world's largest stone aqueduct, built in 1861 to transport water from the River Durance to Marseille; continue south along the D9, bear north along the D543, then west along the D65 to find it. Afterwards lunch at **Hôtel-Restaurant Arquier** (☎ 04 42 24 20 45; www.arquier-restaurant-hotel.com; 2980 rte du Petit-Moulin, Roquefavour; mains €18, menus €27-37; ☽ lunch & dinner Tue-Sat, lunch Sun), an inn with plane trees outside and copper pans inside. Walnut bread is home-baked and regional specialities are flagged on the menu with a *marmite* (casserole pot): eg pikeperch in creamy *calisson* sauce followed by a sweet *calisson moelleux* (melt). Terrace tables proffer a slither view of the stone arches.

and get set to cruise along narrow vine-laced lanes, roof open, in a mythical 2CV. An inspired idea, the classic car launched in the 1950s as the ultimate economy vehicle can be rented for the day from **2CV Experience.com** (☎ 06 06 43 75 43; www.2cvexperience.com; Villa Le Morandière, 21 chemin des Petites Plaines, chemin des Nouradons; rental day/weekend/week €159/259/599; ⊗ 9am-noon & 3-9pm), 16km west of Aix in Ventabren. Rates include suggested one-day 150km-long driving itineraries and, for one-day rentals, a picnic hamper.

THE CAMARGUE

3 PERFECT DAYS

❦ DAY 1 // VAN GOGH'S ARLES

Celts, Greeks and Romans shaped this colourful city, but the most indelible modern legacy is that of Van Gogh (p89). See his canvases come to life on the banks of the Rhône, on place du Forum with its yellow café, and in the mighty Roman amphitheatre best visited during a bullfight (see boxed text, p90).

❦ DAY 2 // NATURE FEST

Grab your binoculars and flock with the birds to the southeast corner of this extraordinary wetland: study its flora at La Capelière (p97) and watch flamingos wade through springtime irises at Salin de Badon (p97). End the nature fest with a horse trek through purple-flowered sea lavender and carp-pocked lakes at Domaine de la Palissade (p98).

❦ DAY 3 // A CULINARY TOUR

Cycle along the Digue à la Mer to Stes-Maries de la Mer for mussels on the sand (p95). Or head to Salin de Giraud for a salt-pan tour and lunch on a bull farm (p98) or at sheepfold La Chassagnette (p91). Taste wine and rice (p98) in the afternoon and at dusk dine on local *tellines* (tiny clams) dressed in cream and garlic (p93).

THE CAMARGUE

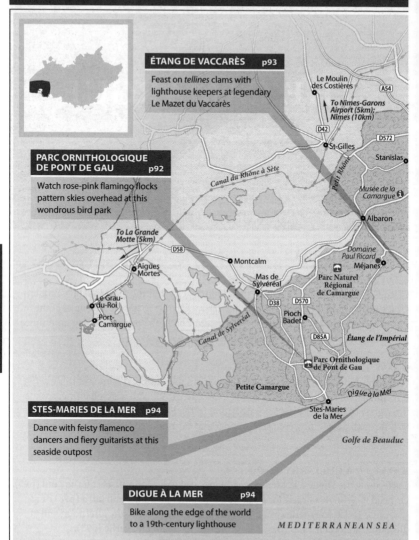

ÉTANG DE VACCARÈS   p93

Feast on *tellines* clams with lighthouse keepers at legendary Le Mazet du Vaccarès

PARC ORNITHOLOGIQUE DE PONT DE GAU   p92

Watch rose-pink flamingo flocks pattern skies overhead at this wondrous bird park

STES-MARIES DE LA MER   p94

Dance with feisty flamenco dancers and fiery guitarists at this seaside outpost

DIGUE À LA MER   p94

Bike along the edge of the world to a 19th-century lighthouse

Le Moulin des Costières

A54

To Nîmes-Garons Airport (5km); Nîmes (10km)

D42

St-Gilles

D572

Stanislas

Petit Rhône

Musée de la Camargue

Albaron

Canal du Rhône à Sète

To La Grande Motte (5km)

D58

Aigues Mortes

Le Grau-du-Roi

Port-Camargue

Montcalm

Mas de Sylvéréal

Domaine Paul Ricard

Méjanes

Parc Naturel Régional de Camargue

D38   D570

Pioch Badet

D85A

Étang de l'Impérial

Canal de Sylvéréal

Parc Ornithologique de Pont de Gau

Petite Camargue

Digue à la Mer

Stes-Maries de la Mer

Golfe de Beauduc

MEDITERRANEAN SEA

GETTING AROUND

Touring this backwater means cruising along narrow lanes with sufficient roadside distraction – flamingo flocks, bull herds – to create the odd hairy moment. Car or bicycle is the way to go. The D36 along Étang de Vaccarès' eastern shore and the D85a north of Stes-Maries de la Mer are particularly picturesque. For the Marseille-bound and Côte Bleue day-trippers, the Bac de Barcarin (€5 one-way) provides a car-ferry link across the Rhône from Salin de Giraud.

THE CAMARGUE

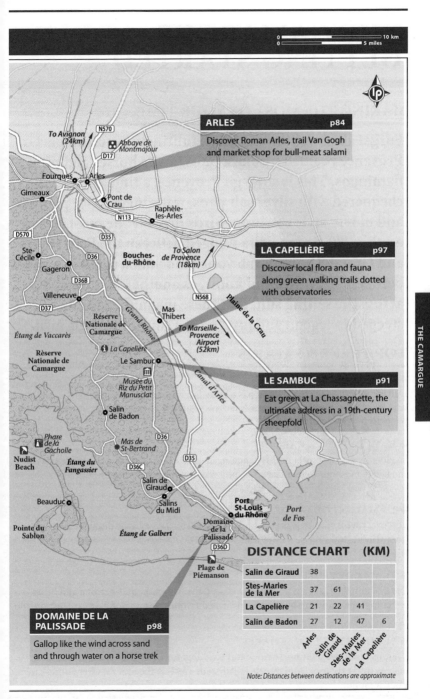

ARLES   p84

Discover Roman Arles, trail Van Gogh and market shop for bull-meat salami

LA CAPELIÈRE   p97

Discover local flora and fauna along green walking trails dotted with observatories

LE SAMBUC   p91

Eat green at La Chassagnette, the ultimate address in a 19th-century sheepfold

DOMAINE DE LA PALISSADE   p98

Gallop like the wind across sand and through water on a horse trek

DISTANCE CHART   (KM)

	Arles	Salin de Giraud	Stes-Maries de la Mer	La Capelière
Salin de Giraud	38			
Stes-Maries de la Mer	37	61		
La Capelière	21	22	41	
Salin de Badon	27	12	47	6

Note: Distances between destinations are approximate

THE CAMARGUE GETTING STARTED

MAKING THE MOST OF YOUR TIME

Forget all about time in this hauntingly beautiful part of Provence roamed by black bulls, white horses and pink flamingos. This is slow-go Provence, a timeless wetland chequered with silver salt pans, waterlogged rice paddies and movie-style cowboys. Birds provide the most action on this 780-sq-km delta wedged between the Petit Rhône and Grand Rhône. Grab your binoculars, squat in a shack between bulrushes and know, as another flamingo flits across the setting sun, that these magnificent waters, steeped in legend and lore, have a soul all of their own.

TOP TREKS & SAFARIS

❦ CAMARGUE DÉCOUVERTE
Delving into the delta by 4WD jeep is a buzz. Safari-style half-day trips can be combined with horseback rambles back at the bull farm. (☎ 06 85 35 10 04; www.camargue-decouverte.com, in French; 24 rue Porte de Laure, Arles)

❦ KAYAK VERT CAMARGUE
Explore by paddle power at this canoeing centre, 14km northwest of Stes-Maries on the D85. One-hour to two-day trips, plus a one-day biking-canoeing adventure. (☎ 04 66 73 57 17; www.kayakvert-camargue.fr; Mas de Sylvéréal, Sylvéréal)

❦ LA MAISON DU GUIDE
Discovery weekends by naturalist Jean-Marie Espuche embrace birdwatching, cycling, horse riding and sunrise nature walks. (☎ 04 66 73 52 30; www.maisonduguide.camargue.fr, in French; Montcalm)

❦ LE MAS DE PEINT
For a countrified take on this gutsy wetland, the flamenco, bull-herding and bird-watching weekends run by this sophisticated farmhouse and bull farm are just the job. (p382 & p98)

❦ LES CABANES DE CACHAREL
Zillions of stables offer horse rides and trekking; for a less Disney approach these stables (p92) are top. Domaine de la Palissade (p98) is the other kosher address to book a mount.

GETTING AWAY FROM IT ALL

The Camargue is getting away from it all full stop. Try these to get even further away:

★ **Overnight in Salin de Badon** Dossing down at this park-run property means a sunset- and sunrise-peek at wildlife you wouldn't otherwise see (p97)

★ **Trek at Domaine de Palissade** Wading thigh-high through water is part of the thrill of horseback trekking on this protected estate (p98)

★ **Les Boucles du 13** These thematic biking itineraries take you off the beaten track; download PDFs at French site www.cg13.fr (search 'Boucles du 13') and rent wheels in Stes-Maries de la Mer (p96)

ADVANCE PLANNING

To ensure a smooth landing, prepare the ground before arrival.

★ **Mosquitoes** Bring a supply of insect repellent. Mosquitoes are savage, and June/July brings scalp-eating harvest mites

★ **Binoculars** Bring some

★ **Arles féria (bullfighting festival) tickets** (p85) They're snapped up fast

★ **Gîte at Salin de Badon** (p97) Barebones but nature rich, this prime real estate fills quickly

★ **La Chassagnette** (p91) Reserve in advance at this scarecrow-guarded garden restaurant

★ **Bicycle rental** Companies in Stes-Maries de la Mer (p96) deliver bikes to your door for free; book ahead if you want to pedal Day 1 or for several days

TOP NATURE TRAILS

❦ DIGUE À LA MER
Dramatic footpath and cycling track atop a windy sea dike (p94)

❦ LA CAPELIÈRE
Its 1.5km-long Tree-frog Trail is perfect for families (p97)

❦ PARC ORNITHOLOGIQUE DE PONT DE GAU
Observation posts and tree-trunk benches lace the 7km-long lakeside loop here (p92)

❦ MUSÉE DE LA CAMARGUE
Lovely 3.5km trail with observation posts (p93)

❦ SALIN DE BADON
Protected salt pans zig-zagged by 4.5km of trails (p97)

❦ DOMAINE DE LA PALISSADE
Three remote trails, 1km to 7km (p98)

RESOURCES

★ **Visit Provence** (www.visitprovence.com) Current event info from the departmental tourist office

★ **Arles Office de Tourisme** (www.tourisme.ville-arles.fr) The works in and around main town Arles

★ **Parc Naturel Régional de Camargue** (www.parc-camargue.fr) Maps, listings, nature, culture and tradition in this regional nature park

★ **Le Tour du Valat** (http://en.tourduvalat.org) Biology research station

THE CAMARGUE

NATURE PARKS & INFORMATION

Travelling around the Camargue is tantamount to having a hay day with a zillion-and-one frolicking mosquitoes in a giant nature park. Almost all its wetlands are protected by the 863-sq-km **Parc Naturel Régional de Camargue** (PNRC), created to preserve its fragile ecosystems by maintaining an equilibrium between ecological considerations and economic mainstays: agriculture, salt and rice production, hunting, grazing and tourism. The Maison du Parc, 4km north of Stes-Maries de la Mer in Pont de Gau, is closed indefinitely but pick up information on walking, birdwatching and other activities at the park-run **Musée de la Camargue** (p93), 10km south of Arles on the D570.

On the periphery, the 600-sq-km lagoon **Étang de Vaccarès** and nearby peninsulas and islands form the 135-sq-km nature reserve, **Réserve Nationale de Camargue** (www.reserve-camargue.org, in French). Get the full low-down on the reserve and its activities at its information centre in La Capelière (p97).

Another 20 sq km between Arles and Salin de Giraud is managed by the **Conservatoire du Littoral** (www.conservatoire-du-littoral.fr), France's Coastal Protection Agency that buys threatened natural areas by the sea to restore and protect.

ARLES

· · · · · ·

pop 53,000
Roman treasures, sultry stone squares and a festive atmosphere that reaches crescendo during bullfights makes Arles a seductive stepping stone into the Camargue. And if its colourful sun-baked houses evoke a sense of déjà vu, it's because you've seen them already on a Van Gogh canvas.

Long before the Dutch artist captured starry nights over the Rhône, the Romans had been won over by the charms of the Greek colony Arelate. The city's prosperity rose meteorically in 49 BC when it backed a winner in Julius Caesar. Not one to be defeated, Caesar seized and plundered Marseille, so much so that Arles eclipsed Marseille as the region's major port. Soon its citizens were living the high life with gladiator fights and chariot races in magnificent open-air theatres. Controversial *corrida* (bullfights), less bloody *courses Camarguaises* (p90) and a rash of street parties take centre stage today.

By 2013 Arles will be graced with a fantastic cultural centre designed by world-renowned architect Frank Gehry: a cinema, book publisher Actes Sud, photography school École National Supérieure de la Photographe, several exhibition spaces, a restaurant and more are already marked on the floor plan of this new space.

ESSENTIAL INFORMATION

TOURIST OFFICES // Tourist office (www.arlestourism.com); city centre (☎ 04 90 18 41 20; esplanade Charles de Gaulle; ◷ 9am-6.45pm Apr-Sep, 9am-4.45pm Mon-Sat, 10am-12.45pm Sun Oct-Mar); train station (☎ 04 90 43 33 57; ◷ 9am-1.30pm & 2.30-4.45pm Mon-Fri Apr-Sep) Both offices organise **walking tours** (adult/6-12yr €6/3; ◷ mid-Jul–Sep) and sell walking maps, cycling itineraries and sightseeing passes (see boxed text, p88).

EXPLORING ARLES

❦ **MUSÉE DÉPARTEMENTAL DE L'ARLES ANTIQUE // ROMAN ARLES: LET THE STORY BEGIN**
For the perfect introduction to the fabulous tale of Roman Arles, dip into this

state-of-the-art **museum** (☎ 04 90 18 88 88; www.arles-antique.cg13.fr; av de la Première Division Française Libre; adult/under 18yr €6/free, free 1st Sun of month; ☺ 9am-7pm Apr-Oct, 10am-5pm Nov-Mar). Inside the contemporary triangular structure exhibitions trace the area's evolution from 2500 BC to the end of antiquity. Highlights include Roman statues, artefacts, mosaics and an assortment of early Christian 4th-century sarcophagi. Temporary exhibitions complete its savvy history-book repertoire. Find the museum on the fringe of the Roman's old chariot racing track, 1.5km southwest of the city-centre tourist office.

☙ LES ARÈNES & THÉÂTRE ANTIQUE // GRAB A PEW, ENJOY THE SHOW!

Slaves and criminals met their dramatic demise before a jubilant 20,000-strong crowd during Roman gladiatorial displays at **Les Arènes** (☎ 04 90 96 03 70; adult/student €6/4.50; ☺ 9am-7pm May-Sep, 9am-6pm Mar, Apr & Oct, 10am-5pm Nov-Feb), built around the late 1st or early 2nd century AD. Adapted over the ages, during the early medieval Arab invasions the arch-laced circular structure, which is 136m long, 107m wide and 21m tall, was topped with four defensive towers to become a fortress. Indeed, by the 1820s, when the Roman amphitheatre was returned to its original use, there were 212 houses and two churches on the site.

Les Arènes is a remarkable space to soak up: wandering inside its thick stone walls under the sizzling sun is electric, as is watching a show. Buy tickets for bloody bullfights, bloodless *courses Camarguaises*, theatre performances and concerts at the **Bureau de Location** (box office; ☎ 08 91 70 03 70; www.arenes-arles.com; Rond-Point des Arènes; ☺ 9.30am-noon & 2-6pm Mon-Fri, 10am-1pm Sat).

Across the street, alfresco music concerts and film screenings enchant summertime audiences in the 1st century BC **Roman theatre** (Théâtre Antique; ☎ 04 90 96 93 30; bd des Lices; ☺ 9am-7pm May-Sep, 9am-noon & 2-6pm Mar, Apr & Oct, 10am-noon & 2-5pm Nov-Feb). You'll notice it is dramatically less intact than its big brother – in fact this 102m-diameter, 12,000-seat theatre was used for centuries as a source of construction materials.

Performances aside, one ticket covers admission to both theatres.

☙ PLACE DU FORUM // HEART OF THE ROMAN ACTION

Just as social, political and religious life revolved around the forum in Roman Arles (spot the remains of a temple embedded in Hôtel Pinus Nord's facade), so this busy plane-tree-shaded square buzzes with café life today. Take your pick of terrace styles (from Provençal old-timer to industrial wi-fi hotspot) and cuisines (bags of quick bites and €15 lunch *menus* but nothing startling), order *un café* or pastis and watch local life unfold around you.

Café Van Gogh (11 place du Forum), otherwise called Café de la Nuit, is the café depicted in Van Gogh's *Café Terrace at Night* (1888). The café is painted sunflower-yellow to re-create the effect used by the artist to suggest bright nighttime lights, and it's always packed with tourists.

Beneath your feet are **Cryptoportiques** (place du Forum; adult/under 18yr €3.50/free; ☺ 9am-7pm May-Sep, 9am-noon & 2-6pm Mar, Apr & Oct, 10am-noon & 2-5pm Nov-Feb), subterranean storerooms carved out by the Romans in the 1st century BC. Access to the horse-shoe-shaped underground galleries, 89m long and 59m wide, is via the **Hôtel de Ville** (Town Hall; plan de la Cour).

THE CAMARGUE

🌿 LES ALYSCAMPS & THERMES DE CONSTANTIN // COMPLETE THE ROMAN TOUR

Van Gogh and Gauguin both painted the necropolis known as **Les Alyscamps** (av des Alyscamps; adult/under 18yr €3.50/free; ⏰ 9am-7pm May-Sep, 9am-noon & 2-6pm Mar, Apr & Oct, 10am-noon & 2-5pm Nov-Feb). Founded by the Romans and adopted by Christians in the 4th century, the cemetery became a coveted resting place – miracle-working Christian martyrs were apparently among its dead.

Last but not least are the **Thermes de Constantin** (rue du Grand Prieuré; adult/under 18yr €3/free; ⏰ 9am-noon & 2-6.30pm May-Sep, 9am-noon & 2-5.30pm Mar, Apr & Oct, 10am-noon & 2-5pm Feb & Nov), private baths built in the 4th century for Roman Emperor Constantin.

🌿 ÉGLISE ST-TROPHIME // GUARDIAN OF BROKEN BISHOP BONES

Arles was an archbishopric from the 4th century until 1790, and this Romanesque-style **church** (place de la République) was once a cathedral. Built in the late 11th and 12th centuries on the site of several earlier churches, it's named after St-Trophime, a late-2nd- or early-3rd-century bishop of Arles. On the western portal's intricately sculpted biblical scene facade, play I Spy to find St-Trophime depicted holding a spiral staff in his right hand. Inside the austere church, the most fascinating feature is the 'treasury', containing pieces of bone of Arles' bishops, later canonised. Many of the broken statues inside were decapitated during the French Revolution.

Across the courtyard, medieval monks slept, ate and studied in living quarters provided by the Romanesque **Cloître St-Trophime** (☎ 04 90 49 36 36; adult/under 18yr €3.50/free; ⏰ 9am-7pm May-Sep, 9am-6pm Mar, Apr & Oct, 10am-5pm Nov-Feb), flanked by highly detailed stone and marble columns. The cloister's two Gothic galleries were added in the 14th century.

🌿 TWO MUSEUMS // A PORTRAIT OF PROVENÇAL LIFE

It was in Arles in the 1890s that Nobel Prize–winning poet and dedicated Provençal preservationist Frédéric Mistral chose to popularise his work by opening the **Museon Arlaten** (☎ 04 90 93 58 11; 29 rue de la République; admission €1; ⏰ 9.30am-12.30pm &

ACCOMMODATION

With its range of accommodation, from Disney-style low-lying ranch complexes to authentic 1950s bull farms and bulrush-thatched *cabanes de gardians* (cowboy cottages), staying in the Camargue is a unique experience – and cheaper than elsewhere. For detailed listings, see the accommodation chapter. Here is a taste of the best:

★ Right up to date, **Le Bélvedère Hôtel** (p381) is the best of Arles' midrange bunch

★ Arles' best-kept secret, **L'Hôtel Particulier** (p381) is a quite-divine boutique hotel

★ Sleep steps from the sea at **Hôtel Méditerranée** (p382), Stes-Maries de la Mer's budget choice

★ A soulful backwater farm, **Hôtel de Cacharel** (p382) perfectly fuses rural authenticity with contemporary comfort

★ Commune with nature and birdwatchers at **Gîte at Salin de Badon** (p97), particularly dreamy at sunrise and sunset

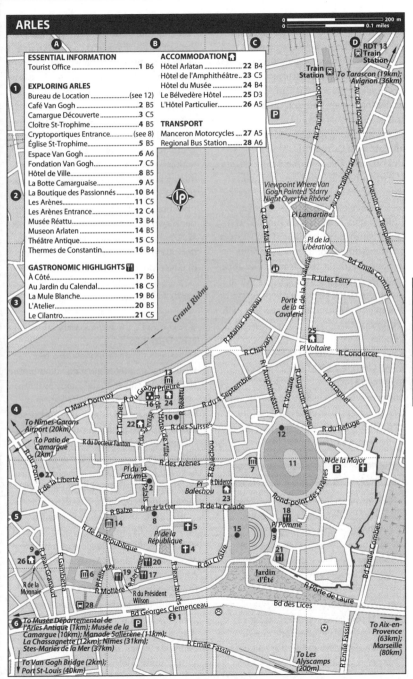

ARLES

0 ———— 200 m
0 ———— 0.1 miles

RDT 13
Train Station
To Tarascon (19km);
Avignon (36km)
Train Station

Viewpoint Where Van
Gogh Painted 'Starry
Night Over the Rhône'
Pl Lamartine
Pl de la
Libération
Bd Émile Combes
R Jules Ferry
Porte
de la R.
Cavalerie
Pl Voltaire
R Condercer

Grand Rhône

R Marius Jouveau
R Chiavary
R du 8 Mai 1945

Q du 8 Mai 1945

Av Paulin Talabot
Av de Hongrie
Chemin des Templiers
Av de Stalingrad
R de la Cavalerie

THE CAMARGUE

R Amphithéâtre
R Voltaire
R Augustin Tardieu
R Portagnel

13
16 24
Réattu
R du Grand Prieuré
Q Marx Dormoy
R Truchet
R du 4 Septembre
10
R des Suisses
R du Refuge
12
Pl de la Major

To Nîmes-Garons
Airport (20km)
To Patio de
Camargue
(2km)
R du Docteur Fanton
22
R de l'Hôtel de Ville
R Balechou

7
11
Rond-point des Arènes

27
R de la Liberté
Pl du
Forum
2
R des Arènes
Pl Diderot
Pl
Balechou
23
R de la Calade
18
Pl Pomme
3
21

26
9
R de la République
14
8
Pl de la
Cour
Plan de la Cour
R Balze
5
4
15
R du Cloître
Jardin
d'Été

R Gambetta
R Jean Granaud
R de la
Monnaie
6
R Félix Rey
19
17
20
R Molière
R du Président
Wilson
R Jean Jaurès
R Porte de Laure
Bd Émile Combes

28
Bd Georges Clemenceau
Bd des Lices
1

To Musée Départemental de
l'Arles Antique (1km); Musée de la
Camargue (10km); Manade Salierène (11km);
La Chassagnette (12km); Nîmes (31km);
Stes-Maries de la Mer (37km)

To Van Gogh Bridge (2km);
Port St-Louis (40km)

R Émile Fassin

To Les
Alyscamps
(200m)

To Aix-en-
Provence
(63km);
Marseille
(80km)

2-6pm Jun-Aug, 9.30am-noon & 2-5.30pm Apr, May & Sep, 9.30am-noon & 2-4.30pm Oct-Mar). Enchanting to visit, the museum remains a vivid expression of traditional culture with its displays of Provençal furniture, crafts, costumes, ceramics, wigs, mythical people-eating amphibious monsters and so on.

Modern-day Provence strikes a pose on dozens of canvases inside the **Musée Réattu** (☎ 04 90 96 37 58; www.museereattu.arles .fr, in French; 10 rue du Grand Prieuré; adult/under 18yr €7/free, free 1st Sun of month; ⏲ 10am-7pm Tue-Sun Jul-Sep, 10am-12.30pm & 2-6.30pm Tue-Sun Oct-Mar), when it reopens in July 2009 after extensive renovations. Two Picasso paintings and 57 of his sketches from the early 1970s, as well as works by 18th- and 19th-century Provençal artists rub shoulders in the permanent collection of this splendid museum, housed in a 15th-century priory.

❦ STREET BEATS // DANCE CAMARGUE FLAMENCO WITH ROMA BANDS

Roma bands such as Los Reyes, the Gypsy Kings (from Arles no less, discovered while busking in St-Tropez), Chico & the Gypsies (the band of former Gypsy King Chico Bouchikki) and Manitas de Plata have all performed on the streets of Arles. For gig flyers and an outstanding collection of tracks by these and other artists, pass by **La Boutique des Passionnés** (☎ 04 90 96 59 93; www.passionnes.com, in French; 14 rue Réattu).

The best time to catch Roma bands performing on the streets – Roma women encircling exclusively male musicians with a flurry of Camargue flamenco – is during Stes-Maries de la Mer pilgrimages (p10). Otherwise catch Roma street beats over a sangria-fuelled *dîner-spectacle* (dinner show) at **Patio de Camargue** (☎ 04 90 49 51 76; www.patiodecamargue.com, in French; 21 bis chemin Barriol; ticket incl dinner €55-70). Hacienda of Chico Bouchikki no less, Chico & the Gypsies are among the big-name Roma bands to play here.

❦ COWBOY LIFE // LEARN HOW TO HERD BULLS

Get a taste of *gardian* life with a one-week *stage de monte gardiane* (Camargue cowboy course) at the **Manade Salierène** (☎ 04 66 86 45 57; www.manadesalierene.com, in French; Mas de Capellane, Saliers), 11km west of Arles. Initiation/perfection courses (€570 including accommodation and meals with the *manadier*'s family) comprise up to seven hours a day on horseback learning how to ride the Camargue's rough terrain and herd bulls.

Buy a pair of Real McCoy cowboy boots from **La Botte Camarguaise** (☎ 04 90 96 20 87; 22 rue Jean Granaud). Not only does Monsieur Vidal make made-to-measure cowboy boots by hand; he has done so for 27 years and is happy to chat, and chat, and chat as the permanent gaggle of *gardians* in his workshop attests. Even if you can't wait for or invest in a pair – count six weeks and €250 – visiting the Camarguais Boot is an experience.

ROMAN COMBO

Decide how many Roman monuments you intend visiting and buy your pass accordingly at the tourist office or any Roman site: A **Passeport Arelate** (€9) covers both theatres, the baths and crypt; a **Passeport Avantage** (€13.50) gets you into Les Alyscamps and the Cloître St-Trophime too; and the **Passeport Liberté** (€9) gives you the choice of five sights total including one museum. Passes are valid for a month and under 18s get in for free.

❦ VAN GOGH WALKING TOUR // TRAIL THE DUTCH ARTIST

Mapped out in a tourist-office brochure (€1 or downloadable for free online), this evocative walking circuit of the city takes in scenes painted by Van Gogh. He painted 200-odd canvases in Arles, but none remain today.

The collection at the **Fondation Van Gogh** (☎ 04 90 49 94 04; 24bis rond-point des Arènes; adult/student €6/4; ☽ 10am-7pm Jul-Sep, 10am-6pm Apr-Jun & Oct, 11am-5pm Tue-Sun Nov-Mar) shows just how widely Van Gogh's influence has been felt in the artistic world. Celebrated artists, including David Hockney and Francis Bacon, pay homage to the artist's distinctive style.

Temporary art exhibitions are held at **Espace Van Gogh** (☎ 04 90 49 39 39; place Félix Rey), the former hospital where Van Gogh had his ear stitched and was later locked up. Van Gogh's little 'yellow house' on place Lamartine, which he painted in 1888, was destroyed during WWII.

POOR OLD VINCENT

Vincent van Gogh may have been poor – he sold only one painting in his lifetime – but he wasn't old. Despite his aged, haggard appearance in his self-portraits, he was only 37 when he died.

Born in 1853, the Dutch painter arrived in Arles in 1888 after living in Paris with his younger brother Theo, an art dealer, who financially supported him from his modest income. Revelling in Arles' intense light and bright colours, Van Gogh painted sunflowers, irises and other vivid subjects with a burning fervour, unfazed by howling mistrals, during which he knelt on his canvases and painted horizontally or lashed his easel to iron stakes driven deep into the ground. He sent paintings to Theo in Paris to try and sell, and dreamed of founding an artists colony here, but only Gauguin followed up his invitation.

Differing artistic approaches and temperaments between Van Gogh and fellow painter Paul Gauguin came to a head with an argument that, fuelled by absinthe, prompted Van Gogh to threaten Gauguin with a cut-throat razor before slicing off part of his own left ear. Van Gogh was hospitalised in Arles, during which he produced, among other works, a portrait of his doctor, Dr Rey, which he presented as a gift. The doctor used it to plug a hole in his chicken coop.

In May 1889, Van Gogh voluntarily entered an asylum in St-Rémy de Provence where he painted another 150-odd canvases, including masterpieces like *Starry Night* (not to be confused with *Starry Night over the Rhône,* painted in Arles).

On 16 May 1890 Van Gogh moved to Auvers-sur-Oise near Paris to be closer to Theo. But on 27 July that year he shot himself, possibly to avoid further financial burden on his brother. Van Gogh died two days later with Theo at his side. Theo subsequently had a breakdown, was committed and died, aged 33, six months after Van Gogh.

Less than a decade later, Van Gogh's talent started to be recognised with major museums acquiring his works. By the early 1950s, he had become a household name. His tormented life is documented in countless books, films, and Don McLean's poignant song, 'Vincent'.

See above for a tour of Vincent van Gogh's Arles.

THE CAMARGUE

FESTIVALS & EVENTS

Féria d'Arles (www.feriaarles.com, in French) This four-day Easter festival in Arles heralds the start of the bullfighting season, which sees bulls in Les Arènes most Sundays in May and June; Easter.

Fête des Gardians Mounted Camargue cowboys parade through Arles; 1 May.

Festival Européen de la Photo de Nu (www.fepn-arles.com, in French) Love this one: Europe's annual one-week nude-photography exhibition; May.

Les Suds (www.suds-arles.com, in French) Vibrant world music festival; one week early July.

L'Abrivado des Bernacles (www.feriaarles .com, in French) An extraordinary spectacle, Camargue *gardians* shepherd bulls for 15km from their paddock to Les Arènes for the season's most prestigious *course Camarguaise*, the **Cocarde d'Or**. Hundreds of aficionados on bike, scooter, foot and horseback follow the *gardians;* first Monday in July.

Les Rencontres d'Arles Photographie (www.rencontres-arles.com) International photography festival; early July .

Féria du Riz (www.feriaarles.com, in French) Bullfights are part and parcel of this week-long festival in Arles marking the start of the rice harvest; September.

GASTROMONIC HIGHLIGHTS

Tickle taste buds with an amble along Arles' Saturday-morning **market** (bd des Lices) where Camargue salt, goats' cheese and *saucisson d'Arles* (bull-meat sausage) scent the air. The scene shifts to bd Émile Combes on Wednesday morning.

👻 À CÔTÉ €€

☎ 04 90 91 07 69; www.bistro-acote.com, in French; 21 rue des Carmes; menus €23 & €29; 🕑 9am-midnight daily

---

A BULLISH AFFAIR

Animal lovers fear not: not all types of bullfights end with blood. The local Camargue variation, the *course Camarguaise,* sees amateur *razeteurs* (from the word 'shave'), wearing skin-tight white shirts and trousers, get as close as they dare to the *taureau* (bull) to try and snatch rosettes and ribbons tied to the bull's horns, using a *crochet* (a razor-sharp comb) held between their fingers – leaping over the arena's barrier as the bull charges, making the spectators' hearts lurch.

Bulls are bred on a *manade* (bull farm) by *manadiers,* who are helped in their daily chores by *gardians* (Camargue cowboys who herd cattle on horseback). These mounted herdsmen are honoured by the **Fête des Gardians** in Arles in May, during which they parade through town on horseback clad in leather hats, checked shirts and boots. *Gardians* traditionally live in *cabanes de gardians* (whitewashed, thatched-roof cottages sealed with a strip of mortar).

Many *manades* also breed the cowboys' best friend: the creamy white *cheval de Camargue* (Camargue horse), recognised as a breed in its own right. Several *manades* open their doors to visitors; tourist offices in Arles and Stes-Maries de la Mer have seasonal information.

A calendar of the *courses Camarguaises* is posted online by the Nîmes-based **Fédération Française de la Course Camarguaise** (French Federation of Camargue Bullfights; ☎ 04 66 26 05 35; www.ffcc.info, in French). *Recortadores* (a type of bull-baiting with lots of bull-jumping and vaulting) can also be seen during the bullfighting season (Easter to September).

Be it breakfast, coffee, lunch, dinner, tapas or a cold meat platter, this modern bistro by genius chef Jean-Luc Rabanel hits the spot every time. Slouch on wood-and-metal slat chairs on the terrace or plump for a contemporary spot inside at the bar. Quintessential bistro dishes – organic roast chicken, *brandade de morue* (mix of crushed salted cod, olive oil and garlic), guinea fowl in a salt crust – are chalked on the blackboard and online.

❦ AU JARDIN DU CALENDAL €

☎ 04 90 96 11 89; www.lecalendal.com, in French; 5 rue Porte de Laure; mains €15; ☺ noon-7pm Apr-Oct; ♿

Rendered in ochre with sky-blue shutters, this lovely old house across from the Théâtre Antique is also a hotel. But it is to its leafy courtyard garden that everyone flocks. Lunch on gourmet salads, revel in tea and cake in the late afternoon or snack on a nut- and seed-topped roll with designer filling from its Öli Pan coffee shop, which also has free wi-fi.

❦ L'ATELIER €€€

☎ 04 90 91 07 69; www.rabanel.com; 7 rue des Carmes; lunch/dinner menus from €45/85, incl wine €85/150; ☺ lunch & dinner Wed-Sun

A beautiful and modern gastronomic experience, dining here is one gorgeous gourmet leap in the dark – around bare wood tables. Opt for a series of seven or 13 edible works of art, sit back and revel in Jean-Luc Rabanel's superbly crafted symphony of fresh organic tastes. No wonder this green-fingered urban chef with his own veggie patch has two Michelin stars.

❦ LA CHASSAGNETTE €€€

☎ 04 90 97 26 96; http://lachassagnette-uk.blogspirit .com; rte du Sambuc, Le Sambuc; lunch/dinner menu €34/54, mains €32; ☺ lunch & dinner Thu-Mon Mar-Dec, daily Jul & Aug

LITERARY CAMARGUE

Immerse yourself in the region with a trio of Camargue-inspired travel titles.

- ★ *Taurine Provence* (Roy Campbell) – Provençal bullfights told by a 1930s matador
- ★ *The Bull that Thought* (Rudyard Kipling) – short story with a twist about bullfighting in Arles, written in 1924 by the 1907 Nobel Prize for Literature winner
- ★ *A Little Tour in France* (Henry James) – vivid portrait of Van Gogh's 19th-century Arles, first visited by James in 1882

Inhaling the scent of sun-ripened tomatoes is one of many pleasures at this 19th-century sheepfold – the ultimate Camargue dine. Alain Ducasse prodigy Armand Arnal cooks up 100% organic, grows much of it himself, woos his guests with a modern mosquito-covered outside terrace and roasts 100% free-range meat open-rotisserie style in the fireplace. Dedicated foodies can lounge in its gourmet library. Look for the fork and trowel sign, 12km southeast of Arles on the southbound D36.

❦ LA MULE BLANCHE €

☎ 04 90 93 98 54; www.restaurant-mule-blanche.com, in French; 9 rue du Président Wilson; lunch menu €17, mains €15; ☺ lunch Tue-Sun & dinner Wed-Sun summer, lunch Tue-Sat & dinner Wed-Sat winter

Jazz is performed at the piano in the White Mule's domed interior. But the hottest tables at this soulful bistro are aboard the pavement terrace – easily the town's prettiest with its violet awning, Saturday-morning market view and lazy mood. Performances by some great street buskers are the icing on the cake.

THE CAMARGUE

❦ LE CILANTRO €€

☎ 04 90 18 25 05; www.restaurantcilantro.com, in French; 29 rue Porte de Laure; mains €35; ☽ lunch & dinner Tue-Fri, dinner Sat & Mon Jul & Aug, lunch & dinner Tue-Fri, dinner Sat Sep-Jun

So subtle is the entrance to this buzzing table that you can easily miss it. A born-and-bred local lad, Arlésian chef Jêrome Laurant combines seasonal Provençal ingredients with world spices to create accomplished dishes such as saddle of lamb in almond oil, or frog leg and watercress soup. For the ultimate tastebud tour, order his six-course *menu dégustation* (€134/99 with/without wine), perfectly paired with a different wine for each course.

TRANSPORT

BUS // From Arles **bus station** (☎ 08 10 00 08 16; 24 bd Georges Clemenceau; ☽ 7.30am-4pm Mon-Sat) there are daily buses to/from Stes-Maries de la Mer (one hour).

TRAIN // The **train station** (av Paulin Talabot) serves Nîmes (€7.30, 30 minutes), Marseille (€13, 45 minutes) and Avignon (€6.40, 20 minutes).

BIKE // **Manceron Motocycles** (Vélo & Oxygène; ☎ 04 90 96 03 77; 15 rue du Pont) rents bikes.

TAXI // Call ☎ 04 90 96 90 03 or ☎ 04 90 52 22 22.

TOWARDS STES-MARIES

· · · · · ·

❦ PARC ORNITHOLOGIQUE DE PONT DE GAU // WATCH FLAMINGOS CLOSE-UP

Pink flamingos pirouette overhead and stalk the watery landscape at this **bird park** (☎ 04 90 97 82 62; Pont de Gau; adult/4-16yr €7/4; ☽ 9am-sunset Apr-Sep, 10am-sunset Oct-Mar), home to every bird species known to set foot in the Camargue and large enough to lose the tourist crowds. Several kilometres of paths wend through reed beds and marshes – the complete loop around the Marais de Gînes is 7km – and trails ensnare hides and observation towers to peek at the area's dazzling array of birdlife. The state-of-the-art ecological loos here are particularly smart, needing neither water nor electricity nor chemical products to flush. Find the park on the D570 in Pont du Gau, 4km north of Stes-Maries.

❦ EXPLORING ON HORSEBACK // SADDLE UP AND TREK THROUGH NATURE

Heaps of roadside farms along route d'Arles (D570) into Stes-Maries de la Mer offer *promenades à cheval* (horse riding) astride white Camargue horses, but a more authentic experience can be had along the parallel rte de Cacharel (D85A): **Les Cabanes de Cacharel** (☎ 04 90 97 84 10, 06 11 57 74 75; www.cabanes decacharel.com, in French; rte de Cacharel) charge the same rates as most other stables – €15/26/38 for a one-/two-/three-hour trek in the marshes and €60 for a day trek and canter on the beach – but is substantially less tacky. It also does horse-and-carriage rides (€12/20 per one/two hours).

Not many stables have smaller ponies for younger children (kids must be at least eight years old to ride a Camargue horse): one sure-thing pony address is ranch theme-park **Domaine Paul Ricard** (☎ 04 90 97 10 62; www.mejanes .camargue.fr; ☽ year-round, by advance reservation only mid-Oct–Easter), on the northwestern bank of the Étang de Vaccarès in Méjanes. Drive 14km south along the D570 from Arles, turn left along the eastbound D37, then right towards Méjanes.

PRETTY IN PINK

The pink or greater flamingo *(Phoenicopterus ruber)* in flight is a breathtaking sight. Equally majestic is the catwalk stance – neck high, breast out – adopted by this elegant, long-legged creature when strutting through shallow waters.

Each year in the Camargue some 10,000 couples nest on the Étang du Fangassier: the 4000-sq-metre island artificial, constructed in 1970 as a flamingo-breeding colony, is one of the rare spots in Europe that guarantees the flamingo protection from its predators.

Flamingo courtship starts in January, with mating taking place March to May. The single egg laid by the female in April or May is incubated in a mud-caked nest for one month by both parents. The young chicks shakily take to the skies when they are about three months old. By the time they reach adulthood (around five years old), their soft grey down has become a fine feather coat of brilliant white or pretty rose-pink.

This well-dressed bird lives to the grand old age of 34 (longer if kept in captivity). It stands between 1.5m and 2m tall and has an average wing span of 1.9m. When the flamingo feels threatened, its loud hiss is similar to the warning sound made by a goose. It feeds on plankton, sucking in water and draining it off with its disproportionately heavy, curved bill.

Come the end of August or early September, several thousand take flight to Spain, Tunisia and Senegal where they winter in warmer climes before returning to the Camargue in February in time for early spring. Some 6000 to 7000 flamingos however remain in the Rhône delta year-round.

THE CAMARGUE

♥ LE MAZET DU VACCARÈS // FISH DINNER WITH A LIGHTHOUSE KEEPER

Gorging on fish in this legendary lakeside cabin, otherwise called **Chez Hélène et Néné** (☎ 04 90 97 10 79; menu €30; ☽ lunch & dinner Fri & Sat, lunch Sun), is a feast for the eyes and belly. Memorabilia from Hélène and Néné's days – all 20 years of them – as lighthouse keepers in Beauduc (until it was automated nine years ago) fill the restaurant with soul: the miniature lighthouse on the huge fireplace, the equestrian paintings, the bull photos, the fish nets, the newspaper cuttings… The jovial couple cook up one fixed *menu* built from the catch of local fishermen Christophe and Florent: *soupe de poissons* (fish soup), *tellines* (tiny clams) plucked fresh from the Golfe de Beauduc and cooked in a creamy garlicky sauce, an entire fresh fish grilled then beheaded at the

table, followed by a simple homemade dessert. Dining, even in summer, is more inside than out (too many mosquitoes). From Domaine Paul Ricard (see opposite), it is a signposted 2.5km drive along potholed gravel.

♥ MUSÉE DE LA CAMARGUE // IMMERSE YOURSELF IN TRADITIONAL DELTA LIFE

Inside an 1812-built sheep shed 10km southwest of Arles on the D570, the **Camargue Museum** (☎ 04 90 97 10 82; Mas du Pont de Rousty; adult/under 18yr €4.50/free; ☽ 9am-6pm Apr-Sep, 10am-5pm Wed-Sat Oct-Mar) paints an exhaustive portrait of traditional life, its exhibitions covering local history, ecosystems, farming techniques, flora and fauna. A 3.5km trail leads to an observation tower with bird's-eye views of the *mas* (farmhouse) and its nature-protected surrounds. The museum is the main information point for the Parc Naturel Régional de Camargue (p84).

STES-MARIES DE LA MER

· · · · · ·

pop 2400

You could be forgiven for thinking you'd crossed into Spain at this remote seaside outpost where whitewashed buildings line dusty streets, bulrush reeds thatch pitched roofs and dancers in gaudy dresses spin flamenco. During its Roma pilgrimages, street-cooked pans of paella fuel chaotic crowds of carnivalesque guitarists, musicians, dancers and mounted cowboys. The mood is fiery and brash.

Away from the small village, 30km of uninterrupted sandy beach bask in the hot midday sun and narrow nature-fringed roads beg to be biked along: the northbound D85A and the D38 are particularly scenic cycling routes.

ESSENTIAL INFORMATION

TOURIST OFFICES // Tourist office (☎ 04 90 97 82 55; www.saintesmaries.com; 5 av Van Gogh; ⏱ 9am-8pm Jul & Aug, to 7pm Apr-Jun & Sep, to 5pm or 6pm Oct-Mar) Guided walking tours (€7) departing 2pm every Tuesday and Friday.

EXPLORING STES-MARIES DE LA MER

❦ ÉGLISE DES STES-MARIES // VENERATE SAINTLY BONES WITH PILGRIMS

This 12th- to 15th-century **church** (place de l'Église) is cinematic with its dark, hushed, candle wax-scented atmosphere and legions of pilgrim Roma who pour

in here to venerate the statue of black Sara, their highly revered patron saint, during the **Pèlerinage des Gitans** (Roma Pilgrimages) on 24 May, and again in mid-October. The relics of Sara along with those of Marie-Salomé and Sainte Marie-Jacobé (see boxed text, p96), all found in the crypt by King René in 1448, are enshrined in a painted wooden chest, stashed in the stone wall above the choir. From the church's **rooftop terrace** (adult/child €2/1.50; ⏱ 10am-8pm Jul & Aug, 10am-12.30pm & 2-6.30pm Mon-Fri, 10am-7pm Sat & Sun Mar-Jun, Sep & Oct, 10am-noon & 2-5pm Wed, Sat & Sun Nov-Feb), a great panorama unfolds.

❦ A SUNSET APÉRO // SLURP OYSTERS AND WHITE WINE ON THE SEAFRONT

As the day's blazing heat fades join the crowds at **La Cabane aux Coquillages** (☎ 06 10 30 33 49; rue Théodore Aubanel), a pocket-sized fish shop on the seafront with crates of crustaceans piled high inside and a gaggle of sea-blue chairs outside. Buy shellfish to savour at home or relax on the packed pavement terrace and indulge in a glass of dry white and half-a-dozen oysters; the privilege costs a mere €6. For dedicated seafood lovers there are larger seafood platters.

❦ DIGUE À LA MER // CYCLE LIKE THE FAMOUS FIVE TO THE LIGHTHOUSE

Don your pedalling legs and free wheel 13km east from Stes-Maries to a 19th-century lighthouse along what feels like the edge of the world: the Digue à la Mer is a 2.5m-high dike built in the 19th century to cut the delta off from the sea. A 20km-long walking and cycling track runs along its length, and footpaths cut down to a couple of lovely sandy beaches. Allow ample time to birdwatch: grey

THE CAMARGUE

herons, little egrets, shelduck, avocet, the Kentish plover, oystercatcher and the yellow-legged gull are among the dozens of species to spot. Walking on the fragile sand dunes is forbidden.

The solar-powered **Phare de la Gacholle** (⊙ 11am-5pm Sat, Sun & school holidays; admission free), dating to 1882, was automated in the 1960s. Inside the former lighthouse keeper's house, a small exhibition focuses on local birdlife and fishing traditions; B&W photos show how *tellines* are caught. You can also buy bottled water here.

By car the closest you can get to the lighthouse is Parking de la Comtesse, a car park 1km from the lighthouse at the eastern end of the dike. The car park, only accessible in dry weather, is reached by a roller-coaster of a muddy, pot-holed 4km-long track. Alternatively, skip the bone-rattling, second-gear drive and park in Parking de la Gacholle instead, from where it is a 5km walk. To reach both car parks, pick up the D36B in Le Paradis, 7km west of Salin de Giraud on the eastern side of the Étang de Vaccarès.

♥ MUSSELS ON THE BEACH // SANDY FROLICS AND SERIOUS CUISINE

Stes-Maries de la Mer is fringed by 30km of fine-sand beaches, easily reached by bicycle (p96). If an all-over tan is your muse, head to the nudist beaches 11km east around the Gacholle lighthouse.

For lunch on the sand **Lou Santen** (☎ 06 30 17 32 49; www.lousanten.com; 21 rue Sadi Carnot; ⊙ May–mid-Sep) is the address. Rebuilt each summer for the new season, the beach restaurant is shaded by a typical reed *loupio*. The catch of the day grilled can feel pricey but stick to a finger-licking bowl of *moules frîtes* (mussels and chips) and value is guaranteed.

♥ A BOAT TRIP // SAIL OUT TO SEA OR ALONG THE RHÔNE

Down on the seafront at Stes-Maries' small Port Gardian (quai des Brumes) boat companies run 1½-hour trips, March to November, along the Petit Rhône and out to sea. Les Quatre Maries II (☎ 04 90 97 70 10; www.bateaux-4maries.camargue .fr, in French; 36 av Théodore Aubanel; adult/child €10/5) depart three or four times daily mid-March to October, and include a guided commentary on the waterside flora and fauna. Ditto for trips aboard **Le Camargue** (☎ 04 90 97 84 72; www.bateau -camargue.com, in French; 5 rue des Launes).

FESTIVALS & EVENTS

Festo Vierginenco (Virgin Festival) This festival, created by Provençal poet Frédéric Mistral in 1904, honours young women donning the traditional Arlésienne costume for the first time. It supposedly takes more than two hours to get dressed in the long full skirt, lacy shawl, cap and elaborate hair style; mid-July.

Pèlerinage des Gitans (Roma pilgrimages) Roma pour into town for three days from 24 May and again on the Sunday closest to 22 October to celebrate their patron saint; see boxed text, p96.

GASTRONOMIC HIGHLIGHTS

Dining choices are unexceptional in this touristy seaside town; Camargue specialities such as *gardianne de taureau* (bull stew) are easy to find alongside giant pans of paella. For self caterers there is one essential stop: the seafront **fish market** (av Van Gogh).

♥ L'AUBERGE CAVALIÈRE €€

☎ 04 90 97 88 88; www.aubergecavaliere.com; rte d'Arles; menus €32 & €42; ⊙ lunch & dinner

As sleek in real life as online, this sophisticated complex of purpose-built

NO WASHED-UP LEGEND

Catholicism first reached European shores in what is now the little township of Stes-Maries de la Mer. So the stories go, Sainte Marie-Salomé and Sainte Marie-Jacobé (some say along with Lazarus, Marie-Madeleine, Martha and Maximin) fled the Holy Land in a tiny boat and were caught in a storm, drifting at sea until washing ashore here in AD 40.

Provençal and Catholic lore diverge at this point: Catholicism believes Sara (patron saint of the gitans Romas, also known as gypsies), travelled with the Maries on the boat; Provençal legend says Sara was already here, and was the first person to recognise their Holiness. (And if you believe Dan Brown's ubiquitous blockbuster *The Da Vinci Code*, Sara was none other than Jesus' and Marie-Madeleine's daughter.) In 1448 skeletal remains said to belong to Sara and the Maries were found in the crypt in Stes-Maries' church.

Finer ficto-historical points aside, it's by no means a washed-up legend: Gitans continue to make the **Pèlerinage des Gitans** here on 24 May for three days (many staying for up to three weeks) of dancing and playing music in the streets, and parading a statue of Sara through town. The Sunday in October closest to the 22nd ushers in a second pilgrimage dedicated to the two saintly Maries.

thatched-roof *cabanes* (cowboy cottages) woos punters with homemade bread, bull steaks and biodynamic produce fresh from its vegetable garden. The perfectly manicured grounds hint at Disney, but dining by the pool or overlooking the private lake is salt-of-the-earth stuff nonetheless. The spa-hotel-restaurant (doubles €140 to €170) is stabled 1.5km north of Stes-Maries de la Mer on the D570.

♥ LE FOURNELET €€

☎ 04 90 97 97 75; 12 av Gambetta; lunch & dinner menus €17.50-33, shellfish platters from €25; ☺ lunch & dinner
It has no view to speak of and its interior is nothing to write home about, but this fish restaurant, with a *menu* translated into several languages, is the address the locals recommend. Whichever crustacean you plump for, include a plate of local aïoli-dressed *tellines* in your choice. Advance reservations recommended.

TRANSPORT

BUS // Stes-Maries de la Mer has no bus station; buses to/from Arles (p92) via Pont du Gau and Mas du Pont

de Rousty use the shelter at the northern entrance to town on av d'Arles (the continuation of rte d'Arles and the D570).

BIKE // Le Vélociste (☎ 04 90 97 83 26; www .leveociste.fr, in French; place Mireille; ☺ Apr-Oct) charges €15/28/34 per one/two/three days for bicycle hire and advises on cycling itineraries. **Le Vélo Saintois** (☎ 04 90 97 74 56; www.levelosaintois .camargue.fr; in French; 19 rue de la République; ☺ Apr-Oct) charges similar prices and has tandems (€30 per day). Both drop off bikes for free at your hotel.

SOUTH-EASTERN CAMARGUE

· · · · · ·

DRIVING TOUR: THE WILD SOUTHEAST

Map p97
Distance: 96km
Duration: one day
For a jaunt to the edge of the world, drive south from Arles along the D570 (direction Stes-Maries de la Mer). After 2.8km, turn left onto the D36 (direction Le Sam-

buc and Salin de Giraud) and within seconds you're in the Parc Naturel Régional de Camargue. Four kilometres on, turn right onto the D36B (direction Gageron) and at the crossroads continue straight.

Soon after the D36B dramatically skims the eastern shores of the **Étang de Vaccarès**. The wetland is at its most savage here and much of the area is off-limits, making the nature trails and wildlife observatories at **La Capelière** (☎ 04 90 97 00 97; adult/12-18yr €3/1.50; ⏱ 9am-1pm & 2-6pm Apr-Sep, 9am-1pm & 2-5pm Wed-Mon Oct-Mar), 18.5km south of Arles, particularly precious. Discover flora and

fauna native to freshwater marshes along its 1.5km-long Sentier des Rainettes (Tree-frog Trail) and play voyeur as little egrets and grey herons frolic in the marshes.

Before leaving La Capelière buy a permit (adult €3, 12 to 18 years €1.50) to visit the observatories and nature trails at **Salin de Badon**, former royal salt pans 7km south. True birders mustn't miss a night in its **gîte** (dorms €12), a two-floor cottage with 20 beds over seven rooms, kitchen, toilet and solar electricity. BYO food, drinking water, bedding and mosquito spray.

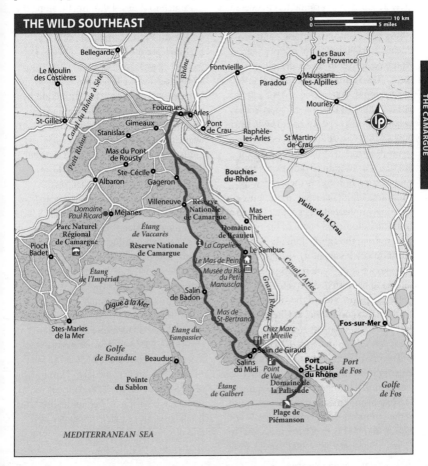

THE WILD SOUTHEAST

Enjoy a rustic lunch nearby at the **Mas de St-Bertrand** (☎ 04 42 48 80 69; rte du Vaccarès; mains €10; ☺ lunch & dinner Wed-Mon mid-Mar–mid-Nov; ☖), 4km south; immediately after Le Paradis turn left towards Salin de Giraud along the D36C to find it. Dining in the old sheepfold, with monumental fireplace and rusty farm-tool sculptures by Madame, is unique. It has three chalets (doubles/quads €45/75), cycling trails (25km, 50km and 75km) and rents bikes (two hours/one day €5/€15).

Next up along the D36C is **Salin de Giraud**, an unexceptional village that grew up from 1856 around its chequered evaporation *salins* (salt pans) covering 100 sq km – Europe's largest – and producing 800,000 tonnes of salt per year. At the ecomuseum inside the village saltworks, **Les Salins de Giraud** (☎ 04 42 86 70 20; place Péchiney, Salin de Giraud; adult/4-13yr/family €8.20/6/24.20; ☺ 9.30am-12.30pm & 2-7pm Jul & Aug, 10.15am-12.15pm & 2-6pm Mar-Jun, Sep & Oct), learn how *sel* (salt) is produced by local *sauniers* (salt farmers) and tour the pans on board a tourist train. Dramatically more soul-stirring however is the windswept panorama of the pans, salt mountains and seemingly toy-sized diggers that unfold a couple of kilometres south of the marsh village along the D36D. Pull up at the **point de vue** (viewpoint), breathe in the salty sea air and, if you're lucky, watch salt being harvested. Afterwards buy salt in the shop and back in the village, lunch on fresh fish and *tellines* at **Chez Marc et Mireille** (☎ 04 42 48 80 08; 2 rue Vanelles, Salin de Giraud; menus €16; ☺ lunch & dinner Thu-Mon).

The final 12km leg of this southbound journey is unforgettable. Drive slowly to watch pink flamingos wade through water. Just over 5km south of the viewpoint is the **Domaine de la Palissade** (☎ 04 42 86 81 28, 06 87 84 33 72; rte de la Mer; adult/under 11yr €3/free; ☺ 9am-5pm or 6pm Apr-Oct, 9am-5pm Wed

& Sun Nov-Feb), a nature centre that organises fantastic forays into the marshes on foot and horseback; call ahead to book **horse treks** (1 hr adult/8-12 yr €15.50/12.50, 2 hr €25.50/22.50). The ticket desk rents binoculars (€2) and has free maps of the estate's three marked walking trails (1km to 8km) through scrubby glasswort, flowering sea lavender (August) and flooded lagoons.

The road reaches the Med and **Plage de Piémanson** 3.7km south. Not quite the natural paradise it could be, campervans park overnight on the sand and litter spots the wild, untended beach.

Return to Arles, 48km north, along the D36. In Petit Manusclat the tiny **Musée du Riz du Petit Manusclat** (☎ 04 90 97 20 29; www.heureuse-camargue.com; admission €5; ☺ 9am-12.30pm & 2-6pm Tue Mar-Nov, 9am-12.30pm & 2-6pm Tue & Thu Jul & Aug) explores the local rice industry, a key part of the economy since the 13th century: the Camargue grows 70% of French rice, including that heavenly nutty organic red rice (p371).

Just 500m north, south of Le Sambuc, is **Le Mas de Peint** (☎ 04 90 97 20 62; www.masdepeint.com, in French; menus €36, €44 & €57; ☺ dinner Tue & Thu, lunch & dinner Fri-Mon Sep-Nov & Mar-Jun, lunch & dinner Thu-Tue, lunch Wed Jul & Aug), the upmarket sleeping-eating quarters of one of the Camargue's oldest family bull farms, 550-hectare **Manade Jacques Bon** (☎ 04 90 97 28 50). Call ahead to book horse-riding and jeep tours (both €60 per two hours) or a table for lunch.

A fitting final stop on the return journey to Arles is **Domaine de Beaujeu** (☎ 04 90 97 22 30; www.domainedebeaujeu.com; rte du Sambuc; ☺ 9.30am-noon & 2-5.30pm Fri & Sat, 2-5.30pm Wed), an organic farm 7km north of Le Sambuc on the D36. Wine is its mainstay (€9 for a 3L bag in the box) but it sells organic red rice (€3.80 per kg) and olive oil too, in its farm shop. Out of shop hours, ring the bell.

AVIGNON AREA

3 PERFECT DAYS

🌱 DAY 1 // ROMAN RELICS

Choose one of three towns to explore a rich selection of Roman ruins. Make gourmet St-Rémy de Provence home to investigate the ruins of Glanum (p133), an atmospheric Gallo-Roman town built around a sacred spring. Orange contains the best-preserved Roman theatre (p115) in Europe, and is also close to France's largest archaeological site at Vaison-la-Romaine (p117). Pont du Gard (p143), the three-tiered aqueduct beloved of Provence's poster-makers, is easily accessed from Nîmes, which also contains the superb amphitheatre Les Arènes (p140).

🌱 DAY 2 // CYCLING IN THE DENTELLES

The jagged limestone Dentelles, dotted with sleepy villages, were just made for exploring by bicycle. Pick up a route map from the tourist office at Vaison-la-Romaine (p117), then pedal southeast to Le Barroux to admire its castle and working monastery (p121). Stop for lunch in Beaumes de Venise (p122), famous for its golden Or Blanc wine. Heading north, Gigondas (p122) is also great for wine lovers, with producers handily scattered round the village square.

🌱 DAY 3 // THE RIVER SORGUE SPECIAL

Get to Fontaine de Vaucluse first thing to contemplate the River Sorgue's mysterious birthplace (p129). As kingfishers and dragonflies dance by, take a lazy two-hour canoe trip (p129) downstream, followed by lunch at the Partage des Eaux (p128). Then stroll along a flowery lane into L'Isle-sur-la-Sorgue to admire its 18th-century canals and still-turning waterwheels, dripping with moss, before antique shopping (p127), then dining at the Michelin-starred Le Vivier (p128) to round the evening off.

AVIGNON AREA

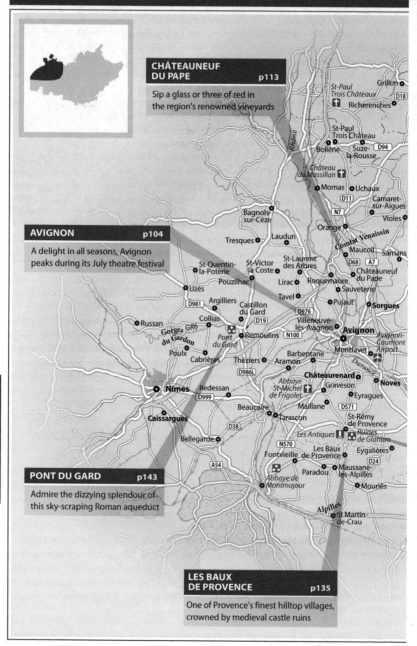

CHÂTEAUNEUF DU PAPE p113

Sip a glass or three of red in the region's renowned vineyards

AVIGNON p104

A delight in all seasons, Avignon peaks during its July theatre festival

PONT DU GARD p143

Admire the dizzying splendour of this sky-scraping Roman aqueduct

LES BAUX DE PROVENCE p135

One of Provence's finest hilltop villages, crowned by medieval castle ruins

Grillon
St-Paul Trois Châteaux
Richerenches
D18
St-Paul Trois Château
Bollène
Suze-la-Rousse
D94
Château de Massillan
Mornas
Uchaux
D11
Camaret-sur-Aigues
N7
Orange
Violès
Comtat Venaissin
Bagnols-sur-Cèze
Maucoil
Sarrians
Laudun
D68
A7
Tresques
St-Laurent des Arbres
Châteauneuf du Pape
St-Quentin-la-Poterie
St-Victor la Coste
Roquemaure
Sauveterre
Pouzilhac
Lirac
Pujaut
Sorgues
Uzès
Tavel
D981
Argilliers
Castillon du Gard
D976
Villeneuve-lès-Avignon
Avignon
Collias
D19
Remoulins
N100
Avignon-Caumont Airport
Russan
Gorges du Gardon
GR6
Pont du Gard
Montfavet
Durance
Poulx
Cabrières
Théziers
Aramon
Barbentane
Châteaurenard
Noves
D986L
Abbaye St-Michel de Frigolet
Graveson
Eyragues
Redessan
Maillane
D571
Nîmes
D999
Beaucaire
St-Rémy de Provence
Caissargues
Tarascon
Les Antiques
Ruines de Glanum
D38
N570
Bellegarde
Fontvieille
Les Baux de Provence
Eygalières
A54
Paradou
Maussane-les-Alpilles
D24
Abbaye de Montmajour
Mouriès
Alpilles
St-Martin-de-Crau

Rhône

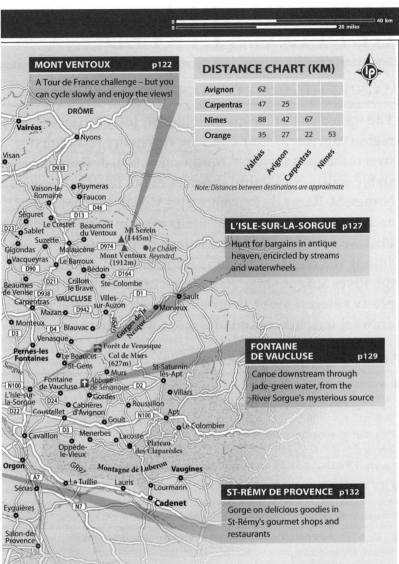

0 — 40 km
0 — 20 miles

MONT VENTOUX   p122

A Tour de France challenge – but you can cycle slowly and enjoy the views!

DISTANCE CHART (KM)

	Valréas	Avignon	Carpentras	Nîmes
Avignon	62			
Carpentras	47	25		
Nîmes	88	42	67	
Orange	35	27	22	53

Note: Distances between destinations are approximate

L'ISLE-SUR-LA-SORGUE   p127

Hunt for bargains in antique heaven, encircled by streams and waterwheels

FONTAINE DE VAUCLUSE   p129

Canoe downstream through jade-green water, from the River Sorgue's mysterious source

ST-RÉMY DE PROVENCE   p132

Gorge on delicious goodies in St-Rémy's gourmet shops and restaurants

DRÔME
Valréas
Nyons
Visan
D938
Vaison-la-Romaine
Puymeras
Faucon
D46
Séguret
D13
Le Crestet
Beaumont du Ventoux
Mt Serein (1445m)
D23
Sablet
Suzette
Malaucène
D974
Le Chalet Reynard
Gigondas
Vacqueyras
Le Barroux
Mont Ventoux (1912m)
D90
Bédoin
D164
Beaumes de Venise
D21
Crillon le Brave
Ste-Colombe
D938
Carpentras
VAUCLUSE
Villes-sur-Auzon
D1
Sault
Mazan
D942
Monieux
Monteux
D4
Blauvac
D3
Venasque
Gorges de la Nesque
Pernes-les-Fontaines
Forêt de Venasque
Le Beaucet
Col de Murs (627m)
St-Saturnin-lès-Apt
Sorgue
St-Gens
Murs
Fontaine de Vaucluse
Abbaye de Sénanque
D2
N100
Villars
L'Isle-sur-la-Sorgue
D24
Gordes
D22
Coustellet
Cabrières d'Avignon
Roussillon
Apt
Goult
N100
Le Colombier
Cavaillon
D3
Menerbes
Lacoste
Oppède-le-Vieux
Plateau des Claparèdes
Orgon
GR97
Montagne de Luberon
Vaugines
A7
La Tuillie
Lauris
Lourmarin
Sénas
Cadenet
Eyguières
N7
Salon-de-Provence

AVIGNON AREA

GETTING AROUND

Beyond the big towns, transport is hit-and-miss or nonexistent – a hire car is recommended for exploring the Enclave des Papes, the Dentelles de Montmirail, the towns along the River Sorgue and the Alpilles. A fine road for driving/cycling is the wiggly D90 from Malaucène to Suzette, with wonderful views of Mont Ventoux and the Dentelles. Avignon, Nîmes and Orange have train stations with good connections; surprisingly, the only way to get to/from Carpentras on public transport is by bus.

AVIGNON AREA GETTING STARTED

MAKING THE MOST OF YOUR TIME

The walled city of Avignon holds this joyfully jumbled region together. Allow two days to explore its tangled streets and papal palace. Spinning outwards from its stable centre, you'll find superb Roman relics at Orange, Nîmes, St-Rémy de Provence and Vaison-la-Romaine, each worthy of a day. Time melts away in the peaceful Enclave des Papes; hilltop castles and hamlets hide among the ragged limestone Dentelles and Alpilles; and the River Sorgue sings glass-green lullabies to its brood of pretty villages. Mont Ventoux, Provence's highest peak, draws skiers, hikers and bikers according to the season.

TOP TOURS & COURSES

☙ AVIGNON WINE TOUR

Visit the region's vineyards with a knowledgable guide who does all the driving, leaving you free to enjoy the wine. (☎ 06 28 05 33 84; www.avignon-wine-tour.com; per person €75)

☙ LA TRUFFE DU VENTOUX

Glimpse into the clandestine world of the 'black diamond' on a truffle hunt near Carpentras. (☎ 04 90 66 82 21; www.truffes-ventoux.com; La Quinsonne, 634 chemin du Traversier, Monteux; ☾ Oct–mid-Mar)

☙ 'LE MARMITON' COOKING SCHOOL

Avignon's loveliest hotel (p382) arranges cooking classes (€80 to €135) with the region's best chefs. (☎ 04 90 85 93 93; www.la-mirande.fr; Hôtel de la Mirande, 4 place de la Mirande, Avignon; ☾ Sept–Jun)

☙ LES ATELIERS DE L'IMAGE PHOTOGRAPHY WORKSHOPS

Dull holiday snaps? Improve your photography skills with a tailor-made two-day course (from €250) at this design-driven hotel (p386), with on-site darkrooms. (☎ 04 90 92 51 50; www.hotelphoto.com; 36 bd Victor Hugo, St-Rémy de Provence)

☙ AUTOCARS LIEUTAUD SIGHTSEEING TOURS

Themed half- and full-day sightseeing trips across the region – of lavender fields, Roman monuments, vineyards, Van Gogh–associated sites, or anything else you fancy. (☎ 04 90 86 36 75; www.cars-lieutaud.fr; 36 bd St-Roch, Avignon)

GETTING AWAY FROM IT ALL

* **Sneak away on the Visite Palais Secrét** Explore areas of the Palais des Papes (southern France's most-visited monument), normally closed to visitors (p104)

* **Picnic in the peaceful Abbaye St-André gardens** A world away from the crowds of Avignon, but only a tiny hop across the river (p112)

* **Canoe down the Sorgue** You can't get trampled by the herds if you're skimming down the middle of a river... (p129)

* **Hiking Mont Ventoux** It's a popular spot, but with so many tracks and trails, solitude is just around the corner (p124)

ADVANCE PLANNING

If you're around for the region's biggest festivals, booking tickets and accommodation ahead is essential.

* **Festival d'Avignon** (Bureau du Festival; ☎ 04 90 27 66 50; www.festival-avignon.com; Espace St-Louis, 20 rue du Portail Boquier) Avignon's mighty three-week theatre festival takes place in July

* **Les Chorégies d'Orange** (www.choregies .com) During July and August, Orange hosts a series of weekend operas, classical concerts and choral performances

* **Choralies** (www.choralies.fr) This two-week choral festival, held every three years in Vaison-la-Romaine, is Europe's largest. The next recurrence is in August 2010.

* **Féria de Pentecôte** (www.arenesdenimes .com in French) Bull fights and wild partying at Nîmes' annual Spanish-style festivities

TOP MARKETS

Displays of regional food pop up at weekly outdoor markets, generally running from 8am to noon. Covered food markets in Avignon and Nîmes operate daily.

🍄 MONDAY
Bédoin, Fontvieille

🍄 TUESDAY
Tarascon, Vaison-la-Romaine

🍄 WEDNESDAY
Malaucène, Sault, St-Rémy de Provence, Valréas

🍄 THURSDAY
Beaucaire, L'Isle-sur-la-Sorgue, Maillane, Maussane-les-Alpilles, Orange, Villeneuve-lès-Avignon

---

🍄 FRIDAY
Carpentras, Châteauneuf du Pape, Fontvieille, Graveson

🍄 SATURDAY
Pernes-les-Fontaines, Richerenches (truffles; November to March), St-Rémy de Provence, Villeneuve-lès-Avignon

---

🍄 SUNDAY
Beaucaire, L'Isle-sur-la-Sorgue

RESOURCES

* **Avignon & Provence** (www.avignon-et-provence.com) Sleeping and eating suggestions

* **Provence Guide** (www.provenceguide.com) Covering the whole of the Vaucluse region including B&Bs

* **Visit Provence** (www.visitprovence.com) Extensive information on the Alpilles

AVIGNON AREA

AVIGNON & AROUND

......

AVIGNON

pop 92,454

The belle of Provence's ball, Avignon's charm shines through whatever the weather or season. The massive medieval palace, the Palais des Papes, lords it over the walled city; the Pont d'Avignon, that famous nursery-rhyme bridge, spans the river Rhône; ancient streets thread past glamorous boutiques and gourmet restaurants; and in July each year, thousands flood into Avignon for its renowned performing arts festival.

The most fascinating period of Avignon's history began 700 years ago, when this medieval town became the new Vatican. Pope Clement V and his court fled political turmoil in Rome and settled here in 1309. The town grew rapidly, with the immense Palais des Papes (Palace of the Popes) seated at its heart. From within its fortified walls, seven successive French popes ruled until 1377, controlling vast amounts of money and making Avignon one of the most powerful cities in Europe.

ESSENTIAL INFORMATION

EMERGENCIES // Hôpital Général Henri Duffaut (☎ 04 32 75 33 33; 305 rue Raoul Follereau) Marked on maps as Hôpital Sud, 2.5km south of the central train station – take bus 3 or 6. **Police station** (☎ 04 90 16 81 00; bd St-Roch)

TOURIST OFFICES // Tourism office (☎ 04 32 74 32 74; www.avignon-tourisme.com; 41 cours Jean Jaurès; 🕲 9am-6pm Mon-Sat & 9.45am-5pm Sun Apr-Jun & Aug-Oct, 9am-6pm Mon-Fri & 9am-5pm Sat & 10am-noon Sun Nov-Mar, 9am-7pm Mon-Sat & 9.45am-5pm Sun Jul). **Tourism office annex** (rue Ferruce; 🕲 10am-1pm & 2-6pm 9 Apr-Oct).

EXPLORING AVIGNON

Avignon's two big sights are the Palais des Papes and the Pont St-Bénézet, and the walled city itself makes a third. Ticket offices for most sights close half to one hour before overall closing times.

🌱 **PALAIS DES PAPES // EXPLORE AVIGNON'S PAPAL PAST AT THIS UNESCO-RATED GOTHIC PALACE**
The immense **Palais des Papes** (Palace of the Popes; ☎ 04 90 27 50 00; www.palais-des-papes .com; place du Palais; full price/pass €10.50/8.50; 🕲 9am-8pm Jul & early–mid-Sep, 9am-9pm Aug, 9am-7pm mid-Mar–Jun & mid-Sep–Oct, 9am-6.30pm early–mid-Mar, 9am-5.45pm Nov-Feb) is the world's largest Gothic palace and a Unesco World Heritage site. It was built when Pope Clement V abandoned Rome in 1309 and settled in Avignon, which became the centre of papal power for over 70 years. The immense scale of the palace, with its cavernous stone halls and vast courtyards, testifies to the wealth of the popes; the 3m-thick walls, portcullises and watchtowers emphasise their insecurity.

Today, it takes some imagination to picture the former luxury of these vast bare rooms. You can catch whispering glimpses in the wonderful 14th-century chapel frescoes painted by Matteo Giovannetti; in the dark-blue walls of the Pope's bedroom, threaded with dusky red flowers; and in the superb Chambre du Cerf, alive with medieval hunting scenes.

An audioguide directs you from ground level to crenellations: join the gargoyles for superb views, or drink a well-earned coffee in the tiny sky-high café. Exit is via La Bouteillerie wine cellar, where you can sample 55 Côtes du Rhône wines.

The two-hour French-only **Visite Palais Secrét** (Secret Palace Tour; tours €30; ☙ by reservation Sat & Sun) takes you to secret towers and rooftop walkways in unexplored parts of the palace, and feeds you brunch on the Great Dignitaries' Terrace.

Combination tickets (adult/8-17yr Mar-Oct €13/10, Nov–mid-Mar €11/8.50) covering admission to the palace and Pont St-Bénézet are available.

🌶 PLACE DU PALAIS // OTHER HIGHLIGHTS OF THE SQUARE

The palace isn't the only eye-catching building on this massive square. A golden statue of the Virgin Mary (weighing a portly 4.5 tons) stands on the dome of the Romanesque **Cathédrale Notre Dame des Doms** (built 1671–72), outstretched arms protecting the city. Next to the cathedral, the **Rocher des Doms** gardens are a fine place to admire views of the Rhône, Villeneuve-lès-Avignon, Mont Ventoux and Les Alpilles. Opposite the palace, the much-photographed building dripping with outsized carvings of fruit and heraldic beasts is the former 17th-century mint, **Hôtel des Monnaies**.

🌶 PONT ST-BÉNÉZET // DANCE ON AVIGNON'S FAMOUS NURSERY-RHYME BRIDGE

The **Pont St-Bénézet** (☎ 04 90 27 51 16; full price/pass €4.50/3.50) is known to countless kids as the Pont d'Avignon from the chirpy French rhyme. Altogether, now:

Sur le pont d'Avignon
L'on y danse, l'on y danse
Sur le pont d'Avignon
L'on y danse tout en rond…

(On the bridge of Avignon
Everyone is dancing, everyone is dancing
On the bridge of Avignon
Everyone is dancing in a circle…)

According to legend, pastor Bénézet had three saintly visions urging him to build a bridge across the Rhône. Completed in 1185, the bridge linked Avignon with Villeneuve-lès-Avignon, controlling trade at this vital crossroads. It was rebuilt several times, before all but four of its spans were washed away in the mid-1600s. Opening hours are the same as for Palais des Papes (opposite).

ACCOMMODATION

Whether a five-star hotel or a hidden Provençal *mas,* book accommodation well ahead in summer. Check out the detailed listings in our dedicated accommodation chapter.

★ Guests themselves contribute to the artistic vibe at **Lumani** (p383), an Avignon *maison d'hôte*

★ Orange makes a cheap base, with lots of good-value accommodation like the **Hôtel l'Herbier d'Orange** (p384)

★ Romance fills the air of the 15th-century **Hostellerie Le Beffroi** (p383), hidden in the walled medieval city at Vaison-la-Romaine

★ Gardens complete with small swimming pool surround peaceful **La Madelène** (p384), a B&B based in a 12th-century priory outside Malaucène

★ **Fragrance** (p385) in St-Rémy de Provence is a home away from home, filled with crisp linen and fresh flowers, and serving homemade pastries for breakfast

AVIGNON

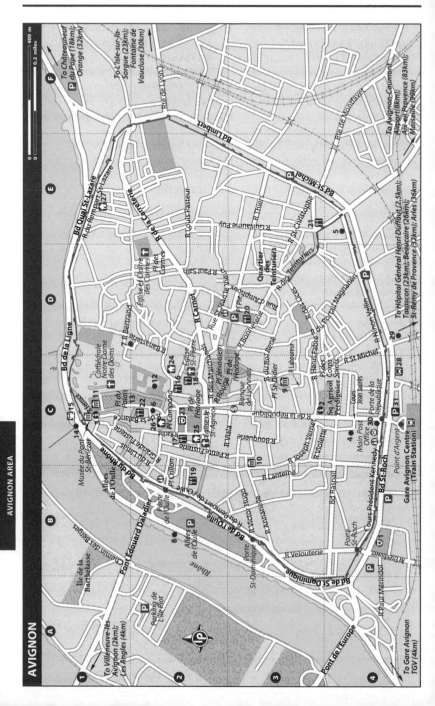

🌱 CITY WALKS // IMMERSE YOURSELF IN THE CITY'S SLOW-BEATING CHARM

One of Avignon's chief joys is to wander aimlessly, peeking into hidden corners of this photogenic old city. Within the embrace of its superbly preserved 14th-century **ramparts** lie crooked streets and leafy squares, bursting with medieval churches, handsome old houses, statues and brightly-painted murals.

For a more structured approach, pick up a free city map from the tourist office showing four different walking routes: around the Palais des Papes; the medieval streets; the university area; and the **Quartier des Teinturiers**, Avignon's old dyers' district where four waterwheels still turn. **Walking tours** (adult/child €17/7) in French and English run at 10am year-round: contact the tourist office for days and starting points.

🌱 FESTIVAL D'AVIGNON & FESTIVAL OFF // THOUSANDS OF THESPIANS WOW THE CROWDS IN JULY

The three-week **Festival d'Avignon** (Bureau du Festival; ☎ 04 90 27 66 50; www.festival-avignon.com; Espace St-Louis, 20 rue du Portail Boquier; tickets €16-50), held annually in July, is one of the world's most well-respected performing arts festivals. Over 40 French and international works of dance and drama play to 100,000-plus spectators, in the town's theatres, streets, historical palaces and churches.

The official festival is paralleled by a fringe event **Festival Off** (Avignon Public Off; ☎ 04 90 85 13 08; www.avignonleoff.com; Bureau du Off, 5 rue Ninon Vallin), with an eclectic – and cheaper – program of experimental performances. La Carte Off (€13) is a discount card giving you 30% off all Festival Off performances.

Tickets for both festivals are also available from FNAC branches.

🌱 MUSEUMS & GALLERIES // UNEARTH AVIGNON'S PAST THROUGH ART AND ARTEFACTS

Charming little **Musée Angladon** (☎ 04 90 82 29 03; www.angladon.com; 5 rue Laboureur; full price/pass €6/4; ⏱ 1-6pm Tue-Sun Apr-Nov, 1-6pm Wed-Sun Jan-Mar, closed Dec) holds, *Railway Wagons*, the only Van Gogh painting in Provence. If you look closely you'll see the 'earth' isn't paint but the bare, underlying canvas. Also displayed are a handful of early Picasso sketches and artworks by Cézanne, Sisley, Manet and Degas.

Epic shipwrecks and dying heroes abound in the dramatic oil paintings at the **Musée Calvet** (☎ 04 90 86 33 84; 65 rue Joseph Vernet; full price/pass €6/3; ⏱ 10am-1pm & 2-6pm Wed-Mon), Avignon's fine arts museum.

There's also an interesting prehistoric collection, translucent 19th-century marble sculptures, silverware, and the elongated landscapes of Avignonnais artist Joseph Vernet.

If you like Madonnas, you'll really love the **Musée du Petit Palais** (☎ 04 90 86 44 58; www.petit-palais.org; place du Palais; adult/under 12yr €6/free; ⊙ 10am-1pm & 2-6pm Wed-Mon), based in a medieval archbishop's palace, which houses a collection of 13th- to 16th-century religious paintings. The most famous work is Botticelli's *La Vierge et l'Enfant* (1470).

❦ **LES GRANDS BATEAUX DE PROVENCE // TAKE A BOAT TRIP ALONG THE MIGHTY RHÔNE**
Les Grands Bateaux (☎ 04 90 85 62 25; www .mireio.net; allées de l'Oulle) runs 45-minute **boat tours** (adult/under 8yr €8/free; ⊙ tours 3pm & 4.15pm Apr-Jun & Sep, 2pm, 3pm, 4pm, 5pm & 6pm Jul-Aug) that weave under the famous bridge before looping to Villeneuve and back.

For a longer **daytime cruise** (with/without lunch from €48/25), hop aboard *Le Mireio*, which sails to Arles, Châteauneuf du Pape or Tarascon year-round. On summer evenings, the company's **dinner cruises** (from €52; ⊙ 8.30pm Jul & Aug) attract older visitors with dancing or live entertainment. See the website for cruise schedules.

GASTRONOMIC HIGHLIGHTS

Place de l'Horloge is a riot of outdoor brasseries from Easter until mid-November: food is average, but it's not bad value and

---

48 HOURS IN AVIGNON

FOR FREE
Avignon's beautiful maze of medieval streets, crammed with ancient buildings, independent shops, statues and murals, requires no spending. For postcard-perfect views of the palace and bridge, take the free **shuttle boat** (⊙ 10am-12.30pm & 2-6.30pm Apr-Jun & Sep, 11am-9pm Jul & Aug, 2-5.30pm Wed, 10am-noon & 2-5.30pm Sat & Sun Oct-Dec) across the Rhône to Île de la Barthelasse, then stroll left along the river bank (to the pontoon adjacent to Pont St-Bénézet).

RAINY DAY
The chambers and chapels of Avignon's number one tourist attraction, the Palais des Papes (p104), are made for bad-weather visits. A quick dash between raindrops will get you to the Musée du Petit Palais (p107), where you can beseech the medieval painted virgins to stop the downpour. Or embrace the wateriness of your day by taking a boat trip (above) along the Rhône.

OUTDOOR AVIGNON
Once you've danced on Avignon's famous bridge (p105), take a 10-minute bus-ride across the river to Villeneuve-lès-Avignon. After a leisurely lunch on the town square, climb the hill to Fort St-André (p112), with its precipitous towers, for marvellous views of Avignon. Round off your day with a long, lazy exploration of the dreamy Jardins de l'Abbaye (p112), one of France's top 100 gardens.

AVIGNON AREA

you'll always find a table. Several hotels (p382) have superb restaurants open to guests and nonguests. **Les Halles food market** (place Pie; ⏰6am-1.30pm Tue-Sun), with its remarkable living-plant facade, contains over 40 stalls.

🍴 CHRISTIAN ÉTIENNE €€€

☎ 04 90 86 16 50; www.christian-etienne.fr; 10 rue de Mons; lunch menu €35, dinner menus €65-125; ⏰lunch & dinner Tue-Sat, daily Jul

One of Avignon's top tables, this elevated restaurant is based in a 12th-century palace, and has a leafy outdoor terrace with a view of the Palais des Papes. Signature seasonal specialities, such as Avignonnaise wild boar stew, tomatoes prepared in numerous ways, and truffle ice cream, are created by its eponymous master chef. The comprehensive wine list is packed with local Côtes du Rhône wines.

🍴 LA FOURCHETTE €€

☎ 04 90 85 20 93; 17 rue Racine; lunch/dinner menus from €27/33; ⏰lunch & dinner Mon-Fri, closed 1st 3 weeks in Aug

An enduring classical French bistro, La Fourchette has been run by the same family for generations. Its dining rooms are large and light, decorated with plaster cicadas and old festival posters, and there's a tempting choice of dishes on its fixed-price *menu*. Along with tender lamb, specialities include marinaded sardines, hearty meat or seafood stews, and a sinful meringue ice cream with praline.

🍴 LE GRAND CAFÉ €€

☎ 04 90 86 86 77; www.legrandcafe-avignon.com; 4 rue des Escaliers Ste-Anne; lunch/dinner menus from €20/30; ⏰lunch & dinner Tue-Sat, also Sun Jun-Aug

Nestled at the foot of the palace, this bistro-bar is part of the arty Manutention cultural centre (p110). Its vibrant,

bohemian atmosphere is enhanced by the chatter of happy diners, all tucking in to full-flavoured meals with a Moroccan-Italian emphasis. The menu changes regularly – if it's available, how about the duck breast, endorsed by locals as 'almost gastronomic' (ie delectable but affordable)?

🍴 L'ÉPICERIE €€

☎ 04 90 82 74 22; 10 place St-Pierre; lunch/dinner menus from €15.50/28; ⏰lunch & dinner, closed Nov-Apr & 1st 2 weeks Aug

Recommended by readers, this tiny restaurant seats only 25, but in summer outdoor tables spread across the cobbled square outside Église St-Pierre. The small menu zings with colourful and flavoursome Mediterranean ingredients – try lamb tajine, spiced beef with vegetable crumble, or the *assiette des épicières* (a plateful of nibbly delights such as salmon muffin, aubergine stack, and tomato-and-basil crème brulée).

☙ LES 5 SENS €€€

☎ 04 90 85 26 51; www.restaurantles5sens.com; 18 rue Joseph Vernet; lunch formule €20, lunch/dinner menu €42/50; ☽ lunch & dinner Tue-Sat, closed 1st 2 weeks Aug

Celebrated chef Thierry Baucher rustles up gastronomic delights at Les 5 Sens, hidden in a courtyard off rue Joseph Vernet. The ingredients are Mediterranean, but imagination renders them into something new and beautiful. Try turbot enlivened with fennel and ginger, tender pigeon breast, or butternut-squash ravioli with snails. A long wine list backs up the food, and there's always one vegetarian option.

☙ NUMÉRO 75 €€

☎ 04 90 27 16 00; 75 rue Guillaume Puy; menus from €18; ☽ lunch & dinner Mon-Sat, daily during Festival

This lovely old building was once the home of absinthe inventor Jules Pernod, who created Pernod here in 1870. It's now one of Avignon's in-spots for Mediterranean cuisine packed with seasonal flavour – if you're looking for value, try the fantastic €18 'chef's suggestion' *menu*. The stately interior glows with a rich, contemporary colour scheme, and in summer you can dine in the charming garden.

☙ RESTAURANT BRUNEL €€

☎ 04 90 85 24 83; 46 rue de la Balance; plat du jour €11, menus from €26; ☽ lunch & dinner Tue-Sat, also Mon Jul

Brunel is a local favourite for authentic Provençal dishes, using seasonal ingredients such as goat's cheese, asparagus, foie gras and lamb – come here on Friday lunchtime to sample the aïoli. There are outstanding deals on lunch main courses (which always include a fish of the day) and freshly prepared desserts. The handful of outdoor tables is hotly contested in warm weather.

NIGHTLIFE

Avignon's nightlife revolves around live music and theatre, rather than wild bars and clubs. Avignon is the theatre capital of France: there are dozens scattered across the city, staging every kind of performance you can imagine. Ask the tourist office for a full list.

☙ AJMI

Association pour Le Jazz & La Musique Improvisée; ☎ 04 90 86 08 61; www.jazzalajmi.com, in French; 4 rue des Escaliers Ste-Anne

This 30-year-old jazz club is inside the arts centre, La Manutention. Most concerts take place on Friday nights, although there are also Tea Jazz sessions (with solo performers and nonalcoholic drinks) at 4.30pm on Sunday. Tickets cost around €15 and can be bought from FNAC; see the website for forthcoming gigs.

☙ OPÉRA THÉÂTRE D'AVIGNON

☎ 04 90 82 81 40; www.operatheatredavignon.fr; place de l'Horloge

The season at the Opéra Théâtre d'Avignon, built in 1847, runs from October to June. It's the city's main classical venue, presenting operas, operettas, plays, symphonic concerts, chamber-music concerts and ballet. Tickets vary in price, depending on performance and seating: book through the website.

☙ CINÉMA UTOPIA

☎ 04 90 82 65 36; www.cinemas-utopia.org, in French; 4 rue des Escaliers Ste-Anne

This four-screen art-house cinema shows films in their original language, with French subtitles. The emphasis is on independent, golden-oldie and foreign films, although it does give an occasional nod to Hollywood blockbusters. Matinee/evening films cost €4/6.

TRANSPORT

GETTING TO/FROM THE AIRPORT
Avignon-Caumont airport (☎ 04 90 81 51 51) Located 8km southeast of Avignon. From around May to late September, carriers Flybe and Jet2.com have direct flights from the UK. There is no public transport into town; a taxi costs about €15. Try **Radio-Taxi Avignon** (☎ 04 90 82 20 20) or **Taxi Bruno Avignon** (☎ 06 07 19 45 21).

GETTING AROUND
PARKING // Narrow streets and a complex one-way system mean you're better off leaving the car outside the walls. **Vinci Park Gare Centre** (☎ 04 90 80 74 40; cnr bd St-Roch & bd St-Ruf; ⏲ 24hr) is a massive car park, which is beneath the train station, and offers free bicycles to customers.

TRAIN // Avignon has two train stations. Gare Avignon TGV, 4km southwest, serves TGV trains to/from Marseille (€26.90, 35 minutes) and Nice (€51.50, 3¼ hours). From early July to early September, there's a direct **Eurostar** (www.eurostar.com) service on Saturdays to/from London (six hours) and Ashford (five hours). Some TGVs to/from Paris (€99, around three hours) also stop at **Gare Avignon Centre** (42 bd St-Roch), which serves local trains, such as those to/from Orange (€5.30, 20 minutes), Arles (€6.40, 20 minutes) and Nîmes (€8.30, 30 minutes).

LOCAL BUSES // Local **TCRA** (www.tcra.fr) bus tickets cost €1.50 each on board. Buses run from 7am to about 7.30pm (8am to 6pm and less frequently on Sunday) from the main post office. *Navettes* (shuttle buses) link Gare Avignon TGV with the centre (13 minutes, twice hourly between 6.15am and 10.30pm). For Villeneuve-lès-Avignon, take bus 11 (bus 70 on Sunday).

REGIONAL BUSES // The underground **bus station** (halte routière; ☎ 04 90 82 07 35; bd St-Roch; ⏲ information window 8am-7.30pm Mon-Sat) is next door to the central railway station. Tickets are sold on the buses. Services include Arles (€7.70, 1½ hours), Carpentras (€4.20, 45 minutes), Marseille (€20, 35 minutes), Nîmes (€7.60, 1¼ hours) and Orange (€3, 45 minutes). Long-haul bus company **Linebus** (☎ 04 90 86 88 67) has an office at the far end of the bus platforms.

AVIGNON PASS

This nifty Avignon Passion pass entitles you to discounts in Avignon and Villeneuve-lès-Avignon, on museum visits, trips and tours. The first place you use the pass costs the full amount, but after that there's a 10% to 50% reduction. It's valid for 15 days, and covers a family of five. Pick up your pass from the tourist office, or any of the tourist sites.

BIKE // Provence Bike (☎ 04 90 27 92 61; www.provence-bike.com, in French; 7 ave St-Ruf; ⏲ 9am-noon & 3-7pm Mon-Sat) rents city bikes for €12/60 per day/week, and mountain bikes from €15/75 per day/week.

VILLENEUVE-LÈS-AVIGNON

pop 12,471
Villeneuve-lès-Avignon gazes across the Rhône at Avignon like a wistful little sister. Entranced by the bigger city's charm, most visitors barely glance at Villeneuve; but frankly, it's our preferred sibling, with monuments to rival Avignon's and none of the crowds. Loiter in the cloisters of a medieval monastery, get high on the views from Fort St-André, or lose yourself in the superb gardens of Abbaye St-André.

ESSENTIAL INFORMATION

TOURIST OFFICES // Tourist office (☎ 04 90 25 61 33; www.villeneuvelezavignon.fr; 1 place Charles David; ⏲ 9am-12.30pm & 2-6pm Mon-Fri, to 5pm Sat Sep-Jun, 10am-7pm Mon-Fri, 10am-1pm & 2.30-7pm Sat & Sun Jul, 9am-12.30pm & 2-6pm daily Aug) Runs guided tours in English in July and August.

EXPLORING VILLENEUVE-LÈS-AVIGNON

The Avignon Passion museum pass (see above) is valid in Villeneuve.

❦ CHARTREUSE DU VAL DE BÉNÉDICTION // IMPRESSIVE NAME OF THE ROSE–STYLE MEDIEVAL MONASTERY

Shaded from the summer heat, the three cloisters, 40 cells, church and chapels, washhouse, and nook-and-cranny gardens of the **Chartreuse du Val de Bénédiction** (☎ 04 90 15 24 24; www.chartreuse.org; 58 rue de la République; full price/pass/under 18yr €7/5.50/ free; ☻ 9am-6.30pm Jul-Sep, 9.30am-6.30pm Apr-Jun, 9.30am-5pm Mon-Fri, 10am-5pm Sat & Sun Oct-Mar) make up the biggest Carthusian monastery in France. Pope Innocent VI founded the monastery in 1352…and was buried here 10 years later in an elaborate mausoleum. Today La Chartreuse acts as a different kind of retreat – for budding playwrights on writing residencies.

❦ TOWERS & TURRETS // PANORAMIC TABLEAUX OF AVIGNON AND THE RHÔNE

With 2m-thick walls, King Philippe le Bel wasn't messing when he built the defensive 14th-century **Fort St-André** (☎ 04 90 25 45 35; full price/pass/under 18yr €5/3.50/ free; ☻ 10am-1pm & 2-6pm mid-May–mid-Sep, 10am-1pm & 2-5.30pm Apr–mid-May & mid-Sep–end Sep, 10am-1pm & 2-5pm Oct-Mar) on the then-border between France and the Holy Roman Empire. Today it's possible to walk a small section of the ramparts, and admire the 360-degree views from the top of the Tour des Masques (Mask Tower) and Tour Jumelles (Twin Towers).

Philippe also commissioned the **Tour Philippe le Bel** (☎ 04 32 70 08 57; full price/pass €2.10/1.60; ☻ 10am-12.30pm & 2-6.30pm Tue-Sun Apr-Sep, 10am-noon & 2-5pm Tue-Sun Oct, Nov & Mar), about 1.5km out of Villeneuve, which controlled traffic over the Pont St-Bénézet to and from Avignon. Steep steps spiral to the top – you're rewarded by another stunning view of the flowing Rhône.

❦ JARDINS DE L'ABBAYE // ITALIANATE GARDENS WITH VERTIGINOUS VIEWS

Within the encircling walls of Fort St-André, the privately owned **Jardins de l'Abbaye** (☎ 06 71 42 16 90; full price/pass €5/4; ☻ 10am-12.30pm & 2-6pm Tue-Sun Apr-Sep, to 5pm Oct-Mar) have splendid views of Avignon from the monumental terrace, built on top of the vaults of a 10th-century abbey. Meandering pathways cross a rose garden, duck under wisteria-covered pergolas, saunter into an olive grove sprinkled with irises, and thread by three ancient ruined churches. One of France's top 100 gardens, this is a place to breathe deep and watch the butterflies.

❦ MUSÉE PIERRE DE LUXEMBOURG // HEAVEN AND HELL FIGHT OVER SINNERS' SOULS

If you're remotely interested in religious art, seek out Enguerrand Quarton's painting *The Crowning of the Virgin* (1453) at the **Musée Pierre de Luxembourg** (☎ 04 90 27 49 66; rue de la République; full price/pass €3.10/2.10; ☻ 10am-12.30pm & 2-6.30pm Tue-Sun Apr-Sep, 10am-noon & 2-5pm Oct-Jan & Mar). Under solemn ranks of saints, angels wrest souls from purgatory – much to the devils' disappointment. Accompanying notes explain the painting's history and underpinning dogma.

GASTRONOMIC HIGHLIGHTS

❦ LA MAGNANERAIE €€

☎ 04 90 25 11 11; www.hostellerie-la-magnaneraie .com; 37 rue du Camp de Bataille; lunch menu €26, dinner menus €35-89; ☻ closed Sun evening & Wed
White-cloth tables and wicker chairs cluster beneath a canopy of lime trees – it's particularly seductive when lantern-lit. Menus change with the seasons, but contain delights such as foie gras marinated in peach wine, caramelised

lamb with pumpkin and artichoke, or stuffed wild hare. La Magnaneraie also has four-star guest rooms (doubles €135 to €235, suites €240 to €450) in shades of cornflower blue, rose and violet – the best have terraces overlooking the garden.

TRANSPORT

BUS // Bus 11 (70 on Sunday) links Villeneuve-lès-Avignon with Avignon (it's only 3km, but is a dull walk).

NORTH OF AVIGNON

· · · · · ·

Beloved of wine connoisseurs, the vineyards of Châteauneuf du Pape unfold above Avignon. Further north and east, Orange and Vaison-la-Romaine are rich in Roman treasures. The region extends up to the rocky Dentelles de Montmirail ridge, and the slopes of Provence's mighty mountain Mont Ventoux.

CHÂTEAUNEUF DU PAPE

pop 2107

Châteauneuf du Pape is a town obsessed with wine. As its name suggests, Pope John XXII (r 1316–34) built himself a castle here in 1317; being a keen oenophile, he planted vineyards around it, which today produce the renowned label. The **castle** is no more than a ruined facade (the German army blew it up during WWII), but there are fine views of the vine-laden countryside from its 118m hilltop.

The best wines of the last *millésime* (vintage) are cracked with gusto around 25 April during the **Fête de la St-Marc**. The **Fête de la Véraison**, held over the

first weekend of August, rejoices in the ripening of the grapes with a medieval festival (music, dance, jousting, markets, a Sunday Mass in Provençal, and plenty of papal wine).

ESSENTIAL INFORMATION

TOURIST OFFICES // Tourist office (☎ 04 90 83 71 08; www.paysprovence.fr, in French; place du Portail; ⏲ 9.30am-6pm Mon-Sat Jun-Sep, 9.30am-12.30pm & 2-6pm Mon, Tue, Thu-Sat Oct-May)

EXPLORING CHÂTEAUNEUF DU PAPE

❦ **WINE TASTING // CELEBRATE CHÂTEAUNEUF'S EARTHY REDS AND LESSER-KNOWN WHITES**
Splashed around town are more than two dozen wine shops offering *dégustation gratuite* (free wine tasting). Tastings are also free at the **Musée du Vin** (☎ 04 90 83 70 07; www.brotte.com; rte d'Avignon; admission free; ⏲ 9am-1pm & 2-7pm mid-Apr–mid-Oct, 9am-noon & 2-7pm mid-Oct–mid-Apr), which has an extensive exhibition about the area's soils, grape varieties and winemaking processes.

The tourist office has a **brochure of estates** in the area, showing which wine producers allow cellar visits and offer free tastings, which have English tours, and which ones require you to make an appointment first (generally Monday to Friday).

If you don't want to drive round the vineyards, the tourist office also has a brochure detailing a 16km **walking circuit**; or you could hire a **bicycle** (per day €18) from chocolate-maker Bernard Castelain (see p114); or even trot round in a **horse-drawn carriage** (☎ 04 90 70 88 42; la.rebousse@wanadoo.fr; 583 chemin St-Laurent).

To get the most out of your wine, try the **École de Dégustation** (Tasting School;

CHÂTEAUNEUF DU PAPE WINES – A BRIEF HISTORY

First of all, thank geology for these world-famous wines. Aeons ago, when the glaciers receded, they left *galets* scattered across the region's red clay soil. These large, smooth pebbles trap the Provençal heat and release it after sunset, ensuring that the grapes ripen quickly in a steady warmth.

The Romans first planted vineyards here some 2000 years ago, but winegrowing took off in earnest when Pope John XXII built a castle in 1317 and planted vineyards to provide the court with wine. From this papally endorsed beginning, wine production flourished.

Disaster struck in 1866, when aphid-like *phylloxera* attacked and the vineyards were devastated. Salvation came by grafting *Vitis vinifera* (the European grape) onto resistant American rootstocks.

Wine fraud then became a growing problem. In 1923, decorated WWI fighter pilot, lawyer and viticulturalist Baron Le Roy de Boiseaumarié defined the boundaries of the region to stop imposters. His framework evolved over 12 years into the national Appellation d'Origine Contrôlée (AOC).

Today, the Châteauneuf du Pape AOC area covers just 32 sq km between Avignon and Orange. Within that space, 320 wine producers conjure up almost 14 million bottles per year. Most are reds; a few are whites; and rosés are forbidden. Strict regulations allow 13 different types of hand-picked grape to be used, stipulate a maximum output of 35 hectolitres, and set the minimum alcohol level as 12½% (maximum 15%).

☎ 04 90 83 56 15; www.oenologie-mouriesse.com; 2 rue des Papes; 2hr courses from €40) where you'll learn to swirl, sniff and savour like a professional – see the website for the course calendar.

☘ **BERNARD CASTELAIN // BUY HANDMADE CHOCOLATES – OR CREATE YOUR OWN!**
Those with sweeter tastebuds should head for artisan *chocolatier* **Bernard Castelain** (☎ 04 90 83 54 71; www.vin-chocolat-castelain.com; rte d'Avignon; admission free; ☽ 9am-noon & 2-7pm Mon-Sat year-round, plus 10am-noon & 2-7pm Sun Jul & Aug), whose specialities include *picholines* (roasted almonds covered in chocolate), and the cream and chocolate-filled Palet des Papes. There are **factory tours** (adult/under 12yr €4/free; ☽ 4pm Mon-Fri) in English during July and August. To discover the secret of a

good ganache, join a **chocolate-making course** (adult/child €75/35). The course is in French; see the website for calendar.

GASTRONOMIC HIGHLIGHTS

☘ **LA MÈRE GERMAINE €€**
☎ 04 90 83 54 37; www.lameregermaine.com; place de la Fontaine; lunch menu €19.50, evening menus €23-105; ☽ restaurant closed Sun dinner
This central village brasserie-restaurant has been providing travellers with classic dishes – *pieds et paquets* (sheep tripe), roast lamb, guinea fowl etc – since 1922, and has a wine list as long as your arm. The *menu Pontifical* includes seven surprise courses accompanied by seven different glasses of papal wine. And the dining room has panoramic vineyard views. Eight Provençal style rooms (doubles €50 to €70) slumber above.

AVIGNON AREA

♥ LE VERGER DES PAPES €€

☎ 04 90 83 50 40; 4 rue du Château; menus €19.50-29; ⏰ lunch & dinner Mar–mid-Dec; ♿

Perched by the castle at the pinnacle of the village, this restaurant is for those who enjoy feasting on stunning views along with their food. Two brothers turn out traditional nourishment – juicy Camargue steaks, duck breast à la pêche, and breads baked in a wood-fired oven. Dishes are paired with wines from the cavernous cellar (where you can order bottles to take home).

TRANSPORT

CAR // Take the A7 north from Avignon, and the A7 south from Orange. Parking isn't a problem in Châteauneuf.

BUS // Transdev Sud-Est (☎ 04 32 76 00 40; www.sudest-mobilites.fr) operates limited services to/from Orange (€2, 15 minutes, two or three Monday to Saturday) and Avignon (€3.50, 40 minutes, one or two Monday to Saturday). Buses use the stop on av du Général de Gaulle.

ORANGE

pop 29,859

Compact and down-to-earth, this friendly little city is home to two of Provence's juiciest Roman treasures: a steep, spectacular theatre and a monumental archway, both Unesco World Heritage sites. Orange is filled with shady plazas, fountains and a cobweb of narrow pedestrian streets…it's more affordable than its Provençal neighbours too.

Orange was a principality of the Holy Roman Empire, only becoming part of France in 1713. The Princes of Orange married into other European monarchies, giving their name to the Dutch royal family (still called the House of Orange-Nassau), and a king, William III (William of Orange), to England.

Orange's train station is 1.5km east of central place de la République, along av Frédéric Mistral then rue de la République.

ESSENTIAL INFORMATION

TOURIST OFFICES // Tourist office (☎ 04 90 34 70 88; www.otorange.fr; 5 cours Aristide Briand; ⏰ 9am-7.30pm Mon-Sat, 10am-1pm & 2-7pm Sun Jul & Aug, to 6.30pm Apr-Jun & Sep, 10am-1pm & 2-5pm Mon-Sat Oct-Mar)

EXPLORING ORANGE

♥ ROMAN RUINS // EUROPE'S BEST-PRESERVED ROMAN THEATRE, PLUS A MONUMENTAL ARCH

Orange's superb Roman theatre, the **Théâtre Antique** (☎ 04 90 51 17 60; rue Madeleine Roch; adult/7-17yr €7.90/5.90; ⏰ 9am-7pm Jun-Aug, 9am-6pm Apr, May & Sep, 9.30am-5.30pm Oct & Mar, 9.30am-4.30pm Jan, Feb, Nov & Dec), is a must-see. Used to spread Roman propaganda, it's easy to imagine how it would have impressed the Empire's conquered subjects, because even today it causes jaws to drop! The steep seats are modern, but the mighty 103m-wide, 37m-high stage wall is the only one still standing in Europe. Designed to seat 9000 spectators, it's thought to have been built during Augustus Caesar's rule (27 BC–AD 14). Admission includes a seven-language audioguide and a weird audiovisual exhibition in the gallery.

The theatre is used as a venue for various theatrical spectacles, including the **Chorégies d'Orange** (☎ 04 90 34 24 24; www.choregies.com; tickets €48-220), an international opera festival that pulls out all the stops in July.

Your ticket also admits you to the **Musée d'Orange** (☎ 04 90 51 17 60; museum only adult/child €4.50/3.50; ⏰ 9.15am-7pm Jun-Aug,

9.15am-6pm Apr, May & Sep, 9.45am-12.30pm & 1.30-5.30pm Mar & Oct, 9.45am-12.30pm & 1.30-4.30pm Nov-Feb), which is opposite, and contains carved friezes from the theatre.

Orange's 1st-century AD **monumental arch**, the Arc de Triomphe, stands on the Via Agrippa, a proud 19m high and wide, and 8m thick. Cleaned up in 2009, its reliefs commemorate Roman victories in 49 BC with carvings of chained and naked Gauls.

GASTRONOMIC HIGHLIGHTS

♥ Á LA MAISON €

☎ 04 90 60 98 83; 4 place des Cordeliers; formule €12.50, dinner menu €18, mains €14; ⊗ closed Sun Sep-Jun; ☜

We heartily recommend this welcoming place, which transforms from a daytime tea salon to a chic fairy-lighted restaurant at night. Superior ingredients are used to create traditional French dishes, all beautifully presented and extremely good value – succulent salmon and moist chocolate *moelleux* (brownie-like cake with a melting raspberry centre) had us drooling. An outdoor terrace looks onto a fountain and a slice of the Roman theatre.

♥ LE FORUM €€

☎ 04 90 34 01 09; 3 rue du Mazeau; www.hotel-orange-provence.com; lunch/dinner menus from €19/22; ⊗ closed Sun evening & Mon year-round, closed late Aug-early Oct & late Dec

The tiny Forum, tucked down a narrow street near the theatre, focuses on seasonal Provençal specialities; for example the springtime asparagus menu where even the sorbet pudding incorporates those delicate green shoots; or autumn dishes based on wild boar, venison,

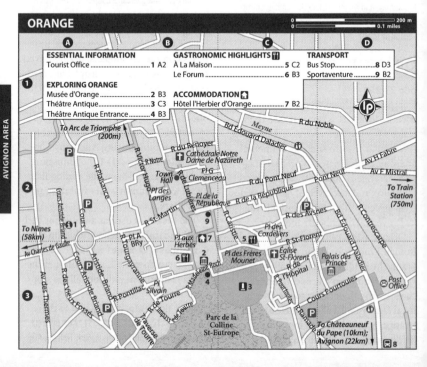

ORANGE

0 — 200 m
0 — 0.1 miles

A	**B**	**C**	**D**

ESSENTIAL INFORMATION
Tourist Office 1 A2

EXPLORING ORANGE
Musée d'Orange 2 B3
Théâtre Antique 3 C3
Théâtre Antique Entrance 4 B3

GASTRONOMIC HIGHLIGHTS 🍴
À La Maison 5 C2
Le Forum 6 B3

ACCOMMODATION 🏠
Hôtel l'Herbier d'Orange 7 B2

TRANSPORT
Bus Stop 8 D3
Sportaventure 9 B2

AVIGNON AREA

To Arc de Triomphe (200m)
R du Renoyer
Cathédrale Notre Dame de Nazareth
Bd Edouard Daladier
R du Noble
Meyne
Av H Fabre
Av F Mistral
Town Hall
Pl G Clemenceau
R du Pont Neuf
Pont Neuf
R Victor Hugo
R Notre
R Plaisance
R Lubières
Pl des Langes
Pl de la République
R de la République
To Train Station (750m)
Cours Aristide Briand
R St-Martin
R Caristie
R des Avènes
Bd Edouard Daladier
R Contrescarpe
To Nîmes (58km)
Cours
R A BRy
R Tourguranne
Pl Aux Herbes
Pl des Cordeliers
Pl des Frères Mounet
Pl R St-Florent
Église St-Florent
R de l'Hôpital
Palais des Princes
Av Charles de Gaulle
Av des Thermes
R des Vieux Fossés
Aristide Briand
R Pontillac
Pl Silvain
R de Impasse de Tourre
Traverse de Tourre
R Madeleine Roch
Parc de la Colline St-Eutrope
R Ramade
Cours Pourtoules
Post Office
To Châteauneuf du Pape (10km); Avignon (22km)

pumpkin and sweet chestnuts. The surroundings are a little cramped and chintzy, but it's a small quibble.

TRANSPORT

TRAIN // Orange's **train station** (☎ 04 90 11 88 03, 3635; av Frédéric Mistral) has direct services south to Avignon (€5.30, 20 minutes) and Marseille (€20.80, 1½ hours) and north to Lyon (€26.20, 2¼ hours).

BUS // Buses stop at the train station and on bd Édouard Daladier (near the post office), and travel to destinations including Avignon (€3, 45 minutes) and Vaison-la-Romaine (€3, 45 minutes).

BIKE // Central bike shop **Sportaventure** (☎ 06 10 33 56 54; www.velolocation-aventure.com; place de la République; half/full days €12/18, week €69) can deliver bicycles within a 20km radius of Orange.

VAISON-LA-ROMAINE

pop 6313
This quintessentially Provençal town has a rich Roman legacy: 20th-century buildings jostle for space with the ruins of France's largest archaeological site. A Roman bridge crosses the glinting River Ouvèze, which divides the Roman/contemporary town from the walled mediaeval city perched on a hilltop, where the counts of Toulouse built their 12th-century castle.

Situated at the crossroads of Provence, Vaison's bustling streets, decent restaurants and varied accommodation make it a good base for jaunts into the Dentelles' villages or an expedition up Mont Ventoux.

ESSENTIAL INFORMATION

TOURIST OFFICES // **Tourist office** (☎ 04 90 36 02 11; www.vaison-la-romaine.com; place du Chamoine Sautel; ☺ 9am-12.30pm & 2-6.45pm daily Jul & Aug, 9am-noon & 2-5.45pm Mon-Sat, 9am-noon Sun Apr-Jun & Sep–mid-Oct, 9am-noon & 2-5.45pm Mon-Sat mid-Oct-Mar)

EXPLORING VAISON-LA-ROMAINE

❦ GALLO-ROMAN RUINS // EXPLORE MANSIONS, COLONNADED SHOPS AND A ROMAN THEATRE

The ruined remains of Vasio Vocontiorum, the Roman city that flourished here from the 6th to the 2nd century BC, have swum to the surface of modernday Vaison. Two neighbourhoods of this once-opulent city, Puymin and La Villasse, are right in the centre of town, one on either side of the tourist office. Admission to both is covered by a single **ticket** (adult/12-18yr €8/3.50), which includes a four-language **audioguide** (collectable from the Puymin museum) covering the Roman ruins, the museum, the Cathédrale Notre-Dame and the medieval city.

Noblemen's houses, mosaics, a workman's quarter, a temple, and the still-functioning 5000-seater theatre can be seen at **Puymin** (☺ 9.30am-6pm Apr-Sep, 10am-12.30pm & 2-5.30pm Mar & Oct, 10am-noon & 2-5pm Nov & late Feb, closed Jan-early Feb). To make sense of the scattered remains, and to pick up your audioguide, head first for the **archaeological museum**, which is open the same hours as the site, and does a great job of explaining Vaison's Roman past. Precious finds on display include the superb peacock mosaic, carvings of theatre masks, and a swag of finely worked statues (such as the silver bust of a 3rd-century patrician, and marble likenesses of Hadrian and his wife Sabina).

The Romans shopped at the colonnaded boutiques and went to the baths and the gym in **La Villasse** (☺ 10am-noon & 2.30-6pm Apr-Sep, 10am-12.30pm & 2-5.30pm Mar & Oct, 10am-noon & 2-5pm Nov & late Feb, closed Jan-early Feb). There are also more mansions, including the Maison au Dauphin, with its splendid marble-lined fish ponds.

Your ticket also includes entry to the peaceful 12th-century Romanesque cloister at **Cathédrale Notre-Dame de Nazareth** (cloister only €1.50; 10am-noon & 2-5pm Nov, 10am-noon & 2-5pm Mar & Oct, 10.30am-12.30pm & 2-6pm Apr & May, 10am-12.30pm & 2-6.30pm Jun-Sep, closed Jan & Feb), a five-minute walk west of La Villasse. This is also a great spot to take refuge from the summer heat.

CITÉ MÉDIÉVALE // TAKE AN UPHILL STROLL INTO THE MIDDLE AGES

Cross the **Pont Romain** (Roman bridge) and follow in the footsteps of frightened medieval peasants, who took refuge in the walled city when things became too warlike in the valley. It's a refreshingly tranquil place, particularly when compared to other Provençal hilltop villages. Paved alleyways known as *calades* carve through the stone walls up to an imposing 12th-century **château** built by the counts of Toulouse, from where there are eagle-eye views.

CYCLE ROUTES // SLEEPY LANES TO HIDDEN MEDIEVAL HAMLETS

Rent bikes at **Mag 2 Roues** (04 90 28 80 46; cours Taulignan; 8.30am-noon & 2-7pm Tue-Sat). The tourist office stocks three excellent free brochures detailing **cycling circuits** that begin in Vaison before soaring and swooping through the surrounding villages. Some highlights:

No 1: Circuit du Pays Voconce (42km) – Threading through Roaix, Rasteau, Sablet and Séguret, this circuit also offers a shorter family route and a 'sports' version for keen cyclists.

No 7: Les Villages des Templiers (36km) – Follow the course of two streams to discover traces of the Knights Templar.

No 8: Les Villages Médiévaux (23km) – A hilly circuit, taking you through the medieval villages of St-Romain, Puyméras, Faucon and Entrechaux.

GASTRONOMIC HIGHLIGHTS

Avoid the average bistros on place Montfort and head for cours Taulignan, which contains quality, well-priced restaurants such as L'Alchimiste (No 32), Au Petit Bedon (No 43) and La Lyriste (No 45).

LE BATELEUR €€

 04 90 36 28 04; www.le-bateleur.com; 1 place Théodore Aubanel; menus €22-45; Tue-Sat Sep-Jun, Mon-Sat Jul & Aug

In two cosy dining rooms, one of which overlooks the rushing river, this is a convivial place for innovative Provençal fare. Mouth-watering morsels of fresh lamb, duck, salmon and beef are sliced, diced, grilled and roasted along with unusual accompaniments, appearing from the kitchen as beautifully presented works of art. If you can find room, order the extravagant local cheese platter.

LE BISTRO DU O €€

 04 90 41 72 90; www.santaduc.fr; rue du Château; menus €19-34; closed Mon lunch & Sun, closed Jan

TOP FIVE

TINY VILLAGES AROUND VAISON-LA-ROMAINE

★ **Le Crestet** – quaint medieval streets with immense views towards Mont Ventoux

★ **Entrechaux** – castle-topped village with a bull-running festival in August

★ **Séguret** – delightfully characterful, with medieval cobbles, chapels and castle ruins

★ **Faucon** – famous for apricots and gingerbread

★ **Sablet** – a village of bookworms, hemmed in by 16th-century walls

High in the medieval city, tucked into a 13th-century vaulted cellar, this gastronomic choice concentrates on modern Mediterranean cuisine. There's just one menu, altered daily according to what's market-fresh. Expect local, organic produce, turned into succulent, unfussy dishes, served with crusty home-baked bread. One of the owners is a wine producer himself, a fact reflected in the long, carefully chosen wine list.

❦ MOULIN Á HUILE €€€
☎ 04 90 36 20 67; www.moulin-huile.com; quai Maréchal Foch; lunch menu €28-40, dinner menu from €60; ☺ lunch & dinner Tue-Sat, lunch Sun
Master chef Robert Bardot refines and redefines the art of gastronomic cooking at this old clementine-coloured oil mill by the river, in the shadow of the Cité Médiévale. Like all great artists, Bardot believes his cooking would be 'insipid if it was not flavoured by a touch of madness'. Sample a cross-section of his Michelin-starred creations with his €75 tasting plate.

TRANSPORT

CAR // There's a large, free car park by the tourist office.
BUS // Vaison's bus station is 400m east of the town centre on av des Choralies. **Lieutaud buses** (☎ Vaison 04 90 36 05 22, Avignon 04 90 86 36 75) runs limited services from Vaison to Orange (€3, 45 minutes) and Carpentras (€3, 45 minutes).

ENCLAVE DES PAPES

Shaped like one of the truffles for which the area is famed (see the boxed text on p121), this bumpy ball of land has been part of the Vaucluse since 1791, despite being buried within the Drôme *département*. Medieval Valréas (population 9732; elevation 250m), 29km north of Vaison-la-Romaine, is the primary town.

ESSENTIAL INFORMATION

TOURIST OFFICES // **Valréas tourist office** (☎ 04 90 35 04 71; www.ot-valreas.fr; av Maréchal Leclerc; ☺ 9am-12.30pm & 3-6.30pm Mon-Sat, 9am-12.30pm Sun mid-Jul–mid-Aug; 9.15am-12.15pm & 2-6pm Mon-Sat Mar-Jun, Sep & Oct, 9.15am-12.15pm & 2-5pm Mon-Fri, 9.15am-12.15pm Sat Nov-Feb)

EXPLORING THE ENCLAVE DES PAPES

❦ MUSÉE DU CARTONNAGE ET DE L'IMPRIMERIE // THE WORLD'S ONLY MUSEUM OF CARDBOARD
A cardboard-and-printing museum may sound as worthwhile as an exhibition of watching paint dry, but actually the **Musée du Cartonnage et de l'Imprimerie** (☎ 04 90 35 58 75; musee-cartonnage-imp@cg84.fr; 3 av Maréchal Foch; adult/12-18yr €3.50/1.50; ☺ 10am-noon & 3-6pm Mon & Wed-Sat, 3-6pm Sun Apr-Oct, 10am-noon & 2-5pm Mon & Wed-Sat, 2-5pm Sun Nov-Mar) is an interesting exploration of Valréas' 19th-century industrial heritage. The printing paraphernalia and box designs will particularly appeal to fans of graphic design and typography.

❦ ENCLAVE DES PAPES CYCLING CIRCUIT // PEDAL THROUGH THREE FORTIFIED VILLAGES, RICH WITH HISTORY
Scattered among undulating purple lavender fields are the fortified villages of **Visan**, **Richerenches** and **Grillon**. Richerenches, with its Knights Templar history and renowned truffle market, is perhaps the most interesting, but these sleepy, honey-stoned communities were made for discovering on a lazy day-long cycle tour, and a ready-made 33.5km route from Valréas takes in all three. Pick up the free cycling brochure *No 10 – Tour de l'Enclave des Papes* from tourist offices in the Vaucluse region,

CHRISTMAS

At dusk on Christmas Eve, Provence celebrates the **Cacho Fio**. A log cut from a pear, olive or cherry tree is placed in the hearth, doused with fortified wine, blessed three times by the youngest and oldest family members, and then set alight. The fire must burn until the three kings arrive on 6 January.

The village of **Séguret** (population 904; elevation 250m) has a unique version of this tradition. Rather than taking place in the villagers' homes, everyone gathers in the Salle Delage (adjoining Chapelle Ste-Thecle on rue du Four) to burn a log together. Later, locals wend their way up to Église St-Denis where, during Li Bergié, real-life shepherds, lambs and a baby in a manger create a living nativity scene. This is followed by midnight Mass in Provençal, after which families hurry home for Caleno vo Careno (see p373).

and hire bicycles from **Chap's Moto** (☎ 04 90 35 18 33; 40 cours du Berteuil; ☾ 9am-noon & 2-7pm Tue-Fri, 9am-noon & 2-5.30pm Sat) in Valréas.

☙ AU DÉLICE DE PROVENCE // THE FOODIES' CHOICE IN VALRÉAS

This delightful **restaurant** (☎ 04 90 28 16 91; audelicedeprovence@gmail.com; 6 la placette, Valréas; menus €18-35; ☾ daily) has a tiny but perfectly formed menu. There are usually just three seasonal dishes on offer – when we visited, it was spring lamb, poultry casserole or scallops stewed with apples – but each is prepared with love and gusto. Between November and March, come here for the truffle menu.

FESTIVALS & EVENTS

Nuit du Petit St-Jean Held since 1504, this endearing festival in Valréas sees a torch-lit procession in medieval dress culminating in the crowning of a three-to five-year-old boy as the new Petit St-Jean (Little St John); 23 June.

TRANSPORT

BUS // Seven buses daily (five Saturday, two Sunday) go from Orange to Valréas (€4, 55 minutes), stopping at Visan (€2, 35 minutes) and Richerenches (€3, 40 minutes).

TAXI TOURS // Taxi Sud Provence (☎ 04 75 46 52 25; www.transports-sudprovence.com) runs themed tours and can customise trips throughout the area.

DENTELLES DE MONTMIRAIL

This 8km-long limestone ridge rises in a sudden, jagged cockscomb from the vineyard-covered plain. Its spikes and spires take their name from the *dentelles* (lace) they resemble. Forty kilometres of footpath wind through the *garrigue* (look out for buzzards, eagles and fluorescent-green lizards), while climbers dangle perilously from the southern face. Around the ridge, tiny slow-paced villages lie scattered like lace-makers' beads, drenched in sunshine and golden wine.

ESSENTIAL INFORMATION

TOURIST OFFICES // Beaumes de Venise tourist office (Maison des Dentelles; ☎ 04 90 62 94 39; www.ot-beaumesdevenise.com; place du Marché; ☾ 9am-noon & 2-7pm Mon-Sat summer, 9am-noon & 2-5pm Mon-Sat winter) Large and well-stocked. **Gigondas tourist office** (☎ 04 90 65 85 46; www.gigondas-dm.fr; place du Portail; ☾ 10am-12.30pm & 2.30-6.30pm Mon-Sat, 10am-1pm Sun Jul & Aug, 10am-12.30pm & 2.30-6pm Mon-Sat Apr-Jun, Sep & Oct, 10am-noon & 2-5pm Mon-Sat Nov-Mar)

AVIGNON AREA

EXPLORING DENTELLES DE MONTMIRAIL

🌿 **LE BARROUX // CASTLE-CROWNED VILLAGE WITH A WORKING MONASTERY NEARBY**

Charming wee **Le Barroux** (population 615; elevation 325m) topples down a hillside from its medieval **Château du Barroux** (☎ 04 90 62 35 21; www.chateau-du-barroux .com; adult/child €4/free; ⏰ 10am-7pm Sat & Sun Apr & May, 2.30-7pm Jun, 10am-7pm Jul-Sep, 2-6pm Oct), whose mighty keep was built in the 12th century to protect the village from Saracen invaders. The castle's fortunes rose and fell, the last indignity being during WWII when the retreating German army set it on fire – it burned for 10 days.

Two kilometres out of Le Barroux along thread-narrow lanes, **Gregorian chants** are sung at 9.30am (10am Sunday and holidays) by Benedictine monks at the **Abbaye Ste-Madeleine** (☎ 04 90 62 56 31; www.barroux.org in French; rte de Suzette), a lavender-surrounded monastery built in Romanesque style in the 1980s. The monastery shop sells delicious monk-made almond cake. Hats, miniskirts, bare shoulders and mobile phones are forbidden in the church.

BLACK DIAMONDS

Provence's cloak-and-dagger truffle trade – operated out of a car boot, with payment exclusively in cold, hard cash – is a real black business.

Little-known Richerenches, a deceptively wealthy village shielded by a medieval Templar fortress, is the setting for France's largest wholesale truffle market. On Saturday mornings during the season (mid-November to mid-March), the main street fills with furtive *rabassaïres* (truffle hunters) selling their weekly harvest to *courtiers* (brokers) who come to buy on behalf of big-time dealers from Paris, Germany, Italy and beyond. If you happen to witness the market, it's unlikely you'll even see a truffle, so covert are the dealings.

Black truffles *(Tuber melanosporum)* can cost up to €1000 per kilogram, making them almost literally worth their weight in gold. Although *trufficulteurs* (truffle growers) try tricks like injecting spores into oak roots, humankind has so far been unable to increase crops of this quasi-mystical fungus. Nature dictates whether it will be a good or bad truffle year, and there's not a thing the grower can do about it.

Richerenches villagers celebrate an annual Truffle Mass in the village church, during which parishioners place truffles in the collection bowl instead of cash. The truffles are then auctioned to raise money for the church. The Mass falls on the closest Sunday to 17 January, the feast day of Antoine, patron saint of truffle harvesters. Contact Richerenches' **Point Tourisme** (☎ 04 90 28 05 34; www.richerenches.fr, in French; rue du Campanile; ⏰ 1.30-5.30pm Mon-Fri, 9.30am-12.30pm Sat mid-Nov–mid-Mar, 2-6pm Mon-Fri mid-Mar–mid-Nov) for details.

If you want to unearth black diamonds yourself, **Dominique and Eric Jaumard** (☎ 04 90 66 82 21; www.truffes-ventoux.com; La Quinsonne) can arrange truffle-hunts in season (prices arranged on inquiry), on their land 7km southwest of Carpentras in Monteux. Pick up fresh truffles at general markets in Vaison-la-Romaine (Tuesday), Valréas (Wednesday) and Carpentras (Friday), and at the specialist truffle shop in St-Rémy de Provence (see boxed text, p135).

AVIGNON AREA

❦ BEAUMES DE VENISE // SAMPLE GOLDEN MUSCAT WINES AND OLIVE OIL

Snugly sheltered from the mistral winds, **Beaumes de Venise** (population 2185; elevation 126m) is best known for its **or blanc** (white gold). These sweet muscat wines are best drunk young and chilled, and are the perfect partner for juicy Cavaillon melons. You can attend tastings at the local co-operative **Balma Vénitia** (☎ 04 90 12 41 00; Quartier Ravel; ☷ 8.30am-12.30pm & 2-7pm Mon-Sat, 9am-12.30pm & 2.30-7pm Sun summer, 8.30am-noon & 2-6pm Mon-Sat, 9am-12.30pm & 2-6pm Sun winter); and the tourist office has a brochure of local estates open to the public.

Taste Beaumes' olive oil at the **Moulin à Huile de la Balméenne** (☎ 04 90 62 93 77; www.labalmeenne.fr; av Jules Ferry; ☷ 9am-noon & 2-7pm daily Apr-Aug, 9am-noon & 2-6pm Mon-Sat Sep-Mar), in business since 1867.

❦ GIGONDAS // GLORIOUS VIEWS AND GREAT RED WINE

Enigmatic outdoor sculptures enhance **Gigondas** (population 598; elevation 282m), whose narrow pathways lead ever upwards to a ruined castle, campanile, church and cemetery, with stunning vistas. The village is famous for its prestigious red wines: cellars cram the central square, and the tourist office has a list of visitable vineyards.

TRANSPORT

BUS // Trans'Cove (☎ 08 00 88 15 23; www.transcove.com) runs three buses per day Monday to Saturday on the Carpentras–Beaumes de Venise–Vacqueras–Gigondas route. You need to telephone the day before to arrange for the minibus to pick you up.

MONT VENTOUX

'The Giant of Provence', Mont Ventoux (1912m) lords it over the northern part of the region and is visible from as far away as Avignon. This noble mountain features regularly in the Tour de France, and is a favourite of amateur cyclists following in the pedals of their heroes. Less sporty types can access the summit by car. Roads generally open between May and October (signs at Bédoin and Ste-Colombe indicate when the summit pass is closed).

Since 1990 the mountain has been protected by Unesco's Réserve de Biosphère du Mont Ventoux (Mont Ventoux Biosphere Reserve). Unique species, including the snake eagle and an assortment of spiders and butterflies, are only found on this isolated peak.

As you ascend the relentless gradients, temperatures can plummet by 20°C, there's twice as much precipitation as on the plains below, and wind speeds of up to 300km/h have been recorded. Bring warm clothes and rain gear, even in summer. Snow blankets the areas above 1300m from December to April; in summer the peak appears snowcapped because of the *lauzes (*broken white stones) covering the top.

ESSENTIAL INFORMATION

TOURIST OFFICES // Bédoin tourist office (☎ 04 90 65 63 95; www.bedoin.org; espace Marie-Louis Gravier; ☷ 9am-12.30pm & 2-6pm Mon-Fri, 9.30am-12.30pm Sat Sep-Jun, plus 9.30am-12.30pm Sun Jul & Aug) The meeting point for summertime walks run by the Office National des Forêts (ONF; National Forests Office). Malaucène tourist office (☎ /fax 04 90 65 22 59; ot-malaucene@wanadoo.fr; place de la Mairie; ☷ 10am-noon & 2.30-4.30pm Mon-Sat) Stocks information on the Mont Ventoux area, but nothing on the Dentelles. Sault tourist office (☎ 04 90 64 01 21; www.saultenprovence.com; av de la Promenade; ☷ 9am-1pm & 2-7pm Jul & Aug, 9am-noon & 2-6pm Mon-Sat, 9.30am-12.30pm Sun May & Jun, 9am-noon & 2-5pm or 6pm Mon-Sat Sep-Apr) Also a good resource for the Gorges de la Nesque (p131).

EXPLORING MONT VENTOUX

❦ VILLAGES AROUND MONT VENTOUX // FIND YOUR HIDEAWAY VILLAGE BASE IN THE MOUNTAINS

Near the southwestern end of the Mont Ventoux massif is the agricultural village of **Bédoin** (population 2974; elevation 295m), sheltered from the mistral and a popular cyclists' base. In July and August, the tourist office runs pleasant walks in the surrounding 6300 hectares of forest.

With a beautiful plane-tree-lined main street, **Malaucène** (population 2691; elevation 377m), 10km south of Vaison-la-Romaine, is a central starting point for sorties into the Dentelles and up Mont Ventoux. Pope Clement V had a second home here in the 14th century: his legacy is the military-style Gothic-Romanesque **Église St-Michel & St-Pierre**, constructed in 1309 on the site of an ancient temple.

At the eastern end of the Mont Ventoux massif, the sweet stone village of **Sault** (population 1285; elevation 800m) has sweeping summertime views over the carpet of purple lavender laid out below. In the village, pop into **André Boyer** (☎ 04 90 64 00 23; place de l'Europe) to stock up on lavender honey and almond nougat made by the family since 1887. Sault's tourist office has a list of other **artisan industries** throughout the area, which often take visitors behind the scenes.

❦ VENTOUX THE TOUR DE FRANCE WAY // KILLER RIDES ON THE SLOPES OF THIS CYCLISTS' MECCA

In summer cyclists labour up the sun-baked slopes of Mont Ventoux, with ascents from Bédoin, Malaucène and Sault.

Tourist offices distribute *Massif du Mont Ventoux: 9 Itinéraires VTT*, a free booklet detailing nine mountain-bike itineraries ranging from an easy 3.9km (one hour) to a gruelling 56.7km (seven to eight hours) tour of Mont Ventoux.

Rent road bikes/mountain bikes/tandems from €25/15/30 per half-day from **Vélo France Locations** (☎ 04 90 67 07 40; www.larouteduventoux.com; rte du Ventoux; ☯ 8am-7.30pm Apr-Nov) in Bédoin, **Ventoux Bikes** (☎ 04 90 62 58 19; www.ventoux-bikes.fr; 1 ave de Verdun; ☯ Apr-Nov) in Malaucène, and **Albion Cycles** (☎ 04 90 64 09 32; www.albioncycles.com; rte de St-Trinit; ☯ closed Mon Sep-Jun) in Sault. All can suggest cycling routes.

The website www.lemontventoux.net (in French) details 16 cycling routes around Ventoux.

❦ WINTER EXHILARATION // HURTLE DOWN THE GIANT OF PROVENCE ON SKIS

December to March, locals ski the slopes of Ventoux, which offer downhill and cross-country trails. **Chalet Reynard** (☎ 04 90 61 84 55; www.chalet-reynard.com, in French), at the intersection of the D974 and the eastbound D164 to Sault, is a small ski station (1440m) on the southern slopes. Two *téléskis* (drag lifts) serve six red and blue runs, with a full-day pass/ski hire costing €10/20. There's a luge that nonskiers can bomb down.

Station de Mont Serein (www.stationdumontserein.com), 5km west of the summit on the colder northern side, is the main ski station (1400m) with 12km of downhill pistes served by nine drag lifts. Skis, lessons, piste maps and passes (€16.70) are available from the **Chalet d'Accueil** (☎ 04 90 63 42 02), in the resort centre. **Chalet Liotard** (☎ 04 90 60 68 38) is a midstation, 100m further uphill, where you can eat a well-earned lunch.

❦ MAKE GREAT STRIDES // HIKE LONG-DISTANCE FOOTPATHS UP VENTOUX'S SLOPES

Running from the River Ardèche west, the GR4 crosses the Dentelles de Montmirail before scaling the northern face of Mont Ventoux, where it meets the GR9. Both trails traverse the ridge before the GR4 branches eastwards to the Gorges du Verdon. Continuing on the GR9 takes you across the Monts du Vaucluse and Luberon Range.

Tourist offices have information on exploring Mont Ventoux on foot. From Bédoin and Malaucène it's possible to make a night-time expedition up the mountain in July and August (over 15 years only) to watch the sun rise over Provence.

TRANSPORT

CAR // Mont Ventoux is reached by car from Sault via the D164 or – in summer – from Malaucène or St-Estève via the switchback D974, which is often snow-blocked until April.

BUS // For information on bus services in the area, see p126.

CARPENTRAS

pop 27,451 / elevation 102m

Plan to be in Carpentras on a Friday morning, when a massive food market spills into the streets.

Carpentras' mouth-watering weekly stalls aside, this slightly rundown agricultural town has a handful of architectural treats. A Greek trading centre and later a Gallo-Roman city, Carpentras' sole Roman remain is a monumental arch. The city became papal territory in 1229, and was also shaped by a strong Jewish presence, as Jews who had been expelled from French crown territory took refuge here. The 14th-century synagogue is the oldest still in use in France.

ORIENTATION

A heart-shaped ring of boulevards replaced the city's fortifications in the 19th century; the largely pedestrianised old city sits inside.

If you're arriving by bus, walk northeastwards to place Aristide Briand, a major intersection at the boulevards' southernmost point, where you'll find the tourist office.

ESSENTIAL INFORMATION

TOURIST OFFICES // Tourist office (☎ 04 90 63 00 78; www.carpentras-ventoux.com; 97 place du 25 Août 1944; 🕙 9am-1pm & 2-7pm Mon-Sat, 9.30am-1pm Sun Jul & Aug, 9.30am-12.30pm & 2-6pm Mon & Wed-Sat, 9.30am-12.30pm & 3-6pm Sun Sep-Jun) Hands out a free English-language *Discover Carpentras* walking brochure, and arranges fabulous tours (€3 to €10), including wine-tasting workshops and truffle hunts (advance booking a must).

EXPLORING CARPENTRAS

❦ SYNAGOGUE // DISCOVER THE CHANGING FORTUNES OF FRANCE'S JEWS

The centre of Jewish life for centuries and still a place of worship today, Carpentras' moving **synagogue** (☎ 04 90 63 39 97; place Juiverie; admission free; 🕙 10am-noon & 3-5pm Mon-Thu, 10am-noon & 3-4pm Fri) was founded in 1367. The wood-panelled prayer hall was rebuilt in the 18th century; below, there's an oven used until 1904 to bake *matzo,* Passover's unleavened bread. Although Jews were initially welcomed into papal territory, by the 17th century they were forced to live in ghettoes established in Avignon, Carpentras, Cavaillon and L'Isle-sur-la-Sorgue. The synagogue is situated opposite the town hall; its deliberately inconspicuous frontage is marked by a stone plaque

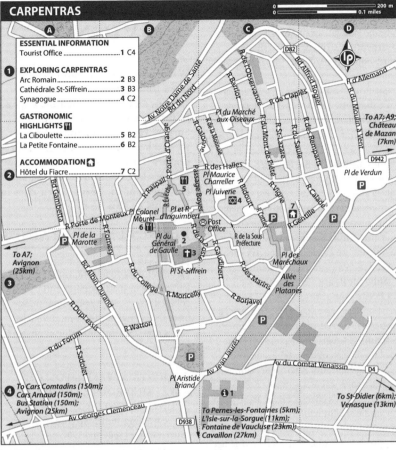

CARPENTRAS

inscribed in Hebrew. The tourist office runs tours on Tuesday, Wednesday and Thursday from April to September.

❤ CATHÉDRALE ST-SIFFREIN // CARPENTRAS' SOARING GOTHIC CATHEDRAL

Carpentras' **cathedral** (place St-Siffrein; 🕙 10am-noon & 2-6pm Tue-Sat) was built in the Méridional (southern French) Gothic style between 1405 and 1519 and is topped by a distinctive contemporary bell tower. Sadly, due to theft, its **Trésor d'Art Sacré** (Treasury of Religious Art)

holding precious 14th- to 19th-century religious relics is now salted away from the public except during the Fête de St-Siffrein on 27 November.

Hidden behind the cathedral, the **Arc Romain**, built under Augustus in the 1st century AD, is decorated with worn carvings of enslaved Gauls.

❤ DINING IN CARPENTRAS // ONE FAMOUS FOOD MARKET, TWO RARIFIED RESTAURANTS

Carpentras bursts into life at its weekly Friday market, which has over 350 stalls laden with breads, honeys, cheeses, olives, blood-red strawberries, brittle almond nougat, a rainbow of *berlingots* (Carpentras' striped, pillow-shaped hard-boiled sweets) and (during winter) truffles.

Sit-down restaurants are scarce. Try **La Ciboulette** (☎ 04 90 60 75 00; 30 place de l'Horloge; lunch/dinner menus from €19/24; ⌖ closed Mon), which focuses on fresh local ingredients, tasting all the better when eaten in the sunshine on the flowered patio. Cinnamon-coloured walls, well-spaced tables and a warm welcome create an easy air, and you can watch your meal being prepared. In season, there's a gourmet truffle menu; year round, old favourites are given new life – try the lavender *crème brulée*, for example.

Solid meals are served with a smile at **La Petite Fontaine** (☎ 04 90 60 77 83; 17 place du Colonel Mouret; menus from €25; ⌖ closed Wed & Sun), a bistro-style restaurant. On a pedestrianised square, it's a pleasant place for lunch, with outside tables next to a splashing fountain. Again, specialities have a Provençal feel – think scallops, foie gras, goat's cheese, crispy fresh salmon, and pungent truffles in winter. The complex, earthy regional flavours are supported by a well-considered wine list.

TRANSPORT

CAR // Carpentras is 25km away from both Orange (on the D950) and Avignon (on the D942). In town, the largest car park is near the tourist office, along av Jean Jaurès.

BUS // The **bus station** (place Terradou) is 150m southwest of the tourist office. There are hourly services to Avignon (€2, 40 minutes) Monday to Saturday (four on Sunday) and infrequent runs to Vaison-la-Romaine (€3, 45 minutes) via Malaucène (€2, 35 minutes) at the southwestern foot of Mont Ventoux. Schedules are available from **Cars Comtadins** (☎ 04 90 67 20 25; 192 av Clémenceau) across the square and from **Cars Arnaud** (☎ 04 90 63 01 82; 8 av Victor Hugo).

EAST OF AVIGNON

· · · · · ·

Water is the abiding motif here: it flows from fountains, surges from springs, and rolls through the region in the form of the glorious River Sorgue. Pernes-les-Fontaines' unspoiled heart dates back to the 13th century; L'Isle-sur-la-Sorgue is one of France's largest antique centres; and the source of the Sorgue itself rises in Fontaine de Vaucluse.

PERNES-LES-FONTAINES

pop 10,410
Famous for its 40 fountains that splash and gurgle in shady squares and narrow cobbled streets, Pernes-les-Fontaines, once the capital of the Comtat Venaissin, is now a sleepy gathering of ancient buildings.

♥ **FOUNTAIN WALK // FOLLOW A WALKING ROUTE THROUGH FOUNTAIN-LINED GINNELS**
A free walking-tour map from the **tourist office** (☎ 04 90 61 31 04; www.ville-pernes-les-fontaines.fr in French; place Gabriel Moutte; ⌖ 9am–noon & 2-6.30pm Mon-Fri, to 5pm Sat Jul & Aug, 9am–noon & 2-6pm Mon-Fri, to 5pm Sat Apr, Jun & Sep, 9am–noon & 2-5pm Mon-Fri, 9am–noon Sat Oct-Mar) offers the choice of a one- or two-hour stroll through the quaint, quiet streets. These swing you past the **Maison du Costume Comtadin** (☎ 04 90 61 31 04; rue de la République; admission free; ⌖ 10am-12.30pm & 2.30pm-6.30pm Wed-Mon Jul & Aug, 2-6.30pm Wed-Mon mid-Apr–Jun & Sep, 2-5pm Wed-Mon Oct–mid-Apr), containing 19th-century Provençal costumes; the gloomy fortified 11th-century **church**; and **Maison Fléchier** (☎ 04 90 61 31 04; pl Fléchier; admission free), with

displays on local crafts and traditions; its opening hours are the same as for Maison du Costume Comtadin. You're then whisked along a spiralling path to the top of the medieval **clock tower** for wonderful panoramic views. The route is lined by monumental fountains like the grandiose, moss-covered **Fontaine du Cormoran**, **Fontaine Reboul** and **Fontaine du Gigot**, built in the 18th century to carry water from the newly discovered Font de Bouvery source.

♥ MAS LA BONOTY // FINE DINING UNDER FRAGRANT PINE TREES
This **farmhouse hotel** (☎ 04 90 61 61 09; www .bonoty.com; chemin de la Bonoty, Pernes-les-Fontaines; lunch/dinner menus €22/41; ⊙ closed Jan–mid-Feb) has built up a reputation as a laudable Provençal restaurant, even though it's owned by two Englishmen! *Menus* feature such meaty delights as thyme-roasted duckling and an unusual lobster served with mango sauce. They also have lovely, light-filled rooms (doubles including breakfast from €85) named after its garden flowers.

L'ISLE-SUR-LA-SORGUE

pop 18,015
A moat of flowing water encircles the ancient and prosperous town of L'Isle-sur-la-Sorgue, paddled by picturesque old waterwheels that trail dripping strands of moss. This 'Venice of Provence' is stuffed to bursting with antique shops, a favourite weekend browsing ground for well-heeled visitors.

L'Isle dates from the 12th century, when local fishermen built huts on stilts above what was then a marsh. By the 18th century, canals lined with 70 giant wheels powered a plethora of silk factories and paper mills.

ESSENTIAL INFORMATION

TOURIST OFFICES // **Tourist office** (☎ 04 90 38 04 78; www.oti-delasorgue.fr; place de la Liberté; ⊙ 9am-noon & 2.30-6pm Mon-Sat, 9am-12.30pm Sun) In the centre of the old town.

EXPLORING L'ISLE-SUR-LA-SORGUE

♥ ANTIQUES VILLAGES // POKE THROUGH A TUMBLE OF MUSEUM-QUALITY CURIOS
If the west wing of your mansion is missing an original Louis XV chandelier, look no further than L'Isle-sur-la-Sorgue! The disused mills and factories along the main road contain seven **antiques villages** (⊙ 10am-6pm Sat-Mon), which house around 300 individual antiques dealers and make for fascinating exploration. But if you're looking for bargains, the giant four-day **antiques fairs** held in mid-August as well as over Easter are a better bet.

♥ THE OLD TOWN // HUNT FOR HISTORY AMONG L'ISLE'S EVOCATIVELY NAMED STREETS
Ask the tourist office for its *Patrimony* brochure, which explains L'Isle's fascinating historical centre. Highlights include the **Collégiale Notre Dame des Anges** (Our Lady of Angels; place de la Liberté; ⊙ 10am-noon & 3-6pm daily Jul-Sep, 10am-noon & 3-5pm Tue-Sat Oct-Jun), graced by a lunar calendar on its facade. The angular exterior offers no clue to the baroque theatricals inside – here you'll find 220 blue-and-gaudy-gold angels, and a magnificent 1648-built organ (on the left as you face the altar; the faux organ, opposite, is purely for symmetry).

The former **Jewish quarter** exists in name only, with the ghetto's synagogue finally being torn down in 1856. The ancient **fisherman's quarter**, a tangle of narrow passageways and dead ends in the eastern corner of L'Isle, retains its town-within-a-town feel. Scattered along the canals are the creaking **waterwheels** – the wheel by the tiny park on ave des Quatre Otages is particularly photogenic.

Museums include the quaint **Musée du Jouet & de la Poupée Ancienne** (Ancient Toy & Doll Museum; ☎ 04 90 20 97 31; 26 rue Carnot; adult/child €3.50/1.50; ☺ 10.30am-6pm Tue-Sun Jun-Sep, 1.30-5pm Sat & Sun Oct-May); and one dedicated to native poet René Char (1907–88), in the 18th-century **Hôtel Donadeï de Campredon** (☎ 04 90 38 17 41; 20 rue du Docteur Tallet; adult/child €6.20/5.20; ☺ 10am-1pm & 3-7pm Tue-Sun Jun-Aug, 10am-12.30pm & 2-5.30pm Tue-Sun Sep-May), which also mounts temporary exhibitions.

☙ PARTAGE DES EAUX // BUCOLIC RIVERSIDE SCENERY, RIPE FOR PICNICS

A country lane runs along the river from the old town to the **partage des eaux** (parting of the waters), a serene spot where the River Sorgue splits into the two arms that embrace the town on its island. It's popular for old-fashioned, low-key, family-centric afternoons: skip stones, snooze by the calming flow, watch kingfishers, beavers and herons, and indulge in ice cream at one of the waterside cafés…

☙ CANOEING ON THE RIVER SORGUE // A GENTLE DESCENT FROM FONTAINE DE VAUCLUSE

Canoë Kayak (☎ 04 90 38 33 22; www.canoe-sur-la-sorgue.com; ave Charles de Gaulle; adult/under 12yr €19/13) drive you to Fontaine de Vaucluse, 8km upstream, so that you can shoot back into town in style on a two-hour canoe trip (see opposite for details).

GASTRONOMIC HIGHLIGHTS

L'Isle-sur-la-Sorgue has plenty of decent restaurants, although you'll need to trundle a short way out of town for some.

☙ LE VIVIER €€€

☎ 04 90 38 52 80; 800 cours Fernande Peyre; lunch/dinner menus from €28/43; ☺ lunch Tue-Thu & Sun, dinner Tue-Sat, closed mid-Feb–mid-Mar

Hidden out of town in a bland modern building, the Michelin-starred 'Fishpond' seems a little bashful…but its imaginative, contemporary menu should be advertised from the rooftops. Sourced from numerous local farms, prime ingredients are used in dishes such as smoked eel with glazed apple, or roasted rabbit with artichoke ravioli. The inviting interior combines sharp lines with glowing colours, and the terrace has restful river views.

☙ L'OUSTAU DE L'ISLE €€

☎ 04 90 20 81 36; 147 chemin du Bosquet; lunch/dinner menus from €18/28; ☺ Thu-Mon, closed Jan & Nov

In an old farmhouse 1.5km out of town, L'Oustau has been a firm Pays de Sorgues favourite for 12 years. Its flowery gardens, airy terrace and light uncluttered dining room (where diners are eyeballed by giant Modigliani paintings) are perfect for a leisurely lunch. The chef is a foie gras enthusiast, and his special wintertime dish is pigs' trotters with truffles. Off the N100 towards Apt.

Also recommended:

Le Carré d'Herbes (☎ 04 90 38 23 97; 13 ave Quatre Otages; lunch/dinner menus from €15/25) Tucked among the antique villages, with a lovely patio, market-fresh *menus*, and occasional live jazz.

Le Jardin du Quai (☎ 04 90 20 14 98; 91 ave Julien Guigue; lunch/dinner menus €30/40; ☺ Thu-Mon) Customers are presented with a fixed three-course *menu* at this gastronomic restaurant, opposite the train station.

AVIGNON AREA

TRANSPORT

CAR // Car parks are scattered around the edges of the canals (the historic centre is largely vehicle-free); free spaces are rare at weekends.

BUS // Voyages Raoux (☎ 04 90 33 95 75) runs at least four buses daily to/from Avignon (€2, 40 minutes) and Carpentras (€2, 30 minutes).

TRAIN // Five services per day run to Marseille (€14.20, 1 hour 25 minutes), and six to Avignon (€4.20, 32 minutes) from the SNCF train station on ave Julien Guigue.

BIKE // Christophe Tendil (☎ 04 90 38 19 12; 10 av Julien Guigue; per day adult/child €15/10; ⊕ closed Sun & Mon) has a small number of road bikes for hire.

FONTAINE DE VAUCLUSE

pop 671

France's most powerful spring surges out of nowhere above the pretty little village of Fontaine de Vaucluse. The miraculous appearance of this crystal-clear flood draws 1.5 million tourists each year – aim to arrive early in the morning before the trickle of visitors becomes a deluge.

A tumble of mini-attractions caters to the crowd, ranging from the serious-minded Musée d'Histoire: 1939–1945, to biscuit-makers, glass-blowers and paper-manufacturers all vying for the contents of your wallet.

Underneath the tourist tackiness, you can still glimpse the peace and beauty that inspired Italian poet Petrarch (1304–74) to write his most famous works here – the sonnets to his never-to-be-attained love, Laura.

ESSENTIAL INFORMATION

TOURIST OFFICES // Tourist office (☎ 04 90 20 32 22; www.oti-delasorgue.fr; chemin de la Fontaine; ⊕ 9.30am-12.30pm & 1.30-5.30pm Tue-Sat Sep-May, 10am-1pm & 2-6pm) On the pedestrianised pathway to the spring.

EXPLORING FONTAINE DE VAUCLUSE

❧ LA FONTAINE // THE MYSTERIOUS BIRTHPLACE OF THE RIVER SORGUE

At the foot of a craggy cliff 1km above the village, the River Sorgue first surges from the depths of the earth. All the rain that falls around Apt, as well as melting snow, combine somewhere in subterranean passageways before making a surprise appearance at La Fontaine. The spring is at its most dazzling after heavy rain, when the water is an azure blue, and gushes from the ground at an incredible 90 cu metres per second. Jacques Cousteau was one of many who attempted to plumb the spring's depths before an unmanned submarine eventually touched base (315m down) in 1985.

❧ CANOE TO L'ISLE-SUR-LA-SORGUE // GO WITH THE FLOW ON A CANOE TRIP

The beautiful Sorgue is a gem of a river to drift down on a summer's day. Two canoe companies based near Fontaine de Vaucluse operate guided two-hour trips (adult/child €17/12, including the minibus back) to L'Isle-sur-la-Sorgue, 8km downstream, between late April and October.

Canoë Évasion (☎ 04 90 38 26 22; www.canoe -evasion.net; rte de Fontaine de Vaucluse) Next to Camping de la Coutelière on the D24 towards Lagnes.

Kayak Vert (☎ 04 90 20 35 44; www.canoefrance .com; Quartier la Baume) By the aqueduct, 1km out of town on the D25. Also hires canoes for self-guided trips.

❧ MUSÉE D'HISTOIRE: 1939-1945 // A MOVING EXPLORATION OF WWII FRANCE

It sits at odds with the sunshine-and-ice cream tourist mayhem outside, but the **Musée d'Histoire: 1939-1945** (☎ 04 90 20 24 00; chemin de la Fontaine; adult/12-16yr €3.50/1.50; ☉ 10am-6pm Wed-Mon Jun-Sep, 10am-noon & 2-6pm Wed-Mon Apr & May, 10am-noon & 2-5pm Wed-Mon Oct, 10am-noon & 2-5pm Sat & Sun Mar, Nov & Dec) is an excellent examination of life in occupied France during WWII, with thoughtful displays, and artefacts from wine-cork bicycle tyres to disturbing anti-semitic propaganda to radios used by the Vaucluse resistance. Allow a couple of hours. In French only.

❦ ST VÉRAN // TRACE THE SAINT'S LIFE THROUGH TWO MEDIEVAL BUILDINGS

Fontaine was once plagued by the Couloubre, a vile half-dragon, half-serpent, until St Véran dealt with the beast. Today a statue outside the 11th-century Romanesque **Église St-Véran** commemorates the slaying, and a **castle** was built on the clifftop to protect the saint's tomb. The current ruins date from the 13th century – climb up for superb views of the valley.

❦ PÉTRARQUE ET LAURE // ENJOY A MEAL IN A PLEASANT COURTYARD

Next door to the 11th-century church, **Pétrarque et Laure** (☎ 04 90 20 31 48; place Colonne; lunch/dinner menus from €16.30/25.30)

serves meat- and fish-based traditional Provençal food (with the odd piece of kangaroo thrown in) – try the trout, fresh from the Sorgue. Fontaine de Vaucluse's restaurants tend towards the *touristiques*, and this one is no exception. However, although it's obviously used to catering for coach parties, it still manages to produce good-quality food at a decent price. The pleasant tree-shaded courtyard looks onto an original waterwheel slowly spinning in the river.

TRANSPORT

CAR // Fontaine de Vaucluse, 21km southeast of Carpentras and 7km east of L'Isle-sur-Sorgue, is most easily reached by car.

BUS // Some buses on the Avignon–Cavaillon route, run by **Voyages Raoux** (☎ 04 90 33 95 75), stop at Fontaine de Vaucluse. There are at least four buses daily to/from Avignon (€3, one hour) and a couple more to/from L'Isle-sur-la-Sorgue (€1, 10 minutes).

PARKING // Parking costs €3 per day.

PAYS DE VENASQUE

The seldom-visited yet beautiful 'Venasque Country' is a strange little corner of the region. A cluster of hilltop villages perch above a forested landscape, scattered over with hundreds of *bories* (domed stone huts originating in the Bronze Age). It's famous for its ruby-red

∼ WORTH A TRIP ∼

Follow the course of a vanished underground river through the **Grottes de Thouzon** (☎ 04 90 33 93 65; www.grottes-thouzon.com; 2083 rte d'Orange, Le Thor; adult/5-11yr €7.90/5.40; ☉ 10am-6.30pm Jul & Aug, 10am-noon & 2-6pm Apr-Jun, Sep & Oct, 2-6pm Sun Mar), a 230m-long cave accidentally discovered in 1902 during mining works. Marvels include a mound of 5000-year-old bat poo, thousands of 'macaroni' stalactites, odd mineral formations like folds of waxy skin, and a 40-ton flint boulder suspended from a limestone thread. Access is by 45-minute guided tour, with the last running half an hour before closing time. The cave lies a short car-ride from L'Isle-sur-la-Sorgue, 2km outside the village of Le Thor on the D16.

cherries, ripe between mid-May and mid-July.

ESSENTIAL INFORMATION

TOURIST OFFICES // Venasque tourist office (☎ 04 90 66 11 66; www.tourisme-venasque .com; Grande Rue; ⏱ 3-7pm Mon, 10am-12.30pm & 3-7pm Tue-Sat Jul & Aug, 2-6pm Mon, 10am-noon & 2-6pm Tue-Sat Apr-Jun & Sep-Oct, closed Nov-Mar) Has information on the entire area.

EXPLORING PAYS DE VENASQUE

❦ PERCHED VILLAGES // A TRIO OF SKY-HIGH SETTLEMENTS WITH RAVISHING VIEWS

Tiny **Venasque** (population 1131; elevation 320m) teeters on an exposed rocky spur, its twisting streets and ancient buildings weathering the winds. It has a well-deserved 'beau village' status, which will have you reaching for your camera at every corner. Sights include an ancient **baptistry** (☎ 04 90 66 62 01; adult/under 12yr €3/free; ⏱ 9.15am-noon & 1-5pm or 6.30pm Jan–mid-Dec), built in the 6th century on the site of a Roman temple; and a compact **Romanesque church** (⏱ 9.15am-5pm) containing the pride of the village, an unusual painting of the crucifixion (1498) in which Marie-Madeleine (Mary Magdalene) takes centre stage.

The fortress village of **Le Beaucet** (population 362; elevation 300m) perches 6km south via the winding D314. In the hamlet of **St-Gens**, 2km south along chemin des Oratoires, is a small Romanesque basilica. The hermit Gens, who lived with wolves and performed rain-making miracles, died here in 1127.

The third hilltop village is **La Roque-sur-Pernes** (population 450; elevation 290), less dramatic but worth a glance if you're passing.

❦ FORÊT DE VENASQUE // WANDER THROUGH OAK WOODS ON WELL-MARKED TRAILS

The **Forêt de Venasque**, criss-crossed by walking trails including the long-distance GR91, lies east of Venasque. Heading across the Col de Murs (627m) mountain pass to the pretty village of **Murs**, you can see remains of **Le Mur de la Peste** (Plague Wall), built in 1720 in a vain attempt to stop the plague from entering papal territory. You could also walk into the Luberon from here, calling at Gordes (p152) and the Abbaye Notre-Dame de Sénanque (p153). The map *Balades en forêts du Ventoux de Venasque et St-Lambert* (€8) outlines several family walks.

❦ GORGES DE LA NESQUE // EXPLORE THIS DRAMATIC RAVINE WITH A DONKEY COMPANION

Following the GR91 north through the Forêt de Venasque leads you to the steep-sided 20km-long **Gorges de la Nesque**. A fun way of exploring this spectacular canyon (or nearby Mont Ventoux) is alongside a patiently plodding donkey hired from **Les Ânes des Abeilles** (☎ 04 90 64 01 52; anesdesabeilles@wanadoo.fr; Col des Abeilles). Donkeys carry up to 40kg (ie small children or bags) and amble along at 3km to 4km an hour; a day/weekend costs from €45/80.

❦ LES REMPARTS // GORGEOUS SCENERY AND PLATEFULS OF SCRUMPTIOUS GRUB

Diners have a dilemma at the strongly recommended **Les Remparts** (☎ 04 90 66 02 79; rue Haute, Vénasque; lunch/dinner menus from €19.50/24.50; ⏱ May–mid-Nov) – should they focus on the astounding panorama or the mouth-watering food? A glassed-in terrace and a tiny open patio float high above the Plateau de Vaucluse, and the Provençal dishes are packed with flavour and beautifully presented. Vegetarians may not believe this – they have their own dedicated menu. In season, try the cherry juice.

LES ALPILLES

• • • • • •

This silvery chain of almost-mountains, strung between the rivers Durance and Rhône, is worthy of several days' exploration. Bon vivants should base themselves in delightful St-Rémy de Provence, with its far-reaching reputation for fine food. The whole region is filled with gastronomic delights (AOC olive oil, vineyards, Michelin-starred restaurants and truffles), all guarded by

magnificent ruined castles, the remnants of medieval feuds. One of Provence's best Roman sites, the city of Glanum, lies just outside St-Rémy.

ST-RÉMY DE PROVENCE

pop 10,203

Chic, stylish St-Rémy has an unfair share of gourmet shops and restaurants. In keeping with the town's most famous son, prophecy-maker Nostradamus, we predict that you'll need to add another notch or two to your trouser belt. Aside from gluttony, one of France's most atmospheric Roman sites, the sacred city of Glanum, sits on the outskirts of town, next door to the hospital where Van Gogh painted some of his best-known works.

The websites www.alpilles.com and www.alpilles.fr (in French) list information on the region.

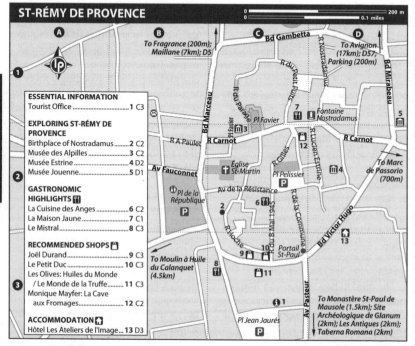

ST-RÉMY DE PROVENCE

ESSENTIAL INFORMATION
Tourist Office 1 C3

EXPLORING ST-RÉMY DE PROVENCE
Birthplace of Nostradamus 2 C2
Musée des Alpilles 3 C2
Musée Estrine 4 D2
Musée Jouenne...............................5 D1

GASTRONOMIC HIGHLIGHTS
La Cuisine des Anges 6 C2
La Maison Jaune.............................7 C1
Le Mistral 8 C3

RECOMMENDED SHOPS
Joël Durand.....................................9 C3
Le Petit Duc 10 C3
Les Olives: Huiles du Monde
/ Le Monde de la Truffe..........11 C3
Monique Mayfer: La Cave
aux Fromages...........................12 C2

ACCOMMODATION
Hôtel Les Ateliers de l'Image...13 D3

ESSENTIAL INFORMATION

TOURIST OFFICES // Tourist office
(☎ 04 90 92 05 22; www.saintremy-de-provence
.com; place Jean Jaurès; ☺ 9am-12.30pm & 2-7pm
Mon-Sat, 9am-noon Sun mid-Jun–mid-Sep, 9am-noon
& 2-6pm Mon-Sat mid-Sep–mid-Jun) Runs numerous
guided tours in English and French (adult/12-18yr €8/5)
between Easter and October, including nature rambles
in the Alpilles.

EXPLORING ST-RÉMY DE PROVENCE

❦ GLANUM // THE HAUNTING RUINS OF A GALLO-ROMAN CITY

The vast **Site Archéologique de Glanum** (☎ 04 90 92 23 79; rte des Baux-de-Provence;
adult/under 18yr/pass €7/free/5.50; ☺ 9.30am-6.30pm
Apr-Sep, 10am-5pm Oct-Mar, closed Mon Sep-Mar, last
entry 30min before closing), dating back to the
3rd century BC, is this author's favourite archaeological site. Walking up the
main street towards the sacred spring
around which Glanum grew, you pass
the poignant remains of a once-thriving
city, complete with baths, forum, marketplace, temples and houses. For a free
panorama, have lunch at the **Taberna
Romana** (☎ 04 90 92 65 97; www.taberna-romana
.com; rte des Baux; menus €16-26; ☺ 10am-6.30pm
Tue-Sun Apr-Sep) by the entrance, with tasteful Roman-inspired *menus* (including
honeyed red wine).

By the car park are **Les Antiques**, a
spectacular pair of Roman monuments
comprising a **triumphal arch** (AD 20)
and **mausoleum** (30 BC to 20 BC).

The site is 2km from St-Rémy town
centre. Parking costs €2.20.

❦ MONASTÈRE ST-PAUL DE MAUSOLE // THE ASYLUM OF VAN GOGH

Van Gogh admitted himself to the
Monastère St-Paul de Mausole (☎ 04 90

FINE VIEWS

★ Orgon – this tiny village is guarded
   by Notre Dame de Beauregard, a
   19th-century church perched high on
   a needle of rock

★ Les Baux de Provence – take a
   commanding view of the countryside
   from the castle walls

★ Eyguières – close to this village is the
   Alpilles' highest point (493m)

92 77 00; www.cloitresaintpaul-valetudo.com, in French;
adult/12-16yr/pass €4/3/3; ☺ 9.30am-7pm Apr-Sep,
10.15am-5.15pm Oct-Mar) between 1889 and
1890. The security of the asylum led to
his most productive period – he completed 150-plus drawings and about 140
paintings here, including his famous irises. A reconstruction of Van Gogh's room
is open to visitors, as are the gardens and
Romanesque cloister that feature in several of his works. St-Paul remains a psy-
chiatric institution: an exhibition room
sells artwork created by patients.

For its time, the 19th-century asylum
was quite enlightened: Van Gogh was
allowed to roam up to a mile away to
paint, if accompanied by a member of
staff. From the monastery entrance, a
walking trail is marked by colour panels
showing where the artist set up his easel.

The tourist office runs a **guided Van
Gogh tour** (per person €8; ☺ 10am Tue, Thu, Fri
& Sat, Easter-Oct) in English and French. For
more about Van Gogh see the boxed text,
p89.

❦ ST-RÉMY ROOTS // CUSTOMS, CULTURE AND A KOOKY ASTROLOGER'S HOUSE

The area's rich heritage is scrutinised at
the solid little **Musée des Alpilles** (☎ 04
90 92 68 24; 1 place Favier; adult/child/pass €3/2/2;

🕐 10am-12.30pm & 2-7pm Tue-Sat Jul & Aug, 10am-noon & 2-6pm Tue-Sat Mar-Jun, Sep & Oct, 2-5pm Tue-Sat Jan, Feb, Nov & Dec, plus 1st Sun each month), which has comprehensive coverage of a pleasing tangle of topics, including fossils, traditional crafts, bull-fighting, Augustin Gonfond's painstaking illuminations, and contemporary engraving, plus absorbing temporary exhibitions.

The **Musée Estrine** (☎ 04 90 92 34 72; 8 rue Lucien Estrine; adult/pass €3.20/2.30; 🕐 10.30am-12.30pm & 2-6pm Tue-Sun mid-Mar-Nov) curates changing modern-art exhibitions, as does the private **Musée Jouenne** (☎ 04 32 60 00 51; www.michel-jouenne.com, in French; 20 bd Mirabeau; adult/under 12yr €4/free; 🕐 10am-12.30pm & 3-7pm Tue-Sat, 3-7pm Sun).

The **birthplace of Nostradamus** (1503–66) can be found on rue Hoche.

FESTIVALS & EVENTS

Fêtes des Peintres (Painters' Festival) Some 200 artists sell their works in the streets; one Sunday each month May to September.
Féria de St-Rémy Bull-running, festivities and fireworks; mid-August
Fête Votive de St-Rémy Six-day celebration of the town's patron saint, with bull fights and parades; late September.

GASTRONOMIC HIGHLIGHTS

🌱 LA CUISINE DES ANGES €€

☎ 04 90 92 17 66; 4 rue du 8 Mai 1945; lunch/dinner menu €12.50/26; 🕐 lunch Mon-Sat, dinner daily Jun-Aug, lunch & dinner Thu-Sat, dinner Sun Sep-Oct & Dec-May, closed Nov
The 'kitchen of angels' is attached to the cute-as-pie *chambre d'hôte* Le Sommeil des Fées. Here, Hélène Ricard cooks up light, summery Provençal dishes like grilled sea bass and honey-glazed duck, with ingredients from the local market. The warm, wood-floored dining room is decorated with bright paintings and

quirky statues; in fine weather, you can dine in the suntrap courtyard.

🌱 LA MAISON JAUNE €€€

☎ 04 90 92 56 14; 15 rue Carnot; menus €35-64; 🕐 lunch & dinner Wed-Sun, dinner Tue summer, lunch Sun, lunch & dinner Tue-Sat winter, closed Jan & Feb
This discreet Michelin-starred restaurant, hidden on the 1st floor of a 16th-century building, is home to one of the most buzzing tables in town. Chef François Perraud constantly comes up with winning creations, like saffron-roasted free-range chicken or Camargue steak with crushed herbs and garlic; but the best way to sample a selection is with his five-course Provençal *dégustation menu* (€54).

🌱 MARC DE PASSORIO €€€

☎ 04 90 92 04 40; www.restaurant-marcdepassorio.fr; chemin Canto Cigalo; menus from €58
Adding to St-Rémy's foodie fervour, this refined place (in the Hostellerie du Vallon de Valrugues) received its first Michelin star in 2009. The eponymous chef combines Provence's best ingredients with wildly unusual flavours to thrill your tastebuds. Even the puddings are a wonder – try the strawberry sorbet with candied olives. An attached bistro with a more relaxed atmosphere opens for lunch (€29).

TRANSPORT

CAR // The D57 runs from Avignon to St-Rémy. From Nîmes, take the D99.

ST-RÉMY PASS

This free pass offers a small entrance discount to Glanum, the Monastère St-Paul de Mausole, and the town's museums – ask for it at these sites.

PARKING // St-Rémy gets very busy: try the car parks on the northern edge of town.

BUS // **Allô Cartreize** (☎ 08 11 88 01 13) is responsible for Avignon-bound buses (€4.40, 40 minutes, six per day Monday to Saturday, four Sunday), stopping at Eyrargues (€1.50, 10 minutes). From June to September, there are four buses daily to Les Baux (€2.80, 15 minutes). They also operate a service to Tarascon and Arles (two Monday to Saturday). Buses depart from place de la République.

BIKE // If you're based within 15km of St-Rémy, contact **Telecycles** (☎ 04 90 92 83 15; www.telecycles -location.com; 1/3/7 days €19/39/72), who will deliver a mountain bike to your door.

AROUND ST-RÉMY DE PROVENCE

Rows of grapevines and silvery-green olive groves line the valleys, while the land around rises to craggy heights, covered in scented herbal *garrigue*. Scattered throughout you'll find rugged castles, ancient olive-oil mills, a troglodyte monastery, and the weird son-et-lumière of the Cathédrale d'Images.

LES BAUX DE PROVENCE

pop 381 / elevation 245m
Clinging precariously to an ancient limestone *baou* (Provençal for 'rocky spur'), this fortified hilltop village is one of the most visited in France. It's easy to see why – tiny car-free streets wend past ancient houses, up to a splendid castle. The **tourist office** (☎ 04 90 54 34 39; www .lesbauxdeprovence.com; ☻ 9.30am-5pm Mon-Fri, 10am-5.30pm Sat & Sun) has information on the few accommodation options.

☙ **CHÂTEAU DES BAUX // DEVOUR THE VIEWS FROM THESE IMPRESSIVE CASTLE RUINS**
The town's high-point attraction in both senses, the dramatic ruins of the **Château des Baux** (☎ 04 90 54 55 56; www.chateau-baux-provence.com; adult/student

---

◣ **TOP FIVE**

GOURMET GOODIES
St-Rémy's specialist food shops usually open until 7pm daily in summer.

★ **Joël Durand** (☎ 04 90 92 38 25; www.chocolat-durand.com; 3 bd Victor Hugo) One of France's top 10 chocolate makers, utilising Provençal herbs and plants like lavender, rosemary, violet and thyme, along with out-of-the-box flavours such as Earl Grey, and coffee-and-barley

★ **Le Petit Duc** (☎ 04 90 92 08 31; www.petit-duc.com; 7 bd Victor Hugo) Historical biscuits baked by food historian Anne Daguin using old Roman, Renaissance, Alpine and Arlésien recipes

★ **Monique Mayfer: La Cave aux Fromages** (☎ 04 90 92 32 45; 1 place Joseph Hilaire) Fabulous cheese shop with a 12th-century ripening *cave* (cellar)

★ **Moulin á Huile du Calanquet** (☎ 04 32 60 09 50; www.moulinducalanquet.fr; Vieux Chemin d'Arles; ☻ till 6pm or 6.30pm) Brother-and-sister-run olive-oil mill 4.5km southwest of St-Rémy, offering tastings and homemade tapenade, fruit juice and jam

★ **Les Olives: Huiles du Monde/Le Monde de la Truffe** (☎ 04 90 15 02 33; 16 bd Victor Hugo) Taste 30 different oils at its *bar à huiles* (oil bar) or breathe in the pungent aroma of truffle products

€7.70/5.70; 9am-8.30pm Jul & Aug, 9am-6pm Mar-Jun & Sep-Nov, 9.30am-5pm Dec-Feb) dominate the surrounding countryside. Thought to date back to the 10th century, the castle was largely destroyed during the reign of Louis XIII in 1633. Explore its 7 hectares of maze-like ruins with the free audioguide, or just run wild through deep dungeons and up crumbling towers (from where there are out-of-this-world views). The reconstructed siege weapons – trebuchets, ballistas, and battering rams – are demonstrated several times daily in summer.

❦ CATHÉDRALE D'IMAGES // UNEARTHLY CINEMATIC PROJECTIONS IN A DISUSED QUARRY

One of the region's weirdest attractions is the **Cathédrale d'Images** (☎ 04 90 54 38 65; www.cathedrale-images.com; rte de Maillane; adult/7-17yr €7.50/3.50; 10am-7pm Apr-Sep, 10am-6pm Mar & Oct-Dec, closed Jan-Feb), a few minutes' stroll north of the village. In the chilly halls of a former limestone quarry, gigantic projections flicker on the rough walls, accompanied by swells of music. The show (Picasso-themed at the time of writing) changes each year. It's hard to describe, pretty unique, and definitely recommended – but wear warm clothes.

❦ L'OUSTA DE BAUMANIÈRE // TWO MICHELIN STARS ATTRACT TASTE-CONSCIOUS DINERS

The legendary **L'Ousta de Baumanière** (☎ 04 90 54 33 07; www.oustaudebaumaniere.com; menus €95-150) serves rarefied cuisine, including a (*très* gourmet) vegetarian menu, with ingredients plucked from its own organic garden. A minimum of two diners is required. There is also fine accommodation available (doubles from €290). Head chef and owner Jean-

André Charial's kingdom also includes the Michelin-star restaurant and luxury rooms of La Cabro d'Or, also in Les Baux. Reservations are imperative for both.

TRANSPORT

CAR // Driving is the easiest way of getting here, but parking is hellish! There are metered spaces all the way down the hill from the edge of the village, and free parking outside the Cathédrale d'Images, but prepare to fight for a place.

BUS // For info on bus services in Les Alpilles, see p135.

TARASCON & BEAUCAIRE

Tarascon (population 13,376) and **Beaucaire** (population 15,099) glower at each other across the River Rhône, each backed up by a mighty castle. Both have a distinctly down-to-earth, untouristy feel, refreshing in much-visited Provence, yet their well-preserved medieval centres are a pleasure to wander. Tarascon has churches, a cloister, a tiny Jewish quarter, and remnants of its ancient wall and gates, while bulls stampede through Beaucaire's streets during the week-long **Foire de Beaucaire** in mid-July.

ESSENTIAL INFORMATION

TOURIST OFFICES // Tarascon Tourist Office (☎ 04 90 91 03 52; www.tarascon.org; bd de la République; 9am-1pm & 2-6pm Mon-Sat, 9.30am-12.30pm Sun Jul & Aug, 9am-12.30pm & 2-6pm Mon-Sat, 9.30am-12.30pm Sun Jun & Sep, 9am-12.30pm & 2-5.30pm Mon-Sat Oct-May) **Beaucaire Tourist Office** (☎ 04 66 59 26 57; www.ot-beaucaire.fr; 24 cours Gambetta; 8am-12.15pm & 2-6pm Mon-Fri, 9.30am-12.30pm & 3-6pm Sat Easter-Sep, plus 9.30am-12.30pm Sun Jul, 8.45am-12.15pm & 2-6pm Mon-Fri Oct-Easter)

❧ CHÂTEAUX OF TARASCON & BEAUCAIRE // A TALE OF TWO CASTLES

A beauty of a castle, the 15th century **Château de Tarascon** (☎ 04 90 91 01 93; adult/12-17yr/18-25yr €6.50/2.50/4.50; ☼ 9.30am-5.30pm Apr-Sep, 10.30am-noon & 2-5pm Oct-Mar) includes a wonderful mossy inner courtyard, a dainty chapel, corbelled latrines, carved grotesques, and a wide flat roof with stunning views. The castle was built by Louis II to defend Provence's frontier, marked by the River Rhône. After losing battles and suffering a lengthy imprisonment, Louis' son King René (r 1434-80) turned away from politics and towards the arts, writing poetry, decorating the castle in rich Renaissance style, organising courtly tournaments and instigating the **Fêtes de la Tarasque**, an Easter parade to celebrate St Martha's taming of Tarasque, a monstrous lion-headed, tortoise-shelled, fish-bellied beast that legend says once lurked in the river. This colourful festival still takes place today.

Across the Rhône, the ruined 11th-century **Château de Beaucaire** (☎ 04 66 59 26 72; www.aigles-de-beaucaire.com; place du Château; adult/5-11yr €10/7; ☼ 3 afternoon shows Mar-Nov, closed Wed) can only be entered during 45-minute falconry displays (in French).

❧ ABBAYE DE ST-ROMAN // FRANCE'S ONLY TROGLODYTIC MONASTERY

Burrowing into a limestone outcrop, this strange little **monastery** (☎ 04 66 59 19 72; www.abbaye-saint-roman.com; adult/child €5.50/free; ☼ 10am-1pm & 2-7pm Jul & Aug, 10am-1pm & 2-6pm Apr-Jun & Sep, 2-5pm Tue-Sun Mar & Oct, 2-5pm Sun Nov-Feb) covers only a small area but is quite fascinating – a chapel, the monks' cells, higgledy-piggledy stairways and interconnecting passageways, and even the graves were all painstakingly carved into the rock from the 5th century onwards. The abbey lies 5km north of Beaucaire, off the D999; once you've parked, it's a further 1km walk up a winding path through *garrigue*.

❧ MAS DES TOURELLES // TASTE ROMAN WINE OFF THE VIA DOMITIA

Learn how Romans made wine at the **Mas des Tourelles** (☎ 04 66 59 19 72; www.tourelles.com; adult/5-16yr €4.90/1.50; ☼ 10am-noon & 2-7pm Mon-Sat, 2-7pm Sun Jul & Aug, 2-6pm Apr-Jun, Sep & Oct, 2-5pm Sat Nov-Mar), a farm southwest

---

OLIVE OIL MILLS

The Alpilles' southern edge contains some of Provence's best-known *moulins d'huile* (oil mills), where four different types of olives, freshly harvested between November and January, are pummelled and pressed into silken AOC Vallée des Baux-de-Provence oil.

In Maussane-les-Alpilles, the cooperative **Moulin Jean-Marie Cornille** (☎ 04 90 54 32 37; www.moulin-cornille.com; rue Charloun Rieu; ☼ shop 10am-12.30pm & 1.30-6pm Mon-Sat) deals direct to the public, though its 200,000L can sell out by mid-August. Between June and September, you can also take a guided tour of the mill (€2; 11am Tuesday and Thursday).

At Mouriès, 6km southeast of Maussane, pop in for a taste of exceptional olive oil milled at the **Moulin Coopératif** (☎ 04 90 47 53 86; www.moulincoop.com; Quartier Mas Neuf; ☼ 9am-12.30pm & 2-7pm Mon-Fri, 9am-12.30pm & 3-7pm Sat, 3-7pm Sun Jul–mid-Sep, 9am-noon & 2-6pm Mon-Sat, 2-6pm Sun mid-Sep–Jun). The village celebrates a **Fête des Olives Vertes** (Green Olive Festival) in mid-September and the arrival of the year's new oil with a **Fête des Huiles Nouvelles** in early December.

of Beaucaire on the D38. There are explanations about classical winemaking techniques, followed by tastings of the domaine's Roman *mucsum* (honeyed wine) and *defrutum* (grape juice) alongside its modern vintages.

TRANSPORT

BUS // Bus 71 from Nîmes (around six per day Monday to Saturday, more during term-time) stops at Beaucaire (40 minutes) and Tarascon (50 minutes), with some services continuing to Avignon. Navettes between Avignon TGV station (at least eight daily) and Arles also stop at Tarascon train station.

NÎMES & AROUND

· · · · · ·

NÎMES

pop 144,092

Nîmes' unusual coat of arms – a crocodile, chained to a palm tree – is a reference to its Roman history. It recalls the retiring Roman legionaries who fought with Caesar during his River Nile campaign, and were granted land here as their reward. Nîmes is famous for three major Roman monuments: Les Arènes, a spectacular amphitheatre; the Tour Magne watchtower; and a temple, the Maison Carrée. It also makes a good base for excursions to the Unesco-blessed Pont du Gard aqueduct (p143), 23km to the northeast, which supplied the Roman city with water.

Nîmes' 'big three' and the Musée d'Art Contemporain can be seen in a day or two. After that, we recommend a leisurely exploration of this laidback city – the narrow streets in the old town are packed with interesting shops, while cafés and bars spill onto sunny squares.

ORIENTATION

Everything, including traffic, revolves around Les Arènes. Just north of the amphitheatre, the fan-shaped, largely pedestrianised old city is bounded by bd Victor Hugo, bd Amiral Courbet and bd Gambetta. Southeast of Les Arènes is esplanade Charles de Gaulle, a large open square, from where av Feuchères leads southeast to the train and bus stations.

∼ WORTH A TRIP ∼

Eager gourmets are attracted to the charming Alpilles village of **Eygaliéres** (population 1955; elevation 134m) by the incomparable **Chez Bru: Le Bistrot de L'Eygalières** (☎ 04 90 90 60 34; http://chezbru.com; rue de la République; menus €95-120; ☯ lunch Wed-Sun, dinner Tue-Sun; ⌘). Here you can savour mind-blowing flavours like cream of foie gras with fig confit and saffron mousse in Wout and Suzy Bru's cosy dining room (twin Michelin-starred, no less), and retreat to seven stunning *chambre d'hôte* doubles (from €130) and suites (from €200).

Also in Eygalières, the fascinating **Jardin de l'Alchimiste** (Alchemist's Garden; ☎ 04 90 90 67 67; www.jardin-alchimiste.com; Mas de la Brune; adult/concession/child €7/5/2; ☯ 10am-6pm May, 3-6pm Mon-Fri, 10am-6pm Sat & Sun Jun-Sep), inspired by the nearby 16th-century house of an alchemist, is planted out in arcane medieval patterns and filled with blossoming trees and herbs, all holding mystical properties. Fall asleep under an almond tree and you'll dream the solution to your financial problems – maybe someone should tell the bankers?!

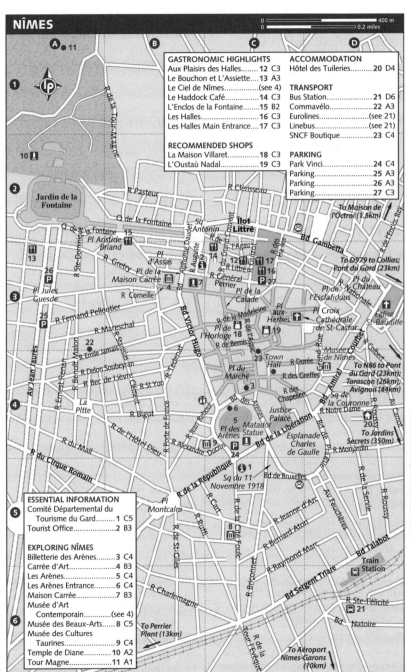

NÎMES

0	400 m
0	0.2 miles

GASTRONOMIC HIGHLIGHTS
Aux Plaisirs des Halles........**12** C3
Le Bouchon et L'Assiette....**13** A3
Le Ciel de Nîmes................(see 4)
Le Haddock Café................**14** C3
L'Enclos de la Fontaine......**15** B2
Les Halles.........................**16** C3
Les Halles Main Entrance....**17** C3

RECOMMENDED SHOPS
La Maison Villaret...............**18** C3
L'Oustaù Nadal..................**19** C3

ACCOMMODATION
Hôtel des Tuileries..........**20** D4

TRANSPORT
Bus Station....................**21** D6
Commavélo...................**22** A3
Eurolines.....................(see 21)
Linebus........................(see 21)
SNCF Boutique..............**23** C4

PARKING
Park Vinci.....................**24** C4
Parking.........................**25** A3
Parking.........................**26** A3
Parking.........................**27** C3

ESSENTIAL INFORMATION
Comité Départemental du
  Tourisme du Gard........**1** C5
Tourist Office................**2** B3

EXPLORING NÎMES
Billetterie des Arènes.........**3** C4
Carrée d'Art....................**4** B3
Les Arènes.....................**5** C4
Les Arènes Entrance..........**6** C4
Maison Carrée.................**7** B3
Musée d'Art
  Contemporain............(see 4)
Musée des Beaux-Arts......**8** C5
Musée des Cultures
  Taurines.....................**9** C4
Temple de Diane............**10** A2
Tour Magne..................**11** A1

AVIGNON AREA

ESSENTIAL INFORMATION

TOURIST INFORMATION // Comité
Départemental du Tourisme du Gard
(☎ 04 66 36 96 30; www.tourismegard.com; 3 rue
de la Cité Foulc; ☺ 8am-8pm Mon-Fri, 9.30am-noon
Sat Jul & Aug, 8.45am-6pm Mon-Fri, 9.30am-noon Sat
Sep-Jun) Information on the Gard *département*. **Tourist office** (☎ 04 66 58 38 00; www.ot-nimes.fr; 6
rue Auguste; ☺ 8.30am-8pm Mon-Fri, 9am-7pm Sat,
10am-6pm Sun Jul & Aug, 8.30am-7pm Mon-Fri, 9am-
7pm Sat, 10am-6pm Sun Apr-Jun & Sep, 8.30am-6.30pm
Mon-Fri, 9am-6.30pm Sat, 10am-5pm Sun Oct-Mar) City
information.

EXPLORING NÎMES

♥ LES ARÈNES // THE WORLD'S BEST-PRESERVED ROMAN AMPHITHEATRE

Impressively intact, and retaining its upper storey, Nîmes' Roman **amphitheatre**
(www.arenes-nimes.com; places des Arènes; adult/10-
16yr €7.70/5.90; ☺ 9am-7pm Jun-Aug, 9am-6.30pm
Apr, May & Sep, 9am-6pm Mar & Oct, 9.30am-5pm
Nov-Feb) was once the setting for wild-animal hunts, executions and, of course, gladiator fights. Built around AD 100 to seat 24,000 spectators, the interior has four seating tiers and a system of exits and passages designed so that patricians never had to rub shoulders with the plebs up top. An excellent free audioguide brings the amphitheatre's dramatic history to life.

Year-round, Les Arènes stages plays, music concerts and bullfights (for ticket details see opposite).

♥ TOUR MAGNE // GET A BIRD'S-EYE VIEW FROM THIS IMPERIAL WATCHTOWER

In 15 BC, the emperor Augustus built 7km of walls around Nîmes, guarded by 80 towers. The crumbling 37m-high **Tour Magne** (adult/child €2.70/2.30; ☺ 9.30am-

COMBO SAVER

Save on Nîmes' three major Roman sites
with a **combination ticket** (adult/child
€9.80/7.50).

7pm Jun-Aug, 9.30am-6.30pm Apr & May, 9.30am-1pm
& 2-6pm Mar, Sep & Oct, 9.30am-1pm & 2-4.30pm
Nov-Feb) is almost all that remains of those prestigious defenses. A spiral staircase of 140 steps leads to the top, from where there are fabulous views. The tower lies a 10-minute walk uphill through the Jardins de la Fontaine.

♥ MAISON CARRÉE // A CLASSICAL TEMPLE STRAIGHT FROM ROME

Six Corinthian columns stand guard at the entrance of the **Maison Carrée**
(Square House; place de la Maison Carrée; adult/11-16yr
€4.50/3.70; ☺ 10am-7.30pm Jun-Aug, 10am-7pm
Apr, May & Sep, 10am-6.30pm Mar & Oct, 10am-1pm &
2-5pm Jan-Feb), a beautifully proportioned Roman temple and one of the few to have survived completely intact from antiquity. It was built around AD 5 to honour Augustus' adopted heirs, Gaius and Lucius; but how honoured they would be by the cinema inside, showing a tacky 20-minute 3D film entitled *Héros de Nîmes*, is debatable…

♥ NÎMES MUSEUMS // BONE UP ON THE CITY'S HISTORY AND CUSTOMS

Contrasting yet complementing the Maison Carrée temple (directly opposite) is the glass-and-steel **Carrée d'Art** (Square of
Art; 15 place de la Maison Carrée), a beautiful airy building which is the brainchild of British architect Lord Norman Foster (1935–).
Its 2nd floor is home to the **Musée d'Art Contemporain** (Contemporary Art Museum; ☎ 04
66 76 35 35; adult/11-16yr €5/3.70; ☺ 10am-6pm
Tue-Sun), which features some ingenious

works from the 1960s to 1990s, and is a great excuse to appreciate this stunning building from the inside out.

Bone up on bovine history and culture at the **Musée des Cultures Taurines** (Museum of Bullfighting Culture; ☎ 04 66 36 83 77; 6 rue Alexandre Ducros; adult/10-16yr €5.50/3.80; ⌚ 10am-6pm Tue-Sun late May-Oct).

Nîmes' biggest and best **Roman mosaic** illustrates the myth of Alcestis, who could only marry if her future husband Admetus rolled up in a chariot pulled by a wild boar and a lion. The mosaic was discovered in 1883 during the construction of the city's indoor market, and is displayed in the **Musée des Beaux-Arts** (☎ 04 66 67 38 21; 20-22 rue de la Cité Foulc; adult/11-16yr €5.50/3.80; ⌚ 10am-6pm Tue-Sun) along with Flemish, Italian and French sculptures and paintings.

❧ JARDINS DE LA FONTAINE // HANDSOME GARDENS PERFECT FOR A STATELY STROLL

Marble statues line the green waterways of the monumental 18th-century **Jardins de la Fontaine** (Fountain Gardens), laid out around the Source de la Fontaine. This was the site of a spring, temple and baths in Roman times, although only the enigmatic **Temple de Diane**, to the left of the main entrance, remains.

❧ FÉRIAS DE NÎMES // FESTIVALS WITH SPANISH SPIRIT: PARTIES, PROCESSIONS AND BULLFIGHTS

Nîmes goes wild at the five-day **Féria de Pentecôte**, a Spanish-flavoured Whitsuntide festival that draws almost a million visitors. The celebrations begin with the Pégoulade, a parade-cum-conga that winds through Nîmes' streets and boulevards before finishing up at Les Arènes. After this, the focus is on music, partying and bulls, with *abrivados* (bull-running),

corridas (bull-fighting, with the bulls killed) and *courses Camarguaises* (a kind of non-fatal bull-taunting – see the boxed text, p90). Reserve tickets (from €20 to €100) several months ahead via the **Billetterie des Arènes** (☎ 04 66 02 80 90; www.arenes denimes.com, in French; 4 rue de la Violette). Similar antics occur at the lower key, three-day **Féria des Vendanges** (Wine Harvest Féria), held over the last weekend in September.

❧ CITY TOURS // EXPLORE NÎMES' CORE BY TAXI OR ON FOOT

The tourist office runs city tours (€5.50) in French: pick up the *Laissez-vous conter Nîmes* brochure for details. They also hire out audioguides (€10) in French, German and English for self-guided walks.

Taxi TRAN (☎ 04 66 29 40 11) negotiate Nîmes' merry-go-round traffic on your behalf: their city driving tours (from €35 per hour for up to six people; pick-up by arrangement) have recorded commentaries in six languages including English.

GASTRONOMIC HIGHLIGHTS

Place aux Herbes, place du Marché, and the western side of place de la Maison Carrée buzz with café life. Several cosy dining spots are hidden away on place de l'Esclafidous. The vast covered food market **Les Halles** (rue Guizot, rue Général Perrir & rue des Halles; ⌚ 6.30am-1pm) is the city's 'gourmet soul'.

DENIM ORIGINS

Nîmes' name is a household one, thanks to Bavarian tailor Levi Strauss. During the California goldrush, Strauss struck riches himself by outfitting miners with durable trousers made from the traditional blue *serge de Nimes,* nowadays shortened to 'denim'.

❦ AUX PLAISIRS DES HALLES €€€

☎ 04 66 36 01 02; 4 rue Littré; lunch menu €21.50, dinner menus €27-60; ☺ Tue-Sat

Tucked down a pedestrianised alley, the seating here is split fifty-fifty between a simple, slightly 1970s interior and a pretty shaded courtyard. The restaurant is proud of its Nîmois heritage, using local delicacies such as *brandade de Nîmes* (salted cod paste), and draws every ounce of flavour from its fresh ingredients. The puddings are especially pretty, and the lunchtime menu is great value.

❦ LE BOUCHON ET L'ASSIETTE €€

☎ 04 66 62 02 93; 5bis rue de Sauve; lunch menu €17, dinner menus €27-45; ☺ Thu-Mon, closed early Jan, mid-Jul–mid-Aug

This restaurant, with its warm colour scheme, rough stone walls and bordering-on-the-chintz lampshades, offers a homey atmosphere and an excellent quality:price ratio. Salmon, lamb and guinea fowl are cooked to time-honoured recipes, supplemented by local specialities like *brandade* as well as those from other French regions, like the creamy *faisselle* (curd cheese with honey, almonds, hazelnuts and raisins) offered for dessert.

TREATS TO EAT

The city's most famous culinary speciality is *brandade de Nîmes* – cod poached in milk, then whipped into a paste with olive oil. Buy it from **l'Oustaù Nadal** (☎ 04 66 67 80 18; 4 rue des Marchands).

Caladons (Nîmes' almond-studded honey biscuits) are sold at most pâtisseries. Rival *croquants Villaret* (rock-hard finger-shaped almond biscuits) have been baked by the Villaret family at **La Maison Villaret** (☎ 04 66 67 41 79; 13 rue de la Madeleine) since 1775.

❦ LE CIEL DE NÎMES €€

☎ 04 66 36 71 70; place de la Maison Carrée; mains €12/25; ☺ 10am-6pm Tue-Sun year-round, 7-11.30pm Fri & Sat Apr-Sep

Beneath a metallic-covered terrace, this chic rooftop hang-out at the Carrée d'Art is favoured by fashionable Nîmois. Reasons for making your way here are threefold: to admire the stunning view of Nîmes' Roman temple and city panorama; to take a break from sightseeing with afternoon tea and sinfully delicious cakes; or to sample the small but exemplary lunch and dinner menus.

❦ LE HADDOCK CAFÉ €

☎ 04 66 67 86 57; 13 rue de l'Agau; menus around €20; ☺ 11am-3pm Mon-Fri & 7pm-1am Mon-Sat

A highlight of Nîmois nightlife, this bohemian café-bar has an affordable and atmospheric restaurant with brimming bowls of *moules et frites* (mussels and fries; €10) on Wednesday at lunchtime. When we visited, this large, packed-out bistro was being ably attended to by a single waiter – a miraculous sight! It hosts changing art exhibitions and extremely popular cabaret-style concerts, from conjurors and karaoke to jazz and blues bands (table reservations are a must).

❦ L'ENCLOS DE LA FONTAINE €€€

☎ 04 66 21 90 30; www.hotel-imperator.com; quai de la Fontaine; menu €55, mains €22-28; ☺ lunch & dinner

At Nîmes' most beautiful garden restaurant (part of the Hôtel Imperator Concorde), chef Victor dos Santos delights with creations like sea bass and wild fennel, followed by a mouth-watering selection of farm-fresh *fromage* (cheese). *Picholine* olive oil is used in all the cooking, alongside other Nîmes' specialities.

Afterwards the literary-minded can pop into the Hemingway Bar.

TRANSPORT

AIR // **Nîmes-Garons airport** (☎ 04 66 70 49 49) is 10km southeast on the A54 to Arles, and is served by Ryanair flights to/from England (Liverpool and London-Luton) and Brussels. An airport bus (€5, 30 minutes), leaving from the train station, meets all flights. Ring ☎ 04 66 29 52 00 to confirm times. Bus drivers sell tickets.

CAR // The A9 runs between Nîmes and Orange; turn off at junction 23 onto the N100 for Avignon. The D999 runs due east to Tarascon and Beaucaire. Nîmes' narrow streets and demonic one-way system make it a pig to drive around: prepare to take several turns around the city before getting the right road!

PARKING // There are several large underground car parks, the largest being **Park Vinci** (☎ 04 66 67 88 95; place des Arènes; per 1/5/24hr €1.60/7.30/11; ☺ 24hr), which offers free bicycles to its customers.

BUS // Buses run to the Pont du Gard (see p144) from the **bus station** (☎ 04 66 29 52 00; rue Ste-Félicité). International bus operators **Eurolines** (☎ 04 66 29 49 02) and **Linebùs** (☎ 04 66 29 50 62) have offices at the far end of the terminal.

TRAIN // The city's **train station** (bd Talabot) is at the southeastern end of av Feuchères. In town, tickets are sold at the **SNCF Boutique** (11 rue de l'Aspic; ☺ 8.30am-6.30pm Tue-Sat). Destinations include Avignon Centre (€8.30, 45 minutes, 10 or more daily) and Arles (€7.30, 30 minutes, nine daily). A number of SNCF trains head to Aigues-Mortes (€6.90, 45 minutes).

BIKE // **Commavélo** (☎ 04 66 29 19 68; www .commavelo.com; 28 rue Emile Jamais; ☺ Mon-Sat, by arrangement Sun) hires out road bikes, mountain bikes and tandems (per half/full day from €9/15).

PONT DU GARD

The Romans didn't do anything on a small scale, and this awe-inspiring three-tiered aqueduct – the highest in the world at 50m – is no exception.

❧ PONT DU GARD // MARVEL AT THIS 2000-YEAR-OLD ROMAN AQUEDUCT

A Unesco World Heritage site, the exceptional **Pont du Gard** was once part of a 50km-long system of canals. It was built around 19 BC by Agrippa, Augustus' son-in-law, to bring water from the Eure Springs in Uzès, 25km away, to Nîmes, using the power of gravity alone. The aqueduct's arches, looping 275m across the valley, were built from massive limestone blocks – incredibly, without the use of mortar! It would have taken 1000 workers five years to build, and it remained in use until the 3rd century, in its heyday carrying 35,000 cu metres of water a day.

It's possible to **walk the bridge's topmost tier** (€6) with a guide between mid-June and mid-September (advance bookings are essential for this). Heading from the car parks on either side of the river, you can take a walk along the road bridge, which runs parallel with the aqueduct's lowest tier. In summer, you can also **swim** in the river upstream from the aqueduct. An open-air exhibition on the left bank, **Mémoires de Garrigue**, also makes a pleasant 1.5km walking route. The bridge is lit by a spectacular **light show**, nightly from July to mid-August.

Admission to the river and the aqueduct is free. Visitor numbers here reach a punishing 15,000 daily in July and August. The **Accueil du Pont du Gard** (☎ 08 20 90 33 30; www.pontdugard.fr; Le Portal, rte du Pont du Gard; ☺ 9.30am-5.30pm Oct-Apr, 9.30am-7pm May-Sep, closed Mon morning year-round) visitor centre includes a **museum** (admission €7), a 25-minute **film** (with English version €4) and **Ludo** (admission €5), which is a fun children's education centre. Parking costs are reimbursed if you purchase a **combination ticket** (adult/child €12/9) or **family ticket** (2 adults & up to 4 children under 17yr €24).

❦ CANOEING ON THE RIVER GARD // SWEEP DOWNSTREAM, THROUGH THE PONT DU GARD'S ARCHES

Arrive at the Pont du Gard (€20 per person, two hours) aqueduct in style by paddling 8km downriver from Collias, 4km west of the D981. **Kayak Vert** (☎ 04 66 22 80 76; www.canoe-france.com/gardon) and **Canoë Le Tourbillon** (☎ 04 66 22 85 54; www.canoe-le-tourbillon.com), both based near the village bridge, rent out kayaks and canoes from March/April to October.

Longer descents through the watery Gorges du Gardon (€34, full day) are also possible between March and mid-June.

TRANSPORT

CAR // The Pont du Gard is 21km northeast of Nîmes and 26km west of Avignon. From the A9, take exit 23 at Remoulins, and head towards Uzès. There are giant **car parks** (€5; ⊗ 7am-1am) at the site, on both the left and right banks of the River Gard.

BUS // Buses to/from Nîmes (€6.50, 45 minutes, six Monday to Saturday, two Sunday) normally stop 1km north of the bridge. In summer, some make a diversion to the Pont du Gard car park. A similar service runs from Avignon.

THE LUBERON

3 PERFECT DAYS

♥ DAY 1 // EXPLORE OCHRE COUNTRY

Start in Rustrel for a morning walk through the fiery-ochre rock formations of the Colorado Provençal (p158). Seek sustenance at Le Table de Pablo (p155) then swing your handlebars or steering wheel west to Gargas to visit Europe's only operational ochre quarry (p154). Continue on to rust-coloured Roussillon (p153) to amble along its ochre trail and take an ochre workshop (p154).

♥ DAY 2 // FROM MOUNTAINS TO BOUTIQUES

Marvel at the views from Saignon (p162) before heading through lavender fields into the Luberon mountains to explore Buoux (p162) and find lunch at magnificent Ferme Auberge Le Castelas (p163). Then plunge through the Combe de Lourmarin to reach lively Lourmarin (p164). Stroll through olive groves around town and then dip into the village to take a literary tour or explore the streets lined with boutiques and *ateliers*. Sup at an outstanding restaurant, like Le Moulin de Lourmarin (p165).

♥ DAY 3 // HILLTOP VILLAGES AND HAUTE CUISINE

Wind your way around the hillsides to Bonnieux (p158) to scuttle up 86 steps to its 12th-century church, and stroll in its cedar forest. Lunch in style at one of the village's excellent restaurants (p159). Then push west to Lacoste (p159) to gaze out over the former château of the Marquis de Sade. Finish in Ménerbes (p160), calling in at the quirky corkscrew museum (p161) before charting a course through the higgledy-piggledy village to learn about wine and truffles (p161) and feast on Laurent Jouin's delicious fare at Véranda (p161).

THE LUBERON

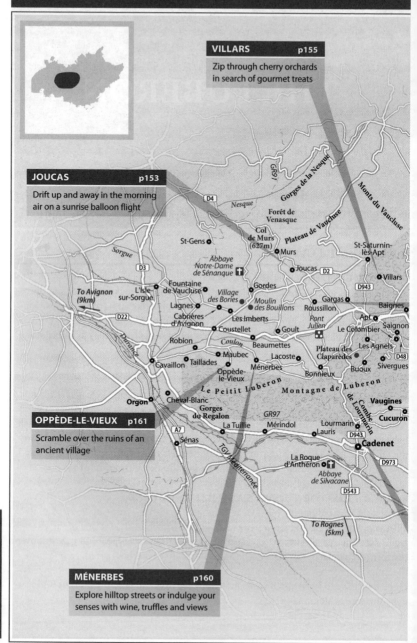

VILLARS   p155

Zip through cherry orchards in search of gourmet treats

JOUCAS   p153

Drift up and away in the morning air on a sunrise balloon flight

OPPÈDE-LE-VIEUX   p161

Scramble over the ruins of an ancient village

MÉNERBES   p160

Explore hilltop streets or indulge your senses with wine, truffles and views

THE LUBERON

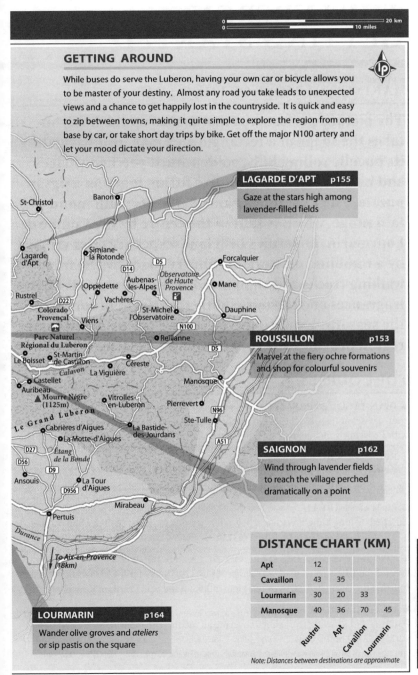

GETTING AROUND

While buses do serve the Luberon, having your own car or bicycle allows you to be master of your destiny. Almost any road you take leads to unexpected views and a chance to get happily lost in the countryside. It is quick and easy to zip between towns, making it quite simple to explore the region from one base by car, or take short day trips by bike. Get off the major N100 artery and let your mood dictate your direction.

LAGARDE D'APT   p155

Gaze at the stars high among lavender-filled fields

ROUSSILLON   p153

Marvel at the fiery ochre formations and shop for colourful souvenirs

SAIGNON   p162

Wind through lavender fields to reach the village perched dramatically on a point

LOURMARIN   p164

Wander olive groves and *ateliers* or sip pastis on the square

DISTANCE CHART (KM)

	Rustrel	Apt	Cavaillon	Lourmarin
Apt	12			
Cavaillon	43	35		
Lourmarin	30	20	33	
Manosque	40	36	70	45

Note: Distances between destinations are approximate

THE LUBERON

THE LUBERON GETTING STARTED

MAKING THE MOST OF YOUR TIME

The picture-perfect area that makes up the Luberon takes the shape of a rectangle on a map. But navigating its bucolic rolling hills, golden-hued perched villages and hidden valleys is a bit like fitting together a jigsaw puzzle. The Luberon is named after its main mountain range, which is split in the centre by the Combe de Lourmarin. Luberon's lush landscapes are criss-crossed by a rambling network of country roads, waymarked walking tracks and signposted cycling routes. Its hues, fragrances and flavours subtly transform in tune with the seasons. Exploring even a piece of this picturesque region provides an ever-changing spectacle.

TOP COURSES

❦ JEAN-JACQUES PRÉVÔT
Half-day sessions (€135/110 with/without market visit) focus on a seasonal product with Provence's melon-mad chef. Pâtisserie classes for children are available (p151).

❦ REINE SAMMUT
Cooking classes and lunch with Michelin-starred chef Reine Sammut (€145) or her staff (€75 to €95), include baking for children (p164).

❦ LE MAS PERRÉAL
Elisabeth, a long-time French teacher, offers lessons to guests (€30 per hour) at her gorgeous *chambre d'hôte* (☎ 04 90 75 46 31; www.masperreal.com; Lieu-dit la Fortune, St-Saturnin-lès-Apt).

❦ CONSERVATOIRE DES OCRES ET DE LA COULEUR
A mind-boggling array of art workshops (€119/114/104/99 for the first/second/third/fourth day). Using natural dyes and pigments from the ochre earth in Roussillon (p154).

❦ L'ATELIER DORÉ
Painting and drawing workshops covering all media (two-hour session adult/child €20.50/17, 20 hours €195/140) by Jean-Claude Lorber in an 18th-century *mas* (farmhouse) (☎ 04 90 06 29 60; www.mas-des-amandiers.com, in French; 48 chemin des Puits Neufs, Cavaillon).

THE LUBERON

GETTING AWAY FROM IT ALL

* **Have Sunday brunch in the mountains** Burrow deep into the Combe de Lourmarin to Auberge de l'Aiguebrun for lovely Sunday brunches (p159)
* **Find the hidden ice-cream shop** Ply the back roads of the Pays d'Aigues to find L'Art Glacier, the artisan ice-creamery with a hilltop view (p165)
* **Stargaze at Observatoire la Sirene** Drive high into the foothills of the Alps for clear night views at this observatory run entirely by volunteers (p155)
* **Walk semi-inhabited ruins** Explore the hilltop ruins of Oppède-le-Vieux, where only a handful of artists live today (p161)

ADVANCE PLANNING

* **Couleur Pass Luberon** Sold at local tourist offices, this pass (€5) gives a discount of up to 50% on 16 major tourist sites and activities in the region
* **Abbaye Notre-Dame de Sénanque** (p153) Book ahead to take a tour of this famous abbey
* **Château de Tour d'Aigues** (p166) Buy tickets for an outdoor concert in a restored château in the Pays d'Aigues
* **Festival de Lacoste** (p159) Buy tickets for July events held in the 9th-century Château de Lacoste, former home of the notorious Marquis de Sade
* **Ferme Auberge Le Castelas** (p163) Make a reservation here or, in summer, at any other restaurant in which you have your heart set on eating

TOP MARKETS

The Luberon's food markets take place from around 8am to 1pm unless otherwise noted.

MONDAY
Cadenet, Cavaillon, Lauris

TUESDAY
Apt (farmers market April to December), Cucuron, Gordes, Lacoste, La Tour d'Aigues, St-Saturnin-lès-Apt

WEDNESDAY
Coustellet (from 5.30pm June to August), Gargas, Mérindol, Pertuis

THURSDAY
Allemagne-en-Provence, Allos, Les Salles-sur-Verdon, Montagnac, Roussillon, Sospel

FRIDAY
Bonnieux, Lourmarin, Pertuis

SATURDAY
Apt, Cadenet (farmers market May to October), Lauris (2pm to 5pm winter, 5pm to 8pm summer), Manosque, Oppède, Pertuis, Vaugines

SUNDAY
Coustellet (April to December), Vaugines, Villars (June to September)

RESOURCES

* **Parc Naturel Régional du Luberon** (www.parcduluberon.fr) Regional information
* **Bienvenue à la Ferme** (www.bienvenue-a-la-ferme.com) Find out about farm visits
* **Départment de Vaucluse** (www.vaucluse.fr) Bus schedules and fares

THE LUBERON

CAVAILLON
· · · · · ·

pop 25,200

In France and beyond, Cavaillon is tantamount to its sweet cantaloupe melons, often referred to simply as 'Cavaillons', regardless of where they're grown. Masses of melons fill Cavaillon's early morning Monday market from May to September and abound during the four-day Fête du Melon in July.

ESSENTIAL INFORMATION

TOURIST OFFICES // Cavaillon Tourist Office (☎ 04 90 71 32 01; www.cavaillon-luberon .com, in French; place François Tourel; ⏰ 9am-12.30pm & 2-6.30pm Mon-Sat mid-Mar–mid-Oct plus 10am-noon Sun Jul & Aug, 9am-noon & 2-6pm Mon-Fri, 10am-noon Sat mid-Oct–mid-Mar) Information on western Luberon and arranges tours: melon tasting (adult/child €6/free), hilltop villages (€3) or wine tasting with farm-house brunch (€35).

EXPLORING CAVAILLON

♥ MUSEUMS // EXPLORE THE HISTORY OF CAVAILLON

Cavaillon's beautiful **synagogue** (1772–74) houses the **Musée Juif Comtadin** (Jewish Museum; ☎ 04 90 76 00 34; rue Hébraïque; adult/child €3/free; ⏰ 9.30am-12.30pm & 2.30-6.30pm Wed-Mon May-Sep, 9am-noon & 2-5pm Wed-Mon Oct, 9am-noon & 2-5pm Mon & Wed-Sat Nov-Apr), inside the former bakery of the Jewish community (women worshipped beneath the synagogue's wooden floor in the bake-house). The same ticket is also good for the **Hôtel-Dieu** (☎ 04 90 76 00 34; porte d'Avignon; ⏰ 9.30am-12.30pm & 2.30-5.30pm Wed-Mon May-Oct, by reservation Nov-Apr), at the old town's northern edge, which covers

---

PEDAL POWER

Jaunty blue signs mark the way for the **Autour du Luberon**, a 236km cycling itinerary through the region that leads from one picturesque village to the next. Tourist offices have maps for it, as well as **Les Ocres en Vélo** (www.ocresenvelo.com), another route through ochre country. Also, the railway tracks that have been unused since the 1960s are slowly being turned into an extensive **cycleway** that will allow riding completely free of traffic. At the time of writing, 20km of the route was open near Apt. Bicycle club **Vélo Loisir en Luberon** (☎ 04 92 79 05 82; www .veloloisirluberon.com) has loads of info.

Cavaillon's former Celtic settlement and has archaeological exhibits.

♥ LIVE THEATRE // CATCH A PLAY OR A ROCKIN' BAND

Little Cavaillon has two of the Luberon's main theatres. The **Théâtre du Cavaillon** (☎ 04 90 78 64 64; www.theatredecavaillon.com; La Scéne Nationale, rue du Languedoc) books international and national tours of drama and dance. **Le Grenier à Sons** (☎ 04 90 06 44 20; www.grenier-a-sons.org; 157 av du Géneral de Gaulle) holds concerts of regional and local acts – lots of reggae and rock.

♥ DOMAINE FAVEROT // TASTE AWARD-WINNING WINES

Just west of Maubec on the road to Robion, this former silk farm now houses a medal-winning winery: **Domaine Faverot** (☎ 04 90 76 65 16; www.domainefaverot .eu; 771 rte de Robion, Maubec). Using no chemicals, the Domaine produces 25,000 bottles a year, which guests (and anyone passing by) can snap up before they're exported around the world. If it's quiet, Sally and François can give a behind-the-scenes tour. Four cottages look out across the vineyards (doubles per week from €850).

GASTRONOMIC HIGHLIGHTS

♥ CÔTÉ JARDIN €€

☎ 04 90 71 33 58; 49 rue Lamartine; lunch/dinner menus from €12/24; ☺ lunch Mon-Sat, dinner Tue-Sat Apr-Oct, lunch & dinner Wed-Sat Nov-Mar

Behind a melon-coloured wooden facade, family-run Côté Jardin has sage-coloured wicker chairs and its stencilled walls open to a charming little courtyard. Frédéric Toppin's aubergine, tomato and goats'-cheese tart is a treat, as is the salmon and St-Jacques accompanied by a feather-light vegetable flan.

♥ LE CLOS GOURMAND

☎ 04 90 78 05 22; 8 place du Clos; ☺ 8.15am-12.30pm & 3-7pm Mon-Sat

Quench your thirst with a taste of Provence: *sirop au mimosa* (a nonalcoholic fizzy mimosa drink), a shot of *crème au melon* (a melon liqueur) or a glass of *délice de Cavaillon* (a melon-flavoured *apéritif*) from this *épicerie fine* (gourmet grocery).

♥ L'ÉTOILE DU DÉLICE

☎ 04 90 78 07 51; 57 place Castil-Blaze; ☺ 7am-7.30pm Mon-Tue, Thu, Fri & Sat, to 1pm Sun

Yannick Jaume – *chocolatier-pâtissier-glacier* – also does inventive things with melons at his cheery sweet-stacked shop. Friendly staff will help you to make creations like *melonettes* (a unique chocolate ganache with a melon essence) and melon ice cream.

♥ PRÉVÔT €€€

☎ 04 90 71 32 43; 353 av de Verdun; lunch menus €25-30, dinner menus €55-85; ☺ lunch & dinner Tue-Sat, closed early-late Aug

Melon memorabilia artfully adorns the dining room of Prévôt, Cavaillon's most prestigious restaurant. May to September Jean-Jacques Prévôt conjures up melon-inspired *menus*. He also works his thematic magic on truffles (January and February), game and chocolate (November and December), asparagus (March and April) and artichokes and aubergines (May to November). He offers classes (p148).

♥ SOLE E PAN €

☎ 04 90 78 06 54; 61 cours Bournissac; plat du jour €8.50; ☺ 7am-7.30pm Wed-Mon

Formerly Chez Auzet, Sole e Pan turns out dozens of varieties of bread including walnut and Roquefort, along with sandwiches and dishes such as duck with raspberries, and zucchini flowers with basil, tomato and thyme.

TRANSPORT

BIKE // Cyclix Cavaillon (☎ 04 90 78 07 06; 166 cours Gambetta; ☺ 9am-12.15pm & 3-7pm Tue-Sat) rents bikes (from €16/78 per day/week). Bikes can be delivered (€0.61 per kilometre return).

BUS // From the bus stop beside the train station, Express de la Durance (☎ 04 90 71 03 00) and Transalex (☎ 04 90 78 16 96) offer daily services including L'Isle-sur-la-Sorgue and Aix-en-Provence.

TRAIN // From the train station (place de la Gare), there are services to Marseille and Avignon centre.

GORDES & AROUND

· · · · · ·

Some of Provence's most quintessential sights – impossibly pretty villages, beehive-shaped *bories* (primitive dwellings built from dry limestone), lavender fields and a stunning

THE LUBERON

Cistercian abbey – are all just a few kilometres apart in this picturesque patch of the Luberon.

ESSENTIAL INFORMATION

TOURIST OFFICES // Gordes Tourist Office (☎ 04 90 72 02 75; www.gordes-village.com; place du Château; ◷ 9am-noon & 2-6pm, 10am-noon & 2-6pm Sun) **Roussillon Tourist Office** (☎ 04 90 05 60 25; www.roussillon-provence.com, in French; place de la Poste; ◷ 10am-noon & 1.30-5pm Mon-Sat)

EXPLORING GORDES & AROUND

♥ GORDES // SEE ONE OF PROVENCE'S MOST FAMOUS VILLAGES

Forming an amphitheatre over the Rivers Sorgue and Calavon, the tiered village of **Gordes** sits spectacularly on the white rock face of the Vaucluse plateau. Gordes has top billing on many tourists' must-see lists (particularly those of high-profile Parisians) so high season sees attendants ushering a cavalcade of tour coaches and cars into parking bays. Early evenings, the village is theatrically lit by the setting sun, turning the stone buildings a shimmering gold. Motorists must park in the car park (€3).

WINE TASTING

The Luberon is graced with three main wine appellations: the Côtes du Ventoux, the Côtes du Luberon and the Coteaux de Pierrevert (p167). Upon arrival to the region, head to your nearest tourist office and pick up the map detailing all of the growers, cooperatives and wine cellars. Then, as you traipse through the countryside, you'll know just where to pull over and take a tipple.

ACCOMMODATION

Everything about the Luberon drips with charm and the lodging is no exception. For complete listings, see the accommodation chapter. Here are a few of our favourites.

★ Dig into fresh quince jelly during bodacious breakfasts at relaxing **La Magnanerie** (p388)

★ **Domaine des Andéols** (p386) sequesters you in comfortable luxury in the midst of exceptional natural beauty

★ Rainbows occasionally arc over the valley views at bustling **Auberge de Presbytère** (p388)

★ Escape the masses teeming in Gordes at quiet, cosy **Le Mas de la Beaume** (p387)

★ Stay over the night before Apt's booming Saturday market at **Le Couvent** (p387)

♥ MUSEUMS // STUDY THE LIFE OF PAINTERS AND OLIVE-OIL MAKERS

Apart from celebrity-spotting, Gordes' star attraction is its 11th-century château housing the **Musée Pol Mara** (☎ 04 90 72 02 75; place du Château; adult/child €4/free; ◷ 10am-noon & 2-6pm), dedicated to Flemish painter Pol Mara, who lived in Gordes.

Heading 3.5km south along rte de St-Pantaléon (D148) you hit the fabulous museum **Moulin des Bouillons** (☎ 04 90 72 22 11; rte de St-Pantaléon; adult/10-17yr €5/0.50; ◷ 10am-noon & 2-5pm or 6pm Feb-Oct), an oil mill with a 10m-long Gallo-Roman press weighing seven tonnes – said to be the oldest such press in the world. There is also an interesting on-site stained-glass museum.

THE LUBERON

❧ HOT-AIR BALLOONING PROVENCE // FLOAT OVER THE LUBERON

Just outside Gordes, 6km northeast in Joucas, you can take off for a blissful balloon flight over the Luberon with **Hot-Air Ballooning Provence** (☎ 04 90 05 76 77; www.montgolfiere-provence-ballooning.com; 1½hr flights from €245).

❧ VILLAGE DES BORIES // EXPLORE A SURREAL CONGREGATION OF STONE HUTS

You'll spot beehive-shaped *bories* while you're buzzing around Provence (1610 have been counted to date), but the **Village des Bories** (☎ 04 90 72 03 48; adult/child €6/4; ☽ 9am-sunset), 4km southwest of Gordes, has hoards of them.

Reminiscent of Ireland's *clochàn*, these dry-walled huts constructed from slivers of limestone were first built in the area in the Bronze Age. Their original purpose isn't known, but over time they've been used as homes, workshops, wine cellars and silkworm huts. This 'village' contains about 20 *bories*, best visited early in the morning or just before sunset for the interplay of light and shadow.

❧ ABBAYE NOTRE-DAME DE SÉNANQUE // ESCAPE TO ANOTHER TIME

Framed by fields of lavender in July, this picture-postcard Cistercian **abbey** (☎ 04 90 72 05 72; guided tour in French adult/child €7/3; ☽ tours by reservation, shop 10am-6pm Mon-Sat, 2-6pm Sun Feb–mid-Nov, 2-6pm mid-Nov–Jan), 4km northwest of Gordes off the D177, sits in a magical valley. The abbey was founded in 1148 and is inhabited by a few monks who celebrate mass at noon, Tuesday to Saturday, and 10am Sunday. A 1½-hour walk will get you to or from Gordes.

❧ CABRIÈRES D'AVIGNON & AROUND // EAT WELL SOUTH OF GORDES

Cabrières d'Avignon was one of the most unfortunate Waldensian villages (see the boxed text, p164). Pine and cedar forests, criss-crossed with paths and picnic tables, shroud the northern village fringe.

Herbs and flowers are used to flavour honey made at the village honey house and the dishes cooked up at **Le Vieux Bistrot** (☎ 04 90 76 82 08; Grande Rue; d from €65; lunch menu €15, dinner menus €28-35; ☽ lunch & dinner 5.30-7.30pm Jun-Sep, closed lunch Sat & Sun Oct-May). Downstairs, soft jazz plays in the crimson '20s-inspired dining room and upstairs are six cosy *chambres d'hôtes*.

Near Lagnes, 5km west, enjoy a quintessential Provençal sleeping and eating experience at **Le Mas des Grès** (☎ 04 90 20 32 85; www.masdesgres.com; rte d'Apt; d from €150, half-board per person €38; P ☒ ☒), a farmhouse with rooms in warm hues of ochre and gold. Nonguests can also join Nina and Thierry's extravagant *table d'hôte* (€38). Thierry runs a range of cooking courses between March and November, including classes for kids.

❧ ROUSSILLON // REVEL IN THE BRILLIANT RED VILLAGE

Some two millennia ago, the Romans used the ochreous earth around the

---

HONEY HOUSES

Bees collect the nectar from dozens of different flowers including *bruyerè* (heather), *tilleul* (linden), *châtaignier* (chestnut), *garrigue* (aromatic ground cover) and *lavande* (lavender) to make the area's many *miels* (honeys).

Tourist offices have lists of **miellers** (honey houses), and you'll see signs by the roadside reading '*miel*'.

THE LUBERON

spectacular village of **Roussillon**, set in the valley between the Plateau de Vaucluse and the Luberon range, for producing pottery glazes. These days the whole village – even gravestones in the cemetery – is built of the reddish stone. Motorists must park in car parks (€2) outside the village, a 300m walk away.

From the town, take a 45-minute walk along the **Sentier des Ocres** (Ochre Trail; adult/child €2.50/free; ☺ 9am-7.30pm Jul & Aug, to 5pm Mar-11 Nov). Within fairy-tale groves of chestnuts, maritime pines and scrub the trail leads you through a stunning sunset-coloured paint palette of ochre formations.

♥ CONSERVATOIRE DES OCRES ET DE LA COULEUR // ENJOY A COLOUR EXPLOSION

This unique nonprofit celebrates everything about colour, in a conscientious, sustainable way. **Conservatoire des Ocres et de la Couleur** (Ochre & Colour Conservatory; ☎ 04 90 05 66 69; www.okhra.com, in French; rte d'Apt; guided tours adult/student €6/4, combined ticket with Sentier des Ocres €6.80; ☺ 9am-7pm Jul & Aug, to 6pm Wed-Sun Sep-Jun; ⚐), located in an old ochre factory on the D104 east towards Apt, holds workshops (some in English), explores the colouring properties of ochre, and has a fantastic shop. Tours depart every half-hour between 10am to noon and 2pm to 6pm in July and August; call for tour times the rest of the year.

♥ LES MINES D'OCRE DE BRUOUX // EXPLORE AN OTHER-WORLDLY OCHRE MINE

In Gargas, 4km northwest of Apt, visit Europe's last remaining **ochre quarry** (☎ 04 90 06 22 59; admission €7.50; ☺ 10am-8pm Jul & Aug, to 7pm May-Jun & Sep-15 Oct, 10am-1pm & 2-6pm 15 Oct-15 Nov, closed 15 Nov-Apr). It produces

around 1000 tonnes of ochre a year, 45% of which is exported. The parts of the 45km of mines that are open to the public seem like a natural, serene mineral church full of spires and chambers.

♥ ST-SATURNIN-LÈS-APT // SKIP OFF TO THE QUIETER SIDE OF THE LUBERON

Rooftop views of **St-Saturnin-lès-Apt**, 9km north of Apt, and the surrounding Vaucluse hilltops can be enjoyed by climbing to the **ruins** atop the village or from the **17th-century windmill**, 1km north of the village off the D943 to Sault. Follow signs for Le Château Les Moulins.

On the edge of the village, discover how olives are turned into oil at the **Moulin à Huile Jullien** (☎ 04 90 75 56 24; rte d'Apt; ☺ 2-6pm Mon-Sat, also 10am-noon Easter-Aug). Lunch at the welcoming **Le Restaurant L'Estrade** (☎ 04 90 71 15 75; 6 av Victor Hugo; menus from €13; ☺ lunch) run by friendly women who prepare a seasonal menu.

OCHRE

Although ochre has been used in the Luberon since Roman times, it wasn't until 1785 that large deposits of the hydrated oxidised iron-and-clay sands were mined industrially. In 1929, the peak of the ochre industry, some 40,000 tonnes of ochre were mined around Apt, 90% of which was exported to other parts of Europe and America. Traditionally used as a pigment to colour pots and buildings, ochre comes in over 25 shades ranging from delicate yellow to vivid orange and fire red. Discover these vibrant hues firsthand along walking trails in Roussillon's Sentier des Ocres (left), Gargas' ochre quarry (left) or Rustrel's Colorado Provençal (p158).

THE LUBERON

🌱 **OBSERVATOIRE SIRENE & CHÂTEAU DU BOIS // LEARN ABOUT THE STARS AMID FLOWERING LAVENDER**

In **Lagarde d'Apt**, 20km northeast of Apt, volunteers at the **Observatoire Sirene** (☎ 04 90 75 04 17; www.obs-sirene.com, in French; day/night/child €10/40/free; ⌚ by reservation year-round; 🅰) teach you about astronomy amid the lavender fields by day, but the best time to visit is during an all-night star-gazing session sustained by coffee and goats' cheese.

Lagarde d'Apt is also home to a 800,000-sq-metre lavender farm, **Château du Bois** (☎ 04 90 76 91 23; www.lechateaudu bois.com) where a 2km-long lavender trail blazes from late June until mid-July when the sweet-smelling flower is harvested.

GASTRONOMIC HIGHLIGHTS

🌱 HOSTELLERIE LE PHÉBUS // JOUCAS €€€

☎ 04 90 05 78 83; rte de Murs, Joucas; menus from €60; ⌚ noon-1.30pm & 7.30-9.30pm, closed mid-Oct–mid-Mar

Located in an exquisitely renovated hotel, the light-filled dining room sparkles with sunshine in the day and candlelight at night. Silver-maned master chef Xavier Mathieu is originally from Marseille and has won a Michelin star for his inventive cuisine that combines the freshest local ingredients. Specialities include an *escabeche* of red mullet and tender beans. Or try his *barigoule*, another traditional Provençal dish, which combines braised artichokes with pattypan squash in a white-wine broth.

🌱 LE MAS TOURTERON // LES IMBERTS €€€

☎ 04 90 72 00 16; chemin de St-Blaise, Les Imberts; www.mastourteron.com; menus from €45

Dining at the lilac-clothed tables in the stone dining room or amid the flourishing gardens of chef Elisabeth Bourgeois-Baique and her sommelier husband Philippe's welcoming Le Mas Tourteron is like eating at the home of friends. Elisabeth's seasonally changing *menus* and her legendary desserts marry with wines hand picked by Philippe from over 200 vintages. Find it 3.5km south of Gordes, signposted off the D2. Check their website for opening hours.

🌱 LE TABLE DE PABLO // VILLARS €€

☎ 04 90 75 45 18; Hameau Les Petits Cléments, Villars; lunch/dinner menu from €16/28; ⌚ noon-1.30pm & 7.30-10pm, closed Wed, lunch Thu & Sat

On the heels of his first Michelin mention, young chef Thomas Gallardo wows with inventive gastronomic creations like a delectable maize soup with chestnuts and *tasso*, or a frappé of soft, white cheese. He has created a comfortable,

THE LUBERON

modern dining room decorated with local art and it is well worth the excursion through the rolling cherry orchards. Gallardo also offers cooking courses.

❦ LES GRANDS CAMPS // LE CHÊNE €€

☎ 04 90 74 67 33; Le Chêne; menu adult/under 10yr incl wine & coffee €26/13; ☽ lunch Sun, dinner Mon, Wed, Fri & Sat Jul & Aug, lunch Sun, dinner Fri & Sat Sep-Jun; ♿

Eat under the willow trees at unpretentious working *ferme auberge* Les Grands Camps. Not far from Gargas' ochre quarry, they serve up heaping feasts of farm-fresh duck, lamb and the like. Take the signposted dirt road north from the hamlet Le Chêne.

❦ MAS DES HERBES BLANCHES // JOUCAS €€€

☎ 04 90 05 79 79; rte de Murs, Joucas; lunch/dinner menus from €39/75; ☽ 12.15-1.30pm & 7.15-9.30pm, closed Tue & Wed Mar-Jun & Sep-Dec, all of Jan & Feb

Extravagant Mas des Herbes Blanches brought in new executive chef Akhara Chay in March 2009. Born in Paris of Thai and Cambodian descent, Chay trained with Ducasse and now combines Provençal and Asian flavours in his excellent creations. Handmade gnocchi with soy and sesame glaze comes with artichokes seasoned in citrus and saffron, and the foie gras is accompanied by a mango and Szechuan-pepper chutney.

APT
· · · · · ·

pop 11,500 / elevation 250m
At the centre of the Luberon's cherry-laden orchards is its capital, Apt. The agricultural town's festive spirit comes alive at its Saturday-morning market, brimming with cherries, grapes, and candied and crystallised fruits; and peaks during its wine and jazz festivals.

ESSENTIAL INFORMATION

TOURIST OFFICES // Apt Tourist Office (☎ 04 90 74 03 18; www.ot-apt.fr, in French; 20 av Philippe de Girard; ☽ 9am-7pm Mon-Sat, 9.30am-12.30pm Sun Jul & Aug, 9am-noon & 2-6pm Mon-Sat, 9.30am-12.30pm Sun May, Jun & Sep, 9am-noon & 2-6pm Mon-Sat Oct-Apr) **Parc Naturel Régional du Luberon Maison du Parc** (see p159)

EXPLORING APT

❦ SEEING APT // EXPLORE THE TOWN AND ITS FRUITY HISTORY

Apt's tourist office has information on strolls around town. The 11th-century **Ancienne Cathédrale Ste-Anne** (rue Ste-Anne; ☽ 8.30am-6pm Mon-Sat), houses the relics of St Anne and 11th- and 12th-century illuminated manuscripts.

Gain an appreciation of Apt's artisan and agricultural roots at the **Musée de l'Aventure Industrielle du Pays d'Apt** (Industrial History Museum; ☎ 04 90 74 95 30; 14 place du Postel; adult/under 12yr €4/free; ☽ 10am-noon & 3-6.30pm Mon-Sat, 3-7pm Sun, closed Sun & Tue Oct-May). In an old candied-fruit factory, the museum interprets the candied-fruit trade as well as ochre mining and earthenware production from the 18th century.

Thirty tonnes of cherries a day are candied at the **Confiserie Kerry Aptunion** (☎ 04 90 76 31 43; rte Nationale 100, quartier Salignan; ☽ shop 9am-12.30pm & 1.30-6.30pm Mon-Sat, tours by reservation), the world's largest crystallised-fruits factory, 2.5km west of town. They offer a free film, tastings and tours.

Fondation Blachère (☎ 04 32 52 06 15; 384 av des Argiles; admission free; ⊗ 2-6.30pm Tue-Sun) runs a series of interesting art exhibitions.

❧ **EATING IN APT // FIND UNPRETENTIOUS TREATS ALL OVER TOWN**
Saturday market aside, stop in at **Le Fournil du Luberon** (☎ 04 90 74 20 52; place de la Bouquerie; ⊗ 7am-7pm Tue-Sat, 7am-1pm Sun), directly across from the tourist office, for Apt's best bakery. Loaves include one made from a heritage local grain called *blé*. West of Apt, local winery **Sylla** (☎ 04 90 74 95 80; N100; ⊗ 9am-7pm Mon-Sat) serves cheese and light meals with its wine.

For a sit-down meal in the town centre, try **Thym, te Voilà** (☎ 04 90 74 28 25; 59 rue St-Martin; mains €10; ⊗ 11.30am-6pm Tue-Sat). On Saturday a fresh-as-it-gets market soup bubbles aromatically in its open kitchen. **L'Intramuros** (☎ 04 90 06 18 87; 120 rue de la République; menus €24-30; ⊗ lunch & dinner Tue-Sat) is beloved by locals for its 'instinctive Provençal' cooking in a 19th-century grocery shop filled with nostalgic bric-a-brac. Aptois frequent **Les Délices de Léa** (☎ 04 90 74 32 77; 87 rue de la République; mains €10; ⊗ lunch & dinner Tue-Sat) for Léa's tender green salads and inventive *plats du jour*.

FESTIVALS & EVENTS

Luberon Jazz Festival (☎ 04 90 74 55 98; www.luberonjazz.net) Held each May.
Wine Festival Held on the Ascension (May or June).

TRANSPORT

BIKE // Sport 2000 (☎ 04 90 04 30 00; 669 av Victor Hugo; ⊗ 10am-12.30pm & 2.30-7pm Mon-Sat) rentals start at €12/115 per day/week.

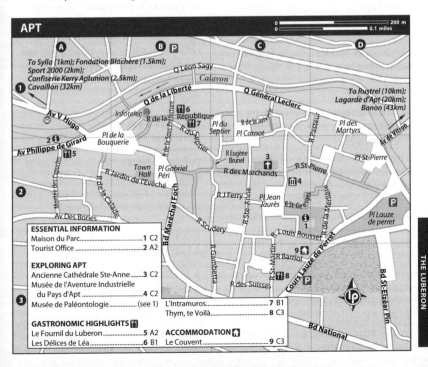

BUS // From the **bus station** (☎ 04 90 74 20 21; 250 av de la Libération) east of the centre buses serve Avignon, Digne-les-Bains and Cavaillon.

RUSTREL & AROUND

· · · · · ·

The russet village of Rustrel, 10km northeast of Apt, is the threshold to the other-worldly ochre formations of the Colorado Provençal. The eastbound D22 and D33 link Rustrel with Viens, a starting point for forays into the limestone canyon Gorges d'Oppedette. From Viens the 3km-long Circuit des Bories takes afternoon strollers past several *bories*; yellow markers flag the footpath.

In Roman times the Via Domitia passed through Céreste (population 1045; elevation 380m), 8km south. Just outside Céreste on the D31, visit the family-run lavender farm **Le Frigoulet** (☎ 04 92 79 05 87; humannfrigoulet@aol.com; ☺ by reservation).

🌱 **COLORADO PROVENÇAL //
EXPLORE THE DRAMATIC OCHRE
LANDSCAPE**
Discover the vibrant hues of the ochreous mountainsides firsthand along short walking trails in Rustrel's **Colorado Provençal** (☎ 04 32 52 09 75; ☺ 9am-dusk). The savage landscape of red-ochre sand has extraordinary rock formations like the fiery upright **Cheminée de Fée** (Fairy Chimney). It was part of a quarry where ochre was mined from the 1880s until 1956.

Colour-coded trails – the 'blue' **Sentier de Cheminée de Fée** (1km) and the 'red' **Sentier du Sahara** (1.5km) – can be picked up in the car park, signposted

south of Rustrel village off the D22 to Banon. Parking costs €3 (free November to March) and a map €3.

Let a horse carry you with **Pars Monts et par Chevaux** (☎ 06 80 42 82 40; per 2hr €35).

Nearby **Colorado Aventures** (☎ 06 78 26 68 91; www.colorado-aventures.com, in French; adult/child €18/14; ☺ closed Jan; ♿) is a Tarzan-style obstacle course rigged between red rocks in a forest. The site, signposted off the D22, is a rocky 15-minute walk from the car park. Kids need to be 150cm tall.

LE PETIT LUBERON

· · · · · ·

South of the N100, the deep Combe de Lourmarin carves a north–south divide through the Luberon massif. Le Petit Luberon (Little Luberon) sits on the western side and its rocky landscape is sprinkled with cake decoration–like *villages perchés* (perched villages) overlooking thick cedar forests and Côtes du Luberon vineyards.

ESSENTIAL INFORMATION

TOURIST OFFICES // Bonnieux Tourist Office (☎ 04 90 75 91 90; www.tourisme -en-luberon.com, in French; 7 place Carnot; ☺ 9.30am-12.30pm & 2-6.30pm Mon-Fri, 2-6.30pm Sat)

EXPLORING LE PETIT LUBERON

🌱 **BONNIEUX & AROUND // SEE A QUINTESSENTIAL HILLTOP VILLAGE**
Bonnieux burst onto cinema screens in 2006 as the village where Russell Crowe's character Max Skinner, a British finan-

cier, finds *joie de vivre* in the vineyards of Provence. Based on the 2004 novel *A Good Year,* by Peter Mayle, its filming was a good year for Crowe and his wife, whose second child, so locals proudly proclaim, was conceived in Bonnieux (apparently the mayor has offered baby Crowe honorary citizenship).

Navigating Bonnieux is a little jigsaw puzzle in itself. The village straddles several levels: from place de la Liberté, 86 steps lead to the 12th-century **Église Vieille du Haut**, while the history of bread-making is raised at the **Musée de la Boulangerie** (☎ 04 90 75 88 34; 12 rue de la République; adult/12-18yr €3/1.50; ☻ 10am-noon & 2.30-6pm or 6.30pm Wed-Mon Apr-Oct).

South of Bonnieux is **Forêt des Cèdres**, a protected cedar forest through which runs a **botanical trail**. Heading north, you can taste and buy local wine in the village cooperative, **Caves des Vignerons de Bonnieux** (☎ 04 90 75 80 03; La Gare de Bonnieux; ☻ 9am-12.30pm & 2.30-6.30pm Mon-Sat).

☙ GOURMET BONNIEUX // FOOD TO SUIT ANY MOOD

Le Fournil (☎ 04 90 75 83 62; 5 place Carnot; lunch/dinner menu €22/42; ☻ lunch & dinner Wed-Sun) is a cut above the average village restaurant – literally. Its glass-and-steel interior is sliced into a rock face. Creations like courgette cake with tiny prawns are consistently first-rate.

At **Auberge de l'Aiguebrun** (☎ 04 90 04 47 00; www.aubergedelaiguebrun.fr; d €175-205; ☒ ☒ ☒) dine at stone tables on a cobbled terrace with riverside views (lunch/dinner *menu* €27/45), and stroll through gardens graced with peacocks, a greenhouse and dovecote. The inn is hidden in the dramatic heart of the Combe de Lourmarin, 6km southeast of Bonnieux off the D943.

The magnificently restored **La Bastide de Capelongue** (☎ 04 90 75 89 78; www.capelongue.com; lunch/dinner menus from €70/120; ☻ closed mid-Nov–mid-Mar), high above Bonnieux, is the brand-new bastion of wunderkind chef Édouard Loubet, who moved here with his two Michelin stars from Le Moulin de Lourmarin (p165). The hotel (which also has doubles from €160) is impeccably decorated by Édouard's mother, and his grandmother is the inspiration for many of his renowned recipes.

☙ LACOSTE // THRILL IN A SPOOKY INTERLUDE

Its name may be unrelated to the clothing label's crocodile emblem, but Lacoste,

LUBERON'S REGIONAL PARK

Egyptian vultures, eagle owls, wild boars, Bonelli's eagles and Etruscan honeysuckle are among the species that call the 1650-sq-km **Parc Naturel Régional du Luberon** home. Created in 1977 and recognised as a Biosphere Reserve by Unesco in 1997, the park encompasses dense forests, unexpected gorges and 67 villages with a combined population of 155,000. The GR6, GR9, GR92 and GR97 walking trails all cross it, as does a 236km-long **cycling route** (see the boxed text, p150).

Information, maps, workshops and guides are available in Apt at the **Maison du Parc** (☎ 04 90 04 42 00; www.parcduluberon.fr, in French; 60 place Jean Jaurès, Apt; ☻ 8.30am-noon & 1.30-7pm Mon-Sat Jul-Sep, 8.30am-noon & 1.30-6pm Mon-Fri Oct-Mar). Its **Musée de Paléontologie** (Palaeontology Museum; adult/child €1.50/free) provides an historical framework, with prehistoric flora and fauna displays.

THE LUBERON

LITERARY LUBERON

There's more on the list than the classic *A Year in Provence* (Peter Mayle), regaling the Mayles' move to the Luberon and renovation of a *mas* in Ménerbes (below).

★ 'The Man Who Planted Trees' (Jean Giono) – a jewel-like short story from this much-loved Manosque writer, many of whose works are available in English

★ *Confessions of a French Baker* (Peter Mayle and Gerard Auzet) – the secret behind successful bread-making, revealed by Cavaillon-based baker Auzet

★ *Seeking Provence* (Nicholas Woodsworth) – the myths and ways of everyday life in Provence

★ *Village in the Vaucluse* (Lawrence Wylie) – published in the mid-1970s, this amusing account of life in red-rock Roussillon was written by Wylie in the 1950s, decades before all and sundry jumped on the travelogue bandwagon

★ *The Luberon Garden* (Alex Dingwall-Main) – an English garden designer uproots his family from London to landscape a garden in Ménerbes

6.5km west of Bonnieux, does have couturier connections. Earlier this decade, designer Pierre Cardin purchased the 9th-century **Château de Lacoste**, where the notorious Marquis de Sade (1740–1814) retreated when his writings became too scandalous for Paris.

The erotic novels penned by the marquis (who gave rise to the term 'sadism'), including *120 Journées de Sodome* (120 Days of Sodom; 1785), were only freely published after WWII. De Sade spent chunks of his childhood in Provence where his family had owned Château de Lacoste since 1627. In 1771 he moved here with his wife and children, engaging in a salacious lifestyle before he was tried on charges of sodomy and attempted poisoning. He spent 27 years in prison. The château was looted by revolutionaries in 1789, and subsequently seized and sold.

The 45-room palace remained an eerie ruin until Cardin transformed part of it into a 1000-seat theatre and opera stage hosting July's month-long **Festival de Lacoste** (www.festivaldelacoste.com). In the village, **Espace La Costa** (☎ 04 90 75 93 12)

sells festival tickets (€15 to €150) and has information on guided tours of the château (including the incredible Roman quarry beneath it). Don't miss the powerful statue of de Sade by Alexandre Bourganov.

Upping the town's tiny population are students of the US-based art school Savannah College of Art & Design.

🌿 MÉNERBES // SEE WHAT ENCHANTED PETER MAYLE

Scaling the steep streets to the boat-shaped village **Ménerbes**, moored on a hilltop, rewards you with uninterrupted views. The maze of streets conceals a 12th-century village **church** and a fabulous museum (opposite).

The village captured the attention of millions of armchair travellers when it was memorably rendered by British author Peter Mayle. The lavishly detailed books *A Year in Provence* and *Toujours Provence* recount renovating a *mas* just outside the village in the late 1980s. Mayle subsequently sold up and moved abroad, though the Luberon's charm has recently lured him back to Lourmarin.

His former home, 2km southeast of Ménerbes on the D3 to Bonnieux, is the second house on the right after the football pitch.

♥ DINING IN MÉNERBES // TWO OF LUBERON'S FINEST, HIDDEN IN THE VILLAGE

Ménerbes' tobacconist-newsagent-bar, **Café du Progrès** (☎ 04 90 72 22 09; place Albert Roure; menus €13-16; ☿ lunch, bar 6am-midnight), run by good-humoured Patrick, hasn't changed much since it opened a century ago. This utterly authentic spot is great for a lunch stop and taking in a spectacular sweep of the countryside.

Well-travelled chef Laurent Jouin is doing impressive things in the kitchen of **Véranda** (☎ 04 90 72 33 33; 104 av Marcellin Poncet; lunch mains €10-13, dinner menu €38; ☿ lunch & dinner Tue-Sat, lunch Sun) his excellent establishment high up in the village, with views overlooking the valley. Effortlessly elegant, the magnificent meals are built from seasonal fresh fruit and vegetables. The smoked salmon ravioli is to die for.

♥ WINE // STUDY IT, TASTE IT, BUY IT – LOVE IT!

In Ménerbes, the wonderful **Maison de la Truffe et du Vin** (House of Truffle & Wine; ☎ 04 90 72 52 10; www.vin-truffe-luberon.com; place de l'Horloge; ☿ 10am-12.30pm & 2.30-6pm daily Jul & Aug, 10am-12.30pm & 2-5pm Thu-Sat Apr-Jun, Sep & Oct, 3-7pm Thu-Sat Nov-Mar) is housed in the former hospice on the cobbled square. The head office for the Brotherhood of Truffles and Wine of Luberon represents 60 domaines, and sells all their wines at rock-bottom prices. In July and August it organises two-hour wine-tasting sessions (€20) and truffle workshops (€95).

Without a corkscrew, the best Côtes du Luberon wines are nothing but ornaments. A shrine to the gadgets, the **Musée du Tire-Bouchon** (Corkscrew Museum; ☎ 04 90 72 41 58; adult/child €4/free; ☿ 9am-noon & 2-7pm Apr-Sep, 9am-noon & 2-5pm Mon-Fri, 2-5pm Sat Oct-Mar), sits in the Domaine de la Citadelle, a wine-producing estate on the D3 to Cavaillon. Sample Côtes du Luberons and marvel over 1000 different corkscrews.

♥ PARC AUX ESCARGOTS & MUSÉE DE LA LAVANDE // FROM SLIMY SNAILS TO SAUCY SCENTS

Also near Ménerbes, some 30,000-odd gastropods live on the family-run **Parc aux Escargots** (☎ 04 90 72 22 26; Les Grès; 1hr guided visit adult/child €5/3; ☿ 9am-12.30pm & 5.30-8pm Jun-Sep), signposted off the D24, which specialises in snail cuisine.

Musée de la Lavande (Lavender Museum; ☎ 04 90 76 91 23; www.museedelalavande.com; N100; adult/child €6/free; ☿ 9am-noon & 2-6pm or 7pm Feb-Dec), just a bit north in Coustellet celebrates the purple flower. There's an audioguide and a short video (in English) that explains how the lavender is harvested and distilled. Also see stills used to extract the essential oil and buy lavender-scented products at its boutique.

♥ OPPÈDE-LE-VIEUX // WALK A UNIQUE HILLTOP RUIN

This medieval hilltop village 6km southwest of Ménerbes was abandoned in 1910 by villagers who moved down the valley to the cultivated plains to earn their living. A handful of artists (population 20) lives here today. From the car parks (€2) a precarious path leads to flower-dotted cottages and the hillside **ruins**, with views all around. The 16th- to 18th-century **church**, under constant restoration, hosts concerts during August and celebrates mass in honour of Oppède's patron saint on 10 August.

THE LUBERON

Visit two of the artists at **L'Atelier des Cendres** (☎ 04 90 76 75 10) with its gorgeously glazed ceramic creations.

Signs also direct you from the car parks to the **Sentier Vigneron d'Oppède**, a 1½-hour winegrowers' trail through olive groves, cherry orchards and vineyards. Panels interpret grape varieties, show how to train a vine 'lyre' style etc.

Oppède-les-Poulivets (or just Oppède), the new village (population 1250), is 1km north of Oppède-le-Vieux and home to **La Bastide des Minguet** (☎ 04 32 52 17 85; ⏱ 9am-7pm Jul & Aug), which sells 40 varieties of farm-made jams and condiments.

LE GRAND LUBERON

· · · · · ·

Marking the great divide between Le Petit and Le Grand Luberon, the deep Combe de Lourmarin cuts a near-perpendicular swathe through the massif from Bonnieux to Lourmarin. To its east, Le Grand Luberon takes in dramatic gorges, grand fortresses and lavender fields.

☙ BUOUX // EAT LIKE ROYALTY IN A REMOTE HAMLET

Dominated by the hilltop **ruins of Fort de Buoux**, the tiny village of **Buoux** (the 'x' is pronounced softly) sits across the divide from Bonnieux, and less than 8km south of Apt. As a traditional Protestant stronghold, Buoux was destroyed in 1545 and again in 1660. Explore on foot the fort and old village ruins, perilous in places due to loose rocks. Painted white arrows mark an optional return route via a spectacular spiralling staircase cut in the rock.

Local climbing club **Améthyste** (☎ 04 90 74 05 92; http://amethyste1901.free.fr, in French) organises rock climbing and walks.

Beneath cliffs in the Vallée de l'Aiguebrun, the rambling *gîte d'étape*, **Auberge des Seguins** (☎ 04 90 74 16 37; www .aubergedesseguins.com; dm/d with half-board per person €36/56; ⏱ Mar–mid-Nov; ⌨) is a thrilling 2.5km descent from Buoux. Dine on duck breast with fresh cherries on the shaded veranda (menus from €25).

Amid flowery gardens, the **Auberge de la Loube** (☎ 04 90 74 19 58; lunch/dinner menu from €22/28; ⏱ closed Mon, Thu & Jan) remains true to its roots serving wicker trays overflowing with *hors d'oeuvres Provençaux* like *tapenade* (olive dip), *anchoïade* (anchovy sauce), quail eggs, melon slices and fresh figs. Leave room for the succulent roast lamb, and allow plenty of time to savour the experience, especially during legendary Sunday lunches. Payment is cash-only (there are no ATMs in Buoux). Reservations are essential.

☙ SAIGNON // TRIP THROUGH LAVENDER FIELDS

Purple lavender carpets the **Plateau de Claparèdes** area between Buoux (west), Sivergues (south), Auribeau (east) and picture-postcard **Saignon** (north). Cycle, walk or motor through the lavender fields and along the northern slopes of **Mourre Nègre** (1125m). Stop for views of gorgeous Saignon before you wander its precipitous streets.

Husband and wife artists Kamila Regent and Pierre Jaccaud are the creative force behind amazing **Chambre de Séjour avec Vue** (☎ 04 90 04 85 01; www.chambre avecvue.com, in French; Saignon; table d'hôte €25) – a 16th-century village house turned *chambre d'hôte*-art studio (doubles/studio including breakfast €80/100) and stunningly decorated with artwork. Cross a little wooden bridge to the garden where bronze sculptures lounge beneath trees.

The D113 climbs to idyllic **Les Agnels**, where Jean-Claude Guigou distils lavender, cypress leaves and rosemary at the 1895-established **Distillerie Les Agnels** (☎ 04 90 74 34 60; rte de Buoux, btwn Buoux & Apt; free tours mid-Jul–mid-Aug; ☺ shop open year-round). Stock up on all manner of lavender goodies for a song.

♣ FERME AUBERGE LE CASTELAS // LIVE A DREAM

Although the isolated **Ferme Auberge Le Castelas** (Chez Gianni; ☎ 04 90 74 60 89; Sivergues; menus incl wine €25-30; ☺ lunch & dinner by reservation only Mar-Dec) is well off any track, beaten or not, celebs such as Catherine Deneuve drop in via helicopter to pass around heaping platters at long shared timber tables. Fresh-from-the-farm feasts include bite-sized toast topped with *tomme* (a mild cows'-milk cheese) and whole, roasted pigs. The farm (doubles including half-board are €70 per person) sits on a hill between two breathtaking valleys and the mood gets down-right convivial as the sangria makes it way down the tables. To get here (sans helicopter), follow the only road through the village of Sivergues; ignore the *fin de la route* ('end of the road') sign at the village entrance. Continue 1.5km along the potholed track until you see the goats in the corral.

SOUTH OF THE LUBERON MOUNTAINS

· · · · · ·

Skimming the Petit Luberon's southern boundary, southeast of Cavaillon, the busy D973 delineates the river Durance and the valley it carves. As you work your way north of the D973, you'll find easily accessible villages full of life.

ESSENTIAL INFORMATION

TOURIST OFFICES // **Lourmarin Tourist Office** (☎ 04 90 68 10 77; www.lourmarin.com; av Philippe de Girard; ☺ 10am-12.30pm & 3-6pm Mon-Thu & Sat, 10am-1.30pm & 3-6pm Fri) Leads guided walks (adult/child €4/free) dedicated to Camus (10am Tuesday), Bosco (10am Wednesday) and exploring the village (10am Thursday).

EXPLORING SOUTH OF THE LUBERON MOUNTAINS

♣ CAVAILLON TO CADENET // SEE LOCAL FLORA AND FAUNA

Spot some 243 species of birds at the **Observatoire Ornithologique**, a bird centre run by the Parc Naturel Régional du Luberon (see the boxed text, p159) near the Mérindol-Mallemort dam (signposted 1.5km from the roundabout at the entrance to Mérindol on the D973). Spot herons and great cormorants along the 3km-long **bird sanctuary trail** (1½ hours) marked with yellow blazes.

Lauris, 10km further east, is a regal hilltop village crowned with an 18th-century **château** surrounded by terraced gardens. Tinctorial plants, many rare, grow in the **Jardin Conservatoire de Plantes Tinctoriales** (☎ 04 90 08 40 48; adult/child €7/free; ☺ 2-5pm Wed-Mon late May & Oct, 3.30-7pm Jun-Sep, by appointment Nov-Mar). Workshops explore dyes traditionally made from these plants. Lauris' **tourist office** (☎ 04 90 08 39 30; 12 place de l'Église) has details on July's **Hot Jazz Festival** held around the château.

THE LUBERON

Wickerwork is the mainstay industry of **Cadenet**, 7km upstream (east). Learn about the cultivation of *osier* (wicker) on the river banks and its artisan applications in the **Musée de la Vannerie** (☎ 04 90 68 24 44; av Philippe de Giraud; adult/child €3/free; ☽ 10am-noon & 2.30-6.30pm Wed-Sat, 2.30-6.30pm Sun Apr-Oct).

❧ ABBAYE DE SILVACANE // ENJOY A CLASSICAL CONCERT IN A SYLVAN SETTING

South of the Durance, 7km southwest of Cadenet, **Abbaye de Silvacane** (☎ 04 42 50 41 69; adult/child €6.50/4.50; ☽ 10am-6pm Jun-Sep, to 1pm & 2-5pm Wed-Mon Oct-May) is one of a trio of medieval Provençal abbeys built by Cistercian monks in an austere Romanesque style. Constructed between 1175 and 1230, today it hosts **classical concerts** and three colonies of bats in its cloister.

❧ AUBERGE LA FENIÈRE // EAT THE MEAL OF A LIFETIME

Visit this restored old post office for an excellent meal or an idyllic night's stay. **Auberge La Fenière** (☎ 04 90 68 11 79; www .reinesammut.com; rte de Cadenet; s/d from €150/180; ☽ lunch & dinner; ☏ � ☷) is the exquisite domain of Michelin-starred Reine Sammut. She grows her own kitchen garden to supply her outstanding restaurant (restaurant lunch/dinner menus from €46/80, bistro menus from €35) and her simpler, but equally wonderful bistro. Classes (€75 to €145) demonstrate how to achieve such perfect puff pastries or such delectable *andouillette* (a breaded sausage).

❧ LOURMARIN // CRUISE AN EASY, STYLISH VILLAGE

At the base of the Combe de Lourmarin and, unlike many of the Luberon's precarious hilltop townships, easily accessed, the alluring village of **Lourmarin** makes for a lovely stroll. Explore the olive groves and herb gardens (see p344) alongside its Renaissance **château** (☎ 04 90 68 15 23; adult/child €5.50/2.50; ☽ 10am-noon & 2.30-6pm Jul & Aug, Feb-Jun & shorter hours Sep-Dec) – the first of its kind built in Provence. It houses a wine cooperative chock-full of local vintages.

Today home to author Peter Mayle, charming streets, cafés and a lively Friday morning **market**, Lourmarin was

MARTYR VILLAGES

People of eleven Luberon villages were brutally massacred on 9 and 10 April 1545 under the terms of the Arrêt de Mérindol, a bill passed by the Aix parliament condemning anyone of Waldensian faith to death. In Cabrières d'Avignon alone more than 700 men were killed, and the women were locked in a straw barn and burnt alive.

The Waldenses (Vaudois) were a minority Protestant group who sought refuge in the Luberon hills (and other remote parts of France and Italy) following the excommunication of their leader Pierre Valdès from the Catholic Church in 1184. What remains of the original castrum in **Mérindol** guards a memorial to the estimated 3000 murdered and 600 sent to the galleys in the two-day massacre.

Tours (€3) covering Waldensian history depart from **Mérindol's tourist office** (☎ 04 90 72 88 50; rue du Four) at 9.30am on Thursday, and include a visit to the town's olive-oil mill.

La Muse (☎ 04 90 72 91 64; 3 rue du Four; ☽ call for hours), in Mérindol, is a Waldensian library and research centre.

the final home of Nobel Prize-winning writer Albert Camus (1913–60) and his wife, who are buried in the village cemetery. Also buried in the cemetery is the writer Henri Bosco (1888–1976), another Lourmarin local (see p163 for tour information).

Stop in at one of the many *ateliers* and boutiques, like **Les Habits Neufs** (☎ 06 07 50 18 79) with clothes and bags made from vintage material. **La Boutique du Moulin** (☎ 04 90 68 82 97) carries deluxe Provençal design and **Espace Karas** (☎ 04 90 68 14 25) hangs contemporary art.

♥ WINING & DINING IN LOURMARIN // PICK YOUR HEAVENLY POISON

Given its tiny population, Lourmarin has a trove of gastronomic gems, unearthed by a stroll around town. Reservations are recommended, and the tourist office has a list of the many local wineries.

Although chef extraordinaire Édouard Loubet is now based in Bonnieux (see p159) he still keeps the wheels turning at **Le Moulin de Lourmarin** (☎ 04 90 68 06 69; www.moulindelourmarin.com; d/ste from €120/350; Ⓟ Ⓧ 🛜 Ⓡ), a restored 17th-century olive-oil mill. His decadent restaurant (*menus* from €26) is housed in the cavernous old pressing room and dreamy rooms line elegant corridors.

In the heart of the village, its oldest bar, the convivial **Café de l'Ormeau** (☎ 04 90 68 02 11; place de l'Ormeau; dishes €4–10; 🕑 6.30am–11.30pm) has a pavement terrace perfect for sipping *pastis* and sitting with the locals watching the eye candy stroll by.

♥ VAUGINES & CUCURON // BUILD UP AN APPETITE AND THEN SATE IT

From Lourmarin the D56 shadows the GR97 walking trail 5km east to **Vaug-**ines, where Claude Berri's Pagnol films *Manon des Sources* and *Jean de Florette* (1986) were partly shot with the village's horse-chestnut tree as a backdrop.

Cucuron, 2km further east, is the starting point for walks up **Mourre Nègre** (1125m) and a one-hour walk through vineyards. Get maps from the tourist office. Once you're good and hungry, don't miss excellent **La Petite Maison de Cucuron** (☎ 04 90 68 21 99; place de l'Etang; menus €40–60; 🕑 lunch & dinner Wed-Sun, closed Jan-Apr) with its Michelin-starred cuisine and cooking classes. Or for great breads, visit **Boulangerie Gastaldi** (☎ 04 90 77 28 98; rue de la Place) where Christophe learned to bake at the hands of his father.

♥ ANSOUIS // DISCOVER ARTISAN ICE CREAM OR THE GRAND CHÂTEAU

Labelled one of France's 'most beautiful villages' (and it is), **Ansouis** shelters the **Musée Extraordinaire** (☎ 04 90 09 82 64; adult/under 16yr €3.50/1.50; 🕑 2-6pm or 7pm), set up by Provençal painter and diver Georges Mazoyer, whose passion for the sea is reflected in the museum's fossilised exhibits and art. The palatial **Château d'Ansouis** (☎ 04 90 09 82 70; adult/6-18yr €6/3; 🕑 call for hours) is still inhabited but can be visited by guided tour. Classical-music concerts fill its hedged courtyards in August.

Go further afield to find **L'Art Glacier** (☎ 04 90 77 75 72; Les Hautes Terres hamlet; 🕑 call for hours) where ice cream is an art. Michel and Sigrid Perrière handcraft mind-boggling varieties of the sweet stuff: from lavender to sesame to cassis. The ice-creamery sits between Ansouis and La Tour d'Aigues on a hilltop off the D9 (look for the signs posted on roundabouts) and has views all around.

For a delightful dinner back in Ansouis, reserve a table at **La Closerie** (☎ 04 90 09 90 54; bd des Platanes; menus from €21; ✆ lunch Tue-Sun, dinner Tue-Sat).

💚 LA TOUR D'AIGUES // TAKE IN AN OPEN-AIR CONCERT
La Tour d'Aigues is dominated by the 12th- to 15th-century **Château de Tour d'Aigues** (☎ 04 90 07 50 33; www.chateau-latour daigues.com, in French; adult/8-18yr €4.50/2; ✆ 10am-1pm & 2.30-6pm Jul–mid-Aug, 2.30-6pm Sun & Mon, 10am-1pm Tue, 10am-1pm & 2.30-6pm Wed-Sat Apr-Jun & mid-Aug–Oct, 2-5pm Sun & Mon, 10am-noon Tue, 10am-noon & 2-5pm Wed-Sat Nov-Mar). Burned down in 1792, it was restored in 1974 and now holds outdoor concerts and a **Musée des Faïences** full of 18th-century earthenware.

MANOSQUE
· · · · · ·

pop 20,309 / elevation 387m
Manosque's industrial belt wraps around its cobblestone old town. Provençal writer Jean Giono (1895–1970) was born here, and has an arts centre dedicated to him. To the north, Mont d'Or looks out over the town's red-tiled roofs to the hills. Mont Furon (600m), 10km west, also has lavish Luberon views. Twenty-odd kilometres southwest of Manosque adjoining St-Paul-lès-Durance is the nuclear research centre, Cadarache.

ESSENTIAL INFORMATION

TOURIST OFFICES // Manosque Tourist Office (☎ 04 92 72 16 00; www.manosque-tourisme .com, in French; place du Docteur Joubert)

EXPLORING MANOSQUE

💚 L'OCCITANE EN PROVENCE // GO TO LAVENDER CENTRAL
The town's biggest employer is the natural cosmetics company **L'Occitane en Provence** (☎ 04 92 70 19 50; Zone Industrielle St-Maurice; ✆ boutique 10am-7pm Mon-Sat), on the southeastern outskirts, which utilises Provençal flowers and herbs in its internationally exported products. There are free one-hour guided visits of the operations. Tours must be booked at Manosque's tourist office.

💚 LA BASTIDE DE L'ADRECH // GET AWAY FROM IT ALL
On Manosque's southwestern fringe, 2km from the centre, the grand manor house-turned-*chambre d'hôte* **La Bastide de L'Adrech** (☎ 04 92 71 14 18; www.bastide-adrech.com; av des Serrets; d incl breakfast €68, table d'hôte incl wine & coffee €26) languished empty for over a century until its resurrection by Géraldine and Robert Le Bozec. Amid heritage-listed trees, they host *tables d'hôtes* beside the crackling fireplace and its five guest rooms are stocked with L'Occitane products. L'Oustau de Baumaniére–trained chef Robert also runs cooking classes (from €30 for three hours) and gourmet weekends themed around local specialities like truffles.

💚 AROUND MANOSQUE // HAVE A HORTICULTURAL-VINTNER'S DAY
Northwest of town, **Maison de la Biodi-versité** (☎ 04 92 87 74 40; chemin de la Thomassine; adult/child €4/free; ✆ 10.30am-1pm & 3-6.30pm Tue-Sat Jul-Sep, 10am-12.30pm & 2-4.30pm Wed Oct-Jun), part of the Parc Natural Régional du Luberon (p159), has over 500 varieties of plants from prairie flowers to roses and

THE LUBERON

heirloom herbs. Guided tours explain it all.

Or if you want to focus on one plant – the grape – go 6km southwest of Manosque, to the village of **Pierrevert**, the centre of the Coteaux de Pierrevert AOC. More than 75% of its wine production takes place at the village's co-op, the **Cave des Vignerons** (☎ 04 92 72 19 06; 1 av Auguste Bastide), where you can have a free tasting and stock up at producers' prices. Call one day ahead for a free behind-the-scenes winery tour.

HAUTE-PROVENCE

3 PERFECT DAYS

❦ DAY 1 // LAVENDER FIELDS FOREVER

Living is easy in Provence, when summer brings postcard images to life with row upon serried row of lavender colouring the countryside. Pack a picnic in Forcalquier (opposite), then cycle or drive with the windows down to the scented gardens of Mane's beautiful 13th-century priory, Prieuré de Salagon (p174), and visit its on-site lavender museum. Cross the River Durance and traverse the little-trafficked D6 along the Plateau de Valensole, where Provence's greatest concentration of farms create purple ribbons intertwined with white-gold wheat.

❦ DAY 2 // DELICATE POTTERY AND DELICIOUS DINING

Start the day by exploring the winding streets and myriad pottery shops in beautiful Moustiers Ste-Marie (p179). Tour one of the *ateliers* (workshops) to see how the local *faïence* (earthenware) is made. Then choose from one of the area's excellent restaurants (p180) for a culinary journey: foie gras wrapped in ever-so-sweet quince at La Ferme Ste-Cécile, homemade pasta at Les Comtes, or one of Alain Ducasse's latest creations at La Bastide de Moustiers.

❦ DAY 3 // MOUNTAIN WALKS AND LOCAL WOLVES

Immerse yourself in the majesty of the Hautes-Alpes around Le Boréon (p187). During summer, trails criss-cross the hillside, and in winter those same routes turn into perfect snowshoeing territory. Stop in at Alpha (p188) to learn about the grey wolves roaming the area and spot them in their natural habitat.

VALLÉE DE LA DURANCE

······

At the western edge of Haute-Provence, the winding waters of the 324km-long River Durance, an affluent of the Rhône, follow the Via Domitia, the road from Italy that allowed the Romans to infiltrate the whole of France.

The Vallée de la Durance spreads southwest from Sisteron to the western side of Parc Naturel Régional du Verdon. The three main towns along this 100km stretch are Manosque, on the eastern edge of the Luberon (p166); industrial Château-Arnoux St-Auban with its 16th-century castle and foodie enclave; and Sisteron.

ESSENTIAL INFORMATION

TOURIST OFFICES // **Banon** (☎ 04 92 73 36 37; banon.accueil@wanadoo.fr; place de la République; ⏰ 9am-12.30pm & 3-6pm Tue-Sat year-round, also 10am-noon Sun Jul & Aug) **Forcalquier** (☎ 04 92 75 10 02; www.forcalquier.com; 13 place du Bourguet; ⏰ 9am-noon & 2-6pm Mon-Sat) Information about walks, ballooning and cycling. **Sisteron** (☎ 04 92 61 12 03; www.sisteron.fr; Hôtel de Ville; ⏰ 9am-7pm Mon-Sat, 10am-1pm Sun mid-Jul–mid-Aug, 9am-noon & 2-6pm Mon-Sat mid-Aug–Nov & May–mid-Jul, 9am-noon & 2-5pm Mon-Sat Nov-Apr) Information on concerts and poetry slams.

EXPLORING VALLÉE DE LA DURANCE

☘ WANDER FORCALQUIER // TRAIPSE THROUGH A TRAIL OF ATELIERS TO THE CITADEL

Pays de Forcalquier, delightfully off mass-tourism's radar, shelters sweet hill-top villages and wildflower-strewn countryside. At its heart, the town that bears its name sits atop a rocky perch. Steep steps lead to the gold-topped citadel and octagonal chapel, where carillon concerts are held most Sundays from 11.30am to 12.30pm. On the way up, peruse the local artists workshops packed with pottery and furniture.

☘ LOCAL LIQUEURS // TRY A COLLECTION OF REGIONAL SPIRITS

Fiery liqueurs such as Bigarade (bitter orange), La Farigoule (thyme), Amandine (almond) and pastis (see p55) have been distilled at Forcalquier's Distilleries et Domaines de Provences since 1898. Taste and buy at its **Espace Dégustation** (☎ 04 92 75 15 41; 9 av St-Promasse; ⏰ 10am-12:30pm & 2-6pm Mon & Wed-Sat Apr-Dec).

☘ FORCALQUIER'S FOOD // STUDY, BUY AND FEAST ON AREA GOODIES

Forcalquier's Monday market draws locals from throughout the region. Winding city streets teem with trolleys and trays stacked with every cheese or knick-knack you can imagine.

If the market has made you curious to know more about the local produce, head to the edge of town to **Ecomusée l'Olivier** (☎ 04 92 72 66 91; www.ecomusee-olivier.com, in French; Ancienne rte de Forcalquier; adult/child €4/free; ⏰ 10am-12.30pm & 2-6pm Mon-Fri, 2-6pm Sat, closed Jan) to get an in-depth look at local olive oil production. And if you're here during the first weekend in February, don't miss the **Fête de la Truffe à Forcalquier**, with lectures, music, dance and exhibitions to honour the vaunted fungus.

Signs for yoga classes and Chinese Tao healing adorn hip, cosy café, **Salon de**

(Continued on page 174)

HAUTE-PROVENCE

HAUTE-PROVENCE

HAUTE-PROVENCE

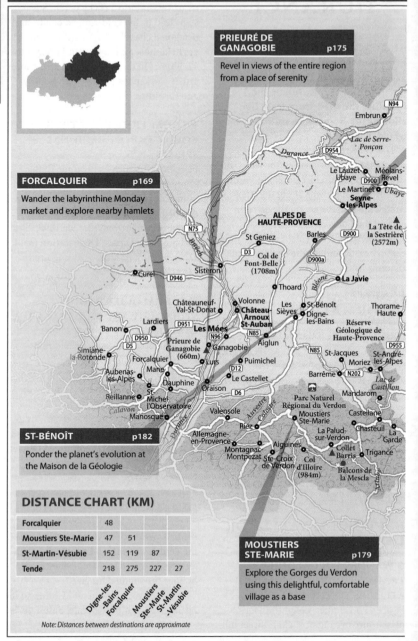

PRIEURÉ DE GANAGOBIE p175

Revel in views of the entire region from a place of serenity

FORCALQUIER p169

Wander the labyrinthine Monday market and explore nearby hamlets

ST-BÉNOÎT p182

Ponder the planet's evolution at the Maison de la Géologie

MOUSTIERS STE-MARIE p179

Explore the Gorges du Verdon using this delightful, comfortable village as a base

DISTANCE CHART (KM)

	Digne-les-Bains	Forcalquier	Moustiers Ste-Marie	St-Martin-Vésubie
Forcalquier	48			
Moustiers Ste-Marie	47	51		
St-Martin-Vésubie	152	119	87	
Tende	218	275	227	27

Note: Distances between destinations are approximate

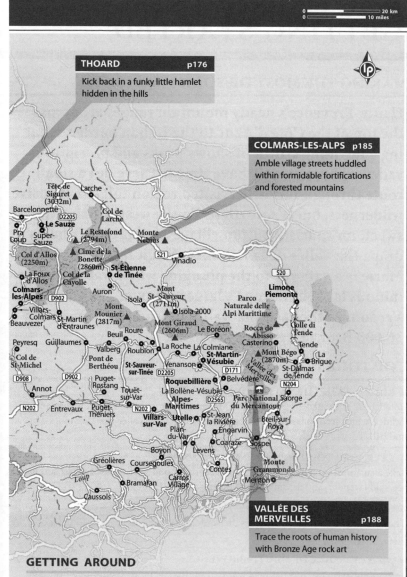

THOARD p176

Kick back in a funky little hamlet hidden in the hills

COLMARS-LES-ALPS p185

Amble village streets huddled within formidable fortifications and forested mountains

VALLÉE DES MERVEILLES p188

Trace the roots of human history with Bronze Age rock art

GETTING AROUND

Haute-Provence is really best seen when using your own wheels. The tiny roads and unplanned diversions that carry you into the heart of the countryside make for scenic drives and daily adventures. Plan plenty of extra time for any of the mountainous driving, as even short distances can take hours when the route is filled with switchbacks. Always be prepared for falling rocks. On the other hand, criss-crossing the Vallée de la Durance and the Plateau de Valensole is a breeze.

HAUTE-PROVENCE GETTING STARTED

MAKING THE MOST OF YOUR TIME

Haute-Provence's heady mountain ranges arc across the top of the Côte d'Azur to the Italian border, creating a far-flung crown of snowy peaks and precipitous valleys. You may only have time to carve out a small route through this little-visited region full of expansive wilderness, but it's worth it. To the west, a string of sweet, un-touristy hilltop villages and lavender fields drape the Vallée de la Durance. Magical Moustiers Ste-Marie is a gateway to the plunging white waters and luminous lakes of Europe's largest canyon, the Gorges du Verdon. In the east, the 'valley of wonders' wows with 36,000 Bronze Age rock carvings.

TOP TOURS

❦ ROCK ART IN THE VALLÉE DES MERVEILLES
Book ahead with the Parc National du Mercantour or with the Escapade Bureau des Guides, which lead walks through the petroglyphs in the Vallée des Merveilles. (p189 and p187)

❦ LAVENDER TOUR WITH RANDO LAVANDE
Take a customised walk through the mountains around Digne-les-Bains. In summer see wild lavender, and in winter strap on snowshoes. (p182)

❦ GUIDES AVENTURE
They'll take you through the Gorges du Verdon any way you like – by foot, by boat, by bike, by horse. (p178)

❦ OBSERVATOIRE DE HAUTE-PROVENCE
Take a guided tour of this national research centre, full up with information on stargazing and planet-finding. It's a perfect chance to ask any of your nagging questions: why is the sky blue? what is a crab nebula? (p175)

❦ WALKING TOUR OF SISTERON
Get the full story on Sisteron's spectacular citadel on the 1¼-hour walking tour of this town at the top of the Vallée de la Durance. (p175)

GETTING AWAY FROM IT ALL

Haute-Provence can already feel like a get-away, especially compared to the coast. Even sweeter, therefore, are these quiet spots:

★ **Sleep over at Le Vieil Aiglun** This is your chance to stay in an ancient Celtic village that has been restored to house a pastoral inn (p388)

★ **Sunday lunch, Domaine d'Aiguines** Join the locals who come with grandma and the kids for a decadent country meal in a hidden valley (p181)

★ **Prieuré de Ganagobie** The monks here stick by two main tenets, one of which is 'listen': share their serenity (p175)

ADVANCE PLANNING

To make the most of local cultural activities and sightseeing, check schedules and book in advance during summer.

★ **Prieuré de Salagon** Plan ahead to be there, with tickets, for their summer program of concerts and exhibitions (p174)

★ **Festival des Nuits de la Citadelle** (www.nuitsdelacitadelle.fr, in French) Book tickets to open-air classical-music concerts held in Sisteron's mighty citadel (p175) from mid-July to mid-August

★ **Chemins de Fer de Provence** Prepare to board le Train des Pignes for a ride on the narrow-gauge mountain railroad from Digne to Nice (p183)

★ **La Bastide de Moustiers** Because of Ducasse's celebrity, this elegant restaurant can require reservations in the busy season (p180)

TOP MARKETS

Markets generally start early and end by noon or 1pm.

✤ **MONDAY**
Forcalquier

✤ **TUESDAY**
Breil-sur-Roya, Colmars-les-Alpes

✤ **WEDNESDAY**
Barcelonnette, Castellane, Digne-les-Bains, La Foux d'Allos, La Palud-sur-Verdon, Riez, Sisteron, St-André-les-Alpes, Tende

----

✤ **THURSDAY**
Allemagne-en-Provence, Allos, Les Salles-sur-Verdon, Montagnac, Sospel

----

✤ **FRIDAY**
Colmars-les-Alpes, Entrevaux, Moustiers Ste-Marie, Quinson, Seyne-les-Alpes

----

✤ **SATURDAY**
Barcelonnette, Castellane, Digne-les-Bains, Riez, Sisteron, St-André-les-Alpes

----

✤ **SUNDAY**
Bauduen (summer only), Castellane, La-Palud-sur-Verdon (summer only)

✤ **DAILY**
St-Martin-Vésubie

RESOURCES

★ **Parc National du Mercantour** (www.parc-mercantour.com, in French) Maps, listings and culture

★ **La Route Napoléon** (www.route-napoleon.com) Learn about Bonaparte's route to Paris

(Continued from page 169)

Thé Sud Attitude (☎ 06 81 28 72 86; 23 bd des Martyrs; menus €12; ☽ lunch; ♿); the outdoor terrace is the place to be seen. Tuck into organic quiches and salads or a home-made sweet. Or try one of Forcalquier's best-loved bistros, **Restaurant L'Establé** (☎ 04 92 75 39 82; 4 place du Bourget & Impasse Louis Andrieux; menus from €23; ☽ lunch & dinner), which feels like an intimate wine cellar.

❦ PRIEURÉ DE SALAGON // STROLL GARDENS AND GALLERIES

There are few more peaceful places in Provence than the 13th-century **Prieuré de Salagon** (☎ 04 92 75 70 50; www.musee-de-salagon.com, in French; adult/12-18yr €6/3.60; ☽ 10am-7.30pm Jun-Aug, 10am-12.30pm & 2-6.30pm May & Sep, 2-5pm Oct & Feb-Apr, 2-5pm Sun Nov & Dec,

---

ACCOMMODATION

Little-touristed, Haute-Provence har-bours many a ho-hum hotel and prices are lower than elsewhere in Provence. But if you look hard enough, you'll find stunners like these. For detailed listings, see the accommodation chapter.

★ **Le Vieil Aiglun** (p388) was marvellously renovated out of a Celtic village

★ Friendly, friendly, friendly **Le Petit Ségriès** (p389) perches on a hillside near Moustiers Ste-Marie

★ Like living in a sprawling villa, **Mas Saint-Joseph** (p389) is run by a welcoming family

★ Gaze at stars above hilltop **Auberge de la Banette** (p388) and feast on farm-raised meals

★ **Gîte de Chasteuil** (p389) is as close as you can get to staying in the Gorges du Verdon, but in comfort

---

closed Jan; ♿), 4km south of Forcalquier outside the walled city of Mane. A multi-lingual audioguide tours a medieval herb garden, Provençal lavenders, mints and mugworts and a showcase of world plants. Stone buildings house concerts and exhibitions on metalwork and lav-ender. The excellent bookshop features a wonderful children's section.

❦ HERBS & PERFUMES // EXPERIENCE THE POWER OF LOCAL PLANTS

For a curative little detour, go 800m south of Mane to the Hôtel Mas du Pont Roman, then turn right and go 3km along a bumpy dirt track to the Église de Châteauneuf, a remote, centuries-old church on the hillside. The *prêtre* (priest) can concoct natural remedies from his rambling garden. Locals swear the cures – for anything from hay fever to arthritis – work wonders.

Re-create the scents of the region when you get home by way of candles, essential oils and more from the factory of **Terre d'Oc** (☎ 04 92 79 40 20; Zone Artisanale; ☽ 9am-7pm Mon-Sat), 13km southeast of For-calquier in Villeneuve, where everything including packaging is done by hand.

❦ MOUNTAIN VILLAGE ROAD TRIP // BEAUTIFUL DRIVE TO RENOWNED CHEESE-PRODUCING VILLAGE, BANON

For fabulously authentic cheese, fol-low the D950 25km northwest from Forcalquier to **Banon** (population 940, elevation 760m), renowned for its *chèvre de Banon*, made from goats' milk and wrapped in chestnut leaves. On the way, pass through **Simiane-la-Rotonde**, host to the international music festival **Les Riches Heures Musicales** in August.

In Banon, the **Fromagerie de Banon** (☎ 04 92 73 25 03; rte de Carniol) sells its cheeses at the Tuesday-morning market and at the wonderful cheese-and-sausage shop **Chez Melchio** (☎ 04 92 73 23 05; place de la République; ⏰ 7.30am-12.30pm & 2.30-7pm Wed-Sun). Banon's tourist office has a list of farms where you can sample cheese. In May the town celebrates its annual **Fête du Fromage**.

Bibliophiles can stop in at the town's enormous bookshop **Le Bleuet** (☎ 04 92 73 25 85; place St Just; ⏰ 9.15am-8pm).

❦ ST-MICHEL L'OBSERVATOIRE // STARGAZE IN THE COUNTRYSIDE

In **St-Michel l'Observatoire**, a stroll up to the hilltop overlook passes along winding walkways and tiny *ateliers*. After the 12th-century Église Haute, arrive at a 360-degree view from the Luberon to the Alps.

The **Observatoire de Haute-Provence** (☎ 04 92 70 64 00; www.obs-hp.fr, in French) is a national research centre at the end of the D305 near St-Michel l'Observatoire. Buy tickets for the 30-minute **guided tour** (☎ 04 92 76 69 09; adult/6-12yr €2.50/1.50; ⏰ tours 1.15-4.15pm Wed & Thu Jul & Aug, 2-3.30pm Wed Apr-Jun & Sep, 3pm Wed Oct-Mar; ♿) from the ticket office in St-Michel's village square. The tour includes the only close-up look at an actively used high-tech 193cm telescope in France, and a film about the centre's research.

From St-Michel l'Observatoire, the eastbound D5 flashes past **Centre d'Astronomie** (☎ 04 92 76 69 69; Plateau du Moulin à Vent; adult/6-16yr €8.75/7; ⏰ 9pm Fri & Sat Jul & Aug), an astronomy centre that organises star-filled multimedia events and educational workshops.

For more earthly pleasures, go to friendly **Hôtel-Restaurant l'Observatoire** (☎ /fax 04 92 76 52 27; place de la Fontaine, St-Michel l'Observatoire; menu €17; ⏰ lunch Tue-Sun, dinner Tue-Sat, closed late Oct–early

Nov) for delicious food including duck polenta, and you can eavesdrop on village gossip at the little bar. There are also welcoming rooms (singles €41, doubles €49).

❦ GANAGOBIE // TRUE SERENITY IN A SILENT EYRIE

Ten kilometres south of Les Mées, stroll the quiet hilltop grounds of the 10th-century Benedictine **Prieuré de Ganago-bie** (☎ 04 92 68 00 04; ⏰ 3-5pm Tue-Sun) to soak up the ethereal magic of this working monastery. The chapel is the only enclosed section of the monastery open to visitors. Its exquisite 12th-century floor mosaic is the largest of its kind in France. The shop stocks handmade soaps, honeys and the like – all made by the monks – and houses a small collection of artefacts found on-site.

❦ SISTERON // EXPLORE A CITADEL AND HOW TIME IS MEASURED

Sisteron's stunner is its spectacular **citadel**, an imposing 3rd- to 16th-century fortress perched on a rock above a transverse valley. The town itself has a lived-in feeling and there's not a whiff of the tourist trap. The tourist office conducts 1¼-hour walking tours (€1) and open-air classical-music concerts are held during the **Festival des Nuits de la Citadelle** from mid-July to mid-August.

In the centre of town the **Musée Terre et Temps** (Museum of Earth & Time; ☎ 04 92 61 61 30; www.resgeol04.org, in French; 6 place Général de Gaulle; ⏰ 10am-1pm & 3-7pm Jul & Aug, 9.30am-12.30pm & 2-6pm Thu-Mon Apr-Jun, Sep & Oct; ♿), inside a former 17th-century chapel, explores human time and geologic time. Displays include a Foucault's pendulum, sundials and a water clock.

TOP FIVE

VIEWS

Almost anywhere you turn in Haute-Provence you'll be met by a magnificent view. Here are a few of our favourite areas:

★ **Arboretum Marcel Kroenlein** in Roure (p186)

★ **Thoard** (below)

★ **Colmars-les-Alps** (p185)

★ **Belvédère de l'Escalès** (opposite)

★ **La Madone d'Utelle** (p187)

❧ THOARD // ESCAPE TO ANOTHER TIME

From Sisteron, follow the **rte du Temps** (Time Rd), a marked itinerary along the D3 to remote St-Geniez, from where it climbs over the **Col de Font-Belle** (1708m) before swooping south to the medieval fortified village of **Thoard**. Information panels en route highlight geological sights.

In Thoard, the 2km **Balade de Suy** is a signposted walking tour through the village and its environs. **Le Petit Musée des Cuivres** (☎ 04 92 31 57 46; adult/child €3/free; ⚘ by appointment) is a small shrine to brass instruments, including a sax signed by eponymous Adolphe Sax.

The gorgeously situated lavender **Distillerie du Siron**, up a tiny lane leading out of the village centre, offers free guided tours in summer (see p344). If you make reservations, you can enjoy the heaping farm-raised feasts (*menu* €22) served up at **Auberge de la Banette** (p388). Both have lodgings.

❧ DONKEY DISCOVERY // GUIDED TREK AND FARMSTAY

Ramble through the lavender-strewn mountains with a donkey from **Poivre d'Âne** (☎ 04 92 34 87 12; poivre.ane.free.fr; La Bastide des Férauds; treks from €58; ⚘ closed Jan–Mar; ⚘), 1km north of Thoard on the D3. To discover more about these endearing creatures stay on the donkey farm in *chambre d'hôte* rooms (doubles including breakfast €58) and feast on farm-fresh *tables d'hôtes* (€18).

❧ EAT WELL // EXCELLENT EATERIES LINE THE VALLEY

Fabulous *ferme auberge* (farmhouse restaurant) **Danse L'Ombre** (☎ 04 92 62 05 86; Les Remises; plat du jour €12, menu €22; ⚘ by reservation), in a secluded valley 26km west of Sisteron, creates organic feasts from farm-raised meats and farm-grown vegetables. Find it in the hamlet of Curel, 200m off the D946.

Or relax in the understatedly elegant dining room of newcomer and recent Logis de France award-winner **La Magnanerie** (☎ 04 92 62 60 11; www.la-magnanerie.net; N85, 1km north of Château-Arnoux St-Auban; menus €17–50; ⚘ lunch & dinner). Magnificently presented dishes include duck cooked to perfection with a drizzle of raspberry reduction. Stay over in stylish rooms (doubles from €59). Chef Patrick Chassy works his magic at neighbouring **L'Oustaou de la Foun** (☎ 04 92 62 65 30; N85, Château-Arnoux St-Auban; menus €17–50; ⚘ lunch & dinner). Specialties include duck breast with olives and apple gnocchi or delicacies like kangaroo with a morel cream sauce.

As you approach Les Mées, 20km south of Sisteron, you can't miss the other-worldly **Rocher des Mées**, a row of rocky pinnacles jutting 100m straight up. Legend claims that they were once a gaggle of monks who were turned to stone for lusting after Saracen women. Indulge your own hungers at **Restaurant La Marmite du Pêcheur** (☎ 04 92 34 35 56; Les Mées; menus €20–56; ⚘ lunch & dinner Thu–Mon) at the base of the rocks. Chef Christophe Roldan prepares decadent multicourse *menus* rich in foie gras and tender, slow-cooked lamb.

PARC NATUREL RÉGIONAL DU VERDON

· · · · · ·

Under the protection of the Parc Naturel Régional du Verdon since 1997, Europe's largest canyon, the plunging Gorges du Verdon, slices a 25km swathe through Provence's limestone plateau. Along with a wealth of whitewater sports, there's also breathtaking birdwatching, including the chance to see the canyon's very own colony of reintroduced griffon vultures.

The main gorge begins at Rougon near the confluence of the Verdon and the Jabron Rivers, and then winds westwards until the Verdon's green waters flow into Lac de Ste-Croix. At a dizzying 250m to 700m deep, the gorge's floors are just 8m to 90m wide, and its overhanging rims are from 200m to 1500m apart. The two main jumping-off points for exploring the gorges are the villages of Moustiers Ste-Marie in the west and Castellane, east of Rougon. The deep floors are only accessible by foot or raft. Motorists, horse riders and cyclists can take in staggering panoramas from two vertigo-inducing cliffside roads.

ESSENTIAL INFORMATION

DANGERS & ANNOYANCES // The river can rise very suddenly if hydroelectric dams upstream are opened, making it difficult or impossible to cross. Check water levels and weather forecasts before setting out. Roads close due to rock falls and/or snow; watch for falling rocks year-round. There are few petrol stations.

TOURIST OFFICES // Castellane (☎ 04 92 83 61 14; www.castellane.org; rue Nationale; ◷ 9am-12.30pm & 2-6.45pm Mon-Sat Mar-Oct, also 10am-12.30pm Sun Jul & Aug, 9am-noon & 2-5pm Mon-Fri Nov-Feb) Moustiers Ste-Marie (☎ 04 92 74 67 84; www.moustiers.fr; place de l'Eglise; ◷ 10am-12.30pm & 2-5.30pm Mar & Oct, to 6pm Apr & May, to 6.30pm Jun & Sep, 9.30am-12.30pm & 2-7pm Jul & Aug, 10am-noon & 2-5pm Nov-Feb) Wi-fi available (per hr €6).

DRIVING TOUR: GORGE EXPLORER

Map p178
Distance: 140km
Duration: two days

The largest gorge on the entire continent, the mighty **Gorges du Verdon** (left) is often referred to as the Grand Canyon du Verdon. Cycling or driving around the gorge's precarious rimside roads gives you a dramatic introduction to its tortuous topography.

Before setting out from **Moustiers Ste-Marie** (p179), warm up your calf muscles climbing to its cliffside chapel, then give your energy levels a boost with lunch at **Les Comtes** (p180). Afterwards, follow the **Route des Crêtes** (D952 & D23; ◷ closed Nov-Feb) along the northern rim. The best view from the northern side is from **Belvédère de l'Escalès**. Steel your nerves for the stunning drop-off into the gorge. The belvedere is also one of the best places to spot vultures wheeling overhead. After rejoining the D952, the road corkscrews past **Point Sublime**, which offers a fish-eye-lens view of serrated rock formations falling away to the river below. At the D952's eastern end, the narrow D317 scales 3km to the quaint village of

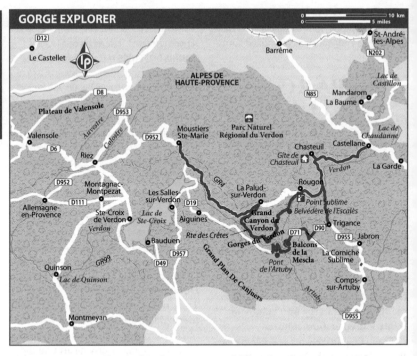

GORGE EXPLORER

Rougon. Rest up in Chasteuil at charming **Gîte de Chasteuil** (p389).

Start day two in **Castellane** (p180), which has a rock-perched church of its own.

You can return to Moustiers Ste-Marie along another heart-palpitating road, **La Corniche Sublime** (the D955 to the D71 to the D19). It twists along the southern rim, taking in landmarks such as the **Balcons de la Mescla** (Mescla Terraces) and **Pont de l'Artuby** (Artuby Bridge), the highest bridge in Europe.

EXPLORING PARC NATUREL RÉGIONAL DU VERDON

❦ WALKING // TAKE A LONG HIKE OR A SHORTER DAY WALK

In addition to canyon descents, dozens of blazed **trails** fan out from Castellane

and Moustiers through untamed countryside. The excellent English-language book *Canyon du Verdon* (€4.20), available at the tourist offices, lists 28 walks in the gorges.

You can walk most of the canyon along the often-difficult GR4, a route covered by Didier-Richard's 1:50,000 map No 19, *Haute-Provence-Verdon*. The full route takes two days, though short descents into the canyon are possible. Bring a torch (flashlight) and drinking water. Camping on gravel beaches is illegal. Check with tourist offices before embarking.

❦ WATER SPORTS, BUNGEE JUMPING & PARACHUTING // GET AN ADRENALINE KICK

Castellane is the main base for watersports companies; all offer similarly priced trips (April to September by reservation). **Guides Aventure** (☎ 06 85 94 46 61; www.guidesaventure.com) runs canyoning (€45/70 per half-/full day), rock climbing and rafting (€55/75) and 'floating' (€45/90) – river running with only a buoyancy bag strapped to your back.

If that's not enough, hurtle through the air on a death-defying jump from Europe's highest bungee site, the 182m Pont de l'Artuby (Artuby Bridge), with self-described 'dealers in adrenaline', **Latitude Challenge** (☎ 04 91 09 04 10; www .latitude-challenge.fr, in French; €105; ⏲ by appointment). Too tame? Free fall instead with the company's parachuting program.

❧ LACS DE STE-CROIX & DE QUINSON // DIP INTO HISTORY AROUND TWO OF VERDON'S LAKES

The largest of the lakes in Parc National Régional du Verdon, Lac de Ste-Croix, southwest of Moustiers Ste-Marie, was formed in 1974. Scads of summertime rentals include windsurfers, canoes and kayaks. Pretty Bauduen sits on its south-eastern banks.

Lac de Quinson lies at the southern-most foot of the lower Gorges du Verdon. In the village of Quinson, hi-tech **Musée de la Préhistoire des Gorges du Verdon** (☎ 04 92 74 09 59; rte de Montmeyan; adult/6-18yr/family €7/5/20; ⏲ 10am-8pm Jul & Aug, 10am-7pm Wed-Mon Apr-Jun & Sep, 10am-6pm Wed-Mon Feb, Mar & Oct–mid-Dec, closed mid-Dec–end Jan; ♿) explores the gorges' prehistoric past and archaeological treasures. In July and August it organises expeditions to Grotte de la Baume Bonne, a prehistoric cave.

Nearby Allemagne-en-Provence is named after Roman goddess of fertility Alemona. Her likeness appears on the village's centrepiece, the turret-topped 12th- to 16th-century **Château d'Allemagne** (☎ 04 92 77 46 78; guided tours adult/child €7/free; ⏲ tours 4pm & 5pm Tue-Sun Jul–mid-Sep, 4pm & 5pm Sat & Sun Easter-Jun & mid-Sep–Oct), a fairy-tale castle where would-be princes and princesses can also sojourn (doubles €80 to €140).

❧ RIEZ // HAVE LUNCH IN A BUSTLING VILLAGE

Take the D952 on a charming jaunt to simple Riez. The pretty road passes ceramic-tiled roofs and arrives at the village's surreal Roman columns. This is a fun stop on market days (Wednesday and Saturday) but it's worth stopping any day to lunch at **Le Rempart** (☎ 04 92 77 89 54; 17 rue du Marché; menus from €15; ⏲ lunch & dinner) at the foot of the clock tower. People-watch on the sunny, wooden deck with bright tablecloths and tuck into dishes like grilled salmon with truffles.

❧ MOUSTIERS STE-MARIE // A GORGEOUS GATEWAY VILLAGE

Dubbed the *Etoile de Provence* (Star of Provence), the charming little village Moustiers Ste-Marie (population 635, elevation 634m) makes a fair claim to the title. Tucked between two limestone cliffs, it overlooks open fields and far-off mountains. A 227m-long gold chain bearing a shining star is suspended over the town, so legend claims, by the Knight of Blacas, grateful to have returned safely from the Crusades. Twice a century the weathered chain gives way and the star is replaced.

Beneath the star, clinging to a cliff ledge, 14th-century **Chapelle Notre Dame de Beauvoir** (guided tours adult/child €3/free; ⏲ 10am Tue & Thu Jul-Aug), is built on the site of an AD 470 temple. A trail climbs up to the chapel and its waterfall, passing 14 stations of the cross en route. On 8 September, Mass is held at 5am to celebrate the nativity of the Virgin Mary,

HAUTE-PROVENCE

followed by flutes, drums and a breakfast on the square.

♥ MOUSTIERS' FAÏENCE // EVERY KIND OF EARTHENWARE YOU CAN IMAGINE

When silverware was reclaimed by the French kingdom and melted down to mint currency, Moustiers' decorative *faïence* graced Europe's palaces. Today there are 15 *ateliers* in Moustiers, all with their own styles, from lyrical poppy paintings to abstract splashes of colours.

Husband-and-wife artisans Martial and Françoise Baudey and their son Sylvain have a shop at the top of the village on place Pomey (closed January), and the **Atelier St-Michel** (☎ 04 92 74 67 73; tours €3) at the bottom of the village in the St-Michel quarter. Workshop tours show step-by-step how they craft the intricate pieces. Antique masterpieces are housed in the **Musée de la Faïence** (☎ 04 92 74 61 64; rue de la Bourgade; adult/child €3/free, free Tue Jul-Aug; ☺ 10am-12.30pm & 2-7pm Jul & Aug, 10am-12.30pm & 2-6pm Wed-Mon Apr-Jun, Sep & Oct) adjacent to Moustiers' town hall.

♥ MOUSTIERS' GASTRONOMIC GEMS // FORGET ROUGHING IT, DINE IN STYLE!

Get one of Haute-Provence's best meals at **La Ferme Ste-Cécile** (☎ 04 92 74 64 18; D952, quartier St-Michel; menus €26-35; ☺ lunch & dinner, closed Mon & mid-Nov–Dec). Among the delicious culinary surprises served on the terrace of this authentic *ferme auberge* find the thinnest slice of Roquefort and pear warmed in filo pastry, or foie gras wrapped in sweet quince. Everything on the menu is seasonal: like the exquisite crème brûlée with fresh truffles!

Meals at low-key **Les Comtes** (☎ 04 92 74 63 88; rue de la Bourgade; mains €16-28; ☺ lunch

Tue-Sun, dinner Tue-Sat, closed Nov-Feb) start with a mountain fruit aperitif. Follow up with dishes like squid-ink tagliatelle with saffron. In summer, dine in the sunshine, in winter the mosaicked dining room.

Some of France's finest chefs get their start at Alain Ducasse's **La Bastide de Moustiers** (☎ 04 92 70 47 47; www.bastide-moustiers.com; menus €55-75; ☺ lunch & dinner, closed Nov-Mar). Inside the rose-draped archways and thick stone walls of this old potter's studio, local produce is used in service to the master. Outside, baby deer scamper on the grounds, and yes, there's a place to park the helicopter. They also have elegant rooms (doubles from €240).

♥ CASTELLANE & CHAPELLE NOTRE DAME DU ROC // A CHAPEL THAT SERVED AS A SAFE HAVEN

The small, cobbled streets of **Castellane** (population 1539, elevation 723m) are beautiful in the off-season but are teeming in summer, when the tourist facilities and water-sports shops open. **Chapelle Notre Dame du Roc** is perched spectacularly above town on a needlelike rock. In 812, Castellan was destroyed by Saracen invaders and survivors sought refuge on this pinnacle. The first church was built in the 13th century, but the one standing now dates from 1703. Each year on 15 August (Assumption Day) a procession of pilgrims goes by torchlight up the rock to celebrate Mass.

Another highlight here, **La Fête du Pétardier**, on the last Saturday in January, honours Judith Andrau, a villager who protected the town from Protestant invaders in the 16th century. The brave lass poured boiling water onto the attacking general. Residents re-enact the battle and indulge in medieval games and food.

❦ CASTELLANE'S MUSEUMS // GO FROM MERMAIDS TO WWII

Study mermaid mythology and fossil facts at the **Musée Sirènes et Fossiles** (☎ 04 92 83 19 23; www.resgeol04.org, in French; place Marcel Sauvaire; adult/child €4/2; ⏲ 10am-noon & 2-5pm Wed-Sun May-Sep, 9am-noon & 2-5pm Wed-Sun Apr & Oct). In the same building (with the same opening hours) the **Musée du Moyen Verdon** celebrates local history and culture.

The captivating **Musée de la Résistance** (☎ 04 92 83 78 25; rte de Digne; adult/child €3/1.50; ⏲ Apr-Sep by appointment), about 1.5km along the road to Digne, is a private collection dedicated to heroes of the Resistance.

❦ DETOUR FOR DELICACIES // WHERE LOCALS GO FOR A SPECIAL MEAL

Head 5km east of Castellane to La Garde for the area's best eats. Locals flock to intimate, roadside **Auberge du Teillon** (☎ 04 92 83 60 88; D4805 to Grasse; menus €22-34; ⏲ lunch & dinner Wed-Mon Jul-Aug, lunch Tue-Sun & dinner Tue-Sat mid-Mar–Jun & Sep–mid-Nov, closed mid-Nov–mid-Mar) for housemade pâtés or tender-roasted pigeon. Save room for *tarte tatin au foie gras*.

❦ VERDON'S EASTERN LAKES // SNACK ON CHARCUTERIE WHILE WATCHING PARAGLIDERS

At the eastern end of the Gorges du Verdon, **Lac de Chaudanne** has steep-sided banks, but **Lac de Castillon** has gently sloping beaches and waters ideal for swimming and paddle-boating. **St-André-les-Alpes**, on the banks of Lac de Castillon, is France's leading paragliding centre.

Students of **Aérogliss** (☎ 04 92 89 11 30; chemin des Iscles) paraglide into local fields. Walks in the nearby hills like the one up Stue Hill (965m), across the lake from town, give views of the lake and the para-

gliders. Make a picnic at **Maison du Saucisson** (House of Sausages; ☎ 04 92 89 03 16; place de Verdun; ⏲ closed Mon winter & all of Jan), where the 30 types of sausage include donkey, ostrich and wild boar. They also have pâtés, *terrines* and cheeses.

❦ CITÉ STE-DE MANDAROM SHAMBHASALEM // RETREAT INTO AN AUMIST ENCLAVE

From Lac de Castillon, single-lane D402 goes to the walled **Cité Ste-de Mandarom Shambhasalem** (☎ 04 92 83 63 83; www.aumisme.org; adult/10-18yr €5/2; ⏲ 10-11.15am & 3-4.30pm Jul & Aug, 3-4.30pm Sat & Sun Sep-Jun), glittering with a 22m Buddha statue, a giant statue of Christ, and temples representing the word's major religions. The holy city is the home of Aumism, founded in 1969 by Gilbert Bourdin (1923–98), aka the Holy Lord Hamsah Manarah, as the 'Religion of the Unity of God's Faces'. Visitors must dress modestly.

❦ DOMAINE D'AIGUINES // DINE ON DUCKS, DUCKS AND MORE DUCKS

Though this is a **duck farm** (☎ 04 92 34 25 72; St-Jacques; menus €22-29; ♿), you may be greeted by their peacock. Nestled in a rolling valley with views of the mountains all around, this family-run off-the-beaten-path hideaway cooks up farm-made foie gras, pan-fried duck salad and other duck dishes. Follow the N202 for 13km west from St-André-les-Alpes and go north just before Barrême, along the narrow D118 to the hamlet of St-Jacques. Opening hours vary, so reserve ahead.

TRANSPORT

BIKE // In Castellane, rent bicycles at **Aqua Viva Est** (☎ 04 92 83 75 74; 12 bd de la République; per half-day €12). Just outside Moustiers Ste-Marie, rent from **Le Petit Ségriès** (☎ 04 92 74 68 83; per half-day €19).

RÉSERVE GÉOLOGIQUE DE HAUTE-PROVENCE

· · · · · ·

Footprints of prehistoric birds, out-sized ammonites and ram's-horn spiral shells are among the amazing fossil deposits found throughout the 1900-sq-km Réserve Géologique de Haute-Provence. You'll need a detailed regional map (sold at tourist offices) and your own transport to get to the 18 sites, most of which are found around Barles and Barrême to the south. An impressive limestone slab with some 500 ammonites sits 3km north of Digne on the road to Barles. The reserve also runs museums in Sisteron and Castellane.

ESSENTIAL INFORMATION

EMERGENCIES // Hôpital Digne (☎ 04 92 30 15 15)

TOURIST INFORMATION // Digne-les-Bains (☎ 04 92 36 62 62; www.ot-dignelesbains.fr; place du Tampinet; ☺ 8.45am-12.30pm & 1.30-6.30pm Jul & Aug, 8.45am-noon & 2-6pm Mon-Sat, 10am-noon Sun Sep-Jun) Seasonal guided tours of a lavender distillery. **Relais Départemental des Gîtes de France** (☎ 04 92 31 30 40; www.gites-de-france .com; ☺ 9am-noon & 1-5pm Mon-Fri, 9am-noon Sat) Adjacent to the tourist office.

EXPLORING RÉSERVE GÉOLOGIQUE DE HAUTE-PROVENCE

❧ MAISON DE LA GÉOLOGIE // TRACE HISTORY ON EARTH

Find time to visit the fascinating **Maison de la Géologie** (☎ 04 92 35 09 34; www.resgeol04 .org, in French; Parc St-Bénoît; adult/7-14yr €4.60/2.75; ☺ museum 10am-1pm & 2.30-6.30pm Wed-Sun mid-Jun–mid-Sep, park 8am-7pm Apr-Oct, 8am-7pm Mon-Fri Nov-Mar) in St-Bénoît, 2km north of Digne-les-Bains off the road to Barles. Trails lead to a museum containing aquariums, insect displays, and fossils and plants put into evolutionary context.

❧ DIGNE-LES-BAINS // A BUSY TOWN SURROUNDED BY LAVENDER

Both wild and cultivated lavender carpet the mountains and plains around **Digne-les-Bains** (population 17,680, elevation 608m), which rests at the foot of the Alps. For more than 50 years the five-day **Corso de la Lavande**, in August, has heralded the lavender harvest. Musicians flock to town, colourful floats parade through the streets and torch-lit celebrations continue into the night.

Digne hugs the eastern bank of the shallow River Bléone. Stroll or bike the riverfront promenade and bd Gassendi to take in town life.

Rando Lavande (☎ 04 92 32 27 44; www .chez.com/randolavande, in French; 7 rue de Provence; from €20) organises customised walks through the mountains' wild lavender in summer and snowshoeing expeditions in winter.

❧ DIGNE'S MUSEUMS // A SURPRISING BREADTH FROM TIBET TO GOLDSWORTHY

Tibetan culture is celebrated at the **Fondation Alexandra David-Néel** (☎ 04 92 31 32 38; www.alexandra-david-neel.org; 27 av Maréchal Juin; admission free; 2hr tours 10am, 2pm & 3.30pm), in memory of the Paris-born writer and philosopher who made an incognito voyage in the 1900s to Tibet before settling in Digne. **Journées Tibetaines** (Tibetan Days), an annual celebration of Tibetan culture, is held here in August.

ALONG THE MOUNTAIN RAILWAY

Chugging between the mountains and the sea, narrow-gauge railway **le Train des Pignes** (the Pine Cone Train) is one of Provence's most picturesque trips. Conceived in 1861 and fully inaugurated in 1911, the line was initially serviced by steam train, which still puffs between **Puget-Théniers** and **Annot** in summer. Endearing theories abound (such as pine cones falling into the train one Christmas Eve when it had run out of coal), but no one knows the history behind the name.

Rising to 1000m altitude, with breathtaking views, the 151km track passes through 50 tunnels and over 16 viaducts and 15 metal bridges on its precipitous journey, stopping at villages en route. You can buy direct tickets to the place you want to visit or, if you're travelling the whole route, it's possible to hop out, explore, and join a later train.

The entire trip from Digne-les-Bains to Nice takes 3¼ hours (€18 one way). Find updated schedules on the website of **Chemins de Fer de Provence** (☎/fax 04 92 31 01 58; www.trainprovence.com; av Pierre Sémard, Digne-les-Bains).

Musée Gassendi (☎ 04 92 31 45 29; place des Récollets; adult/child €4/free; ☟ 11am-7pm Apr-Sep, 1.30-5.30pm Oct-Mar, closed Tue), in the town centre, displays everything from modern art by Andrew Goldsworthy to exhibits on natural history or the 16th-century philosopher-scientist-painter Pierre Gassendi.

♥ **ÉTABLISSEMENT THERMAL //
CHILL OUT IN WARM WATERS**
Ahhhh...float in the thermal pool, wrap yourself in seaweed or luxuriate in a lavender bath at **Établissement Thermal** (☎ 04 92 32 32 92; 20min spa/massage from €45; ☟ 8am-noon & 3-5pm Mon-Sat, Mar-early Dec). Digne is named for these curative thermal springs, which are visited annually by around 11,000 people seeking cures for rheumatism and other ailments. Find it 2km east of Digne's centre in a quiet valley surrounded by stone pinnacles.

♥ **A SKI DETOUR // HIT THE SLOPES
NORTH OF DIGNE-LES-BAINS**
Like a little swatch of Switzerland, the **Vallée de la Blanche** (www.valleedelablanche .com), 50km north of Digne, has more than 110km of ski runs split between three resorts. The main one, well set up for families, is the 1350m **St-Jean Montclar** (passes €16 to €20 per day). The area is the home of Montclar spring water, but you won't need to buy it while you're here – just turn on the tap.

TRANSPORT

BUS // The **bus station** (☎ 04 92 31 50 00; place du Tampinet; ☟ 9am-12.30pm & 3-6.30pm Mon-Sat) in Digne serves Nice via Castellane, Marseille and Apt.
TRAIN // Digne's train station (☎ 04 92 31 00 67; av Pierre Sémard; ☟ ticket windows 8.15am-12.30pm & 1-8pm Mon-Fri, 8.15am-12.30pm & 1.45-4.45pm Sat) serves Marseille (€25, 2½ hours). Digne-les-Bains is the northern terminus of le Train des Pignes (above).

PARC NATIONAL DU MERCANTOUR

· · · · · ·

Ringed by a roller coaster of rugged mountains, the Mercantour National Park is Provence at its most majestic. Europe's highest mountain pass, Col de Restefond la Bonette (2802m), coils through the Vallée de l'Ubaye, the park's most northerly and wildest area. Ski trails criss-cross the Vallées de l'Ubaye, du Haut Verdon and de la Tinée. A short hop from the Côte d'Azur, the Vallées de la Vésubie, des Merveilles and de la Roya span gorges, ageless rocks and white waters.

The park is home to a dazzling array of birds, including the golden eagle. Its higher-altitude plains shelter marmot, mouflon and chamois, as well as the *bouquetin* (Alpine ibex), reintroduced into the region in the early 1990s. In lower wooded areas, red and roe deer are common. Wild boar roam throughout, and wolves prowl the park once more.

The park's headquarters are in Nice but permanent Maison du Parc offices (www.parc-mercantour.fr) scatter the park; see essential information sections for details. They provide information on all aspects of the park and sell maps and guides. Camping in the park is not allowed.

VALLÉE DE L'UBAYE

Desolate and wild, the Ubaye Valley is crossed by the D900, which closely shadows the banks of the River Ubaye. Winter skiing and summer white-water rafting are its two main activities.

ESSENTIAL INFORMATION

TOURIST OFFICES // Barcelonnette (☎ 04 92 81 04 71; www.barcelonnette.net, in French; place Frédéric Mistral; ☼ 9am-noon & 2-7pm Jul & Aug, 9am-noon & 2-6pm Mon-Sat Sep-Jun) **Parc National du Mercantour Visitors Centre Barcelonnette** (☎ 04 92 81 21 31; ☼ 9am-noon & 2-6pm)

EXPLORING VALLÉE DE L'UBAYE

❦ BARCELONNETTE // FIND MEXICO IN THE ALPS

The valley's only town, **Barcelonnette** (elevation 1135m), has a fascinating Mexican heritage, resulting in some exceptional, very un-alpine architecture. From the 18th century until WWII, some 5000 Barcelonnettais emigrated to Mexico to seek their fortunes in the silk- and wool-weaving industries, building mansions throughout the town upon their return. One of the most spectacular now houses the **Musée de la Vallée** (☎ 04 92 81 27 15; 10 av de la Libération; adult/child €3.30/free; ☼ 10am-noon & 2.30-7pm mid-Jul–Aug, 2.30-6pm Tue-Sat Oct–mid-Jul, closed mid-Nov–mid-Dec), which explores the town's colourful history.

❦ GETTING OUTDOORS // CYCLING, WALKING AND SKIING THE VALLEY

The Vallée de l'Ubaye is linked to the outside world by seven mountain passes. Cyclists tough enough to conquer them all are given a medal. Outfitters in **Le Martinet** rent mountain bikes and arrange guided rides. One of these outfitters, **River** (☎ 04 92 85 53 99; www.river.fr, in French), also has a mini mountain-bike (VTT) course for kids. Barcelonnette's tourist office has a list of guides who organise walks and cycling and canoeing trips.

Rising 8.5km southwest of Barcelonnette are the twin ski resorts of **Pra Loup 1500** (sometimes called Les Molanes) and **Pra Loup 1600** (which has more infrastructure and nightlife). Both are connected by a lift system with the ski resort of **La Foux d'Allos**. In summer it's a hiker's heaven.

VALLÉE DU HAUT VERDON

The dizzying Col d'Allos (2250m and snow-blocked in winter) links the Vallée de l'Ubaye with the Vallée du Haut Verdon. The River Verdon has its source here at La Tête de la Sestrière (2572m).

ESSENTIAL INFORMATION

TOURIST OFFICES // Colmars-les-Alpes
(☎ 04 92 83 41 92; www.colmars-les-alpes.fr; Ancienne Auberge Fleurie; ☷ 8am-12.30pm & 2-6.30pm Jul & Aug, 9am-12.15pm & 2-5.45pm Mon-Sat Sep-Jun).

EXPLORING VALLÉE DU HAUT VERDON

♥ LA FERME GIRERD-POTIN // SOJOURN IN A SECLUDED AUBERGE

Mountain hospitality will warm your heart at the restored 16th-century working *ferme auberge* **La Ferme Girerd-Potin** (☎ 04 92 83 04 76; www.chambredhotes-valdallos .com; rte de la Foux). Within rough-hewn stone walls, thaw out with casseroles made from farm-raised poultry and rest up in wood-beamed *chambre d'hôte* rooms

(half-board per person from €38). Find it 1.8km south of La Foux d'Allos and 5km north of Allos.

♥ LAC D'ALLOS // ENJOY SPECTACULAR ALPINE LAKE SERENITY

It's well worth the trek to reach the stunning natural mountain **Lac d'Allos** (2226m; closed in winter). Drive 12km to the end of the bumpy D226 through Colmars-les-Alpes, then follow the 40-minute walking trail that leads to the lake from the car park. Route maps and walking information are available from the **Parc National du Mercantour hut** (☎ 06 32 90 80 24), which operates from the car park in July and August.

♥ COLMARS-LES-ALPES // STROLL A ONE-OF-A-KIND MOUNTAIN STRONGHOLD

The Vauban-fortified village **Colmars-les-Alpes** (elevation 1250m) sits in the southern part of the valley. Colmars' maze of quaint streets is tethered between high thick walls, surrounded by magnificent mountainscapes. Colmars was at the frontier of Savoy in the 14th

---

∽ WORTH A TRIP ∽

Straddling the Haute-Provence–Hautes-Alpes border, Europe's largest manmade lake, **Lac de Serre-Ponçon**, sits high in the mountains and flows into Ubaye Valley. The lake district's main town, **Embrun** (elevation 870m), was the Roman capital of the Alps and later a bishopric. Its enchanting tangle of cobblestone streets lead to the dramatic black-and-white stone cathedral **Notre Dame du Réal**. In town, pack a lakeside picnic from the farm produce at **La Ferme Embrunaise** (☎ 04 92 43 01 98; place Barthelon); and the chocolatier-pâtisserie of **Luc Eyriey** (☎ 04 92 43 01 37; place Barthelon), run by his family since 1902. Luc has also opened a small on-site chocolate museum.

Hidden deep in the forest, 3km uphill from the lake's eastern bank, the beautiful 12th-century **Abbaye de Boscodon** (☎ 04 92 43 14 45; Crots; admission €3.50; ☷ 8.30am-7pm Mon-Sat, 12.15-7pm Sun) fell to ruin and was inhabited by sheep; it has been magnificently resurrected by the community.

century and today its Savoy fort can be visited via a little **museum** (place Joseph Girieud; adult/child €3/free; ☺ 10am-noon & 3-6.30pm Jul–mid-Sep).

VALLÉE DE LA TINÉE

The Col de Restefond la Bonette (2802m) links the Vallée de l'Ubaye with the tamer, more southern Vallée de la Tinée. In winter, when the snowy pass is closed, the 149km-long valley can only be accessed up its southern leg from Nice. The valley is marked by sharp drops, dramatic mountain faces and striated burgundy, mauve, and pink rock formations.

ESSENTIAL INFORMATION

TOURIST INFORMATION // **Parc National du Mercantour Information Centre Valberg** (☎ 04 93 02 58 23; rue Jean Mineur; ☺ 9am-noon & 2-6pm). **St-Étienne de Tinée** (☎ 04 93 02 42 27; quartier de l'Ardon; ☺ Jul & Aug). **St-Sauveur-sur-Tinée** (☎ 04 93 02 10 33; 11 av des Blavets; ☺ Jul & Aug). **Valberg** (☎ 04 93 23 24 25; www.valberg.com; place du Quartier; ☺ 9am-noon & 2-6pm Thu-Tue).

EXPLORING VALLÉE DE LA TINÉE

☙ TUNNELS & GORGES // GET CARRIED AWAY IN GORGEOUS GORGES

Guillaumes (elevation 800m), around 13km west of Valberg, is the starting point for forays into the **Gorges de Dalius**, which is chiselled from wine-coloured rock. Seventeen tunnels burrow through these outcroppings.

Vertiginous **Pont de la Mariée**, an 80m-high stone footbridge crosses the gorges and **Pont de Berthéou**, another bridge 8km south of Guillaumes on the D2202, is the starting point for

the scenic **Sentier du Point Sublime** (4km, 1½ hours), an invigorating walk through oak and pine forest and past red rock formations to panoramic 'Sublime Point'.

☙ SKI & APRÉS-SKI // VISIT A BUSY HAUTE-PROVENCE SKI RESORT

Valberg (elevation 1700m) is a ski resort that lures walkers and mountain bikers in summer. At the **Espace Valberg Aventure** (☎ 04 93 23 24 25; ☺ Jul & Aug; ⑤) scale trees and monkey around dozens more Tarzan-inspired obstacles. Valberg also has a summer **luge** (1/3 rides €3/8).

Le Valbergan (☎ 04 93 02 50 28; 2 av Valberg; menus from €22; ☺ lunch & dinner Tue-Sat, lunch Sun; ⑤), at the foot of the slopes, serves up mountain cuisine guaranteed to warm your cockles. Specialities include *raclettes* (melted cheese over boiled potatoes, served with pickles and ham). Their *crêperie* downstairs (crêpes from €6) is perfect for the kiddies.

☙ MOUNTAINTOP VILLAGE & ARBORETUM // FEEL ON TOP OF THE WORLD

Drive up to **Roure**, a few hair-raising kilometres west of St-Sauveur off the D30. The breathtaking, narrow road leads to this village atop a pinnacle with fantastic views all around. **Chapelle St-Sebastien** has a unique sideways-facing clock tower, and a sculpture of a youth atop poles hanging over the abyss. From the 1920s until 1961, villagers used a 1850m-long cable to transport things up the mountain; you can still see the cable today. Continue along for a few precarious kilometres to reach the unique **Arboretum Marcel Kroenlein** (☎ 04 93 57 38 02; adult/child €5/free; ⑤) and its six peak-top hectares of mountain flora from around the world.

**❧ HIGH MOUNTAIN DRIVE //
EXPLORE THE REMOTE ALPS**

East of Valberg, the spectacular D30 takes you through tiny **Beuil** (elevation 1450m), tucked in a hanging valley, from where you can access the **Gorges du Cians**, carved from burgundy-coloured rock. Continue 24km east, past waterfalls, to wonderful **Roubion**, a cliff-hugging village set among rocky spires.

At **St-Sauveur-sur-Tinée** (elevation 490m) the D2205 twists north through beautiful gorges to Isola and then the lovely Alpine village **St-Étienne de Tinée** (population 1684). There are endless walking opportunities in summer around the **Cime de la Bonette** (2860m).

VALLÉE DE LA VÉSUBIE

Sporty cars reappear in the Vésubie, a dead-end valley accessed from the south, often referred to as 'Nice's Switzerland' due to its proximity to the Côte d'Azur.

ESSENTIAL INFORMATION

TOURIST INFORMATION // Parc National du Mercantour Visitors' Centre St-Martin-Vésubie (☎ 04 93 03 23 15; ⏲ 9am-noon & 2-6pm) St-Martin-Vésubie (☎ 04 93 03 21 28; www.saintmartinvesubie.fr, in French; place Félix Faure; ⏲ 9am-7pm Jul & Aug, 9am-noon & 2-6pm Mon-Sat, 2-6pm Sun Sep-Jun) Has a list of mountain guides.

EXPLORING VALLÉE DE LA VÉSUBIE

❧ VALLEY VIEWS // SEARCH OUT SPECIAL PERCHES

For a stunning aerial view of the **Gorges de la Vésubie** and its surroundings, head for **La Madone d'Utelle** (1181m), a pilgrimage site settled by Spanish sailors in the 9th century and crowned with a chapel. From the mountain village of

St-Jean la Rivière (on the D2565), a stone bridge crosses the River Var, from where a steep, winding mountain pass (the D32) leads west to **Utelle** (population 489), 6km northeast of La Madone.

About 18km north of St-Jean along the D2565, just past the turning for **La Bollène-Vésubie** (elevation 964m), you arrive at a crossroads. Snake east along the D171 to **Belvédère** (elevation 820m), a hilltop village where you can learn how milk is made in the tiny **Musée du Lait** (Milk Museum; ☎ 04 93 03 51 66).

❧ GETTING OUT IN THE VALLEY // WALK, BIKE OR SKI IN TRANQUILLITY

In St-Martin-Vésubie, **Escapade Bureau des Guides** (☎ 04 93 03 31 32; www.guidescapade.com; place du Marché; ⏲ Jul & Aug) organises guided walks, climbs (€35) and canyoning (€30 to €60) and leads walks into the Vallée des Merveilles (see p188). In nearby La Colmiane, the **Bureau des Guides** (☎ /fax 04 93 02 88 30) charges similar rates and **Colmiane Sports** (☎ 04 93 02 87 00) and **Ferrata Sport** (☎ 04 93 02 80 56) lead walks and hire mountain bikes.

VIA FERRATA

During WWI Italian troops moved swiftly and safely through the Dolomites – the natural frontier between Italy and Austria – using iron-rung ladders and steel cables bolted into the mountainside. Today, similar routes known as via ferrata (meaning 'iron way' in Italian) allow adventurous tourists to scale the rock faces.

Haute-Provence sports a clutch of *via ferrata* courses (see www.viaferrata.org), rigged at dizzying heights. First-timers can tackle short sections. Equipment hire, guides and tickets are generally handled by local tourist offices.

The small ski station of **La Colmiane**, 7km west of St-Martin-Vésubie, has one chairlift to **Pic de la Colmiane** (1795m) and 30km of ski slopes and walking and mountain-bike trails. You can also rent cross-country skis and snowshoes at **Alpha** (below) in Le Boréon.

♥ THERMES DE BERTHEMONT LES BAINS // FIND AN OASIS OF RELAXATION

A great place to soak weary bones, or just loll in luxury, the **Thermes de Berthemont Les Bains** (☎ 04 93 03 47 00; www.valvital.eu; Roquebillière; ☺ Apr-Oct) offers an enormous range of massages (starting at €25) and baths. Or simply relax in the thermal pool and sauna (€10). Find this rare bastion of mountaintop pampering south of St-Martin-Vésubie in **Roquebillière**.

♥ ART & GASTRONOMY // CREATURE COMFORTS IN ST-MARTIN-VÉSUBIE

While in picturesque **St-Martin-Vésubie** (elevation 1000m), the valley's main outdoor-activity base, feed your eyes and your belly. **J Huttler Atelier 58** (☎ 04 93 03 29 24; 58 rue Cagnoli) is packed with brightly coloured modernist interpretations of local landscapes.

The family-run village restaurant **La Trappa** (☎ 04 93 03 29 23; place du Marché; menus from €18; ☺ lunch & dinner Tue-Sat, lunch Sun) is tucked into a small, peaceful inner square. Sup on snails in garlic butter, game *terrine*, herb-infused lamb and other 'mountain' food.

VALLÉE DES MERVEILLES

♥ BRONZE AGE ROCK ART // EXPLORE THE VALLEY OF WONDERS

The 'Valley of Wonders' contains one of the world's most stupendous collections of **Bronze Age petroglyphs**. They date from between 1800 and 1500 BC and are thought to have been made by a Ligurian cult. Effectively an open-air art gallery, wedged between the Vésubie and Roya Valleys, it shelters more than 36,000 rock engravings of human figures, bulls and other animals spread over 30 sq km around **Mont Bégo** (2870m).

The main access route into the valley is the eastbound D91 running from St-Dalmas de Tende in the Vallée de la Roya to Castérino, where the Parc National du Mercantour has a summertime-only **park office** (☎ 04 93 04 89 79). Alternatively, go via the dead-end D171, which leads north to the valley from Roquebillière in the Vallée de la Vésubie. As the area is snow-covered much of the year, the best

THE GREY WOLF

Sustained hunting over 1000 years led to the eventual disappearance of the wolf *(Canis lupus)* from France in 1930. But in 1992 two 'funny-looking dogs' were spotted near Utelle. Since then wolves have been making a natural return, loping across the Alps from Italy. Summer leaf coverage makes them hard to spot and in warmer weather they usually pad back to Italy. Unlike the beasts of fairy tales, these wolves are wary animals and will run in the opposite direction if they sniff you – although they do feed on sheep. Learn how man is learning to live with the wolf and watch wolves roam wild at Wolf Watch at **Alpha** (☎ 04 93 02 33 69; www.alpha-loup.com; Le Boréon; adult/child €10/8). You can visit year-round, but opening hours vary; call ahead or visit their website for details.

time to visit, unless you are snow-shoeing, is July to September.

Access is restricted to protect the precious artworks: walkers should only visit with an official guide; see Parc National du Mercantour Visitors Centre, below and Escapade Bureau des Guides, p187.

VALLÉE DE LA ROYA

The Roya Valley once served as a hunting ground for King Victor Emmanuel II of Italy. Occupied by the Italians during WWII, it became part of France in 1947.

The pretty medieval township of Breil-sur-Roya (population 2023, elevation 300m) sits just 62km northeast of Nice. Panoramic views unfold from the Col de Brouis (879m), which links Sospel (population 2937), 21km south, with the Roya Valley. In July the valley celebrates Les Baroquiales, a baroque art and music festival with period markets, 17th-century restaurant menus and a series of concerts.

ESSENTIAL INFORMATION

TOURIST INFORMATION // **Parc National du Mercantour Visitors Centre** Castérino (☎ 04 93 04 89 79; ☽ Jun-Aug) Tende (☎ 04 93 04 67 00) **Sospel** (☎ 04 93 04 15 80; www.sospel-tourisme .com, in French; 19 av Jean Medecin; ☽ 10am-2.30pm & 1.30-5.30pm Mon-Sat, 10am-12.30pm Sun) **Tende** (☎ 04 93 04 73 71; www.tendemerveilles.com, in French; av du 16 Septembre 1947; ☽ 9am-noon & 2-5pm Mon-Sat, 9am-noon Sun)

EXPLORING VALLÉE DE LA ROYA

❦ SOSPEL // PLAY LIKE A LOCAL
Sweet Sospel sits at a junction of several valleys. The simple village is bustling with a lived-in feel year-round and is well worth a break and a stroll. Criss-cross the river to explore the tiny walking streets and find cheery **Atelier Habana** (☎ 04 89 98 99 93; place St-Nicolas) behind Le Pont-Vieux, whose B&W photographs of the region make wonderful mementos.

Locals flock to **Restaurant Côté Cuisine** (☎ 04 93 79 81 37; av Jean Medecin; lunch/dinner menus from €34/52, ☽ lunch & dinner Thu-Sun), the area's premier spot for elegant meals. Friendly, young hosts Claire and Edmond grow most of the produce for the restaurant on their nearby organic farm.

Or chill out to the tunes of Desmond Dekker in colourful, tiny **Au Café Bleu** (☎ 04 93 04 24 23; 13 rue St-Pierre; mains €14-18, ☽ lunch Mon-Fri & dinner Thu-Sat). The lamb shank is so tender it falls straight off the bone, and the braised carrot so sweet it tastes like candy.

❦ SAORGE // WIND THROUGH A GORGE TO A FRANCISCAN MONASTERY
Gashed into the landscape, the dramatic **Gorges de Saorge**, 9km north of Breil-sur-Roya, lead to fortified **Saorge** (elevation 520m). The vertiginous village is plastered on the wall of the mountain and is a maze of tangled streets and 15th- to 17th-century houses. Franciscan **Monastère de Saorge** (☎ 04 93 04 55 55; ☽ 10am-noon & 2-5pm Wed-Mon) has nine sundials and a baroque church with frescos of the life of St Francis.

❦ TENDE // DIP INTO THE VALLEY'S CULTURAL CENTRE
In Tende (population 1890, elevation 830m), the **Musée des Merveilles** (☎ 04 93 04 32 50; av du 16 Septembre 1947; admission free; ☽ 10am-6.30pm May–mid-Oct, 10am-5pm mid-Oct–Apr, closed mid–late Mar & mid–late Dec) explains the archaeological and natural history of the valley and of the Vallée Des Merveilles.

The small but sweet **Maison du Miel et de l'Abeille** (House of Honey & Bees; ☎ 04 93 04 76 22; place Lieutenant Kalck; ⊙ Jun-Sep) shows how the region's honey is made. For more treats, try the wonderful cheeses, hams and freshly baked breads that are sold at several artisan shops on rue de France and av du 16 Septembre 1947. Try the **Fiori delle Alpi** (☎ 04 93 04 55 05; av du 16 Septembre 1947; ⊙ 7.30am-8pm) for fresh sausage, cheese, walnuts and fruit.

A cheerful trio of gents runs the dining room at **Le Miramonti** (☎ 04 93 04 61 82; 5-7 rue Vassalo; menus from €17; ⊙ lunch & dinner Tue-Sat, lunch Sun, closed Nov; ⑤). Families flock here for pizzas and the space to let the kids roam, but the restaurant's specialties are Piedmontese. They also have spartan rooms (doubles from €45).

South of Tende, the eastbound D143 leads from St-Dalmas de Tende to **La Brigue** (elevation 770m) and 4km further on to **Notre Dame des Fontaines**, dubbed the 'Sistine Chapel of the southern Alps', with beautifully preserved frescos by 15th-century Piedmontese painters Jean Canavesio and Jean Baleison.

Just 5km north of Tende, the **Tunnel de Tende** – engineered in 1882 – provides a vital link into Italy.

♣ WALKING, BIKING & PADDLING THE VALLEY // HIT THE TRAILS OR THE RIVER

Tende's tourist office has information on guided archaeological walks to **Mont Bégo** and the **Maison de la Montagne et des Sports** (☎ /fax 04 93 04 77 73; mmstende@aol.com; 11 av du 16 Septembre 1947) hires bikes and can give you the inside track on 23 bike trails. Alternatively, contact the **Bureau des Guides** (☎ 04 93 04 67 88; www.berengeraventures.com, in French; 6bis rue Grandis). In Sospel, cycling club **Sospel**

VTT (☎ 06 70 76 57 05; www.sospelvtt.net, in French; per half-day €11) rents wheels.

Breil-sur-Roya is the valley's watersports base. **Roya Évasion** (☎ 04 93 04 91 46; www.royaevasion.com, in French; 1 rue Pasteur) organises kayaking, canyoning and rafting trips on the River Roya, as well as walks and mountain-bike expeditions.

TRANSPORT

TRAIN // Trains (www.ter-sncf.com/paca) run several times per day along the Nice–Turin line, stopping in Sospel, Breil-sur-Roya, St-Dalmas de Tende and Tende.

NICE, MONACO & MENTON

3 PERFECT DAYS

❦ DAY 1 // NICE, BELLE OF THE CÔTE D'AZUR

Wake up to Vieux Nice's vibrant market scene. Enjoy the buzz of the market from a café terrace on cours Saleya (p197) and get some picnic supplies from the groaning stalls. Head to the Colline du Château (p201) to feast on views and delicacies. In the afternoon, arty types shouldn't miss Nice's Musée Matisse (p201) or the Musée d'Art Moderne et d'Art Contemporain (MAMAC; p202). For something more active, rent out skates and zoom along the Promenade des Anglais (p201).

❦ DAY 2 // SCENIC RIVIERA

Make your way to Èze (p216), the coast's most stunning perched village. Wander about Jardin d'Èze (p216) for breathtaking views of the coast and lunch at Château Eza (p217) to revel in style in this exceptional panorama. Head back down to the coast and spend the afternoon at the eccentric Villa Ephrussi (p213) or admiring Jean Cocteau's frescoes at Villa Santo Sospir (p214) in St-Jean-Cap Ferrat.

❦ DAY 3 // HIT MONACO

Start with a visit of the Jardin Exotique (p224), from where there are stupendous views of the principality. Lunch at one of Monaco's excellent Italian restaurants before heading to Le Rocher (p221) for the afternoon. A couple of hours should do justice to Monaco's outstanding Musée Océanographique (p223). You can then head to Monte Carlo for an evening of fun: drinks at Karé(ment) (p229) and a gamble at the casino (p223).

NICE, MONACO & MENTON

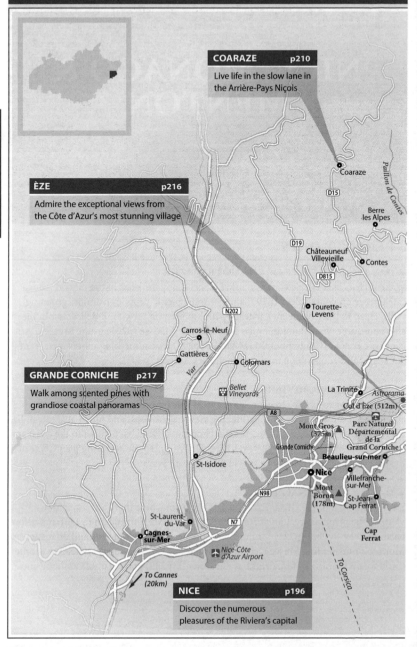

COARAZE   p210
Live life in the slow lane in the Arrière-Pays Niçois

ÈZE   p216
Admire the exceptional views from the Côte d'Azur's most stunning village

GRANDE CORNICHE   p217
Walk among scented pines with grandiose coastal panoramas

NICE   p196
Discover the numerous pleasures of the Riviera's capital

Coaraze

Berre les Alpes

Châteauneuf Villevieille

Contes

Tourette-Levens

Carros-le-Neuf

Gattières

Colomars

Bellet Vineyards

La Trinité

Astrorama

Col d'Èze (512m)

Parc Naturel Départemental de la Grand Corniche

Mont Gros (375m)

Grande Corniche

Beaulieu-sur-mer

St-Isidore

Nice

Villefranche-sur-Mer

Mont Boron (178m)

St-Jean-Cap Ferrat

St-Laurent-du-Var

Cagnes-sur-Mer

Cap Ferrat

Nice-Côte d'Azur Airport

To Cannes (20km)

To Corsica

Var

Paillon de Contes

N202

D15

D19

D815

A8

N98

N7

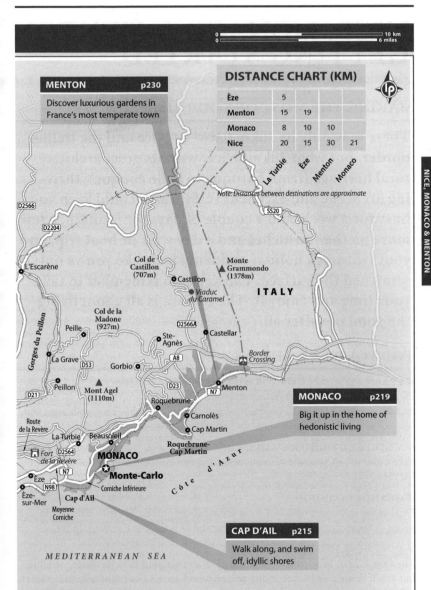

MENTON p230

Discover luxurious gardens in France's most temperate town

DISTANCE CHART (KM)

	La Turbie	Èze	Menton	Monaco
Èze	5			
Menton	15	19		
Monaco	8	10	10	
Nice	20	15	30	21

Note: Distances between destinations are approximate

MONACO p219

Big it up in the home of hedonistic living

CAP D'AIL p215

Walk along, and swim off, idyllic shores

GETTING AROUND

Public transport is excellent along the coast, with numerous buses and trains shuttling between Nice and Menton and stopping everywhere in between, including Monaco. Distances are short so travel times are very reasonable, even at rush hour. All bus journeys in the area cost just €1, making it a bargain to get around. For the arrière-pays and the Grande Corniche, a car is essential. There is little traffic and numerous opportunities to drive off the beaten track.

NICE, MONACO & MENTON GETTING STARTED

MAKING THE MOST OF YOUR TIME

There may only be 30km between Nice and the Italian border, but what 30km! Nice, with its great architectural heritage (from baroque to belle époque), thriving art scene and excellent restaurants could keep you busy for a week; add a couple of days for Monaco, a few more on the Corniches and a day walk or boat trip, and your two-week holiday suddenly feels like you've only scratched the surface. The key is to remember to take your time and enjoy it. The Riviera is all about living the good life after all.

TOP TOURS & COURSES

❦ LEARN HOW TO COOK WITH GASTRONOMIC STARS
Eating at a Michelin-starred restaurant is one thing but learning how to cook in one is quite another! Try it at La Recette Magique's highly individual cooking lessons with some of the Riviera's biggest names. (p204)

❦ VISIT LE CORBUSIER'S CABANON
Take a tour of Le Corbusier's famous beach hut and learn the saga behind its origins. (p215)

❦ GRANDE CORNICHE
Drive along this iconic road and enjoy breathtakingly beautiful views of the Med and a picnic in the scenic Parc Naturel Départemental de la Grande Corniche. (p219)

❦ DOLPHINS AND WHALE TOURS
The Côte d'Azur is better known for its glitz and glamour than its marine wildlife, but you'll be amazed by how many dolphins and whales live in these coastal waters. (p212)

❦ TRAM ART
The city of Nice commissioned 14 original works of art to liven up its new tram (anything from daring visual works to funky sound bites). Discover this innovative approach to urban planning on a dedicated guided tour. (p203)

GETTING AWAY FROM IT ALL

Head for the Riviera hills for unforgettable landscapes and life on the Côte d'Azur without the razzmatazz.

- ★ **Arrière-Pays Niçois** Just 20km from Nice yet a world away from city life, with deserted perched villages, unspoilt countryside and wonderful walks (p209)

- ★ **Parc Naturel Départemental de la Grande Corniche** Retreat from the D2564 road to the scented slopes of this nature reserve for breathtaking panoramas and a picnic under the pines (p219)

- ★ **Ste-Agnès & Gorbio** Visit the vertigo-inducing village of Ste-Agnès before walking to Gorbio and working up an appetite for lunch at Beau Séjour (p234)

ADVANCE PLANNING

The events and festivals schedule (Nice p204; Monaco p226; Menton p233) is packed on this stretch of coast. Many make fantastic excursions during a holiday; you just need to plan ahead both in terms of booking tickets and finding accommodation.

- ★ **Monaco Grand Prix** At the end of May, this is an accommodation nightmare. Prices go up 10-fold and rooms are generally booked up months in advance within a 50km radius. If you're going to the Grand Prix, start looking the second you have tickets.

- ★ **Guided tours** Tours in Nice (p197) or La Recette Magique cooking lessons (p204) don't run every day so make sure you check exact dates to avoid disappointment.

TOP 'LIVING THE HIGH LIFE' ATTRACTIONS

♥ MONACO GRAND PRIX
Formula One meets high society. (p227)

♥ SOIREE AT VILLA EPHRUSSI
Spend an unforgettable evening sipping Champagne and enjoying alfresco opera. (p213)

♥ CASINO DE MONTE CARLO
Risk it all at the original casino. (p223)

♥ HELICOPTER FLIGHT
Fly from Nice to Monaco, just like the stars would. (p226)

♥ TERRES DE TRUFFES
Feast on 'black diamond' at every course at this truffle restaurant. (p207)

RESOURCES

- ★ **www.nicetourisme.com** Tourist office website

- ★ **http://holiday.monacoeye.com** Alternative guide to Monaco

- ★ **www.monaco-montecarlo.com** Five-language site loaded with practical info

- ★ **www.monaco-tourisme.com** The tourist office

- ★ **www.monaco-spectacle.com** Browse Monaco's busy performance schedule and book tickets online

- ★ **Guides Randoxygène** Essential for anyone who loves walking. *Rando Pays Côtier* and *Rando Moyen Pays* both cover walks in this chapter. Available in all tourist offices.

NICE & AROUND

······

NICE

pop 347,060

With its unusual mix of real-city grit, old-world opulence, year-round sunshine and exceptional location, Nice's appeal is universal. Everyone from backpackers to romance-seeking couples and families will love sitting at a café on cours Saleya in Vieux Nice or a bench on the legendary Promenade des Anglais for an epic sunset. Eating options are some of the best you'll find in France, the nightlife is buzzing and the art scene thriving. You could happily spend a week here and still be hungry for more.

ESSENTIAL INFORMATION

EMERGENCIES // **Central police station** (☎ 04 92 17 22 22; 1 av Maréchal Foch; ☺ 24hr) **Foreign Tourist Department** (☎ 04 92 17 20 63; ☺ 8am-noon & 2-6pm) Part of the central police station; translators are at hand to help. **Hôpital St-Roch** (☎ 04 92 03 33 75; ☺ 24hr) In the centre of town.

TOURIST OFFICES // **Nice Tourist Office** (☎ 08 92 70 74 07; www.nicetourisme.com); Airport information desk (Terminal 1; ☺ 8am-9pm Jun-Sep, 8am-9pm Mon-Sat Oct-May); Main tourist office (5 promenade des Anglais; ☺ 8am-8pm Mon-Sat, 9am-7pm Sun Jun-Sep, 9am-6pm Mon-Sat Oct-May); Train station annexe (av Thiers; ☺ 8am-8pm Mon-Sat, 9am-7pm Sun Jun-Sep, 8am-7pm Mon-Sat, 10am-5pm Sun Oct-May).

ORIENTATION

Av Jean Médecin runs south from near the main train station to place Masséna, close to the beach and old town. The bus station is two blocks east of place Masséna.

From the airport, 6km west, promenade des Anglais runs along the curving beachfront (Baie des Anges), becoming quai des États-Unis near the old town. Vieux Nice (Old Nice) is crunched into a 500-sq-metre area enclosed by bd Jean Jaurès, quai des États-Unis and the hill known as Colline du Château.

The wealthy residential neighbourhood of Cimiez, home to some outstanding museums and belle époque architecture, is north of the centre.

ACCOMMODATION

This stretch of coast is fairly compact and well served by public transport so you can easily base yourself in one place and radiate from there for a week or two. Find our full accommodation listings in the accommodation chapter.

★ Self-caterers will love **Nice Pebbles'** (p391) gorgeous boutique flats, many of them right in the centre of Vieux Nice

★ For a romantic stay in the tranquil *arrière-pays,* nothing beats **La Parare** (p392), with its exquisite rooms (each with a fireplace) and rambling Provençal gardens

★ Hip travellers will love the arty **Hôtel Normandy** (p392), a 15-minute walk from the idyllic and very trendy Mala beach, and a mere 10 minutes by bus from glitzy Monaco

★ For superb views, anywhere on the Grande Corniche will do. **Le Roquebrune** (p393) on the Corniche Inférieure, also has plunging views of the Med; brilliantly, each room has its own terrace so that you can make the best of the panorama

NICE, MONACO & MENTON

48 HOURS IN NICE

CULTURE VULTURES

It seems that whatever art you're into, Nice will have it. Architecture buffs shouldn't miss the excellent themed **guided tours** (p200) run by the tourist office and the Centre du Patrimoine: choose from baroque, belle époque or neoclassical. Fans of 20th-century art will be overwhelmed by the sheer amount to see, from dedicated **museums** to **Matisse** (p201) and **Chagall** (p201), to the avant-garde **MAMAC** (p202) featuring works by many local artists. Finish the day with a night tour of the unique **contemporary art** dotted about town along the **tram line** (p203).

GOURMET

Vieux Nice is all about its markets: check out the flower market and fruit and veg stalls on **cours Saleya** (below), sample a portion of *socca* (chickpea flour and olive oil batter fried on a large griddle, served with pepper) with a chilled glass of rosé at **Thérèsa's** stand (p207), and watch the action at the **fish market** (below). Gourmets will love Nice's flurry of **gastronomic shops** (p209), while wine amateurs shouldn't miss the **Bellet vineyards** (p202), one of France's smallest.

STROLLERS' HEAVEN

Nice was made for strolling: not only is it stunning, pedestrians also run the show in the centre: from **Vieux Nice**'s labyrinthine lanes (below) to the glorious and newly pedestrianised **place Masséna** (p201) to the legendary **promenade des Anglais** (p201) on the seafront. For unparalleled views of the Baie des Anges, scale the slopes of **Parc du Château** (p200), before ambling down to the pretty **Port Lympia** (p201).

NICE, MONACO & MENTON

EXPLORING NICE

All museums in the city are free, with the exception of Musée Chagall.

♥ VIEUX NICE // EXPLORE NICE'S THRIVING HISTORICAL AND GOURMET HEART

Nice's old town, a mellow-hued rabbit warren, has scarcely changed since the 1700s. Retracing its history – and therefore that of the city – is a highlight, although you don't need to be a history buff to enjoy a stroll in this atmospheric quarter. Vieux Nice is as alive and prominent today as it ever was. Cue the **cours Saleya**: this joyous, thriving market square hosts a daily **flower, fruit and vegetable market** (☾ 7am-1pm Tue-Sun), a staple of local life. Antiques take over on Mondays, and the spill over from bars and restaurants seems to be a permanent fixture.

Much of Vieux Nice has a similar atmosphere to cours Saleya, with delis, food shops, boutiques and bars crammed in its tiny lanes. Rue de la Boucherie and rue Pairolière are excellent for food shopping. You'll also find a daily **fish market** at place St François.

For a gastronomic tour of Vieux Nice, **Les Petits Farcis** (☎ 06 81 67 41 22; www .petitsfarcis.com) organises Niçois cooking lessons centred on Nice's strong market and street-food tradition. Run by longtime Nice resident Rosa Jackson, courses

NICE

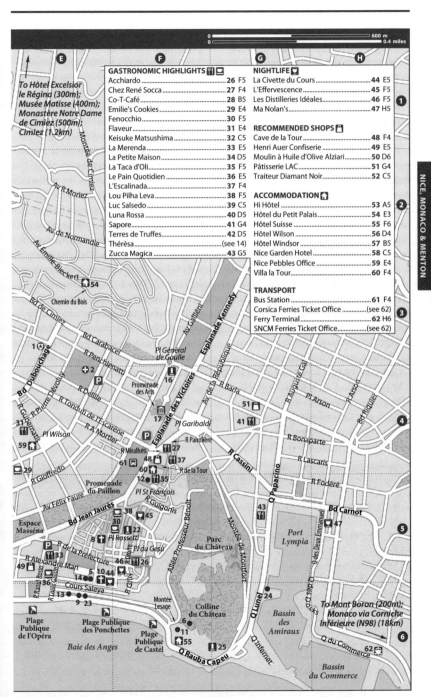

GASTRONOMIC HIGHLIGHTS

Acchiardo	**26** F5
Chez René Socca	**27** F4
Co-T-Café	**28** B5
Emilie's Cookies	**29** E4
Fenocchio	**30** F5
Flaveur	**31** E4
Keisuke Matsushima	**32** C5
La Merenda	**33** E5
La Petite Maison	**34** D5
La Taca d'Oli	**35** F5
Le Pain Quotidien	**36** E5
L'Escalinada	**37** F4
Lou Pilha Leva	**38** F5
Luc Salsedo	**39** C5
Luna Rossa	**40** D5
Sapore	**41** G4
Terres de Truffes	**42** D5
Thérèsa	(see 14)
Zucca Magica	**43** G5

NIGHTLIFE

La Civette du Cours	**44** E5
L'Effervescence	**45** F5
Les Distilleries Idéales	**46** F5
Ma Nolan's	**47** H5

RECOMMENDED SHOPS

Cave de la Tour	**48** F4
Henri Auer Confiserie	**49** E5
Moulin à Huile d'Olive Alziari	**50** D6
Pâtisserie LAC	**51** G4
Traiteur Diamant Noir	**52** C5

ACCOMMODATION

Hi Hôtel	**53** A5
Hôtel du Petit Palais	**54** E3
Hôtel Suisse	**55** F6
Hôtel Wilson	**56** D4
Hôtel Windsor	**57** B5
Nice Garden Hotel	**58** C5
Nice Pebbles Office	**59** E4
Villa la Tour	**60** F4

TRANSPORT

Bus Station	**61** F4
Corsica Ferries Ticket Office	(see 62)
Ferry Terminal	**62** H6
SNCM Ferries Ticket Office	(see 62)

include a market tour, cooking class and lunch (€200); you can add a post-lunch gourmet stroll (€290) to make a day of it. Rosa also runs a Meet the Producers day tour in the surrounding area, where you can visit olive oil or wine producers, tomato or citrus growers, farms etc (€290 including transport and lunch).

Much harder to spot because of the narrow lane it sits on is the baroque **Palais Lascaris** (☎ 04 93 62 05 54; 15 rue Droite; admission free, guided visit €3; ☺ 10am-6pm Wed-Mon, guided visit 3pm Fri), a 17th-century mansion housing a frescoed orgy of Flemish tapestries, *faïence* and gloomy religious paintings. On the ground floor is an 18th-century pharmacy. Baroque aficionados shouldn't miss Nice's other architectural gems such as **Cathédrale Ste-Réparate** (place Rossetti), honouring the city's patron saint or the exuberant **Chapelle de la Miséricorde** (cours Saleya).

The best way to discover this incredibly rich heritage is to take a guided tour. The **Centre du Patrimoine** (☎ 04 92 00 41 90; centre.patrimoine@ville-nice.fr; 75 quai des États Unis; adult/child €5/2.50) runs a two-hour **Vieux Nice Baroque tour** (Tuesday afternoon) while the tourist office runs a 2½-hour **old town tour** in English (adult/child €12/6), departing from the beachfront office at 9.30am on Saturday. The Centre du Patrimoine also runs tours on other themes including art deco, neoclassical and belle époque Nice.

♥ PARC DU CHÂTEAU & PORT LYMPIA // VIEW NICE FROM A DIFFERENT PERSPECTIVE

Vieux Nice's eastern extremity is flanked by **Parc du Château** (Castle Park; ☺ 8am-8pm Jun-Aug, to 7pm Apr, May & Sep, to 6pm Oct-Mar), a towering 92m-high rock offering a cinematic panorama of Nice and the Baie des Anges on one side, and the port on the other. The 12th-century castle was razed by Louis XIV in 1706; only the 16th-century **Tour Bellanda** remains.

The park is fabulous for picnics. Its other simple attractions include **Cascade Donjon**, an 18th-century artificial waterfall crowned with a viewing platform, and kids' playgrounds.

To get here, ride the **Château Lift** (Ascenseur du Château; rue des Ponchettes; single/return €0.90/1.20; ☺ 9am-8pm Jun-Aug, 9am-7pm Apr, May & Sep, 10am-6pm Oct-Mar) from beneath Tour Bellanda, or hike up the staircases on

---

SIGHT SAVINGS

All museums in Nice are free, with the exception of the Chagall Museum. There are still plenty of attractions that you have to pay for however, in Nice and along the Riviera. The **Nice Riviera Pass** (www.frenchrivierapass.com) includes access to a number of these sights and costs €24/36/54 for a one-/two-/three-day pass.

Sights included are, in Nice, the Chagall Museum, Nice Le Grand Tour bus, the Cathédrale Orthodoxe Russe St Nicolas and tourist office or Centre du Patrimoine guided tours (see above); along the coast, the Musée Renoir in Cagnes (p254), the Musée National Fernand Léger in Biot (p254), the Jardin d'Èze (p216), the Jardin Exotique in Monaco (p224), and even the Marineland in Antibes (p251) for the three-day pass.

The pass also includes discounts at local restaurants and shops. It is worth buying if you plan to visit most of the above sights. It is available online or at the Nice tourist office (p196).

montée Lesage or the eastern end of rue Rossetti in Vieux Nice. From the port, follow montée Montfort.

Nice's **Port Lympia**, with its beautiful Venetian-coloured buildings, is often overlooked, but a stroll along its quays is lovely, as is the walk to get here: come down through the **Colline du Château** or follow **quai Rauba Capeu**, the atmospheric headland at the end of the promenade where a massive **war memorial** hewn from the rock commemorates the 4000 Niçois who died in both world wars.

♥ PROMENADE DES ANGLAIS & PLACE MASSÉNA // REVEL IN NICE'S GLORIOUS ARCHITECTURE AND NATURAL SETTING

Palm-lined promenade des Anglais, paid for by Nice's English colony in 1822, is a fine stage for a stroll. It's particularly atmospheric in the evening, with Niçois milling about and epic sunsets over the sea. Don't miss the magnificent facade of **Hôtel Negresco**, built in 1912 for Romanian innkeeper Henri Negresco, or art deco **Palais de la Méditerranée**, saved from demolition in the 1980s and now part of a four-star palace.

The promenade follows the whole Baie des Anges (4km) and has a cycle and skating lane. For a fantastic family outing, rent skates or scooters at **Roller Station** (☎ 04 93 62 99 05; www.roller-station.com; 40 quai des États-Unis; skate per hr/half-day €4/6, scooter €3/6; ☼ 9.30am-8pm Apr-Sep, 10am-6.30pm Oct-Mar) and whizz along the Prom. You'll need some ID as a deposit. Rentals include protective gear (helmet and pads).

A block back from the Promenade, behind the Jardin Albert 1er and opposite beautiful fountains sits the grand **place Masséna**, with early-19th-century, neoclassical arcaded buildings painted in Tuscan shades of red. Now largely pedestrian, following the completion of the tram line, it's an atmospheric square.

♥ CIMIEZ // RETRACE MATISSE'S STEPS

Located about 2km north of the centre in the leafy quarter of Cimiez, the **Musée Matisse** (Matisse Museum; ☎ 04 93 81 08 08; www.musee-matisse-nice.org; 164 av des Arènes de Cimiez; ☼ 10am-6pm Wed-Mon) houses a fascinating assortment of works by Matisse (p36) documenting the artist's stylistic evolution. Its permanent collection is displayed in a red-ochre 17th-century Genoese villa overlooking the olive-tree-studded **Parc des Arènes**. Temporary exhibitions are hosted in the futuristic basement building.

Matisse lived nearby in the 1940s, in the monumental **Régina** building at 71 bd de Cimiez. Originally Queen Victoria's wintering palace, it had been converted and Matisse had two apartments that he used as his home and studio. He died there in 1954.

The artist is buried in the cemetery of the **Monastère Notre Dame de Cimiez** (☎ 04 93 81 00 04; ☼ 8.30am-12.30pm & 2.30-6.30pm), which adjoins the **Église Notre Dame**. His grave is signposted *'sépulture Henri Matisse'* from the cemetery's main entrance (next to the monastery church on av Bellanda). Raoul Dufy is also buried here. There are towering views from the delightful **Jardin du Monastère**, which surrounds the buildings.

Take bus 15 or 22 from the bus station to the Arènes stop.

♥ CHAGALL MUSEUM // PONDER THE SPIRITUAL MESSAGE IN CHAGALL'S WORK

The small **Musée National Message Biblique Marc Chagall** (Marc Chagall Biblical Message Museum; ☎ 04 93 53 87 20; www.musee-chagall.fr; 4 av Docteur Ménard; adult/child €6.50/

free, plus €2 for temporary exhibitions; 10am-6pm Wed-Mon May-Oct, to 5pm Nov-Apr) houses the largest public collection of works by Belarusian painter Marc Chagall (1887–1985).

The main hall contains 12 huge interpretations (1954–67) of stories from Genesis and Exodus. In an antechamber, an unusual mosaic of Elijah in his fiery chariot, surrounded by signs of the zodiac, is viewed through a plate-glass window and reflected in a small pond.

Take bus 15 or 22 to the Musée Chagall stop, or walk (signposted from av de l'Olivetto).

🌿 MODERN ART IN NICE //
EXPLORE THE CITY'S SPECIAL
RELATIONSHIP WITH MODERN
ART
European and American avant-garde works from the 1950s to the present are the focus of Nice's **Musée d'Art Moderne et d'Art Contemporain** (MAMAC; Museum of Modern & Contemporary Art; ☎ 04 97 13 42 01; www.mamac-nice.org; promenade des Arts; 10am-6pm Tue-Sun). Highlights among the permanent 2nd- and 3rd-floor exhibits include items wrapped by Christo; a red model-T Ford crunched into a 1.6m-tall block by Marseillais sculptor César; and the mundane objects (rubbish, letters, children's toys) encased in Perspex containers by Nice-born Arman. Temporary exhibitions fill the ground and 1st floors, and atop the building, humpbacked wooden bridges connect the four marble towers, crowned with a rooftop garden and gallery featuring pieces by city son Yves Klein (see also p331).

East of the museum is the giant square head of **La Tête Carrée** (2002). The massive 30m-tall sculpture designed by Sacha Sosno is, in fact, a building (the

---

∼ WORTH A TRIP ∼

High in the hills northwest of Nice is one of France's smallest vineyards, **Bellet** (www.vinsde bellet.com). The appellation dates back to 1941 but vines have been grown in the area for more than 2000 years. Bellet wines are now very sought after, but because of the tiny size of the vineyard – there are just 15 producers – you'll only find them in a few select restaurants (luckily, a number are in Nice) and rarely in wine shops.

Whites use Rolle grapes, a typical Nice variety, while reds and rosés rely on Folle Noire ('crazy black', so named because of its erratic yields) and Grenache. Because of the terrain (small terraces called *restanque*), the vintage is done by hand.

The only domaine (estate) that is regularly open to the public is **Château de Crémat** (☎ 04 92 15 12 15; www.chateau-cremat.com; 442 chemin de Crémat; Mon-Sat 9am-12.30pm & 1.30-5.30pm) 9km from the centre of Nice. It organises one-hour **tours** (per person €15, minimum 4 people; Mon-Fri, booking required) of its vineyard, cellars and sprawling estate with a tasting at the end (white, red and rosé). Visitors can also turn up for **tastings** (€5; deductible from purchases) during opening hours.

Twice a year, Bellet producers hold an open-door weekend when visitors can freely wander the vineyards, talk to winemakers and taste wines from each domaine. The tourist office in Nice has details.

To get to the vineyard, head north along rte de Grenoble (D6202). The vineyard is signposted (brown signs) just before you get to Nice St-Isidore.

offices of the city's public library are inside).

Building on its long artistic tradition, the city of Nice decided to integrate **art with the tram** (www.tramway-nice.org, in French) and commissioned a number of renowned artists to add their touch to the project (the tram was launched in November 2007). As well Jaume Plensa's glow-in-the-dark *Conversation* on place Masséna, there are 13 more works to discover along the way, including original sound bites at each stop, the calligraphy of the tram's stops by Niçois artist Ben and more visual works. The best way to appreciate this artistic input is to take the tourist office's two-hour **Art dans la Ville guided tour** (adult/child €8/3, plus €2 for transport; ☺ tours 7pm Fri), which travels along the tram track to visit all 14 works. The tour is in French and English.

♥ NICE & THE BELLE ÉPOQUE // STEP BACK IN TIME TO NICE'S WINTERING HEYDAY

Nice retains a number of stunning belle époque buildings from its wintering days. And what better place to find out about this illustrious history than the beautiful **Musée Masséna** (☎ 04 93 91 19 10; 65 rue de France; ☺ 10am-6pm Wed-Mon), housed in a marvellous Italianate neoclassical villa (1898). The museum explores the city and Riviera history from the early 19th century to WWII. It's a fascinating journey, with a roll call of monarchs, a succession of nationalities (British, Russians, Americans), the advent of tourism, the prominence of the carnival and much more. History is told through an excellent mix of furniture, objects, art deco posters, early photographs and paintings and the lovely setting – the city of Nice still uses the ground floor rooms for official occasions.

BUS TOURS

If you're struggling to fit everything Nice has to offer into your schedule, you might find the open-topped double-decker bus **Nice Le Grand Tour** (☎ 04 92 29 17 00; www.nicelegrandtour.com; 1-day pass adult/child €20/5) a godsend. Buses go round the port, up to Cimiez, and along promenade des Anglais. Hop on or off at any one of 14 stops, including the Cathédrale Orthodoxe Russe St Nicolas, the Chagall Museum, place Garibaldi and the train station. Commentaries are available in seven languages. Drivers and tourist offices sell passes.

Another distinctive piece of belle époque history is the **Cathédrale Orthodoxe Russe St Nicolas** (☎ 04 93 96 88 02; av Nicolas II; admission €3; ☺ 9am-noon & 2.30-6pm Mon-Sat, 2.30-6pm Sun May-Sep, to 5.30pm Oct & mid-Feb–Apr, 9.30am-noon & 2-5pm Nov–mid-Feb). Built between 1902 and 1912 to provide a big enough church for the growing Russian community, the cathedral, with its colourful onion domes and rich, ornate interior, is the biggest Russian Orthodox church outside Russia. Shorts, miniskirts and sleeveless shirts are forbidden.

♥ BEACHES & BOATS // MAKE THE BEST OF THE AZURE WATERS

Nice's beaches are all pebbly; sensitive behinds should therefore opt for a comfy mattress at one of its 14 **private beaches** (per day €15-20; ☺ Apr-May). Out of the free **public sections of beach** (with lifeguards, first-aid posts and cold showers), **Plage Publique des Ponchettes**, opposite Vieux Nice, is the most popular.

To escape the crowds, take a scenic cruise along the coast with **Trans Côte d'Azur** (☎ 04 92 00 42 30; www.trans-cote-azur.com; quai Lunel; ☺ Mar-Oct). The company

NICE, MONACO & MENTON

MICHELIN-STARRED COOKING LESSONS

What better way to learn how to cook than from the very best? **La Recette Magique** (The Magic Recipe; www.larecettemagique.com; 3hr lesson plus by 3-course meal incl wine €100-250) runs themed, seasonal cooking classes with local Michelin-starred chefs such as a spring class on asparagus and morels, an Easter chocolate special, a Valentine's macaroon class or a more traditional, seasonal three-course meal preparation. Among La Recette Magique's chefs are Alex Wagner (Château Eza in Èze Village; p217), Yannick Fauries (Le Paris-Rome in Menton; p233), Christophe Dufau (Les Bacchanales in Vence; p256) and Pascal Lac (LAC in Nice; p209).

Courses take place in the restaurant itself, and each chef has a different approach: some are very hands on, others are generous with tips and advice. No matter who you work with, you're guaranteed to have a good time and you'll go home with a bound copy of the day's recipes, a very full tummy (you'll eat what you've prepared, accompanied by some fine wine), a funky apron and the course organiser will email you pictures. Most chefs speak English, as does the Recette Magique organiser, who attends all courses.

runs daily (except Monday) one-hour trips along the Baie des Anges and the Rade de Villefranche (adult/child €15/9) from May to October (four times a week in March and April). From mid-June to mid-September it also runs weekly excursions to Île Ste-Marguerite (€32/23, crossing one hour), St-Tropez (€53/40, crossing 2½ hours) and Monaco (€30/22, crossing 45 minutes). Reservations are essential.

FESTIVALS & EVENTS

Carnaval de Nice (Nice Carnival; www.nicecarnaval.com) Held each year around Mardi Gras (Shrove Tuesday) since 1294 – highlights include the *batailles de fleurs* (battles of flowers), and the ceremonial burning of the carnival king on promenade des Anglais, followed by an enormous fireworks display; February

Nice Jazz Festival (www.nicejazzfestival.fr) France's original jazz festival, in the beautiful outdoor setting of Cimiez's Arènes gardens; July

Les Nuits Musicales de Nice Classical music concerts in the cloister of the Monastère Notre-Dame de Cimiez; August

GASTRONOMIC HIGHLIGHTS

Foodies will love Nice: there are dozens of excellent restaurants catering to all budgets and tastes. Vieux Nice and the Prom have the usual mix of hidden gems and tourist traps.

🍃 ACCHIARDO €

☎ 04 93 85 51 16; 38 rue Droite; mains €8-15; ☺ lunch & dinner Mon-Fri

This Nice institution is beloved by all who come here: locals stop by to gossip and sip a glass of red or rosé (€1.80) by the counter while visitors wolf down classics such as lamb cutlets and French beans, a juicy steak with pepper sauce and home-made *frites* (French fries) or good ol' beef ravioli. The atmosphere is gregarious and the service very friendly; it's often full but the turnover is swift so you're generally in with a chance to get a table.

🍃 CO-T-CAFÉ €

☎ 04 93 16 09 84; 11bis rue Meyerbeer; salads €6.50; ☺ 8am-6pm

With its tiny terrace and funky coloured chairs, this small café in Nice's shopping district packs a punch. Counters groan with hearty salads topped with marinated chicken and salmon, tasty-looking wraps and beautifully presented fruit salads with yoghurt and granola, all going for about €6. And since you're just a couple of blocks from the promenade, Co-T-Café is the perfect takeaway for lunch on the beach.

❤ EMILIE'S COOKIES €

☎ 04 93 13 89 58; 9 rue Alberti; cookies from €1.80, sandwiches & salads around €5; ⏰ 8am-6.30pm Mon-Fri, from 9am Sat

As the name suggests, Emilie does a mean cookie (we like the 'intelligent cookie' with Smarties and the 'space cookie' with Mars bar). But not only: there are also muffins, cheesecakes, fabulous bagels, gorgeous salads (top pick is the Vespa with Parma ham, sundried tomatoes, artichokes, goats' cheese, pine kernels and olives) and great coffee to savour throughout the day. Take it away on your city ventures or enjoy in one of the comfy armchairs in the café.

❤ FENOCCHIO €

☎ 04 93 80 72 52; 2 place Rossetti; 1-/2-/3-scoop cone €2.20/3.70/4.80; ⏰ 9am-midnight Feb-Oct

Dither too long over the 70-plus flavours of ice cream and sorbet at this unforgettable *glacier* (ice-cream shop) and you'll never make it to the front of the queue. Eschew predictable favourites and indulge in a new taste sensation: black olive, tomato-basil, rhubarb, avocado, rosemary, *calisson* (almond biscuit frosted with icing sugar), lavender, ginger or liquorice.

❤ FLAVEUR €€

☎ 04 93 62 53 95; 25 rue Gubernatis; lunch/dinner menu from €15/30, mains €20-28; ⏰ lunch & dinner Tue-Fri, dinner Sat

Flaveur in French refers to the combined sensation of both taste and smell. The brainchild of a young team of three (two chefs and a sommelier), this new restaurant strives to take customers on a culinary journey. Dishes are innovative and work the fusion niche, with particularly surprising desserts (candied grapefruit with pistachio cake and grapefruit sorbet). Enjoy it in the funky dining room with candlelit tables, original prints on the chairs and modern wooden sculptures.

❤ KEISUKE MATSUSHIMA €€€

☎ 04 93 82 26 06; 22ter rue de France; lunch/dinner menu from €35/50; ⏰ lunch & dinner Tue-Sat, dinner Mon

Japanese hotshot Keisuke Matsushima, alias Kei, makes heads turn at a minimalist space dedicated to his trademark cuisine: Mediterranean (lots of Italian influence in there) with a subtle dash of the Orient (braised pork with honey, Szechuan pepper and ginger, or chocolate and banana dome with banana sorbet). The presentation is a work of art and the content of the cellar is as stellar as the food (and exclusively French).

❤ LA MERENDA €€

4 rue Raoul Bosio; mains €14; ⏰ lunch & dinner Mon-Fri

Simple, solid Niçois cuisine by former Michelin-starred chef Dominique Le Stanc draws the crowds to this pocket-sized bistro (you'll be rubbing back and shoulders with fellow customers). The tiny open kitchen stands proud at the back of the room, and the equally small menu is chalked on the board. Quintessential dishes to try include *tripes à la Niçoise* (tripe) with *panisse* (potato-sized chunks of fried chickpea) and stockfish (dried-cod stew with aniseed). No credit cards.

☙ LA PETITE MAISON €€€

☎ 04 93 92 59 59; 11 rue St-François de Paule; mains €30; ☽ lunch & dinner Mon-Sat

A sterling reputation props up this ode to contemporary Niçois cuisine, framed in a stylish clean-cut interior with concrete floor, potted olive trees, crisp white tablecloths and art on the walls. Whet your appetite with a shared plate of seven Niçois starters (€20, purple artichokes, *petits farcis*, Nice olive tapenade etc), followed by the house signature *loup en croûte de sel* (seabass in salt crust) or a decadent portion of grilled blue lobster.

☙ LA TACA D'OLI €€

☎ 04 93 80 70 93; 35 rue Pairolière; menu €24, mains €17; ☽ lunch & dinner Fri-Tue

The owner is economical with words but his cuisine speaks volumes: try the *bagna cauda* (raw mixed veg dipped into a pot of warm tangy anchovy paste known as *anchoïade*) or the *bagna pan* (raw red mullet and sea bream fillets dipped in hot fish soup), the house speciality for nearly 20 years. Any of the dishes featuring on the menu (homemade gnocchi, fish kebabs etc) will see you right though. The trademark here is freshness and great value for money, hence its undying popularity.

☙ LE PAIN QUOTIDIEN €

☎ 04 93 62 94 32; 3 rue Louis Gassin; breakfast €6-8, salads €10-15, tartines €6-8.50; ☽ 7am-7pm

Choose between six different breakfast formulas (with cereals, yoghurts, cereal breads, pastries, and a self-service jam bar that includes two chocolate spreads, milk and dark), lavishly topped lunchtime *tartines* (toasted bread) or sinful pastries (including waffles topped with chocolate from the chocolate fountain) at this popular café near cours Saleya.

Sit on solid, dining room–sized wooden tables inside or on the street terrace.

☙ L'ESCALINADA €€

☎ 04 93 62 11 71; 22 rue Pairolière; menu €23, mains €17; ☽ lunch & dinner daily mid-Dec–mid-Nov

This enchanting old-town *auberge* (inn) has been one of the best places in town for Mediterranean favourites for the last half-century: melt-in-your-mouth homemade gnocchi with tasty *daube* (Provençal beef stew), grilled prawns with garlic and herbs, Marsala veal stew, and for gastronomic adventurers, breaded sheep testicles. The staff are delightful and the welcome kir is on the house; get in early (or late) for a table on the candle-lit street-side terrace. No credit cards.

☙ LUC SALSEDO €€€

☎ 04 93 82 24 12; 14 rue Maccarani; lunch/dinner menu from €26/44 ☽ lunch Fri & Sun-Tue, dinner Thu-Tue Sep-Jun, dinner Jul & Aug

The cuisine of Salsedo, another relatively young chef who's built a fine reputation, is local and seasonal. His menu (which, unusually, caters well for vegetarians) changes every 10 days to reflect the mood of the market stalls. The food is delightful and served without pomp on plates, rustic boards or authentic cast-iron pots. The wine list is another hit, with an all French cast from white to red and rosé.

☙ LUNA ROSSA €€

☎ 04 93 85 55 66; 3 rue Chauvain; mains €15-25; ☽ lunch & dinner Tue-Fri, dinner Sat

Luna Rossa is like your dream Mediterranean dinner come true: fresh pasta, exquisitely cooked seafood (pan-fried John Dory, grilled sea bass, sautéd king prawns), sun-kissed vegetables (artichoke hearts, sun-dried tomatoes, asparagus tips etc) and divine meats (beef carpaccio with truffle and parmesan shavings). Try the Poêlée Luna Rossa, a seafood stir-fry served in garlic, basil and fresh linguine, served in a cast-iron pan; it is simply divine. And wash it down with one of the excellent bottles of red or rosé from the cellar.

☙ SAPORE €€

☎ 04 92 04 22 09; 19 rue Bonaparte; menu €30; ☾ dinner Tue-Sat

Inquisitive gourmets will love this place: the menu is a fixed eight-course meal of bite-size dishes, each a riot of taste inspired by the chef's culinary travels and the season's products (think pea soup, aïoli, beef and foie gras sauce, passionfruit zabaglione with banana). A hip, discerning crowd nibbles on these modern tapas in the stylish dining room featuring stone walls, wooden beams and ambient coloured lighting. Don't forget to book if you'd like to join them.

☙ TERRES DE TRUFFES €€€

☎ 04 93 62 07 68; 11 rue St-François de Paule; menu from €48; ☾ lunch & dinner Mon-Sat

Bruno Clément is the name behind this exclusive deli-bistro where the much-acclaimed truffle chef prepares the region's famous fungi in every imaginable form. How does goats' cheese roasted in truffle honey, followed by leg of lamb with truffles sound? And make sure you leave space for the cheesecake with its fruit compote and truffle caramel. The deli also sells some of Clément's star products (truffle olive oil, truffle foie gras etc).

☙ ZUCCA MAGICA €€

☎ 04 93 56 25 27; 4bis quai Papacino; menu €29; ☾ lunch & dinner Tue-Sat; Ⓥ

You'll either love it or you'll hate it…the idea of someone else deciding what you eat. Bursting with vegetarian surprises and guaranteed to thrill, the 'Magic Pumpkin' is the work of top Italian chef Marco Folicardi, and the only one of its kind on the Riviera. Dinner is a fixed

NICE, MONACO & MENTON

NIÇOIS NIBBLES

Perfect for filling a hungry moment coming from the beach (or any time of day) are a bunch of battered local specialities, especially common in Vieux Nice where **Chez René Socca** (☎ 04 93 92 05 73; 2 rue Miralhéti; ☾ Tue-Sun 9am-9pm, to 10.30pm Jul & Aug) and **Lou Pilha Leva** (☎ 04 93 13 99 08; place Centrale; ☾ 8am-midnight or 1am) dole them out to a merrily munching, family-friendly, fun-loving crowd packed around shared bench seating on the street. Order drinks separately from a passing drinks waiter.

Take your pick while standing in the cacophonous queue. A portion of *beignets d'aubergines* or *beignets de courgettes* (battered aubergine or courgette slices) sets you back between €2 and €6, as do *beignets de sardines* (battered sardines) – a guaranteed taste of the sea. *Petits farcis* (stuffed vegetables), *pissaladière* (traditional onion tart topped with black olives and anchovies), and *salade niçoise* (green salad with boiled egg, tuna and anchovy) are other must-haves.

Essential tasting for every visiting palate is *socca,* a savoury, griddle-fried pancake made from chickpea flour and olive oil, sprinkled with a liberal dose of black pepper. The *socca* cooked up by the flamboyant **Thérèsa** (cours Saleya market; socca €3; ☾ 8am-1pm Tue-Sun) at her market stall with plastic tables beneath the awning is legendary. Order a glass of rosé to have with it.

five-course menu, dictated simply by the market and *la fantasie du chef*. Seating is amid a fabulous collection of pumpkins and fairy lights. Bring along a gargantuan appetite.

NIGHTLIFE

Any of the café-terraces on cours Saleya are lovely for an early evening *apéritif*. Vieux Nice's bounty of pubs attracts a noisy, boisterous crowd but there are plenty of more sophisticated or low-key establishments too.

❦ LA CIVETTE DU COURS

☎ 04 93 80 80 59; 1 cours Saleya; ☺ 8am-1am

Sprawling across cours Saleya, La Civette is *the* place to hang out if you're cool, regardless of age – it's all about aspiration here! Dark shades nurse a hangover with a cappuccino in the morning sun, locals kick back with a pre-lunch *pastis* and a portion of *socca* (chick pea flour pancake, a typical Niçois snack) at weekends and friends come here in the evenings for a kir or a beer.

❦ L'EFFERVESCENCE

☎ 04 93 80 87 37; 10 rue de la Loge; ☺ 6pm-midnight Tue-Sat

If you love a glass of bubbly and the sound of popping corks, L'Effervescence is for you. This Champagne bar offers all the big names (Bollinger, Ruinart, Bruno Paillart etc) as well as vintages from the Loire valley, Spain and Italy. They're all available by the glass or bottle (or magnums). Make it a night with some of the bar's delicious (and very filling) nibbles. The €49 'formule couple' includes half a bottle of Champagne, six savoury nibbles, two plates of either sushi, foie gras, smoked fish or cheese and six dessert nibbles. Happy hour is from 6.30pm to 7.30pm.

❦ LES DISTILLERIES IDÉALES

☎ 04 93 62 10 66; 24 rue de la Préfecture; ☺ 9am-12.30am

Whether you're after an espresso on your way to the cours Saleya market or an *apéritif* (complete with cheese and charcuterie platters, €4.90) before trying out one of Nice's fabulous restaurants, Les Distilleries, in the heart of Vieux Nice, is one of the most atmospheric bars in town. Tables on the small street terrace are ideal for watching the world go by. Happy hour is from 6pm to 8pm.

❦ MA NOLAN'S

☎ 04 93 80 23 87; 5 quai des Deux Emmanuel; ☺ noon-midnight Mon-Fri, 11am-midnight Sat & Sun

This Irish pub made its name with its cours Saleya establishment – it is now *the* pub of reference for all foreigners in town. With live music, big sport events and pub grub (sausage and mash, English breakfast etc), it's a pretty rowdy place. The new Ma Nolan's by the port has a more relaxed feel and the terrace is the perfect place to enjoy a pint in the sun. It also hosts regular live music sessions. Happy hour is from 6pm to 8pm.

TRANSPORT

TO/FROM THE AIRPORT

BUS // Buses 98 and 99 link Nice Gare Routière and Nice train station respectively with both terminals of Nice-Côte d'Azur airport (€4, 30 minutes, every 20 minutes). Bus 110 (€18, hourly) links the airport with Monaco (40 minutes) and Menton (one hour). Bus 210 goes to Cannes (€14.70, 50 minutes, half-hourly).
CAR // The airport is 6km west of the city centre on the seafront.

GETTING AROUND

Buses and trams in Nice are run by **Ligne d'Azur** (www.lignedazur.com). Tickets cost just €1 and include one connection, including intercity buses within the Alpes-Maritimes *département*. A new tram line linking place Masséna with the airport along promenade des Anglais is planned for 2012.

TRAM // Nice's sleek new tram is great for getting across town, particularly from the train station to Vieux Nice and the bus station. Trams run from 4.30am to 1.30am.

WALKING // The centre is quite spread out but because of the traffic, walking is definitely the easiest, and nicest, way to get around.

BUS // For areas beyond the station–Masséna–Vieux Nice triangle within Nice, the bus is the way forward. Night buses run from around 9pm until 2am.

GETTING THERE & AWAY

AIR // Nice-Côte d'Azur airport (NCE; ☎ 08 20 42 33 33; www.nice-aeroport.fr) is France's second airport and has numerous international flights to Europe, North Africa and even the US with regular as well as low-cost companies. The airport has two terminals (1 and 2), linked by a free shuttle.

BUS // TAM (www.randoxygene.fr/transport/trans ports-tam.html) runs excellent intercity services. Bus 100 goes to Menton (1½ hours) via Monaco (40 minutes) and the Corniche Inférieure, bus 200 goes to Cannes (1½ hours), bus 400 to Vence (1¼ hours) via St-Paul de Vence (one hour), bus 500 to Grasse (1½ hours). There are also services to Haute-Provence villages such as ski resort Isola 2000 (buses 740 and 750). All journeys cost €1.

TRAIN // From Nice Ville station, there are services to Monaco (€3.30, 25 minutes), Menton (€4.40, 35 minutes), Cannes (€5.80, 30 minutes), every 20 minutes or so. Trains to Grasse (€8.40, one hour), St-Raphaël (€10.30, 1¼ hours) and Marseille (€31.50, 2½ hours) leave hourly. The mountain railway operated by **Chemins de Fer de Provence** (www .trainprovence.com) takes the scenic route to Digne from Nice's Gare du Sud.

CAR // Driving in Nice is a pain. It is often slow, and the one-way system can be difficult to navigate for visitors. The A8 motorway skirts the northern edge of the city.

PARKING // Parking in Nice is maddening. If you don't want to drive around the block for an hour, opt for one of the many underground car parks instead.

FERRY // Nice is the main port for ferries to Corsica. **SNCM** (www.sncm.fr) and **Corsica Ferries** (www.corsica-ferries.fr) are the two main companies.

ARRIÈRE-PAYS NIÇOIS

You'd never believe you're just 20km from Nice. This little-known corner of the Côte d'Azur is so quiet and unaffected by tourism that Niçois themselves come here to spend a weekend away from the urban rush.

NICE, MONACO & MENTON

TOP FIVE

GASTRONOMIC SHOPS IN NICE

★ Crystallised fruit based on family recipes dating back to 1820 from **Henri Auer Confiserie** (☎ 04 93 85 77 98; www.maison-auer.com; 7 rue St-François de Paule)

★ Olive oil fresh from the mill at **Moulin à Huile d'Olive Alziari** (☎ 04 93 62 94 03; www .alziari.com.fr; 14 rue St-François de Paule); from €17 per litre for extra virgin

★ Benjamin Bruno's truffle creations make for a very gourmet take-away from **Traiteur Diamant Noir** (☎ 04 93 89 69 60; www.diamantnoir.fr; 22 rue Maréchal Joffre)

★ Wine from *cavistes* (cellarmen) who know what they're talking about: **Cave de la Tour** (☎ 04 93 80 03 31; 3 rue de la Tour), run by the same family since 1947

★ Decadent cakes and chocolates from chef patissier Pascal Lac at his mouth-watering **Pâtisserie LAC** (☎ 04 93 55 37 74; 18 rue Barla)

Attractions are pretty low-key: a walk in the hills, a stroll in isolated perched villages or a long lunch in an excellent restaurant.

🌱 CHÂTEAUNEUF-VILLEVIEILLE // ROAM ANCIENT RUINS IN STUNNING SCENERY

It's not the actual village so much as the **ruins** of the former medieval village that are worth the detour. Find them at the top of a hill near Col de Châteauneuf, about 1.5km from Châteauneuf-Villevieille in the direction of Tourrette-Levens on the D815.

The ruins are pretty overgrown but extensive and in the most incredible location: perched on a rock, with **panoramic views** of the surrounding valleys and hills, the sea at one end and the snowy peaks of the Alps at the other. You can wander freely; there are also a number of **walking trails** in the area. The Guides Randoxygène *Rando Pays Côtier* has a **three-hour walk** around Crête du Mont Macaron starting from the ruins.

To access the site, you can either park at the *col* (mountain pass; there is a car park) and follow the signs up the hill (about 20 minutes' walk) or drive directly to the ruins along a narrow road. The fields near the ruins are wonderful for picnics.

🌱 AUBERGE DE LA MADONE // FINE DINING IN SPLENDID PEILLON

At the foot of the spectacular hilltop village of **Peillon** is this superb gastronomic **restaurant** (☎ 04 93 79 91 17; Peillon village; lunch menu €32, dinner menus €49 & €62; 🕑 lunch & dinner Thu-Tue Feb-Oct) that draws diners from far and wide. In the grand Provençal dining room in winter or on the panoramic terrace in summer, father and son chef

duo Christian and Thomas Millo serve a divine Provençal cuisine, a refined mix of traditional staples with a dash of modernity (Swiss Chard tart with fresh herbs, cod fillet in spice crust, Muscat pan-fried strawberries with an almond biscuit and strawberry sorbet). There are some fine wines on offer too.

Take a leisurely digestive stroll around the village – its *nid d'aigle* (eagle's nest) location is quite dramatic. The more energetic can opt for longer walks; the Guides Randoxygène *Rando Pays Côtier* has suggestions.

🌱 CONTES & COARAZE // EXPLORE INTACT PERCHED VILLAGES

There is not an art gallery, souvenir shop or café in sight in Coaraze. The silence here is deafening.

The village's main 'attractions' are its six modern **sundials**, including one by Jean Cocteau. They don't exactly draw crowds of tourists though, so you can look forward to a quiet, contemplative wander in a maze of 11th-century lanes.

The area is well known for **walking**. The Guides Randoxygène *Moyen Pays* has itineraries nearby.

If the walks have whetted your appetite, the nearest, and thankfully, excellent restaurant is **Fleur de Thym** (☎ 04 93 79 47 33; 3 av Charles Alunni, Contes; lunch/dinner/seasonal menu €18/29/46, mains €18-26; 🕑 lunch & dinner Thu-Mon, lunch Tue). Don't be put off by the neighbouring petrol station and garage: the talented young chef cooks up a punchy, great-value cuisine. Lunch features the *bœuf du jour* (beef of the day) and dinner is as good *à la carte* (duck cooked with cherries and polenta, panfried cod with chorizo and tomatoes) or themed (a fixed, four-course menu based on foie gras in winter, morels in spring, truffle in summer and lobster in the autumn).

The village of **Contes** itself is not as pretty as Coaraze but its location, clinging to a rocky outcrop, is spectacular.

THE THREE CORNICHES

· · · · · ·

Three parallel roads offering unparalleled views link Nice and Menton, passing quaint perched villages, epic monuments and the principality of Monaco on the way. The Corniche Inférieure (aka Basse Corniche, the Lower Corniche and the N98) sticks closely to the nearby train line and villa-lined waterfront. The Moyenne Corniche (the N7) is the middle road, clinging to the hillside and affording great views if you can find somewhere to pull over. The Grande Corniche leaves Nice as the D2564 and is the most breathtaking.

TRANSPORT

CAR // The Corniche Inférieure is very scenic; traffic can be heavy at rush hour (7.30am to 9.30am and 4pm to 7pm).

BUS // Bus 100 (every 15 minutes between 6am and 8pm) runs the length of the Corniche Inférieure between Nice and Menton, stopping at all the villages along the way, including Villefranche-sur-Mer (15 minutes), Beaulieu-sur-Mer (20 minutes), Cap d'Ail (35 minutes) and Cap Martin (1¼ hours). Bus 81 serves Villefranche (20 minutes) and St-Jean-Cap Ferrat (30 minutes).

TRAIN // Nice–Ventimiglia (Italy) trains (every 15 to 30 minutes, 5am to midnight) stop at Villefranche-sur-Mer (€1.50, seven minutes), Beaulieu-sur-Mer (€1.80, 10 minutes), Cap d'Ail (€2.80, 18 minutes) and Roquebrune-Cap Martin (€3.90, 30 minutes).

CORNICHE INFÉRIEURE

Heading east from Nice to Menton, the Corniche Inférieure, built in the 1860s, passes through the towns of Villefranche-sur-Mer, St-Jean-Cap Ferrat, Beaulieu-sur-Mer, Èze-sur-Mer, Cap d'Ail and Roquebrune-Cap Martin.

VILLEFRANCHE-SUR-MER

pop 6610

Heaped above a postcard–perfect harbour, this picturesque village overlooks the Cap Ferrat peninsula and, with its ultradeep *rade* (harbour), is a prime port of call for *Titanic*-sized cruise ships (Nice harbour isn't deep enough for the biggest cruise liners so they moor here and passengers get ferried to/from Nice in smaller boats).

♥ THE MEDIEVAL TOWN // GET FAMILIAR WITH VILLEFRANCHE'S DEFENSIVE PAST

Villefranche's 14th-century old town with its tiny, evocatively named streets, broken by twisting staircases and glimpses of the sea, is reason enough to visit. Don't miss eerie arcaded **rue Obscure**, a historical monument a block in from the water.

The imposing citadel **Fort St-Elme** (place Emmanuel Philibert) was built by the duke of Savoy between 1554 and 1559 to defend the gulf. Nowadays the walls shelter a scattering of cultural doodahs, including the town hall, some well-combed public gardens and a clutch of museum collections: the **Musée Volti** (☎ 04 93 76 33 27; admission free; ⊗ 9am-noon & 2.30-7pm Mon & Wed-Sat, 2.30-7pm Sun Jul & Aug, to 6pm Mon & Wed-Sat Jun & Sep) displays voluptuous bronzes by Villefranche sculptor Antoniucci Volti (1915–89).

A coastal path runs around the citadel to Port Royal de la Darse, fortified between 1725 and 1737, and today shel-tering pleasure boats. En route there are good views of Cap Ferrat and the wood-ed slopes of the Golfe de Villefranche (Gulf of Villefranche), a Russian naval base in the 19th century during their conflicts with the Turks.

The **tourist office** (☎ 04 93 01 73 68; www .villefranche-sur-mer.com; Jardin François Binon; ⏳ 9am-7pm Jul & Aug, 9am-noon & 2-6.30pm Mon-Sat Jun & Sep, 9am-noon & 2-6pm Mon-Sat Oct-May), at the top of the historical centre, off the Corniche Inférieure, runs two-hour **guided tours** (€5; ⏳ 10am Fri) of the citadel and old town.

❦ CHAPELLE ST-PIERRE // DECIPHER COCTEAU'S SYMBOLISM IN THIS HUMBLE FISHERMEN'S CHAPEL

Villefranche was a favourite of Jean Cocteau (1889–1963), who sought sol-ace here in 1924 after the death of his companion Raymond Radiguet. Several years, holidays and friends later, Cocteau managed to convince local fishermen to let him paint the neglected, 14th-century **Chapelle St-Pierre** (☎ 04 93 76 90 70; admis-sion €2.50; ⏳ 10am-noon & 3-7pm Tue-Sun Mar-Sep, 10am-noon & 2-5pm Tue-Sun Oct-Feb). Until then (1957–58), the chapel had been used to store nets. Cocteau transformed it into a mirage of mystical frescoes with scenes of angels and St Peter's life interspersed with references to his cinematographic work (notably the drivers from *Orpheus*) and friends (Francine Weisweiller, whose villa Cocteau also decorated; see p214).

❦ NAUTICAL PLEASURES // ADMIRE THE MED'S WILDLIFE AND NATURAL BEAUTY

Weekly two-hour **boat tours** to Monaco (adult/child €16/10; June to September), and one-hour trips around the *rade* and

Cap Ferrat (€11/6; July and August) are organised by **Affrètement Maritime Villefranchois** (☎ 04 93 76 65 65; www.amv -sirenes.com; Port de la Santé; ⏳ 9am-noon & 2-6pm Tue-Sun Jun-Sep). Boats leave from Port de la Santé, at the western end of quai Amiral Courbet.

The same company also runs **dol-phin- and whale-watching expeditions** from June to September. Boats sail sev-eral times weekly and expeditions last four hours (adult/child €44/30). Since the creation of an international marine mammal sanctuary between France, Monaco and Italy in 1999, a number of cetaceans frequent the waters off the French Riviera. Dolphins are common sights; more occasional are sperm whales and fin whales. For more information on Mediterranean cetaceans, check www .dauphin-mediterranee.com.

❦ LA MÈRE GERMAINE // FEAST ON SEAFOOD AT THIS TIME-OLD ESTABLISHMENT

Open in 1938, the great-grandmother of Villefranchois cuisine, **La Mère Ger-maine** (☎ 04 93 01 71 39; 7 quai Amiral Courbet; menu €41; ⏳ lunch & dinner, Christmas–mid-Nov), is a quintessential Villefranche address. Seafood, fish and more seafood is the or-der of the day. Crack open freshly caught shells or try the legendary *bouillabaisse* (€65; to be ordered 24 hours in advance). The menu also lists some fine whites to accompany this decadent meal. Book-ings are essential to guarantee one of the prized tables on the water's edge.

ST-JEAN-CAP FERRAT

pop 2170

Once a drowsy fishing village, yacht-laden St-Jean-Cap Ferrat sits on the fringe of Cap Ferrat, a stunning wooded peninsula glittering with millionaire mansions. Famous former residents read like a *Who's Who* of the 19th and 20th centuries: Somerset Maugham, Charlie Chaplin, Winston Churchill, Jean Cocteau and many more.

♥ VILLA EPHRUSSI DE ROTHSCHILD // MARVEL AT ARISTOCRATIC WHIMS AND ECCENTRICITY

A decadent, totally over-the-top belle époque confection, **Villa Ephrussi de Rothschild** (☎ 04 93 01 33 09; www.villa-ephrussi.com; adult/child €10/7.50; ☺ 10am-7pm Jul & Aug, to 6pm Feb-Jun, Sep & Oct, 2-6pm Mon-Fri, 10am-6pm Sat & Sun Nov-Feb) was commissioned by the eccentric Baroness Béatrice Ephrussi de Rothschild in 1912, and took 40 architects seven years to build. Pink is everywhere (the Baroness' favourite animals were flamingos because of their colour). Fragonard paintings, frilly Louis XVI furniture and flowery porcelain heighten the sugary effect. The 1st floor costs a further €3 to see (tour only), and includes the Monkey Room, decorated with painted monkey friezes on the panelled walls and filled with Béatrice's collection of cheeky porcelain chimps.

Out of this world are the villa's nine themed **gardens**. Stroll through Spanish, Japanese, Florentine, stone, cactus and pink rose areas, before entering the romantic French garden, landscaped to resemble a ship's deck (the Baroness had her 30 gardeners dress as sailors to complete the effect). A stream flows from the Temple of Love to a pool at the heart of the complex, where musical fountains dance every 20 minutes.

A combined ticket with Villa Kérylos in Beaulieu costs €15/10.70 per adult/child. Bus 81, which links Nice and St-Jean-Cap Ferrat, stops at the foot of the driveway leading to the villa (stop Passable).

A divine way of discovering the villa is to visit on a balmy August night during the two-week **Les Azuriales** (www.azurial opera.com) festival, when the villa becomes

TALK TO A FISHERMAN

His father fished alone at sea until the grand old age of 90 – as did his father, and his father. And Jean-Paul Roux, fourth generation fisherman, 60 years old and still going strong, is no exception to the family rule.

'My father fished every single day of his life. He had to eat every day – so he fished every day. That is the essential principle of the fisherman.

'The sea is my passion. It has to be. Fishing is a very hard trade and if you're not passionate about it, you wouldn't do it. I get up at 3am, am at sea from 4.30am until around 10am and work until at least noon sorting out my nets, the boat. There are different nets for every fish; at the moment it's the season for *chapon* and *bouille* (both used in *bouillabaisse*).

'My parents lived in Villefranche; my grandfather did. It is my town, although there are few Villefranchois left – just two or three fishermen like me.'

Jean-Paul can be found every morning from 10am to noon plucking seaweed from his nets aboard his traditional *pointu* (fishing boat), moored next to the quay opposite Hôtel Welcome. Most of the morning's catch goes straight into the kitchen of his daughter's waterfront restaurant, **La Fille du Pêcheur** (www.lafilledupecheur.com). What's left he sells from a makeshift stall on the quay in front of his boat.

an open-air opera stage. Visitors can enjoy productions of *Cosi Fan Tutte* or *La Bohème* during intimate soirées. Tickets cost €138; to make it even more of a special occasion, you can have dinner at the villa after the performance. A three-course meal including wine and coffee costs €100.

♥ WALKING // DISCOVER UNSPOILT SHORES BEHIND THE MILLIONAIRES' VILLAS

There are some 14km of eucalyptus-scented walking paths around the cape, with magnificent views and wonderful coastline all the way. There are various itineraries but all of them are easygoing. The longest walk links the fine-shingle **Plage de Passable** on the western side with the café-lined **Port de Plaisance** on the east (6km). You can otherwise opt for the shorter loop around Pointe Saint Hospice (3km) or the paved, oleander-lined 2.5km stroll between the port and the **Baie des Fourmis** in Beaulieu. The **tourist office** (☎ 04 93 76 08 90; www.saintjean capferrat.fr; 59 av Denis Séméria; ☾ 8.30am-6pm Mon-Fri, 10am-5pm Sat & Sun) has maps.

♥ VILLA SANTO SOSPIR // DISCOVER COCTEAU'S FAMOUS 'TATTOOED' VILLA

The elegant **Villa Santo Sospir** (☎ 04 93 76 00 16; 14 av Jean Cocteau) belongs to the Weisweiller family. Francine Weisweiller (1918–2003) was a Parisian socialite and fervent admirer and patron of Jean Cocteau. The pair met on the set of Cocteau's famous film *Les Enfants Terribles* (1949) and the connection was immediate. Weisweiller used her wealth (her husband was American millionaire Alec Weisweiller) and influence to support Cocteau; she notably published most of his books. In 1950, she asked the artist to

decorate the doors of her villa in St-Jean-Cap Ferrat. Cocteau got carried away and soon the house was covered with mythological frescoes; Weisweiller liked to say he'd 'tattooed' rather than painted her house. Cocteau amateurs can now visit the villa; it is still a private property so 45-minute **guided tours** (€10) must be booked at least the day before by ringing the villa.

♥ ZOO // MEET FROLICKING MONKEYS, PLAYFUL LEMURS AND LOUD PARROTS

On the western side of the cape, **Zoo Parc du Cap Ferrat** (☎ 04 93 76 07 60; www .zoocapferrat.com; adult/child €15/11; ☾ 9.30am-7pm summer, to 5.30pm winter), a small but well-landscaped botanical park with 500 animals to discover, provides easy entertainment for parents with small children in tow. There are feeding sessions throughout the day.

♥ RESTAURANTS WITH A VIEW // GORGE ON SEAFOOD AND SCENERY

The secret is out, and the crowds are in. **Le Sloop** (☎ 04 93 01 48 63; Port de Plaisance; menu €32, mains €18-25; ☾ lunch & dinner Thu-Tue), with its elegant red-and-blue nautical decor and port-side terrace within grasp of the bobbing yachts, is a cut above the rest on this popular restaurant strip. Its seafood and shellfish are uberfresh and good value; try sea bass *à la plancha* with sun-dried tomatoes, or opt for the blue lobster salad. And drink to the good Cap Ferrat life with a glass of chilled white. **Restaurant du Port** (☎ 04 93 76 04 46; 7 av Jean Mermoz; menu €21, mains from €12; ☾ lunch Wed-Mon) looks like every village café on every village square in France, except that this is St-Jean-Cap Ferrat. Inside the gregarious local crowd feasts on excellent

TOP FIVE

GARDENS OF THE RIVIERA

With its mild winters and never-ending sunshine, the Côte d'Azur has been a prime territory for gardeners. *Hivernants* (19th- and 20th-century wintering residents) were quick to spot this potential and many of the most luxuriant gardens date back at least a century.

- ★ **Jardin d'Èze** (p216) – thousands of cacti, the history of Èze and the most enthralling, sweeping views of the Mediterranean

- ★ **Jardin Exotique de Monaco** (p224) – stroll among century-old cacti and thousands of succulent plants, with stunning views of the principality

- ★ **Jardin Botanique Exotique du Val Rahmeh, Menton** (p232) – the original botanical garden, beautifully maintained, and home to one of the last Easter Island trees (extinct on the island)

- ★ **Villa Ephrussi de Rothschild, St-Jean-Cap Ferrat** (p213) – nine different gardens, all exquisite, in the grounds of this early 20th-century folly

- ★ **Medieval gardens, Ste-Agnès** (p234) – small and slightly surreal, dramatically perched at the top of Ste-Agnès

quality homemade fare – grilled sardines, steaks, fish carpaccio – and catches up on gossip with a drink. Sit at the table by the window for a lovely port view (and cooling sea breeze) or on the tiny but highly prized terrace.

BEAULIEU, CAP D'AIL & CAP MARTIN

These three coastal resorts don't have much in the way of attractions apart from their good looks. Cap d'Ail (which translates as Cape of Garlic but actually derives from the Provençal 'Cap d'Abaglio', meaning 'Cape of Bees') and Cap Martin are particularly noteworthy for their relatively well-preserved coastline.

♥ CABANON LE CORBUSIER // LEARN THE INCREDIBLE STORY BEHIND THIS ICONIC HUT

Le Corbusier (1887–1965) first came to Cap Martin in the 1930s to visit friend Eileen Gray, an Irish designer. Le Corbusier loved the area and visited often. It was during one of his stays, when Gray wasn't around, that Le Corbusier took the liberty of painting the interior of her villa. Gray was furious: Le Corbusier's paintings had ruined the perspectives of her design, and Gray was offended by the subject matter (kissing women; Gray was a lesbian).

Dejected, she left the villa and Le Corbusier was no longer welcome as a guest. He returned in 1949, but as a tenant; it was during that stay that he met Robert Rebutato, owner of **L'Étoile de Mer**, the next-door café where he ate his meals. Friendship blossomed between the two men and in 1951, they agreed on the construction of a *cabanon* (a small beach hut) next door to L'Étoile de Mer so that Le Corbusier could have his own space.

The **Cabanon** was designed using the Modulor, a mathematical benchmark based on the height of a man with his arms held up. Le Corbusier moved in as soon as it was completed, in August 1952; he spent many happy holidays there until his death in 1965.

NICE, MONACO & MENTON

The Cabanon and L'Étoile de Mer, which still belongs to the Rebutato family, can both be visited on excellent two-hour **guided tours** (€8; ⏰ 10am Tue & Fri) run by the Roquebrune-Cap Martin **tourist office** (☎ 04 93 35 62 87; www.roquebrune-cap -martin.com; 218 av Aristide Briand, Cap Martin; ⏰ 9am-7pm Mon-Sat, 10am-5pm Sun Jul & Aug, 9am-12.30pm & 2-6.30pm Mon-Sat Jun & Sep, to 6pm Oct-May).

❧ SENTIER DU LITTORAL // ENJOY PRISTINE COASTLINES AND SCENIC VIEWS

With the exception of Monaco, you can walk the 13km between Cap d'Ail and Menton without passing a car. The **Sentier du Littoral** follows the rugged coastline from the hedonistic **Plage Mala** in Cap d'Ail (a tiny gravel cove where a couple of restaurants double up as private beach and cocktail bars) to **Plage Marquet** in the Fontvieille neighbourhood of Monaco. The path then picks up at the other end of Monaco, in Larvotto, from where you can walk to Menton along the beaches and wooded shores of **Cap Martin**, including the beautiful **Plage Buse**.

The walk is easygoing but visitors should note that the stretch of coast between Monaco and Cap d'Ail is inaccessible in bad weather. The path is well signposted and you can easily walk small sections or make a day trip out of it, including beach stops and lunch in Monaco (see our recommendations p226). If you don't fancy walking through Monaco you can catch bus 6, which takes you from Larvotto to Fontvieille.

❧ VILLA GRECQUE KÉRYLOS // TRAVEL BACK IN TIME IN THIS ATHENIAN VILLA

Eccentric and beautiful in equal measure is **Villa Grecque Kérylos** (☎ 04 93 01 01 44; www.villa-kerylos.com; impasse Gustave Eiffel; adult/child €8.50/6.30; ⏰ 10am-6pm Feb-Oct, 2-6pm Mon-Fri, 10am-6pm Sat & Sun Nov-Jan), a seven-years-in-the-making mansion designed by scholar-archaeologist Théodore Reinach (1860–1928) and architect Emmanuel Pontremoli (1865–1956) in 1902. Rooms and everything in them are based on ancient Greek models. The result: a perfect reproduction of a 1st-century Athenian villa. Audioguides lead you through this astonishing house, complete with Greek-style recliners and stunning mosaic floors.

A combined ticket with the Rothschild villa costs €15/10.70 per adult/child.

MOYENNE CORNICHE

Cut through rock in the 1920s, the Moyenne Corniche takes drivers from Nice past the Col de Villefranche (149m), Èze and Beausoleil (the French town bordering Monaco's Monte Carlo).

Bus 82 serves the Moyenne Corniche from Nice all the way to Èze Village (20 minutes); bus 112 carries on all the way to Beausoleil (40 minutes, Monday to Saturday).

❧ ÈZE VILLAGE // GAZE AT AWE-INSPIRING VIEWS

This rocky little village perched on an impossible peak is the jewel in the Riviera crown. The main attraction is the medieval village itself, which is exceptionally well preserved, with small higgledy-piggledy stone houses and winding lanes. There are plenty of art galleries, cafés and shops.

Steep streets lead to Èze's crowning glory, the old Château ruins and the stunning **Jardin d'Èze** (☎ 04 93 41 10 30; adult/child €5/2.50; ⏰ 9am-8pm Jul & Aug, to 7pm Sep & Jun, to 6pm Apr, May & Oct, to 5pm Nov-Mar).

There are hundreds of unusually shaped cacti and sweet-scented plants, phenomenal views of the Mediterranean, Cap Ferrat and neighbouring Corniches, and even a relaxing area with wooden lounges from where to take it all in.

Perfumery Fragonard (p262) has a **factory** (☎ 04 93 41 05 05; admission free; ⊗ 8.30am-6.30pm Feb-Oct, 8.30am-noon & 2-6.30pm Nov-Jan) that you can visit on the eastern edge of Èze, and a small shop in the village.

The village gets very crowded between 10am and 5pm; if you'd prefer a quiet wander, come first thing in the morning or late in the afternoon.

You can walk down from the village to Èze-sur-Mer on the coast via the chemin de Nietzsche (45 minutes); the German philosopher started writing *Thus Spoke Zarathustra* while staying in Èze and enjoyed this path.

❦ CHÂTEAU EZA // FINE DINING AND EXTRAORDINARY VIEWS
This is one of the Côte d'Azur's finest tables, both in terms of cuisine and setting. Right in the medieval village, **Château Eza** (☎ 04 93 41 12 24; www.chateaueza.com; rue de la Pise; lunch menu €39 & €49, dinner menu €105, mains €39-49; ⊗ lunch & dinner) is perched on the edge of the village, with out-of-this-world views of the deep-blue Med. Chef Axel Wagner prepares a colourful mix of seasonal and local meats and seafood (pan-fried red mullet with red Camargue rice and wild garlic, roast lamb from the Alps with aubergine mousse, scallops and solen with asparagus).

GRANDE CORNICHE

Hitchcock was sufficiently impressed by Napoléon's cliff-hanging Grande Corniche to use it as a backdrop for his film *To Catch a Thief* (1956), starring Cary Grant and Grace Kelly. Ironically, the Hollywood actor, who met her Monégasque Prince Charming while making the film, died in 1982 after crashing her car on this very same road.

Bus 116 links La Turbie with Nice (35 minutes, Monday to Saturday), bus 114 with Monaco (30 minutes, Monday to Friday only).

EXPLORING GRANDE CORNICHE

❦ ROQUEBRUNE // STEP BACK IN MEDIEVAL TIMES
The medieval half of the town of Roquebrune-Cap Martin, Roquebrune sits 300m-high on a pudding-shaped lump. The village is delightful, free of tacky souvenir shops but kept alive by its wonderful castle and excellent restaurants (see p218).

Château de Roquebrune (☎ 04 93 35 07 22; www.roquebrune-cap-martin.com; place William Ingram; adult/child €3.70/2.70; ⊗ 10am-12.30pm year-round, plus 3-7.30pm Jul & Aug, 2-6.30pm Apr-Jun & Sep, 2-6pm Feb, Mar & Oct, 2-5pm Nov-Jan) dates back to the 10th century. The four floors are atmospheric, with simple but evocative props of life in medieval times. Views are sensational.

Of all Roquebrune's steep and tortuous streets, rue Moncollet – with its arcaded passages and stairways carved out of rock – is the most impressive. Architect Le Corbusier (whose holiday *cabanon* you can visit in Cap Martin, p215) is buried in the cemetery at the top of the village. Down from the cemetery, you'll also find a rare, **1000-year-old olive tree** (signposted 'Olivier Millénaire').

Roquebrune and Cap Martin are linked together by a steep path with innumerable steps.

🌱 OBSERVATOIRE DE NICE & ASTRORAMA // FROM CLEAR BLUE SKIES TO SPACE

French architects Gustave Eiffel and Charles Garnier designed Nice Observatory (☎ 04 92 00 31 12; www.obs-nice.fr; Grande Corniche; guided tours adult/child €6/3), a 19th-century monument 5km northeast of Nice amid 35 hectares of landscaped parkland atop Mont Gros (375m). When the observatory opened in 1887, its telescope – 76cm in diameter – was among Europe's largest. Guided tours take place at 2.45pm on Wednesday and Saturday. They last two hours and are not suitable for children under 12.

Much more child-friendly is Astrorama (☎ 04 93 85 85 58; www.astrorama.net, in French; rte de la Revère, Èze; adult/child €9/7; ⏰ 7-11pm Tue-Sat Jul & Aug, Mar-Jun, Sep & Oct, Fri & Sat Sep-Jun), a planetarium and astronomy centre where you can watch the skies. You must book to attend but the evening is then yours to enjoy, with telescope observations, mini-rocket launches and loads of interactive sessions about anything and everything space-related. Some of the staff speak English but you'll need to ring ahead to guarantee they're here the night you attend.

🌱 TROPHÉE DES ALPES // CONTEMPLATE A PIECE OF LOCAL HISTORY

Teetering dramatically on a promontory above Monaco, the Trophée des Alpes (Trophy of the Alps; ☎ 04 93 41 20 84; 18 av Albert Ier; adult/child €5/free; ⏰ 9.30am-1pm & 2.30-6.30pm Tue-Sun mid-May–mid-Sep, 10am-1.30pm & 2.30-5pm Tue-Sun mid-Sep–Mar), a 2000-year-old triumphal monument built by Emperor Augustus in 6 BC, sits on the highest point of the old Roman road. The 45 Alpine tribes the Roman leader conquered are listed on the inscription carved on the western side of the monument. There is a small museum on site. Last admission is half an hour before closing time.

GASTRONOMIC HIGHLIGHTS

🌱 AU GRAND INQUISITEUR // ROQUEBRUNE €

☎ 04 93 35 05 37; 18 rue du Château; lunch/dinner menu €14/25; ⏰ lunch & dinner Wed-Sun

In a windy lane leading up to the castle, this pocket-sized restaurant sits snug in a sumptuous vaulted stone dining room. The atmosphere is medieval romantic, with candles and coloured glass windows. Diners tuck into the simple but super fresh dishes (toasted goat's cheese with walnuts and rosemary, lemon red mullet filets with polenta), carried to your table from the kitchen across the street!

🌱 CAFÉ DE LA FONTAINE // LA TURBIE €

☎ 04 93 28 52 79; 4 av Général de Gaulle; mains €13-18; ⏰ lunch & dinner Tue-Sun Oct-Apr, every day May-Sep

Those not in-the-know wouldn't give this inconspicuous village bistro a second glance. What they don't know is that it is Michelin-starred chef Bruno Cirino's baby – somewhere for him to go back to his culinary roots with stunningly simple yet delicious dishes. Try his *osso bucco à la Niçoise* (a beef stew) with fresh tagliatelle, or a wonderfully lemony-buttery pan-fried sole, with a creamy *fraisier* (a traditional strawberry gateau) for dessert. Hmmm.

🌱 FRAISE ET CHOCOLAT // ROQUEBRUNE €

☎ 04 93 28 99 00; place des Deux Frères; sandwiches €5-6; ⏰ 8am-6pm Sat-Thu

Run by the same family as Les Deux Frères, Fraise et Chocolat (Strawberry and Chocolate) is a lovely café with an old-fashioned deli feel. Stop here for a drink or a quick bite (sandwiches and quiches) on the way back from your village ventures. You might find you'll stay longer than intended: the two gorgeous terraces, one on the village square or the flowered patio with lovely views at the back, were made for contemplative breaks.

🍃 LES DEUX FRÈRES //
ROQUEBRUNE €€

☎ 04 93 28 99 00; place des Deux Frères; lunch/dinner menu €28/48; 🕑 lunch & dinner Wed-Sat, lunch Sun, dinner Tue

This gourmet restaurant, perched dramatically at the edge of the village on a panoramic terrace, is a stylish choice. Waiters wear formal black, and mains (huge pieces of meat or whole fish for two, delicate fish filets in hollandaise sauce or spinach and basil olive oil)

come hidden beneath silver domed platters. In winter, guests lunch or dine in the minimalist dining room with its contemporary fireplace. The lunch menu, including a half-bottle of wine, is good value.

MONACO

· · · · · ·

pop 32,000 / ☎ 377
Squeezed into just 1.95 sq km, this confetti principality might be the world's second-smallest country (the Vatican is smaller), but what it lacks in size it makes up for in attitude. Glitzy, glam and screaming hedonism, Monaco is truly beguiling.

With zero natural resources to rely on, this sovereign state has made pampering

NICE, MONACO & MENTON

∼ WORTH A TRIP ∼

If you're touring the Grande Corniche, the **Parc Naturel Départemental de la Grande Corniche**, a protected area that stretches along the D2564 from Col d'Èze to La Turbie, makes a wonderful stop for a stroll or a picnic. The views from these lofty hills are awe-inspiring.

Plateau de la Justice, signposted from Col d'Èze, is fabulous for scenic walks among the scented *garrigue* (typical Mediterranean groundcover of aromatic plants) and a picnic amidst the pines (there are a couple of dedicated picnic areas with tables and benches too).

For mighty coastal views stretching beyond Cap Ferrat to Cap d'Antibes, the Îles de Lérins and the Ésterel, it doesn't get much better than Fort de la Revère (675m), a fort built on top of a barren rocky outcrop in 1870 to protect Nice. An orientation table tells you what's what: the panoramic view is the best on the coast. Picnic at tables beneath plane trees here, or follow the footpath around the fort signposted 'Maison de la Nature et Animations Nature' into the *garrigue*. On your left, a small rocky path leads to an observation point, from which bird enthusiasts can watch more than 80-odd species of migratory birds at work and play, including the osprey and falcon (both late August to mid-October), European bee-eater (mid-August to mid-September) and black stork (mid-October).

There are a number of walking trails leading to nearby villages: the Guides Randoxygène *Rando Pays Côtier* (available in tourist offices) has suggestions.

the super-rich its speciality. Back in the 1930s Somerset Maugham had already famously dubbed Monaco 'a sunny place for shady people'. Yet 'decadent hideout for dodgy characters' is not a designer label reigning monarch Prince Albert II likes. In the wake of his coronation in 2005, the prince promised to clean things up. Monaco had been formally identified as a tax haven by the OECD in 2000 and included in a list of uncooperative countries in 2002, after failing to comply with transparency requirements. But in 2009, Monaco agreed to exchange information on all tax matters with the EU and members of the G20 in accordance with international standards, a move welcome by the OECD.

Since the 13th century, Monaco's history has been that of the Grimaldi family whose rule began in 1297. Charles VIII, king of France, recognised Monégasque independence in 1489. But during the French Revolution France snatched Monaco back and imprisoned its royal family. Upon release, they had to sell what few possessions they still owned to survive and the palace became a warehouse.

The Grimaldis were restored to the throne under the 1814 Treaty of Paris. But in 1848 they lost Menton and Roquebrune to France, and Monaco swiftly became Europe's poorest country. In 1860 Monégasque independence was recognised for a second time by France, and a monetary agreement in 1865 sealed the deal on future cooperation between the two countries.

Rainier III (r 1949–2005), nicknamed *le prince batisseur* (the builder prince), expanded the size of his principality by 20% in the late 1960s by reclaiming land from the sea to create the industrial quarter of Fontvieille (see opposite). In 2004 he doubled the size of the harbour with a giant floating dike as part of an ambitious project to place Port de Monaco (Port Hercules) among the world's leading cruise-ship harbours. Upon Rainier's death in 2005, son Albert II became monarch.

Monaco's economic status is unusual. Although not a member of the European Union, because of its continuing special relationship with France, Monaco participates in the EU customs territory (meaning no border formalities crossing from France into Monaco) and uses the euro as its currency.

MONÉGASQUES

Citizens of Monaco (Monégasques), of whom there are only 7600, don't pay taxes. They have their own flag (red and white), their national anthem and national holiday (19 November).

The traditional dialect is Monégasque (broadly speaking, a mixture of French and Italian), which children of the 107 different nationalities living in Monaco are taught in schools alongside French, Monaco's official language. Many street signs are bilingual.

The ruling prince is assisted by a national council of 18 democratically elected members. Only Monégasques aged 21 or over can vote; elections are held every five years.

The telephone country code for Monaco is ☎ 377.

ESSENTIAL INFORMATION

EMERGENCIES // Hospital (Centre Hospitalier Princesse Grace; ☎ 97 98 97 69; www.chpg.mc, in French; 1 av Pasteur) **Police** (☎ 93 15 30 15; 3 rue Louis Notari)

WANTED: LAND

Wedged between sheer cliffs and the Med, Monaco has had few options to expand: upwards (hence the forest of skyscrapers) and at sea. The neighbourhood of Fontvieille was built on 30 hectares of land reclaimed from the sea between 1966 and 1973.

The principality was planning further expansion with the multi-billion-dollar creation of an artificial island but plans were shelved at the end of 2008 because of the global financial crisis, much to the relief of environmentalists, who argued the project would damage local marine ecosystems.

TOURIST OFFICES // Tourist office (☎ 92 16 61 16; www.monaco-tourisme.com; 2a bd des Moulins; ☺ 9am-7pm Mon-Sat, 10am-noon Sun) From June to September additional tourist information kiosks open at the harbour and train station.

ORIENTATION

Monaco can be divided into five neighbourhoods: Monaco Ville, a rocky outcrop crowned by the Palais Princier on the southern side of Port de Monaco; Monte Carlo, north of the port; La Condamine, the flat area around the port; Fontvieille, the industrial area southwest of Monaco Ville; and Larvotto, the beach area east of Monte Carlo. The French town of Beausoleil is three streets up the hill from Monte Carlo, and Moneghetti borders Cap d'Ail's western fringe.

EXPLORING MONACO

❧ LE ROCHER // VISIT THE HISTORIC HEART OF MONACO

Monaco Ville, also called Le Rocher, thrusts skywards on a pistol-shaped rock. It's this strategic location overlooking the sea that became the stronghold of the Grimaldi dynasty.

Built as a fortress in the 13th century, the **palace** (☎ 93 25 18 31; www.palais.mc; place du Palais) underwent a number of transformations over the centuries. It is now the private residence of the Prince (if the Grimaldi standard is flying from the palace tower, the Prince is at home). The palace is protected by an elite company of 112 guards, the Carabiniers du Prince. At 11.55am daily a tourist scrum scrambles to watch the pristine soldiers parade outside the palace during the **changing of the guard**.

From April to October, you can sneak a peak at royal life with an audioguide tour of the **state apartments** (combined ticket with Musée des Souvenirs Napoléoniens et Archives Historiques du Palais adult/child €9/4.50; ☺ 10am-6.15pm Apr-Oct).

Another important Grimaldi site is the **Cathédrale de Monaco** (☎ 93 30 87 70; 4 rue Colonel Bellando de Castro; ☺ 8am-7pm summer, to 6pm winter). Visitors flood to this Romanesque-Byzantine cathedral (built in 1875) to view the flower-covered graves of fairy-tale couple Princess Grace (1929–82) and Prince Rainier III.

To access Le Rocher, visitors can walk up the 16th-century red-brick **Rampe Major** from place aux Armes (where the daily **fruit and veg market** takes place) in the Condamine area. Alternatively, take a nautical stroll around the **Port de Monaco** to check out some of the yachts

DRESS CODE

By law, it's forbidden to inline skate or walk around town bare-chested, barefooted or bikini-clad. In the evening, many restaurants, bars and entertainment venues will require smart outfits (jacket and tie for men).

NICE, MONACO & MENTON

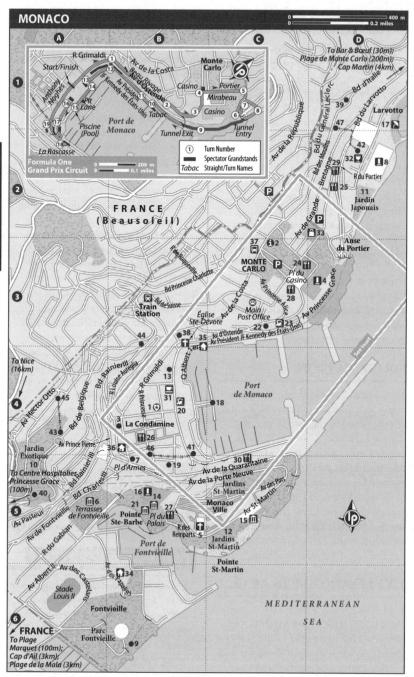

MONACO

Formula One Grand Prix Circuit

Turn Number
Spectator Grandstands
Tabac Straight/Turn Names

Monte Carlo

Start/Finish
R Grimaldi
Av de la Costa
Beau Rivage
Av d'Ostende
Av du Président JF Kennedy des États-Unis
Casino
Portier
Mirabeau
Casino
Tabac
Anthony Noghes
Pit Lane
Piscine (Pool)
Port de Monaco
Tunnel Exit
Tunnel Entry
La Rascasse

FRANCE (Beausoleil)

Monte Carlo
Train Station
Bd de Suisse
Bd Princesse Charlotte
R de Roqueville
R Louise Aureglia
Bd de Belgique
Bd du Jardin Exotique
Bd Rainier III
Av Hector Otto
To Nice (16km)
To Centre Hospitalier Princesse Grace (100m)
Jardin Exotique
Av Prince Pierre
Pl d'Armes
Av Pasteur
Bd Charles III
Bd du Jardin Exotique
R du Gabian
Av Albert II
Av des Castelans
Stade Louis II
Fontvieille
Parc Fontvieille
To Plage Marquet (100m); Cap d'Ail (3km); Plage de la Mala (3km)

Port de Fontvieille
Pointe Ste-Barbe
Terrasses de Fontvieille
Pl du Palais
R des Remparts
Jardins St-Martin
Pointe St-Martin
Monaco Ville
Av St-Martin
Av des Pins

La Condamine
R Grimaldi
R Princesse
Q Albert Ier
Église Ste-Dévote
Main Post Office
Av de la Costa
Av Princesse Alice
Av d'Ostende
Av Président JF Kennedy des États-Unis
Av Princesse Grace
Port de Monaco
Av de la Quarantaine
Av de la Porte Neuve

MONTE CARLO
Pl du Casino
Anse du Portier
Bd de Grande Bretagne
Bd des Moulins
Bd du Général Leclerc
Av de la République
Av de Grande Bretagne
Bd d'Italie
Bd du Larvotto
Larvotto
R du Portier
Jardin Japonais
To Bar & Bœuf (30m); Plage de Monte Carlo (200m); Cap Martin (4km)

See Inset

MEDITERRANEAN SEA

FRANCE

NICE, MONACO & MENTON

moored along the quays; from its southern end a path winds along the coast and up through the shady **Jardins St-Martin** to Monaco Ville.

☙ MUSÉE OCÉANOGRAPHIQUE // EMBARK ON A VOYAGE OF MARINE DISCOVERY

Stuck dramatically to the edge of a cliff since 1910, the world-renowned **Musée Océanographique de Monaco** (Oceanographic Museum; ☎ 93 15 36 00; www.oceano.mc; av St-Martin; adult/child €13/6.5; ⏲ 9.30am-7.30pm Jul & Aug, to 7pm Apr-Jun & Sep, to 6pm Oct-Mar), which is a Prince Albert I (1848–1922) creation, is a stunner. Its centrepiece is its aquarium, with a 6m-deep lagoon where sharks and marine predators are separated from colourful tropical fishes by a coral reef. Ninety smaller tanks contain a dazzling 450 Mediterranean and tropical species, sustained by 250,000L of freshly pumped sea water per day. Kids will love the **tactile basin** (2-12yr €3; ⏲ school holidays); tickets for the 30-minute feel-the-fish sessions are sold at the entrance.

Upstairs, two huge colonnaded rooms retrace the history of oceanography and marine biology. Displays recount Prince Albert's explorations, and the cetacean skeletons, fossils and other pickled specimens give an insight into the trials of these now-established fields.

Make sure you pay a visit to the rooftop terrace too for sweeping views of Monaco and the Med.

☙ CASINO DE MONTE CARLO // RISKING IT ALL AT THE ORIGINAL CASINO

The drama of watching the poker-faced gamble in Monte Carlo's grand marble-and-gold **casino** (☎ 92 16 20 00; www.montecarlocasinos.com; place du Casino; ⏲ from noon Jul & Aug, from 2pm Mon-Fri & noon Sat & Sun Sep-Jun) makes the stiff admission fees, stakes and obligatory cloakroom 'tips' almost bearable. The **Salon Ordinaire** (admission €10) has European roulette (minimum stake €5) and *trente-et-quarante* (minimum stake €20); and the **Salons Privés** (admission €20; ⏲ from 4pm) offer baccarat, craps, English roulette and chemin de fer.

To enter the casino, you must be at least 18, have a passport for ID, and be dressed relatively smartly (no shorts, trainers, flip flops etc). A jacket and tie are required to enter the Salons Privés and the Salon Ordinaire in the evening.

🌳 GARDENS OF MONACO // RELAX IN THE PRINCIPALITY'S GREEN OASES

Amidst the skyscrapers' maze, you'll find some wonderful gardens in Monaco, the highlight of which is the **Jardin Exotique** (☎ 93 15 29 80; www.jardin-exotique.mc; 62 bd du Jardin Exotique; adult/child €7/3.70; ☼ 9am-7pm mid-May–mid-Sep, 9am-6pm or dusk mid-Sep–mid-May). Home to the world's largest succulent and cactus collection, from small *echinocereus* to 10m-tall African candelabras, the gardens tumble down the slopes of Moneghetti through a maze of paths, stairs and bridges. Views of the principality are spectacular and the gardens are delightful.

Your ticket also gets you a 35-minute guided tour round the **Grottes de l'Observatoire**, a prehistoric cave network stuffed with stalactites and stalagmites, 279 steps down inside the hillside; strangely, it's the only cave in Europe where the temperature rises as you descend.

Also commanding dreamy sea views are the cliffside Mediterranean **Jardins St-Martin** (☼ 7am-6pm Oct-Mar, to 8pm Apr-Sep) in Monaco Ville. The gardens stretch all the way from the cathedral to the port, a lovely, cool walk on hot days.

Much smaller but equally pleasant is the **Jardin Japonais** (Japanese Garden; av Princesse Grace; ☼ 9am-7pm Apr-Oct, to 6pm Nov-Mar), next to the Grimaldi Forum conference centre, complete with ornamental carps, bonsai trees, rock pools and footbridges. It was blessed by a Shinto high priest, and quiet contemplation and meditation is encouraged.

🌳 QUIRKY MUSEUMS // BROWSE MONACO'S ECCENTRIC COLLECTIONS

Kids of all ages should not miss the **Collection de Voitures Anciennes** (☎ 92

DYNASTY

Monaco's longest-ruling monarch, reigning for 56 years, Rainier III (1923–2005), won the heart of the nation with his fairy-tale marriage to Grace Kelly in 1956. The legendary Philadelphia-born actress made 11 films in the 1950s, including Alfred Hitchcock's *To Catch a Thief* (1955). The movie took Kelly to Cannes and Monaco for a photo shoot, where she met Rainier. Tragically, she died in a car crash in 1982.

The soap-opera lives of the couple's children – Prince Albert (b 1958), monarch since 19 November 2005, Caroline and Stéphanie – take centre stage today. Prince Albert is as well-known for his sporting achievements (he's a black belt in Judo and played in the national soccer team) as he is for his two illegitimate children, neither of whom are in line for the throne.

Indeed, until Prince Albert marries and fathers an heir, older sister Caroline (b 1957) remains next in line. She has four children and is married to Prince Ernst of Hanover, a cousin of Britain's Queen Elizabeth (her first husband died in 1990 in a boat accident).

With her tumultuous love life and brief dealing with pop music (including the 1986 hit *Ouragan*), wild child Princess Stéphanie (b 1965) has been prime tabloid fodder for the last 20 years. She was in the same crash that killed her mother in 1982 but has always denied rumours that she was the driver.

05 28 56; www.palais.mc; Terrasses de Fontvieille; adult/child €6/3; ☺ 10am-6pm), the former collection of Prince Rainier III. Highlights include a Rolls Royce Silver Cloud, a wedding present from local shopkeepers, a black London cab (Austin 1952) fitted out for Grace Kelly, and the first F1 racing car to win the Monaco Grand Prix – the Bugatti 1929. Fire engines, WWII jeeps, legendary Americans (Buick, Cadillac etc) and 19th-century carriages complete the collection. It's just a shame there is so little in the way of explanation.

Fans of historic memorabilia should head to the **Musée des Souvenirs Napoléoniens et Archives Historiques du Palais** (Museum of Napoleonic Souvenirs & the Palace's Historic Archives; www.palais.mc; place du Palais; adult/child €4/2; ☺ 10am-6.15pm Apr-Oct, 10.30am-5pm Dec-Mar), where an assortment of princely bric-a-brac (medals, coins, uniforms and swords), Napoléon's socks and other random objects form yet another intriguing collection. Tickets for the Palais Princier include entrance to the Musée des Souvenirs.

❦ PERFORMING ARTS // ENJOY WORLD-CLASS BALLET, OPERA AND MUSIC

The Grimaldis have a long tradition of art patronage. Already back in the 18th century, the palace regularly opened its doors to offer music performances to its subjects.

The tradition continues with summer concerts performed by the **Monte Carlo Philharmonic Orchestra** (www.opmc.mc) in the Cour d'Honneur (Courtyard of Honour) at the Palais Princier. Tickets (€18 to €80), sold at the **Atrium du Casino** (☎ 98 06 28 28; place du Casino; ☺ 10am-5.30pm Tue-Sun) in the casino, are like gold dust. In winter, the orchestra regularly plays at the Salle Garnier (1892), a confection of neoclassical splendour adjoining Monte Carlo Casino and the permanent home of the renowned **Opéra de Monte Carlo** (☎ 92 16 22 99; www.opera.mc; place du Casino).

LOSER RISKS ALL

The beautiful belle époque decor of Monte Carlo Casino – Europe's oldest – is as extravagant as those who play in it. The casino was built in several phases, the earliest being the Salon de l'Europe, built in 1865 and splendidly lit with eight 150kg crystal chandeliers from 1898. The second phase saw French architect Charles Garnier, who'd just completed the Paris opera house, move to Monte Carlo to create the luxurious fresco-adorned Salle Garnier in 1878. The main entrance hall, with its 28 marble columns and flurry of gamblers and voyeurs, opened the same year. The third part, the Salle Empire, was completed in 1910.

Monaco's Prince Charles III, who saw the casino as the solution to the principality's financial troubles, was nevertheless concerned about the malign effect of gambling on his subjects. He therefore made it illegal for his family, or any Monégasque, to set foot in the precincts!

Monte Carlo Casino remains in the hands of its founding owner, the **Société des Bains de Mer** (SBM; Sea Bathing Society; www.montecarloresort.com), established in 1863 and Monaco's largest corporation today, owning the principality's priciest hotels, restaurants and spa. Original shareholders included Charles III, and the state remains the leading shareholder today.

GARDEN SAVER

The *Jardins de Monaco et de la Côte d'Azur* booklet, available at the tourist office in Monaco, gives visitors reductions at **Jardin Exotique de Monaco** (€5.30 instead of €7, see p224), **Jardin de la Serre de la Madone** in Menton (€5 instead of €8; see p232) and **Villa Ephrussi de Rothschild** in St-Jean-Cap Ferrat (€9 instead of €10, see p213).

Another world-class act is the **Monte Carlo Ballet** (www.balletsdemontecarlo.com). Performances take place at the Salle des Princes at the **Grimaldi Forum** (☎ 99 99 30 00; www.grimaldiforum.mc; tickets from €25; 10 av Princesse Grace).

Jacket and tie for men is obligatory at all performances.

**♥ HELICOPTER FLIGHTS //
FLY FROM NICE TO MONACO,
IN STYLE**
If you've never flown in a helicopter, seize the day! Where would it be more appropriate to arrive in a helicopter than in Monaco? **Héli-Air Monaco** (☎ 92 05 00 50; www.heliairmonaco.com) operates regular flights between Nice Côte d'Azur airport and **Héliport de Monaco** (☎ 92 05 00 10; av des Ligures) in Fontvieille. Flights cost €120/210 one way/return, last seven minutes and offer fantastic views of the coast.

♥ BEACHES & SPAS // INDULGE IN MONACO'S CREATURE COMFORTS
Plage du Larvotto and **Plage de Monte Carlo**, both in Larvotto, have private, paying sections where you can hire sun lounges and parasols.

Beautiful swimmers frequent **Stade Nautique Rainier III** (☎ 93 30 64 83; quai Albert 1er; adult/child €4.80/2.90; ☽ 9am-6pm May,

Jun, Sep & Oct, 9am-6pm Mon, 9am-8pm Jul & Aug), the Olympic-sized outdoor sea-water pool with water slide and sun lounges and parasols (€4.20 each) at the port.

For the ultimate pampering experience, head to the prestigious **Thermes Marins de Monte-Carlo** (☎ 92 16 49 46; www.montecarlospa.com; 2 av de Monte Carlo; ☽ 8am-8pm), with its 29°C sea-water pool, solarium and endless list of treatments from seaweed wraps to four-hand massages. One-day packages, including three or four treatments, start at €150.

FESTIVALS & EVENTS

Monaco has a packed events schedule, and with a little planning ahead, they can be surprisingly accessible, both in terms of price and availability.

Festival International du Cirque (www.montecarlofestival.mc) Hold your breath during world-class acrobatics or laugh out loud at the clowns; late January

Tennis Masters Series (www.mccc.mc) Fast becoming a key fixture on the professional circuit, with all the big players involved; April

Formula One Grand Prix (www.acm.mc) The one and only, the race every F1 driver dreams of winning. Tickets can be hard to get, but nowhere near as hard as reasonably priced accommodation; end of May

Fête de la St Jean To celebrate midsummer, dancers in folk costume leap around Bonfires on place du Palais; 23 June

International Fireworks Festival (☎ 93 15 28 63) A showdown of pyrotechnic expertise in the port area. The winner gets to organise the fireworks on 18 November, eve of the national holiday; July and August

GASTRONOMIC HIGHLIGHTS

Eating in Monaco is as diverse as its population. Everything from Monégasque (a variant of Niçois) to Italian, Japanese and gastronomic French cuisine is available, and like most things in the principality, it's rather expensive.

♥ BAR & BŒUF €€€

☎ 98 06 71 71; Le Sporting, 26 av Princesse Grace; full meal around €150; ☻ dinner mid-May–mid-Sep

Style-setters hobnob in a minimalist wood-and-glass interior designed by Philippe Starck at this Ducasse venture overlooking the sea. Bar & Bœuf specialises in just that – sea bass *(bar)* and beef *(bœuf)*, cooked in whatever style takes the chef's fancy (Mediterranean with poached seabass and beef carpaccio, Asian with beef stir-fry etc). Gentlemen, note that a jacket is required. Bookings are essential.

♥ CAFÉ DE PARIS €€

☎ 92 16 20 20; place du Casino; starters/salads €15, mains €25-50; ☻ 8am-2am

Monaco's best-known café has been in business since 1882 and is *the* place in Monte Carlo to people-watch. You'll find all the typical *brasserie* fare (*croque monsieur,* French onion soup, steak tartare with fries etc) at Monaco prices. Service is brisk and rather snobbish but don't be fazed: if lunch isn't on the cards, you can just have a coffee and enjoy the front-row view of the casino's razzmatazz.

♥ COSMOPOLITAN €€

☎ 93 25 78 68; 7 rue du Portier; lunch menu €19.50, mains €16-27; ☻ lunch & dinner

THE FORMULA ONE GRAND PRIX   *TONY WHEELER*

If there's one trophy a Formula One driver would like to have on the mantelpiece, it would have to be from the most glamorous race of the season, the Monaco Grand Prix. This race has everything. Its spectators are the most sensational: the merely wealthy survey the spectacle from Hôtel Hermitage, the really rich watch from their luxury yachts moored in the harbour, while the Grimaldis see the start and finish from the royal box at the port. Then there's the setting: the cars scream around the very centre of the city, racing uphill from the start/finish line to place du Casino, then downhill around a tight hairpin and two sharp rights to hurtle through a tunnel and run along the harbourside to a chicane and more tight corners before the start/finish. To top it all off there's the race's history: it was first run in 1929, and the winners' list features a roll-call of racing greats right down to Michael Schumacher's five victories between 1994 and 2001.

But despite its reputation, the Monaco Grand Prix is not really one of the great races. The track is too tight and winding for modern Grand Prix cars, and overtaking is virtually impossible. The Brazilian triple world champion Nelson Piquet famously described racing at Monaco as like 'riding a bicycle around your living room'. Piquet clearly rides a much faster bicycle than most of us; Monaco may be the slowest race on the calendar, but the lap record is still over 160km/h and at the fastest point on the circuit cars reach 280km/h. Even the corner in the gloom of the tunnel is taken at 250km/h (over 150mph).

The 78-lap race happens on a Sunday afternoon in late May, the conclusion of several days of practice, qualifying and supporting races. Tickets (€70 to €400) are available from **Automobile Club de Monaco** (ACM; ☎ 93 15 26 00; www.acm.mc) and the official T-shirt, loo seats et al from **L@Boutique** (☎ 97 70 45 35; laboutique@acm.mc; 46 rue Grimaldi) and **Boutique Formule 1** (☎ 93 15 92 44; 15 rue Grimaldi).

A recent, and welcome, addition to the dining scene in Monaco, Cosmopolitan serves excellent value international cuisine. The menu features timeless classics from all corners of the world such as fish and chips, three-cheese gnocchi or veal cutlets in Béarnaise sauce, all re-visited by Cosmo's talented chefs. The result is refreshingly good and unpretentious, and tastes even better with one of the *many* wines on offer (including a dozen available by the glass).

❦ HUIT ET DEMI €€

☎ 93 50 97 02; 4 rue Langlé; pizza €10.50-12.50, pasta €15, meat dishes €16-20; ☾ closed Sat lunch & Sun

Eight and a Half is a chic, clean-cut place with a cabaret-like interior with red walls and glamorous black-and-white celebrity portraits. Outside, its pavement terrace fills an entire street running off rue Princesse Caroline and buzzes with activity every lunch time. The fare is a mix of Italian (lots of pasta) and local (think *bagna cauda,* or lamb with Sospel olives).

❦ LE CASTELROC €€

☎ 93 30 36 68; place du Palais; menu €35, mains €27; ☾ lunch daily, dinner Tue-Sat May-Sep

Opposite the palace with an entrance ensnared by T-shirt and souvenir shops it might be, but, incredibly, Le Castelroc is no tourist trap. Spilling out onto an alfresco terrace, its twin dining rooms are the best place around to try authentic Monégasque specialities such as *barbajuan* (a spinach and cheese–stuffed shortcrust parcel) and *stockfish* (a distinctive dish made with rehydrated dried cod and flavoured with aniseed).

❦ LOUIS XV €€€

☎ 92 06 88 64; Hôtel de Paris, place du Casino; mains from €100; ☾ lunch & dinner Thu-Mon Jan-Nov, plus dinner Wed Jul–mid-Aug

Set jewel-like inside the opulent Hôtel de Paris, the dining room of Alain Ducasse's famous establishment looks as though it's been teleported from 17th-century Versailles. Nice-born head chef Franck Cerutti uses seasonal ingredients in his themed French dishes, with dashes of Italy, Bavaria, Scotland and the Far East to keep things peppy. The restaurant contains the world's largest wine cellar: 250,000 bottles of wine (many priceless) stashed in a rock cave. Reservations are essential, as is the jacket and tie for men.

❦ PULCINELLA €€

☎ 93 30 73 61; 17 rue du Portier; ☾ lunch & dinner

One of Monaco's long-standing Italian establishments, Pulcinella is the place to indulge in *scaloppina di vitello alla milanese* (veal escalope in bread crumbs) or *spaghetti alle vongole veraci* (spaghetti with clams) and other divine Italian fare. The staff is charming and the traditional bistro-style decor now a tad passé, but no matter, local businesspeople can't get enough of it for their power lunches. It's a little more informal in the evening.

❦ STARS 'N' BARS €€

☎ 97 97 95 95; 6 quai Antoine 1er; mains €13-25; ☾ 7.30am-2am Jun-Sep, to midnight Tue-Sun Oct-May

Every star worth his or her reputation has partied at this long-standing American bar-restaurant. The portside terrace remains one of Monaco's sexiest – as does its interior plastered with sporting memorabilia (from F1 helmets to football shirts) and celebrity portraits. Tex-Mex platters, buffalo wings, burgers and a generous dose of vegetarian dishes plump out a family-friendly menu. The weekend brunch with its stacks of pancakes and monster English breakfasts is another hit.

☙ SUPERMARCHÉ CASINO €

17 quai Albert 1er; pizza slices & sandwiches from €3;
☯ 8.30am-midnight Mon-Sat summer, 8.30am-10pm
Mon-Sat winter)

It's not so much the supermarket that's
worth knowing about as its excellent
street-side bakery and pizzeria. Huge,
freshly-prepared sandwiches and tasty
pastries line the shelves of the bakery
on one side whilst a permanent queue
hungrily waits for freshly-baked pizzas to
come out of the wood-fired oven on the
other. A saviour for those keen to watch
the pennies.

☙ ZELOS €€

☎ 99 99 25 50; Grimaldi Forum, 10 av Princesse
Grace; ☯ lunch & dinner

With enormous chandeliers, intensely
blue walls, a ceiling fitted with hundreds
of star-like lights and uninterrupted sea
views, it's hard to say which makes more
of an impression, the setting or the food.
Indeed, the wow factor comes on the
plate too, with modern dishes such as
the trio of Carpaccio (sea bass, king crab
and salmon) and creative desserts such
as the Venezuelan chocolate fondant
with milk chocolate sauce and after-eight
ice-cream.

NIGHTLIFE

Much of Monaco's superchic drinking
goes on in its designer dines and luxury
hotels. Otherwise, the following are
pretty popular too.

☙ COSMOPOLITAN

☎ 93 25 78 68; 7 rue du Portier; ☯ 5.45pm-1am

Whether you're after cocktails or excellent wine, Cosmopolitan should see you
right. With its chocolate-orange decor,
contemporary furniture and *The Big
Chill* music, it's a nice place to ease yourself into a night out with a mojito or enjoy a late-night bottle of Malbec or Bellet
(or another of the 100-plus references on
offer) with tasty nibbles.

☙ KARÉ(MENT)

☎ 99 99 20 20; Grimaldi Forum, 10 av Princesse Grace;
☯ 5.30pm-dawn Jun-Aug, Thu-Sat Sep-May

One glimpse of the stunning waterside
terrace and you'll be fighting for one of
the giant alfresco cushion-lounges or
kitsch plastic Louis XV armchairs at this
celebrity-cool lounge bar. Fashion shows,
DJ mixes and cultural happenings are
held here in a blur of lava lamps, dim
lights, spotlights and mirrors. Drinks are
nothing fancy (vodka Red Bull, gin and
tonic etc) leaving the setting to work its
magic. The nightclub gets going around
midnight.

☙ NI BAR

☎ 97 97 51 51; 1bis rue Grimaldi; ☯ 6pm-1am

This new venue in the historical Condamine district looks like a cross between a giant disco-ball and the movie
set of *Star Trek* or *Star Wars*. It's pretty
cool actually, and Ni specialises in the
finer things in life: nothing but the very
best spirits, rare vintages and liquors
(here you can drink absinthe for instance). The giant mouth-shaped urinals
are baffling.

☙ SASS CAFÉ

☎ 93 25 52 00; 11 av Princesse Grace; ☯ 7pm-3am

A favourite of former F1 driver David
Coulthard, piano-bar Sass buzzes with
a fun-loving crowd most nights of the
week. The atmosphere is reminiscent of
old-school cabarets, with its shiny bar
counter, lacquered grand piano (live jazz
every night), padded red walls and intimate lighting. Rums and whiskeys take
the lion's share of drinks on the bar's

NICE, MONACO & MENTON

shiny shelves and merry punters spill out onto the terrace on busy nights.

🍷 STARS 'N' BARS

☎ 97 97 95 95; 6 quai Antoine 1er; ⏰ 7.30am-2am Jun-Sep, to midnight Tue-Sun Oct-May

The drinks menu is as long as the food menu at this Monaco party institution: cocktails (piña colada, margarita, mojito, Long Island iced tea, you name it) are shaken or stirred by handsome bar staff, beer flows by the bottle or tap and even kids can share in the fun with coke or ginger floats (coke or ginger beer with a scoop of ice cream) and milkshakes.

RECOMMENDED SHOPS

Monaco's streets drip with couture and designer shops, many of which congregate in Monte Carlo. Av des Beaux Arts and av de Monte Carlo, close to the casino, are where to go for all your haute couture needs (from Chanel to Yves Saint Laurent). For chic boutiques and a few more designer brands, head to the Métropole Shopping Centre. The annual 150-page *Monaco Shopping* guide, free at the tourist office, lists them all. From mid-July to mid-August, boutiques are open on Sunday too.

TRANSPORT

BUS // Bus 100 (€1, every 15 minutes) goes to Nice (45 minutes) and Menton (40 minutes) along the Corniche Inférieure. Bus 110 (€18, hourly) goes to Nice Côte d'Azur airport (40 minutes). Both services stop at place d'Armes and the casino stop on bd des Moulins. Monaco's urban bus system has five lines, bizarrely numbered one to six without the three. Line 2 links Monaco Ville to Monte Carlo and then loops back to the Jardin Exotique. Line 4 links the train station with the tourist office, the casino and Plage du Larvotto. Tickets are €1.

TRAIN // Services run about every 20 minutes east to Menton (€2.30, 15 minutes) and Ventimiglia (Vintimille in French; €3.70, 25 minutes) in Italy, and west to Nice (€3.30, 25 minutes). Access to the station is through pedestrian tunnels and escalators from 6 av Prince Pierre de Monaco, pont Ste-Dévote, place Ste-Dévote and bd de la Belgique.

CAR // Only Monaco and Alpes-Maritimes (06) registered cars can access Monaco Ville. Elsewhere, traffic is often dense but straightforward. The Corniche Moyenne (N7) links Monaco to the A8 motorway.

PARKING // Park in one of the numerous underground car parks as street-side parking is limited. The first half-hour is free, the second costs €2.60, and every subsequent 20 minutes is €0.60.

LIFTS // A system of escalators and public lifts links the steep streets. They operate either 24 hours or 6am to midnight or 1am.

MENTON & AROUND

· · · · · ·

Lemons, lemons, hilltop villages, the most fabulous gardens on the Riviera and more lemons are the main attractions of this privileged coastal pocket, a pebble's throw from Italy.

MENTON

pop 27,655

You'd have thought Eve was in enough trouble. But just before she was chucked out of Eden, she stole one of the garden's Golden Fruits. Upon arriving in lush, subtropical Menton, she was reminded of paradise so much that she instantly planted the fruit's seeds – ensuring a famed and fabulous bounty of lemons for Menton ever since. Frenzied citrus worship has accompanied the two week–long Fête des Citrons in February since the 1930s.

ESSENTIAL INFORMATION

**TOURIST OFFICES // Menton Tourist
office** (☎ 04 92 41 76 76; www.menton.fr; Palais
de l'Europe, 8 av Boyer; ☺ 9am-7pm Jun–mid-Sep,
8.30am-12.30pm & 2-7pm Mon-Sat, 9am-12.30pm Sun
mid-Sep–May) **Service du Patrimoine** (☎ 04
92 10 97 10; 24 rue St-Michel; ☺ 10.30am-12.30pm &
2-6pm) Runs guided tours of the town and gardens.

ORIENTATION

Menton's old town and port are wedged
between Baie de Garavan to the east and
Baie du Soleil, which stretches 3km west
towards Roquebrune-Cap Martin. Promenade du Soleil and its continuations,
namely quai Général Leclerc and quai de
Monléon, skirt the length of Menton's
gravel beach. There are more beaches
fringing the coast directly northeast of
the old port, as well as east of Port de Garavan, Menton's pleasure-boat harbour.

EXPLORING MENTON

Menton's old town, with its cascade of
terracotta-coloured buildings, looks
better from afar. Inside its labyrinthine

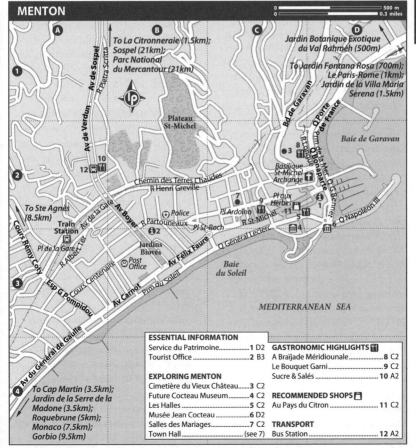

MENTON

ESSENTIAL INFORMATION			
Service du Patrimoine	1 D2	**GASTRONOMIC HIGHLIGHTS** 🍴	
Tourist Office	2 B3	A Braïjade Méridionale	8 C2
		Le Bouquet Garni	9 C2
EXPLORING MENTON		Sucre & Salés	10 A2
Cimetière du Vieux Château	3 C2		
Future Cocteau Museum	4 C2	**RECOMMENDED SHOPS** 🛍	
Les Halles	5 C2	Au Pays du Citron	11 C2
Musée Jean Cocteau	6 D2		
Salles des Mariages	7 C2	**TRANSPORT**	
Town Hall	(see 7)	Bus Station	12 A2

lanes, there is little to see. There are great views from the **Cimetière du Château** towards the top of the hill. The town's epicentre is the area from pedestrian **rue St-Michel**, where ice-cream parlours and souvenir shops jostle for space, to the sea-facing covered market **Les Halles** (quai de Monléon; 5am-1pm Tue-Sun).

COCTEAU & MENTON // ADMIRE COCTEAU'S LEGACY

Poet, artist, novelist and filmmaker Jean Cocteau loved Menton. It was following a stroll along the seaside that he got the idea of turning the disused 17th-century seafront bastion into a monument to his work. Cocteau restored the building himself, decorating the 2m-thick alcoves, outer walls and reception hall with pebble mosaics. This **Musée Jean Cocteau** (☎04 93 57 72 30; Vieux Port; adult/child €3/free; 10am-noon & 2-6pm Wed-Mon) now houses a number of his Mediterranean works (crayon drawings, tapestries, ceramics, photos etc).

In 1957, Cocteau decorated Menton's **Salle des Mariages** (Registry Office; ☎04 92 10 50 00; place Ardoïno; adult/child €1.50/free; 8.30am-12.30pm & 2-5pm Mon-Fri), inside the **town hall**, with scenes of mythological Orpheus' and Eurydice's wedding, galloping horses and starry local lovers.

In 2005, avid Cocteau collector Séverin Wunderman donated some 1500 Cocteau works to Menton, on the condition that the town build a dedicated Cocteau museum. Works started in 2009 and the new museum is scheduled to open in 2011. Until then, works from the Wunderman collection will appear at the bastion on a rotating basis.

BEAUTIFUL GARDENS // STROLL THROUGH MENTON'S BOTANIC WONDERS

Menton's myriad gardens, each with a different horticultural appeal and histori-cal charm, are a true Eden. The most high-profile are open to the public year-round, but there are many more that are only accessible to guided tours or during **Rendez-Vous aux Jardins** (www.rendezvous auxjardins.culture.fr), a four-day festival in June during which rare and elusive gardens across the country open their doors to the public.

Most wonderful perhaps is the **Jardin Botanique Exotique du Val Rahmeh** (☎04 93 35 86 72; av St-Jacques; adult/child €6/1; 10am-12.30pm & 3.30-6.30pm Wed-Mon Apr-Sep, 10am-12.30pm & 2-5pm Wed-Mon Oct-Mar). Laid out in 1905 for Lord Radcliffe, governor of Malta, the terraces overflow with exotic fruit-tree collections and subtropical plants, including the only European specimen of the Easter Island tree *Sophora toromiro,* now extinct on the island.

Equally exuberant but more unkempt is the **Jardin de la Serre de la Madone** (☎04 93 57 73 90; www.serredelamadone.com; 74 rte de Gorbio; adult/child €8/free; 10am-6pm Tue-Sun Apr-Oct, to 5pm Dec-Mar, guided tour 3pm Tue-Sun). It was American gardener Lawrence Johnston who planted dozens of rare plants here, picked up from his travels around the world. Abandoned for decades, it is slowly being restored. Take bus 7 to the 'Serre de la Madone' stop.

Garden buffs might also want to make time for the following, with guided tours from the Service du Patrimoine (see p231).

Jardin Fontana Rosa (av Blasco Ibañez; admission €5; tour only 10am Mon & Fri) Created by Spanish novelist Vicente Blasco Ibañez in the 1920s and decorated with fanciful benches, pergolas and ceramics.
Jardin de la Villa Maria Serena (21 promenade Reine-Astrid; admission €5; tour only 10am Tue) France's most temperate garden – known for its palm, olive and citrus trees – framing the grandiose Villa Maria Serena, designed by Charles Garnier.

La Citronneraie (Colline de l'Annonciade, 69 corniche André Tardieu; admission €8; ☺ tour only, several per month) The 350 citrus trees – think lemons, oranges, clementines, grapefruit – date to the 1950s, but the olive grove is at least 600 years old.

☙ FÊTE DU CITRON // CELEBRATE MENTON'S FAVOURITE FRUIT

Menton's quirky two-week **Fête du Citron** (Lemon Festival; www.feteducitron.com) in February sees sculptures and decorative floats made from 115 metric tonnes of lemons (plus another five tonnes used to replace damaged fruit during the festival) weave processions along the seafront. Afterwards, the monumental lemon creations are dismantled and the fruit sold off at bargain prices in front of Palais de l'Europe. Each year the festival follows a different theme (Asterix, Alice in Wonderland, world carnivals). Accommodation gets booked up weeks in advance so plan ahead.

GASTRONOMIC HIGHLIGHTS

☙ A BRAÏJADE MÉRIDIOUNALE €€

☎ 04 93 35 65 65; 66 rue Longue; menu €28, mains €18; ☺ lunch & dinner Thu-Tue Sep-Jun, dinner Jul & Aug

In a beautiful stone-walled dining room framed by heavy wooden beams, A Braïjade is the only restaurant in the old town and has made the best of it. The house speciality is the original flambé skewers: orange-marinated chicken and pesto-marinated prawns flambé with cognac, for instance. Not only does it taste good, it also looks fabulous (the kebab is flambéed at your table). The menu, which includes an *apéritif*, glass of local wine and digestive, is excellent value.

☙ LE BOUQUET GARNI €

☎ 04 93 35 85 91; 1 rue Palmaro; mains €15; ☺ lunch & dinner Tue-Sat

What you see is what you get at bouquet garni (think a bunch of Provençal herbs), a dead-simple bistro down an alley off the main pedestrian street. Delicious Italian staples (gnocchi, seafood spaghetti etc) feature heavily, as does more local fare such as *brochette de volaille à l'estragon* (poultry skewer with tarragon) or *sole meunière* (pan-fried lemon sole).

☙ LE PARIS-ROME €€€

☎ 04 93 35 73 45; 79 av Porte-de-France; lunch menu €35, 3-/4-course dinner menu €55/70; ☺ lunch & dinner Wed-Sun, dinner Tue

Menton was in dire need of a gastronomic star – it finally got one in the shape of Yannick Fauries. Newly consecrated with a Michelin star, this young chef is infusing some fun in Menton's dining scene with immaculately turned out dishes such as coffee-glazed veal sweetbreads with green asparagus and cardamom ice cream. Le Paris-Rome has also embraced the concept of informal eating: all hail the gastronomic picnic hamper (to order, €35), and the nibble menu (€19), available in the lounge bar for both lunch and dinner.

☙ SUCRE & SALÉS €

☎ 04 93 35 11 45; 8 promenade Maréchal Leclerc; cakes/sandwiches €3/5; ☺ 7.30am-8pm Mon-Sat

Conveniently located opposite the bus station, Sucre & Salés is a contemporary

NICE, MONACO & MENTON

LEMON TREATS

Limoncello, lemon-infused olive oil, lemon preserve, lemon wine, or lemon syrup (for squash) are just some of the delicious products you'll be able to sample and buy at the family-run **Au Pays du Citron** (☎ 04 92 09 22 85; www.aupaysducitron .fr; 24 rue St Michel; ☺ 10am-7pm). Products are also available online.

spot to enjoy a coffee, cake or well-stuffed baguette sandwich. Their desserts are a work of art, with mousses, charlottes and fruit tarts a welcome change from the traditional brownies. The pâtisserie also serves breakfast (€5). A lunch formula of sandwich, dessert and drink is €8.

TRANSPORT

BUS // Bus 100 (€1, every 15 minutes) goes to Nice (1½ hours) via Monaco (40 minutes) and the Corniche Inférieure. Bus 110 links Menton with Nice-Côte d'Azur airport (€18, one hour, hourly).

TRAIN // There are regular services (every 20 minutes) to Ventimiglia in Italy (€2.60, 12 minutes), Monaco (€2.30, 13 minutes) and Nice (€4.40, 35 minutes).

AROUND MENTON

A string of mountain villages peer down on Menton from the surrounding hills. The stunning Parc National du Mercantour (p183), a prime walking area, is a mere 20km away. But there are some fantastic excursions even closer to home. The Guides Randoxygène *Rando Pays Côtier* (available at tourist offices) features a number of walks within a 10km to 15km drive from Menton.

💗 **STE-AGNÈS & GORBIO // EXPLORE THE RUGGED HEIGHTS OF MENTON'S HINTERLAND** Ste-Agnès' claim to fame – Europe's highest seaside village – is not for nothing: sitting snug on a rocky outcrop at

---

LITERARY NICE, MONACO & MENTON

Beach reads set in Nice, Monaco and Menton.

★ *High Season in Nice* (Robert Kanigel) – 'How one French Riviera town has seduced travellers for 2000 years' is the tag line of this fascinating portrait of Nice

★ *The Mystery of the Blue Train* (Agatha Christie) – Hercule Poirot investigates a mysterious murder aboard the *Blue Train* to the Riviera

★ *The Doves' Nest* (Katherine Mansfield) – short story, published the year the tuberculosis-stricken author died in Menton, about a group of lonely women living in a villa on the French Riviera

★ *The Rock Pool* (Cyril Connolly) – 1930s decadence on the French Riviera

★ *The Long Afternoon* (Giles Waterfield) – the tale of the Williamsons and their quest for a quiet retirement, in Menton: told through letters, extracts from literature, and travel guides

★ *Loser Takes All* (Grahame Greene) – short novel written in 1955 in which a young couple are manipulated into honeymooning at the Hôtel de Paris in Monte Carlo and end up risking all at the casino

★ *Collected Short Stories* (Somerset Maugham) – includes 'The Facts of Life', a short story about a tennis player taking to the gambling tables at Monte Carlo; and 'Three Fat Women from Antibes', inspired by the many years Maugham lived on Cap Ferrat

★ *Mademoiselle of Monte Carlo* (William Le Queux) – drama around Monte Carlo's 'suicide table', written in 1921 by the British writer said to have inspired Fleming's 007

780m, the village looks spectacular and commands dramatic views of the area. For the most breathtaking panorama, climb the 200 or so steps to the rubbly 12th-century **Château ruins** (admission by donation; 🕑 10am-6pm) with its intriguing flower beds, based on allegorical **gardens** found in medieval French poetry.

The drawbridged entrance to the huge underground **Fort Ste-Agnès** (☎ 04 93 35 84 58; adult/child €4/2; 🕑 3-6pm Jun-Sep, 2.30-5.30pm Sat & Sun Oct-May) sits at the top of the village. The 2500-sq-metre defence was built between 1932 and 1938 as part of the 240km-long Maginot line, a series of fortifications intended to give France time to mobilise its army if attacked. The fort is in good nick; it was maintained throughout the Cold War as a nuclear fallout shelter!

A well-signposted path leads to the neighbouring village of **Gorbio**, another pretty Provençal village. Just 2km as the crow flies from Ste-Agnès, it is much more convoluted to get there by car, so walking is a good option. Allow one hour on the way down, and 1¼ hours back up, particularly if you've had lunch at the exquisite **Beau Séjour** (☎ 04 93 41 46 15; place du Village, Gorbio; 🕑 lunch/dinner menu €25/30, mains €25; 🕑 lunch & dinner Thu-Tue Apr-Oct). The stuff of Provençal lunch dreams, Beautiful Stay serves up local fare in a buttermilk house overlooking the village square. Inside, the dining room, which looks like it is straight out of a glossy design magazine, proffers panoramic views of the tumbling vale. No credit cards.

NICE, MONACO & MENTON

CANNES AREA

3 PERFECT DAYS

❧ DAY 1 // STARSTRUCK
No stay on the Riviera would be complete without a stroll along Cannes' La Croisette (opposite) gawping at the palaces and scanning the beach for celebrities. If you'd like to indulge in creature comforts, plump yourself on the immaculate lounges of Z Plage (p244), the beach of Hôtel Martinez. Or if you'd like a more active approach, head to Cap d'Antibes where a walk around the headland (p251) will reveal row upon row of millionaires' villas.

❧ DAY 2 // ART TRAIL
Retrace the steps of famous 20th-century artists. Start with a tour of the Musée Picasso in Antibes (p250), before driving to Renoir's cherished home (p254) in Cagnes-sur-Mer. Head to La Colombe d'Or for lunch in St-Paul de Vence, where impoverished artists once paid for their meals with works of art. Digest amongst Miró sculptures and Chagall mosaics at the brilliant Fondation Maeght (p257), and finish the day with a visit to Matisse's masterpiece, the Chapelle du Rosaire (p256) in Vence.

❧ DAY 3 // NATURAL WONDER
Spend a day exploring the stunning and unspoilt Massif de l'Estérel (p269). Active types should opt for the Sentier du Littoral (p216), or tackle the red spires of Cap Roux (p270) and feast on picnic and panoramic views at the summit. Beach bums will have the chance to seek out their own secret cove and snorkel the afternoon away in crystal-clear waters. Crown the day with a Provençal meal fit for a king at Villa Matuzia (p270).

CANNES TO NICE

· · · · · ·

CANNES

pop 70,610

Walking along the couture shops and palaces of La Croisette, you'd be forgiven for thinking that the economic recession of the late noughties was all media hype. There is as much wealth and glamour as ever and admiring Ferraris and Porsches, or celebrity-spotting on the liner-sized yachts are still favourite pastimes.

For those who aren't seduced by Cannes' hedonistic air, there's enough natural beauty to make a trip worthwhile: the harbour, the bay, the clutch of islands off the coast and the old quarter, Le Suquet, all spring into life on a sunny day.

As for the world-famous eponymous film festival (see the boxed text, p245), it is unfortunately not the most visitor-friendly event: think stratospheric prices and insider-only attendance. It is however, celebrity-spotting at its very best!

ESSENTIAL INFORMATION

EMERGENCIES // SOS Médecins (☎ 08 25 00 50 04; ☺ 24hr) Emergency doctor service.
TOURIST OFFICES // Cannes Tourist Office (www.cannes.fr); Main tourist office (☎ 04 92 99 84 22; bd de la Croisette; ☺ 9am-8pm Jul & Aug, 9am-7pm Sep-Jun) On the ground floor of Palais des Festivals; Train station annexe (☎ 04 93 99 19 77; rue Jean Jaurès; ☺ 9am-1pm & 2-6pm Mon-Sat Sep-Jun, 9am-7pm Jul & Aug).

ORIENTATION

Don't expect glitz'n'glamour the second you hop off the train: things don't glam up until rue d'Antibes, the main shopping street a couple of blocks south. A couple more blocks south again is Palais des Festivals, east of Vieux Port at the start of Cannes' famous promenade, bd de la Croisette, which follows the shore eastwards along Baie de Cannes to Pointe de la Croisette.

Perched on a hill just to the west of Vieux Port and of the bus station is the old quarter of Cannes: the quaint, pedestrianised Le Suquet.

EXPLORING CANNES

❦ LA CROISETTE // STROLL ALONG THE WORLD-FAMOUS PROMENADE

The multi-starred hotels and couture shops that line the famous **bd de la Croisette** (aka La Croisette) may be the preserve of the rich and famous, but anyone can enjoy the palm-shaded promenade and take in the atmosphere. In fact, it's a favourite even amongst Cannois (natives of Cannes). The views of the bay and nearby Estérel mountains are beautiful, as is the art-deco architecture of the seafront palaces, such as the **Martinez** (see p394) or the legendary **Carlton InterContinental**; its twin cupolas were modelled on the breasts of the courtesan La Belle Otéro, infamous for her string of lovers – Tsar Nicholas II and Britain's King Edward VII among them.

Not so elegant but imposing nonetheless is the **Palais des Festivals** (Festival Palace; ☎ 04 93 39 01 01; bd de la Croisette) at the western end of the prom, an ugly concrete beast and unlikely host of the world's most glamorous film festival (see the boxed text, p245). Climb the red carpet, walk down the auditorium, tread the stage and learn about cinema's most glamorous event and its numerous anecdotes on a **Palais des Festivals guided**

(Continued on page 243)

CANNES AREA

CANNES AREA

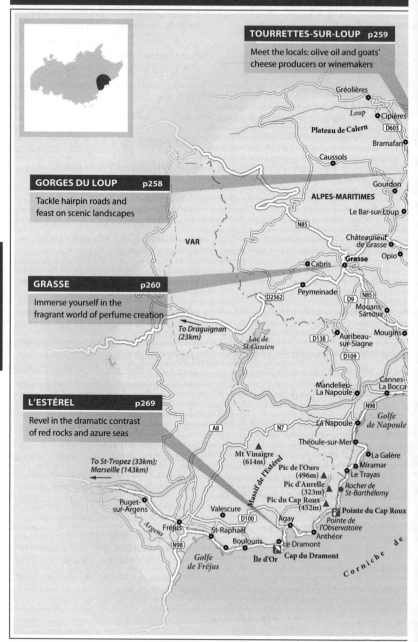

TOURRETTES-SUR-LOUP p259

Meet the locals: olive oil and goats' cheese producers or winemakers

Gréolières

Loup

Cipières

D603

Plateau de Calern

Bramafan

Caussols

GORGES DU LOUP   p258

Tackle hairpin roads and feast on scenic landscapes

Gourdon

ALPES-MARITIMES

Le Bar-sur-Loup

N85

Châteauneuf de Grasse

Opio

VAR

Cabris   **Grasse**

GRASSE   p260

Immerse yourself in the fragrant world of perfume creation

Peymeinade

D2562

D9   N85

Mouans-Sartoux

To Draguignan (23km)

Lac de St-Cassien

D138   Auribeau-sur-Siagne   Mougins

D109

Mandelieu-La Napoule   Cannes-La Bocca

N98

L'ESTÉREL   p269

Revel in the dramatic contrast of red rocks and azure seas

La Napoule   *Golfe de Napoule*

A8   N7

Théoule-sur-Mer   La Galère

To St-Tropez (33km); Marseille (143km)

Mt Vinaigre (614m)   Miramar

Pic de l'Ours (496m)   Le Trayas

Pic d'Aurelle (323m)   *Rocher de St-Barthélemy*

Puget-sur-Argens   Pic du Cap Roux (452m)   **Pointe du Cap Roux**

Pointe de l'Observatoire

Valescure   D100   Agay   Anthéor

Fréjus   St-Raphaël

N98   Boulouris   Le Dramont

Golfe de Fréjus   Île d'Or   Cap du Dramont

Corniche de

Massif de l'Estérel

Argens

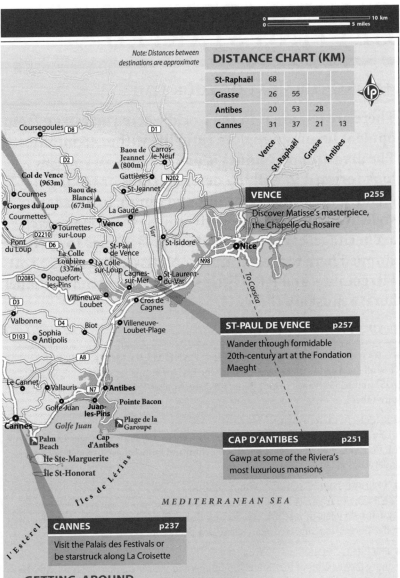

	Vence	St-Raphaël	Grasse	Antibes
St-Raphaël	68			
Grasse	26	55		
Antibes	20	53	28	
Cannes	31	37	21	13

Note: Distances between destinations are approximate

DISTANCE CHART (KM)

VENCE p255

Discover Matisse's masterpiece, the Chapelle du Rosaire

ST-PAUL DE VENCE p257

Wander through formidable 20th-century art at the Fondation Maeght

CAP D'ANTIBES p251

Gawp at some of the Riviera's most luxurious mansions

CANNES p237

Visit the Palais des Festivals or be starstruck along La Croisette

GETTING AROUND

Public transport (bus and train) is pretty good between towns of the Alpes-Maritimes *département* but pretty thin on the ground in more rural areas such as the Gorges du Loup or the Estérel – you'll definitely need your own wheels to explore these scenic spots. Driving in the more populated Cannes–Grasse–Antibes triangle is relatively straightforward (good signposting) but dense at rush hour (between 7.30am and 9.30am in the morning and 4.30pm and 7.30pm in the evening).

CANNES AREA

CANNES AREA GETTING STARTED

MAKING THE MOST OF YOUR TIME

There are few areas in the world where you can go from opulent luxury to remote rural life within 45 minutes. The area around Cannes is one of them, so you can look forward to walking deserted trails or talking to an olive-oil producer by day and dining in decadent style by night. Equally captivating is the region's rich art heritage: every 20th-century great seems to have stopped here for inspiration – Matisse, Picasso, F Scott Fitzgerald – and left a little something behind (a chapel here, a museum there…).

TOP TOURS & COURSES

❧ TRAIL PICASSO, MATISSE, CHAGALL AND MANY MORE
They all lived and worked here – retrace the Riviera' iconic artists' steps in St-Paul (p257 and p258), Vence (p256), Biot (p255) or Antibes (p250) and discover what inspired them.

❧ SNORKELLING TOURS
Meet the Côte d'Azur's marine residents – sea anemone, sea urchin, starfish and more fish than you could name – under the watchful and knowledgeable goggles of your underwater guide. (p268)

❧ ATELIER DE LA CUISINE DES FLEURS
You'll wow your guests at your next dinner party once you've learned how to add crystallised violets or rose preserve to your dish. Try these cooking classes with a twist in the Gorges du Loup. (www.la-cuisine-des-fleurs.com, p259)

❧ ESTÉREL CRUISE
Admire the red cliffs of the Estérel mountains and their incredible contrast with the forest's intense green and deep transparent blue of the water from out at sea. (p243)

❧ PERFUME CREATION WORKSHOP
A touch of rose, a hint of bergamot and voilà, your perfume is ready! Or so you might think – try your hand (nose) at the incredibly skilful art of fragrance creation in Grasse. (p262)

GETTING AWAY FROM IT ALL

The Côte d'Azur is relentlessly popular, so much so that a far from the madding crowd joker is a must! Thankfully there are some great ones to choose from.

★ **Massif de l'Estérel** Pristine forests, deserted tracks and sterling views of the Med, it doesn't get much better than that for a quiet day (p269).

★ **Ste-Marguerite** With its seaweed-covered coves and forest tracks, this little island is definitely more Robinson Crusoe than Marilyn Monroe – and just a 20 minute-boat ride from Cannes (p247).

★ **Col de Vence & Around** Admire the coast from the deserted heights of the Pays Vençois (p260).

ADVANCE PLANNING

Many of the most fun activities in the region only take place on certain days of the week or month.

★ Check dates ahead for **perfume workshops** (p262).

★ the Palais des Festivals **guided tours** in Cannes (p237), the quirky **Antibes tours** (p250), **Grasse guided tours** (p264) and **cooking courses** (p259 and p266).

★ **Festival de Cannes** (p245) Though fabulously glamorous, this festival (in May) is a bit of a nuisance for visitors: accommodation is booked up months in advance and prices soar. The festival is also mostly off-limits to industry outsiders – celebrity-spotting is the best it offers.

TOP RESTAURANTS

♣ **MANTEL**
Divine cuisine at affordable prices (p245)

♣ **LE BROC EN BOUCHE**
Gourmet bistro with vintage atmosphere (p253)

♣ **LES BACCHANALES**
Michelin-starred cuisine at its most creative (p256)

♣ **L'HOSTELLERIE DU CHÂTEAU**
Wonderfully original and divine, with sweeping panoramas on the side (p260)

♣ **LES CHARAVINS**
Where wine matters at least as much as food (p268)

♣ **VILLA MATUZIA**
Exquisite flavours, best enjoyed on the sun-drenched terrace or by the fireplace (p270)

RESOURCES

★ **www.guideriviera.com** Excellent regional guide run by Côte d'Azur tourism professionals

★ **www.cannes.com** The city's official web portal

★ **www.antibes-juanlespins.com** Online info about Antibes and Juan-les-Pins

★ **Guides Randoxygène** Essential for anyone who loves walking. *Rando Pays Côtier* and *Rando Moyen Pays* both cover walks in this chapter; available in all tourist offices

CANNES AREA

CANNES AREA

CANNES

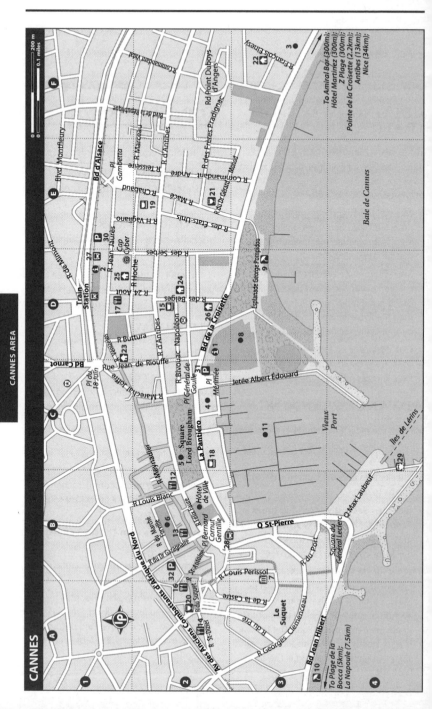

(Continued from page 237)

tour (€2.50; 1½ hr; ⏰ 2.30pm). The tourist-office-run tours take place several times a month, except in May. Check dates on the offices' website (visits in English are sometimes available). Tickets must be bought at 2pm on the day.

After posing for a photograph on the 22 steps leading up to the cinema entrance, wander along **allée des Étoiles du Cinéma**, a path of celebrity hand imprints in the pavement.

❦ THE VIEUX PORT & LE SUQUET // CANNES' HEART AND SOUL, GLAM AND GLITZ-FREE

On the western side of the Palais des Festivals lies the real Cannes. The yachts that frame the **Vieux Port** are the only reminder that this is where celebrities holiday but they don't seem to impress the pensioners playing *pétanque* (a game like lawn bowls) year-round on shaded **square Lord Brougham**. Half the town hangs out here: kids ride the merry-go-round, teens drink shakes outside McDonald's and a **flower market** blooms across the northern side of the square each morning.

Northwest of the square, a couple of blocks back, is **Marché Forville** (⏰ 7am-1pm Tue-Sun), one of the most important markets in the region and the supplier of choice for restaurants. Snaking up hilly **Le Suquet**, the city's oldest quarter, is restaurant-crammed **rue St-Antoine**, where many of the town's better establishments can be found.

Atop the hill, you could spend as long studying the beautifully presented ethnographic collections of **Musée de la Castre** (☎ 04 93 38 55 26; adult/18-25yr €3.20/2; ⏰ 10am-7pm Jul & Aug, 10am-1pm & 2-6pm Tue-Sun Apr, Jun & Sep, 10am-1pm & 2-5pm Tue-Sun Oct-Mar) as you would admiring the glorious views of the Baie de Cannes and the Estérel summits.

❦ BOAT TRIPS // ADMIRE THE COAST FROM OUT AT SEA

From June to September, **Trans Côte d'Azur** (☎ 04 92 98 71 30; www.trans-cote-azur.com, in French; quai Laubeuf) runs day trips to St-Tropez (adult/child €40/26.50 return) and Monaco (€42.50/26.50), an ideal way to avoid congested roads to these popular spots and relax among scenic landscapes instead. Panoramic cruises taking in the dramatic contrasts of the Estérel's red cliffs, green forests and intense azure waters are another must (€23/14).

❦ BEACHES // PAYING OR NOT, BE A BEACH BUM

Cannes is blessed with sandy beaches, although much of the stretch along bd de la Croisette is for guests of top-notch hotels or those prepared to pay for the luxury of having a strip of carpet leading to the water's edge: rates range from €15/19 per half-/full day for a mattress and yellow-and-white parasol on **Plage du Gray d'Albion** (☎ 04 92 99 79 99; 10am-6pm) – it has a water-skiing school – to €31/27/35 for the pearl-white lounges on the front row/other rows/pier of the super-stylish **Z Plage** (9.30am-6pm), the beach of Hôtel Martinez.

This arrangement leaves only a small cheap strip of sand near the Palais des Festivals for the bathing hoi polloi, although free public beaches **Plage du Midi** and **Plage de la Bocca** stretch for several kilometres west from Vieux Port along bd Jean Hibert and bd du Midi.

ACCOMMODATION

Unsurprisingly, there are some exceptional, and unusual, hotels to choose from in this area. What's more, many are relatively affordable outside of summer months. For a complete list of recommendations, see the accommodation chapter.

★ An essential sleepover for any modern art lover is **La Maison du Frêne** (p395), where the owners' private collection adorn the house

★ Green souls will love the tree houses and eco-pool at **Les Cabanes d'Orion** (p396)

★ Revel in eccentric luxury at **Hôtel 3.14** (p394) and make the best of the exotic rooftop garden and pool

★ For the perfect location, head to the small but perfectly formed **Hôtel La Jabotte** (p395) between Antibes and the cape

GASTRONOMIC HIGHLIGHTS

ASTOUX & BRUN €€
☎ 04 93 39 21 87; 21 rue Félix Faure; seafood platters €25-39, mains €20-25; lunch & dinner

Every type and size of oyster is available alongside lobster, crab, sea urchins, scallops, winkles and stuffed mussels at this temple to seafood founded in 1953. If you've never had the chance to try a seafood platter, this is *the* place to do it, washed down with an ice-cold bottle of white. Watch the deft chefs crack oysters open on the street-side kitchen: you'd never know from their speed that it is actually quite tricky!

AUX BONS ENFANTS €€
80 rue Meynadier; menu €24; lunch & dinner Tue-Sat

A people's-choice place since 1935, this informal restaurant cooks up wonderful regional dishes such as aïoli *garni* (aïoli with vegetables), *daube* (a Provençal beef stew), and *rascasse meunière* (pan-fried rockfish), all in a convivial atmosphere. Make no plans for the afternoon after lunching here. No credit cards.

BARBARELLA €€
☎ 04 92 99 17 33; 16 rue St-Dizier; menu €25-35; dinner Tue-Sun

The reputation of this gay-friendly establishment perched on top of the Suquet owes as much to its superbly eccentric, slightly retro, Philippe Starck–style decor (see-through coloured plastic chairs, psychedelic lighting, latest techno-lounge sounds) as to its top-notch fusion food (sweet-and-sour duck, foie gras and exotic fruit chutneys, fruit sushi etc). Eating out made fun.

LA TARTERIE €
☎ 04 93 39 67 43; 33 rue Bivouac Napoléon; tart slices €4-5, with salad €9; 8.30am-6.30pm Mon-Sat

STARRING AT CANNES

For 10 days in May, all eyes turn to Cannes, centre of the cinematic universe where more than 33,000 producers, distributors, directors, publicists, stars and hangers-on descend to buy, sell or promote more than 2000 films. As the premier film event of the year, the **festival** (www.festival-cannes.com) attracts some 4000 journalists from around the world.

At the centre of the whirlwind is the colossal, 60,000-sq-metre Palais des Festivals, where the official selections are screened. The palace opened in 1982, replacing the original Palais des Festival – since demolished. The inaugural festival was scheduled for 1 September 1939, as a response to Mussolini's Fascist propaganda film festival in Venice, but Hitler's invasion of Poland brought the festival to an abrupt end. It re-started in 1946 – and the rest is history.

Over the years the festival split into 'in competition' and 'out of competition' sections. The goal of 'in competition' films is the prestigious Palme d'Or, awarded by the jury and its president to the film that best 'serves the evolution of cinematic art'. Notable winners include Francis Ford Coppola's *Apocalypse Now* (1979), Quentin Tarantino's cult film *Pulp Fiction* (1994) and American activist Michael Moore's anti–Bush administration polemic *Fahrenheit 9/11* (2004). More recent winners include Michael Haneke's disturbing *White Ribbon,* set in pre-WWI Germany, and *La Classe* (2008), a film by Laurent Cantet about teaching in tough Parisian suburbs.

The vast majority of films are 'out of competition'. Behind the scenes the **Marché du Film** (Film Market; www.marchedufilm.com) sees nearly one-billion dollars' worth of business negotiated in distribution deals. And it's this hard-core commerce combined with all the televised Tinseltown glitz that gives the film festival its special magic.

Tickets to the Cannes film festival are off-limits to average Joes. What you can get are free tickets to selected individual films, usually after their first screening. Invitations must be picked up on the day at **Espace Cannes Cinéphiles** (☎ 04 97 06 45 15; La Pantiéro; ⊙ 9am-5.30pm) and are limited. Alternatively, take a tour of the Palais des Festivals (see p237) to find out what goes on behind and on the scene.

Hearty salads, tasty quiches, fancy fruit tarts and clafoutis (a batter cake with fruit) ensure there's always a queue at this good-value tart house. It's ideal for a quick and affordable sit-down lunch but you can also take your goodies away – so much more satisfying than a sandwich!

♥ MANTEL €€

☎ 04 93 39 13 10; 22 rue St-Antoine; lunch/dinner menus from €25/36; ⊙ lunch Fri-Mon, dinner Thu-Tue
Discover why Noël Mantel is the hotshot of the Cannois gastronomic scene at his refined old-town restaurant. Service is stellar and the seasonal cuisine divine: try the wonderfully tender glazed veal shank in balsamic vinegar or the original poached octopus *bourride*-style. Best of all though, you get not one but two desserts from pastry-chef wonder Christian Gonthier, who bakes the bread, and prepares the sweets served with coffee.

♥ NEW MONACO €€

☎ 04 98 38 37 76; 15 rue du 24 Août; lunch/dinner menu €14.50/23; ⊙ lunch Tue-Sat, dinner Thu-Sat
The New Monaco is proof of the pudding that simple is best. Phil and Délia serve generous portions of delicious

staples such as juicy leg of lamb with creamy *gratin dauphinois* (potato gratin), tasty *andouillette* (pork tripe sausage), delicate apple tart and homemade tiramisus, all with a smile on the side. Cannois have been quick to spot the bargain: it's a full-house every lunch time and evening.

☕ PHILCAT €

☎ 04 93 38 43 42; La Pantiéro; sandwiches or salads €5; ⏰ 8.30am-5pm

Don't be put off by Phillipe and Catherine's unassuming prefab cabin on the Pantiéro: this is Cannes' best lunch house. Huge salads, made to order, are piled high with fresh lettuce and tomatoes, goat's cheese, Parma ham, tuna, marinated peppers and more. Or if you're *really* hungry, try one of their phenomenal *pan bagna* (a moist sandwich bursting with Provençal flavours). Take away or savour at their little terrace with a view of the yachts.

☕ VOLUPTÉ €

☎ 04 93 39 60 32; 32 rue Hoche; snacks €5, mains €14-17; ⏰ 9am-8pm Mon-Sat

With its 140 different types of teas, all neatly stocked in red-and-white tins spanning an entire wall, this elegant tearoom has become something of a mundane hot spot. Young and beautiful things come here to sip rare Chinese white teas and nibble on bresaola (cured salted beef) and parmesan *tartines* (a slice of bread with toppings). There is also a good selection of (healthy!) salads and mouth-watering treats to undo all the healthy work.

NIGHTLIFE

Bars around the 'magic square' (the area bordered by rue Commandant André, rue des Frères Pradignac, rue du Batégui-

er and rue du Dr Gérard Monod) tend to be young, trendy and pretty rowdy. For a more sophisticated atmosphere, try the beach or top hotel bars. Pick up the free monthly *Le Mois à Cannes* for full event listings.

☕ AMIRAL BAR

☎ 04 92 98 73 00; 73 bd de la Croisette; ⏰ 11am-2.30am

A cocktail from the extensive – and expensive – selection of the Martinez' legendary piano bar is a must when in town. Punters enjoy live music every night, from the mellow jazz notes of the grand piano to full-on bands playing the last 30 years' hits.

☕ CARIGNAN

☎ 04 93 39 71 14; 26 rue du Suquet; ⏰ 5pm-12.30am

Taste wine safe in the knowledge that Léandre Piquet (a former sommelier at the Majestic) is an authority. Find him behind the bar in his pocket-sized *bar à vins* (wine bar) atop the hill in Le Suquet and let him guide you through some of his 100-plus references, from big vintages to organic productions. Make it the perfect *apéritif* with a cheese board or charcuterie selection.

☕ LE SUN 7

☎ 04 93 39 38 70; 5 rue du Dr Gérard Monod; ⏰ 9pm-2.30am

The cocktail list is one arm long (literally), and it doesn't even include the 350 whiskies and many draught beers also served at this happening bar. The crowd is young on weekend nights, when DJs spin their stuff, but much more mellow and eclectic during the week.

TRANSPORT

TRAIN // Cannes is well connected to Nice (€5.80, 30 minutes), Antibes (€2.50, 10 minutes), Monaco (€8, one hour) and St-Raphaël (€6.10, 40 minutes), with services every 20 minutes or so. There are trains to Marseille (€28.10, two hours) half-hourly.

BUS // The electric **Elo Bus** (€1) follows a loop that takes in the bus station on place Cornut Gentille, the Croisette, rue d'Antibes and the train station. It has no set stops, just flag it down as it passes. **TAM** (www.randoxygene.fr/transport/transports-tam.html) runs express services to Nice (bus 200, €1, 1½ hours, every 15 minutes) and Nice airport (bus 210, €14.70, 50 minutes, half hourly). Bus 600 (€1, every 20 minutes) for Mougins and Grasse leaves from the bus station next to the train station.

CAR // The A8 motorway, that follows the coast from Italy to St-Raphaël, passes above Le Cannet. It is fast but expensive (with tolls). For cheaper but slower travel, follow the green *'par bord de mer'* signs.

PARKING // Street parking is limited to two hours in the centre. Opt for car parks instead, there are plenty (Palais des Festivals, Forville, train station).

ÎLES DE LÉRINS

The two islands making up Lérins – Île Ste-Marguerite and Île St-Honorat – lie within a 20-minute boat ride of Cannes. Tiny and traffic-free, they're oases of peace and tranquillity, a world away from the hustle and bustle of the Riviera.

Camping is forbidden; there are no hotels and only a couple of eating options so bring a picnic and a good supply of drinking water.

Boats for the islands leave Cannes from quai des Îles, at the end of quai Laubeuf on the western side of the harbour. **Riviera Lines** (☎ 04 92 98 71 31; ww.riviera-lines.com) run ferries to Île Ste-Marguerite (adult/child €11/5.50 return), while **Compagnie Planaria** (☎ 04 92 98 71 38; www.cannes-ilesdelerins.com) operates boats going to Île St-Honorat (adult/child €11/5.50 return).

In St-Raphaël, **Les Bateaux de St-Raphaël** (see p268) also runs excursions to Ste-Marguerite.

❧ ÎLE STE-MARGUERITE // UNSPOILT SHORES, FAR FAR FROM THE MADDING CROWD

Covered in sweet-smelling eucalyptus and pine, Ste-Marguerite, just 1km from the mainland, makes a wonderful day trip from Cannes. Its shores are an endless succession of castaway beaches and fishing spots ideal for picnics, and there are numerous walking trails.

The island served as a strategic defence post for centuries. **Fort Royal**, built by Richelieu in the 17th century and later fortified by Vauban, today houses **Musée de la Mer** (☎ 04 93 38 55 26; adult/18-25yr €3.20/2; ☉ 10am-5.45pm Jun-Sep, 10am-1.15pm & 2.15-5.45pm Apr & May, 10.30am-1.15pm & 2.15-5.45pm Oct-Mar), with exhibits on the island's Greco-Roman history. You can also visit the cells of the former **state prison**, whose most famous inmate, the Man in the Iron Mask, has puzzled historians for centuries (see p248).

❧ ÎLE ST-HONORAT // DISCOVER ONE OF FRANCE'S OLDEST MONASTIC COMMUNITIES

Forested St-Honorat was once the site of a powerful monastery founded in the 5th century. Now it's home to 25 Cistercian monks who own the island but welcome visitors. At 1.5km by 400m, St-Honorat is the smallest (and most southerly) of the two Lérins islands.

The **Monastère Fortifié** (☎ 04 92 99 54 00; www.abbayedelerins.com, in French) guarding the island's southern shores is all that remains of the original monastery. Built in 1073 to protect the monks from pirate attacks, its entrance stood 4m above ground level and was accessible only by ladder (later replaced by the stone staircase evident today). The elegant arches of the vaulted prayer cloister on the 1st floor date from the 15th century, and

CANNES AREA

THE MAN IN THE IRON MASK

The Man in the Iron Mask was imprisoned by Louis XIV (r 1661–1715) in the fortress on Île Ste-Marguerite from around 1687 until 1698, when he was transferred to the Bastille in Paris. Only the king knew the identity of the man behind the mask, prompting a rich pageant of myth and legend to be woven around the ill-fated inmate.

More than 60 suggested identities have been showered on the masked prisoner, among them the Duke of Monmouth (actually beheaded under James II), the Comte de Vermandois (son of Louis XIV, said to have died from smallpox in 1683), and Molière. Some theorists claimed the Man in the Iron Mask was actually a woman.

In 1751, political and social satirist Voltaire (1694–1778) published *Le Siècle de Louis XIV* in which he claimed the prisoner was the king's brother – a twin or an illegitimate older brother.

With the 1850 publication of Alexandre Dumas' novel *Le Vicomte de Bragelonne,* the 'royal crime' became written in stone: in 1638 Anne of Austria, wife of Louis XIII (r 1617–43) and mother of Louis XIV, gives birth to twins; one is taken away from her, leaving her to bear the secret alone until the terrible truth is discovered.

there's a magnificent panorama of the coast from the *donjon* terrace.

In front of the *donjon* is the walled, 19th-century **Abbaye Notre Dame de Lérins**, built around a medieval cloister. In the souvenir shop you can buy the 50% alcohol Lérina, a ruby-red, lemon-yellow or pea-green liqueur concocted from 44 different herbs. The monks also produce wine from their small vineyard.

ANTIBES AREA

pop 75,820
With its boat-bedecked port, 16th-century ramparts and narrow cobblestone streets festooned with flowers, lovely Antibes is the quintessential Mediterranean town. Picasso, Max Ernst and Nicolas de Staël were captivated by Antibes, as was a restless Graham Greene (1904–91) who settled here with his lover, Yvonne Cloetta, from 1966 until the year before his death.

Greater Antibes embraces Cap d'Antibes, an exclusive green cape studded with luxurious mansions, and the modern beach resort of Juan-les-Pins.

The latter is known for its 2km-long sandy beach and its nightlife, a legacy of the sizzling 1920s when Americans swung into town with their jazz music and oh-so-brief swimsuits.

The southwestern tip of the cape is crowned by legendary Hôtel du Cap – Eden Roc. Dating from 1870, it hit the big time just after WWI when a literary salon held here one summer (previous guests had come for the winter season only) was attended by Hemingway, Picasso et al. The icing on the cake was the immortalisation of the hotel (as the thinly disguised, fictional Hôtel des Étrangers) by F Scott Fitzgerald in his novel *Tender Is the Night* (1934).

ESSENTIAL INFORMATION

TOURIST OFFICES // Antibes Juan-les-Pins Tourist Office (www.antibesjuanlespins .com) Antibes (☎ 04 92 90 53 00; 11 place du Général de Gaulle; ◷ 9am-7pm Jul & Aug, 9am-12.30pm & 1.30-6pm Mon-Fri, 9am-noon & 2-6pm Sat, 10am-12.30pm & 2.30-5pm Sun Sep-Jun); Juan-les-Pins (☎ 04 92 90 53 05; 55 bd Charles Guillaumont; ◷ 9am-7pm

CANNES AREA

Jul & Aug, 9am-noon & 2-6pm Mon-Sat Sep-Jun) **Accueil Touristique du Vieil Antibes** (☎04 93 34 65 65; 32 bd d'Aguillon; ☺10am-noon & 1-6pm Mon-Sat Sep-Jun, 10am-9pm Jul & Aug).

ORIENTATION

Antibes is divided into three areas: the commercial centre around place du Général de Gaulle, Vieil Antibes (Old Antibes) south of Port Vauban and the Vieux Port, and Cap d'Antibes to the southwest, including the contiguous community of Juan-les-Pins.

Av Robert Soleau links Antibes train station with place du Général de Gaulle, where the tourist office is. From here, Juan-les-Pins is a straight 1.5km walk along bd du Président Wilson, which runs southwest off Antibes' central square.

EXPLORING ANTIBES AREA

Vieil Antibes is a pleasant maze of food shops, boutiques and restaurants. The **Marché Provençal** (☺7am-1pm Tue-Sun Sep-Jun, daily Jul & Aug) on place Masséna, at the top of the old town, is an institution.

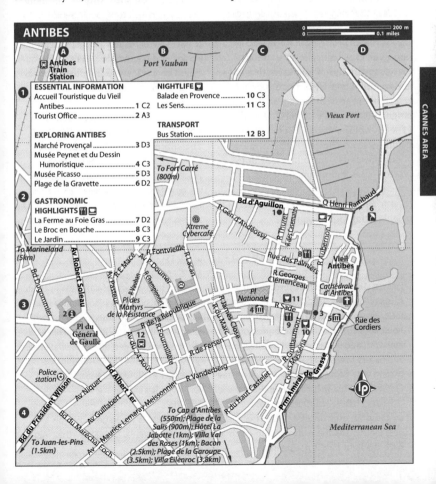

❤ MUSÉE PICASSO // ONCE PICASSO'S STUDIO, NOW A UNIQUE COLLECTION

> If you want to see the Picassos from Antibes, you have to see them in Antibes.
>
> *Pablo Picasso*

Spectacularly positioned overlooking the sea, 14th-century Château Grimaldi served as Picasso's studio from July to December 1946. What is now Antibes' star museum, the **Musée Picasso** (☎ 04 92 90 54 20; Château Grimaldi, 4 rue des Cordiers; adult/ concession €6/3; ☻ 10am-6pm Tue-Sun mid-Jun–mid-Sep, 10am-noon & 2-6pm Tue-Sun mid-Sep–mid-Jun) houses an excellent collection of the master's paintings, lithographs, drawings and ceramics, as well as a photographic record of the artist at work. Particularly poignant is Picasso's *La Joie de Vivre* (The Joy of Life), one in a series of 25 paintings from *The Antipolis Suite*. The young flower girl, surrounded by flute-playing fauns and mountain goats, symbolises Françoise Gilot, the 23-year-old lover of Picasso, with whom he lived in neighbouring Golfe-Juan.

❤ VIEIL ANTIBES GUIDED TOURS // HISTORY WITH A TWIST

Antibes has a rich and complex history: not only does it go back a very long way (more than 25 centuries), it has also played host to illustrious visitors who brought with them their fare share of anecdotes. Try the tourist office's 1½-hour **Artists and the Mediterranean Sea guided tour** (adult/couple/child €7/12/3.50) to understand what inspired the likes of Graham Greene, Picasso, Prévert or F Scott Fitzgerald. Or join the Accueil Touristique du Vieil Antibes' two-hour **Quirky Antibes tour** (adult/child €7/free) to find out about James Bond's appearance at Fort Carré, Sydney Bechet's wedding parade and Nicolas de Staël's tragic suicide. These weekly tours must be booked ahead and days of the visits vary.

❤ FORT CARRÉ // TESTIMONY TO ANTIBES' HISTORICAL HEYDAY

The impregnable 16th-century **Fort Carré** (☎ 06 14 89 17 45; rte du Bord de Mer; guided tour only adult/child €3/free; ☻ 10am-6pm Tue-Sun mid-Jun–mid-Sep, 10am-4.30pm Tue-Sun mid-Sep–mid-Jun), enlarged by Vauban in the 17th century, dominates the approach to

---

∼ WORTH A TRIP ∼

Picasso (1881–1973) discovered ceramics in the small potters' village of **Vallauris** in 1947. Attracted by its artistic vibe, he settled in Vallauris between 1948 and 1955. During that time, Picasso produced some 4000 ceramics (many on display at the Musée Picasso in Antibes, above) as well as his last great political composition, the **Chapelle La Guerre et La Paix** (War and Peace Chapel), a collection of dramatic murals painted on plywood panels and tacked to the walls of a disused 12th-century chapel. It is now the **Musée Picasso La Guerre et la Paix** (☎ 04 93 64 71 83; www.musee-picasso-vallauris.fr; place de la Libération; adult/child €3.25/free; ☻ 10am-12.15pm & 2-6pm Wed-Mon mid-Jun–mid-Sep, to 5pm mid-Sep–mid-Jun).

Picasso left Vallauris another gift: a dour bronze figure clutching a sheep, **L'Homme au Mouton**, now on place Paul Isnard (adjoining place de la Libération). But his biggest legacy was the revival of the ceramics industry in Vallauris, an activity that might have died out had it not been for the 'Picasso effect'.

Antibes from Nice. It served as a border defence post until 1860 when Nice, until then in Italian hands, became French. Tours depart half-hourly and guides speak English.

☙ MUSÉE PEYNET ET DU DESSIN HUMORISTIQUE // CONTEMPLATE THE ART AND POWER OF CARTOONS

You'll find more than 300 pictures, cartoons, sculptures and costumes by veteran cartoonist Raymond Peynet at the eponymous **museum** (☎ 04 92 90 54 30; musee .peynet@ville-antibes.fr; place Nationale; adult/child €3/free; ⏰ 10am-noon & 2-6pm Tue-Sun, to 8pm Wed & Fri Jul & Aug). Best known for his *Lovers* series, and a long-time resident of Antibes, you'll realise you know Peynet when you see his work. In addition, the museum runs fantastic temporary exhibitions by other illustrators and cartoonists.

☙ MARINELAND // AMUSEMENT PARK-STYLE MARINE ZOO

Killer-whale and dolphin shows, a shark tunnel, aquariums, sea lions, turtles and otters, **Marineland** (☎ 08 92 30 06 06; www .marineland.fr; N7; adult/child €35/26; ⏰ 10am-10.30pm Jul & Aug, 10am-8pm Sep-Dec & Feb-Jun) will have kids squealing with delight. The site is big, with shows and interactive sessions (feeding time, training etc) throughout the day. There are picnic areas as well as restaurants.

On the same site, **Aquasplash** (a water park with slides), **La Petite Ferme du Far West** (a cowboy-themed farm with amusements) and **Adventure Golf** (crazy golf) provide additional entertainment, although it's hard to squeeze in more than two parks in a day. Combined tickets for two are available.

Take bus 10 from Antibes bus station to the Marineland stop. The nearest

BARGAIN BOX

If you intend to visit all of Antibes' museums, buy a **combined ticket** (€10). It's valid for seven days and can be purchased from the museums or the tourist office.

train station is Biot. For those driving, Marineland is on the D4 in the direction of Biot, off the N7 between Antibes and Nice. Parking is a hefty €5 no matter how long you stay.

☙ A WALK AROUND THE CAPE // CAP D'ANTIBES IN A NUTSHELL

Starting from the pretty but relentlessly popular **Plage de la Garoupe**, a scenic and signposted **path** skirts the shores to **Cap Gros**, the cape's southeastern-most tip. The contrast between the ruggedness of the coastline on one side and the manicured, CCTV'd lawns of the millionaire's mansions on the other are typical of the cape.

Further along the cape is the stunning 11-hectare landscaped park of **Villa Eilenroc** (☎ 04 93 67 74 33; av de Beaumont; admission free; ⏰ villa 9am-noon & 1.30-5pm Wed Sep-Jun, park 9am-noon & 1.30-5pm Tue & Wed Sep-Jun). The villa was designed by Charles Garnier (architect of the Paris Opera) in 1867 for rich Dutchman Hugh Hope Loudon, who reversed the name of his wife Cornélie to come up with the villa's name.

The gardens are a fragrant maze of cypress and pine trees, herbs and wild flowers overlooking the sea. The **rose garden** in particular is worth visiting: more than 1500 rose varieties with poetic names – Peynet's lovers, Normandy Sweetness, Gold Symphony – are cultivated, many of them collectors' items only grown here.

CANNES AREA

Signs on chemin des Douaniers and av de Beaumont take you back to Plage de la Garoupe along the cape's mansion-lined avenues.

♥ CHAPELLE DE LA GAROUPE // POIGNANT HISTORY AND SWEEPING VIEWS

Pilgrims have walked up to the plateau of La Garoupe at Cap d'Antibes for centuries. There are still 14 shrines marking the way up chemin du Calvaire from Plage de la Salis, and the **Chapelle de la Garoupe** (http://garoupe.free.fr; chemin du Phare; ☯ 10am-noon & 2.30-5pm) atop the hill, remains an important site for local worshippers: there are more than 300 *ex votos* inside the chapel – photos, model boats and marble plaques expressing gratefulness for protection from the elements, accidents or diseases.

The adjoining **lighthouse** is the modern-day version of what has been an observation point for centuries. Records show that a wooden observation tower already existed in the 16th century. And you can see why: 360-degree views sweep from St-Tropez to Italy and the Alps.

♥ BEACHES // SEA, SAND, SNORKEL AND SUN

Right in the centre of Antibes, you'll find **Plage de la Gravette**, a small patch of sand by the *remparts* (ramparts). Twenty minutes out of town is **Plage de la Salis**, with unbeatable views of old Antibes and the Alps. For a more party-like atmosphere, opt for **Juan-les-Pins**.

The stretch of coast between Plage de la Salis and Cap d'Antibes, especially the section around **Pointe Bacon**, is fringed with rocks coves from which snorkellers frolic in clear waters. On the cape itself, **Plage de la Garoupe** was famously first raked clear of seaweed in 1922 by Cole

Porter and American artist Gerald Murphy to create a sandy beach. Far from an idyllic paradise today, it is packed with **sun-lounges** (per day from €21).

FESTIVALS & EVENTS

July is *the* party month in Antibes and Juan-les-Pins. The headline event is Juan's jazz festival but a number of fringe music festivals are also picking up. **Musiques au Cœur** (www.antibesjuanlespins .com) Held in the beautiful Villa Eilenroc in Cap d'Antibes, this festival celebrates lyrical music and opera; early July **Jazz à Juan** (www.antibesjuanlespins.com) This major festival in mid-July will be celebrating its 50th edition in 2010. Every jazz great has performed here, and Jazz à Juan continues to attract big music names.

GASTRONOMIC HIGHLIGHTS

♥ BACON // CAP D'ANTIBES €€€

☎ 04 93 61 50 02; bd de Bacon, Cap d'Antibes; menus lunch/dinner €49/79, mains €80; ☯ lunch & dinner Wed-Sun, dinner Tue

Nothing to do with pork – rather fish, lots of it, either grilled with fennel, steamed or cooked in a *papillote* (a greased wrapping of parchment paper in which the fish is baked) and dressed in warm olive oil, basil butter, chive butter or broth. *Bouillabaisse* (Marseillais fish stew) is the other dish to revel in at this known-far-and-wide fish restaurant on Pointe Bacon.

♥ LA FERME AU FOIE GRAS // ANTIBES €

☎ 04 93 34 26 50; 35 rue Aubernon; sandwiches €5; ☯ 9am-6pm Tue-Sun

Now, this is our idea of what a good sandwich should be like: filled with foie gras or smoked duck breast, onion chutney or fig jam, truffle cheese and fresh salad. And many people seem to think the same: a queue snakes down from the tiny counter of La Ferme every lunch time. The adjoining shop is where to buy all the delicious fillings to take home with you (130g of foie gras costs €22).

☻ LE BROC EN BOUCHE // ANTIBES €€
☎ 04 93 34 75 60; 8 rue des Palmiers; mains €20-25; ◔ lunch & dinner Thu-Mon, lunch Tue

No two chairs, tables or lights are the same at this lovely bistro: instead, every item has been lovingly sourced from antique shops and car boot sales, giving the place a sophisticated but cosy vintage feel. The charming Flo and Fred have put the same level of care and imagination into their cuisine, artfully combining Provençal and oriental flavours. Highly recommended is the *assiette gourmande,* a selection of starters including foie gras (the house speciality), warm goat's cheese and exotically dressed salads.

☻ LE JARDIN // ANTIBES €€
☎ 04 93 34 64 74; 5 rue Sade; menus €19.50-33.50, mains €20; ◔ lunch & dinner

A stalwart of Antibes' restaurant scene, Le Jardin, as its name suggests, has a delightful garden for alfresco dining, the perfect setting for the restaurant's resolutely southern cuisine. The menu changes with the seasons but is always imaginative and the dishes beautifully presented: pumpkin cappuccino with chestnut froth, sea bream crumble, scallops with sweet-potato blinis, winter yoghurt sorbet with a warm chocolate liqueur. Mediterranean dining with flair.

NIGHTLIFE

In Antibes, pedestrian bd d'Aguillon heaves with merrily piddled Anglophones falling out of the busy 'English' and 'Irish' pubs.

☻ BALADE EN PROVENCE
☎ 04 93 34 93 00; 25 cours Masséna; ◔ 6pm-2am

Flirt with the green fairy at this dedicated absinthe bar in the vaulted basement of an olive oil shop. It is the only one of its kind in France, with an original 1860 zinc bar, five round tables and all the accessories (four-tapped water fountain, sugar cubes etc). Pick from 25 brain-pickling absinthe varieties (€4 per glass) and let the hugely knowledgeable staff debunk some of the myths shrouding this much reviled spirit.

☻ LES SENS
☎ 04 93 74 57 06; 10 rue Sade; ◔ 10am-midnight

Wine shop by day and wine bar by night, Les Sens is a 21st-century cellar: the decor is more designer shop than vaulted basement with its lime green walls, mezzanine bar and lounge music, but the advice is excellent all the same, with a great selection of local and French wines. Make it a night out with tapas-style cheese and charcuterie assortments.

TRANSPORT

TRAIN // Antibes' train station is on the main line between Nice (€3.90, 25 minutes, five hourly) and Cannes (€2.50, 10 minutes, five hourly).

BUS // The TAM (www.cg06.fr/transport) Nice–Cannes service (bus 200, €1) stops by the tourist office. Local bus services (€1) for Opio, Vence and St-Paul de Vence leave from the bus station off rue de la République.

CAR // Vieil Antibes is mostly pedestrianised so park outside the centre and walk in.

PARKING // There are several car parks along the port on av de Verdun. The only free car park is a 20-minute walk from town behind Fort Carré.

BIOT

pop 8800

This charming 15th-century hilltop village was once an important pottery-manufacturing centre specialising in large earthenware oil and wine containers. Metal containers brought an end to this, but Biot is still active in handicraft production, especially glassmaking. The village was also the one-time headquarters (1209–1387) of the Knights Templars, then the Knights of Malta: the picturesque **place des Arcades**, dating from the 13th and 14th centuries, is a reminder of this illustrious past.

Apart from its quaint medieval streets, Biot's main attractions, the Musée Léger and the Verrerie, are located outside the village.

🌱 **MUSÉE NATIONAL FERNAND LÉGER // MAKING SENSE OF LÉGER'S COLOURS AND SHAPES**

Atop a landscaped hill sits the rather imposing, mosaic-covered **Musée Léger** (☎ 04 92 91 50 30; www.musee-fernandleger.fr; chemin du Val de Pome; adult/concession €6.50/5; 🕙 10am-6pm Tue-Sun Jun-Oct, to 5pm Nov-May). Founded by Léger's wife after his death in 1957, the museum presents a thorough overview of Léger's work and life: his brush with cubism, his ongoing interest in architecture and cinema, and the influence of his stays in America. As well as works by Léger himself, the museum contains coloured glass, sculptures and mosaics by other artists based on Léger's work. The museum is located 1.5km from Biot in the direction of Antibes and

CANNES AREA

∾ WORTH A TRIP ∾

Except for their historic centres, the sprawling towns of Villeneuve-Loubet and Cagnes lack charm. Two cultural highlights make it worth the detour however. Le Domaine des Collettes, today the **Musée Renoir** (☎ 04 93 20 61 07; chemin des Collettes, Cagnes-sur-Mer; adult/concession €4/2; 🕙 10am-noon & 2-6pm Wed-Mon May-Sep, to 5pm Oct-Apr), was home and studio to an arthritis-crippled Renoir (1841–1919), who lived here with his wife and three sons from 1907 until his death.

Works of his on display include *Les Grandes Baigneuses* (The Women Bathers; 1892), a reworking of the 1887 original, and rooms are dotted with photographs and personal possessions. The magnificent olive and citrus groves are as much an attraction as the museum itself. Many visitors set up their own easel to paint.

Equally wonderful but in a completely different genre is the **Musée Escoffier de l'Art Culinaire** (Escoffier Museum of Culinary Arts; ☎ 04 93 20 80 51; www.fondation-escoffier.org; 3 rue Auguste Escoffier, Villeneuve-Loubet Village; adult/concession €5/2.50; 🕙 2-7pm Jul & Aug, to 6pm Sun-Fri Sep-Jun), which retraces the history of modern gastronomy. Escoffier (1846–1935), inventor of the *pêche Melba* and dried potato among other things, was France's first great chef and a celebrity amongst Europe's well heeled. The museum includes beautiful period furniture and 'appliances', hilarious period cartoons that ridiculed the notion of cooking as an art, and a fascinating wall chronology retracing the history of cooking and chefs from prehistory to nowadays (alas in French only).

signposted (in brown). Bus 10 between Antibes and Biot stops nearby (at stop Musée Fernand Léger).

❦ RESTAURANT DES ARCADES // A PIECE OF BIOT'S HISTORY

Dining at this lovely **hotel-restaurant** (☎ 04 93 65 01 04; 16 place des Arcades; mains €25-30; 🕓 lunch & dinner Tue-Sat, lunch Sun) on Biot's oldest and most charming square, is a unique occasion: not only is the regional food fabulous, you also get to enjoy Mimi and Dédé Brothier's unique art collection. It is the result of 50 years of friendship between the bistro owners and the many artists living in Biot in postwar years, such as César, Novaro, Vasarely and Léger. Many of the works they donated (paintings, sculptures, mosaics, photographs) are displayed in the dining room and basement galleries. Some have also made their way to the hotel's rooms (see p395).

❦ VERRERIE DE BIOT // WATCH BIOT'S FAMOUS BUBBLED GLASS TAKE SHAPE

Biot's famous bubbled-glass is produced by rolling molten glass into baking soda; bubbles from the chemical reaction are then trapped by a second layer of glass. You can watch skilled glass-blowers at work at the **Verrerie de Biot** (☎ 04 93 65 03 00; www.verreriebiot.com; chemin des Combes; admission free, 45min guided tour €6; 🕓 9.30am-8pm Mon-Sat, 10.30am-1.30pm & 2.30-7.30pm Sun Jul & Aug, 9.30am-6pm Mon-Sat, 10.30am-1.30pm & 2.30-6.30pm Sun Sep-Jun), 1km from the centre at the foot of the village. The *verrerie* also has a couple of art galleries and a shop where you can buy glasses, vases etc made on site. Find it 1km downhill from the village, linked by a free shuttle or a small path.

THE ARRIÈRE-PAYS

· · · · · ·

The 'coast' in Côte d'Azur is what many people come to see, but the *arrière-pays* (hinterland) has a charm of its own. Less crowded and incredibly varied, it has something for everyone: from keen walkers to culture vultures and foodies.

VENCE

pop 18,930
Despite its well-preserved medieval centre, visitors often skip Vieux Vence altogether to head straight to Matisse's otherworldly Chapelle du Rosaire. Yet Vence deserves more than a flying visit. It's worth spending a little time here, if only to appreciate its comparatively quiet medieval streets and enjoy some of its gastronomic gems.

The **tourist office** (☎ 04 93 58 06 38; www .ville-vence.fr; 8 place du Grand Jardin; 🕓 9am-7pm Mon-Sat, 10am-6pm Sun Jul & Aug, 9am-6pm Mon-Sat Sep, Oct & Mar-Jun, 9am-5pm Mon-Sat Nov-Mar) has several good leaflets for self-guided tours in and around Vence.

A fruit and veg market fills place du Jardin several mornings a week, with antiques on Wednesday.

EXPLORING VENCE

❦ THE VIEUX VENCE // BOLD MODERN ART AND MEDIEVAL HISTORY

Much of the historical centre is very old indeed (as old as the 13th century) so it's a neat surprise to find the daring **Fondation Émile Hugues** (☎ 04 93 24 24 23; 2 place du Frêne; adult/concession €5/2.50; 🕓 10am-12.30pm & 2-6pm Tue-Sun), with its wonderful 20th-century art exhibitions, inside the imposing **Château de Villeneuve**.

The **Romanesque cathedral** on the eastern side of the square was built in the 11th century on the site of an old Roman temple. It contains Chagall's **mosaic** of Moses (1979), appropriately watching over the baptismal font.

♥ CHAPELLE DU ROSAIRE // MATISSE'S LAST AND MOST POIGNANT MASTERPIECE

> This work required four years of exclusive and relentless attention, and it is the fruit of my whole working life. Despite all its imperfections, I consider it my masterpiece.
>
> *Henri Matisse*

Matisse was 81 when he completed **Chapelle du Rosaire** (☎ 04 93 58 03 26; 466 av Henri Matisse; adult/6-16yr €2.80/1.50; ⌚ 2-5.30pm Mon, Wed & Sat, 10-11.30am & 2-5.30pm Tue & Thu, plus 2-5.30pm Fri during school holidays, Sunday mass 10am, closed mid-Nov–mid-Dec), floodlit by the most extraordinary stained-glass windows, in 1951.

An ailing Matisse moved to Vence in 1943 where he fell under the care of his former nurse and model Monique Bourgeois, who had since become a Dominican nun. She persuaded him to design the extraordinary chapel for her community: it took Matisse four years to do so and the Dominican nuns of the Rosary still use it today.

From the road, all that you can see are the blue-and-white ceramic roof tiles and a wrought-iron cross and bell tower. Inside, light floods through the glorious stained-glass windows, painting stark white walls with glowing blues, greens and yellows.

A line image of the Virgin Mary and child is painted on white ceramic tiles on the northern interior wall. The western wall is dominated by the bolder *Chemin de Croix* (Stations of the Cross). St Dominic overlooks the altar. Matisse also designed the chapel's stone altar, candlesticks, cross and the way-out priests' vestments (displayed in an adjoining hall).

GASTRONOMIC HIGHLIGHTS

♥ LA LITOTE €€

☎ 04 93 24 27 82; 5 rue de l'Évêché; menus €20-35, mains €18; ⌚ lunch & dinner Tue-Sat, lunch Sun
Dining here is a treat, whether alfresco on a little square at the back of the cathedral or inside the stone-wall dining room with its open fire. In an area where the bar is set very high, young chef Stéphane Furlan still manages to surprise and delight diners with a regularly changing menu that favours quality rather than quantity. The foie gras crème brûlée with rhubarb-and-endive gratin will stay in this author's food memory for a long time.

♥ LES BACCHANALES €€€

☎ 04 93 24 19 19; 247 av de Provence; lunch €34, dinner menus €50, €60 & €70; ⌚ lunch & dinner Thu-Mon
Chef Christophe Dufau has moved lock, stock and barrel from his tiny bistro in Tourrettes to this elegant 1930s town house. Nothing has been lost in his cuisine – it's still as creative, seasonal and divine as ever and guaranteed to challenge your culinary curiosity. There's more room for guests, and space to accommodate his passion for art: the walls, garden and hall feature daring original works.

TRANSPORT

BUS // Bus 400 to and from Nice (€1, 1¼ hours, at least hourly) stops on place du Grand Jardin.

CAR // Medieval Vence is pedestrian; you can park on place du Grand Jardin or in the streets leading to the historical centre.

ST-PAUL DE VENCE

pop 3340

Once upon a time, St-Paul de Vence was a small medieval village atop a hill looking out to sea. Then came the likes of Chagall and Picasso in postwar years, followed by showbiz stars such as Yves Montand and Roger Moore, and St-Paul shot to fame. The village is now home to dozens of art galleries as well as the exceptional Fondation Maeght.

The village's tiny cobbled lanes get overwhelmingly crowded in high season – come early or late to beat the rush.

EXPLORING ST-PAUL DE VENCE

♥ THE VILLAGE // MOOCH AROUND THIS HILLTOP MEDIEVAL WONDER

Strolling the narrow streets is how most visitors pass time in St-Paul. The village has been beautifully preserved and the panoramas from the ramparts are stunning. The main artery, rue Grande, is lined with **art galleries**. The highest point in the village is occupied by the **Église Collégiale** (containing a hotchpotch of religious icons). The adjoining **Chapelle des Pénitents Blancs** was redecorated by Belgian artist Folon and inaugurated in 2008.

Many more artists such as Folon lived or passed through St-Paul de Vence, amongst them Soutine, Léger, Cocteau, Matisse and Chagall. The latter is buried with his wife Vava in the **cemetery** at the village's southern end. The **tourist office** (☎ 04 93 32 86 95; www.saint-pauldevence.com; 2 rue Grande; ☽ 10am-7pm Jun-Sep, 10am-6pm Oct-May) runs informative daily 1½-hour **themed guided tours** (€8) that delve into this illustrious past.

Across from the entrance to the fortified village, the **pétanque** pitch, where many a star has had a spin, is the hub of village life. The tourist office rents out balls (€2) and runs *pétanque* discovery tours (€8, one to 1½ hours).

♥ FONDATION MAEGHT // MODERN ART AT ITS MOST CREATIVE

The region's finest art museum is **Fondation Marguerite et Aimé Maeght** (☎ 04 93 32 81 63; www.fondation-maeght.com; adult/concession €11/9; ☽ 10am-7pm Jul-Sep, to 6pm Oct-Jun). Inaugurated in 1964, the building was designed by Josep Lluís Sert and is a masterpiece in itself, integrating the works of the very best: a Giacometti courtyard, Miró sculptures dotted across the terraced gardens, coloured-glass windows by Braque and mosaics by Chagall and Tal-Coat. And that's before you've even seen *inside* the museum: its collection of 20th-century works is one of the largest in Europe. It is exhibited on a rotating basis, which, along with the excellent temporary exhibitions, guarantees you'll rarely see the same thing twice. Find the *fondation* 500m downhill from the village.

GASTRONOMIC HIGHLIGHTS

♥ CAFÉ DE LA PLACE €

☎ 04 93 32 80 03; place de Gaulle; plat du jour €12; ☽ lunch Sep-Jun, lunch & dinner Jul & Aug
If you'd rather watch than take part in the latest round of *pétanque,* settle down at this quintessential village caf' overlooking the pitch. Ice-cold *pastis* (an aniseed drink and regional tipple of choice

CANNES AREA

in the South) flows from 11am onwards, and the *raviolis à la Daube* (the English translation of 'ravioli served in rich beef gravy' really doesn't do it justice!) or delicious *salade niçoise* are fantastic value.

☙ LA COLOMBE D'OR €€€

☎ 04 93 32 80 02; www.la-colombe-dor.com, in French; place de Gaulle, St-Paul de Vence; mains €30-55; ☺ lunch & dinner mid-Dec–Oct

A Léger mosaic here, a Picasso painting there, a doodle by Charlie Chaplin in a corner: these are just some of the original modern artworks at the Golden Dove, a legendary world-renowned restaurant where impoverished artists paid for meals with their creations – today forming one of France's largest private art collections. Dining is beneath fig trees in summer or in the art-filled dining room in winter, and the cuisine is surprisingly uncomplicated (terrines, rabbit stew, beef carpaccio). Book well ahead. They also have rooms (see p395).

☙ LE TILLEUL €€

☎ 04 93 32 80 36; place du Tilleul; menu €25, mains €20; ☺ lunch & dinner

Under the shade of a big lime blossom (linden) tree, Le Tilleul is a gem. Considering its location on the *remparts*, it could have easily plumbed the depths of a typical tourist trap; instead, dishes such as saffron mussel gratin served with melting leeks or roasted duckling cooked in cider and apple sauce grace your table, all beautifully presented and tasting divine. Enjoy them with one of the St-Paul vintages featured on the wine list.

TRANSPORT

BUS // St-Paul is served by bus 400 running between Nice (€1, one hour, at least hourly) and Vence (€1, 15 minutes).

CAR // St-Paul is closed to traffic.

PARKING // There are several car parks surrounding St-Paul (€2 per hour); finding a space in July and August can be nigh impossible.

AROUND VENCE

The Pays Vençois is an enticing mix of fertile land, rocky heights and quirky attractions. A car is essential to get around.

EXPLORING AROUND VENCE

☙ GORGES DU LOUP // DISCOVER THE DRAMATIC LANDSCAPES OF THE HINTERLAND

A combination of perilously perched villages, sheer cliffs, waterfalls, densely wooded slopes and gushing river, the Gorges du Loup is a scenic and surprisingly unspoilt place. People come here mostly for the **spectacular drive** and **great walking trails**. The Guides Randoxygène *Rando Pays Côtier* and *Rando Moyen Pays* (available at tourist offices) have excellent walk suggestions.

The highlight of the western side of the gorges (the D3) is the outstanding village of **Gourdon**. The panorama from **Place Victoria** sweeps 80km of coastline from Nice to Théoule-sur-Mer. Inside the 18th-century **Château de Gourdon** (☎ 04 93 09 68 02; www.chateau-gourdon.com; place du Château) is the remarkable **Musée des Arts Décoratifs et de la Modernité** (admission €10; ☺ 1½hr guided tour by appointment only) featuring great art deco works, such as pieces from designer Eileen Gray. In summer, guided tours take you round the exceptional **gardens** (€5; ☺ tours 3pm & 5pm Jul & Aug): Italian, French and Provençal, as well as a medieval medicinal garden.

On the eastern side, on the D2210, is the small hamlet of **Pont du Loup**. Standing over the Loup River at the bottom of the gorges, under what's left of the old railway bridge (bombed during WWII), this is where villagers from Gourdon used to come and cultivate flowers and fruit trees. Access to Gourdon was via the **chemin du Paradis**, a track that still exists and is very popular with walkers.

Testimony to this fertile past is sweet factory **Confiserie Florian** (☎ 04 93 59 32 91; www.confiserieflorian.com; ☺ 9am-noon & 2-6pm), where jasmine jam, candied clementines and crystallised flowers such as violets or roses are cooked up in a 19th-century flour mill. Free 10-minute tours show you how and finish in the factory shop where you can sample the goods.

Further down Le Pont du Loup, on the D2210, hilltop **Le Bar-sur-Loup** pops onto the horizon. Bitter orange trees are cultivated in terraces around the beautifully intact medieval village. There are some great **walks** from the village and the friendly **tourist office** (☎ 04 93 42 72 21; www.lebarsurloup.fr; place Francis Paulet) has put together a leaflet with three itineraries in English.

❦ ATELIER DE LA CUISINE DES FLEURS // LEARN HOW TO COOK WITH FLOWERS

If the unusual flavours of the Confiserie Florian's treats (above) have piqued your curiosity, try the cooking classes of **Atelier de la Cuisine des Fleurs** (The Flowers' Cooking Workshop; ☎ 04 92 11 06 94; www.la -cuisine-des-fleurs.com; 1-/3-course-meal lesson €45/80) run by chef Yves Terrillon. The original menus change monthly according to flowers (violet in March, centifolia rose in May, verbena in August etc). Lessons are fun, very hands-on and take place in Yves' airy, first-floor kitchen, where great views of the Gorges are certain to get your creative juices flowing.

L'Atelier also runs great kids' class where little ones (from aged eight) can learn to bake their own birthday cake or prepare funky sandwiches for picnics.

❦ TOURRETTES-SUR-LOUP // LIFE IN THE SLOW ARRIÈRE-PAYS LANE

Dubbed the 'city of violets' for the numerous flower fields that surround the village, Tourrettes is a postcard-perfect 15th-century hilltop village overflowing with art galleries and boutiques selling violet tea, ice cream, melon syrup etc. Its **Fête des Violettes** (Violet Festival) on the first or second Sunday in March closes with a flower battle.

Walking around the **medieval village** won't take you more than an hour, but there are many more **walks** to do in the surrounding countryside, most with superb panoramas. *Promenades & Randonnées Balisées* (in French) is a useful leaflet produced by the **tourist office** (☎ 04 93 24 18 93; www.tourrettessurloup.com; 2 place de La Libération; ☺ 9.30am-12.30pm & 2.30-6.30pm May & Jun, 10am-6.30pm Mon-Sat, 10am-6pm Sun Jul & Aug, 9.30am-12.30pm & 2.30-6.30pm Mon-Sat Sep-Apr) with 14 itineraries ranging from an easy 1½-hour stroll to heartier walks to local summits or neighbouring villages. Also good is the Guides Randoxygène *Rando Pays Côtier* (available at tourist offices), with a great selection of itineraries in the Pays Vençois section.

Tourrettes is also a good base to visit local producers and discover a life that revolves around seasons of the nontouristy kind. **Domaine Saint-Joseph** (☎ 04 93 59 38 04; 160 chemin des Vignes; ☺ 9am-noon & 2.30-7pm Mon-Sat) is a small winery and olive-oil producer and the friendly owners will happily show you round the estate and answer questions about wine and olive-oil production. You can then taste and/or buy their wines (red, white and rosé) and excellent olive oil (part of Nice AOC; Appelation d'Origine Contrôlée certifies the origin and quality of the oil). The Domaine is 2km southwest of Tourrettes, signposted off rte de Grasse.

Also off the D2210 to Grasse, you'll find organic goats'-cheese producer **La Ferme des Courmettes** (☎ 04 93 59 31 93; www.chevredescourmettes.com; rte des Courmettes; ☺ 9am-12.30pm & 4-6pm). This small family affair welcomes visitors year-round for tastings and visits of the farm. Mornings are better for watching the cheese production process; milking otherwise takes place early morning or late afternoon. The cheeses are absolutely divine and incredibly diverse in tastes. Find the farm 4km up rte des Courmettes, signposted off the D2210, about halfway between Tourrettes and Pont du Loup.

♥ COL DE VENCE & AROUND // DISCOVER THE ARID LANDSCAPES OF THE ARRIÈRE-PAYS

The northbound D2 from Vence leads to the **Col de Vence** (963m), a mountain pass 10km north offering good views of the *baous* (rocky promontories) typical of this region. At the foot of the pass is the **Baou des Blancs** (673m), crowned by the stony remains of the **Bastide St-Laurent**, inhabited by the Templars in the 13th century. The landscape across these lofty plateaux is very arid, a far cry from the orchards and lush valleys around the Loup River. A number of trails criss-cross the area, linking villages such as photogenic **Coursegoules** (at the end of the D2), a hilltop village with 11th-century castle ruins and fortifications, and **Courmes**, where time seems to be on standby. Walkers should use the Guides Randoxygène *Rondo Pays Côtier* and *Rondo Moyen Pays* (available at tourist offices).

GASTRONOMIC HIGHLIGHTS

♥ LE RELAIS DES COCHES €€

☎ 04 93 24 30 24; 28 rte de Vence, Tourrettes-sur-Loup; plat du jour €12-28, lunch menu €16, dinner menus €25 & €38; ☺ lunch & dinner Tue-Sun

After local nightlife legend Wayne sold it lock, stock and barrel in 2009, Le Relais had a lot to live up to. But the new management at this atmospheric medieval house, with a delightful village-facing terrace, has done well: sunny dishes, such as sea bream filets with basil, or roasted lamb in aromatic herbs and confit tomatoes, are beautifully cooked and served on gigantic plates. Service is charming, and with perfectly bilingual staff at that.

♥ L'HOSTELLERIE DU CHÂTEAU €€

☎ 04 93 42 41 10; 6-8 place Francis Paulet, Le Bar-sur-Loup; 2-/3-course menu, lunch €22/26, dinner €33/39; ☺ lunch & dinner Wed-Sun

Lunch around orange bistro tables on the village square or dine on the spectacular terrace of Le Bigaradier, L'Hostellerie du Château's superb restaurant. The menu is a great combination of high-brow, creative gastronomy (roasted scallops with balsamic butter pan-fried Granny Smith apples and carrots) and timeless classics such as steak tartare or homemade ravioli with parmesan cream and parsley. Kids also get tailor-made menus (€15), without a frozen burger or chip in sight. You can also stay the night in one of their six rooms (see p396).

GRASSE

pop 48,800

It is the abundance of water up in the hills that helped turn Grasse into a perfume centre. Tanners, who needed reliable water supplies to clean their hides, first settled here in the Middle

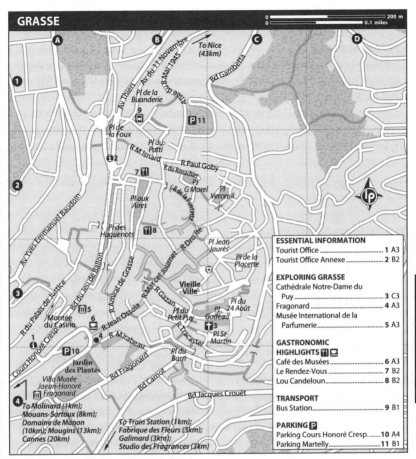

GRASSE

ESSENTIAL INFORMATION
Tourist Office	1 A3
Tourist Office Annexe	2 B2

EXPLORING GRASSE
Cathédrale Notre-Dame du Puy	3 C3
Fragonard	4 A3
Musée International de la Parfumerie	5 A3

GASTRONOMIC HIGHLIGHTS
Café des Musées	6 A3
Le Rendez-Vous	7 B2
Lou Candeloun	8 B2

TRANSPORT
Bus Station	9 B1

PARKING
Parking Cours Honoré Cresp	10 A4
Parking Martelly	11 B1

Ages. With the advent of perfumed gloves in the 1500s, the art of perfumery took shape. Glove-makers split from the tanners and set up lucrative perfumeries. New irrigation techniques allowed flower growing to boom, sealing Grasse's reputation as the world capital of fragrance.

Today, Grasse is still surrounded by jasmine, centifolia roses, mimosa, orange blossom and violet fields but the industry, which counts some 30 perfumeries, is rather discreet, with only a handful offering tours of their facilities.

ESSENTIAL INFORMATION

TOURIST OFFICES // **Grasse Tourist Office** (☎ 04 93 36 66 66; www.grasse.fr; ☺ 9am-7pm Mon-Sat, 9am-1pm & 2-6pm Sun Jul-Sep, 9am-12.30pm & 2-6pm Mon-Sat Oct-Jun) Main office (Palais des Congrès, cours Honoré Cresp); Annexe (place de la Foux).

ORIENTATION

Because of its hilly topography, sprawling centre and one-way street system, Grasse can be hard to navigate. The medieval old town is relatively compact and fairly central. The bus station is

TOP FIVE

SCENIC WALKS

A secluded cove, an exceptional panorama or a particularly secluded villa: these are the preserve not of the rich, but of walkers. The Riviera still has many unspoilt corners so make sure you pack some sturdy shoes to go explore. These are some of our favourite trails.

* ★ **Sentier du Littoral** (p269) – these 11km of stunning coastline alternate with long beaches, tiny coves and spectacular cliffs, all along the tantalising azure waters

* ★ **Balcon du Loup** – admire from up high the dramatic landscape of the Gorges du Loup (p258) with this mighty walk perched high on the plateaux; some of it follows the old railway line (some tunnels and galleries) – make sure you make the detour to the fabulous goat's-cheese producer La Ferme des Courmettes (p260)

* ★ **Ste-Marguerite** (p247) – just 20 minutes by boat from Cannes, yet a world away from the city's hustle and bustle; the island is only 3km long so you can just lose yourself in its fragrant woods without worrying about maps

* ★ **Tour du Cap Roux** (p270) – the view atop Pic du Cap Roux' 453m is breathtaking: neighbouring red peaks, the Med stretching out as far the eye can see and a green, rolling hinterland

* ★ **Cap d'Antibes** (p251) – a hedonist mix of luxurious villas, beautiful gardens and stunning shores, in fine Riviera tradition

CANNES AREA

north of the old town, the train station 2km south. Many of the town's sights congregate in the southwest, around place du Cours. Most perfumeries are out of town.

EXPLORING GRASSE

Attractions in Grasse focus on its celebrated perfume industry, a nice change from traditional sights and activities.

❦ THE PERFUMERIES // HOW PERFUMES ARE MADE, FROM FLOWER TO BOTTLE

Most of Grasse's *parfumeries* are unknown: they sell their essences for aroma in foodstuff and toiletries, and to couture houses for their perfumes.

The few that produce their own fragrances are better-known and run free guided tours. You're taken through every stage of perfume production, from extraction and distillation to the work of the 'nose'. Visits end in the perfumery's showroom where you can buy fragrances (much cheaper than couture perfumes, where 60% of what you pay is packaging). Tours leave every 15 to 30 minutes and are available in a number of languages.

Fragonard (☎ 04 93 36 44 65; www.fragonard .com; 20 bd Fragonard; ⊙ 9am-6pm Feb-Oct, 9am-12.30pm & 2-6pm Nov-Jan) Very central, with a small museum about perfume through the ages.

Galimard (☎ 04 93 09 20 00; www.galimard .com; 73 rte de Cannes; ⊙ 9am-6.30pm Jun-Sep, 9am-12.30pm & 2-6pm Oct-May) About 3km from Grasse centre on the southbound N85.

Molinard (☎ 04 93 36 01 62; www.molinard.com; 60 bd Victor Hugo; ⊙ 9am-7pm Jul & Aug, to 6.30pm Apr-Jun & Sep, 9.30am-12.30pm & 2-6pm Mon-Sat Oct-Mar) Only 1km out of town, with a sumptuous showroom.

❦ PERFUME CREATION WORKSHOPS // DABBLE IN THE ART OF PERFUME CREATION

It can take months, sometimes years, for a 'nose' (perfumers who, after 10 years' training, can identify up to 3000 smells) to create a perfume. And you'll understand why once you sit down in front of a mind-boggling array of essences: the number of combinations is dizzying. Perfume workshops won't turn you into a perfumer overnight, but the olfactory education they offer is fascinating – and great fun.

Molinard runs a 90-minute **workshop** (incl 50mL bottle of perfume €40) in its Grasse factory (see opposite) where you can create your own perfume (minimum two people). A professional perfumer guides you through the structure of the perfume (base, heart and head notes) and helps you through the more subtle blends and associations.

Galimard runs a similar workshop at its **Studio des Fragrances** (☎ 04 93 09 20 00; 5 rte de Pégomas; 2hr workshop incl 100mL bottle of perfume €45), 3km out of town.

❦ MUSÉE INTERNATIONAL DE LA PARFUMERIE // DISCOVER PERFUME'S HISTORY IN FULL INTERACTIVE GLORY

After four years of extensive renovations, the **Musée International de la Parfumerie** (International Perfumery Museum; ☎ 04 97 05 58 00; www.museesdegrasse.com; 2 bd du Jeu de Ballon; adult/child €3/free; ☯ 10am-7pm Jun-Sep, 11am-6pm Wed-Mon Oct-Mar) finally reopened in 2008, in a style fit for the 21st century. The 18th-century mansion has been beautifully renovated and daringly enlarged

CORINNE MARIE-TOSELLO, PERFUMER IN GRASSE

Corinne Marie-Tosello has two routes to work: one through olive groves, the other one through fields overlooking the sea. Most people would revel in the view, but Corinne revels in their smells. Corinne is chief training officer at the prestigious Grasse perfumery Fragonard. She is in charge of the 'olfactory education' of the perfumery's staff (scent identification, production process, types of perfumes etc) and she runs the sought-after perfume workshops where perfume-fanatics get a shot at producing their own scents. Life therefore revolves around her nose. She also works as an olfactory consultant (yes, they do exist) where she advises on scents destined to be used as incense, candles, air fresheners and so on.

So what's the best thing about living in Grasse? Grasse is very authentic – the perfumery industry is world-famous but it remains very understated and hidden from the public. Many people don't believe us when we tell them it's so prominent. I also love Grasse's theatre; it puts on very original plays and films, although my teenage daughters prefer going out in glitzy Cannes! On the downside, driving is a nightmare because of the one-way system, and since the city is built on a hill, everything goes up and down; it's exhausting.

What do you like doing in the area? I love walking through flower fields (do the same at Domaine de Manon, p266): May roses and violets in the spring, lavender in early summer and jasmine between August and October. I've taken Fragonard's staff on a couple of occasions so that they could see where the essences we work with come from. I also love going to St-Honorat (see p247): it's an olfactory paradise with eucalyptus, pine trees, dry wood and vine.

Favourite smells? Vetiver and galbanum (a resin produced from a Persian plant).

Least favourite smells? Anything that has been smoked, and artificial marine smells.

with a modern glass structure. There are rather too many perfume bottles to look at but the interactive features – including fragrant garden, a film testing your sense of smell and the reproduction of a 19th-century perfume shop – are great, as is the overview of perfume's millennia-old history. The museum also offers interesting insights into the perfume industry and modern production techniques (including the use of synthetic essences).

❦ TOURS OF THE OLD TOWN // FOLLOW THE GUIDE THROUGH GRASSE'S RICH HERITAGE

Grasse's old town was neglected for many years; the medieval centre therefore looks rather shabby. It's a shame because Grasse has a long history and interesting monuments bearing witness to this complex past, such as the **Cathédrale Notre-Dame du Puy**. Built in the 13th century in Roman tradition with an austere stone nave, it was then extended in the 18th century in a vividly contrasting baroque style.

Things are slowly getting better, and the tourist office offers some excellent two-hour **guided tours** (€2), traditional or themed. Fans of Patrick Suskind's novel *The Perfume* will be hooked by the Retracing the Steps of Jean-Baptiste Grenouille tour, which takes in locations visited by the character in the novel, including the old market square **Place aux Aires**. Ring ahead for dates and bookings.

GASTRONOMIC HIGHLIGHTS

❦ CAFÉ DES MUSÉES €

☎ 04 92 60 99 00; 1 rue Jean Ossola; plat du jour €12; ☽ 8am-6pm

Sit on a *citron*-yellow Jacobsen chair in this stylish café and lunch on a Mediterranean-inspired no-fuss platter: pasta of the day, Milanese veal escalope

or toasted goat's cheese salad. There are some wonderful sweet treats too, with macaroons, fruit tarts and almond biscuits. Perfect for dessert or a gourmet coffee break (pastry with coffee or tea €7.50) after touring the sights.

❦ LE RENDEZ-VOUS €

☎ 04 93 77 25 54; 35 place aux Aires; plat du jour/mains/menu €11/15/19; ☽ lunch & dinner Mon-Sat, lunch Sun

The new kid on the restaurant block, this modern bistro on the town's most atmospheric square has proved a hit with Grassois (natives of Grasse). The decor is sleek, with designer furniture, artistic lamps and exuberant bouquets. The cuisine – modern European, with the odd fusion concession – is reliably good and excellent value. Tables on the square are particularly popular at lunchtime so arrive early or book.

❦ LOU CANDELOUN €€

☎ 04 93 60 04 49; 5 rue des Fabreries; lunch menu €17, dinner menu €29-55; ☽ lunch & dinner Tue-Sat, lunch Mon

Tucked down the most unassuming alleyway, this is the gourmet choice in Grasse. With its intimate dining room, charming welcome and delicious cuisine, Lou Candeloun has honed the art of dining out to perfection. Chef Alexis Mayroux changes his menu every three weeks to match the mood of market stalls. So whatever season you're in town, you'll be in for a treat, and always with a great wine to match.

TRANSPORT

BUS // Bus 600 goes to Cannes (€1, 50 minutes, every 20 minutes) via Mouans-Sartoux (25 minutes) and Mougins (30 minutes). Bus 500 goes to Nice (€1, 1½ hours, hourly).
TRAIN // The station is out of town but linked by free shuttle. There are regular services to Nice (€8.40, one hour, hourly) via Cannes (€3.70, 25 minutes).

CAR // Grasse's one-way street system is maddening and often congested so park as soon as you can and walk.
PARKING // If arriving from Nice, park at Parking Martelly. If arriving from Cannes, park at Parking Cours Honoré Cresp.

AROUND GRASSE

This part of the Riviera is densely populated and not as scenic as the Pays Vençois, but it does harbour some real gems, including the picture-perfect village of Mougins and a daring contemporary art museum.

EXPLORING AROUND GRASSE

🌱 **MOUGINS // A PICTURE-PERFECT VILLAGE WITH A PICASSO LEGACY** Pinprick Vieux Mougins looks almost too perfect to be real. Picasso discovered the medieval village in 1935 with lover Dora Marr, and lived here with his final love, Jacqueline Roque, from 1961 until his death. Mougins has since become something of an elite location with prestigious hotel-restaurants, the country's most sought-after international school and Sophia Antipolis nearby (France's Silicon Valley).

For visitors, the small but fabulous **Musée de la Photographie** (Photography Museum; ☎ 04 93 75 85 67; Porte Sarrazine; admission free; ⏱ 10am-8pm Jul-Sep, 10am-6pm Mon-Fri, 11am-6pm Sat & Sun Oct & Dec-Jun) has some fascinating black-and-white photos of Picasso, snapped by celebrated photographers such as André Villers and Jacques Henri Lartigue.

The friendly **tourist office** (☎ 04 93 75 87 67; www.mougins-coteazur.org; 18 bd Courteline; ⏱ 9am-7pm Jul & Aug, 9am-5.30pm Mon-Fri, 9.30am-5pm Sat Sep-Jun) has an explanatory map of the village.

CANNES AREA

LITERARY CANNES AREA

- ★ *Perfume* (Patrick Süskind) – evocation of the horrors of the 18th-century perfume industry in steamy Grasse: a quest to create the perfect perfume from the scent of murdered virgins

- ★ *Tender Is the Night* (F Scott Fitzgerald) – a vivid account of life on the Riviera during the decadent 1920s jazz age; set on Cap d'Antibes with day trips to Cannes

- ★ *Bits of Paradise* (F Scott and Zelda Fitzgerald) – twenty-one short stories by one of the Riviera's most notorious couples; 'Love in the Night' (1925), set in Cannes, is the ultimate romance

- ★ *Perfume from Provence, Sunset House* and *Trampled Lilies* (Lady Fortescue) – a lady's life, stretching from the purchase of a house outside Grasse to her final flight back to the UK at the start of WWII

- ★ *May We Borrow Your Husband* (Grahame Greene) – a collection of short 'comedy of sexual life' stories, kicking off with two homosexuals' pursuit of a newly-wed groom while honeymooning in Antibes with his virgin wife; written in Antibes

- ★ *Super Cannes* (JG Ballard) – fast-paced action in Eden-Olympia (aka Sophia Antipolis), a work-obsessed technology park on the Med near Cannes; an insightful, satirical, essential read by one of the most important names in contemporary British literature

🌑 ESPACE DE L'ART CONCRET // MODERN ART AT ITS BOLDEST

Modern art and architecture lovers shouldn't miss the **Espace de l'Art Concret** (Centre of Concrete Art; ☎ 04 93 75 71 50; www .espacedelartconcret.fr; place Suzanne de Villeneuve, Mouans-Sartoux; adult/child €5/free; ☺ 11am-7pm Jul & Aug, noon-6pm Wed-Sun Sep-Jun) in the sleepy village of Mouans-Sartoux. The contemporary art centre is housed in the 16th-century **Château de Mouans** and in the purpose-built **Donation Albers-Honegger** extension, a brilliant and brilliantly controversial lime-green concrete block ferociously juxtaposed with its historic surroundings. All the old familiars (Eduardo Chillida, Yves Klein, Andy Warhol, César, Philippe Starck) are here, along with lesser-known practitioners and temporary exhibitions.

🌑 ROSE & JASMINE FLOWER FIELDS // VISIT THE SOURCE OF GRASSE'S FAMOUS ESSENCES

Curious noses can combine a perfumery session with a (literal) field trip in season to see rose and jasmine meadows, cultivated for three generations, at **Domaine de Manon** (☎ 04 93 60 12 76; www.domaine-manon.com; 36 chemin du Servan; ☺ guided tours of rose fields Tue 3pm May–mid-Jun, jasmine Tue 9am Aug-Oct), a flower farm 15km southeast of Grasse in the village of Plascassier. Guided tours last an hour and cost €6 per adult, and are free for child under 12.

GASTRONOMIC HIGHLIGHTS

With its Michelin-starred chefs and excellent bistros, Mougins is the place to eat in the area.

🌑 LE MAS CANDILLE €€€

☎ 04 92 28 43 43; bd Clément Rebuffel; lunch/dinner menu from €54/90; ☺ lunch & dinner

Le Mas Candille's reputation is starting to travel as far as chef Serge Gouloumès has: originally from Gascony (the foie gras *tatin* with Armagnac is his trademark dish), his culinary career has taken him to faraway climes, an experience that has enriched his Mediterranean cuisine with exotic flavours. The setting couldn't be more idyllic too: in the grand dining room of the *mas* (old Provençal house) or on the shaded terrace, with spectacular views of Grasse and the surrounding hills. Courses are also offered.

🌑 LE RENDEZ-VOUS DE MOUGINS €

☎ 04 93 75 87 47; place du Commandant Lamy; lunch/dinner menu €15.20/19.80, mains €16; ☺ lunch & dinner

At the heart of the old village, guarded by a mighty plane tree, Le Rendez-Vous is without a doubt the best value restaurant you'll find in this neck of the woods. The sun-kissed cuisine is fresh, generous and mostly sourced at the Marché Forville in Cannes: try the marinated sardines with its assortment of peppers and sun-dried tomatoes or the glacé nougat with lavender honey and citrus coulis.

TRANSPORT

BUS // Bus 400 (€1, every 20 minutes) between Cannes and Grasse stops in Mougins and Mouans-Sartoux.
CAR // The old town in Mougins is pedestrian; there is plenty of free parking on the outskirts.

MASSIF DE L'ESTÉREL

· · · · · ·

This range of red porphyritic rock scented with pines, oak and eucalyptus trees is one of the coast's most stunning natural features. Find it southwest of

Cannes, wedged between Mandelieu-La Napoule (to the north) and St-Raphaël (to the south).

ST-RAPHAËL

pop 33,800

Once upon a time this was a fishing hamlet...until along came mayor Félix Martin (1842–99), who took advantage of the new railway to promote his seaside town and lure in the tourists. It worked. By the 1920s St-Raphaël was a fabulous place to be seen: F Scott Fitzgerald wrote *Tender Is the Night* here, while wife Zelda spent her time drink-diving. During WWII St-Raphaël was also a primary landing base for US and French troops.

Following a few postwar years of identity-searching, the town of St-Raphaël reinvented itself as a prime outdoor destination, making the most of its stunning natural setting (the Massif de l'Estérel sits mostly within St-Raphaël's boundaries). Water sports are the big draw, and the opportunity to explore the Estérel hills is another.

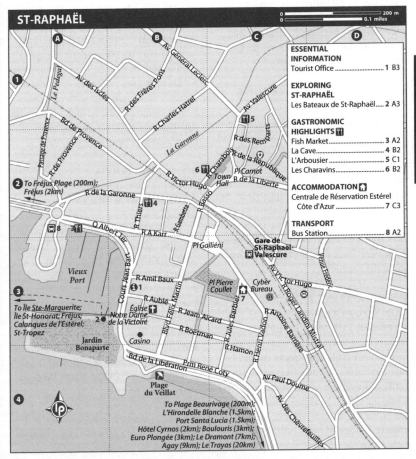

ST-RAPHAËL

0 — 200 m
0 — 0.1 miles

CANNES AREA

ESSENTIAL
INFORMATION
Tourist Office 1 B3

EXPLORING
ST-RAPHAËL
Les Bateaux de St-Raphaël..... 2 A3

GASTRONOMIC
HIGHLIGHTS
Fish Market........................ 3 A2
La Cave............................. 4 B2
L'Arbousier........................ 5 C1
Les Charavins..................... 6 B2

ACCOMMODATION
Centrale de Réservation Estérel
Côte d'Azur 7 C3

TRANSPORT
Bus Station......................... 8 A2

ESSENTIAL INFORMATION

TOURIST OFFICES // Tourist office (☎ 04 94 19 52 52; www.saint-raphael.com; 99 Quai Albert 1er; ☽ 9am-7pm Jul & Aug, 9am-12.30pm & 2-6.30pm Mon-Sat Sep-Jun)

EXPLORING ST-RAPHAËL

Life in St-Raphaël revolves around the sea. Witness the daily **fish market** (Cours Jean Bart) on the quayside of the old port. The fishing community honours its patron saint, St Peter, every August with a two-day **Fête de la St-Pierre des Pêcheurs**. Local fishermen, dressed in traditional costume, joust Provençal-style from flat-bottomed boats moored in the harbour. Visitors too will find themselves drawn to the sea.

♥ BOAT EXCURSIONS // CRUISE ALONG THE MED

Leave the car at home and take to the seas instead: **Les Bateaux de St-Raphaël** (☎ 04 94 95 17 46; www.bateauxsaintraphael.com; Quai Nomy, Vieux Port; ☽ Apr-Oct) runs boat services to St-Tropez (adult/child €23/13, crossing time one hour) and Ste-Marguerite in the Îles de Lérins (full day adult/child €24/13, half-day €18/10, crossing time 1¼ hours) as well as scenic cruises to the Calanques de l'Estérel (adult/child €15/9, 1¼ hours) along the Corniche.

♥ SNORKELLING & DIVING // DON YOUR GOGGLES AND EXPLORE THE MED'S DEPTHS

St-Raph' is a leading dive centre. With numerous WWII shipwrecks and pristine waters, it's a prime area for underwater exploration. Much of the coast along the Corniche is protected too so the fauna and flora is some of the best around. The good news is that you don't need to go the whole diving hog to make the best of it: **Euro Plongée** (☎ 04 94 19 03 26; www.europlongee.fr; Port de Boulouris; ☽ Mar-Nov) now runs great two-hour **snorkelling tours** (€25) along with its traditional diving activities. They're fantastic for families: kids will love spotting starfish, sea anemones, urchins and other colourful Mediterranean residents.

GASTRONOMIC HIGHLIGHTS

♥ LA CAVE €€

☎ 04 94 95 79 62; cnr rue Thiers & rue de la Garonne; menus €29 & €39, mains €27; ☽ lunch & dinner Tue-Sat, lunch Sun Sep-Jun, dinner Jul & Aug
A striking modern facade makes the Cellar stand out. Inside, an equally contemporary, minimalist design is the setting for a creative modern European cuisine with dishes such as venison with potato cakes, seasonal fruit compôte and bilberry or sea bass filet with carbonara bulgur. Standards are as high on the wine list, with some 200 references, many of them available by the glass.

♥ L'ARBOUSIER €€€

☎ 04 94 95 25 00; 4 av Valescure; lunch menu €30, dinner menus €44 & €59; ☽ lunch & dinner Wed-Sun
Its fabulous flowery garden is equal to the reputation of the town's top gastronomic choice. Chef Philippe Troncy cooks up traditional seasonal fare in a staunchly traditional setting. Shellfish is the big draw, and in winter, truffles from the *arrière-pays* (hinterland) populate the menu in the most unexpected ways (pan-fried John Dory with truffle and coconut). And wine enthusiasts will love the sommelier's selection of four different wines (€20) to match the four-course evening menu.

♥ LES CHARAVINS €€

☎ 04 94 95 03 76; 36 rue Charabois; mains €18-26; ☽ dinner Thu-Tue, lunch Thu, Fri, Mon & Tue

Dining at this jolly wine bar, run by the formidable Philippe Furnémont, a former Michelin-starred chef and wine connoisseur, is all about having a good time enjoying the finer pleasures of life. The cuisine is resolutely French, traditional, and cooked to perfection: try the homemade foie gras with shallot jam or the oversized macaroni with *poutargue* (a sausage made from salted and dried fish roe) and sea urchin, and don't even think about turning down Philippe's wine suggestion, it would be akin to lese-majesty!

TRANSPORT

TRAIN // There are regular trains to Nice (€10.30, one hour, every 30 minutes), Cannes (€6.10, 40 minutes, half-hourly), Les Arcs Draguignan (€4.90, 15 minutes, hourly) and Marseille (€22.20, 1½ hours, hourly). Some services stop at the villages along the Corniche de l'Estérel.

BUS // Bus 4 goes to Fréjus old town (€1.10) from St Raphaël bus station. Bus 8 links St Raphaël with villages along the coast between Boulouris and Le Trayas (€1.10). There are also services to St Tropez (€10.90, 1¼ hours, eight daily, more in summer) via Grimaud (€9.70, one hour).

CORNICHE DE L'ESTÉREL

A walk or drive along the winding Corniche de l'Estérel (also called Corniche d'Or, 'Golden Coast'; the N98) is not to be missed and is an attraction in its own right. In fact it was one of the reasons the road was opened by the Touring Club de France in 1903. The views are spectacular, and small summer resorts and dreamy inlets (perfect for swimming), all of which are accessible by bus or train, are dotted along its 30km length. The most dramatic stretch is between Anthéor and Théoule-sur-Mer, where the tortuous, narrow N98 skirts through sparsely built areas. But make sure you take the time to stop, be it for a quick dip or a walk taking in the incredible scenery.

❦ SENTIER DU LITTORAL // STUNNING COASTLINE AND MOMENTOUS HISTORY

Running 11km between Port Santa Lucia (the track starts behind the naval works) and Agay, this coastal path (yellow markers) takes in some of the most scenic spots in the area. It takes roughly 4½ hours to complete, but from May to October, you could make a day out of it by stopping at some of the idyllic beaches scattered along the way.

You can also choose to walk smaller sections; the most scenic is around **Cap Dramont**, crowned by a semaphore, which you can do as a loop from **Plage du Débarquement**. This long sandy beach is where the 36th US Infantry Division landed on 15 August 1944. The large **memorial park** has a car park easily accessible from the N98.

From the beach, the path takes you to the tiny **Port du Poussaï**, before scaling the cape. From the top, views of the coast are stunning. Tintin fans will recognise the nearby **Île d'Or** (Golden Island): this pinprick island, uninhabited bar a mock 'medieval' tower, is thought to have inspired Hergé's design for *The Black Island*. The path snakes back down from the semaphore to Plage du Camp Long, from where a tarmac path takes you back to Port du Poussaï. Yellow markers otherwise continue to Agay.

❦ WALKING IN THE ESTÉREL // REVEL IN THE CONTRASTS OF NATURE'S PALETTE

With its lush green Mediterranean forests, intensely red peaks and sterling sea views, the Estérel is a walker's paradise. Dozens of trails criss-cross the massif;

buy a decent map such as IGN's Carte de Randonnée (1:25,000) No 3544ET *Fréjus, Saint-Raphaël & Corniche de l'Estérel*, if you're planning to explore off the signposted tracks. The tourist office in St-Raphaël has a leaflet detailing the most popular walks, including **Pic de l'Ours** (496m) and **Pic du Cap Roux** (452m), which offer breathtaking panoramas. Access to the range is generally prohibited on windy or particularly hot days because of fire risks, so check with the tourist office before setting off.

Those preferring a more informed wander can opt for a three-hour **guided walk** (adult/child €9/7) with a forest ranger from the Office National des Forêts (National Forestry Office).

❦ BEACHES // SANDY, PEBBLY OR SECRET COVE, TAKE YOUR PICK

With its 36km of coastline, the Corniche has more than 30 **beaches** running the gamut of beach possibilities: sandy, pebbly, cove-like, you name it. But wherever you go, the sea remains that crystal-clear turquoise and deep-blue, an irresistible invitation to swim.

Best for activities (beach volleyball, kids' clubs, water sports etc) are **Plage d'Agay** and **Plage Beaurivage**. For a scenic swim off a sandy beach, the beaches along the **Rade d'Agay** (such as the tiny but lovely Plage du Pourrousset) are perfect, while the section of coast between Anthéor and Le Trayas is famed for its jewel-like **calanques** (tiny coves). The landscape here is much more rugged, with many coves only accessible by boat.

❦ CHÂTEAU DE LA NAPOULE // VISIT ONE OF THE RIVIERA'S MOST ECCENTRIC FOLLIES

Wonderfully bizarre, turreted, 14th-century **Château de la Napoule** (☎ 04 93 49 95 05; www.chateau-lanapoule.com; av Henry Clews, La Napoule; château & gardens adult/child €6/4, gardens only €3.50; ⏰ 10am-6pm Feb-Oct, 2-6pm Mon-Fri, 10am-6pm Sat & Sun Nov-Jan) forms the centrepiece of this small seaside resort. American eccentrics Henry and Marie Clews arrived on the coast in 1918 and spent 17 years rebuilding the sea-facing Saracen tower and decorating it in twisted-fairy-tale style: the effect is Gormenghast-by-the-Sea.

The château's interior can only be visited by guided tour (at 11.30am, 2.30pm, 3.30pm and 4.30pm), but the beautiful gardens (with tearooms and a treasure hunt for kids), designed by Marie in a classic French formal style, can be wandered freely. Dozens more of Henry's creations sit alongside challenging works by contemporary sculptors in the château and gardens.

❦ VILLA MATUZIA // ENJOY MEDITERRANEAN FLAVOURS IN A GORGEOUS SETTING

In **Villa Matuzia** (☎ 04 94 82 79 95; bd Ste Guitte, Agay; menu €24, mains €18, Provençal specialities €30-60; ⏰ lunch & dinner Wed-Sun), his pretty Provençal house renovated with peachy colours and exquisite taste, Hugues Liberato cooks up a storm. His cuisine is Mediterranean, with inspiration from near and distant shores. He also specialises in the greats of French Mediterranean cuisine: *bouillabaisse, bourride* (fish stew) or poached capon (a traditional Christmas meal). These must be ordered in advance. Enjoy them by the fireplace in winter or alfresco on the terrace in summer for an unforgettable meal.

TRANSPORT

CAR // The Corniche gets very busy in summer: if you need to go somewhere as opposed to enjoy a scenic drive, take the inland N7 or the A8 motorway.

BUS // Bus 8 runs between St Raphaël and Le Trayas; stops include Le Dramont, Agay and Anthéor. Tickets cost €1.10.

TRAIN // Mandelieu-La Napoule, Le Trayas, Agay, Le Dramont and Boulouris all have stations on the St Raphaël-Nice line but only a handful of services a day stop there. Trains to Nice (€10.30, 1¼ hours) are hourly.

FRÉJUS

pop 51,530

Roman ruins are the trump card of Fréjus, settled by Massiliots (Greek colonists from Marseille) and colonised by Julius Caesar around 49 BC as Forum Julii. Its appealing old town is a maze of pastel buildings, shady plazas and winding alleys, climaxing with extraordinary medieval paintings in an episcopal complex wedged between market-busy squares.

ESSENTIAL INFORMATION

TOURIST OFFICES // Fréjus Tourist Office (☎ 04 94 51 83 83; www.frejus.fr; 249 rue Jean Jaurès; ☿ 9am-7pm Jun-Sep, 9.30am-noon & 2-6pm Mon-Sat & 9.30am-noon Sun Oct-Mar, 9.30am-6pm Mon-Sat & 9.30am-noon Sun Apr & May)

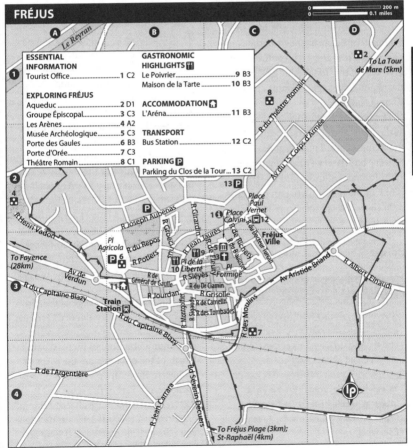

ORIENTATION

Fréjus comprises hillside Fréjus Ville, 3km from the seafront, and Fréjus Plage, on the Golfe de Fréjus. The Roman remains are in Fréjus Ville.

EXPLORING FRÉJUS

❦ GROUPE ÉPISCOPAL // MARVEL AT THE CHIMERICAL IMAGINATION OF MEDIEVAL CHRISTIANS

Fréjus' star sight is the **Groupe Épiscopal** (Cathedral Close; ☎ 04 94 51 26 30; 48 rue de Fleury; adult/child €5/free; ☺ 9am-6.30pm Jun-Sep, 9am-noon & 2-5pm Tue-Sun Oct-May), slap bang in the centre of town on the foundations of a Roman temple. At the heart of the complex is an 11th- and 12th-century **cathedral**, one of the first Gothic buildings in the region (although it retains certain Roman features).

The beautiful carved wooden doors at the main entrance were added during the Renaissance. The octagonal 5th-century **baptistery** (which incorporates eight Roman columns into its structure) is one of the oldest Christian buildings in France, and is exceptionally well preserved.

Stairs from the narthex lead up to the **cloister**, which looks onto a fine court-yard with a well-tended garden and well. Here you'll find the most stunning feature of the complex – its utterly unique 14th- and 15th-century painted **wooden ceiling panels**; 500 of the original 1200 survive. Angels, devils, hunters, acrobats, monsters and a cheery-looking man riding a pig gallivant round the vivid comic-book frames: bring binoculars for a better view or rent a pair at the ticket desk for €1.

❦ ROMAN HERITAGE // EXPLORE THE VESTIGES OF FRÉJUS' SETTLERS

Fréjus' **Roman ruins** (☺ 9.30am-12.30pm & 2-6pm Tue-Sun mid-Apr–mid-Oct, until 5pm rest of year) are not as well preserved as those found in the rest of Provence such as Arles, Orange or Nîmes, but their abundance bears witness to the importance of Forum Julii at the time, with its strategic location on Via Aurelia and military port. See the boxed text, left, for information about admission.

West of the old town, past the ancient **Porte des Gaules**, is the mostly rebuilt 1st- and 2nd-century **Les Arènes** (Amphitheatre; ☎ 04 94 51 34 31; rue Henri Vadon). It was one of Gaul's largest amphitheatres (seating 10,000 spectators). The site has been damaged by archaeological digs but a comprehensive renovation program hopes to breathe new life back into it.

At the southeastern edge of the old city is the 3rd-century **Porte d'Orée** (rue des Moulins), the only remaining arcade of monumental Roman thermal baths. North of the old town are the ruins of a **Théâtre Romain** (☎ 04 94 53 58 75; rue du Théâtre Romain). Part of the stage and the theatre's outer walls are all that remain.

Northeast, towards La Tour de Mare, you pass a section of a 40km-long **aq-**

CENT SAVER

A seven-day **Fréjus Pass** (€4.60) covers admission to the Roman amphitheatre and theatre, archaeological museum, and Cocteau's chapel (otherwise, it's €2 per sight). To visit the Groupe Épiscopal as well buy a seven-day **Fréjus Pass Intégral** (€6.60) instead. Participating sights sells passes, except the Groupe Épiscopal.

ueduc (aqueduct; av du 15 Corps d'Armée), which once carried water to Roman Fréjus.

Adjoining Fréjus' episcopal complex is the small **Musée Archéologique** (☎ 04 94 52 15 78; place Calvini), displaying everyday objects along with some exceptional pieces such as the two-headed statue of Hermes and a magnificent 3rd-century leopard mosaic. It also puts on temporary exhibitions of finds from archaeological digs.

The tourist office runs weekly two-hour **guided tours** (adult/child €5/3) of all the Roman sites. Visits are in French only however.

GASTRONOMIC HIGHLIGHTS

❧ LE POIVRIER €€

☎ 04 94 52 28 50; 52 place Paul Albert Février; lunch/dinner menu €15/28; ⏲ lunch & dinner Tue-Sat

Tucked away on one of Fréjus' pretty market squares, you'd never guess from the cute alfresco set up that downstairs is a grandiose vaulted dining room with a monumental fireplace. A Templar's cross on the wall suggests this was a garrison room many centuries ago. Nowadays, Le Poivrier is a wonderful address serving exquisitely fresh dishes inspired from local traditions and faraway climes (the owner is an avid traveller) such as duck breasts in crusty spice or cod stew with lemongrass.

❧ MAISON DE LA TARTE €

☎ 04 94 51 17 34; 33 rue Jean Jaurès; ⏲ 6am-7pm Mon-Sat Aug-Jun

If you're planning a picnic, stop at this mouth-watering bakery. Tarts of every kind (lemon meringue, pear and chocolate, apricot, almond etc), sold by the slice for €2.50, fill the front window and back shelves. Inside, you'll also find

the usual breads and pastries as well as sandwiches.

TRANSPORT

BUS // Bus 4 links Fréjus' humble bus station on place Paul Vernet with St-Raphaël bus station (tickets €1.10).
TRAIN // The main station in the area is St-Raphaël-Valescure, in St-Raphaël.
PARKING // Parking du Clos de la Tour, on the edge of the old town, is free.

CANNES AREA

ST-TROPEZ TO TOULON

3 PERFECT DAYS

🌱 DAY 1 // ST-TROPEZ STYLE

In St-Tropez mooch around place des Lices (opposite) with its marvellous jam-packed market, followed by a coffee and croissant at Sartre's Sénequier (p281) and a poetic stroll along the coastal path (p283). Devote the afternoon to art (p281) and shopping (p286), and come dusk motor through vineyards to Plage de Gigaro, where Couleurs Jardin (p289) beckons for a beautiful dinner on the sand.

🌱 DAY 2 // TRAVEL TO EAT

This fertile area was created for gourmets: enjoy a luxuriant morning pottering around the hilltop village and market of Ramatuelle (p287), then lunch on grilled fish by the sea at Chez Camille (p288) or between vines at Auberge de l'Omède (p288). Drive inland through the Massif des Maures (p295) to taste sweet chestnuts in Collobrières (p295). Dine rustic at La Petite Fontaine (p296) or Auberge de la Môle (p298). If it is winter and truffles turn you on, delve instead into the Northern Var: meander Aups truffle market (p292) and dine at Chez Bruno and/or Les Chênes Verts (p293).

🌱 DAY 3 // A WINE-LOVER'S TRAIL

Discover matchless Appellation d'Origine Contrôlée (AOC) reds of Bandol (p312) or bear southeast to La Londe, where the Route des Vins de la Londe (p308) escorts wine lovers by bike through vineyards. As the sun sinks, sail to Île de Porquerolles (p300) for a romantic dinner amid the largest wine-producing estate on the vine-rich island at luxuriant Mas du Langoustier (p303). Or spend the night afloat (p304).

PRESQU'ÎLE DE ST-TROPEZ

· · · · · ·

Jutting out into the sea, between the Golfe de St-Tropez and the Baie de Cavalaire, is the St-Tropez peninsula.

From swanky St-Tropez on the northern coast, fine-sand beaches of buttercream yellow and gold – easily the loveliest on the Côte d'Azur – ring the peninsula. Inland, the flower-dressed hilltop villages of Gassin and Ramatuelle charm the socks off millions.

ST-TROPEZ

pop 5690

Pouting sexpot Brigitte Bardot came to St-Tropez in the '50s to star in *Et Dieu Créa la Femme* (*And God Created Woman;* 1956) and transformed the peaceful fishing village overnight into a sizzling jet-set favourite. Tropeziens have thrived on their sexy image ever since: at the Vieux Port, yachts like spaceships jostle for millionaire moorings, and an infinite number more tourists jostle to admire them.

Yet there is a serene side to this village trampled by 100,000 visitors a day in summer. Out of season the St-Tropez of mesmerising quaint beauty and 'sardine scales glistening like pearls on the cobblestones' that charmed Guy de Maupassant (1850–93) comes to life: meander cobbled lanes in the old fishing quarter of La Ponche, sip pastis at a place des Lices café, watch old men play *pétanque* (boules) beneath plane trees, or walk in solitary splendour from beach to beach along the coastal path.

Whatever the season, if you want to be seduced by the mirage of a brooding 17th-century citadel, glowing terracotta roofs and an Italianate church tower topped by Provençal campanile that so charmed pointillist Paul Signac in 1890, arrive by boat.

ESSENTIAL INFORMATION

EMERGENCIES // Pôle de Santé (☎ 04 98 12 53 08; www.ch-saint-tropez.fr) Nearest hospital, 11km from St-Tropez on D559 in Gassin **Police Station** (☎ 04 94 12 70 00; rue François Sibilli)

TOURIST OFFICES // Tourist Office (☎ 08 92 68 48 28; www.ot-saint-tropez.com; quai Jean Jaurès; ⓨ 9.30am-8.30pm Jul & Aug, 9.30am-12.30pm & 2-7pm Apr-Jun, Sep & Oct, 9.30am-12.30pm & 2-6pm Nov-Mar, closed Sun Jan & Nov).

EXPLORING ST-TROPEZ

❦ PLACE DES LICES // THE LIFE AND SOUL OF ST-TROPEZ

Studded with plane trees, cafés and (when the market's not on) *pétanque* players, this is St-Tropez's legendary and very charming central square. Simply sitting on a café pavement terrace watching the world go by or jostling with the crowds at its extravaganza of a twice-weekly **market** (place des Lices; ⓨ 8am-1pm Tue & Sat), jam-packed with everything from fruit and veg to antique mirrors and flip-flops, is an integral part of the St-Tropez experience.

Artists and intellectuals have met for decades in St-Tropez's famous Café des Arts, now simply called **Le Café** (☎ 04 94 97 44 69; www.lecafe.fr; place des Lices): don't confuse it with the newer, green-canopied Café des Arts on the corner of the square. Le Café's dimly lit historic interior with nicotine-coloured ceiling, dating to 1789, is a sight in itself, as is a cream-oozing slab of *tarte tropézienne* (sponge-cake sandwich topped with sugar) served by suitably surly waiters on its pavement terrace. Aspiring *pétanque*

(Continued on page 281)

ST-TROPEZ TO TOULON

ST-TROPEZ TO TOULON

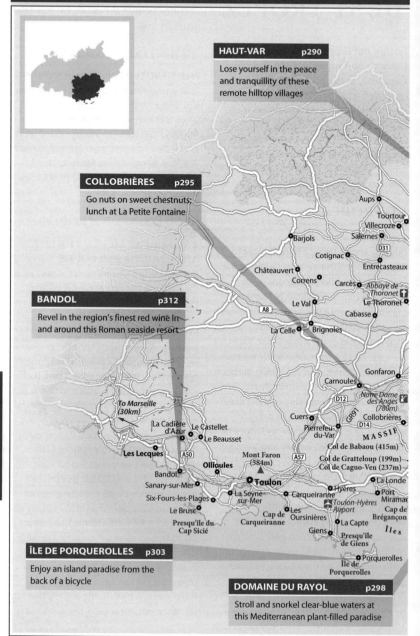

HAUT-VAR   p290

Lose yourself in the peace and tranquillity of these remote hilltop villages

COLLOBRIÈRES   p295

Go nuts on sweet chestnuts; lunch at La Petite Fontaine

BANDOL   p312

Revel in the region's finest red wine in and around this Roman seaside resort

ÎLE DE PORQUEROLLES   p303

Enjoy an island paradise from the back of a bicycle

DOMAINE DU RAYOL   p298

Stroll and snorkel clear-blue waters at this Mediterranean plant-filled paradise

Aups
Tourtour
Villecroze
Salernes
D31
Barjols
Cotignac
Entrecasteaux
Châteauvert
Correns
Carcès
Abbaye de Thoronet
Le Val
Le Thoronet
Cabasse
A8
La Celle
Brignoles

Gonfaron
Carnoules
Notre Dame des Anges (780m)
D12
Collobrières
Cuers
D14
Pierrefeu-du-Var
MASSIF
Col de Babaou (415m)
Col de Gratteloup (199m)
Col de Caguo-Ven (237m)
GR91

To Marseille (30km)
La Cadière d'Azur
Le Castellet
Le Beausset
Les Lecques
A50
Ollioules
Mont Faron (584m)
A57
Bandol
Sanary-sur-Mer
Toulon
La Seyne-sur-Mer
Hyères
La Londe
Port Miramar
Six-Fours-les-Plages
Carqueiranne
Toulon-Hyères Airport
Cap de Brégançon
Îles
Le Brusc
Les Oursinières
Presqu'île du Cap Sicié
Cap de Carqueiranne
La Capte
Giens
Presqu'île de Giens
Porquerolles
Île de Porquerolles

ST-TROPEZ TO TOULON

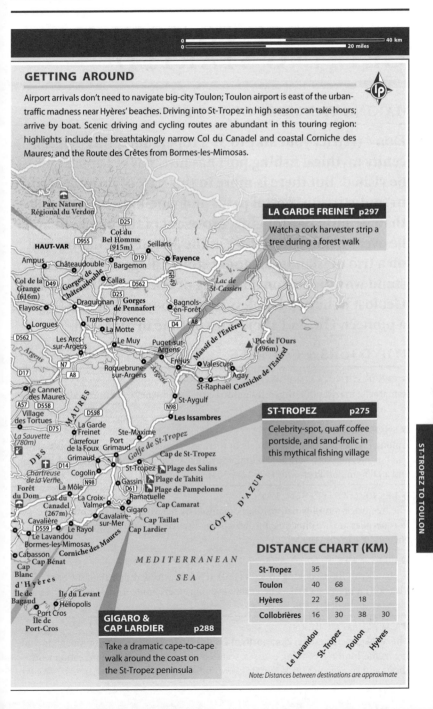

GETTING AROUND

Airport arrivals don't need to navigate big-city Toulon; Toulon airport is east of the urban-traffic madness near Hyères' beaches. Driving into St-Tropez in high season can take hours; arrive by boat. Scenic driving and cycling routes are abundant in this touring region: highlights include the breathtakingly narrow Col du Canadel and coastal Corniche des Maures; and the Route des Crêtes from Bormes-les-Mimosas.

LA GARDE FREINET p297

Watch a cork harvester strip a tree during a forest walk

ST-TROPEZ p275

Celebrity-spot, quaff coffee portside, and sand-frolic in this mythical fishing village

GIGARO & CAP LARDIER p288

Take a dramatic cape-to-cape walk around the coast on the St-Tropez peninsula

DISTANCE CHART (KM)

	Le Lavandou	St-Tropez	Toulon	Hyères
St-Tropez	35			
Toulon	40	68		
Hyères	22	50	18	
Collobrières	16	30	38	30

Note: Distances between destinations are approximate

ST-TROPEZ TO TOULON

ST-TROPEZ TO TOULON
GETTING STARTED

MAKING THE MOST OF YOUR TIME

Don't restrict your stay to St-Tropez. Sure, this magnificently mythical fishing port has lure, has sex appeal, must be visited. But there is more to this part of Provence, rife in soul-stirring coastal paths and vine-knitted peninsulas, than Brigitte Bardot glitz. Move out of the limelight and be overwhelmed by nature in the Massif des Maures and on a trio of islands. Meander stone villages and understand why the seasonal moving of flocks is still celebrated. Get lost in hilltop hamlets in backcountry Var and feel like a pioneer. Oh, and allow bags of time to dine well.

TOP TOURS & COURSES

❦ PENINSULA NATURE WALKS

Ramatuelle tourist office organises guided coastal and vineyard nature walks (adult/8 to 12 years €8/4) (p287).

❦ SNORKELLING

Among Hyères tourist office's excellent thematic guided tours – evening walks, salt-pan birdlife, markets – are snorkelling tours (€26). There is a guided trail in Le Rayol and a DIY trail on Port-Cros (p298 & p304).

❦ LES RENCONTRES DU PARC

The free twice-monthly nature hikes organised by the Maison du Parc on Île de Porquerolles are breathtaking: birdwatching, discovering bats, peregrine falcons, ancient fig varieties (p300).

❦ LE LIBERTY

September to June, cooking courses (€50) at this beachside fish restaurant-bar on Plage de Pampelonne make fine Friday-evening entertainment (☎ 04 94 79 80 62; liberty .plage@wanadoo.fr; rte de Tamaris, Ramatuelle).

❦ CHÂTEAU DE BERNE

This winegrowing estate, 2km north of Lorgues, offers various entertainment, including truffle-hunting, cooking courses, watercolour-painting, perfume-creation workshops and jazz picnics (☎ 04 94 60 43 53; www.chateauberne.com; chemin de Berne, Lorgues; ☙ Mar–Oct).

ST-TROPEZ TO TOULON

GETTING AWAY FROM IT ALL

Finding peace and serenity amid pea-green vines, golden coastline and deep-blue sea is not hard in this nature-rich part of Provence.

* **Domaine du Rayol** These extraordinary sea gardens are among the Mediterranean's most fabulous and are large enough to lose the crowds (p298)

* **Île de Porquerolles & Île de Port-Cros** Despite the seasonal crowd on the boat, these two paradise islands are remote; hike on Port-Cros, bike around Porquerolles (p300)

* **Haut-Var** Devote at least a few days to motoring or cycling in solitude around this wonderful area, a reminder of how other parts of Provence were a few decades ago (p290)

ADVANCE PLANNING

Tips and tricks for getting the most out of this inspiring part of southern France.

* **Getting to St-Tropez** People who do wrong in life are made to drive to St-Tropez in high season after they die: roads in July and August are chock-a-block; arrive by boat instead (p287).

* **St-Tropez market** Depending on your interest, either plan to be in or avoid St-Tropez Tuesday and Saturday mornings

* **Domaine du Rayol** Book tickets well in advance for its evening concerts and July/August snorkelling trail

* **Île de Porquerolles** Many walking trails on the island are closed in July and August when forest fire threatens

TOP MARKETS

MONDAY
Bormes-les-Mimosas, Port Grimaud

TUESDAY
Bandol, Callas, Fayence, Hyères, St-Tropez, Toulon

WEDNESDAY
Bormes-les-Mimosas, Draguignan, La Garde Freinet, Salernes, Sanary-sur-Mer, Toulon

---

THURSDAY
Aups (truffle market November to March), Bargemon, Callas, Collobrières (July and August), Fayence, Grimaud, Hyères, Le Lavandou, Les Arcs-sur-Argens, Port Grimaud, Ramatuelle, Toulon

---

FRIDAY
Le Rayol (April to October), Port Grimaud, Toulon

SATURDAY
Cogolin, Draguignan, Fayence, Hyères, St-Tropez, Toulon

SUNDAY
Cavalière (all-day flea market), Collobrières, Gassin (April to October), La Garde Freinet, La Londe, Port Grimaud, Ramatuelle, Salernes, Toulon

---

RESOURCES

* **Pays des Maures** (http://en.maures.latitude-gallimard.com) Handy guide to the Massif des Maures area

* **Provence Verte** (www.provenceverte.fr) Wine tours, gastronomy, heritage and itinerary planning for villages in Haut-Var

ST-TROPEZ TO TOULON

ST-TROPEZ

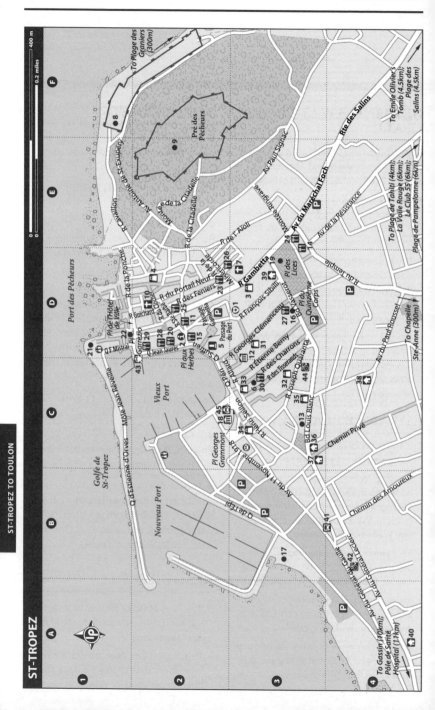

(Continued from page 275)

players can borrow a set of boules from the bar or buy their own at **La Palanquée** (☎ 04 94 97 41 41; bd Louis Blanc).

Locals hang out on the opposite non-sunny side of the square at the brasserie-style **Le Sporting** (☎ 04 94 97 00 65; place des Lices) and neighbouring **Le Clemenceau**: this is as down-to-earth as you get in St-Tropez.

♥ VIEUX PORT // IMMERSE YOURSELF IN TIMELESS TRADITION

Weave your way through the history-laden old city streets to feel St-Tropez's timeless traditions and culture. Start at the **Old Port** where the **Bailli de Suffren statue** (quai Suffren), cast from a 19th-century cannon, peers out to sea. The bailiff (1729–88) was a sailor who fought with a Tropezien crew against Britain and Prussia during the Seven Years War.

As much of an institution as the bailiff is portside café **Sénéquier** (☎ 04 94 97 00 90; www.senequier.com; quai Jean Jaurès), where Sartre wrote parts of *Les Chemins de la Liberté* (The Roads to Freedom). In business since 1887, the café is red-hot with boaties, bikers and tourists watching the world razz by: look for the terrace crammed with pillar-box-red tables and director chairs.

Le Gorille (☎ 04 94 97 03 93; www.legorille.com; 1 quai Suffren), the other eminent portside bistro, gets its name from its 1950s owner, the short, muscular and apparently very hairy Henri Guérin, aka Gorilla! In the 1930s when it first opened it was called Bar Suffren. Duck beneath the archway opposite, next to the tourist office, to uncover St-Tropez's morning **fish market** (☺ daily summer, Tue-Sun winter), packed between stone walls on place aux Herbes.

♥ MUSÉE DE L'ANNONCIADE // GET DOTTY WITH POINTILLISTS SIGNAC AND MATISSE

In a gracefully converted 16th-century chapel, this small but famous **art museum** (☎ 04 94 97 04 01; place Georges Grammont; adult/12-25yr €5/free; ☺ 10am-1pm & 3-7pm Jul-Sep, 10am-noon & 2-6pm Wed-Mon Oct & Dec-Jun) showcases an impressive collection of modern art infused with that legendary Côte d'Azur light. It's a great opportunity to understand what it was about St-Tropez that captivated so many of these painters: the pointillist collection includes Signac's *St-Tropez, Le Quai* (1899), *St-Tropez, Les*

ST-TROPEZ TO TOULON

Pins Parasol aux Canoubiers (1897) and his *St-Tropez, Coucher de Soleil au Bois de Pins* (1896), which hangs juxtaposed against a view of contemporary St-Tropez through the window. Artists like Vuillard, Bonnard, Maurice Denis and Vallotton (the self-named 'Nabis' group) have a room to themselves, and there are wild works by the fauvists: Matisse spent the summer of 1904 in St-Tropez, starting preliminary studies for *Luxe, Calme et Volupté*. Cubists George Braque and Picasso are also represented.

❦ LA PONCHE // DIP INTO ST-TROPEZ'S OLD FISHING QUARTER

Shrug off the hustle of the port in St-Tropez's ramshackle fishing quarter, northeast of the Vieux Port. From quai Suffren, walk to the northern end of its continuations, quai Jean Jaurès and quai Frédéric Mistral, and at 15th-century

ACCOMMODATION

For detailed listings, see the accommodation chapter. Here are some of the best picks for the area:

★ Hidden in Seillans in the Haut-Var, **Hôtel des Deux Rocs** (p295) is your classic village inn with the dreamiest terrace restaurant ever

★ St-Tropez's **Hôtel Lou Cagnard** (p398) is a boutique hotel with pretty fairy-light-lit garden

★ **Hôtel Le Méditerranée** (p401) near the beach in Hyères is everything a solid midrange choice should be

★ **Les 3 Îles** (p399), a *maison d'hôtes* straight out of a design magazine

★ If it's a real château you want: **La Grande Maison des Campaux** (p399)

HIDDEN GEM

Chapelle Ste-Anne (av Augustin Grangeon), built in 1618, sits south of place des Lices. Its marvellous collection of ex-votive paintings and centuries-old miniature boats can be viewed just once a year – on St Anne's feast day (26 July).

Tour du Portalet, turn right to the sandy fishing cove. From here, you can take the coastal path (opposite), which snakes the peninsula.

From the southern end of quai Frédéric Mistral, place Garrezio sprawls east from 10th-century **Tour Suffren** to place de l'Hôtel de Ville. From here, rue Guichard leads southeast to sweet-chiming **Église de St-Tropez** (place de l'Ormeau), a St-Trop landmark built in 1785 in Italian baroque style. Inside is the bust of St-Torpes, honoured during Les Bravades des Espagnols (p284). Follow rue du Portail Neuf south to **Chapelle de la Miséricorde** (rue de la Miséricorde), built in 1645 with a pretty bell tower and colourful tiled dome.

❦ ATELIER IVAN HOR // BUY A BOAT TO SAIL AT HOME

Origami sailing boats are the forte of gregarious Hungarian-born artist Ivan Hor, who fled Budapest for Paris in 1956 and studied art in the capital before moving to St-Tropez in 1968. Today, hundreds of tableaux – monumental to minuscule in size and featuring at least one (but invariably thousands) of his signature paper boats – reflect his life. You can view them (or buy them – his work starts at €20 for a pint-sized piece and goes up to €40,000 for a piece to fill a wall) at his twinset of workshops: **Atelier Ivan Hor** (☎ 06 11 80 12 42; www.ivanhor .com; 20 rue des Remparts & 40 rue Gambetta).

ST-TROPEZ TO TOULON

🌺 LA MAISON DES PAPILLONS // GET ALL AFLUTTER AT THE HOUSE OF BUTTERFLIES

Another St-Tropez character, the gregarious Dany Lartigue (b 1921), son of Riviera photographer Jacques Henri Lartigue (1894–1986), created the **House of Butterflies** (☎ 04 94 97 63 45; 9 rue Étienne Berny; adult/under 8yr €3/free; ⏰ 2.30-6pm Mon-Sat Apr-Oct), where some 4500 butterflies he collected are pinned to the walls. Painter in his own right, Dany spent his heyday (1948–70) in Montmartre, Paris, only later moving to St-Tropez into the house where his mother (Madeleine 'Bibi' Messager, the first wife of Jacques Lartigue) lived.

🌺 STYLISH BEACH BUM // POSE ON MYTHICAL MEDITERRANEAN SAND

About 4km southeast of town is the start of **Plage de Tahiti** and its continuation, **Plage de Pampelonne**, studded with St-Tropez's most legendary drinking and dining haunts: what started out in the '50s as a simple canteen for the crew of *And God Created Woman* is now **Le Club 55** (☎ 04 94 55 55 55; www.leclub55.fr; 43 bd Patch; meals €60; ⏰ lunch Mon-Sun Apr–early Nov), the hippest jet-set joint on the beach. Lunch at tightly packed tables beneath sails strung from trees, drink on white sofas on the sand, and be a stylish beach bum on a white cushioned mattress beneath a *paillote* (straw shack). Rumbling tummies with no reservation can opt for a salad or sandwich at the twig-topped beach bar nearer the water.

The other mythical address is **La Voile Rouge** (The Red Sail; ☎ 04 94 79 84 34; chemin des Tamaris; ⏰ lunch Apr-Sep), where the first topless bathers and later G-string bikinis were sighted in the '60s. The beach restaurant with animal-print seat-

HEADLESS HERO

A grisly legend provided St-Tropez with its name in AD 68. After beheading a Roman officer named Torpes for becoming a Christian, the emperor Nero packed the decapitated body into a small boat, along with a dog and a rooster who were to devour his remains. Miraculously, the body came ashore in St-Tropez un-nibbled, and the village adopted the headless Torpes as its saint.

ing and loungers on the sand remains hot stuff; find it at the northern end of Pampelonne on Mooréa Plage. No credit cards.

Closer to St-Tropez, **Plage des Salins** is a long, wide sandy beach 4.5km east of town at the southern foot of Cap des Salins. Follow route des Salins to its end, passing **La Treille Muscate** (Wine Trellis) en route, a rambling villa framed with red-ochre columns wrapped in honeysuckle. Here in 1927 Colette wrote *La Naissance du Jour* (Break of Day), evoking a 1920s unspoilt St-Tropez. She left town in 1938.

At the northern end of Plage des Salins, on a rock jutting out to sea, is the **tomb of Émile Olivier** (1825–1913), who served as first minister to Napoleon III until his exile in 1870. It looks out towards **La Tête de Chien** (Dog's Head), named after the legendary dog who declined to eat St Torpes' remains. Further south, **Pointe du Capon** is a beautiful cape crisscrossed with walking trails.

🌺 SENTIER DU LITTORAL // PICNIC IN STYLE ALONG ST-TROPEZ'S COASTAL PATH

A **coastal path** wends its way past rocky outcrops and hidden bays 35km south from St-Tropez, around the Presqu'île de

ST-TROPEZ TO TOULON

BEST BEACHES

- ★ Plage de Pampelonne – this utterly divine 9km stretch of golden sand is St-Tropez's most legendary, complete with a clutch of fabulous addresses (p283)

- ★ Plage du Layet, Cavalière – nudist beach with legendary shabby-chic beach restaurant, Chez Jo (p299)

- ★ Port-Cros and Porquerolles – two islands with ample unspoilt golden sand to romp on (p300)

- ★ Plage d'Hyères – a favourite for its fabulous restaurant with tables over the water (p309)

St-Tropez to the beach at Cavalaire-sur-Mer and beyond to Le Lavandou (60km).

In St-Tropez the yellow-flagged coastal path starts at **La Ponche**, immediately east of Tour du Portalet, and curves around Port des Pêcheurs, past St-Tropez's **citadel** (☎ 04 94 97 59 43; adult/under 18yr €2.50/free; 10am-6.30pm Apr-Sep, 10am-12.30pm & 1.30-5.30pm Oct-Mar), built in 1602 to defend the coast against Spain. The path then leads past the walled **Cimitière Marin** (marine cemetery) to the tiny **Plage des Graniers** and beyond. From Tour du Portalet count 50 minutes to the Baie des Cannebiers (2.7km), 2½ hours to Plage des Salins (8.5km) and around 3½ hours to Plage de Tahiti (12km).

From Plage des Graniers on, rocks abound for sunbathing lizardlike and wetting your toes in the Med. Coastal views increase in magnificence as the path wends it way between rocks and high-walled properties of magnificent proportions. Before leaving St-Tropez stock up on picnic supplies at the place des Lices market and everything gour-

ST-TROPEZ TO TOULON

met (caviar, Champagne and foie gras included) at **Benoît Gourmet & Co** (☎ 04 94 97 73 78; 6 rue des Charrons).

♥ A BOAT TRIP // SAIL AROUND ST-TROPEZ'S STARRY BAYS AND GLAM CAPES

Boat trips around the glamorous Baie des Cannebiers (dubbed the 'Bay of Stars' after the many celebrity villas dotting the coast) are advertised on billboards along quai Suffren at the Vieux Port. April to September **Les Bateaux Verts** (☎ 04 94 49 29 39; www.bateauxverts .com) runs various trips departing from quai Jean Jaurès, including around the Baie des Cannebiers (adult/child 4 to 12 years €9/5), Calanques de l'Estérel (€18.50/11.10); Caps Camarat, Taillat and Lardier (€18.50/11.10); Cannes (€32/20.60); Îles de Lérins (€32/20.60); Port-Cros (€32/20.60) and Porquerolles (€36/23.20). The same company runs shuttles between St-Tropez, St-Raphaël, Ste-Maxime and Port Grimaud; see p287 for details.

FESTIVALS & EVENTS

Les Bravades (Provençal for 'bravery') Since 1558 Tropeziens have turned out in traditional costume to watch their *capitaine de ville* (town captain) and an ear-splitting army of 140 musket-firing *bravadeurs* parade through the street carrying a bust of the town's patron saint Torpes; 16, 17 & 18 May.

Les Bravades des Espagnols Blazing guns, fluttering flags and colourful processions led by the town captain celebrate St-Tropez's victory over the 21 Spanish galleons that attacked its port on 15 June 1637; 15 June.

GASTRONOMIC HIGHLIGHTS

No greasy spoons in St-Tropez. Prices are higher than elsewhere on the coast; the glamour-dust sprinkled on fish and chips doesn't come cheap!

Quai Jean Jaurès is lined with restaurants touting €30 *menus* and a strategic view of the yacht brigade's silverware and Champagne. At the northern end of rue des Remparts in the old town, less flash places overlook Port des Pêcheurs at La Ponche.

Don't leave town without sampling *tarte tropézienne*, a decadent sponge-cake sandwich filled with custard cream and topped with sugar.

❦ AU CAPRICE DES DEUX €€€

☎ 04 94 97 76 78; www.aucapricedesdeux.com; 40 rue du Portail Neuf; menu €58; ⊗ lunch & dinner Thu-Sun

This traditional *maison de village* (old stone terraced house) with coffee-coloured wooden shutters is a real McCoy old-time favourite with locals – so much so you might just feel a tad out of place here. Its intimate interior is as traditional as its French cuisine: think sole filets, and beef filet with truffles or duck. Find it tucked down a backstreet off rue de la Citadelle.

❦ BRASSERIE DES ARTS €€

☎ 04 94 40 27 37; www.brasseriedesarts.com; 5 place des Lices; main €20, menu €29; ⊗ lunch & dinner

Wedged in a line-up of eating/drinking terraces jockeying for attention on St-Tropez's people-watching square (p275), BA, as it is known, is where the locals go. Out of season ask for a table at the back to experience the real vibe (and admire the kitsch glitter-sprinkled, velvet-covered back wall). Unless you're feeling flush, skip à la carte: the fixed three-course *menu* is gourmet and excellent value.

❦ CHEZ FUCHS €

☎ 04 94 97 01 25; 7 rue des Commerçants; lunch menu €19.50, mains €25; ⊗ lunch & dinner mid-Feb–mid-Jan

Two bar stools propped precariously on the pavement outside set the tone of this

---

BEACH READS

★ *The Hairdressers of St-Tropez* (Rupert Everett) – comedy of hairdressers and talking dogs opening on St-Tropez's Pampelonne beach in 2042

★ *Jigsaw* (Sybille Bedford) – an autobiographical novel inspired by the author's years spent in Toulon during the 1920s and 1930s; her earlier novel, *A Compass Error* (1968), uses the coast as a backdrop for a love triangle of lesbian and heterosexual encounters

★ *Travels with Virginia Woolf* (Jan Morris) – entertaining extracts from the playwright's journals, including observations made during visits to her sister's home in Cassis

---

fabled address, one of the last stalwarts of 'authentic bistro' in glossy St-Tropez. It was created by the Fuchs sisters fifty-something years ago but was bought up by Christophe Leroy (see p286) in 2008. So far little has changed: cuisine remains firmly Provençal in the form of stuffed courgettes, artichokes *à la barigoule* (artichokes braised in a tangy white wine broth) and so on.

❦ LA DAME DE CŒUR €€

☎ 04 94 97 23 16; 2 rue de la Miséricorde; starter/main €18/28; ⊗ lunch & dinner

The Queen of Hearts – dollhouse-sized with mustard walls and a fireplace – has been around for years, and its authentic 'kitchen' feel has real charm. Copper pots sit on the hearth, the sound of steaks sizzling interject conversation and there are only four tables (one seats 12), meaning you could well end up sharing with strangers. Cuisine is classic and meaty: the beef carpaccio is hand-cut sufficiently thick for the lady of the house to warn you about it, and the *côte de bœuf* only comes one way – blue. Finish on a high with Cathy's unforgettable *tarte tatin*.

♥ LA TABLE DU MARCHÉ €€

☎ 04 94 97 85 20; www.christophe-leroy.com; 38 rue Georges Clémenceau; lunch/dinner menu €19.50/29; ⏱ lunch & dinner

With sister 'market tables' in Alpine ski resort Avoriaz and Marrakech, this simple bistro by St-Tropez's savviest chef, Christophe Leroy, is a success story. The lobster gratin and truffle and celery-stuffed ravioli are unforgettable and, for once, vegetarians are properly catered for. If sweet things are your passion in life, visit Leroy's cake shop and tearoom, **Maison Fetter** (21bis rue Allard).

♥ L'ESCALE JOSEPH €€€

☎ 04 94 97 00 63; www.joseph-saint-tropez.com; 9 quai Jean Jaurès; mains €30-50; ⏱ noon-3am Tue-Sun

This celebrity-loved portside restaurant with floor-to-ceiling glass front, mirrored walls and sand on the floor is the last word in hip dining. Fish and seafood is what the menu is all about – sea bass in a salted crust, *simplement un beau torteau* (simply a handsome crab) or scallops with asparagus and a truffle *tartare* are some of the fishy delights. Lobsters swim around in the tank waiting to be eaten. You need to look good to dine here, one of a handful of hip Joseph addresses in town (Le Quai, a few doors down, has black sand on the floor).

♥ SALAMA €€

☎ 04 94 97 59 62; www.restaurant-salama.com, in French; 1 rue des Tisserands; couscous €21-39, tajines €25-30; ⏱ dinner daily

One of those fashionable addresses that just doesn't seem to lose its charm with Tropeziens, this hip Moroccan den hid-

VINE DINING

★ Auberge de l'Omède (p288) – refined, stylish and very gastronomic

★ Domaine de la Maurette (p293) – hearty dining, vineyard-worker style

★ Le Mas du Langoustier (p303) – vines, an island and the ultimate romance

★ Domaine de Terrebrune (p313) – lunch with a Bandol winemaker

den down an alley is still going strong. Lounge about amid cushioned exotic furnishings, share an assortment of appetisers (€29.50) between a trio of friends, wash down heavenly scented couscous and *tajines* with fresh mint tea, and finish with a lime sherbet.

RECOMMENDED SHOPS

St-Tropez is loaded with voguish boutiques, gourmet food shops and galleries overflowing with bad art. For designer vintage, browse **Le Dépôt** (☎ 04 94 97 80 10; 24 bd Louis Blanc) and **De l'Une à l'Autre** (☎ 04 98 12 66 14; 6 rue Joseph Quaranta).

♥ ATELIER RONDINI

☎ 04 94 97 19 55; www.rondini.fr; 16 rue Georges Clémenceau

Traditional Tropezienne sandals, supposedly inspired by a simple leather pair brought by Colette from Greece to show her cobbler, are all part of the St-Tropez myth. Expect to pay around €74 for a pair of kids strappy sandals and €115 for an adults pair at this traditional shoemaker, in business since 1927.

♥ L'ATELIER DES SPARTIATES TROPÉZIENNES K JACQUES

☎ 04 94 97 41 50; www.kjacques.com; 25 rue Allard & 16 rue Seillon

ST-TROPEZ TO TOULON

St-Tropez's other cobbling family. This one has hand-crafted the same strappy sandals since 1933. Celebrity clients at their two locations include Jean Cocteua, Picasso, Brigitte Bardot and the Baba Cool Generation. Take your pick from silver leather, crocodile, black patent and so on. Prices range from €145 to €220 a pair.

TRANSPORT

BIKE // Rent a bicycle from **Mas Location 2 Roues** (☎ 04 94 97 00 60; 3-5 rue Joseph Quaranta; ☽ Apr-Oct). Daily rates for a city/mountain bike are €10/12; a 50cc scooter is €34. **Holiday Bikes** (☎ 04 94 96 27 17; www.holiday-bikes.com; 12 av du Général Leclerc) charge similar rates.

BOAT // **Les Bateaux Verts** (p284) runs shuttle boats to/from Port Grimaud (single/return €6/11.50, 20 minutes) April to early October, and boats to/from Ste-Maxime (one-way/return €6.60/12, 30 minutes) year-round. Boats depart from quai Jean Jaurès at the Vieux Port. **Les Bateaux de St-Raphaël** (☎ 04 94 95 17 46; www.tmr-saintraphael.com) runs two to six boats daily from St-Tropez to St-Raphaël (adult/2-9yr single €14/9) April to August, twice-weekly in September and October. Boats depart from the Nouveau Port.

BUS // From the **bus station** (☎ 08 25 00 06 50; av du Général de Gaulle), buses serve Ramatuelle (€3.70, 25 minutes), Gassin (€3.70, 25 minutes), St-Raphaël (€10.90, 1¼ hours, at least eight daily) via Grimaud and Port Grimaud, and Fréjus (€9, one hour). Buses to Toulon (€20.90, 2¼ hours, seven daily) stop at Le Lavandou (€11.80, one hour), Hyères (€17.10, 1½ hours) and Toulon-Hyères airport (€22.20, 1½ hours). All services are less frequent in winter.

TAXI // For a boat taxi call **Taxi de Mer** (☎ 06 09 53 15 47); for a regular motorised vehicle, go to the **taxi rank** (☎ 04 94 97 05 27; place Georges Grammont) at the Vieux Port in front of the Musée de l'Annonciade.

THE PENINSULA

South of St-Tropez slumbers a priceless oasis of peace with manicured vineyards, quiet narrow lanes and the odd château or solitary stone *bastide* (country house). Along its southern side spills the golden sand of France's most chic beach, Plage de Pampelonne (p283).

Cap Lardier, the peninsula's southernmost cape, is protected by the Parc National de Port-Cros (p304). Cap Taillat, 1km northeast, is similarly guarded by the Conservatoire du Littoral. The tiny spit of sandy land today supports a range of important habitats, from seashore to wooded cliffs, and hides some of France's rarest plant species as well as a population of Hermann tortoises (see also p296).

EXPLORING THE PENINSULA

♥ GASSIN & RAMATUELLE // AN EXCLUSIVE TWINSET OF PHOTOGENIC VILLAGES

In medieval **Gassin**, 11km southwest of St-Tropez atop a rocky promontory, narrow streets wend up to the village church (1558). The village's most wowing feature is the 360-degree panoramic view of the peninsula, St-Tropez bay and the Maures forests.

From Gassin, rte des Moulins de Paillas snakes 3km southeast to **Ramatuelle**, a labyrinthine walled village with a tree-studded central square and lovely vine-covered café terrace at **Café de l'Ormeau** (place du Village). Its unusual name is thought to come from 'Rahmatu'llah', meaning 'Divine Gift', a legacy of the 10th-century Saracen occupation. Jazz and theatre fill the tourist-packed streets during August's **Festival de Ramatuelle** (www.festivalderamatuelle.com) and **Jazz Fest** (www.jazzfestivalramatuelle.com).

The fruits of the peninsula's vineyards – Côtes de Provence wine – can be tested at various châteaux along the D61; **Ramatuelle tourist office** (☎ 04 98 12 64 00; www.ramatuelle-tourisme.com, in French;

place de l'Ormeau; 9am-1pm & 3-7.30pm Mon-Fri, 10am-1pm & 3-7pm Sat & Sun Jul & Aug, shorter hr rest year) has a list of estates where you can taste and buy. Most require an advance RDV (rendez-vous; appointment).

🌱 SÉMAPHORE DE CAMARAT // REVEL IN A GIDDY BIRD'S-EYE PENINSULA VIEW

Pampelonne stretches for 9km from **Cap du Pinet** to **Cap Camarat**, a rocky cape dominated by France's second-tallest lighthouse, operational since 1861, electrified in 1946 and automated from 1977. Next to it towers the 110m-tall **Sémaphore de Camarat**, a military installation built in 1861. June to September you can scale it for a giddy view of St-Tropez and its peninsula. Visits are by free guided tour only (bring your passport) and must be booked in advance at Ramatuelle tourist office. The **Sentier du Littoral** (coastal path; p283) snakes right by here.

🌱 GIGARO & CAP LARDIER // A SEASIDE WALK ON THE WILD SIDE

From the roundabout at the southern end of uninspiring La Croix-Valmer at the southwestern tip of the Presqu'île de St-Tropez, the last exit strikes east to the pinprick seaside hamlet of **Gigaro**, with its sandy beach, couple of lovely eating and sleeping options, and a water-sports school. From the far end of the beach, a board maps the **Sentier du Littoral** (coastal path) that works its way around the coast to Plage des Brouïs (2.4km, 40 minutes), Cap Lardier (4.7km, 1½ hours), Plage de Briande (7km, 2¼ hours) and beyond past Cap Taillat to L'Escalet (9km, 2¾ hours). Bikes are not allowed along the well-signposted trail; the information hut at its start opens July and August.

From Gigaro, the narrow but drop-dead gorgeous D93 winds inland over the Col de Collebasse (129m) to Ramatuelle – a good ride for mountain bikers. **L'Escalet**, accessible by a 2.5km road signposted off the D93, is a pretty little rocky cove with plenty of chanting cicadas and dried seaweed along the shoreline.

GASTRONOMIC HIGHLIGHTS

🌱 AUBERGE DE L'OMÈDE // RAMATUELLE €€€

☎ 04 94 44 11 11; www.aubergedeloumede.com; chemin de l'Oumède, Ramatuelle; mains €39-59; dinner Mon-Sun Jul & Aug, dinner Tue-Sat Apr-Jun, Sep & Oct

Epicureans come from far and wide to sample Jean-Pierre Frezia's Provençal cuisine served in a sea of vineyards akin to paradise: red mullet and spinach cannelloni, grilled catch of the day *aux ceps de vigne* and sensational desserts, all accompanied by some very fine wines. Dining at this isolated *bastide* down a single-lane track is indeed a rare treat and it even has seven rooms and a pool (doubles low/high season from €195/245) – handy should you really not want to leave.

🌱 CHEZ CAMILLE // RAMATUELLE €€

☎ 04 98 12 68 98; www.chezcamille.fr; rte de Bonne Terrasse, Ramatuelle; mains €20-40; lunch & dinner Wed-Mon

Deep terracotta walls hide this blue-and-white tiled fishing cottage dating from 1913. Now into its fourth generation of cooks, the beachside restaurant cooks up just one thing over a wood-fuelled grill – fish. Guillaume's great-grandparents lived here as fishermen, his grandparents began the restaurant and Guillaume continues to woo punters with the tastiest grills on the Côte d'Azur. Reserve at least a week in advance, especially for summer evenings. From the D93 follow signs for Bonne Terrasse; Chez Camille is 4km north of Ramatuelle village.

❦ COULEURS JARDIN // GIGARO €€

☎ 04 94 79 59 12; Plage de Gigaro, Gigaro; mains €25; ⏰ lunch & dinner Apr-Sep

Eclectic and hip, this imaginative beach-side space is *the* place to dine and/or drink. Loll on cushioned seating beneath the trees or pick a table on the terrace with nothing between you and the deep blue sea (except sand). Cuisine is fish- and market-fuelled – grilled sardines or the catch of the day, followed by straw-berry and pineapple soup spiced with a dash of local wine, make a handsome lunch. Reservations are crucial.

GOLFE DE ST-TROPEZ

❦ PORT GRIMAUD // CRUISE ALONG 'VENETIAN' WATERWAYS PAST RAINBOW COTTAGES

It's hard to believe this so-called 'Venice of Provence' stands on top of what was a mosquito-filled swamp in the 1960s. Inside the high wall that barricades the pleasure port from the busy N98, colour-ful cottages stand gracefully alongside yacht-laden waterways. On Thursday and Sunday mornings a **market** fills place du Marché, from where a bridge leads to Port Grimaud's modernist **church**, with stained-glass window de-signed by Vasarely. Red rooftops fan out from atop its **bell tower** (admission €1).

François Spoerry (1912–99), the Al-satian architect who went on to design Port Liberty in New York, fought for four years to get the authorities to agree to his proposal, which was inspired by pictures of prehistoric lagoon towns.

> ## TOP FIVE
>
> ### LUNCH ON THE SAND
>
> ★ **Le Club 55** (p283) – the place to be seen since the days of Brigitte Bardot
>
> ★ **Couleurs Jardin** (left) – the peninsula's 'insider' address, full of understated chic
>
> ★ **Chez Camille** (opposite) – good-old seafaring tradition
>
> ★ **Chez Jo** (p299) – the alternative address for alternative bathers
>
> ★ **L'Endroît** (p309) – fashionable dusk dining

Now 400,000 visitors a year come to gape at his work, with its mighty 12km of quays, 7km of canals and mooring space for 3000 luxury yachts. Cars are forbidden inside the walls; *tenue correcte* (correct dress) is insisted upon (except on the wide sandy beach accessible from Grand Rue); and wealthy bronzed resi-dents cruise around in speedboats. For the less privileged, two kiosks across the bridge from the church run 20-minute Port Grimaud **boat tours** (adult/3-12yr €5/3; ⏰ 10am-8pm daily Mar-Oct) and rent four-man **electric boats** (per 30 min €20; ⏰ Easter to mid-Nov). June to September shuttle boats sail every 20 minutes on Tuesday and Sat-urday from Port Grimaud to St-Tropez (adult return €10).

Port Grimaud is jam-packed with res-taurants, most of which leave you feeling you've paid over the odds. Those with a soft spot for seafood won't do better than highly regarded restaurant **La Table du Mareyeur** (☎ 04 94 56 06 77; www.mareyeur.com; 10-11 place Artisans; mains €35-50, seafood platters €50; ⏰ lunch & dinner Mar-Nov).

The **tourist office** (☎ 04 94 56 02 01; quai des Fossés; ⏰ 9am-12.30pm & 2.30-6.15pm Mon-Sat

Jun–mid-Sep), outside the village on the N98, is a two-second walk from the main pedestrian entrance into Port Grimaud. Buses link Port Grimaud with Grimaud (€1.40, 10 minutes) and St-Tropez (€3.70, 15 minutes).

♥ GRIMAUD // DELVE INTO PORT GRIMAUD'S MEDIEVAL HALF

Port Grimaud's medieval sibling is a postcard-perfect hilltop village 3km inland. Crowned with the dramatic shell of **Château du Grimaud**, its past is bloody – the castle was built in the 11th century, fortified in the 15th century, destroyed during the Wars of Religion (1562–98), rebuilt in the 17th century, and wrecked again during the French Revolution. Evening concerts held on the stage within the ruins here during the music fest, **Les Grimaldines**, in July and August, are magical.

Grimaud **tourist office** (☎ 04 94 55 43 83; www.grimaud-provence.com; 1 bd des Aliziers; ☺ 9am-12.30pm & 2.30-6.15pm Mon-Sat), at the foot of the village on the D558, has information on walks with or without a guide. South of the village along the St-Tropez-bound D61, enjoy the fruity aroma of local wine at **Caves des Vignerons de Grimaud** (☎ 04 94 43 20 14; 36 av des Oliviers), a cooperative where you can stock up on Vin de Pays du Var for little more than €2 a litre.

HAUT-VAR

· · · · · ·

What a difference a few miles can make! The northern half of the Var *département* **(generally agreed to be everything north of the noisy A8** *autoroute***) – otherwise known as the Northern or Upper Var – is a vastly different kettle of fish from its coastal counterpart: in this rural hinterland there's not a grain of sand or an oiled body in sight.**

Rather, peaceful hilltop villages drowse beneath the midday sun, creating a glorious mirage of an unspoilt Provence *verte* (green Provence). Main town Draguignan, the hard nut in the chocolate box, is a hard-nosed town where the French army maintains its largest military base. The only way to get around: your own wheels or boots.

EXPLORING HAUT-VAR

♥ MOULIN DE CALLAS // GEN UP ON, TASTE AND BUY OLIVE OIL

A nosedive south of Bargemon (p295) is this **oil mill** (☎ 04 94 39 03 20; www.moulinde callas.com; ☺ 10am-noon & 2-6pm Mon-Sat), where Nicole and Serge's family have cultivated olives to make oil since 1928. The mill turns at the southern foot of Callas village, pressing the freshly harvested olives of 400-odd local olive farmers. Learn about olive oil and buy in the on-site shop; for a greater insight, see p372. Afterwards, make your way uphill past the **tourist office** (☎ 04 94 39 06 77; ot.callas@ wanadoo.fr; place du 18 Juin 1940) to the central village square for a stunning panorama of the red-rock Massif de l'Estérel (p269).

♥ CHEZ BRUNO // PIG OUT ON BLACK TRUFFLES

France's most famous truffle restaurant can be found in a country house 2.5km east of the tiny backwater village of Lorgues, on the D562 towards Les Arcs. In his Michelin-starred restaurant, celebrity chef **Bruno Clément** (☎ 04 94 85 93 93; www.restaurantbruno.com; rte de Vidauban; menus €65, €85, €95, €100 & €135; ☺ lunch & dinner Jun–mid-Sep, lunch & dinner Tue-Sat, lunch Sun mid-Sep–Apr) cooks almost exclusively with those knobbly, pungent delicacies: he gets through an incredible 1000kg of the world's most expensive foodstuff every year, some from Provence, many from Alba in northern Italy. Should you not be able to move after your decadent black-diamond feast – it is incredibly rich – stay in one of Bruno's six lovely rooms (doubles from €110).

🌱 ABBAYE DE THORONET // CONTEMPLATE THE SERENITY OF SACRED ARCHITECTURE

The third in a trio of great Cistercian abbeys (the other two are Silvacane and Notre-Dame de Sénanque), **Abbaye de Thoronet** (☎ 04 94 60 43 90; http://thoronet .monuments-nationaux.fr; adult/under 18yr €7/free; ☽ 10am-6.30pm Mon-Sat, 10am-noon & 2-6.30pm Sun Apr-Sep, 10am-1pm & 2-5pm Mon-Sat, 10am-noon & 2-5pm Sun Oct-Mar), 12km southwest of Lorgues, is remarkable for its ultra-austere architecture: pure proportions, perfectly dressed stone and the subtle fall of light and shadow are where its beauty lies. The chapter house, where the monks met to discuss community problems, is more ornate as the only secular room in the complex. Built between 1160 and 1190, the pointed arches show early Gothic influences. Sunday mass is celebrated at noon and concerts are held in summer.

🌱 CORRENS // WINE AND DINE IN FRANCE'S WHOLLY ORGANIC VILLAGE

A few years back no one made it to this tiny backwater village, 25km west of Le Thoronet on the banks of the River Argens. Now a handful of people meander its sun-baked, fountain-pricked streets wedged in all sides by vines – organic since 1997, when the village mayor, himself a wine producer, in an enlight-ened move, decided to make Correns' 200 hectares of AOC Côtes de Provence vineyards organic in order to boost the appeal of its vintage.

It worked. A decade on, Correns wine (30% white, 50% rosé and 20% red) has made a name for itself while several other local farmers have turned organic to produce organic honey, chicken, eggs, olive oil and goats'-milk cheese. Local kids dine on organic meals at the school canteen, and the town hall has in-house expertise in ecofriendly architecture to help villagers 'green' their homes.

Meander the village's peaceful higgledy-piggledy lanes and lunch well – and predominantly organic – at **Auberge du Parc** (☎ 04 94 59 53 52; www.aubergeduparc .fr; 34 place du Général de Gaulle; menu €35; ☽ lunch & dinner Wed-Mon Jul-Aug, closed Sun evening & all day Mon-Tue Apr-Jun & Sep-Oct), a typical *maison de village*, with cream facade and burgundy wooden shutters, a footstep off the main square. Cuisine is innovative and market-driven, the wine list naturally features the local wine and mains are as sizeable as the five elegant guestrooms up top (doubles €100 to €130). For a digestive walk, try the wonderfully cool **Vallon Soun**, where the green waters of the Argens flow peacefully.

Or indulge in a spot of wine tasting in the vineyards ensnaring the village. Correns **tourist office** (☎ 04 94 37 21 31; www .correns.fr; 2 rue Cabassonne; ☽ 9am-noon & 2-5.30pm Mon-Thu, 2-5.30pm Fri, 9am-noon Sat) has a list of estates where you can taste and buy wine. The most prestigious of these, **Château de Miraval** (www.miraval.com), unfortunately shut its tasting doors to passers-by since Brad Pitt, Angelina and kids moved into the dreamy gold-stone property on the vast 400-hectare estate in summer 2008. Miraval was a monastery in the 13th century, and its wine cellars were built in the

19th century by inventor of reinforced concrete, Frenchman Joseph Lambot. Between 1970 and 1992 French jazz pianist Jacques Loussier owned Miraval and built the legendary Miraval recording studio, where Pink Floyd recorded part of *The Wall* in 1979; zillions of artists followed in its heyday, the Cure, Wham, UB40, Sade and the Cranberries included. To peek at the celebrity pad, a scenic 6.5km drive from the village, head north out of Correns on the D45 towards Châteauvert, cross the bridge and turn right onto the D554 towards Le Val; the walled estate looms up large 5km later on the right.

Taste and buy Château de Miraval and other big names such as **Domaine de la Grande Pallière** (www.legrandpalliere.com) at wine cooperative and shop **Vignerons de Correns** (☎ 04 94 59 59 46; chemin de l'Église; ⏰ 3.30-7pm Mon-Fri, 10am-12.30 & 3.30-7pm Sat), which has a second boutique inside the **Hôtel des Vins** (☎ 04 94 86 40 96) on the main roundabout (intersection of D554 and D562) in Le Val, 10km south of Correns. At the lovely **Domaine des Aspras** (☎ 04 94 59 59 70; www.aspras.com; Les Aspras, Correns; ⏰ 10am-noon & 3-7pm Mon-Sat Jun–mid-Sep, 9am-noon & 2-4pm Tue-Sat rest of year) you can taste in situ and, should you fancy it, rent a six-bedroom *bastide* on the estate.

♥ AUPS // SHOP FOR TRUFFLES AT THE VILLAGE MARKET

November to late February, those alien-looking nuggets of black fungus can be viewed at the Thursday morning **truffle market** on the central plane-tree-studded square in Aups. Truffle-hunts and pig-snouting demonstrations lure a crowd on the fourth Sunday in January during Aups' **Journée de la Truffe** (Day of the Truffle). The **tourist office** (☎ 04 94 84 00 69; www.aups-tourisme.com, in French; place Frédéric Mistral; ⏰ 9am-12.30pm & 3.30-7pm Mon-Sat, 9am-12.30pm Sun Jul & Aug, shorter hr rest year), on the central square, has information on other gastronomic festivities and a list of local truffle hunters.

♥ MAISON DES VINS CÔTES DE PROVENCE // TASTE THE PICK OF 700 WINES

This bacchanalian House of Wines, 2.5km south of Les Arcs-sur-Argens on the westbound N7, is a one-stop shop to taste, learn about and buy Côtes de Provence wines. Each week 16 different Côtes de Provence wines are selected for tasting – 'changeover day' is Wednesday – at the **Maison des Vins Côtes de Provence** (☎ 04 94 99 50 20; www.vinsdeprovence.com; ⏰ 10am-6pm Mon-Sat, 10am-5pm Sun). Knowledgeable multilingual staff can advise you on the dream dish to eat with each wine and you can buy 700 different wines from 250 wine estates at producers' prices. The cheapest bottle is €3; the most expensive €30.

A prestigious *cru classé* wine, produced since the 14th century, can be sampled and bought at **Château Ste-Roseline** (☎ 04 94 99 50 30; www.sainte -roseline.com), 4.5km east of Les Arcs-sur-Argens. A 1975 mosaic by Marc Chagall illuminates the estate's 13th-century Romanesque **Chapelle de Ste-Roseline** (⏰ 2.30-6pm Tue-Sun), which contains the corpse of St Roseline. Roseline was born at the château in Les Arcs in 1263 and became a Carthusian nun. She experienced numerous visions during her lifetime and was said to be able to curtail demons. Upon her death in 1329, her eyes were taken out and separately preserved. Piano recitals and musical concerts are held in the chapel in July and August.

GASTRONOMIC HIGHLIGHTS

Not to be missed: the fountain-pierced restaurant terrace of **Hôtel des Deux Rocs** (p295), well worth the drive for the longest of delicious lunches.

❦ DOMAINE DE LA MAURETTE // LA MOTTE €€

☎ 04 94 45 92 82; rte de Callas, La Motte; weekday lunch €14, menus €24 & €32; ☺ lunch & dinner Tue-Sun, lunch Mon

For an authentic Provençal feast, head east out of La Motte, the first village in Provence to be liberated after the August 1944 Allied landings, along the D47 to this rustic wine estate on the intersection of the D47 and the D25. Taste and buy wine, and dine on a vine-covered terrace in its *ferme auberge*, a roadside inn where the atmosphere of chattering people dining on wholesome, homemade food is nothing short of electric.

❦ HOSTELLERIE DE L'ABBAYE DE LA CELLE // LA CELLE €€€

☎ 04 98 05 14 14; www.abbaye-celle.com; 19 place du Général de Gaulle, La Celle; lunch menus €45, dinner menus €62 & €82

Top chefs Bruno Clément and Alain Ducasse are the creative energies behind this refined four-star restaurant-hotel in La Celle, a tiny village with a medieval Benedictine abbey, 40km southwest of Le Thoronet. Its alfresco dining oozes panache – definitely the woo-your-lover variety – and if you (or your loved one) have a penchant for bathtubs with legs, check into the Cedar Tree for the night.

❦ LES CHÊNES VERTS // TOURTOUR €€€

☎ 04 94 70 55 06; rte de Villecroze, Tourtour; mains €45-78, menu €56; ☺ lunch & dinner Thu-Mon Aug-May

It might seem odd that this walled property, 1.5km downhill from Tourtour village on the D51 to Villecroze, shuts up shop in June and July. But there is good reason. The Green Oaks is famed far and wide for its luxurious truffle cuisine, hence the stiff waiters in bow ties and eclectic decor that is hardly wow-factor material. But the cuisine is irreproachable and chef Paul Bajade's seasonal truffle *menu* (€145) is a rare gastronomic treat, experience and privilege.

DRIVING TOUR: HAUT-VAR HILLTOP VILLAGES

Map p294
Distance: 95km
Duration: one or two days

West of Draguignan the rich 'Hills of the High Country', aka the Haut-Var (Upper Var) – easily accessible from the Gorges du Verdon (p177) or after a stroll around the Abbaye de Thoronet (p291) perhaps – embrace lush vineyards, earthy black truffles and a bounty of gastronomic delights. Your own transport is essential for exploring this solitary highland, studded with sleepy unspoilt villages teetering on hilltops, so remote you feel you're the first to visit. Throw in a long lazy lunch (see left for recommendations) and a generous dose of pullover gasp-at-view stops and you might well find yourself spending a couple of days here. Accommodation options are predictably tempting (p399).

On the D562, pick up the northbound D31 towards Entrecasteaux and Salernes. Round the bend and drive past pretty vineyards with typical drystone walls, olive trees and that vivid burnt-orange soil so typical to this harsh winegrowing climate. After 1.5km pass **Domaine de Roucas** (☎ 04 94 04 48 14), a

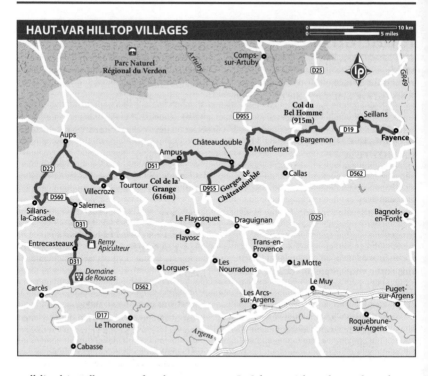

HAUT-VAR HILLTOP VILLAGES

well-lived-in yellow-stone farmhouse, which welcomes wine tasters. Just 4km down the road, hilltop **Entrecasteaux** looms large with its giant 17th-century château with box-hedge garden, old stone houses sun-baked every shade of gold, and fountain-clad square. Grab a coffee at the green-canopied **Bar Central** (☎ 04 94 04 43 53) – you won't get more local than this.

Cross the village and bear right along the D31 towards Salernes and Aups. Stop to buy honey at *miellerie* (honey house) **Remy Apiculteur** (☎ 04 94 04 45 87), 2km north, then drive another wiggly 6km to **Salernes**, where handmade terracotta tiles called *terres cuites* (literally 'baked earth') have been manufactured since the 18th century. The **tourist office** (☎ 04 94 70 69 02; www.ville-salernes.fr; place Gabriel Péri) has a list of workshops to visit.

In Salernes pick up the westbound D2560 and subsequent D560 to **Sillans-la-Cascade**, a golden gem of a fortified village, turrets firmly in place, 5km west on the banks of the River Bresque. The 5km drive is not that riveting but round the bend and the vision of this little-visited toylike village easily compensates. Then it's 9km north along the D22 to **Aups** (p292) and another 10km southeast past olive groves and lavender gardens to the typical 'eagle nest' gold-stone village of **Tourtour**. Buy olive oil in the village and, post–olive harvest in mid-December, watch olives being pressed in its 17th-century **moulin à huile**; the **tourist office** (☎ 04 94 70 59 47; www.tourisme-tourtour.com; montée de St-Dénis) runs guided tours of the mill. On the cuter-than-cute main street, overwhelmingly friendly **L'Alechou** (☎ 04 94 70 54 76; 16 Rue Grande; ◷ 11.30am-10pm daily) is a perfect spot for lunch between flower pots any time of day.

Speed 6km further east along the D51 to **Ampus** and continue east 9km to **Châteaudouble**, an astonishing village perilously clinging to a cliff edge. Hook 2km down to the D955 and if you still have stamina left for a few more bends, detour south a tad to soak up the full splendour of the **Gorges de Château-double** and the village dramatically threatening to tumble down on you.

Backtrack north and turn right onto the D19. Just 7km east of here is **Bargemon**, a village with plenty of medieval streets and ramparts to stroll; it hit the headlines when the Beckhams bought a pad here in 2004. Market day is Thursday and the **tourist office** (☎ 04 94 47 81 73; www.ot-bargemon.fr; av Pasteur; ☽ 8.30am-12.30pm & 2-5pm Mon-Fri) has information on the entire area. It also rents bikes for those who fancy a day cycling.

Seillans, a scenic 12km drive east, is an irresistibly pretty, typical Provençal village with cobbled lanes coiling to its crown and a village inn only the stone-hearted will be able to resist. A boutique hotel with fig-flower Fragonard soap in the bathrooms, a fine collection of old B&W family photos and miniature birds tweeting in a cage in the drawing room, **Hôtel des Deux Rocs** (☎ 04 94 76 87 32; www.hoteldeuxrocs.com; 1 place Fon't d'Amont, Seillans; ☽ mid-Feb-Dec) wins the prize hands-down for most atmospheric village inn. Scipion, knight of the Flotte d'Agout, lived here in the 17th century. Today, the soulful *bastide* is home to Julie and Nicolas Malzac, who run this 13-room hotel (doubles €73 to €135) and gourmet restaurant with extraordinary panache. Divine summer dining, never to be forgotten, is alfresco around a fountain beneath trees.

True hilltop-village fiends can continue 5km east to medieval **Fayence**, yet another picturesque spot with an overdose of English-speaking estate agents, a weathered **bell tower** with fabulous panoramic views, and plenty of eating options.

MASSIF DES MAURES

· · · · · ·

Wild boar roam the forests of the Massif des Maures (from the Provençal word _maouro,_ meaning 'dark pine wood'), whose towns, villages and walking trails are little oases of peace. Traditional industries – chestnut harvests, cork, pipe-making – are their lifeblood, a pleasant surprise in the tourist-economied south of France.

The D14 runs through Collobrières, the largest town in the massif and chestnut capital of the universe. This road is particularly popular with cyclists and is graced with fine panoramas. Similarly dramatic is the D39 from Collobrières, which winds and soars up to Notre Dame des Anges (780m) before plunging down to Gonfaron. The parallel N98, which skims through vineyards and cork oak plantations, runs from St-Tropez to Bormes-les-Mimosas and on to Hyères.

Along the Corniche des Maures, the southern extent of the massif, chestnut trees give way to sand at Le Lavandou and smaller beach resorts to the east.

EXPLORING THE MASSIF

🌳 **COLLOBRIÈRES CHESTNUTS // GO NUTS OVER THE FOREST'S SWEETEST TREAT**
Hidden in the forest, the leafy village of Collobrières is the place to taste chestnuts.

A small **Musée de la Fabrique** (admission free; 9.30am-1pm & 2-7pm or 8pm) opposite **Confiserie Azuréenne** (☎ 04 94 48 07 20; www.confiserieazureenne.com) explains the art of making *marrons glacés* (candied chestnuts), after which you can stock up on *glaces aux marrons glacés* (chestnut ice creams), *crème de marrons* (chestnut cream), *marrons au sirop* (chestnuts in syrup), *liqueur de châtaignes* (chestnut liqueur) and so on in its shop.

Across the 11th-century bridge, the **tourist office** (☎ 04 94 48 08 00; www.collo brieres-tourisme.com; bd Charles Caminat; 10am-12.30pm & 3-6.30pm Mon-Sat Jul & Aug, 10am-noon & 3-6pm Tue-Sat Sep-Jun) can help you join in the October chestnut harvest or join a guided walk through cork oak forest. Three short walking trails, including a 200m trail to a *châtaigneraie* (chestnut grove), are mapped on the noticeboard outside.

Treat taste buds to farm-made chestnut ice cream and grand massif views at **Ferme de Peïgros** (☎ 04 94 48 03 83; fermedepeigros@wanadoo.fr; Col de Babaou; menu €22, no credit cards; lunch & dinner Jul & Aug), a goat farm 1.8km along a gravel track from the top of the Col de Babaou (8km from Collobrières). In Collobrières village **La Petite Fontaine** (☎ 04 94 48 00 12; place de la République; menus €26 & €30; lunch & dinner Tue-Sat, lunch Sun Apr-Sep, lunch Mon-Sat, dinner Fri & Sat Oct-Mar) is a highly regarded address for miles around. Sit at a tree-shaded table outside, feast on seasonal forest mushrooms and chestnuts, and pride yourself on snagging a table at one of southern France's most charming village inns (the type where the happy patron throws in a complimentary digestive for those who conquer a *menu)*. Walls inside are exposed stone, the menu outside is stuck on the trunk of a plane tree and the fruit tarts for dessert…out of this world.

The smell of warm, sweet, roasted chestnuts wafts through the streets of Collobrières the last three Sundays in October during its **Fête de la Châtaigne** (Chestnut Festival).

❦ CHARTREUSE DE LA VERNE // LEARN HOW NUNS LIVE IN THE FOREST

Majestic, 12th- to 13th-century **Monastère de la Verne** (☎ 04 94 43 45 51; http://la.verne.free.fr, in French; adult/8-14yr €5/3; 11am-5pm Wed-Mon Feb-May & Sep-Dec, 11am-6pm Jun-Aug) is in a dramatic forest setting, 12km southeast of Collobrières. The Carthusian monastery was founded in 1170, possibly on the site of a temple to the goddess Laverna, protector of the bandits who hung out in the Maures. The Huguenots destroyed most of the original charterhouse in 1577. Since 1982 the solitary complex has been home to 15 nuns, of the Sisters of Bethlehem.

One of the old monks' cells has been fully restored, complete with a small formal garden, workshop and covered corridor, where the monk would pray as he paced. Other interesting features include the use of serpentine (a stripy green stone) as decoration. Walking trails lead from the monastery into its forested surroundings.

From Collobrières, follow rte de Grimaud (D14) east for 6km, then turn right (south) onto the D214 and drive another 6km to the monastery; the final section of the single-track road is unpaved.

❦ VILLAGE DES TORTUES // ADOPT A THREATENED SPECIES

About 20km north of Collobrières on the northern tip of the massif is this **tortoise village** (☎ 04 94 78 26 41; www.villagetortues.com, in French; adult/5-16yr €10/6; 9am-7pm Mar-Nov, to 6pm Dec-Feb), where one of France's rarest and most endangered species can be seen. The Hermann tortoise *(Testudo hermanni)*, once common along the Mediterranean coastal strip, is today found only in the Massif des Maures and Corsica.

The **Station d'Observation et de Protection des Tortues des Maures** (SOP-TOM; Maures Tortoise Observation and Protection Station) was set up in 1985 by French film-maker Bernaud Devaux, and an English biologist, to ensure survival of the Hermann. A well-documented **trail** (captions in English) leads visitors around the centre: from the tortoise clinic, where wounded tortoises are treated and then released into the Maures; to the quarantine quarter and reproduction enclosures; and to the tropical conservatory, egg hatcheries and nurseries, where the young tortoises (a delicacy for preying magpies, rats, foxes and wild boars) spend the first three of their 60 to 100 years. There's also a great **palaeontology trail**, where vicious-looking models of the tortoise's ancestors lurk among the bushes.

In summer the best time to see the tortoises is in the morning and late afternoon (they tend to shelter from the heat during the day). Watch tortoises hatch from mid-May to the end of June; from November through to early March they hibernate.

🌿 CONSERVATOIRE DU PATRIMOINE DU FREINET // TREK IN THE FOREST AND WATCH CORK HARVESTING
A stark, rocky spur props up the 13th-century **ruins of Fort Freinet** (450m), from where there is a fantastic red-roof panorama of the small medieval town of La Garde Freinet. Local traditions and customs unfold in the village at the **Conservatoire du Patrimoine du Freinet** (☎ 04 94 43 08 57; www.conservatoiredufreinet.org; Chapelle St-Jean, place de la Mairie; adult/under 12yr €1.50/free; 🕒 10am-12.30pm & 2.30-5.30pm Tue-Sat), an environment-driven set-up that hosts exhibitions on flora, fauna, cork harvesting and so on, and organises fascinating discovery walks (in chestnut groves and cork oak forest, a day with a shepherd, sifting rivers for gold) and workshops

A MENHIR DETOUR

With your walking boots firmly laced, set off from the old bridge in Collobrières, walking uphill into town along rue Camille Desmoulins, rue Blanqui and rue Galilée. Follow the signs for the campground and ruined 15th-century Église St Pons, which will lead you onto the GR90.

It's a steep climb out of town and into the woods, composed of oak trees (including cork oak), pine, heathers and ferns, then the path ascends more gradually to about 450m above sea level, before levelling off as it reaches Plateau Lambert.

The trail comes out onto a forest road; follow it to the left for 150m and it will lead you to the *garde forestière* (forest ranger) Ferme Lambert. Ask permission from the forest ranger before crossing the field to see the two biggest **menhirs** in the Var region, now heritage-listed monuments. Each one is over 3m high, and they were raised some time between 3000 BC and 2000 BC. Another super sight is the **Châtaignier de Madame**, the biggest chestnut tree in Provence, with a mighty 10.4m circumference.

The walking detour should take you around four hours there and back.

(art in nature, dry-stone walls, basketry, honey-making, forest photography). Not to be missed are its monthly **treks on horseback** (adult/10-16yr €45/22) and **donkey rambles** (adult/6-12yr €12/9) through the massif, and its weekly walks in the forest to see cork being harvested (p342). Themed walks typically cost €8 per adult, €4 for children aged 8 to 12; workshops vary (free to €22).

🌱 AUBERGE DE LA MÔLE // LUNCH WITH LOCALS ON LEGENDARY TERRINES

Tradition rules fierce and strong at this no-frills village inn, which doubles as the local *bar-tabac* (café-tobacconist). Once the village petrol station (the old pump outside is stuck on 333), the place found international fame in 1990 as a recommended address in Peter Mayle's *A Year in Provence*. The fans might have come and gone, but for locals **Auberge de la Môle** (☎ 04 94 49 57 01; place de l'Église, La Môle; lunch/dinner menu €23/55; 🕐 lunch & dinner Tue-Sat, lunch Sun) remains *the* place for hearty appetites to feast on legendary terrines, pâtés and feisty jars of pickles. No credit cards and no à la carte, just the full-monty *menu*. Find the inn next to the church in the tiny hamlet of La Môle.

🌱 CORNICHE DES MAURES // COAST-CURVE TO STUNNING MEDITERRANEAN GARDENS

From La Môle, the breathtakingly narrow **Col du Canadel** (D27) dives dramatically to the coast – 12km of scenic but nail-biting driving – dishing up unbeatable views of the Massif des Maures, coastline and its offshore islands en route. The coastal road, the **Corniche des Maures** (D559), stretches southwest from La Croix-Valmer to Le Lavandou

along a shoreline trimmed with sandy beaches ideal for swimming, sunbathing and windsurfing. Tiny **Plage du Rayol** and **Plage de l'Escale** are particularly enchanting: they're backed by pine trees and have a restaurant on the sand.

From Le Rayol, a narrow road dips south to the stunning **Domaine du Rayol** (☎ 04 98 04 44 00; www.domainedurayol.org; av des Belges; adult/8-16yr €8/6; 🕐 9.30am-7.30pm Jul & Aug, 9.30am-6.30pm Apr-Jun, Sep & Oct, 9.30am-5.30pm Nov-Mar), a lush Mediterranean garden rescued from abandonment in 1989. Flowers are at their best in April and May, but it's always worth a visit. In addition to freely exploring, there are delightful three-hour themed **nature walks** (adult/under 10yr €9/5; advance reservation) and, for the truly garden-mad, in-depth **workshops and lectures** (€60/day; advance reservation).

In summer the pink-towered **Café des Jardiniers** serves light organic lunches (mains €11) and refreshing hibiscus-peach and ginger-apple infusions beneath trees, and off the estate's gem of a beach you can observe underwater flora and fauna with an experienced guide along the **Sentier Marin** (Marine Trail; adult/8-18yr incl admission & equipment €17/14; 🕐 mid-Jun–mid-Sep), or further afield along the **Corniche des Maures** (€40/34; 🕐 Sun morning Jul & Aug). Advance bookings are essential for snorkelling, as they are for the atmospheric open-air musical concerts (€28) the estate hosts in summer.

🌱 BORMES-LES-MIMOSAS // SHOP FOR OLIVES IN A FLOWER-FILLED MEDIEVAL VILLAGE

This green-fingered, 12th-century village (pop 6399, elevation 180m) is spectacularly flowered with mimosas in winter, deep-fuchsia bougainvilleas in summer, and its **tourist office** (☎ 04 94 01 38 38; www .bormeslesmimosas.com; 1 place Gambetta; ☺ 9am-12.30pm & 3-6.30pm daily Apr-Sep, Mon-Sat only Oct-Mar) takes bookings for botanical walks (€9) and hikes (€7) with a forest warden in the nearby **Forêt du Dom**.

Main street rue Carnot is a pedestrian delight for browsing boutiques brimming with traditional Provençal products, natural soap and essential oils, printed tablecloths, espadrilles, sun dials and so on. At the olive-themed cellar shop **Maison d'Olive** (☎ 04 94 46 60 45; www .maison-de-lolive.fr; 5 rue Carnot) buy flavoured olive oils (truffle, lemon, basil, tomato), vinegars and various alcoholic aperitifs (pastis and mimosa, fig or melon liqueur) *en VRAC* – meaning take your own bottle to fill or grab one at the shop. Vinegars cost €13 per half-litre, oils €16.50 to €19.50. Lunch afterwards in natural splendour at the **Relais du Vieux Sauvaire** (below).

❤ CHEZ JO // LEGENDARY BOUILLABAISSE ON A SIZZLING BEACH

Buzzing with bare-footed, overly bronzed, sarong-clad beach lovers with a fondness for bathing in the nude and piercings in the most unexpected of places, this sizzling beach restaurant is hot stuff. Flamboyant, gregarious and not a sign in sight to tell you it's here, **Chez Jo** (☎ 04 94 05 85 06; Plage du Layet, Cavalière; ☺ lunch May-Sep) is one of those rare 'in the know' addresses, around for a good 30 years already. Dining is around four or five tables on the sand or on a wooden deck above the water. Don't bother dressing up; regulars don't. Cuisine is straight from the sea and comes out from the shack of a kitchen, snug against the rocks, on oversized cork platters: the grilled *langouste* (crayfish) with spaghetti and *bouillabaisse* (€55) are legendary; order both 24 hours in advance.

∼ WORTH A TRIP ∼

For breathtaking views of the islands, follow **Route des Crêtes** as it winds its way through *maquis*-covered hills some 400m above the sea. From Bormes-les-Mimosas, follow the D41 uphill (direction Collobrières) past the Chapelle St-François and, 1.5km north of the village centre, turn immediately right after the sign for Col de Caguo-Ven (237m). Actually a paved forest track, the Route des Crêtes is signposted A32-Protection Incendie-Piste des Crêtes.

Thirteen kilometres and dozens of bends and photo stops later, you arrive at the sensational **Relais du Vieux Sauvaire** (☎ 04 94 05 84 22; Route des Crêtes; mains €20; ☺ lunch & dinner May-Sep), with 180-degree views you could only dream of. Owner Roland Gallo has been here since 1960 and has no intention of moving. The food is as sunny as the views: pizzas cooked in a wood-stoked oven, melon and parma ham, whole seabass in salt crust; and there's a pool to cool off in.

After the restaurant, Route des Crêtes corkscrews down to Le Rayol, hooking up on the way with the final leg of the panoramic **Col du Canadel** (opposite) 6km east of Relais du Vieux Sauvaire. On the *col* (mountain pass), turn left to plunge into the heart of the forested Massif des Maures, via La Môle, or turn right to continue the dramatic drive and gorge on breathtaking views to the sea and coastal Corniche des Maures (D559).

❦ **LE LAVANDOU // SET SAIL FOR 'ISLANDS OF GOLD' OR ST-TROPEZ**
Once a fishing village, Le Lavandou is a family beach-resort with a small but intact old town and 12km stretch of golden sand. The turreted pink-brick faux castle on the seafront is the **tourist office** (☎04 94 00 40 50; www.lelavandou.com; quai Gabriel Péri; 9am-noon & 2.30-6.30pm Mon-Sat).

Opposite, boats sail from the **Gare Maritime** (quai des Îles d'Or) to the Îles des Hyères (below); tickets are sold 30 minutes before departure. **Vedettes Îles d'Or et Le Corsaire** (☎04 94 71 01 02; www.vedettes ilesdor.fr; 15 quai Gabriel Péri) runs seasonal boats to and from Île du Levant (adult/4 to 12 years €24.50/20.30, 35 minutes), Île de Porquerolles (€31.70/24.70, 50 minutes) and Île de Port-Cros (€24.50/20.30, 35 minutes). For La Croisiè Bleue tour (combined ticket for all three islands €46.60/38) and twice-weekly boats to St-Tropez (€46.60/38, two hours), advance reservations are required.

ÎLES D'HYÈRES & ÎLES DU FUN

· · · · · ·

Legend says gods turned a bunch of swimming princesses into the Îles d'Hyères – and they are magical. Their mica-rich rock, which glitters and gleams in the sunlight, gives them their other name, the Îles d'Or (Islands of Gold).

Porquerolles, at 7km long and 3km wide, is the largest island; Île de Port-Cros in the middle is a national park; and its eastern sister, Île du Levant, is a nudist colony. Wild camping and cars are forbidden throughout the archipelago.

Dubbed the Îles du Fun, Bendor and Embiez, west of the Îles d'Hyères off

Toulon's shores, are more sub-Disney than the stuff of myth.

Islanders refer to the rest of France as the 'continent'.

ÎLE DE PORQUEROLLES

pop 250
Despite the huge influx of day trippers (up to 6000 a day in July and August), beautiful Porquerolles is wholly unspoilt: 10 sq km of its sandy white beaches, pine woods, *maquis*, fig trees and eucalyptus are protected by the Parc National de Port-Cros. Everywhere a wide variety of indigenous and tropical flora thrive, including the requien larkspur, which grows nowhere else in the world. In winter blossoming mimosas splash the green island with colour. April and May are the best months to spot some of its 114 bird species.

Pottering along the island's rough unpaved trails on foot or by bicycle, breaking with a picnic lunch on the beach and a dip in crystal-clear turquoise water, is heavenly. Avoid July and August, when the risk of forest fire makes the interior of the island and some trails inaccessible; it is also the time when the owners of Porquerolles' numerous *résidences secondaires* (second homes) return to the island, increasing the population sixfold.

Smoking is forbidden outside the village.

ESSENTIAL INFORMATION

TOURIST INFORMATION // Tourist Office
(☎04 94 58 33 76; www.porquerolles.com; 9am-5.20pm Mon-Sat, 9am-1pm Sun Apr-Nov, 9am-1pm Fri-Wed Dec-Mar) Look for the glass box at the port. Sells island maps (€2) marked with *pistes cyclables* (cycling paths) and *sentiers pédestres* (footpaths); and the plastic *Guide Sous-Marin des Espèces Méditerranéenes* for

ÎLE DE PORQUEROLLES

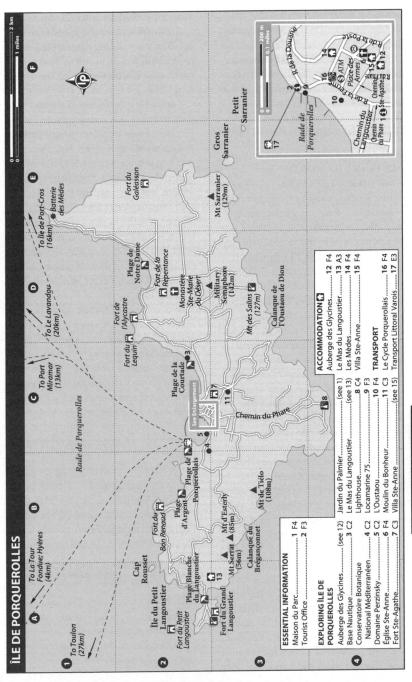

ESSENTIAL INFORMATION

Maison du Parc............................ **1**	F4
Tourist Office............................... **2**	F3

EXPLORING ÎLE DE PORQUEROLLES

Auberge des Glycines..........(see 12)	
Base Nautique............................ **3**	C2
Conservatoire Botanique National Méditerranéen.......... **4**	C2
Domaine Perzinsky...................... **5**	C2
Église Ste-Anne.......................... **6**	F4
Fort Ste-Agathe......................... **7**	C3
Jardin du Palmier.................(see 1)	
Le Mas du Langoustier.......(see 13)	
Lighthouse................................. **8**	C4
Locamarine 75........................... **9**	F3
L'Oustaou................................ **10**	F4
Moulin du Bonheur................. **11**	C3
Villa Ste-Anne......................(see 15)	

ACCOMMODATION

Auberge des Glycines.............. **12**	F4
Le Mas du Langoustier............ **13**	A3
Les Mèdes............................... **14**	F4
Villa Ste-Anne........................ **15**	F4

TRANSPORT

Le Cycle Porquerollais............ **16**	F4
Transport Littoral Varois........ **17**	E3

ST-TROPEZ TO TOULON

snorkellers to identify underwater flora (€20). **Maison du Parc** (☎ 04 94 58 07 24; www.portcros parcnational.fr, in French; rue de la Ferme; ⏰ 9.30am-12.30pm & 2-6pm Feb–late Oct) Porquerolles maps, itineraries and information from the national park office; excellent twice-monthly thematic guided walks known as Les Rencontres du Parc (free; p278).

EXPLORING PORQUEROLLES

💚 PLACE D'ARMES & AROUND // REVEL IN THE HUB OF PORQUEROLLAIS LIFE

A tree-shaded *pétanque* pitch dominates central **place d'Armes**. Music concerts fill **Église Ste-Anne** on its southern side in summer, and festivities frolic through church and square on 25 July when islanders celebrate their patron saint's day. Day in, day out, this hub of Porquerollais life buzzes with outdoor cafés and fruit stalls, ice cream stands and a zillion and one cyclists pedalling to and fro. Come dusk, once the last of the day-tripper boats has sailed home, a Zen lull falls across the square. Indulge in an aperitif of pastis and *petit friture* (tiny deep-fried fish dipped in spicy *rouille*) at **Villa Ste-Anne** (see also p400), oven-baked mussels à la Provençale at **Auberge des Glycines** (see also p400), or a basket of vegetables dipped in *anchoïade* (anchovy paste with garlic and olive oil) at the funkier **L'Oustaou** (☎ 04 94 58 30 09; www .oustaou.com, in French; place d'Armes) – all recommended dining addresses on the square – and enjoy the peace.

From place d'Armes, walk 10 minutes south uphill along chemin Ste-Agathe (between Villa Ste-Anne and Auberge des Glycines) and at the top of the track turn right to 16th-century **Fort Ste-Agathe** (☎ 04 94 00 65 41; adult/5-17yr €4/2; ⏰ 10am-noon & 2-6pm mid-May–Sep), the only fortification open to visitors. It contains historical and natural-history

exhibits, and admission includes access to the tower with lovely island views. Much of the building dates from between 1812 and 1814, when Napoleon had it rebuilt after the British destroyed it in 1793.

Turning left at the top of chemin Ste-Agathe brings you to the postcard-perfect **Moulin du Bonheur** (adult/5-17yr €4/2; ⏰ 10am-noon & 2-6pm mid-May–Sep), a windmill where flour was made in the mid 1700s. Restored by a passionate group of islanders, it is a typical Provence-mill construction: 12m tall and 12m in diameter, with 1m-thick stone walls, on top of which the hefty mechanism and a witch-hat wooden roof rests. From 2010 the islanders plan to start making flour again. One ticket covers admission to mill and fort.

Back on place d'Armes, rue de la Ferme leads to the **Maison du Parc** (left) and **Jardin du Palmier** (☎ 04 94 58 07 24; chemin du Phare; admission free; ⏰ 9.30am-12.30pm & 2-6pm Feb–late Oct), a wonderful ornamental garden planted with magnificent palm varieties, cypress, vanilla and grenadier trees, cactus and bamboo, every herb known to grow under the Provençal sun, sweetly scented jasmine, glycerine and so on.

Keen botanists can continue the green trail at the **Conservatoire Botanique National Méditerranéen** (☎ 04 94 58 07 24), 700m west; continue along rue de la Ferme, turn right at the crossroads and the conservatoire is the large rundown

TRUE LOVE

Three toasters and a towel set just weren't enough. In 1911, newly married Mrs Fournier received the perfect wedding present from hubby François: the island of Porquerolles!

building on the right. The national research centre can't be visited, but its Mediterranean garden and collector orchards embracing dozens of ancient varieties of palm, olive, almond, fig, peach, lemon and orange trees, laurier rose and more can be freely strolled.

❦ CYCLING & WINE TASTING // FEAST ON THE ISLAND'S RICHES SANS CROWDS

An admirable **picnic** of juicy cherries, peaches, cold meats, fresh goat's-milk cheese and so on can easily be built from the fruit stands on place d'Armes, and the small grocery store here or at the port; note that just after noon they all close for a good two-hour lunch break. Then pedal away into the island's thickets. About 3km along rue de la Ferme and chemin du Phare, past fig tree orchards and olive groves, is the island's 82m-tall **lighthouse** on the tip of the cape. Northeast of here, a **military semaphore** (142m) marks the highest point of the island. Neither can be visited.

Porquerolles' vineyards cover a square kilometre of the western part of the island, and are tended by three wine producers. Each offers *dégustation* (tasting) sessions of their predominantly rosé wines. Framed by a fabulous formation of parasol pines, **Domaine Perzinsky** (☎ 04 94 58 34 32; ☉ 10am-12.30pm & 3.30-7.30pm) is an easy stop en route to Plage d'Argent (see right) and unusually requires no advance reservation. Luxurious **Le Mas du Langoustier** (p400) is the ultimate wining and dining experience on the island.

The map sold at the tourist office has four cycling itineraries, 6.5km to 13.8km long. More detail is included in the *Guide de Randonnées dans l'Île de Porquerolles* (€6), available at the Maison du Parc (opposite).

❦ BEACHES & BOATS // PADDLE AND SWIM IN CLEAR TURQUOISE WATERS

Porquerolles' northern coast is laced with beautiful sandy beaches, including **Plage de la Courtade**, a mere 800m walk east from the port (follow the track uphill behind the tourist office). Porquerolles' largest and most beautiful beach, **Plage de Notre Dame**, is 2.5km further east along the same track.

West of the village, **Plage d'Argent**, a good 2km walk or bike ride along a pot-holed track past vineyards, is popular with families because of its summer beachside café-restaurant, lifeguards and toilets; follow rue de la Ferme, past the Maison du Parc, and at the crossroads turn right following signs for Le Hameau and Plage d'Argent.

More secluded is **Plage Blanche du Langoustier**, a former lobster farm 4.5km from the village on the northern shores of the Presqu'île du Langoustier. It's called 'white' beach in contrast to the black sand that darkens the peninsula's southern shores around Port Fay – the legacy of a 19th-century soda-processing plant, which produced potash and soda from sulphuric acid and sea salt between 1828 and 1876.

Cliffs line the island's more dangerous southern coast, where swimming and diving is restricted to **Calanque du Brégançonnet** to the east and **Calanque de l'Oustau de Diou** to the west. Both are accessible by bicycle or foot.

Paddling around in a sea kayak is a wondrous way to see the staggering coastline and its sandy bays. Speedboat-rental outlet **Locamarine 75** (☎ 04 94 58 35 84; www.locamarine75.com, in French), at the port, also takes bookings for kayaks (half-day €35, full day €45 for two adults and child), which set out from **Plage de**

ST-TROPEZ TO TOULON

ALL AFLOAT

Nothing could possibly be more romantic that waking at sunrise afloat – with full-frontal view of a paradise island to boot. That is what you get sleeping aboard *Ysé*, a luxurious two-cabin yacht, with hot and cold water, fridge, heating and other nautical creature-comforts, that can be rented with or without a skipper for two nights or more; contact **Bateaudhote.fr** (☎ 06 82 15 93 76; www.bateaudhote.fr, in French) for details.

Less swish but equally palatable is a night with **Via Skipper** (☎ 06 03 17 23 67; www .viaskipper.com, in French), either moored at the port in Porquerolles (double including breakfast €150) or out at sea (€300), meaning breakfast with a perfect island view.

Porquerollais, a tiny shingle beach immediately behind the yacht club at the port. Alternatively, pick one up from the **Base Nautique** (☎ 06 60 52 37 06; www.ileo -porquerolles.fr; 1/3/6 hr €17/35/45) on Plage de la Courtade.

TRANSPORT

BIKE // There is a plethora of bike rental outlets at the port, and on and around place d'Armes, all open February to mid-November. **Le Cycle Porquerollais** (☎ 04 94 58 30 32; www.cycle-porquerollais.com; 1 rue de la Ferme) opens year-round. Pay €10/13 per half-/full day for an adult bike, €8/10 for a kid's bike, €22/30 for a tandem and €10/13 for a buggy to pedal two tots around.

BOAT // Year-round boats run by **Transport Littoral Varois** (TLV; ☎ 04 94 58 33 76; www.tlv-tvm .com) link La Tour Fondue near Hyères with Porquerolles (adult/bike/4-10yr return €16.50/12/14.30). June to September, weekly boats sail to/from Toulon (p312), St-Tropez (p287), Le Lavandou (p300) and Port Miramar near La Londe.

ÎLE DE PORT-CROS

France's smallest national park, Parc National de Port-Cros was created in 1963 to protect the 7-sq-km island of Port-Cros and a 13-sq-km zone of water around it. Until the end of the 19th century, the islanders' vineyards and olive groves ensured their self-sufficiency. Today, tourism is their sustenance. Palm trees and tobacco plants imported from Argentina line the pretty port.

The island can be visited all year, but walkers must stick to the 30km of marked trails. Fishing, fires, camping, dogs, motorised vehicles and bicycles are not allowed, and smoking is forbidden outside the portside village. Bring picnic supplies and drinking water with you; there are a few bistros at the port open mid-March to mid-November but nothing elsewhere. Out of season the island is dead – and beautiful.

The national park also protects Île de Bagaud, the fourth of the Îles d'Hyères, whose 40 hectares of dense vegetation are used for scientific research and are off limits to tourists.

EXPLORING PORT-CROS

❦ **PORT TO FORT // LOOP THE ISLAND ALONG A BOTANICAL WALKING TRAIL**
At the port, the **Maison du Parc** (☎ 04 94 01 40 70; www.portcrosparcnational.fr) has walking, diving and snorkelling information. It also sells an island map marked with the island's four main trails and also various guides (in French) to underwater fauna and flora. Its opening hours coincide with boat arrivals.

From the portside post office, a track leads inland, from where 30km of footpaths crisscross the island. The 15th-century **Fort du Moulin** is the starting point for the **Sentier des Plantes** (Botanical Trail; 4km; 1½ to two hours), a lovely aromatic trail that wends its way past wild lavender and rosemary, sage and the thyme-like *herbe aux chats* (so called because of its strong cat odour) to **Plage de la Palud** (30 minutes), a beautiful beach on the island's northern shore. A 35-minute **Sentier Sous-Marin** (Underwater Trail; admission free; ✪ mid-Jun–mid-Sep) here allows snorkellers to peer up close at marine life, including 500 algae species and 180 types of fish. Rent mask, snorkel and flippers from portside diving school **Sun Plongée** (☎ 04 94 05 90 16; www.sun-plongee.com, in French). The Sentier des Plantes also takes in imposing 16th-century **Fort de l'Estissac** (admission free; ✪ 10.30am-12.30pm & 1.30-5.30pm May, Jun & Sep,

10.30am-6pm Jul & Aug), host to summer exhibitions. Climb the tower for an island outlook.

From Plage de la Palud, more ambitious walkers can pick up the **Circuit de Port-Man** (four hours), a longer circular trail that follows the coastline to secluded **Plage de Port-Man** on the island's far northeastern tip before looping back inland.

☙ CREST TO CREST // DON HIKING BOOTS FOR A NATURE WATCH

The demanding **Sentier des Crêtes** (Crests Trail; 7.5km; three hours) explores the southwest corner of the island and climaxes atop Mont Vinaigre (194m), from where there is a stunning coastal panorama and the rare chance of seeing a peregrine falcon swooping overhead. Pack binoculars and plenty of

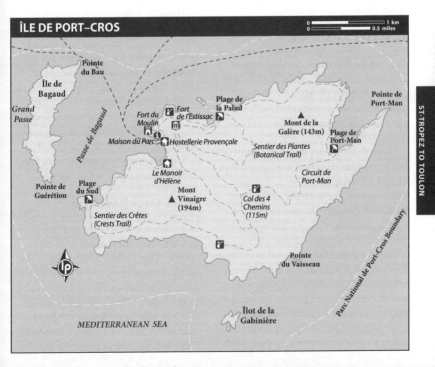

ÎLE DE PORT–CROS

Pointe du Bau

Île de Bagaud

Grand Passe

Passe de Bagaud

Fort du Moulin

Fort de l'Estissac

Plage de la Palud

Pointe de Port-Man

Maison du Parc   Hostellerie Provençale

Mont de la Galère (143m)

Plage de Port-Man

Sentier des Plantes (Botanical Trail)

Le Manoir d'Hélène

Circuit de Port-Man

Mont Vinaigre (194m)

Col des 4 Chemins (115m)

Pointe de Guérétion

Plage du Sud

Sentier des Crêtes (Crests Trail)

Pointe du Vaisseau

Parc National de Port-Cros Boundary

MEDITERRANEAN SEA

Îlot de la Gabinière

0   1 km
0   0.5 miles

water for this lovely walk: nature-watching opportunities are rife, especially in spring when there is a good chance of spotting Cory's shearwaters nesting in the cliffs. During the reproduction season, the Îles des Hyères shelter 90% of France's Yelkouan shearwaters and 25% of Cory's shearwaters. The final leg of the walk, dipping down to **Plage du Sud**, is accompanied by the frenetic buzz of cicadas.

Pick up a map at the Maison du Parc (p304), and the trail head from the western end of the port past Le Manoir d'Hélène (for accommodation details, see p401).

TRANSPORT

BOAT // Le Lavandou (p300) and Hyères (p310) are the main stepping stones to Port-Cros. Seasonal boats sail to/from Toulon (p312), St-Tropez (p284), Port Miramar, La Croix-Valmer and Cavalaire-sur-Mer.

ÎLE DU LEVANT

Oddball Île du Levant, an 8km strip of an island, has a split personality. Ninety percent of it is a closed military camp and the remaining pocket of **Héliopolis** (on the island's southwestern tip) is a nudist colony.

Boats dock at **Port de l'Ayguade** near the **tourist information hut** (☎ 04 94 05 93 52; www.iledulevant.com.fr, in French; ☼ hours vary Easter–mid-Sep). The post office, cafés and hotels are clustered around the central square, place du Village, 1km uphill along rte de l'Ayguade. From place du Village a nature trail leads east into the **Domaine des Arbousiers**, a nature reservation in the eastern part of the colony sheltering rare island plants. The tourist office has information on guided tours.

Baring all is not obligatory except on sandy **Plage Les Grottes**, the main nudist beach east of Port de l'Ayguade. From the port, walk in the direction of Plage de Sable Levant along **Sentier Georges Rousseau**, a rocky coastal path. Signs reading Nudisme Intégral Obligatoire mark the moment you have to strip.

Île du Levant is 10 minutes by boat from Port-Cros. Frequent boats sail year-round from Le Lavandou (p300) and Hyères (p310), and in July and August from Port Miramar (La Londe), La Croix-Valmer and Cavalaire-sur-Mer.

ÎLE DE BENDOR

A place of exile during the 17th century, desolate pinprick Bendor was subsequently abandoned for 250 years. Then in 1951 along came Paul Ricard, a pastis millionaire, who transformed the islet into one of the most sanitised spots on the south coast.

The islet, 300m offshore from Bandol, 19km east of Toulon, is now filled with buildings that look like a Disney movie-set gone bad; the port itself, with its shrunken toy-town buildings and meticulously planned alleys and squares, is quite surreal. Seasonal **exhibitions** (check www.bendor.com) are held on the island and its shallow-sloping **beach**, with lifeguards, is great for tiny kids.

Sail to Bendor year-round from Bandol (€8 return); contact ☎ 04 94 10 75 93.

ÎLES DES EMBIEZ

Not content with owning just one island, in 1958 Paul Ricard also bought the largest of the Embiez archipelago, 1km off the Presqu'île du Cap Sicié between Sanary-sur-Mer and Toulon. It is home to the **Institut Océanographique Paul Ricard** (☎ 04 94 34 02 49; www.institut-paul-ricard .org; adult/4-11yr €4.50/2; ☼ 10am-12.30pm & 1.30-5.30pm Jul & Aug, closed Sat morning Sep-Jun & Wed

& Sun morning Nov-Mar), with a very small aquarium where Mediterranean species swim around in tanks. The rest of the 95-hectare island is occupied by a vast pleasure port, pine forest, *maquis*, vineyards, apartment blocks and a couple of posh hotels.

Boats (www.les-embiez.com; adult/2-12yr return €10/6; ☻ hourly Jul-Sep, less frequent Oct-Jun) sail year-round from the small port at Le Brusc (10 minutes), a beach resort 5km south of Sanary-sur-Mer. June to September four daily **boats** (adult/2-12yr return €10/6) sail to and from Bandol.

TOULON & AROUND
· · · · · ·

LA LONDE

Relatively unspoilt coastline turns increasingly urban as you head west to Toulon and Marseille. A final pocket of blue and green surrounds La Londe (population 8840), midway between Le Lavandou and Hyères. Explore its olive groves, vineyards and flower gardens on guided walks organised by the **tourist office** (☎ 04 94 01 53 10; www.ot-lalondelesmaures .fr) or hire a bike and wine taste by pedal power (see p308).

HYÈRES

pop 52,000

With its overdose of palm trees, its casino, and medieval Vieille Ville (Old Town) perched on a hillside north of its new town, Hyères retains much of the charm that made it the Côte d'Azur's first resort. Tolstoy took a winter 'cure' here in 1860; Robert Louis Stevenson claimed it was the only place he was ever truly happy (he worked on *Kidnapped*

here in 1886); and Queen Victoria breezed through in 1892.

The city's real asset however is the **Presqu'île de Giens** (Giens Peninsula), launch pad for day trips to the Îles d'Hyères (p300) and a walker's and spotter's paradise: the protected wetland area harbouring amazing birdlife, including pink flamingos, herons, terns, egrets, sandpipers, teals and cormorants.

ESSENTIAL INFORMATION

TOURIST OFFICES // City Centre (☎ 04 94 01 84 50; www.hyeres-tourisme.com; 3 av Ambroise Thomas; ☻ 9am-6pm Mon-Fri, 10am-4pm Sat) Fabulous guided walks.

EXPLORING HYÈRES

❦ **LA CAPTE & PRESQU'ÎLE DE GIENS** // **WATCH BIRDS AND CYCLE IN SALT PANS**
Pink flamingos add a splash of colour to the otherwise barren landscape of **La Capte,** two narrow sand bars supporting the **Salins des Presquiers** salt pans and a lake, 4km south of Hyères centre. A 1½-hour cycling itinerary (12.5km) loops the salt pans and the tourist office runs guided **bird discovery nature walks** (adult/under 18yr €5/free) around them. Particularly spectacular is the western sand bar road dubbed the **rte du Sel** (Salt Rd), only accessible in summer.

The northern section of the eastern bar road (the D42) is graced with a two-lane cycling track that runs for 2km from the beach resort of **L'Ayguade** to the roundabout in front of Toulon-Hyères airport; the tourist office stocks a pamphlet outlining a 1½-hour cycling route (13km) around L'Ayguade.

Boats operated by **Transport Littoral Varois** (TLV) set sail to Île du Levant and Port-Cros from pleasure-port **Port**

PEDAL-POWERED WINE TASTING

From La Londe, follow the main street south, and at the traffic lights turn onto av Général de Gaulle following signs for Le Port-les Îles-les Plages-Fort de Brégançon. Continue for 400m, cross the roundabout, and carry on for 700m to **Syril Bikes** (☎ 04 94 15 92 99; bike/tandem per day €12/30; 9am-noon & 2-7pm), where you can pick up wheels and La Londe's pea-green cycling track. Soon after, scenic views of perfectly kempt, symmetrical rows of vines – a vibrant green against the arid red soil – kick in. At the next roundabout, detour 1km to **Plage d'Argentière** for a dip in the sea and snorkel along an **aquatic nature trail** (May-Sep), or continue east along the D42a following signs for Fort de Bregançon.

You're now plump on the **Route des Vins de la Londe**, with pretty **Château des Bormettes** (☎ 04 94 66 81 35; www.chateaudesbormettes.com; rte de Brégançon), framed by nine sky-high palm trees. The oldest of the 70 hectares of vines at this lumbering château, owned by the Faré family (they live in Paris, holiday here), were planted in 1929. Pedal 2km down the silky-smooth lane and you come to another dreamy château with sage-green shutters, where **Clos Mireille** (☎ 04 94 01 53 50; www.domaines-ott.com; rte de Brégançon), one of the region's most highly regarded wines, has been produced since 1896.

At the next junction bear right towards the fort and Bormes-les-Mimosas. Two needle pines mark the entrance to **Domaine de la Sanglière** (☎ 04 94 00 48 58; www .domaine-sangliere.com, in French; 3886 rte de Léoube), where you can buy tasty wild boar and hazelnut terrine alongside your wine. Some 200m further east is the entrance to **Plage du Pellegrin**, the private beach of vast **Château de Léoube**, 1.7km further down the road. Stock up on fresh seasonal fruit at the fruit stall 700m east of the château and carry on 200m to **Parc de l'Esagnot** (☎ 04 94 64 78 76; www.estagnol.com; per car/bicycle €8/1) for a picnic on its white sandy beach. Lunch done, jump back on the saddle and pedal 500m to **Château de Brégançon** (☎ 04 94 64 80 73; www.chateaudebregancon.fr, in French; 639 rte de Léoube), a shabby old château with 40-year-old vines covering 52 hectares. Its Reserve du Château white makes a brilliant marriage with shellfish.

Don't confuse the château with 16th- to 18th-century **Fort de Brégançon**, signposted 500m further east down the road along the D42d on the western side of **Cap de Brégançon**. Once in front of the heavily guarded entrance to the fort, where the president of France summers (he's done so since 1968), park up and flop out on the rocky cape's gorgeous beach, sandy **Plage de Cabasson**.

d'Hyères on La Capte's eastern shore. Two-island **tours** cost €27 return.

At the foot of La Capte is **Presqu'île de Giens**, a beach-fringed peninsula, which briefly became an island in 1811 after huge storms. A fantastic and tough-in-places **Sentier du Littoral** (Coastal Path) loops the peninsula and you can take a TLV boat to **Île de Porquerolles** from **La Tour Fondue**, the port on the

peninsula's southeastern corner. Two-island Porquerolles/Port-Cros **tours** (adult return €28) depart weekdays in July and August only.

🌱 LA BALEINE // DINE AT THE PLEASURE PORT ON LA CAPTE

Of the dozens of appealing waterside restaurants you can find at the port cooking up €11 mounds of *moules frites* (mussels and fries) and other catch of the day, **The Whale** (☎ 04 94 57 59 21; 19 av du Docteur Robin, Port d'Hyères; mains €16-30; ☽ lunch & dinner) is the pick of the shoal. Its wood-decking, boat-facing terrace is stylish; its interior touts tables floating on water inside the whale's belly; and its menu is fish-driven, modern and creative. It is the type of place where you get a complimentary *amuse-bouche* (small appetiser). Follow with deep-fried sardines and lemon-laced fennel, then a simple plate of spaghetti, perhaps studded with *palourdes* (clams) or sea-urchin veins in a crustacean sauce. The *soupe de poisson* (fish soup; €22) is a meal in itself and the ratatouille-filled *encornets* (squid), served with langoustine claws and crushed tomatoes, quite divine.

🐚 L'ENDROÎT // LUNCH ON THE BEACH

What a dreamy place to eat, drink and ponder the sea. Slap on the sand with tables perched on trendy decking above the water – literally – **L'Endroît** (The Place; ☎ 04 94 58 00 97; 1 allee Emile Gerard, Hyères Plages; mains €20; ☽ lunch & dinner daily Jun-Sep, closed Sun dinner & Mon low season) is the fashionable place in Hyères to lunch, relax over an aperitif or dine at dusk. Concrete-sofa seating staring out to sea ensures a hip crowd in the bar; hardcore hipsters drink on the roof terrace; and cuisine in the restaurant catches the imagination with a welcome fusion of Provençal, Thai and Moroccan. Ginger-spiced monkfish, prawn red curry, squid salads, banana spring rolls swimming in chocolate…. Find it at the far end of Hyères Plage, two seconds from the Bona bus stop (bus 67 from the bus or train station). Advance reservations, especially in high season, are essential.

🐚 AN OLD-TOWN STROLL // MARKET STALLS, CAFÉ TERRACES AND CITY GATES

A jumble of furniture, floor tiles, clothes, olives, lavender-spiced marmalade, fruit and vegetables fills **place Georges Clemenceau** during its Saturday morning market. On the square's western side, 13th-century **Porte Massillon** (look for the clock) is the entrance to the Old Town. West along cobbled rue Massillon (don't miss **Poissonerie Massillon**, the fishmonger here) is beautiful arcaded **rue des Porches**, with its polished flagstones and collection of boutiques. **Chez Lucas** (☎ 04 94 28 25 65; 3 rue des Porches; pizza €11-14; ☽ lunch & dinner Tue-Sat, daily Jul & Aug), with its tantalising wood-fired pizza, bruschetta, *pissaladière* (onion, anchovy and olive-topped 'pizza') and *cade* (bite-sized chunks of chickpea pancake) is a tasty lunch spot.

Returning to the market square, walk north to 13th-century **Église St-Louis** to admire its sober, Romanesque architecture. Weave uphill to rue Bourgneuf and west along rue St-Esprit to the limestone arch of **Porte Barruc**. From here, steps pass an iron gate to the rambling hillside grove of **Parc St-Bernard** and **Villa Noailles** (☎ 04 98 08 01 93; www.villanoailles-hyeres.com, in French) below, a cubist maze of concrete and glass designed by Robert Mallet-Stevens in 1923 as a winter residence for devoted lover of modern art, Vicomte Charles de Noailles. Opening hours vary, depending on art exhibitions.

Back downhill, along rue Barbacane, is the oldest city gate, 12th-century **Porte St-Paul**. West of here is **Parc Castel Ste-Claire**, a 17th-century convent converted into a private residence, and home to American writer Edith Wharton from 1927. Today it houses the headquarters of the **Parc National de Port-Cros** (☎ 04 94 12 82 30; www.portcrosparcnational.fr, in French; 50 rue Ste-Claire).

TRANSPORT

TO/FROM THE AIRPORT

BUS // Bus 102 links **Toulon-Hyères airport** (Aéroport de Toulon-Hyères; ☎ 08 25 01 83 87; www .toulon-hyeres.aeroport.fr; bd de la Marine), 3km south of Hyères, with Hyères bus station (€1.40, 10 minutes).

GETTING AROUND

BOAT // **Transport Littoral Varois** (TLV; ☎ 04 94 58 21 81; www.tlv-tvm.com) runs services to Île du Levant (adult return €24.20, 1½ hours, at least once daily year-round) and Port-Cros (adult return €24.20, one hour, at least once daily year-round) from Port d'Hyères; and to Île de Porquerolles (adult/4-10yr return €16.50/14.30, 15 minutes, every 30 minutes May-Sep, six to 10 daily crossings Oct-Apr) from La Tour Fondue.

BUS // From the **bus station** (place du Maréchal Joffre), **Sodetrav** (☎ 08 25 00 06 50) runs daily buses to/from Toulon (€1.40, one hour), Le Lavandou (€7, 30 minutes) and St-Tropez (€15, 1¼ hours). City bus 67 (www.reseaumistral.com, in French) links platform 8 at Hyères bus station with the train station (five minutes), Port d'Hyères (€1.40, 15 minutes) and La Tour Fondue (€1.40, 35 minutes).

TRAIN // From the **train station** (place de l'Europe), local trains chug to/from Toulon (€3.90, 20 minutes). The Marseille–Hyères train (€13.10, 1¼ hours, four daily) stops in Cassis, La Ciotat, Bandol, Ollioules-Sanary and Toulon.

CAP DE CARQUEIRANNE

Immediately west of Hyères, Cap de Carqueiranne is a partly forested stretch of headland, crisscrossed by tiny lanes. The **coastal path** that edges its way from the town of Carqueiranne is a green scenic means of exploring the pretty cape. The lunch address on the cape is **L'Oursinado** (☎ 04 94 21 77 06; www.oursinado .com, in French; chemin du Pas des Gardéens; menu €58; ☺ lunch & dinner Thu-Mon, lunch Tue), hidden on a cliff above the tiny port of Les Oursinières below. Sit on its tree-framed terrace, gaze down at pounding waves and the huge blue sea below and feast on Toulonnais *bouillabaisse* (order 48 hours in advance), the local version of the legendary Marseille fish stew, which has potatoes in it as well as shoals of fish. Don't consider turning up without a table reservation.

TOULON

pop 170,000

Built around a *rade* (a sheltered bay lined with quays), France's second-largest naval port provokes the reaction a tramp might get in St-Tropez: its seedy rough-cut demeanour just doesn't fit in with the glittering Côte d'Azur. But it is not quite as terrible as it once was. Indeed some like its down-to-earth grit, its buskers and street markets, its tatty bar-laden quarter near the water awash with sailors and locals, and its gaggle of fountains reflecting its watery origins: Toulon is named after Télo, a Celtic-Ligurian goddess of springs.

ESSENTIAL INFORMATION

TOURIST OFFICES // City Centre (☎ 04 94 18 53 00; www.toulontourisme.com; 334 av de la République; ☺ 9am-6pm Mon-Sat, from 10am Tue, until 8pm & 10am-noon Sun Jul & Aug)

EXPLORING TOULON

🌿 MONT FARON // VIEW THE PORT FROM AN AERIAL PERSPECTIVE
Overlooking the old city from the northern side is Mont Faron (584m), from where you can see Toulon's red-roofed houses and the epic port in its true magnificence. Not far from the hill's summit rises the **Mémorial du Débarquement de Provence** (☎ 04 94 88 08 09; adult/8-18yr €3.80/1.55; ☺ 10am-noon & 2-4.30pm Tue-Sun), commemorating the Allied landings,

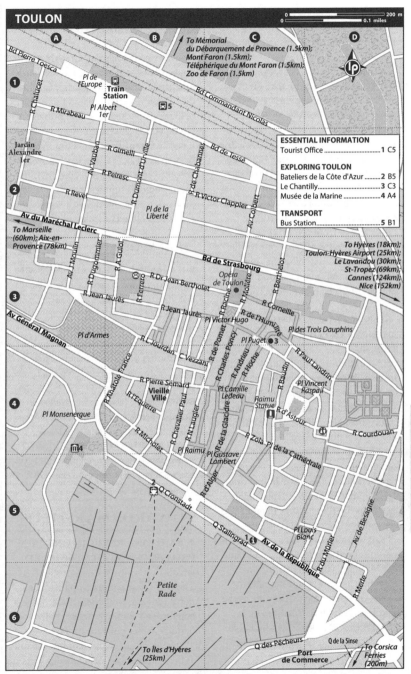

TOULON

ESSENTIAL INFORMATION
Tourist Office 1 C5

EXPLORING TOULON
Bateliers de la Côte d'Azur 2 B5
Le Chantilly 3 C3
Musée de la Marine 4 A4

TRANSPORT
Bus Station 5 B1

ST-TROPEZ TO TOULON

which took place along the coast here in August 1944. Historical displays and a film form part of this fascinating museum.

The Med's only cable car, the **Téléphérique du Mont Faron** (☎ 04 94 92 68 25; www.telepherique-faron.com, in French; bd Amiral Vence; adult/4-10yr €6.60/4.60; ☺ 9.30am-7.45pm Jul & Aug, shorter hr rest of year, closed windy days) climbs the mountain. Kids love **Zoo du Faron** (☎ 04 94 88 07 89; adult/4-10yr €8.50/5; ☺ 2-5pm Mon-Sat, 10am-5pm Sun & school holidays), a wildcat breeding-centre: combination zoo/cable-car tickets cost €12 per adult, €8 for children aged four to 10.

Take bus 40 from central square place de la Liberté to the *téléphérique* (cable car) stop. The tourist office has mountains of information on walking and mountain-bike trails on Mont Faron.

♥ GO NAUTICAL // IMMERSE YOURSELF IN LOCAL SEAFARING CULTURE

Begin the day with a flit around the city's **Musée de la Marine** (Marine Museum; ☎ 04 94 02 02 01; place Monsenergue; adult/under 18yr €5/free; ☺ 10am-6pm Wed-Mon), inside a lovely 18th-century arsenal building. The seafaring museum contains marvellous models of old sailing ships and paintings illustrating Toulon's history: the city only became part of France in 1481, growing in importance after Henri IV established its arsenal. In the 17th century the port was enlarged by Vauban.

Then set sail from quai Cronstadt on a one-hour **boat trip** around the bay and Port Militaire, with French commentary on events that took place here during WWII. Or opt for a cheerier ride to the Îles d'Hyères (p300). **Bateliers de la Côte d'Azur** (☎ 04 94 05 21 14; www.bateliers delacotedazur.com, in French; quai Cronstadt) run both services.

♥ LE CHANTILLY // A QUINTESSENTIAL TOULONNAIS LUNCH

Whether you're here for an early morning breakfast, a mound of *moules-frites* at lunchtime or an evening drink to wind down, you're certain to find this stalwart of local life packed with Toulonnais. Going strong since 1907, the popularity of **Le Chantilly** (☎ 04 94 92 24 37; place Puget; mains €10-25; ☺ 6.30am-11pm) shows absolutely no sign of receding any time soon. Toulon's funniest contemporary product, the lovable comic actor Raimu, particularly liked lunching here.

TRANSPORT

BUS // From the **bus station** (☎ 04 94 24 60 00; www.transports.var.fr, in French; bd de Tessé) bus 103 to St-Tropez (€20.90, 2½ hours, eight daily) runs east along the coast via Hyères (€1.90, 35 minutes) and Le Lavandou (€13.40, one hour). Shuttle buses (€1.40, 30 minutes) link Toulon train station with **Toulon-Hyères airport** (Aéroport de Toulon-Hyères; ☎ 08 25 01 83 87; www.toulon-hyeres.aeroport.fr), 23km east of Toulon.

BOAT // Ferries to Corsica and Sardinia are run by **Corsica Ferries** (☎ 0 825 095 095; quai de la Sinse, Port de Commerce), east of the old town.

TRAIN // From Toulon **train station** (place de l'Europe) there are frequent connections to coastal cities, including Marseille (€13, one hour), Cannes (€20.60, 1¼ hours) and Nice (€24.10, two hours).

TOWARDS MARSEILLE

♥ BANDOL // REVEL IN ONE OF PROVENCE'S MOST RESPECTED REDS

The very name conjures up images of noble reds elevating meat dishes to new heights, and summery rosés chilled to perfection. See p359 for more.

Start wine tasting on Bandol seafront at the excellent **Oenothèque des Vins du**

ST-TROPEZ TO TOULON

Bandol (☎ 04 94 29 45 03; www.maisondesvins-bandol.com; place Lucien Artaud; ⊗ 10am-1pm & 3-7pm Mon-Sat, 10am-1pm Sun), where Pascal Périer, aka a living Bandol encyclopedia, sets up tastings and keeps a well-supplied shop. He can also direct you to châteaux in the surrounding vineyards, which stretch 15km northwest of town, as far as Le Castellet; most require an advance appointment to taste and buy. To enjoy wine tasting as an aperitif, head for the hills to **Domaine de Terrebrune** (☎ 04 94 74 01 30; www.terrebrune.fr; 724 chemin de la Tourelle, Ollioules; ⊗ 9am-12.30pm & 2-6pm Mon-Sat) in Ollioules, where you can taste, buy and then dine on delicious seasonal country fare at **La Table du Vigneron** (☎ 04 94 88 36 19; ⊗ lunch & dinner Tue-Sat), a tasty *auberge* on the estate with alfresco tables overlooking the vines.

Two blocks back from the waterfront, **KV&B** (☎ 04 94 74 25 77; 5 rue de la Paroisse; lunch/dinner menu €15/28; ⊗ lunch & dinner Mon, Tue & Thu-Sat, lunch Sun) is the address to enjoy local wine over tapas in a crisp contemporary *bar à vin* setting (we love the Haribo sweets on the bar). Another recommended address is **L'Assiette des Saveurs** (☎ 04 94 29 80 08; 1 rue Docteur Marçon; menus €15-30; ⊗ lunch & dinner), serving classic recipes with a cheeky fusion twist on a pretty pavement terrace.

Stroll it all off afterwards with a 12km coastal walk along the yellow-flagged **Sentier du Littoral** from Bandol port to La Madrague in St-Cyr-Les-Lecques, passing the stunning **Calanque de Port d'Alon** half-way along.

❦ REGARD DU VIVANT // WATCH DOLPHINS DANCE OFF THE COAST OF SANARY-SUR-MER

Observing various dolphin species from aboard a boat run by exceptional wildlife-photography outfit **Regard du Vivant** (☎ 06 10 57 17 11; www.regard-du-vivant.fr, in French; adult/6-12yr €72/55) is memorable. June to October all-day boat trips depart from Sanary-sur-Mer, 15km west of Toulon, at 9am on Sunday, returning at 6.30pm. Naturalists are aboard to help aspiring naturalists identify marine life and explain what's what.

Sanary itself is a quiet seaside resort with sugary pink-and-white seaside cottages peeping out at shallow sandy beaches. Novelist Aldous Huxley (1894–1963) called the place home in the early 1930s, as did his biographer Sybille Bedford in the late 1930s and a host of German refugees soon after. Thomas Mann and his brother Heinrich sought refuge here, as did the German painter Feuchtwanger.

ST-TROPEZ TO TOULON

BACKGROUND

❦ HISTORY
A tour through the history of Provence: petroglyphs, popes, world wars and the bikini. (p315)

❦ THE ARTS
Designer chapels, exciting architecture, avant-garde art museums and cutting-edge dance – Provence and the Côte d'Azur is a living art museum with a matchless portfolio. (p329)

❦ LYRICAL LANDSCAPES: CORK, LAVENDER & SWEET JASMINE
There's more to Provence than pea-green vineyards, sky-blue seas and blush-red cherry orchards. Its unique riot of colours and scents is electrifying. (p342)

❦ PROVENCE LIVING
Pastis, *pétanque,* celebrity-strewn coastal capes and tall tales about sardines: so just how do people in Provence really spend a Saturday afternoon? (p347)

❦ OUTDOOR INSPIRATION
Fly with the birds, swim with fish, watch for a whale or walk a trail a day. (p352)

❦ PROVENÇAL WINE
L'art de vivre (the art of living) is what those in-the-know Provençal call it. (p359)

❦ A SEASONAL CUISINE
A simple filet mignon sprinkled with olive oil and rosemary fresh from the garden makes the same magnificent Sunday lunch it did a generation ago. (p364)

❦ FOOD GLOSSARY
Read this first to know *socca* is not football and *alouettes sans têtes* has nothing to do with headless larks. (p374)

HISTORY

. . . .

PREHISTORIC MAN

Provence was inhabited from an exceptionally early age and has a bounty of prehistoric sights to prove it. In Monaco the Grottes de l'Observatoire (p224) showcase brilliant prehistoric rock scratchings, carved one million years ago and among the world's oldest. Around 400,000 BC, prehistoric man settled in Terra Amata (present-day Nice).

Neanderthal hunters occupied the Mediterranean coast during the Middle Palaeolithic period (about 90,000 BC to 40,000 BC), living in caves. Provence's leading prehistory museum, the Musée de la Préhistoire des Gorges du Verdon (p179) in Quinson, runs visits to one such cave, the Grotte de la Baume Bonne.

Modern man arrived with creative flair in 30,000 BC. The ornate wall paintings of bison, seals, ibex and other animals inside the decorated Grotte Cosquer in the Calanque de Sormiou (p63), near Marseille, date from 20,000 BC.

> '*Massalia (Marseille) was colonised around 600 BC by Greeks from Phocaea*'

The Neolithic period (about 6000 to 4500 years ago) witnessed the earliest domestication of sheep and the cultivation of lands. The first dwellings to be built (around 3500 BC) were *bories*: visit these beehive-shaped huts at the Village des Bories (p153) near Gordes.

But the star of Provence's prehistoric show is the collection of 30,000 Bronze Age petroglyphs decorating Mont Bégo in the Vallée des Merveilles (p188). Marked walking trails lead to these fascinating rock drawings, which date to between 1800 BC and 1500 BC.

GREEKS TO ROMANS

Massalia (Marseille) was colonised around 600 BC by Greeks from Phocaea in Asia Minor; from the 4th century BC they established more trading posts along the coast at Antipolis (Antibes), Olbia (Hyères), Athenopolis (St-Tropez), Nikaia (Nice), Monoïkos (Monaco) and Glanum (near St-Rémy de Provence). They brought olives and grapevines to the region.

» C90,000 BC	» 600 BC	» 125–126 BC
Neanderthal hunters occupy the Mediterranean coast and starting around 30,000 BC Cro-Magnons start decorating their caves.	The Greeks colonise Massalia and establish trading posts along the coast, bringing olive trees and grapevines to the region.	Romans create Provincia Gallia Transalpina, from which Provence gets its name, and Provence joins the Roman Empire.

BACKGROUND

While Hellenic civilisation was developing on the coast, the Celts penetrated northern Provence. They mingled with ancient Ligurians to create a Celto-Ligurian stronghold around Entremont; its influence extended as far south as Draguignan.

In 125 BC the Romans helped the Greeks defend Massalia against invading Celto-Ligurians. Their victory marked the start of the Gallo-Roman era and the creation of Provincia Gallia Transalpina, the first Roman *provincia* (province), from which the name Provence is derived.

THE GALLO-ROMANS

Provincia Gallia Transalpina, later Provincia Narbonensis, embraced all of southern France from the Alps to the Mediterranean and the Pyrenees. In 122 BC the Romans destroyed the Ligurian capital of Entremont and established the Roman stronghold of Aquae Sextiae Salluviorum (Aix-en-Provence) at its foot.

During this period the Romans built roads to secure the route between Italy and Spain. The Via Aurelia linked Rome to Fréjus, Aix-en-Provence, Arles and Nîmes; the northbound Via Agrippa followed the Rhône from Arles to Avignon, Orange and Lyons; and the Via Domitia linked the Alps with the Pyrenees by way of Sisteron, the

---

DON'T MISS...

HISTORICAL READING

To stay abreast of history in the making in the realm of politics and current affairs check out www.paca.pref.gouv.fr (in French), or the Provence-Alpes-Côte d'Azur region website at www.regionpaca.fr (in French). But for a look further back check out these interesting reads:

★ **Ladder of Shadows: Reflecting on Medieval Vestiges in Provence & Languedoc //** Beautiful lyrical narrative on Roman and early Christian relics in southern France by Gustaf Sobin

★ **Old Provence //** Journalist and travel writer Theodore Andrea Cook's 1905 twist on the region's classic Roman and medieval sights

★ **Operation Dragoon: The Liberation of Southern France //** The liberation of Provence two months after D-Day is the focus of this much-vaunted new title by prolific historian Anthony Tucker-Jones, published December 2009

★ **The French Riviera: A Cultural History //** Twinkling with glamour, Julian Hale's recently published history delves into the modern Côte d'Azur's vibrant past

---

» 118 BC	» C AD 100–300	» 400–900
The Romans build roads, including the Via Domitia connecting Spain to Italy and passing through Provence at Cavaillon, Apt and Gap.	The Romans revel in their heyday with a riot of splendid public buildings: baths, temples and aqueducts of almighty proportions like the Pont du Gard.	Roman Empire collapses and Germanic tribes invade Provence; Franks (hence the name 'France') encourage villagers to move uphill to avert Saracen attacks.

BACKGROUND

Luberon, Beaucaire and Nîmes. Vestiges of these roads – the Pont Julien from 3 BC near Bonnieux and an arch in Cavaillon – remain.

The Roman influence on Provence was tremendous, though it was only after Julius Caesar's conquest of Gaul (58–51 BC) and its consequent integration into the Roman Empire that the region flourished. Massalia, which had retained its independence following the creation of Provincia, was incorporated by Caesar in 49 BC. In 14 BC the still-rebellious Ligurians were defeated by Augustus, who celebrated by building a monument at La Turbie in 6 BC. Arelate (Arles) became the chosen regional capital.

Under the emperor Augustus, vast amphitheatres were built at Arelate (Arles), Nemausus (Nîmes), Forum Julii (Fréjus) and Vasio Vocontiorum (Vaison-la-Romaine). Triumphal arches were raised at Arausio (Orange), Cabelio (Cavaillon), Carpentorate (Carpentras) and Glanum, and a series of aqueducts was constructed. The 275m-long Pont du Gard (p143) was part of a 50km-long system of canals built around 19 BC by Agrippa, Augustus' deputy, to bring water from Uzès to Nîmes. All these ancient public buildings remain exceptionally well preserved and lure sightseers year-round.

Christianity – brought to the region, according to Provençal legend, by Mary Magdalene, Mary Jacob and Mary Salome, who sailed into Stes-Maries de la Mer (p94) in AD 40 – penetrated the region, was adopted by the Romans and continued to spread over the next few hundred years.

MEDIEVAL PROVENCE

After the collapse of the Roman Empire in AD 476, Provence was invaded by various Germanic tribes: the Visigoths (western Goths, from the Danube delta region in Transylvania), the Ostrogoths (eastern Goths, from the Black Sea region) and the Burgundians, of Scandinavian origin. In the 6th century it was ceded to the Germanic Franks.

In the early 9th century the Saracens (an umbrella term adopted locally to describe Muslim invaders such as Turks, Moors and Arabs) emerged as a warrior force to be reckoned with. Attacks along the Maures coast, Niçois hinterland and more northern Alps persuaded villagers to take refuge in the hills. Many of Provence's perched, hilltop villages date from this chaotic period. In AD 974 the Saracen fortress at La Garde Freinet was defeated by William the Liberator (Guillaume Le Libérateur), count of Arles, who consequently extended his feudal control over the entire region, marking a return of peace and unity to Provence, which became a marquisate. In 1032 it joined the Holy Roman Empire.

The marquisate of Provence was later split in two: the north fell to the counts of Toulouse from 1125 and the Catalan counts of Barcelona gained control of the

» 974–1032	» 1309–76	» 1431
William the Liberator extends his feudal control over Provence, which becomes a marquisate and joins the Holy Roman Empire.	Pope Clément V moves the Holy See to Avignon, and nine pontiffs head the Roman Catholic church from there until 1377; 'home' is the Palais des Papes.	Jeanne d'Arc (Joan of Arc) is burnt at the stake in Rouen for heresy; the English are not driven out of France until 1453.

BACKGROUND

southern part (stretching from the Rhône to the River Durance and from the Alps to the sea). This became the county of Provence (Comté de Provence). Raymond Bérenger V (1209–45) was the first Catalan count to reside permanently in Aix (the capital since 1186). In 1229 he conquered Nice and in 1232 he founded Barcelonnette. After Bérenger's death the county passed to the House of Anjou, under which it enjoyed great prosperity.

THE POPES

In 1274 Comtat Venaissin (Carpentras and its Vaucluse hinterland) was ceded to Pope Gregory X in Rome. In 1309 French-born Clément V (r 1305–14) moved the papal headquarters from feud-riven Rome to Avignon. A tour of the Papal palace (p104) illustrates how resplendent a period this was for the city, which hosted nine pontiffs between 1309 and 1376.

The death of Pope Gregory XI led to the Great Schism (1378–1417), during which rival popes resided at Rome and Avignon and spent most of their energies denouncing and excommunicating each other. Even after the schism was settled and a pope established in Rome, Avignon and the Comtat Venaissin remained under papal rule until 1792.

The arts in Provence flourished (see p329). A university was established in Avignon as early as 1303, followed by a university in Aix a century later. In 1327 Italian poet Petrarch (1304–74) encountered his muse, Laura, in Fontaine de Vaucluse (p129). During the reign of Good King René, king of Naples (1434–80), French became the courtly language.

FRENCH PROVENCE

In 1481 René's successor, his nephew Charles III, died heirless and Provence was ceded to Louis XI of France. In 1486 the state of Aix ratified Provence's union with France and the centralist policies of the French kings saw the region's autonomy greatly reduced. Aix Parliament, a French administrative body, was created in 1501.

This new addition to the French kingdom did not include Nice, Barcelonnette, Puget-Théniers and their hinterlands that, in 1388, had become incorporated into the lands of the House of Savoy. The County of Nice, with Nice as its capital, did not become part of French Provence until 1860.

A period of instability ensued, as a visit to the synagogue (p124) in Carpentras testifies: Jews living in French Provence fled to ghettos in Carpentras, Pernes-les-Fontaines,

BACKGROUND

» 1481	» 1530s	» 1545
King of Naples, Good King René's nephew and successor, Charles III, dies heirless and Provence falls to Louis XI of France.	The Reformation sweeps through France, prompting the core of Catholicism to be questioned.	People of 11 Luberon villages are massacred under the terms of the Arrêt de Mérindol, a bill condemning anyone of Waldensian faith to death.

L'Isle-sur-la-Sorgue, Cavaillon or Avignon. All were part of the pontifical enclave of Comtat Venaissin, where papal protection remained assured until 1570.

An early victim of the Reformation that swept Europe in the 1530s and the consequent Wars of Religion (1562–98) was the Luberon. In April 1545 the population of 11 Waldensian (Vaudois) villages in the Luberon were massacred (see the boxed text, p164). Numerous clashes followed between the staunchly Catholic Comtat Venaissin and its Huguenot (Protestant) neighbours to the north around Orange.

In 1580 the plague immobilised the region. Treatments first used by the prophetic Nostradamus (1503–66) in St-Rémy de Provence were administered to plague victims.

The Edict of Nantes in 1598 (which recognised Protestant control of certain areas, including Lourmarin in the Luberon) brought an uneasy peace to the region – until its revocation by Louis XIV in 1685. Full-scale persecution of Protestants ensued. Visit Château d'If (p51) to see where Huguenots were killed or imprisoned.

> *'France's stirring national anthem, La Marseillaise, was born'*

The close of the century was marked by the French Revolution in 1789: as the National Guard from Marseille marched north to defend the Revolution, a merry tune composed in Strasbourg several months earlier for the war against Prussia – *Chant de Guerre de l'Armée du Rhin* (War Song of the Rhine Army) – sprang from their lips. France's stirring national anthem, *La Marseillaise,* was born.

LA ROUTE NAPOLÉON

Provence was divided into three *départements* (administrative divisions) in 1790: Var, Bouches du Rhône and the Basse-Alpes. Two years later papal Avignon and Comtat Venaissin were annexed by France, making way for the creation of Vaucluse.

In 1793 the Armée du Midi marched into Nice and declared it French territory. France also captured Monaco, until now a recognised independent state ruled by the Grimaldi family (see p224). When Toulon was besieged by the English, it was thanks to the efforts of a dashing young Corsican general named Napoléon Bonaparte (Napoleon I) that France recaptured it.

The Reign of Terror that swept through France between September 1793 and July 1794 saw religious freedoms revoked, churches desecrated and cathedrals turned into 'Temples of Reason'. In the secrecy of their homes, people handcrafted thumbnail-sized biblical figurines, hence the inglorious creation of the *santon* (see p54).

» 1539	» 1560	» 1562–98
French (rather than Provençal) is made the official administrative language of Provence.	Nîmes native Jean Nicot (1530–1600) becomes the first to import tobacco into France from Portugal, hence the word 'nicotine'.	The Wars of Religion saw numerous bloody clashes between French Catholics and Protestants (Huguenots).

In 1814 France lost the territories it had seized in 1793. The County of Nice was ceded to Victor Emmanuel I, King of Sardinia. It remained under Sardinian protectorship until 1860, when an agreement between Napoleon III and the House of Savoy helped drive the Austrians from northern Italy, prompting France to repossess Savoy and the area around Nice. In Monaco the Treaty of Paris restored the rights of the Grimaldi royal family; from 1817 until 1860 the principality also fell under the protection of the Sardinian king.

Meanwhile, the Allied restoration of the House of Bourbon to the French throne at the Congress of Vienna (1814–15), following Napoleon I's abdication and exile to Elba, was rudely interrupted by the return of the emperor. Following his escape from Elba in 1815, Napoleon landed at Golfe-Juan on 1 March with a 1200-strong army. He proceeded northwards, passing through Cannes, Grasse, Castellane, Digne-les-Bains and Sisteron en route to his triumphal return to Paris on 20 May. Napoleon's glorious 'Hundred Days' back in power ended with the Battle of Waterloo and his return to exile. He died in 1821.

THE BELLE ÉPOQUE

The Second Empire (1852–70) brought to the region a revival in all things Provençal, a movement spearheaded by Maillane-born poet Frédéric Mistral. Rapid economic growth was another hallmark: Nice, which had become part of France in 1860, was among Europe's first cities to have a purely tourist-based economy. Between 1860 and 1911 it was Europe's fastest-growing city. In the Victorian period the city became particularly popular with the English aristocracy, who followed their queen's example of wintering in mild Nice. European royalty followed soon after. The train line reached Toulon in 1856, followed by Nice and Draguignan, and in 1864 work started on a coastal road from Nice to Monaco. Nice Opera House and the city's neoclassical Palais de Justice were built in fine Second Empire architectural style. For more on the history of Nice and the Riviera, visit Nice's excellent Musée Masséna (p203).

In neighbouring Monaco the Grimaldi family gave up its claim over its former territories of Menton and Roquebrune in 1861 in exchange for France's recognition of its status as an independent principality. Four years later Monte Carlo Casino – a stunning still-operational place that should not be missed (see the boxed text, p225) – opened and Monaco leapt from being Europe's poorest state to one of its richest.

The Third Republic ushered in the glittering belle époque, with art nouveau architecture, a whole field of artistic 'isms' including Impressionism, and advances in sci-

» 1598	» 1720	» 1756–63
Bourbon king Henry IV gives French Protestants freedom of conscience with the Edict of Nantes – to the horror of Catholic Paris.	The Great Plague of Marseille eventually leads to the death of more than half the city's population, and the building of Le Mur de la Peste (Plague Wall).	The Seven Years War is one of a series of ruinous wars pursued by Louis XV, leading to the loss of France's colonies in Canada, the West Indies and India.

ence and engineering. Wealthy French, English, American and Russian tourists and tuberculosis sufferers (for whom the only cure was sunlight and sea air) discovered the coast. The intensity and clarity of the region's colours and light appealed to many painters.

WWI & THE ROARING TWENTIES

No blood was spilled on southern French soil during WWI. Soldiers were conscripted from the region, however, and the human losses included two out of every 10 Frenchmen between 20 and 45 years of age. With its primarily tourist-based economy, the Côte d'Azur recovered quickly from the postwar financial crisis that lingered in France's more industrial north.

The Côte d'Azur sparkled as an avant-garde centre in the 1920s and 1930s, with artists pushing into the new fields of cubism and surrealism, Le Corbusier rewriting the architectural textbook and foreign writers thronging to the liberal coast. Ernest Hemingway, F Scott Fitzgerald, Aldous Huxley, Katherine Mansfield, DH Lawrence and Thomas Mann were among the scores to seek solace in the sun. Guests at Somerset Maugham's villa on Cap Ferrat included innumerable literary names, from TS Eliot to Ian Fleming.

The coast's nightlife gained a reputation for being cutting edge, with everything from jazz clubs to striptease. Rail and road access to the south improved: the railway line between Digne-les-Bains and Nice was completed and in 1922 the luxurious *Train Bleu* made its first run from Calais, via Paris, to the coast. The train only had 1st-class carriages and was quickly dubbed the 'train to paradise'.

> ### THE SKY-BLUE COAST
>
> The Côte d'Azur (literally 'Azure Coast') gained its name in 1887 from the first guidebook published on the region. *La Côte d'Azur* was the work of Stéphane Liégeard (1830–1925), a lawyer-cum-aspiring-poet from Burgundy who lived in Cannes. The guide covered the coast from Menton to Hyères and was an instant hit. Its title, a reflection of the coast's clear blue cloudless skies, became the hottest phrase in town and never disappeared. The Côte d'Azur is known as the French Riviera by most Anglophones.

The roaring twenties hailed the start of the summer season on the Côte d'Azur. Outdoor swimming pools were built, seashores were cleared of seaweed to uncover sandy beaches, and sunbathing sprang into fashion after a bronzed Coco Chanel appeared on

» 1789–94	» 1790–92	» 1795–99
Revolutionaries storm the Bastille, leading to the beheading of Louis XVI and Marie-Antoinette and the Reign of Terror, seeing religious freedoms revoked.	Provence is divided into three *départements;* Papal Avignon and Comtat Venaissin are annexed by France and Vaucluse is created.	A five-man delegation of moderate republicans led by Paul Barras sets itself up as a *Directoire* (Directory) and rules the Republic for five years.

the coast in 1923, draped over the arm of the duke of Westminster. France lifted its ban on gambling, prompting the first casino to open on the coast in the Palais de la Méditerranée (today a hotel) on Nice's promenade des Anglais in 1927. The first Formula One Grand Prix (p227) sped around Monaco in 1929, while the early 1930s saw the arrival of wide pyjama-style beach trousers and the opening of a nudist colony on Île du Levant. With the advent of paid holidays for all French workers in 1936, even more tourists flocked to the region. Second- and 3rd-class seating was added to the *Train Bleu*, which had begun running daily in 1929.

WWII

With the onset of war, the Côte d'Azur's glory days turned grey. Depression set in and on 3 September 1939 France and Britain declared war on Germany. But following the armistice treaty agreed with Hitler on 22 June 1940, southern France fell into the 'free' Vichy France zone, although Menton and the Vallée de La Roya were occupied by Italians. The Côte d'Azur – particularly Nice – immediately became a safe haven from war-torn occupied France; by 1942 some 43,000 Jews had descended on the coast to seek refuge. Monaco remained neutral for the duration of WWII.

On 11 November 1942 Nazi Germany invaded Vichy France. Provence was at war. At Toulon 73 ships, cruisers, destroyers and submarines – the major part of the French fleet – were scuttled by their crews to prevent the Germans seizing them. Almost immediately, Toulon was overcome by the Germans and Nice was occupied by the Italians. In January 1943 the Marseille quarter of Le Panier was razed, its 40,000 inhabitants being given less than a day's notice to pack up and leave. Those who didn't were sent to Nazi concentration camps. The Resistance movement, particularly strong in Provence, was known in the region as *maquis*, after the Provençal scrub in which people hid.

Two months after D-Day, on 15 August 1944, Allied forces landed on the southern coast. They arrived at beaches – all open for bronzing and bathing today – along the Côte d'Azur, including Le Dramont near St-Raphaël, Cavalaire, Pampelonne and the St-Tropez peninsula. St-Tropez and Provence's hinterland were almost immediately liberated, but it was only after five days of heavy fighting that Allied troops freed Marseille on 28 August (three days after the liberation of Paris). Toulon was liberated on 26 August, a week after French troops first attacked the port.

Italian-occupied areas in the Vallée de La Roya were only returned to France in 1947.

MODERN PROVENCE

The first international film festival at Cannes (see boxed text, p245) in 1946 heralded the return to party madness. The coast's intellectuals reopened their abandoned seaside villas, and Picasso set up studio in Golfe-Juan. The 1950s and 1960s saw a succession of society events: the fairy-tale marriage of a Grimaldi prince to Hollywood film-legend Grace Kelly in 1956; Vadim's filming of *Et Dieu Créa la Femme* (And God Created Woman) with Brigitte Bardot in St-Tropez the same year; the creation of the bikini (see below); the advent of topless sunbathing (and consequent nipple-covering with bottle tops to prevent arrest for indecent exposure); and Miles Davis, Ella Fitzgerald and Ray Charles appearing at the 1961 Juan-les-Pins jazz festival.

In 1962 the French colony of Algeria negotiated its independence with President Charles de Gaulle. During this time some 750,000 *pieds noirs* (literally 'black feet', as Algerian-born French people are known in France) flooded into France, many settling in large urban centres such as Marseille and Toulon.

Rapid industrialisation marked the 1960s. A string of five hydroelectric plants was constructed on the banks of the River Durance and in 1964 Électricité de France (EDF), the French electricity company, dug a canal from Manosque to the Étang de Berre. The following year construction work began on a 100-sq-km petrochemical zone and an industrial port at Fos-sur-Mer, southern Europe's most important. The first metro line opened in Marseille in 1977 and TGV high-speed trains reached the city in 1981.

From the 1970s mainstream tourism started making inroads into Provence's rural heart. While a concrete marina was being constructed at Villeneuve-Lourbet-Plage (west of Nice), the region's first purpose-built ski resort popped up inland at Isola 2000. The small flow of for-

ENTER THE BIKINI

Almost called *atome* (French for atom) rather than bikini after its pinprick size, the scanty little two-piece bathing suit was the 1946 creation of Cannes fashion designer Jacques Heim and automotive engineer Louis Réard.

Top-and-bottom swimsuits had existed for centuries, but it was the French duo who plumped for the name bikini – after Bikini, an atoll in the Marshall Islands chosen by the USA in 1946 as a testing ground for atomic bombs.

Once wrapped around the curvaceous rear of 1950s sex-bomb Brigitte Bardot on St-Tropez's Plage de Pampelonne, there was no looking back. The bikini was born.

» 1914–18	» 1920s	» 1939–45
The human cost of WWI is enormous: of the eight million French men called to arms, 1.3 million are killed and almost one million crippled.	The Côte d'Azur sparkles as Europe's avant-garde centre and the luxurious *Train Bleu* (Blue Train) makes its first run from Calais to the Mediterranean coast.	Nazi Germany occupies France, establishing a puppet state led by ageing WWI hero General Pétain in Vichy; Provence is liberated two months after D-Day.

BACKGROUND

eigners that had trickled into Provence backwaters to buy crumbling old *mas* (Provençal farmhouses) at dirt-cheap prices in the late 1970s had become an uncontrollable torrent by the 1980s. By the turn of the new millennium, the region was welcoming nine million tourists annually.

Corruption cast a shady cloud over France's hot south in the 1980s and early 1990s. Nice's mayor, Jacques Médecin (son of another former mayor, Jean Médecin, who governed Nice for 38 years), was twice found guilty of income-tax evasion during his 24-year mayorship (1966–90). In 1990 King Jacques – as the flamboyant mayor was dubbed – fled to Uruguay, following which he was convicted *in absentia* of the misuse of public funds (including accepting four million francs in bribes and stealing two million francs from the Nice opera). Médecin was extradited in 1994 and imprisoned in Grenoble, where he served two years of a 3½-year sentence. Upon being released the ex-mayor, who died in 1998 aged 70, returned to Uruguay to sell handpainted T-shirts.

> 'Following her public denunciation of the Riviera Mafia, the French député was shot'

During 1994 Yann Piat became the only member of France's National Assembly (parliament) since WWII to be assassinated while in office. Following her public denunciation of the Riviera Mafia, the French *député* was shot in her Hyères constituency. Her assassins, dubbed the 'baby killers' by the press after their conviction in 1998, were local Mafia kingpins barely in their 20s.

THE FRONT NATIONAL

In the mid-1990s blatant corruption, coupled with economic recession and growing unemployment, fuelled the rise of the extreme-right Front National (FN). The party's platform posits that immigrants pose a 'mortal danger' to France and immigration should therefore be halted, protecting French culture. They also believe France should return to the franc and give its citizens tax cuts – made possible by ending social benefits for immigrants. Nowhere else in France did the FN gain such a stronghold as in Provence, where it stormed to victory in municipal elections in Toulon, Orange and Marignane in 1995, and Vitrolles in 1997.

Yet the FN, led by Jean Marie Le Pen, legendary for his dismissal of the Holocaust as a 'mere detail of history' in the 1980s and his 'inequality of races' jargon in the late 1990s, never made any real headway in the national arena. Party support for the FN

» 1946	» 1947	» 1946–62
The first international film festival opens at Cannes' old casino, and is a smashing success, helping revive postwar life on the coast.	Vallée de La Roya, in eastern Provence, which had been occupied by the Italians during WWII, is returned to France.	French colonialism ends with war in Indochina (1946–54), followed by the Algerian War of Independence (1954–62), brought to a close with the Accord d'Évian.

BACKGROUND

rose from 1% in 1981 to 15% in the 1995 presidential elections but dropped to 10.4% in 2007. The FN did not secure any seats in the National Assembly. And despite gaining 15.5% of votes in regional elections in 1998 and 14.7% in 2004, the FN never succeeded in securing the presidency of the Provence-Alpes-Côte d'Azur *région*.

Le Pen's incredible success in the first round of presidential elections in 2002 – he landed 16.86% of votes – shocked many people. More than one million protestors took to the streets across France in the days preceding the second round of voting, in which the FN politician was up against incumbent president Jacques Chirac. In response, 80% of the electorate turned out to vote (compared with 41% in the first round) and Chirac won by a massive majority.

Never to be defeated, Le Pen helped his daughter Marine Le Pen achieve appointment as party vice-chairman at the FN party congress in Nice in 2003, despite accusations of nepotism. Though support for the party dropped in the 2007 elections, some say its influence will persist among groups in France who feel disenfranchised by economic globalisation.

ANOTHER MILLENNIUM

France's sea-blue south sped into the 21st century with the opening of the high-speed TGV Méditerranée railway line (p416) and a booming information technology sector. In Marseille, France's third-largest city, Euroméditerranée laid the foundations for a massive 15-year rejuvenation project in the port city. While the arrival by sea of the world's largest floating dike in Monaco doubled the capacity of the already thriving port.

Yet two years on, the tide started to turn. Flash floods devastated northwestern Provence in September 2002, killing 26. A year later floodwaters rose again, this time in Marseille, Avignon, Arles and other Rhône Valley cities, where several died and thousands lost their homes. The floods topped off a year that had seen the Festival d'Avignon (p107) – Europe's premier cultural event with an annual revenue of €15 million – paralysed by striking artists, furious at government proposals to tighten unemployment benefits for arts workers. Strikes peppered much of 2004 and 2005.

Regional elections in March 2004 reflected the national trend: socialist Michel Vauzelle (b 1944) staved off the government-backed centre-right UMP (Union pour un Movement Populaire) candidate to secure a second term in office as president of the 123-strong, Marseille-based Provence-Alpes-Côte d'Azur *conseil régional* (regional council). Among other things, the staunchly left politician – a former justice minister,

» 1956	» 1981	» 1998
Rainier Louis Henri Maxence Bertrand Grimaldi, Count of Polignac, aka Prince Rainier III of Monaco, weds his fairy-tale princess, Hollywood film legend Grace Kelly.	The superspeedy TGV makes its first commercial journey from Paris to Lyon, breaking all speed records to complete the train journey in two hours instead of six.	After resuming nuclear testing in the South Pacific in the early 1990s, France signs the worldwide test-ban treaty, bringing an end to French nuclear testing.

BACKGROUND

NICE TREATY

No pan-European agreement has been more influential on the future map of Europe than the Treaty of Nice, a landmark treaty thrashed out by the then 15 EU member states in the seaside city of Nice in late December 2000. Enforced from February 2003, the treaty laid the foundations for EU enlargement starting in 2004, determined the institutions necessary for its smooth running and – not without controversy – established a new system of voting in the Council of Ministers for the 25 EU countries from 1 November 2004.

Bouches du Rhône MP and mayor of Arles – was a very loud voice in the 'Non' campaign to the proposed EU constitution, which an overwhelmingly disgruntled French electorate rejected in a referendum in May 2005. The next regional elections will be held in 2010.

In October 2005, urban violence across the country – including in Marseille, Cannes, Nice and dozens of other Provençal towns – erupted in response to the death of two teenagers of North African origin. Apparently running from the police, they were electrocuted after hiding in an electricity substation in a northeastern Paris suburb.

Just a year before in multicultural Marseille, part of the city's sizable ethnic population had resorted to street protests following the government's national ban of wearing the Islamic headscarf, Jewish skullcap, Sikh turban, the crucifix and other religious symbols in French schools. Marie-Josée Roig – France's minister for the family and Avignon's mayor – explained to a UN committee for child rights that the law was intended to place schoolchildren on an equal footing in the republican French classroom. But for many Muslims it confirmed feelings that the French state was not prepared to fully integrate Muslims into French society.

Meanwhile, in a privileged pocket of coastal paradise, well away from all this modern-day mayhem, the bachelor son of a Hollywood queen was crowned monarch following the death of his aged father (see boxed text, p224).

THE NATIONAL SCENE

When President Nicolas Sarkozy battled his way into office in a cliff-hanger election in May 2007 he spoke about job creation, lowering taxes, crime crackdown and helping the country's substantial immigrant population. But as early as November 2007, he was beset with fresh conflicts as coastal fishermen began blocking ports, including those on the Mediterranean, to protest rising fuel prices. Demonstrations and block-

» 2000	» 2002	» 2004
European leaders meet in Nice to thrash out future EU expansion. Not without controversy, they establish a new system of voting in the Council of Ministers.	The French franc, first minted in 1360, is dumped on the scrap heap of history as the country adopts the euro as its official currency.	The National Assembly bans the wearing of overtly religious symbols, including the Islamic headscarf and Jewish skullcap, in state schools.

ages continued in May 2008, further disrupting oil terminals near Marseille and along the Mediterranean. That same month, over 500 dock workers in Marseille marched against planned port privatisations, hurling stones and bottles at police.

Then, in the first quarter of 2009, French unemployment soared to 8.7%. In response to Sarkozy's handling of *Le Crise* (The Crisis), as the worldwide financial instability has been dubbed, in January and again in May millions of workers staged massive protests in Marseille and across the country.

The government continues to bail out businesses and in July 2009 draft legislation passed the French lower house to open shops on Sunday in Marseille, Nice and other tourist destinations, despite union opposition. Even the venerable Cannes film festival was not impervious to the economic downturn: 2009 buyer attendance was down 30%, though the red carpet remained asparkle with stars.

A controversial EU proposal in 2009 to broaden methods of rosé wine production by allowing winemakers to simply blend red and white wines to make a pink wine was met with the fury of Provence winemakers.

> '*Marseille was named the European Capital of Culture for 2013*'

France is the number one producer of 'true' rosé, made from lightly macerated red grapes, and Provence is the top producer in France. The EU backed down in June 2009, much to the relief of local vignerons, who largely struggle to eke out a decent living.

Culturally, Provence remains vibrant. In the summer of 2009, for the first time ever, Pablo Picasso's burial place and home from 1959 to 1961, Château de Vauvenargues, near Aix-en-Provence, was opened to the public. His step-daughter, Catherine Hutin, was persuaded to allow tours as part of the Cézanne-Picasso art exposition in Aix. Modern-art pilgrims visited Picasso's tomb, explored rooms in the château, and peeked into his still-paint-splattered studio. The access raised hopes that Hutin could be persuaded to open the château permanently.

While Nice lost out to Annecy in 2009 in its bid to be France's nominee to host the 2018 Winter Olympics, Marseille was named the European Capital of Culture for 2013, beating out Bordeaux, Toulouse and Lyon. Even as in 2009 60 MPs, publicly supported by Sarkozy, called for a national commission to consider outlawing the burka, Marseille highlighted its position as a cultural, economic and religious crossroads, with Bernard Latarjet of the Marseille-Provence 2013 project stressing the city's role in fostering 'the rebirth, in new forms, of mutual understanding and shared diversity'.

» 2004	» 2005	» 2005
A local diver uncovers the wreckage of the plane of Antoine de Saint-Exupéry, author of *Le Petit Prince*, who plunged to his death in July 1944.	The French send the fantastic notion of European unity tumbling out the window with their fierce rejection of the European constitution in a referendum.	After the end of a three-month mourning period for his father, Prince Albert II of Monaco is crowned monarch of the world's second-smallest country.

BACKGROUND

Marseille continues to enhance its cultural facilities in preparation for hosting myriad exhibitions and programs.

Other plans are underway to keep Provence at the fore. A new €15 billion TGV route announced in 2009 will connect Marseille to Nice by 2025 and will thus cut Paris to Nice travel times from 5½ to 3¾ hours. A train tunnel will also be built beneath Marseille, allowing travellers to get from Marseille to Nice in only one hour.

Never a stagnant region, Provence should steam into the future as full of activity, controversy and creativity as ever.

» 2006	» 2008	» 2008
Zinadine Zidane, the superstar footballer from Marseilles and former European footballer of the year, retires after the 2006 World Cup final.	France's 35-hour work week is effectively scrapped as employers are allowed to enforce a longer week on staffers.	Marseille celebrates as it is voted Capital of Culture for 2013, and the city begins to prepare for hosting the big year of events.

THE ARTS

· · · · · · ·

It all started in St-Tropez, that quaint old fishing village on the Mediterranean. Yet those bohemian days of impoverished artists sharing studio space, using their artistic creations as a form of currency to drink and dine very well indeed, are over (although those priceless art collections nonchalantly strung inside St-Paul de Vence's La Colombe d'Or and Biot's Restaurant des Arcades are a lovely lingering reminder). The artistic pace in this artistic-dynamo pocket of southern France today is fast and furious, fuelled by a frenetic, creative energy that finds expression in an orgy of diverse and ground-breaking mediums. One look at the portfolio of Documents d'Artistes (www.documentsdartistes.org), an association in Marseille that catalogues and diffuses the work of contemporary regional artists around the world, proves this: be it tracing a line along the surface of the planet, creating sound installations, or producing inflatable or mechanical art, it is happening here.

> *'The artistic pace in this artistic-dynamo pocket of southern France today is fast and furious'*

The high profile attributed to younger artists echoes the region's natural leaning towards the avant-garde: Avignon has its theatre-driven Festival Off (p107); Marseille has La Friche la Belle de Mai (p55) and La Cité des Arts de la Rue (p330); while legendary Côte d'Azur art centres – Nice, Vence, St-Paul de Vence, Vallauris and Mougins – are rich in one-person *ateliers* (artisan's workshops).

PAINTING & VISUAL ARTS

Contemporary art in the region rides on the back of an extraordinary artistic legacy. For images of the very best of 20th-century art in the region, see p36.

PAPAL PLEASURES TO ROCOCO SILLINESS

In the 14th century Sienese, French and Spanish artists working at the papal court in Avignon created an influential style of mural painting, examples of which can be seen in the city's Palais des Papes – or rather on postcards featuring the paintings that once adorned the palace's now very bare interior.

While the rest of France found itself preoccupied with the Hundred Years' War, art flourished in Nice county, where the School of Nice emerged, led by Louis Bréa. Much exalted as the 'Fra Angelico Provençal', Louis Bréa created the burgundy colour known as *rouge bréa*. View his works at Église Notre Dame in Cimiez (p201). In the Vallée de la Roya, meanwhile, a pair of artists from northern Italy set to work on the beautiful Notre Dame des Fontaines (p190).

Blind-man's bluff, stolen kisses and other courtly frivolities were the focus of Enlightenment artists. Influential Avignon-born Joseph Vernet (1714–89) left a series depicting French ports. Rococo influences brushed the landscapes of Jean-Honoré Fragonard (1732–1806), whose playful and often licentious scenes immortalised his native Grasse. The elevated style of Nice-born Carle van Loo (1705–65) represented rococo's more serious 'grand style'.

19TH CENTURY

The strong empathy with nature expressed in watercolour by François Marius Granet (1775–1849), an Aix-en-Provence artist, was a trademark of early-19th-century Provençal painters.

Landscape painting further evolved under Gustave Courbet (1819–77), a frequent visitor to southern France, where he taught Provençal realist Paul Guigou (1834–71). A native of Villars in the Vaucluse, Guigou painted the Durance plains overdrenched in bright sunlight.

Provence's intensity of light drew the Impressionists, among them Alfred Sisley (1839–99) and Pierre-Auguste Renoir (1841–1919), who lived in Cagnes-sur-Mer from 1903 until his death. Many of his works are displayed in the Musée Renoir (p254), his former home and studio.

Paul Cézanne (1839–1906), celebrated for his still-life and landscape works, spent his entire life in Aix-en-Provence and painted numerous canvases in and around the fountain city (p71).

Southern France was also immortalised by Paul Gauguin (1848–1904). In Arles, Gauguin worked with Vincent van Gogh (1854–90), who spent most of his painting

CONTEMPORARY ART TALK

Nowhere is the dialogue sparkier than in Marseille, where a potent cocktail of street-art projects, artists' residencies and public forums keeps the debate raging.

At La Friche, **Astérides** (www.asterides.org) – an association committed to launching young unknown artists – invites contemporary artists to present their work to an audience of local artists and art-lovers. On top of these twice-monthly vibrant Garage Hermétique sessions, it provides studio space for young artists and hosts contemporary art exhibitions. Installation artist Gilles Barbier (b 1965) is among the well-known local artists behind Astérides; see his work at Nîmes' Carrée d'Art (p140).

In a rejuvenated soap and oil factory complex in Marseille, 'theatrical laboratory' **La Cité des Arts de la Rue** (☎ 04 91 03 20 75; www.lacitedesartsdelarue.net, in French; 225 av des Aygalades, 15e) generates further art talk: emerging artists temporarily reside in studios on the industrial site alongside arts and culture 'diffuser' **Karwan** (www.karwan.info); musical street-theatre **Générik Vapeur** (www.generikvapeur.com); mechanical workshop **Sud Side** (www.sudside.org), where urban installations, stage sets and furniture are created; and **Lézarap'art** (www.lezarapart.com), which, among other things, runs brilliant mechanical-art workshops. La Cité des Arts de la Rue is also home to national centre for the creation of street art **Lieux Public** (www.lieuxpublics.com) and Europe's first further-education establishment dedicated to street art, **FAI AR** (www.faiar.org).

At the other end of the coast in Nice, contemporary art centre **Villa Arson** (☎ 04 92 07 73 73; www.villa-arson.org; 20 av Stephane Liégeard, Nice) fires dialogue and encourages artistic activity with artists' residencies, workshops and some truly fantastic exhibitions.

BACKGROUND

life in Paris and Arles. A brilliant artist, Van Gogh produced haunting self-portraits and landscapes, in which colour assumes an expressive and emotive quality (see also p89). Unfortunately, Van Gogh's talent was largely unrecognised during his lifetime and just one of his paintings remains in the region (in Avignon's Musée Angladon, p107).

Pointillism was developed by Georges Seurat (1859–91), who applied paint in small dots or with uniform brush strokes of unmixed colour. His most devout pupil was Paul Signac (1863–1935), who settled in St-Tropez from 1892. Part of the Musée de l'Annonciade (p281) in St-Tropez is devoted to pointillist works.

20TH CENTURY

On the Côte d'Azur, leading fauvist exponent Henri Matisse (1869–1954) spent his most creative years lapping up the sunlight and vivacity of the coast in and around Nice, where dozens of his works can be enjoyed (p201). The chapel he designed for nuns in Vence (p256) is a particular gem. While in St-Tropez with Signac, Matisse began sketches that produced *Luxe, Calme et Volupté* (Luxury, Calm and Tranquillity). Pointillism's signature uniform brush-strokes were still evident, but were also intermingled with splashes of violent colour. His subsequent painting, *La Gitane* (1906) – displayed in St-Tropez's Musée de l'Annonciade (p281) – is the embodiment of fauvism.

> '*Matisse spent his most creative years lapping up the sunlight and vivacity of the coast*'

Cubism was launched in 1907 by Spanish prodigy Pablo Picasso (1881–1973), for whom Provence – specifically Antibes and Vallauris – had a tremendous importance. As demonstrated in Picasso's pioneering *Les Demoiselles d'Avignon* (The Young Ladies of Avignon), cubism deconstructed the subject into a system of intersecting planes and presented various aspects of it simultaneously. The collage, incorporating bits of cloth, wood, string, newspaper and anything lying around, was a cubist speciality.

After WWI the School of Paris was formed by a group of expressionists, mostly foreign, such as Belarusian Marc Chagall (1887–1985), who lived in France from 1922 and spent his last few years in St-Paul de Vence; his grave can be visited at the town's cemetery (p257). See Chagall works at Nice's Musée National Message Biblique Marc Chagall (p201) and St-Paul de Vence's Fondation Marguerite et Aime Maeght (p257).

With the onset of WWII many artists left and, although some later returned, the region never regained its old magnetism. Picasso moved permanently to the Côte d'Azur, settling first in Golfe-Juan, then Vallauris and finally Mougins, where he died. In 1946 he set up his studio in Antibes' Château Grimaldi (p250) and later painted a chapel (p250).

The 1960s ushered in new realists Arman, Yves Klein and César, and art generated from recycled trash, dirty crockery, crushed cars and scrap metal. Marseille-born César Baldaccini (1921–98), after whom the French cinema awards, the Césars, are named (he created the little statue handed to actors at the awards), was greatly inspired by Michelangelo. He started using wrought iron and scrap metals but later graduated to pliable plastics. From 1960 he crushed motor cars and sculpted the occasional gargantuan thumb (p54).

In 1960 Nice-born Klein (1928–62) produced *Anthropométrie de l'Époque Bleue* – blue imprints made by two naked women (covered from head to toe in blue paint) rolling around on a white canvas – in front of an orchestra of violins and an audience in evening dress. Nice-born Arman (b 1928) became known for his trash-can portraits, made by framing the litter found in the subject's rubbish bin. Another influential realist was Martial Rayasse, born in Golfe-Juan in 1936, renowned for pioneering the use of neon in art. Most notable is his 1964 portrait of *Nissa Bella* (Beautiful Nice) – a flashing blue heart on a human face.

> '*beehive-shaped huts built from dry limestone called bories can be seen near Gordes*'

Hungarian-born Victor Vasarely (1908–97) was in Gordes from 1948, working with geometrical forms juxtaposed in contrasting colours to create shifting perspectives. Works by the avant-gardist hang in Aix-en-Provence's Fondation Vasarely (p72). Stained glass he designed casts patterns across a chapel in Port Grimaud (p289).

The 1970s Supports-Surfaces movement focused on deconstructing the traditional concept of a painting and transforming one of its structural components – such as the frame or canvas – into a work of art instead. The Groupe 70, specific to Nice, expressed an intellectual agitation, typical to Vivien Isnard's 1987 *Sans Titre* (Without Title) and Louis Chacallis' *Tension* (1978). In the 1990s bold paintings of naked angels brought world fame to Arles-born Louis Feraud (1921–99), an artist and couturier who dressed Brigitte Bardot and Ingrid Bergman in the 1950s.

Contemporary works by both foreign and local artists who influence the French-Riviera art scene – including resident Nice artist, Ben (b 1935) – form the backbone of the pioneering tram art project in Nice (p202).

ARCHITECTURE

From old stone villages built on hillocks to cutting-edge glass design: this region covers a fabulous architectural spectrum.

PREHISTORIC TO VILLAGES PERCHÉS

See remnants of stone megaliths at Marseille's Musée d'Archéologie Méditerranéenne in the Centre de la Vieille Charité (p50) and Quinson's Musée de la Préhistoire des Gorges du Verdon (p179). Numerous petroglyphs are evident in the Vallée des Merveilles (p188) and examples of the region's earliest habitats – beehive-shaped huts built from dry limestone called *bories* – can be seen near Gordes (p153).

To view the Romans' colossal architectural legacy look no further than Pont du Gard (p143), gargantuan amphitheatres in Nîmes (p140) and Arles (p85), open-air theatres in Orange (p115) and Fréjus (p272), Nîmes' Maison Carrée (p140) and the triumphal arches at Orange and Carpentras (p124).

Bar the octagonal 5th-century baptistry that can be visited in Fréjus (p272), few churches constructed between the 5th and 10th centuries remain.

BACKGROUND

ROMANESQUE TO RENAISSANCE

A religious revival in the 11th century ushered in Romanesque architecture, so-called because of the Gallo-Roman architectural elements it adopted. Round arches, heavy walls with few windows, and a lack of ornamentation were characteristics of this style, Provence's most famous examples being the 12th-century abbeys in Sénanque (p153), Le Thoronet (p291) and Silvacane (p164). You can visit all three.

Fortresslike sacred buildings also marked this era, as the majestic Chartreuse de la Verne (p296), the older monastery on Île St-Honorat (p247) and the church at Stes-Maries de la Mer (p94) demonstrate. The exceptional dimensions of Digne-les-Bains cathedral (p182) are typical of the late Provençal-Romanesque style.

Provence's most important examples of Gothic architecture are Avignon's Palais des Papes (p104), the Chartreuse du Val de Bénédiction (p112) in Villeneuve-lès-Avignon, and Carpentras' Cathédrale St-Siffrein (p125). Look for ribbed vaults carved with great precision, pointed arches, slender verticals, chapels along the nave and chancel, refined decoration and large stained-glass windows.

The French Renaissance scarcely touched the region – unlike mighty citadel architect Sébastien Le Prestre de Vauban (1633–1707), who thundered in with Antibes' star-shaped Fort Carré (p250), hilltop Entrevaux and constructions at Toulon.

CLASSICAL TO MODERN

Classical architecture fused with painting and sculpture from the end of the 16th to late 18th centuries to create stunning baroque structures with interiors of great subtlety, refinement and elegance: Chapelle de la Miséricorde in Nice, Menton's Italianate Basilique St-Michel Archange and Marseille's Centre de la Vieille Charité are classics.

Neoclassicism came into its own under Napoleon III, the Palais de Justice and Palais Masséna in Nice demonstrating the renewed interest in classical forms that it exhibited. The true showcase of this era, though, is 1878 Monte Carlo Casino (p223), designed by French architect Charles Garnier (1825–98). In 1887 Garnier, together with Gustave Eiffel (1832–1923), of tower fame and who lived in Beaulieu-sur-Mer, came up with the Observatoire de Nice (p218). Elegant Aix-en-Provence's fountains and *hôtels particuliers* (private mansions) date from this period; as do the intricate wrought-iron campaniles.

The belle époque heralded an eclecticism of decorative stucco friezes, trompe l'œil paintings, glittering wall mosaics, brightly coloured Moorish minarets and Turkish towers. Anything went.

Hyères' 1920s concrete-and-glass Villa Noailles (p309) is a stark expression of the cubist movement, which gained momentum in the interwar period. Examples of surrealist interiors designed by Jean Cocteau include Menton's Salles des Mariages, Chapelle St-Pierre in Villefranche-sur-Mer and Cap d'Ail's amphitheatre.

Aix-en-Provence's Fondation Vasarely (p72), designed by Victor Vasarely (1908–97), was an architectural coup when unveiled in 1976. Its 14 giant monumental hexagons reflected what he had already achieved in art: the creation of optical illusion and changing perspective through the juxtaposition of geometrical shapes and colours. This 'father of Op Art' went on to design the town hall in La Seyne-sur-Mer, near Toulon, and the stained-glass windows inside Port Grimaud's church.

BACKGROUND

On the Grande Corniche, east of Nice, Roquebrune's Vista Palace is a marvellous gawp-worthy piece of 1970s architecture.

CONTEMPORARY ARCHITECTURE

Nothing competes with Mouans-Sartoux's lime-green building, designed by Swiss-based architects Annette Gigon and Mike Guyer to complement the village's 16th-century château (p266); or Sacha Sosno's square head in Nice (p202). Other striking examples of contemporary architecture include French architect Rudi Ricciotti's Pavillon Noir in Aix-en-Provence (p340); Monaco's Grimaldi Forum (www.grimaldiforum .com), with several designer dining spaces, two-thirds of which sits beneath sea level; MAMAC in Nice (p202) and the Fondation Maeght (p257). Nîmes' steel-and-glass Carrée d'Art (p140) and the Musée de la Préhistoire des Gorges du Verdon in Quinson (p179) were designed by British architect Sir Norman Foster, who is designing a new five-storey building for Monaco Yacht Club, to open 2012.

Italian architect Vittorio Gregotti's theatre in Aix-en-Provence; the €70 million extension of Riviera legend Grand Hôtel du Cap Ferrat (www.grand-hotel-cap-ferrat. com), by Nice-based hot-shot architect Luc Svetchine (www.lucsvetchine.com); and the cultural centre Frank Gehry is designing for Arles, to be open by 2013 (p84), are all guaranteed stunners.

Urban 20th-century architecture is the focus of Patrimoine XXème, a national government-funded project protecting 33 edifices in the Provence-Alpes-Côte d'Azur region: a 1920s Marseille silo, a dazzling white 1930s summer house in Antibes, Toulon port and a hydroelectric power plant. Read all about it at www.culture.gouv.fr/paca/dossiers/xxeme.

CINEMA

Posing on the steps where many a silver-screen star has stood during the glitzy glam Cannes film festival (p245), or viewing cinema personified on Cannes' bus-station wall are film-buff musts. To sense the grit of regional film-making, tour the film studios at Marseille's La Friche La Belle de Mai (p55), where one of Europe's highest sets stands 17m tall.

With its spectacular light and subtle shadows, southern France was inspirational to cinema: one of the world's first motion pictures, by the Lumière brothers, premiered in Château Lumière in the shipyard resort of La Ciotat, midway between Marseille and Toulon, in September 1895. The series of two-minute reels, entitled *L'Arrivée d'un Train en Gare de La Ciotat* (The Arrival of a Train at La Ciotat Station), made the audience leap out of their seats as the steam train rocketed forward. In March 1899 the brothers opened Eden Théâtre in La Ciotat.

French film flourished in the 1920s, Nice being catapulted to stardom by Hollywood director Rex Ingram, who bought the city's Victorine film studios in 1925 and transformed them overnight into the hub of European film-making.

A big name was Aubagne-born writer Marcel Pagnol, whose career kicked off in 1931 with *Marius,* the first part of his *Fanny* trilogy, portraying prewar Marseille. Pagnol filmed *La Femme du Boulanger* (The Baker's Wife; 1938) in Castellet. These films

TRAILING LE CORBUSIER

Le Corbusier rewrote the architectural stylebook in southern France: track him down in Marseille (where he built the ground-breaking Unité d'Habitation), Cap Martin (where he had a studio) and Roquebrune (where he's buried).

It was the latter part of his life that saw Swiss-born Charles Édouard Jeanneret (1887–1965), alias Le Corbusier, turn to Provence. Of all his architectural achievements, it was the concrete apartment block he designed in Marseille that was the most revolutionary. Built between 1947 and 1952 as a low-cost housing project, **L'Unitè d'Habitation** saw 337 apartments arranged inside an elongated block on stilts. The building was considered a coup by architects worldwide and the façade, communal corridors and rooftop terrace of the block have together been protected as an historical monument since 1986; it can be visited by guided tour (p56). Apartments on the 7th and 8th floors function as a hotel (p378); the rest are private flats.

Le Corbusier frequently visited the coast from the 1930s, often staying with his architect friends, Irish Eileen Gray and Romanian-born Jean Badovici, in their 1920s seaside villa, **E-1027** (www.e1027.org), on Cap Martin. In 1938 Le Corbusier painted a trio of wall frescoes in E-1027, one of which featured three entangled women and offended Gray (a proclaimed lesbian) so much that she broke off her friendship with Le Corbusier and moved to Menton.

After WWII, Le Corbusier befriended Thomas Rebutato, who ran L'Étoile de Mer, a neighbouring shack restaurant. He bought a plot of land from Rebutato and in 1951 created **Le Cabanon**, a cabin containing everything needed for holiday living in 13 sq metres, which he gave to his wife, Monégasque model Yvonne Gallis, as a birthday present. It remained their summer home until 1965 when Le Corbusier had a heart attack while swimming in the sea.

Future plans for Le Cabanon will see the site developed as a museum and architectural research centre, incorporating the cabin, L'Étoile de Mer (p215) and E-1027 (inhabited by squatters from 1990 until 1999). The coastal footpath promenade Le Corbusier leads from Roquebrune-Cap Martin train station to the site; exit the station and bear left along the *sentier littoral* (coastal path; signposted 'Plage de Carnolés').

Le Corbusier is buried with his wife in section J of Roquebrune cemetery (p217). His grave (he designed it before his death) is adorned by a cactus and the epitaph, painted in Le Corbusier's cursive hand on a small yellow, red and blue ceramic tile: *ici repose Charles Édouard Jeanneret (1887–1965)*.

launched the career of France's earliest silver-screen heroes: Toulon-born comic actor Raimu, alias Jules Auguste César Muraire (1883–1946), and 'horse face' Fernandel (1903–71), an honorary citizen of Carry-le-Rouet, where he summered most years. Throughout his career Pagnol stuck to depicting what he knew best: Provence and its ordinary people.

Portraits of ordinary people dominated film until the 1950s, when surrealist Jean Cocteau (1889–1963) eschewed realism in two masterpieces of cinematic fantasy: *La Belle et la Bête* (Beauty and the Beast; 1945) and *Orphée* (Orpheus; 1950). Both starred beautiful blonde-haired Vallauris-born actor Jean Marais (1914–98), who met Cocteau in 1937 and remained his lover until Cocteau's death. Find out more about the film-maker at Menton's Musée Jean Cocteau (p232) and admire frescoes he tattooed inside Villa Santo Sospir (p214) on Cap Ferrat.

Nouvelle Vague (New Wave) directors made films without big budgets, extravagant sets or big-name stars. Roger Vadim turned St-Tropez into the hot spot to be with his *Et Dieu Créa la Femme* (And God Created Woman; 1956), starring Brigitte Bardot. Several French classics filmed in the region followed, among them François Truffaut's *Les Mistons* (The Brats; 1958), filmed exclusively in Nîmes; Jacques Démy's *La Baie des Anges* (The Bay of Angels; 1962); Henri Decoin's *Masque de Fer* (Iron Mask; 1962), parts of which were filmed in Sospel; and Rohmer's *La Collectionneuse* (The Collectors; 1966), again shot in St-Tropez. In 1972 Truffaut filmed part of *La Nuit Américaine* (The American Night; 1972) in the Victorine studios, the Niçois hinterland and the Vésubie Valley.

Generous state subsidies to film-makers focused on costume dramas and heritage movies in the 1980s, prompting a renewed interest in Pagnol's great Provençal classics. Parts of Claude Berri's *Jean de Florette* and *Manon des Sources* were shot in the Massif de la Ste-Baume, and in 1990 Yves Robert directed film versions of Pagnol's *La Gloire de Mon Père* (My Father's Glory) and *Le Château de Ma Mère* (My Mother's Castle).

> *'With its spectacular light and subtle shadows, southern France was inspirational to cinema'*

Big-name stars, slick production values and a strong sense of nostalgia were dominant motifs of the 1998 Hollywood box-office hit *The Man in the Iron Mask*, set in the late 17th century on Île Ste-Marguerite, near Cannes.

Born in L'Estaque near Marseille to an Armenian mother and German docker father, Robert Guédiguian (b 1953) is the region's most successful experimental film-maker. Working with the same actors – including his beautiful wife and muse Ariane Ascaride (who won Best Actress at the 1998 Césars) – is his trademark, as is his commitment to a realist portrayal of Marseille and its inhabitants. Of his many films, *Marius et Jeannette* (1997) and *Marie-Jo et Ses Deux Amours* (Marie-Jo and Her Two Loves; 2002) are the best known. His most recent are cop drama *Lady Jane* (2008) and the powerful *L'Armée du Crime* (The Army of Crime; 2009), which investigates the tragic tale of a group of WWII resistance fighters led by Armenian immigrant Missak Manouchian.

LITERATURE

COURTLY LOVE TO SADISM

Lyric poems of courtly love, written by troubadours solely in Occitan, *langue d'oc,* dominated medieval Provençal literature. Indeed it was traditional Provençal songs and troubadour ballads that imagist poet Ezra Pound took and adapted to suit modern tastes in his two poetry collections, *Provença* (1910) and *Cantos* (1919).

Provençal life featured in the works of Italian poet Petrarch (1304–74), exiled in 1327 to Avignon, where he met Laura, to whom he dedicated his life's works. Petrarch lived in Fontaine de Vaucluse from 1337 to 1353, where he composed his song book

Canzonière and wrote poems and letters about local shepherds, fishermen he met on the banks of the Sorgue, and his pioneering ascent up Mont Ventoux.

Bellaud de la Bellaudière (1533–88), a Grasse native, wrote *Oeuvres et Rîmes* in Occitan. The literary landmark is a book of 160 sonnets drawing on influences by Petrarch and French epic writer Rabelais.

In 1555 the philosopher and visionary writer from St-Rémy de Provence, Nostradamus (1503–66), published (in Latin) his prophetic *Centuries* in Salon de Provence, where he lived until his death (from gout, as he had predicted). Find out why the papal authorities banned his work as blasphemous at Salon de Provence's Maison de Nostradamus (p68).

The 17th-century *grand siècle* (great century) yielded Nicolas Saboly's the *Noëls Provençaux*, poems encapsulating a nativity scene, the pious tone typical of the strait-laced fervour dominating baroque Provençal literature.

TOP 10 FILMS STARRING PROVENCE

* **To Catch a Thief** (1956) Classic Hitchcock suspense starring Cary Grant and Grace Kelly
* **Et Dieu Créa la Femme** (And God Created Woman; 1956) Roger Vadim's tale of the amorality of modern youth made stars out of Bardot and St-Tropez
* **Le Gendarme de St-Tropez** (1964) Fast-paced, farcical and utterly French film in which an ambitious but incompetent police officer is transferred to St-Tropez and makes it his mission to crack down on the local nudists. Meanwhile, daughter Nicole fibs her way into high society by pretending her dad's a high-rolling yacht owner.
* **Herbie Goes to Monte Carlo** (1977) Disney lovable about Herbie the Volkswagen Beetle and his race to Monte Carlo to take part in the Monte Carlo Rally
* **Taxi 3** (2003) Comedy guaranteed to raise a giggle; filmed and set in Marseille
* **Swimming Pool** (2002) A dispirited middle-aged English novelist seeks repose and inspiration in the Luberon at the summer house of her publisher, only for the latter's high-spirited, sexy and very French daughter to show up. Directed by François Ozon.
* **The Statement** (2004) Norman Jewison film set in Vichy France and starring Michael Caine; shot on location in Marseille and in the village of Ste-Anne d'Evenos, northwest of Toulon
* **Brice de Nice** (2005) Hilarious take on cult surfing movie *Point Break*. Surfing dude and poseur Brice, aka charismatic French comic actor Jean Dujardin, waits for *sa vague* (his wave) to come in waveless Nice (great shots of the town).
* **A Good Year** (2006) Ridley Scott's adaptation of the Peter Mayle novel, filmed at Château La Canorgue in Bonnieux. London financier May Skinner inherits his uncle's wine-producing château in the Luberon and, all too predictably, falls in love with the place after hard-heartedly vowing to sell it for the cash.
* **Mr Bean's Holiday** (2007) The lovable Mini Cooper–mad, teddy bear–loving buffoon, Mr Bean, holidays on the Côte d'Azur and somehow gets his video diary entered into the Cannes film festival

BACKGROUND

MISTRAL TO MAYLE

The 19th century witnessed a revival in Provençal literature, thanks to Frédéric Mistral (1830–1914), the only minority-language writer so far to be awarded a Nobel Prize for literature (1904). Born in 1830 in a farmhouse on the outskirts of Maillane, a village 7km northwest of Rémy de Provence, Mistral moved into the centre of the village with his mother following the death of his father. Upon marrying, 46-year-old Mistral left home, only to move with his 19-year-old wife into the house opposite his mother's – a fusty house-museum today – where he lived until his death. Mistral is buried in the village cemetery.

Mistral's passion for Provence and its culture, history and language was awakened by his Avignon tutor Joseph Roumanille (1818–91) who published *Li Margarideto* in 1847. In 1851 Mistral began his epic poem, *Mirèio,* which tells the story of a beauty who flees to Stes-Maries de la Mer when her parents forbid her to marry her true love, only to die of a broken heart on the beach. Three years later, the literary movement Le Félibrige was founded by seven young Provençal poets, including Mistral, who pledged to revive the Provençal dialect and codify its orthography. Between 1878 and 1886 Mistral's most influential work on Provençal culture was published – the monumental Occitan dictionary, *Lou Trésor dou Félibrige.* The 1890s saw Le Félibrige popularise his work with the opening of the Museon Arlaten (p86) and the publication of the *L'Aïoli* journal.

Another outstanding Provençal writer was Nîmes-born Alphonse Daudet (1840–97), who wrote *Lettres de Mon Moulin* (Letters from My Windmill; 1869) in Fontvieille. Daudet is best remembered for his comic novels evoking small-town Tarascon through the eyes of antihero Tartarin: his *Tartarin de Tarascon* trilogy was published between 1872 and 1890.

Parisian novelist Émile Zola (1840–1902) lived in Aix-en-Provence from the age of three to 18. Zola aimed to convert novel writing from an art to a science by the application of experimentation – a theory that, though naive, produced powerful works. Aix-en-Provence is evoked in *La Conquête de Plassans* (The Conquest of Plassans; 1874), and his friendship with Cézanne is the focus of *L'Oeuvre* (The Masterpiece; 1886).

Early-20th-century Provençal literature is dominated by writers depicting their homeland. Jean Giono (1895–1970), from Manosque, blended myth with reality in novels that remain a celebration of the Provençal Alps and their people. British novelist and travel writer Lawrence Durrell (1912–90) settled in Somières, near Nîmes, and dedicated the last 33 years of his literary career to writing about Provençal life.

Surrealism was expressed by Jean Cocteau (1889–1963), French poet and filmmaker who ran away from home to the Côte d'Azur at the age of 15, returned in 1924 and is buried in Menton. His best-known novel, *Les Enfants Terribles* (1955), portrays the intellectual rebellion of the postwar era.

Colette (1873–1954), who thoroughly enjoyed tweaking the nose of conventional readers with titillating novels detailing the amorous exploits of such heroines as the schoolgirl Claudine, lived in St-Tropez from 1927 until 1938. *La Naissance du Jour* (Break of Day) evokes an unspoilt St-Tropez.

BACKGROUND

Roussillon served as a refuge to playwright Samuel Beckett during WWII; he stayed until April 1945 and wrote *Watt* there. The post-WWII years saw the existentialist literary movement develop around Jean-Paul Sartre (1905–80), Simone de Beauvoir (1908–86) and Albert Camus (1913–60). The latter moved to Lourmarin (where he is buried) in 1957; he started his unfinished autobiographical novel *Le Premier Homme* (The First Man) there. The manuscript was found in the wreckage when the Algerian-born writer – son of an illiterate mother – died in a car accident three years later.

Writers who settled in the region in the latter part of their careers include Lawrence Durrell, Dirk Bogarde, James Baldwin, Anthony Burgess and Peter Mayle. Provence-inspired novels written by foreign writers are listed at the start of the regional chapters in this book.

MUSIC

Contemporary music is pretty much a one-stop shop, immigrant life in Marseille *banlieue* (suburbs) proving the inspiration behind a diverse and influential scene enjoyed by an audience far further flung than the beat-hot port city.

The hip hop lyrics of the 1991 smash-hit first album, *de la Planète Mars* ('from Planet Mars', Mars being short for Marseille) by rapping legend IAM – France's best-known rap group from Marseille – nudged rap into the mainstream. Since that time, the city's music scene has transcended its rap roots. 'It has exploded, in all styles. Marseille is a rich place for music; it's not pigeonholed into rap and hip hop any more', says Stéphane Galland, music director of alternative Marseillais radio station, Radio Grenouille (Radio Frog; www.grenouille888.org, in French), on air 24/7 since 1981 and famed across France for broadcasting tomorrow's music. Ten to 15 demo CDs land on Stéphane's desk every day, not to mention a clutch of CDs from record labels, all angling for air space. After their lucky break, many artists return to the Grenouille studios to jam live on the station that launched them.

> 'The 19th century witnessed a revival in Provençal literature, thanks to Frédéric Mistral'

Massilia Sound System is another Marseille-born band: 'They initiated reggae in France,' explains Stéphane, 'using a south-of-France sound as a vehicle for their own identity.' The Rub a Dub trio is involved in dozens of side projects too: lead singer Moussu-T performs blues, calypso, south-of-France and acoustic music and also heads the trio Moussu T e lei jouvants (http://moussut.ohaime.com in French), a band that draws on the musical melting pot of 1930s Marseille – a mix of traditional Provençal, local operettas and imported black music – for inspiration. Its four albums, *Mademoiselle Marseille* (2005), *Foreever Polida* (2006), *Inventé à La Ciotat* (2007) and *Home Sweet Home* (2008) are fabulous.

In world music, 20-something Iranian percussionist Bijan Chemirani stuns with rhythmic playing of the *zarb* (Persian goblet drum), and his debut solo album *Eos* (2002) was hot. *Kismet* (2005) and *Balkanic Jazz* (2008) followed.

BACKGROUND

Cheb Khaled, Cheb Aïssa and Cheb Mami – all from the same multicultural port-side city – have contributed hugely to the development of Algerian rai. 'You can't do rai without passing through Marseille,' says Stéphane whose music knowledge is encyclopedic. 'Marseille is a mecca, but the scene is underground, very community based, in small, low-budget venues, not very visible. You'll always hear guys playing it in cars on the streets, though,' he adds. And on jazz: 'Marseille has a lot of very good jazz – traditional, modern, electro jazz…the whole spectrum.'

Traditional Provençal chants form the root of the powerful percussion-accompanied polyphony by Lo Còr de la Plana (www.myspace.com/locordelaplana), a six-voice male choir born in the La Plaine quarter of Marseille whose Provençal name translates as *la cœur de la Plaine* (the heart of La Plaine). Their album, *Tant deman* (2007), is essential listening.

DANCE

The *farandole* is a Provençal dance, performed at the close of village festivals in and around Arles since the Middle Ages. Men and women take their partner by the hand or remain linked with a cord or handkerchief as they briskly jig, accompanied by a tambourine and *galoubet* (shrill flute with three holes).

Long at the forefront of contemporary dance, Aix-en-Provence is home to France's **Centre Chorégraphique National** (CNN, National Choreographic Centre; rue des Allummettes). Also known as the Pavillon Noir, this glass, steel and black-concrete box has a 378-seat auditorium, roof deck and glass-walled rehearsal studios that allow passers-by to peer in and watch agile dancers at work. At its front end is French-Albanian-born choreographer, Angelin Preljocaj (b 1957) and resident dance company **Ballet Preljocaj** (www

---

DON'T MISS...

DANCE DRAMA

- ★ **Al Masîra** // French-Arabic fusion of contemporary and oriental dance from Marseille; choreography by dancer Virginie Recolin (www.virginierecolin.com)

- ★ **Compagnie Lézards Bleus** // Apt-based company known for its architectural choreography, aka vertical dance performances staged on building facades (www.lezardsbleus.com)

- ★ **Kubilai Khan Investigations** // Mixed-media urban dance company from Marseille with heavy accent on hip hop, photography and video art (www.kubilai-khan-investigations.com)

- ★ **Onstap** // Body percussion is the beat of this Avignon company, whose performers clap out their dance rhythm with their feet, on thighs etc (www.onstap.com)

- ★ **Pascal Montrouge** // Company split between Hyères and Réunion Island, headed by Pascal Montrouge (www.pascalmontrouge.fr)

BACKGROUND

.preljocaj.org), one of Europe's most creative, at times shocking, dance groups, known for pushing dance to its limits.

Avignon meanwhile hosts the annual dance festival, **Les Hivernales** (www.hivernales -avignon.com) each February at Hivernales, the other big choreography centre in the region.

Provence's innovative spirit in contemporary dance echoes the role France played in the development of 19th-century classical ballet – until the centre for innovation shifted to Russia in 1847, taking France's leading talent, Marius Petipa (1818–1910), a native of Marseille, with it. The **Ballet National de Marseille** (www.ballet-de-marseille.com) continues in a classical vein today.

It was in Nice in 1927 that modern-dance icon Isadora Duncan (1878–1927), Paris resident from 1900, died. Her neck was broken in a freak motoring accident on the Riviera when the customary scarf that trailed behind her got caught in the car wheels.

LYRICAL LANDSCAPES: CORK, LAVENDER & SWEET JASMINE
· · · · · · ·

A vibrant paintbox of burnt-orange ochre (see p154), russet-red rock (p266), and golden-stone villages (see p38), landscapes are the soul of Provence and what gives it colour.

Among its unique and vibrant landscapes are the thick cork-oak forest of the Massif des Maures – a wild maze of chocolate brown, gentle ginger and brick-red tree trunks; the spring-green lavender fields of Haute-Provence and the Luberon, which blaze blue in early summer and sit out autumn in a cropped wash of pale grey-blue; and the flower fields of Grasse that blossom with sweet rose and jasmine, from which perfumes are made.

THE CORK HARVESTER

Born-and-bred forest stock, Fabien Tamboloni leads guided hikes in the chestnut- and cork-rich forest around La Garde Freinet for the Conservatoire du Patrimoine et Traditions du Freinet (p297). His unreserved passion for and extraordinary ease in the forest is spellbinding, as I discovered during one of his guided group walks. When he's not captivating cork-curious minds with his axe-chopping, cork-harvesting prowess, the forest technician with earthy good looks and gentle humour is a tree surgeon and researcher at an experimental plantation for France's Centre de Formation Professionnelle Forestière.

'I grew up in the forest, in the Jura, not far from Switzerland. The forest is my home,' he explained, adding 'for me this is not a tree, it's a plane tree' pointing to the *platane* we were standing under on a village square in La Garde Freinet.

DON'T MISS...

COASTAL SCENES

Espaces naturels protégés (protected natural areas) tended by the Conservatoire du Littoral (www.conservatoire-du-littoral.fr) are among the region's most beautiful, oftentimes remote, coastal landscapes.

* ★ **Archipel de Riou //** Cluster of uninhabited limestone islands offshore from Marseille, sheltering 30% of France's Cory's shearwater population (p61)
* ★ **Presqu'île de Port-Miou //** Peninsula laced with *calanques* (rocky inlets)
* ★ **Côte Bleue //** The Blue Coast (p65)
* ★ **Cap Lardier & Cap Taillat //** Wildife-rich capes (p288)
* ★ **Former salt marshes //** On La Capte near Hyères (p307)
* ★ **Massif de l'Estérel //** Red rock massif (p266)
* ★ **Corniche des Maures & Domaine du Rayol //** Lush coastline crammed with Mediterranean flora (p298)
* ★ **The Camargue //** Astonishing birdlife (p79)

BACKGROUND

Introductions done, the long-haired 30-something naturalist with well-used walking boots and a hole in his trousers (don't ask where) lopped his Catalan axe over his shoulder and off we strode up the street, around the corner and 'gosh, here already', into the forest.

Cork oak *(chêne-liège)* trees have grown in the western Mediterranean basin for 60 million years, but it was not until the 17th century, when a Benedictine monk called Dom Pérignon started bottling sparkling wine in glass, that a cork industry emerged. Cutting out cylindrical wedges from the tree's honeycomb-textured bark – cork – and stuffing them in the bottles was quickly found to be the best means of conserving wine.

'Cork is impermeable, lightweight, soft and a great thermal insulator. More importantly, it protects the tree against sun and fire; it doesn't burn,' says Fabien, quick to explain that a cork oak tree – once stripped of its bark – is unprotected from fire for two years. In tracts of forest affected by fire, trunks are charred black but the tree lives.

> *'The suddenly-skinny trunk is gentle ginger in colour, wet, warm and wrinkly.'*

Harvesting cork is a delicate business. It is only allowed mid-June to mid-August when the tree is physiologically active. The bark must be at least 3cm thick, making the tree a minimum of 40 to 60 years old. One wrong move and *la mère* (the mother), the amber-coloured layer beneath the cork, is damaged and the tree's internal balance turned upside-down. 'Cork should only be harvested in the morning – the afternoon is too hot,' Fabien tells us, at this point on his knees, as he deftly pushes his spat-on-and-sharpened axe into the crack of around 1m that he has cut upwards from the foot of the tree. The cork creaks and groans as, inch by inch, he prises it loose from the tree. He has already cut the bevelled *'couronne'* (crown) at the top of the section he is harvesting.

With a macho yank and a flick of the ponytail, Fabien sees the cork come away in two half-pipe sheets. The suddenly-skinny trunk is a gentle ginger in colour, wet, warm and wrinkly. Within a couple of months it will turn brick red; within 12 months, brown; and within 13 years, be ready for the next harvest. But it is the fresh, heady mineral scent it exudes that is the most extraordinary.

Today's cork industry has annual revenue of approximately €1.5 billion: 'No one has ever been able to live only on cork in the Massif des Maures' says Fabien, who spent three years working at France's Mediterranean Institute of Cork where cork oak cultivation is studied, researched and developed. France produces just 1.6% of the world's cork, all of which comes from the Mediterranean, primarily Portugal and Spain. A bumper harvest in 2006 yielded 110,000 tons of raw cork in Portugal, 30,000 tonnes in Spain and between 3500 and 5500 tons in France – of which the Var produced some 50%.

Practically every mountain road in the Massif des Maures takes you through cork oak forest: the D41 between Bormes-les-Mimosas and Collobrières; the D14 from Collobrières to Grimaud; and the painfully wiggle-laced but panoramic D15 from La Garde Freint east across a succession of mountain passes – Col de Vignon (352m), Col de Gratteloup (225m) and Col de Valdingarde (392m) – are particularly cork-oak stunning.

BACKGROUND

THE PERFUME OF PROVENCE

If Provence has one defining fragrance, it is the astringent aroma of purple lavender *(lavande)*, which flowers for a month prior to harvesting between mid-June and mid-August, depending on the region. Lavender fields once seen never forgotten include those surrounding Abbaye Notre-Dame de Sénanque near Gordes and the vast farms sweeping the Plateau de Valensole, framing Largarde d'Apt and strewing the arid Sault region. See p42 for more.

The sweet purple flower is harvested when it is in full bloom, between 15 July and 15 August. It is mechanically harvested on a hot dry day, following which the lorry-loads of cut lavender, known as *paille* (straw), are packed tight in a steam still and distilled to extract the sweet essential oils. The process can be watched at the **Distillerie du Siron** (☎ 04 92 34 61 96, 06 25 12 67 17; www.distilleriesiron-lavande.fr; admission free; ☻ guided tours by advance reservation 10am-noon & 2-5pm daily Jul & Aug, by appointment rest of year), a traditional, family-run distillery and organic flower farm blazing 20 hectares blue near the medieval village of Thoard (p176), northwest of Digne-les-Bains.

All the rage in 1920s Provence, authentic lavender farms such as this are a dying breed today. Since the 1950s lavandin – a hybrid of fine lavender and aspic, cloned at the turn of the century – has been mass produced for industrial purposes. Both are the same vibrant purple when in flower, but lavandin yields five times more oil than fine lavender (which produces 1kg of oil from 130kg of cut straw). Since 1997, *huile essentielle de lavande de Haute Provence* – essential lavender oil from Haute-Provence – has been protected by its own Appellation d'Origine Contrôlée (AOC).

Approximately 80% of Provence's 400 lavender farms produce lavandin today. The few remaining traditional lavender farms – like Château du Bois (p155) in the Luberon – usually colour higher areas. Wild lavender needs an altitude of 900m to 1300m to blossom (unlike its common sister lavandin, which sprouts anywhere above 800m) and its more concentrated essences linger longer. Some 80% of the essential oils produced in the region's 150 distilleries is exported.

For a hand-in-hand stroll through lavender-laced gardens, the 13th-century gardens of the Prieuré de Salagon (p174) are a romantic proposition. A photogenic 2km walking trail wends its way through Château du Bois' lavender fields (see above) and Rando Lavande in Digne-les-Bains organises superb lavender hikes (p172). *Fêtes de la lavande* (lavender festivals) are celebrated to herald the start of the lavender harvest in Valensole (third Sunday in July), Sault (15 August), and Digne-les-Bains and Valréas (both first weekend in August).

In the kitchen lavender is used to flavour ice cream (p165), chocolate (p135), honey (p153), many a sweet dessert and the odd savoury dish.

Several restaurants serve seasonal lavender *menus* (fixed-price menus) or cuisine. In the Luberon near Lourmarin, the use of lavender and other fragrant plants is beautifully explained during one- to 1½-hour tours (in English and French) around organic aromatic plant and herb farm **Ferme de Gerbaud** (☎ 04 90 68 11 83; www.plantes-aromatiques -provence.com; adult/child €5/free; ☻ guided visits 5pm Tue, Thu & Sat Apr-Oct, 3pm Sun Nov-Mar, shop 2-7pm Apr-Nov, Sat & Sun Nov-Mar). Not only that; farm owner Paula cooks herb-infused evening meals on Thursdays; call ahead to reserve.

Whether you want to paint lavender landscapes (p148), amble with a donkey (p176), visit a lavender farm or distillery, help hand-harvest lavender, learn how to cook it, buy luxurious lavender bath salts and creams (p166), or splash out in a lavender spa, **Les Routes de la Lavande** (www.routes-lavande.com) is the ultimate information source.

SWEET JASMINE

I don't wear perfume. Never have. The most I can stomach is a quick dash of Clarins' *Eau Dynamisante* before dashing out. Even then, mood depending, the scent makes me nauseous. So creating my own perfume from the orgy of flowers – sweet rose, jasmine and violets – that bloom like mushrooms after the rain in fields around Grasse (p266) was prime opportunity to hit upon a scent that didn't make me want to leap in the shower after 10 minutes.

Sitting at my allotted 'organ' faced by a mesmerising line-up of 127 'notes' (miniature ginger-glass bottles of scent), I instantly had to pick two of nine – 'quickly, with no hesitation' explained Galimard perfumer Jacques Maurel. A *nez* (nose) for 43 years and more Grassois than Grasse (his grandfather was a *nez*), Monsieur Maurel entered his first factory when he was 22. Professional noses, of which there are 250 worldwide, combine a natural gift with several years of very hard study and a monklike lifestyle (no alcohol, smoking, coffee, garlic and spicy food) to identify – from no more than a whiff – 6000 or so scents.

My choice of two sealed the 'families' of notes my perfume would be created from: *boisée* (woody) and *fleurie* (flowery). From there on, it was a mere matter of selecting three *fond* (base) notes to fix the fragrance and ensure it lingered, three middle (heart) notes to create its unique and naturally irresistible character, and three top (peak) notes to create that vital first impression when the perfume touches the skin.

On paper, the architecture of a perfume is simple. In reality, I'd clearly smoked far too many cigarettes at university, gorged on too much late-night chicken madras, and

LAVENDER BLISS OUT

Lavender baths, algae soaks, shiatsu massages, Mediterranean mudpacks and other pampering pleasures soothe souls at a handful of spas.

* Luxuriate in a bubbling thermal bath laced with essential lavender oil at Établissement Thermal (p183) in Digne-les-Bains

* Go Roman at Thermes Sextius (p72), a spa in Aix-en-Provence, which hits the spot with Zen massages, Camargue-salt skin scrubs and other blissful treatments

* Splurge on a decadent €395 Monte Carlo diamond massage – a body scrub with diamond powder, followed by a massage with rose-scented lotion and topped off with a 'gold and light of Monte Carlo' cream for the ultimate sparkle – at Thermes Marins de Monte-Carlo (p226), the region's most exclusive and luxurious spa

* Hit the heights at Thermes de Berthemont Les Bains (p188), a rare bastion of mountaintop pampering south of St-Martin-Vésubie in Haute-Provence

drunk way over the odds. After five minutes, my nostrils were reeling: green amber, sandalwood, vanilla, hyacinth, lily of the valley, civet (nose shock or what), hare (unpleasant animal smell, extracted from the secretion of a cat's gland, according to the poster on the wall), rose petals (sickly sweet), woody complex, sweet muse, Bavaria mousse, sweet jasmine. The fact that many of the bottles contained not one, but several scents premixed did little to aid my increasing olfactory bewilderment. At the 'organ' behind me, two little girls were picking names for their perfectly honed perfumes: *Les 2 Princesses* (The Two Princesses), *Les Fées* (The Fairies)…

'Add a rose for fullness' commanded Monsieur Maurel, plucking a bunch of rose-based bottles from my organ and plonking them in front of me. Wild rose, oriental rose, rose petals…my nose felt it had roses coming out of its ears. 'Hmm. It's fuller now,' he observed, 5ml of oriental rose into the glass beaker later, before striding off to leave me floundering in heart notes.

It must have been more straightforward for early perfumers. They quite simply left fresh flower petals to swim in animal fat for three months then mixed the fatty mess with alcohol to extract the essences. Unlike today (synthetic products are used in the main), they created perfumes exclusively from flowers: 600kg of fresh flower petals for every 1L of essence.

'Fresh and fruity with strong amber overtones – very modern' was Monsieur Maurel's analysis of my finished fragrance, which, he informed me, actually contained between 100 and 500 different products, most of which would have macerated for a month already. 'Leave it to rest for another 10 days to complete the maceration process,' he added as I jaunted off with my 100ml glass bottle of exclusively designed, one-of-a-kind perfume.

To create a perfume of your own, or to visit a perfumery, head to Grasse (p263 & p262).

PROVENCE LIVING

· · · · · · ·

In a part of the country where foreigners have always come, gone and invariably stayed, regional identity is not clear cut. Less than a smidgen of born-and-bred Provençaux understands or speaks *prouvènçau* (p348), rendering the region's traditional mother tongue useless as a fair expression of regional identity.

Young, old or salt-and-pepper-haired in between, people do share a staunch loyalty to the hamlet, village, town or city in which they live. People in Marseille have a particularly passionate attachment to their city, a port known for its stereotyped rough-and-tumble inhabitants who are famed among French for their exaggerations and imaginative fancies, such as the tale about the sardine that blocked Marseille port.

Markedly more Latin in outlook and temperament, Niçois exhibit a common zest for the good life with their Italian neighbours; while St-Tropez's colourful community is a trendy mix of bronzed-year-round glamour queens, reborn hippies and old-time art lovers. Law-abiding Monégasques dress up to the nines, don't break the law or gossip, and only cross the road on a zebra crossing. In rural pastures where family trees go back several generations and occupations remain firmly implanted in the soil, identity is deeply rooted in tradition.

Affluent outsiders buying up the region are prompting some traditional village communities to question their own (shifting) identities. With 20% of privately owned homes being *résidences secondaires* (second homes), traditional shops in some villages are struggling to stay open year-round, while property prices in many places have already spiralled out of reach of local salaries.

> '*St-Tropez's colourful community is a trendy mix of bronzed-year-round glamour queens, reborn hippies and old-time art lovers.*'

Propped against age-old yellow stone, one hand fondling the water of Châteauneuf du Pape's village fountain, a born-and-bred Provence man ponders this 'them and us' notion: 'I don't see myself or the people living here today as French or Provençal, but as being 'from the south'. People in Provence today have vastly different origins – Italian, African and so on – but we are all from the south. More than a culture, it is a certain way of life here that defines us.'

LIFESTYLE PARADE

Lifestyles in Provence and the Côte d'Azur are dazzlingly different as this cast of local characters shows.

Enter Jeanine Squarzoni, market-stall holder at Marseille's garlic market: 'I've been here 20 years; my mother, Thérèse, has been here for 40 years. I used to help her on the stall, but now I run it.' And will her children continue the family tradition? 'No, they work in an office. It's hard for young people to make a living from farming these days; traditions are no longer being passed on. When my mother started on the market there were 42 stalls. A decade ago there were 14; now there are five', says Jeanine, who reckons the market will have folded within five years (see p60).

BACKGROUND

THE POETRY OF PROVENÇAL

Should you wish to dip into Provençal culture and bone up on the rich lyrics and poetry of *prouvènçau* (Provençal), the region's age-old dialect of *langue d'oc* (Occitan; p427), try one of the Provençal writing workshops at the Frédéric Mistral house-museum in Maillane, north of St-Rémy de Provence.

In Nice, birthplace of subdialect Niçois, **La Remembrança Nissarda** (☎ 04 93 88 32 03; http://remembranca-nissarda.over-blog.com, in French; 1 rue des Combattants) runs weekly lessons in the Niçois language and *chants niçois* (traditional Niçois songs and chants), as well as cultural workshops on Niçois history, carnival traditions and *cuisine nissarde* (local cooking).

Online, glean useful Provençal phrases and old proverbs, such as *fai pas bon travaia quand la cigalo canto* (it is not good to work when the cicada chants), at the portal of Provençal culture, **Lou Pourtau de la Culturo Prouvençalo** (http://prouvenco.presso.free.fr, in French).

Down at the Vieux Port (Old Port) fishmonger Jeanine Vernet stands, merrily dressed in blue-and-white striped top and gumboots, as eels writhe and fish flap in buckets around her. 'Twenty years I've worked here. My husband and sons fish every day and I come here every morning year-round to sell the fish they catch', explains the fisherman's wife, who brings the fish by van from Soumaty, 10.5km north of the Vieux Port in Marseille's 16e, where the family fishing boat is moored.

Next up, what a character! Frédèric Bon, full-time *gardian* (Camargue cowboy) on the family *manade* (bull farm), traditionally assisted at busy times of the year by 'free-lance' or 'amateur' *gardians* who work in exchange for a place to stable their horses, meals etc. But with many a young local lad firmly implanted behind a desk Monday to Friday in Arles these days, casual cowboys are becoming hard to find. Moreover, people are less willing to trade their services and be flexible since the work week was slashed from 39 to 35 hours in 2000, according to the Bon family, who see the shift in work hours as 'spirit changing'. Frédéric's father, Jacques, was born on the farm in 1926, farmed sheep until 1979, when changes in the-then European Economic Community rendered it less profitable, and still rides every day.

Avoiding the midday heat means a 5.30am start for viticulturer Michel Vivet, who grabs a coffee for breakfast and works in the vineyards until noon when the sun drives him in for *une bonne sieste* – a good two-hour snooze. 'Afternoons are spent in the *cave* (cellar), where it's cooler', explains Michel, who describes local lifestyle as a mix of 'outside living and siestas' (as we sit around a tree-shaded table behind the sage green shuttered farmhouse, cicadas making an absolute din in the July heat). Michel runs Domaine Valette in Les Arcs with his father, mother and wife. Bar September's grape harvest, the Vevets do everything themselves on the small 15-hectare holding.

Enter Haute-Provence organic sheep farmers, Luisella and Pierre Bellot. May to November they tend to sheep, chickens and a vegetable garden on their 11-hectare farm, and are ski instructors in winter. 'We dream of just having the farm but we don't make enough money from it. Many people in the mountains have to do this to make a living', says father-of-three Pierre, who grew up on his parent's farm down the road, bought his own farm when he was 18 and laments the decline of mountain farms like his: 'It's why villagers complain about the mess and the smell when they see sheep walking on the village roads. They've forgotten the farming traditions of the region.' Their lifestyle in a nutshell: 'We live with the rhythm of the animals – when days are shorter, we go inside earlier.' And in summer when the sheep are grazing on higher pastures (2000m) with a shepherd? 'We cut dry grass and grow corn.'

Shift to the wealthy Luberon where many a foreigner lives the Provençal dream. Enter Englishwoman Sally Faverot de Kerbrech, who traded in the London smog for a Luberon vineyard in 2000: 'There is everything you could want here…quality of life, music, opera, theatre and art all around,' explains Sally, who tends the vines at Domaine Faverot with husband François, a Frenchman. And with their 'more than abundant' social life, there's a 50% French-/English-speaking split: 'We love going to local markets and to restaurants. There are all sorts of other activities (apart from meeting all sorts of friends and having dinner and musical evenings in all our homes) like walking, cycling, horse riding, tennis, golf. We do a bit of all that. The next thing I'd like to do is to take up painting', says an exuberant Sally, clearly high on Provençal life.

RIVIERA HIGH LIFE

Then, of course, there's the razzmatazz of Riviera high life. From the giddy days of the belle époque to the start of the summer season during the avant-garde 1920s, the Côte d'Azur has always glittered as Europe's most glamorous holiday spot: in 2008 Angelina Jolie and Brad Pitt moved with their brood into Château de Miraval (p291), a gold-stone château on an organic wine-producing estate with a celebrity past (in 1979 Pink Floyd recorded part of *The Wall* in the recording studio here). The Beckhams splurged on the rumoured €2.2-million purchase of a 15-bedroom mansion in Bargemon; their old pal Elton John and film-producer partner David Furnish live next door

> 'Then, of course, there's the razzmatazz of Riviera high life'

with 15 dogs and a constant turnover of showbiz friends at Castel Mont-Alban, a lemon-coloured 600-sq-m villa on Mont Boron near Nice; American film star John Malkovich lives in the Luberon; a €5.3-million wine-producing château near St-Raphaël is F1 superstar Michael Schumacher's summer cup of tea; and Tina Turner, Leonardo DiCaprio, Claudia Schiffer and Bono of U2 are seasonal residents.

Hidden behind high stone walls it might be, but voyeurs can peep in on Riviera high life during a sunlit stroll between dream mansions on Cap Martin and Cap Ferrat; over an *apéritif* on Pampelonne beach or at St-Tropez's yacht-filled old port, where yachtsmen pay close to €100,000 a week to moor; or in Monaco where helipads on pleasure boats are the norm. In Cannes, meanwhile, millionaires congregate once a year at the celebrity city's Millionaire Fair (www.milionairefair.com), a brash celebration of wealth where the world's most luxurious limousines, jewels, homes, private jets, wine, fashions and living concepts are showcased. Target audience: 'consumers in the high-end luxury segment, the rich and famous, CEOs, entrepreneurs and internet-workers, bon vivants, the media, VIPs, business and cultural elite,' quotes its website, footnoting that the 'spiritually rich' can also join in (sort of) the fun. Dress code: *tenue de ville* (jacket and tie) – a key phrase to know should you intend moving in luxury-lifestyle circles.

For essential stops on the Riviera high life circuit see p13. To live the high life firsthand see p195.

THE VILLAGE SQUARE

On the village square a bunch of old men throw *boules* (see opposite) on a dusty patch of gravel beneath trees, lovingly polishing each *boule* between rounds. Yet despite the quintessential image, Provence's national pastime is a serious sport with its own world championships and a museum to prove it.

Pétanque (Provençal *boules*) was invented in La Ciotat, near Marseille, in 1910 when arthritis-crippled Jules Le Noir could no longer take the running strides prior to aiming demanded by the *longue boule* game. The local champion thus stood with his feet firmly on the ground – a style that became known as *pieds tanques* (Provençal for 'tied feet', from which '*pétanque*' emerged).

Big dates on the *pétanque* calendar include France's largest tournament, La Marseillaise, held each year in Parc Borély in Marseille in early July; and the annual celebrity tournament organised in Avignon on the banks of the River Rhône. To have a spin yourself, head for place des Lices in St-Tropez (p275), or the village square in St-Paul de Vence (p257) for a discovery tour organised by the tourist office.

SATURDAY AFTERNOON

Come the weekend, aficionados of the region's two most impassioned sports – football and bullfighting (p90) – pile into the stadium or Roman arena. For fans, these sports are revered as both sport and a celebration of Provençal tradition.

'Merci les bleues!' was the slogan emblazoned on Paris' Arc de Triomphe when the national team, captained by Marseille's beloved Zizou, came home after the dramatic

---

DON'T MISS...

BOOKS

No titles better provide insight into Provençal living, past and present, than these:

★ **Everybody Was So Young, Amanda Vaill** // Beautiful evocation of an American couple and their glam literary friends in the jazzy 1920s

★ **Cote d'Azur: Inventing the French Riviera, Mary Blume** // Fabulous portrait of Riviera life: fantasy, escapism, pleasure, fame, eccentricity…

★ **Provence A – Z, Peter Mayle** // The best, the quirkiest, the most curious moments of the 20-odd years this best-selling author has spent in Provence

★ **Provençal Escapes, Caroline Clifton-Mogg** // Image-driven snoop around beautiful homes in Provence

★ **Words in a French Life: Lessons in Love and Language from the South of France, Kristen Espinasse** // Daily life in Provence through a series of French words

BOULES RULES

Two to six people, split into two teams, can play. Each player has three solid metal *boules* (balls), weighing 650g to 800g and stamped with the hallmark of a licensed *boule* maker. Initials, a name or a family coat of arms can be crafted on to made-to-measure *boules*. The earliest *boules*, scrapped in 1930, were wooden balls studded with hundreds of hammered-in steel nails.

Each team takes it in turn to aim a *boule* at a tiny wooden ball called a *cochonnet* (jack), the idea being to land the *boule* as close as possible to it. The team with the closest *boule* wins the round; points are allocated by totting up how many *boules* the winner's team has closest to the marker (one point for each *boule*). The first to notch up 13 wins the match.

The team throwing the *cochonnet* (initially decided by a coin toss) has to throw it from a small circle, 30cm to 50cm in diameter, scratched in the gravel. It must be hurled 6m to 10m away. Each player aiming a *boule* must likewise stand in this circle, with both feet planted firmly on the ground. At the end of a round, a new circle is drawn around the *cochonnet*, determining the spot where the next round will start.

Underarm throwing is compulsory. Beyond that, players can dribble the *boule* along the ground (known as *pointer*, literally 'to point') or hurl it high in the air in the hope of it landing smack-bang on top of an opponent's *boule*, sending it flying out of position. This flamboyant tactic, called *tirer* (literally 'to shoot'), can turn an entire game around in seconds.

Throughout matches *boules* are polished with a soft white cloth. Players unable to stoop to pick up their *boules* can lift them up with a magnet attached to a piece of string.

final of the 2006 World Cup: high drama indeed, thanks to Zinedane Zidane's headbutt 10 minutes before the end of the match. It was also the end of a brilliant career that saw the Marseille-born midfielder of North African origin captain France to victory in the 1998 World Cup, and transfer from Juventus (Italy) to Real Madrid (Spain) for a record-breaking €75.1 million.

Long the stronghold, not to mention heart and soul, of French football, Marseille at club level was national champion for four consecutive years between 1989 and 1992, and in 1991 Olympique de Marseilles (OM; www.olympiquedemarseille.com) – a team of mythical proportions around since 1899 – became the first French team to win the European Champions League. It reached the UEFA Cup final in 2004 but hasn't got that far since; in 2009 Marseille was knocked out by Ukraine. Club colours are white at home, turquoise away. To witness the side in action, take a trip to the team's hallowed home ground, the 60,000-seat Stade Vélodrome, built in the 1930s initially to host cycling fixtures (hence its name) and magnificently overhauled for the 1988 World Cup. Arsenal manager Arsène Wenger and star striker Thierry Henry both began their careers with the region's other strong club, AS Monaco (ASM).

OUTDOOR INSPIRATION
· · · · · · ·

With its varied landscapes – alpine mountains and cavernous gorges, flamingo-pink wetlands, and a world-famous coastline of sparkling white sand and turquoise water, scattered with offshore islands – Provence has an outdoor activity to match every mood, moment, energy level.

ASTRONOMY

Provence's infamous mistral bites, but it does blow away cloud cover, meaning sunny days and clear, star-filled night skies for stargazers. Large tracts of protected areas, especially across the Luberon and Haute-Provence, give off little artificial light, allowing stars to shine at their brightest.

Observatories welcoming stargazers include the Observatoire de Haute-Provence (p175) west of Manosque, and the nearby Centre d'Astronomie (p175).

Amid Luberon lavender fields in Lagarde d'Apt, watch night stars at the Observatoire Sirene (p155). On the star-studded French Riviera, admire stars at the Observatoire de Nice in La Trinité, and at Astrorama east of Nice (p218)

BALLOONING

Drifting across Provence's patchwork fields in a hot-air balloon is a seductive way to take in the captivating countryside. Balloon flights last one to 1½ hours (allow three to four hours in all for getting to and from the launch pad, inflating the balloon etc) and cost from €230 per person (€305 for a sunrise flight). Flights run year-round but are subject to weather forecasts. Operators include **Montgolfières Luberon** (☎ 04 90 05 76 77; www.montgolfiere-provence-ballooning.com) near Gordes, with flights in the Avignon and Luberon areas; and **Les Montgolfières du Sud** (☎ 04 66 37 28 02; www .sudmontgolfiere.com, in French; 64 rue Sigalon, Uzès), west of Nîmes, whose balloons fabulously float above the Pont du Gard.

> *'Provence has an outdoor activity to match every mood, moment, energy level.'*

BIRDWATCHING

Ornithologists flock to see clouds of pink flamingos in the protected Camargue delta (see p93) and between pink-hued salt pans on the Presqu'île de Giens (p307) near Hyères; and to spot majestic birds of prey in the Parc National du Mercantour (p183).

In Hyères **LPO PACA** (☎ 04 94 12 79 52; http://paca.lpo.fr, in French), the regional branch of the national **Ligue Pour la Protection des Oiseaux** (LPO; League for the Protection of Birds; www .lpo.fr, in French), organises guided birdwatching expeditions, can tell you where to spot what and can put you in touch with LPO-affiliated birdwatching groups in the region. You can download a complete calendar of *sorties natures* (nature outings) from the website.

BACKGROUND

Near Nice on the Côte d'Azur, the Parc Naturel Départemental de la Grande Corniche (p219) provides a precious opportunity to watch extraordinary birdlife against a stunning backdrop.

CANOEING, KAYAKING & RAFTING

Glide on a peaceful paddling expedition beneath the Pont du Gard (p143), along the bird-filled Camargue waterways (p82) or along the River Sorgue between Fontaine de Vaucluse and L'Isle-sur-la-Sorgue (p128). In and around Marseille you can sea kayak (p46) – by moonlight is particularly inspiring – and the green waters of the Gorges du Verdon (p177) are hot with intrepid white-water sport enthusiasts.

CYCLING

With near-endless sunshine and few killing hills to climb, not to mention storybook scenery and enchanting villages en route, the region is ideal two-wheeling territory for professionals and amateurs, adults and kids alike. On the Côte d'Azur the noisy motorway is never far away,

DON'T MISS...

DAY WALKS

★ **Île Ste-Marguerite //** Picnic in cool pine forests and on deserted shores on this Cannois island (p247)

★ **Sentier du Littoral //** Walk the seashore from St Raphaël to Agay (p269); lunch at **Villa Matuzia** (p270)

★ **Balcon du Loup trail //** Explore the Gorges du Loup (p258)

★ **Calanque de Sormiou or Morgiou //** Treat yourself to a *garrigue*-scented stroll from Marseille to one of these rocky little coves (p62)

★ **Cap Lardier's Sentier du Littoral //** Lap up breathtaking coastal views around the St-Tropez peninsula (p288)

★ **Colorado Provençal //** Hike red in Rustrel (p158) then lunch at **Le Table de Pablo** (p155)

★ **Donkey Ramble //** Frolic through lavender-strewn mountains around Thoard (p176)

making cycling a less tranquil affair: coastal cyclists often base themselves in Nice, from where they take a train along the coast each morning with their bicycles to avoid the stress of cycling out of the city. Some walking trails are open to mountain bikes, and those keen to tackle the region's roughest mountain terrain should hightail it to Haute-Provence.

Road and mountain bikes can be easily hired for around €15 a day including helmet, puncture-repair kit and suggested itineraries. Many rental outlets, especially on the coast and in the Luberon, have tandems (€20 to €30 per day), children's bikes (around €12 per day), toddler seats (around €5 per day) and two-seater trailers *(remorques* or *carrioles;* up to €15 per day) to tow little kids and babies along. Some outlets deliver to your door for free. Rental outlets are listed under Transport in the respective regional chapters.

Both on- and off-road cycling itineraries of various lengths and difficulties, compiled by local experts, can be picked up at most tourist offices. The Conseil Général du Var (www.cg83.fr, in French) publishes an excellent cycling *topoguide* for the St-Tropez to Toulon area containing 22 detailed itineraries. For Nice, its coast and hinterland, *Rando VTT: Guide RandOxygène,* published by the Conseil Général des Alpes-Maritimes (www.cg06.fr, in French), maps 30 cycling routes, a gentle 7km to sporty 22km in length. And around Avignon, 13 routes are suggested by the Vaucluse (www.vaucluse.fr, in French) in its *VTT: Loisirs de Plein Air* booklet. Download free PDFs of all these guides (in French) online.

♣ AUTOUR DU LUBERON// NEAR APT AND CAVAILLON

Cyclists can cross the Parc Naturel Régional du Luberon by following a circular 236km-long itinerary. Roads – steep in places – have little traffic and saunter up, down and around photogenic hilltop villages, vineyards, olive groves, lavender fields and fruit farms. Cyclists taking the northern route pedal 111km from Forcalquier to Cavaillon via Apt, Bonnieux, Lacoste and Ménerbes; the southern route links the two towns by way of Lourmarin, Vaugines, Cucuron and Manosque.

Those who enjoy a stiff climb should tackle the northern route east to west (signposted with white markers). Freewheelers should opt for the easier westbound route, which is marked by orange signs. For day trippers in Cavaillon, the 40km round trip to Ménerbes makes for an exhilarating bike ride.

Information boards posted along both routes provide details on accommodation, eating and sightseeing. For more information see www.parcduluberon.fr (in French), or www.veloloisirluberon.com.

♣ BREVET DES 7 COLS UBAYENS // BARCELONNETTE

The seven cols – Allos (2250m), Restefond la Bonette (2802m), Larche (1991m), Vars (2109m), Cayolle (2326m), Pontis (1301m) and St-Jean (1333m) – linking the remote Vallée de l'Ubaye in Haute-Provence with civilisation, form the region's most challenging bike rides. The series of loop rides from Barcelonnette involves 207km of power-pedalling and can only be done May to September when the passes aren't blocked by snow. Cyclists who do all seven get a medal (to prove it, participants have to punch a special card at machines installed on each mountain pass). See p183 and www.ubaye .com for more.

♣ ÎLE DE PORQUEROLLES // PORQUEROLLES

The only means of transport on this paradise island – bar one's feet – is bicycle. Sights are few and distances between beaches are small, making it a hassle-free choice for families happy to spend the day sauntering about by pedal power. In all, 70km of unpaved biking trails zigzag across the island and there are seven rental companies; some provide picnic hampers and they all rent buggies to pedal little kids along. See p300 and www.porquerolles.com.

♣ LE PAYS DE FORCALQUIER ET MONTAGNE DE LURE EN VÉLO // FORCALQUIER

The rough-cut planes of Haute-Provence star on the agenda of this mountainous-in-parts, 78km-long route that can be followed in either direction from Forcalquier; ochre signs mark the eastbound route, blue the west, and brown the 6km *boucle* (loop) that can be picked up in Lurs. Villages passed en route include Aubenas les Alpes,

St-Michel de l'Observatoire and Mane. See www.velopaysforcalquier.com for more details.

❦ LES OCRES EN VÉLO // AROUND APT
This colourful itinerary forms an easy 50km circular route around the land of Luberon ochre (see p154), linking rocky-red Roussillon with Villars (to the north), Rustrel (to the east), Apt (to the south) and Gargas (to the west). The route can be followed in either direction; green signs mark the westbound way from Apt and ochre markers flag its eastbound counterpart. For more information see www.parcduluberon.fr (in French), or www.veloloisirluberon.com.

❦ MONT VENTOUX // MALAUCÈNE AND SAULT
Many cyclists who make it to the summit of the mighty Mont Ventoux do it as something of a tribute to the British world-champion cyclist Tommy Simpson (1937–67), who suffered a fatal heart attack on the mountain during the 1967 Tour de France. There is a moving roadside memorial to Simpson 1km east of the summit, which reads 'There is no mountain too high'. The road ascent from Chalet Reynard on the westbound D974 to the summit is a very painful six kilometres, but a good many cycling enthusiasts only pedal part of the road, often just to see how hard it is!

Tourist offices have information on guided bike rides on the mountain, including night descents by road and daytime mountain-bike descents.

❦ TOULON TO ST-RAPHAËL // TOULON, HYÈRES AND CAVALAIRE-SUR-MER
Between 1905 and 1949 a steam train (poetically named *le macaron* after a local almond cake containing pine kernels extracted from the same pine cones that fuelled the locomotive) huffed and puffed between Toulon and St-Raphaël. Today the same 101km-long coastal stretch is covered by a smooth-as-silk two-lane cycling path *(piste cyclable)* instead. The track winds from Toulon to Hyères via Cap de Carqueiranne past Cavalaire-sur-Mer and St-Tropez to St-Raphaël. Find details in French online at www.cg83.fr.

DONKEY RAMBLING
To ramble amid steep gorges and mountain slopes unencumbered by the weight of a pack on your back, engage a gentle-natured donkey to accompany you on your journey. Farms renting donkeys include Les Ânes des Abeilles (p131), near the Gorges de Nesque, and a couple of other options in Haute-Provence, offering rambles that wend their way through lavender (see p176).

HORSE RIDING
With its famous cowboys, creamy white horses and expansive sandy beaches to gallop along, the Camargue is a wonderful windswept spot to ride (see p92). Aspiring cowboys and gals can learn the ropes on week-long *stages de monte gardiane* (Camargue cowboy courses; p90).

BACKGROUND

Dramatically different but equally inspiring are the donkey and horse treks through lyrical chestnut and cork oak forests in the Massif des Maures, set up by the Conservatoire du Patrimoine du Freinet (p297).

Elsewhere in Provence, tourist offices have lists of stables and riding centres where you can saddle up; a swag of information on horse riding, schools, tours and other equestrian activities in the Provence-Côte d'Azur region is posted on www.terre-equestre.com, in French.

SAILING, SNORKELLING & SEA SPORTS

Sailing is big business on the French Riviera: Antibes, Cannes, Mandelieu-La Napoule and St-Raphaël, as well as Marseille, are large water-sports centres where those without their own boat can hire a set of sails. Tourist offices have a list of sailing centres (*stations violes*) that rent gear and run courses. Count on paying around €50/80 to rent a catamaran for 1½/three hours and up to €50 for a one-hour sailing lesson.

WEATHER CHECK

To get a marine weather forecast before setting sail, call ☎ 3250 or visit www.meteo.fr/marine, in French.

Other sea sports readily available on the beach include windsurfing (around €30 per hour to rent a board), water-skiing and wakeboarding (€25 for around 15 minutes), jet-skiing (around €50 for 30 minutes), parasailing (€45/60 for one/two people for a 10-minute ride), and rides in a hair-raising rubber ring (€20 per person for a 10-minute ride) or fly fish (€30 per person for a 10-minute ride) off the back of a boat.

March to November, surfers ride the best winds of the day on a board propelled by a kite with kite-surf school **Air'X Kite** (☎ 06 60 41 87 34; www.airxkite.com), with schools in **St-Laurent du Var** (Centre Nautique, 416 av Eugène Donadeï) and **Mandelieu-La Napoule** (Centre Nautique, av Général de Gaulle). Emerging kitesurfing and windsurfing hot spots include Hyères' beaches at L'Almanarre, home to **Funboard Center** (☎ 04 94 57 95 33; www.funboardcenter.com), and the Camargue, where thrill-seekers kitesurf wind-whipped seas and speed along flat sands on a kite-powered buggy.

Substantially more soulful are moonlight sea-kayak paddles and canoe forays around stunning turquoise rocky coves near Marseille (see p46).

In summer, underwater nature trails encourage the aquatically curious to discover marine life at Domaine du Rayol (p298) and on Île de Port-Cros (p304).

SKIING & SNOWBOARDING

The few ski resorts in Haute-Provence are refreshingly low-key, with little of the glitz and glamour attached to the Alps' better-known centres such as Chamonix. Provence's slopes are best suited to beginner and intermediate skiers and costs are lower than at their northern neighbours.

Resorts include the larger Pra Loup (straddled between 1500m and 1600m) and La Foux d'Allos (1800m), which share 230km of downhill pistes and 110km of cross-country trails. Smaller sister resorts of Le Sauze (1400m) and Super-Sauze (1700m) in the Vallée de l'Ubaye tend to attract domestic tourists. The concrete-block Isola 2000 (2450m) is the largest and least attractive.

BACKGROUND

These resorts – all in the Parc National du Mercantour (p183) – open for the ski season from December to March/April/May (depending on the snow conditions), and for a short period in July and August for summer walkers. Buying a package is the cheapest way to ski and/or snowboard. For information on lift passes, equipment hire and the like, see the relevant sections in the Parc National du Mercantour section.

North of Digne-les-Bains, near the western edge of the Parc National du Mercantour in the Vallée de la Blanche, the locally patronised resort of St-Jean Montclar (p183) is well set up for families.

Mont Ventoux offers limited downhill and cross-country skiing; Chalet Reynard in Bédoin and Mont Serein are the two ski stations. See p123 for details.

WALKING

The region is criss-crossed by a plethora of *sentiers balisés* (marked walking paths) and *sentiers de grande randonnée* (long-distance paths with alphanumeric names beginning 'GR'). Some of the latter are many hundreds of kilometres long, including the GR5, which travels from the Netherlands through Belgium, Luxembourg and the spectacular Alpine scenery of eastern France before ending up in Nice. The GR4 (which crosses the Dentelles de Montmirail before climbing up the northern face of Mont Ventoux and winding east to the Gorges du Verdon), GR6 and their various diversions also traverse the region. Provence's most spectacular trail, the GR9, takes walkers to most of the area's ranges, including Mont du Vaucluse and Montagne du Luberon. Naturally there are a zillion and one shorter, less challenging walks too.

Between 1 July and 15 September paths in heavily forested areas – such as the section of the GR98 that follows Les Calanques between Cap Croisette (immediately south of Marseille) and Cassis – are closed completely due to the high risk of forest fire. The GR51 crossing the Massif des Maures, paths in the Montagne de Ste-Victoire east of Aix-en-Provence and numerous trails in Haute-Provence are likewise closed in summer due to fire risk.

Many walking guides – predominantly in French – cover the region: an exception is the topoguide *Walks in Provence: Luberon Regional Nature Park* put out by the Fédération Française de Randonnée Pédestre (FFRP; French Walking Federation).

FARM WALKS

No one knows the lay of the land better than those who tirelessly farm it. For a wonderful introduction to a Provençal farm, sign up for a **farmer's itinerary** (www.itineraires-paysans .fr), locally called *itinéraire paysan*, – a two- to three-hour walk with a local farmer through fruit orchards and Alpine pastures, past beehives, along canals, around goat farms and in search of black truffles. Most walks are thematic and usually end with a taste of the farmer's own produce.

Walks can be taken around farms and agricultural land, June to September, in Haute-Provence, the area around Manosque in the Luberon, and in the Var. They cost €7/3.50 per adult/6-16yr and must be booked directly with the farmer at least 24 hours in advance. A full calendar is posted online.

BACKGROUND

Truly outstanding are the walking guides *Guides RandOxygène* (www.randoxygene .org, in French) published by the Conseil Général des Alpes-Maritimes (Alpes-Maritimes General Council): they detail (in French) 60 walks of varying lengths and difficulty, for seaside amblers to serious walkers. In the Alpes-Maritimes *Département: Rando Haut-Pays* covers the Parc National du Mercantour, *Rando Moyen-Pays* tackles the hilltop villages north of Nice and Haute-Provence, and *Rando Pays Côtier* features invigorating coastal walks. Tourist offices stock the guides and have further information, as does the guides' own website.

Almost every tourist office takes bookings for short two- to three-hour guided nature walks in their areas during summer; many are organised by the local branch of the Office National des Forêts (ONF; National Forests Office) or by local mountain guides. Many are featured under Top Tours in the Getting Started planners at the start of each regional chapter. For a list of the best, see p20.

PROVENÇAL WINE

· · · · · · ·

Provençal wines are by no means France's most sought after, but making and tasting them is an art and tradition that bears its own unique and tasty trademark. Each Appellation d'Origine Contrôlée (AOC; trademark body) wine possesses a common ingredient: an exceptionally cold mistral wind and an equally exceptional, hot, ripening sun. Most wines carry the name of the château or domaine they are produced on – unlike Fat Bastard (www.fatbastard.com), a label created by Gigondas oenologist Thierry Boudinaud ('*now zat iz what you call eh phet bast-ard,*' said Thierry allegedly to his English partner Guy Anderson upon tasting the wine, hence the ground-breaking hip name). Using grapes from neighbouring Languedoc, the Gigondas-born wine was the French sensation of the moment when it broke into the US market a couple of years back.

> *'Regionwide it is the northerly mistral wind that plays guardian angel to the vines'*

Wine can be bought direct from the *producteur* (wine producer) or *vigneron* (wine grower), most of whom offer *dégustation* (tasting), allowing you to sample two or three vintages with no obligation to buy. For cheap plonk *(vin de table)* costing €2 or so per litre, fill up your own container at the local wine cooperative; every wine-producing village has one. Lists of estates, *caves* (wine cellars) and cooperatives are available from tourist offices and *maisons des vins* (wine houses) in Avignon (p361), Les Arcs-sur-Argens (p360), Menerbes (p161) and elsewhere.

Organic wine is becoming increasingly hip, with the once little-known winemaking village of Correns in the northern Var gaining a sterling reputation in recent years for its organic whites. Throw in the fact that Brad Pitt, Angelina Jolie and the kids moved into the village's finest wine-producing estate, Château de Miraval, in 2008 and Correns wine suddenly seems really rather glamorous. See p291 for tasting addresses around the village.

Regionwide it is the northerly mistral wind that plays guardian angel to the vines: its dry biting chill protects them from maladies common to more humid areas (see p15).

DON'T MISS...

TOP WINE TASTING ADDRESSES

- ★ **Carignan //** This pocket-sized wine bar is *the* address in Cannes to taste with a first-class sommelier (p246)

- ★ **Les Sens //** Make a night of it at this designer wine cellar in Antibes (p253)

- ★ **KV&B //** Taste Bandol in the resort after which this matchless red is named (p313)

- ★ **Château de Crémat //** Discover Bellet at this Dutch-run wine estate (p202)

- ★ **Domaine de la Brillane //** Dreamy B&B near Aix-en-Provence producing a fine Coteaux d'Aix-en-Provence (p76)

- ★ **Domaine Faverot //** Silk-farm-turned-winery producing a stunning Côtes du Luberon (p150)

BACKGROUND

CÔTES DE PROVENCE

Talk Provence and wine, and bright pink rosé instantly springs to mind. Indeed, there is no more quintessential image of daily life in this hot fertile part of southern France than lounging alfresco beneath a vine-laced pergoda, pre-lunch glass of chilled rosé in hand: *l'art de vivre* (the fine art of living) is what those insightful Provençal call it.

Dating from 1977, Côtes de Provence is the region's largest appellation (and the sixth largest in France), producing 75% of Provençal wine and known predominatly for its rosé, which accounts for 84% of the 130 million bottles the appellation produces each year. Its vineyards carpet 20 hectares between Nice and Aix-en-Provence, and its *terroir* (land) is astonishingly varied. Predominantly sandy coastal soils around St-Tropez produce dramatically different wine to the chalky soils covering subalpine slopes around Les Arcs-sur-Argens. This has led to the creation within the Côtes de Provence appellation of recognised labels like Côtes de Provence Ste-Victoire (22.25 sq km around Cézanne's Montagne Ste-Victoire north of Aix-en-Provence) and Côtes de Provence Fréjus (235 hectares around Fréjus south of Cannes) in 2005, and Côtes de Provence La Londe (441 hectares around La Londe near Toulon) in 2008. Indeed, few other appellations support such a variety of *cépages* (grape varieties) – at least a dozen in all.

Generally drunk young and served at a crisp cool 8°C to 10°C, Côtes de Provence rosé is one of the world's oldest wines. Vines were first planted by the Greeks in Massilia (Marseille) around 600 BC, then came the Romans who likewise demonstrated a penchant for good wine – learn how they made it at the Mas des Tourelles (p137), near Beaucaire. And from the 5th century, monks at Marseille's Abbaye de St-Victor, Abbaye de Lérins on Île St-Honorat, Abbaye du Thoronet in the northern Var, and other monsteries in the region devoted themselves to the art of winemaking. An easy wine to pair with food, rosé usurped its traditional image as a solely summer festive drink long ago, and these days it is drunk year-round with everything from barbecued meats and fish to vegetarian dishes and more wintery seasonal fare.

Lesser known are Côtes de Provence reds, which account for just 13% of the appellation's annual production. Most are drunk young and should be served at 14°C to 16°C. Fresh and fruity, they marry best with herb-scented grilled meat, tomatoes in olive oil, and *tians de legumes*. Older red *vins de garde* are a traditional accompaniment to game, sauced meats, traditionally meaty dishes like *pieds et paquets* and cheese; serve them at 16°C to 18°C.

Despite being the golden friend to fish and seafood when chilled to 8°C, Côtes de Provence white accounts for just 3% of wine production in Côtes de Provence.

For a complete briefing on Côtes de Provence wine, visit the **Comité Interprofessionnel des Vins Côtes de Provence** (www.cotes-de-provence.fr) and its bacchanalian Maison des Vins (p292) in Les Arcs-sur-Argens. An essential port of call on any wine-tasting itinerary, it stocks 700-odd different Côtes de Provence wines.

COTEAUX D'AIX & COTEAUX VAROIS

Both these appellations – Coteaux d'Aix-en-Provence carpeting 42 sq km north of Aix-en-Provence and around the Étang de Berre, and Cotaux Varois covering 25 sq km of notably chalky, higher-altitude land around the Massif des Baumes – produce rosé in the main: red and white account for no more than 15% and 5%, respectively, of each production. Coteaux d'Aix-en-Provence wines are generally dry, oodles of grenache grapes going into the small amount of aromatic and elegant reds made here.

Coteaux Varois-en-Provence is a particularly charming wine to taste in situ: its **Maison des Vins** (☎ 04 94 69 33 18; place des Ormeaux; ✆ 10am-noon & 2-6pm Mon-Sat) is housed in a convent adjoining the lovely 12th-century Benedictine Abbaye de la Celle in the gold-stone village of La Celle. In July and August hauntingly beautiful classical **concerts** (☎ 04 94 69 10 86; www.soireesmusicales-lacelle.com; tickets €23) fill the abbey cloister. Nearby in Correns, Château de Miraval (p291) is one of the most prestigious AOC Coteaux Varois labels.

PALETTE

East of Aix-en-Provence is the bijou vineyard of Palette, age-old vines on its 20 hectares of limestoney soil producing extremely prestigious, well-structured reds. Dating to 1948, the appellation is revered thanks to the extraordinary wines of two estates: **Château Cremade** (☎ 04 42 66 76 80; www.chateaucremade.com; rte de Langesse, Le Tholonet), which cultivates 25 different grape varieties, many ancient and rare; and the larger **Château Simone** (☎ 04 42 66 92 58; www.chateau-simone.fr; Meyreuil), which produces four out of every five Palette bottles.

CÔTES DU VENTOUX & CÔTES DU LUBERON

Vast areas of the region's interior are carpeted with Côtes du Ventoux (69 sq km established in 1973) and Côtes du Luberon (35 sq km dating from 1988) vineyards. The latter has become particularly trendy in recent years thanks to wealthy foreigners and media stars who have bought up its vineyards; Ridley Scott's romantic comedy *A Good Year* (2006) was filmed at **Château La Canorgue** (☎ 04 90 75 81 01; rte du Pont Julien, Bonnieux), a biodynamic winery at the foot of Bonnieux village. The Maison de la Truffe et du Vin (p161) in neighbouring Menerbes provides a prime wine-tasting opportunity.

Both appellations are best known for their red wine, which makes up 80% and 67% of Côtes du Ventoux and Luberon wine respectively. Light and fruity, these reds are generally drunk when young and form the perfect accompaniment to white meats, cheeses and grilled red meats. Production is dominated by cooperatives – taste and buy at cooperatives in Apt, Bonnieux, Goult and Maubec – but the best wines remain the domain of private domaines.

A dreamy way to discover Vins de Pays de Vaucluse, the simple table wine made in this same winegrowing region, is **Musiques dans les Vignes** (www.musiquesdanslesvignes .com), a summertime festival bringing a bounty of classical music concerts to open-air stages in viticultural villages in the area.

CÔTES DU RHÔNE

By far the most renowned vintage in this vast appellation – France's second-largest covering 772 sq km in the Rhône Valley – is Châteauneuf du Pape, a full-bodied wine bequeathed to Provence by the Avignon popes who planted the distinctive stone-covered vineyards, 10km south of Orange. For a short history and tasting addresses see p114 and p113.

Châteauneuf du Pape reds are strong (minimum alcohol content 12.5%) and well-structured masters in their field. Whites account for 7% of total annual production. Châteauneuf du Pape wine growers, obliged to pick their grapes by hand, say it is the *galets* (large smooth, yellowish stones) covering their vineyards that distinguish them from others. Both whites and reds can be drunk young (two to three years) or old (seven years or more). Irrespective of age, whites should be served at 12°C, reds at 16°C to 18°C.

> '*By far the most renowned vintage in this vast appellation is Châteauneuf du Pape*'

Another popular Rhône Valley *grand cru* (literally 'great growth') is red and rosé Gigondas (p122), produced in vineyards around the Dentelles de Montmirail, some 15km east of Orange. The medieval golden-stone village with ruined castle, Provençal campanile and stunning vista is a sheer delight to meander, and its reds are among Provence's most sought after. In nearby Beaumes de Venise (p122) it is the sweet dessert wine, Muscat de Beaumes de Venise, that delights – enjoy it as an aperitif or poured inside half a Cavaillon melon as dessert.

To gen up on the eight different *routes des vins* (wine roads) – colour-coded driving itineraries designed to help discover different areas within the Côtes du Rhône winemaking area – and tasting addresses, visit the **Interprofession des Vins AOC Côtes du Rhône** (☎ 04 90 27 24 00; www.vins-rhone.com; 6 rue des Trois Fauçons) in Avignon.

REPAS DES VENDANGES

Harvesting the grapes is all very good but for *vendangeur* (grape picker) and vigneron (winemaker) it is the *repas des vendanges,* marking the harvest's end, that is the most memorable.

The 'harvest meal' is the culmination of three long weeks spent working hard in the heat of late summer – from around 7.30am to 2am in the case of small-scale wine producer Michel Vivet in Les Arcs, who pretty much works around the clock despite the extra eight *coupeurs* and additional *porteur* he takes on to help him pick and carry grapes on his 15-hectare estate.

The day after the harvest, everyone who's helped harvest joins Michel and his family on the terrace of their green-shuttered farmhouse overlooking vines for an aperitif and lunch, which carries on well into the night: 'It is a fabulous affair. We eat *petit gris de Provence* (snails in tomato sauce), a huge *aïoli* (vegetables, boiled potatoes, boiled eggs and shellfish dunked into a pot of garlic mayonnaise) and plenty of wine.'

For Michel, the *repas des vendanges* evokes the free spirit of his childhood growing up in Les Arcs: 'I looked for mushrooms, I hunted truffles, I took my bike and built tree houses, I walked wherever I wanted to and no one worried about fires. Everyone knew everyone and helped each other. Now, with more and more large industrial domaines run by people who don't actually work on the land, this contact between *paysans* (farmers, country folk) is being lost'.

An inspired address to learn about Rhone Valley wines is the **Académie du Vin et du Goût** (Academy of Wine & Taste; ☎ 04 66 33 04 86; www.academie-du-vin.com; Château de Clary), 15km north of Avignon in Roquemaure. The school runs wine-tasting courses and workshops (two hours to a weekend long), and Accords Mets et Vins (Matching Food with Wine) sessions, at which you can taste six different wines in one appellation with six perfectly married dishes.

BANDOL, CASSIS & BELLET

Bandol is the most respected of Provence's pocket-sized appellations. This winemaking area on the coast near Toulon is known in particular for its deep-flavoured reds produced from the dark-berried *mourvèdre* grape, which needs oodles of sun to ripen – hence its rarity. Sold under their own coveted AOC since 1941, Bandol wines have enjoyed a surprising popularity throughout their 2000-year history. In Roman times, the then Massilia wines were famous across Gaul and their ability to mature at sea meant they travelled far beyond their home shores from the 16th and 19th centuries (Louis XV was rumoured to be an insatiable fan). See p312 for tasting addresses.

Crisp whites, accounting for 75% of production, are drunk in Cassis (p64), often as the ideal companion to the picturesque port's bounty of shellfish and seafood. Then there is Bellet (p202), France's smallest AOC wine and something of a rarity outside its Niçois production area – making a tasting tour of the Bellet vineyards extra fun.

A SEASONAL CUISINE

· · · · · · ·

It was through the humble rhythm and natural cycle of the land that a distinctly Provençal cuisine – laden with sun-filled tomatoes, melons, cherries, peaches, olives, Mediterranean fish and alpine cheese – emerged several centuries ago. Nothing has changed. Farmers still gather at the weekly morning market to sell their fruit and vegetables, olives, garlic plaits and dried herbs displayed in stubby coarse sacks. *À la Provençal* continues to involve a generous dose of garlic-seasoned tomatoes; while a simple filet mignon, sprinkled with olive oil and rosemary fresh from the garden, makes the same magnificent Sunday lunch it did a generation ago.

JANUARY: PIG OUT ON TRUFFLES

Break and beat three eggs, season with salt, pepper and 15g of grated truffle. Leave to rest for 30 minutes, then cook slowly in a bain-marie with a drizzle of olive oil or a knob of butter. Stir regularly, adding a spoon of crème fraîche if necessary. Sprinkle with 15g of grated truffle, stir and serve immediately.

Christian Etienne's recipe for *brouillade de truffes* – a Provençal classic included in many a lavish three- and four-course *menu aux truffes* (truffle menu) served at several restaurants in season – is nothing more than scrambled eggs with truffle shavings.

Simplicity is the basis of many truffle dishes, allowing the palate to revel in the flavour (it's subtle) of Provence's most luxurious and elusive culinary product.

> *'Traditionally snouted out by pigs, truffles these days are hunted by dogs'*

A fungus that takes root underground, usually in symbiosis with the roots of an elm or oak tree, the black truffle *(tuber melanosporum)* is snouted out in modest amounts in the Vaucluse, especially around Carpentras, Vaison-la-Romaine and in the Enclave des Papes, from November to March. January is the height of the season, which climaxes mid-month with a sacred truffle mass in Richerenches (p18). Dubbed *diamants noir* (black diamonds), and at €500 to €1000 per kilogram, truffles are as precious as gold dust.

Traditionally snouted out by pigs, truffles these days are hunted by dogs. 'Dog training is a long activity and requires an enormous amount of patience,' explains fourth-generation *trufficulteur* (truffle farmer) Jean-François Tourrette, from Vénasque. Tourrette, with Youcan, his 10-year-old mongrel, hunts black truffles in winter, and the cheaper, lesser-known and not nearly-as-precious white truffle – often called *truffe d'été* (summer truffle; *tuber aestivum)* – between May and August. Planting oak trees, picking acorns and guarding his oak plantation against 'spring's water excess, summer dryness, autumn's water excess, winter frost and wild boars' are other daily *trufficulteur* tasks.

Truffles form an integral part of the traditional New Year's Day feast in Provence. Families pig out on the biggest *coq* (chicken, rooster; symbolising the coming year) they can find, either stuffed with sausage meat and truffles or chestnuts or – in

DINING DIARY

So what precisely is the dining order of the day for people in Provence? 'My father would start work at 5.30am, stopping around 9am or 10am for a plate of ham, *saucisson* (sausage), radishes from the garden…but breakfast for me is a coffee,' says third-generation wine producer Michel Vivet, at home amid 15 hectares of vines in Les Arcs-sur-Argens. 'At lunchtime it is too hot; our evening meal is the most important,' he says, looking at his wife, who reels off their previous evening's menu: courgette omelette and *saucisson*.

While *petit déjeuner* (breakfast) for urban folk generally entails a short, sharp, black *café* (coffee) or milky *café au lait* and a croissant (no jam or butter) grabbed at a café on the way to work, *petit déj* in agricultural circles is a more imaginative affair: 'I get up at 3.45am to take my melons to the wholesale markets, have a coffee and when I get back at 8am, I have breakfast with my wife,' says Bernard Meyssard, a melon farmer near Cavaillon who kick-starts his dining day with a feast of *jambon cru* (uncooked ham) and melon.

While *déjeuner* (lunch) is the traditional main meal of the day (and a highlight for visitors to Provence), people who work actually dine quite lightly at midday and save the ritual feast of aperitif followed by a hot meal with wine for the evening when it is cooler. 'For lunch I have melon, ham and a tomato salad,' says Bernard, adding, 'A healthy appetite, I always have one,' eyes dancing, when asked which meal – lunch or *dîner* (dinner) – was the more important to him.

In urban climes restaurants get packed out from noon with regulars lunching on a light(er) *plat du jour* (dish of the day), *formule menu* (fixed main course plus starter or dessert) or lunch *menu* (choice of two-course meal) – saving the heavier *menu* for the evening when several hours can be devoted to appreciating an *entrée* (starter), *plat* (main course), *fromage* (cheese) and dessert. Many top-end restaurants serve an *amuse-bouche* (complimentary morsel of something very delicious) between the starter and main course; some also serve a sweet equivalent before dessert, plus petit fours with coffee.

wealthier circles – served alongside 12 partridges (one for each month of the year), truffles (symbolising the nights) and eggs (the day).

For more on truffle culture see p121. Renowned addresses to dine on truffles include Chez Bruno (p290) and Les Chênes Verts (p293). To snout out your own head to Monteux near Carpentras (p102).

FEBRUARY: A FISHY AFFAIR

Slice off the bottom of the spiny ball – anything from deep purple to aubergine, chocolate brown or jet black in colour – and serve like oysters by the dozen or half. Scrape off the foul-looking guts and brown grit to uncover the rusty-orange ambrosia, the roe of the sea urchin exquisitely arranged by nature in five delicate sweet-salty strips. This is what you eat and how they are served in restaurants.

Oursin (sea urchin) is a delicacy that falls in the same love-it-or-hate sphere as oysters and foie gras, and is reason enough to be in Carry-le-Rouet in February, when the quaint fishing port west of Marseille celebrates its sea urchin festival. *Oursins* are fished September to April and are best served with a squeeze of fresh lemon on top and a glass of chilled white Cassis.

Other catches include clamlike *violets* (sea squirts), whose iodine-infused yellow flesh tastes like the sea, and *supions frits* (squid pan-fried with fresh garlic and parsley). Shoals of Mediterranean fish – *merlan* (whiting), *St-Pierre* (John Dory), *galinette* (tub gurnard), *maqueareau* (mackerel), *chapon de mer* (chapon), *congre* (conger eel) and *rascasse* (scorpion fish) – are sold straight from the sea in Marseille at the region's premier fish market.

Assessing whether a fish is fresh hardly takes a genius, says fishmonger Jeanine Vernet with a smile, pointing to the slithering eels and fish flapping noisily in buckets on her market stall at Marseille's Vieux Port (p48). 'You can also tell by the colour; it should be clear,' she continues, citing her favourite way of preparing the day's catch as 'sprinkled with fresh herbs, wrapped in aluminium and baked in the oven'.

Marseillais chef Christian Buffa buys the fish he needs for his highly regarded fish restaurant, Le Miramar (p59), each morning at the Vieux Port market and a wholesale fish market 10km out of town. For him, essential purchases are scorpion fish, white scorpion fish, *vive* (weever), conger eel, chapon and tub gurnard – the six fish types he would not consider making his famous *bouillabaisse* without. King of regional dishes, *bouillabaisse* is a pungent yellow fish-stew, brewed by Marseillais for centuries. It requires a minimum of four types of fresh fish cooked in a rockfish stock with onions, tomatoes, garlic, saffron (hence its colour), parsley, bay leaves, thyme and other herbs. Its name is derived from the French *bouillir* (to boil) and *baisser* (to lower, as in a flame), reflecting the cooking method required: bring it to the boil, let it bubble ferociously for 15 minutes, then serve it: the *bouillon* (broth) first as a soup, followed by the fish flesh, in the company of a local wine. Try it with a white Cassis or dry Bandol rosé.

No two cooks make an identical *bouillabaisse* and the debates about which fish constitute a true *bouillabaisse* are endless. '*St-Pierre* or *lotte* (monkfish) are optional,' says Christian Buffa, who also sometimes throws in a *cigale de mer* (sand lobster), *langouste* (crayfish) or *langoustine* (small saltwater lobster) to transform a bog-standard *bouillabaisse* into *bouillabaisse royale*. In Toulon – shock horror – Toulonnais throw potatoes into the pot; while *bourride,* a cheaper version of *bouillabaisse,* contains no saffron, features cheaper white-fleshed fish, and is served with white aïoli instead of pink *rouille* (garlic mayonnaise with breadcrumbs and crushed chilli pepper; see also boxed text, p368).

Seafood dining standouts include Marseille's *bouillabaisse* restaurants (p59); Le Sloop in St-Jean-Cap Ferrat (p214); Bacon in Cap d'Antibes (p252); La Table du Mareyeur in Port Grimaud (p289); and Chez Jo in Cavalière (p299).

MARCH: OLIVE OIL SHOP

Drink water first. Pour a drop of oil onto a plastic teaspoon, raise it to your lips and taste it. It can have a varying degree of sweetness or acidity, be peppery or fruity and 'green', or it can be clear or murky (which means the oil has not been filtered). Once opened, consume within six months, don't cook with it and keep out of direct sunlight.

BACKGROUND

The secret behind many Provençal dishes, olive oil is a key ingredient in every Provençal sauce; is essential for *socca,* the Niçois chickpea-flour pancake; and is a sheer delight tasted in March with asparagus, the month's seasonal speciality: steam the slender green tips, sprinkle with *fleur de sel* (salt crystals) and drizzle with oil. From the 5th century AD until the French revolution, the kings of France were baptised with olive oil from St-Rémy de Provence.

> *'kings of France were baptised with olive oil from St-Rémy de Provence'*

March is the last chance to shop for that season's *huile d'olive* at the *moulin* (mill), by far the most interesting place to buy it. Some mills are listed in the regional chapters. Most open soon after the winter harvest until March or April (see p372). Sold in glass bottles or plastic containers, olive oil costs around €20 per litre and *dégustation* (tasting) is an integral part of buying.

In the Vallée des Baux and Les Alpilles, *oléiculteurs* (olive growers) adhere to a rigid set of rules to have their bottles stamped with a quality-guaranteed AOC mark. Generally, 5kg of olives yield 1L of oil. Markets and olive oil shops sell oil year-round and several restaurants serve olive-oil *menus.*

APRIL: SPRING CHEESE

Take a round of fresh *chèvre,* drizzle it with local olive oil or honey and bite into what is said to be the finest goat cheese of the year. Serve with bread.

'Our cheese is best in spring because of the lush new grass; the milk tastes the best,' says farm-born Emanuelle Marbezy, technical manager at a small *fromagerie* (cheese shop) in Banon, Haute-Provence, where milk from 12 mountain goat-farms is brought down to the plain and turned into Provence's best-known cheese, Banon (p174).

Instantly recognisable by the five autumnal chestnut leaves it comes wrapped in, Banon cheese has been protected by its own AOC since 2003, the strict rules of which require goats to graze for a minimum of 210 days on the prairies; their milk to stay unpasteurised; and the cheese produced from it to ripen for at least 15 days after being pressed into delicate rounds 7cm to 8cm in diameter.

Banon aside, *chèvre* comes in heart shapes, pyramids, logs and squares. It can be eaten young and *frais* (fresh) – a mild creamy taste – or matured into a tangy, stronger tasting *demi-sec* (semidry) or *sec* (dry) cheese. It can be plain, raisin-studded or coated in crushed peppercorns, *herbes de Provence* (see p370) or black ash. Or you can dip the round in egg and breadcrumbs, fry it and serve it with sweet *miel de Provence* (local honey) or a fruit chutney.

MAY: LAMBS & BULLS

Sprinkle fresh garlic, rosemary and wild thyme over a *gigot d'agneau* (leg of spring lamb), pour over three tablespoons of olive oil and bake in the oven. Or try *pieds et paquets,* sheep trotters wrapped in tripe and cooked with wine and tomatoes.

It is in early May during the traditional transhumance that sheep farmers move their flocks to higher mountain pastures to fatten up on summer's cool, lush grass under the watchful eye of a shepherd. 'My sheep graze on the mountain for 120 days or so. Their return depends on the weather, but it is invariably in October before the first mountain snow,' says Alpilles sheep farmer René Tramier, adding, 'I belong to the "Lamb of Sisteron" Label Rouge (certification of quality), which requires me to kill them when they're 70 to 150 days old.' No wonder lamb from Sisteron, alongside the Alpilles de la Crau, is so tender.

It is a bullish affair in the Camargue where three- or four-year-old bulls who have failed to prove their worth in the arena are slaughtered for their meat to make *guardianne de taureau* (bull-meat stew) and *saucisson d'Arles* (air-dried bull sausage). Bull calves reared specifically for their meat are born in early spring, fattened all summer and packed off to the abattoir in October.

JUNE: RED & GREEN GARLIC

'Crunch a few coffee beans or parsley stems afterwards if your breath smells too aggressively of garlic or, better still, share the aïoli with your friends': wise words of legendary 'cuisine of the sun' chef, Roger Vergé, one of Provence's biggest names from the late 1960s until his new-millennium retirement.

> '*Rub the garlic over the toast, spread the rouille on top, bite it and breathe fire*'

Garlic – harvested and piled high in woven garlands at the markets in June – gives Provençal cuisine its kick, letting rip in a clutch of fantastic strong-tasting sauces, traditionally served to complement *crudités* (raw vegetables), soups and fish dishes. *Anchoïade* is a strong anchovy paste laced with garlic and olive oil and delicious served with *bagna cauda* (raw mixed vegetables); *brandade de morue* is a don't-mess-with-me mix of crushed salt cod, garlic and olive oil; and *tapenade* is a sharp, black-olive-based dip seasoned with garlic, capers, anchovies and olive oil.

Then there is handsome *pistou*, a green crushed-up mix of garlic, basil, pine kernels and olive oil that the Provençal stir into *soupe au pistou* (a vegetable, bean and

INTERVIEW: THE GARLIC FARMER

Tomates à la Provençale (halved tomatoes, sprinkled with crushed garlic, and oven-baked), potatoes cooked in the oven with loads of garlic and herbs, and *bœuf boulettes ail persil* (garlic and parsley-spiced beef balls) are dishes eaten in the family home of garlic-farmer Jeanine Squarzoni, a regular at Marseille's seasonal garlic market.

'The market opens at midsummer on 24 June and runs for a month. People buy garlic to keep for the whole year,' explains Jeanine, who farms near Aix-en-Provence. Garlic is planted in August, plucked from the soil the following June and strewn across the fields to dry for a few days before harvesting.

'I farm two types of garlic: violet, which keeps 10 months and is particularly good raw in salads as it's less strong; and Moulinin or *rouge*, which keeps 12 months,' continues Jeanine, stressing that both garlic taste the same after cooking. Both cost around €3 per kilogram. The strongest-tasting garlic is *vert* (green) garlic, which is harvested in May when it is not fully ripened. But you should eat it quickly; it doesn't keep.

basil soup) or paste on toast. On the coast, aïoli is smeared over many fish dishes and is an essential component of aïoli *Provençal complet* – a mountain of vegetables (including artichokes), boiled potatoes, a boiled egg and *coquillages* (small shellfish), all of which are dunked into the pot of aïoli. Fiery pink *rouille* is best friend to *soupe de poisson* (fish soup), served with bite-sized toasts, a pot of *rouille* – and a garlic clove. Rub the garlic over the toast, spread the *rouille* on top, bite it and breathe fire.

JULY: YELLOW & BLACK TOMATOES

Slice six red tomatoes. Grate two *cébettes* (small white onions) and sprinkle on top. Dress with a vinaigrette of balsamic vinegar, olive oil, salt and pepper; sprinkle with chopped basil or parmesan shavings and *voilà – salade de tomates.*

The humble tomato salad remains a firm favourite of Provençal chef Christian Étienne (p109), who conjures up a magnificent four-course *menu de tomates* at his Avignon restaurant in July, when the region's most quintessential vegetable is at its noble best. 'Tomatoes remind me of my childhood – there were always tomatoes in our garden,' says the burly Avignon-born chef as he waves enthusiastically at the line-up of potted tomato plants on his restaurant terrace.

Tomatoes in this fertile neck of the woods are not all red. Of the region's 2500 known varieties, some are white, some are burgundy, some black, green, orange, yellow and so on. **René Caramela** (☎ 04 90 47 58 40; Mas du Bout des Vignes, Chemin des Poissonniers) grows 30 to 40 different types in her exceptional tomato garden in Mouriès, 15km south of St-Rémy de Provence.

> '*A stroll through the Provençal market in July is a particularly succulent affair*'

Tomato appearance can differ dramatically – coming long and skinny, smooth or crinkled – just as there is a vital difference between '*une belle tomate et une bonne tomate*' (a beautiful tomato and a good tomato). 'My tomatoes are not beautiful but I know they are good,' explains the tomato-mad chef, walking from his steely kitchen to the sun-flooded balcony out back where the 40kg of far-from-uniform tomatoes he will use in two days are stacked in crates. 'Never keep tomatoes in a fridge,' says Monsieur Etienne with horror, 'it dulls their taste'. He adds that there is little point smelling a tomato to check quality: it's the green branch, not the flesh, that exudes that lovely fresh-from-the-garden tomato scent – '*Quel bonheur!*' (What joy!) – familiar to too few these days.

Like every chef in the region, Monsieur Etienne buys his fruit and vegetables at the market and directly from local producers. A stroll through the Provençal market in July is a particularly succulent affair: July is the month for melons, apricots, pomegranates, the first fleshy black figs of the year and the last of the cherries. Francis et Jacqueline Honoré grow 150 fig varieties at **Les Figuières** (www.lesfiguieres.com), an organic farm in Graveson.

The artichoke, another July vegetable, is eaten young and can be stuffed with a salted pork, onion and herb mix, then baked, to become *petits légumes farcis* (little stuffed vegetables); stuffed courgette flowers make an enchanting variation on this. Most vegetables that grow under the Provençal sun can be thrown together into a *tian* (vegetable-and-rice gratin) or eaten as *crudités,* that is, chopped up and served raw with *anchoïade* (anchovy purée), *tapenade* (olive-based dip) or *brandade de morue* (mix of crushed salted cod, olive oil and garlic) with an aperitif.

Staples like onions, tomatoes, aubergines (eggplant) and courgettes (squash or zucchini) are stewed alongside green peppers, garlic and various aromatic herbs to produce that perennial Provençal stew favourite that is known the world over, ratatouille.

AUGUST: HERBAL SCRUB

Distinctive to Provençal cuisine is the use of lavender (see p344), harvested during the hot dry days of August when the aromatic purple flower is still in bloom. Its

INTERVIEW: THE MELON FARMER

Charismatic Bernard Meyssard has plenty of passions in life: 'melons, *la chasse* (hunting), *pétanque,* my wife,' says the 58-year-old melon producer and French *pétanque* champ. Monsieur Meyssard zips around his melon farm in Cheval Blanc, 6km south of Cavaillon, on a quad like a kid, eyes popping out of sockets, frizzy grey locks flying behind him as he revs between greenhouses side-saddle.

A bus driver when he wed Martine in 1969, Bernard traded in the road for agriculture in 1982, quickly establishing himself as one of the largest of the dozen or so small melon-producers farming around Cavaillon. His greenhouses span 20,000 sq metres and yield 2kg to 3.5kg per sq metre of Charentais melons a year (Galia is the other variety rife in these parts). The gentle-hued, sweet-fleshed fruit is harvested and sold at the market late June to early September, although July is the best month.

But life on the melon farm is not a bed of roses: 'It is not as good as it was. The last 10 years have been catastrophic. There are areas now that grow melons like fields of corn while the big buyers fix the prices months before melons are harvested. For us small producers, it is finished,' explains Bernard, bemoaning the industrialisation of the melon trade between sweet mouthfuls of his lovingly grown melon: we are all savouring it around his kitchen table between restrained sips (we *are* all driving) of Beaumes de Venise. 'Melon is my passion – I won't abandon it. But now I grow lettuces November to March and strawberries in spring to make ends meet,' says the man who holidays twice a year ('two weeks in August with my wife on the coast and a gastronomy week in Le Gers with my friends in September before planting the lettuces'). 'Chin chin, *c'est bon,* huh?' Murmurings of contentment rumble around the table as the bottle of Beaumes is drained (there *are* six of us drinking it).

Should you want to meet Bernard in the middle of a melon field and learn more about his trade, enquire at Cavaillon tourist office (p150) or Cheval Blanc tourist office about the farm visits they run in July and August. Otherwise, you can always stop at his roadside stall in front of his farm, 2km south of Cheval Blanc towards Merindol, and buy a Meyssard melon.

For the ultimate melon-dining experience, book a table at Prévôt (p151).

flowers flavour herbal tea, tart up desserts and spice grilled meats. Its leaves float in soups.

Provence's titillating array of aromatic herbs and plants is a legacy of the heavily scented *garrigue* (scrubland) that grows with vigour in the region. Throughout Europe the *herbes de Provence* mix is used abundantly: since 2003 the dried herbal mix has been protected by a Red Label requiring authentic *herbes de Provence* to contain 26% rosemary (a natural ingredient for eternal youth in medieval Provence), 26% savory, 26% oregano, 19% thyme and 3% basil.

In Provence, however, culinary creations rely more on fresh herbs. Fresh basil lends its pea-green colour and fragrance to *pistou* (pesto), although the herb is dried to flavour *soupe au pistou*. Sage is another *pistou* ingredient, and aromatic rosemary brings flavour to meat dishes. Chervil leaves are used in omelettes and meat dishes, and the tender young shoots of tarragon flavour delicate sauces accompanying seafood.

Then there is the sensual aniseed scent of the bulbous fennel. While its leaves are picked in spring and finely chopped for use in fish dishes and marinades, its potent seeds are plucked in late August to form the basis of several herbal liqueurs, including pastis (see p55).

Should you fancy your very own herbal scrub, head to the Église de Châteauneif near the Prieuré de Salagon in Haute-Provence and ask the priest at the church to concoct one for you (p174).

SEPTEMBER: RED RICE

Gourmets rave about the red rice harvested in September in Europe's most northerly rice-growing region – the Camargue. Nutty in taste and borne out of a cross-pollination of wild red and cultivated short-grain rice, the russet-coloured grains are best shown off in a salad or pilaf. They are also delicious simply served with olive oil, salt and herbs or almonds; and marry beautifully with the region's other big product, bull. Risotto-style white and other brown-rice varieties are also cultivated in this wet westerly corner of Provence, where paddies cover 100 sq km and conditions can be unique.

'Flamingos try to eat our rice so we have an automatic gun-sound machine to scare them off,' says Camargue rice-farmer Lucille Bon, whose organic 500-hectare rice plantation yields just 2000kg to 5000kg of rice per hectare (compared to up to 8000kg per hectare on a traditional nonorganic farm).

Rice is planted in a pancake-flat field at the end of April and flooded with water from the Rhône, remaining submerged until 15 days before the September harvest when the water is drained off. Harvesting rice is just like harvesting wheat, after which the field is burned and the rice sent to the cooperative to have its outer husk machine-removed, thus becoming brown rice.

OCTOBER: SWEET CHESTNUTS

Roast chestnuts hot off the coals brighten darker days in October, when the first fresh fruits of the *châtaignier* (chestnut tree) fall – *marrons* (the larger fruits packed

BACKGROUND

singularly in the prickly chestnut burs) and *châtaignes* (the smaller fruits, packed two or more per bur) in culinary terms.

In Collobrières, chestnut capital in the Massif des Maures, the autumnal fruit is made into *marrons glacés, crème de marrons* (sickly sweet chestnut spread, much loved on crêpes) and *liqueur de châtaignes* (chestnut liqueur). The tree's aromatic flowers flavour *gelée de fleurs de châtaignes* (chestnut flower jelly).

> *'Roast chestnuts hot off the coals brighten darker days in October'*

NOVEMBER: THE OLIVE HARVEST

In November, the bulk of the region's succulent, sun-baked black olives – borne from clusters of white flowers that blossom on the knotty old trees in May and June – are harvested. The harvest continues in some parts until January, olives destined for the oil press usually being the last to be picked (see also p366) .

Classic aperitif accompaniments are a simple ramekin of olives marinated in spiced olive oil or a bowl of tangy *tapenade,* a dip described perfectly by Patricia Wells: '*Tapenade* combines the favourite flavours of Provence: the tang of the home-cured black olives in brine, the saltiness of the tiny anchovy, the briny flavour of the caper, the vibrant sharpness of garlic, the heady scent of thyme, the unifying quality of a haunting olive oil'.

Table olives are the first to be harvested and can be black, round and fleshy *(grossane);* green and pointed *(picholine)* or pear-shaped with yellow tints *(salonenque). Olives de Nice* (the Cailletier grape variety) are small, firm and lime, wine, brown or aubergine in colour.

INTERVIEW: THE OLIVE FARMER   *Catherine Le Nevez*

Siblings Anne and Gilles Brun make a formidable team at the family mill, Moulin à Huile du Calanquet, 4.5km southwest of St-Rémy de Provence. Stopped in its tracks following the great frost of 1956, the oil press started turning again in 2001. Lonely Planet author Catherine Le Nevez spoke to the family.

Tell me about a little bit more about the mill and its past. Our family have farmed this property for five generations. Our grandparents ran the oil mill and olive farm but after 1956 production stopped and they grew cauliflowers and potatoes instead. Before 1956 there were five mills in the area; one traded for 10 years afterwards then stopped too, meaning there was nowhere in the northern Alpilles to mill oil.

Provençal and local traditions are important to us. [The mill's name comes from the Provençal word *calan,* a rock used as shelter from the mistral.] After we reopened the mill, we also replanted olive trees where our grandparents' trees were.

What sort of oil do you produce and how much? We cultivate five traditional Alpilles olive varieties which give five types of oil, as well as a blend. Our speciality is separating the different varieties for mono-varietals. Our oils have 0% to 8% acidity, which means they go well with sweet dishes as well as fish. Our 5000 trees produce 100,000kg of olives and 20,000L of oil a year.

When is olive oil at its best? When it's new; the taste and flavour is good.

BACKGROUND

With son Anthony, Nicole and Serge Bérenguier cultivate four varieties of olive at their 10-hectare olive farm and mill in Callas (p290), a four-generation family business founded in 1928 by grandfather Félix and revived by grandson Serge in the 1970s after the 1956 frost froze most olive trees to death. 'October, just before the harvest when the olives change colour, is a magnificent moment. The olives stay green, but they become paler, promising *une belle recolte* (beautiful harvest),' says Nicole, adding that 'early November when the olives fall is also magical'. Just two extra people are taken on to help harvest: green nets are laid out beneath the trees to catch the falling olives, loosened from the tree with special scissors. Annual yield: around 350 tonnes.

DECEMBER: A DOZEN & ONE DESSERTS

December in Provence sees families rush home after Mass on Christmas Eve for Caleno vo Careno, a traditional feast of 13 desserts – symbolising Jesus and the 12 apostles – at least one bite of each to avoid back luck for the coming year. Among the culinary delights are *pompe à huile* (leavened cake baked in olive oil and flavoured with orange blossom), sweet black and white nougats (homemade from honey and almonds), dried figs, almonds, walnuts, raisins, pears, apples, oranges or mandarins, dates, quince jam or paste and *calissons d'Aix* (marzipan-like sweets; see p76).

Not that there's not plenty to keep sweet-tooths appesed year-round. Lavender and thyme flavour milk-based dishes such as crème brûlée as well as jams and honey. Anise and orange blossoms give *navettes* (canoe-shaped biscuits from Marseille) and *fougassettes* (sweet bread) their distinctive flavours. A secret 60 different Mont Ventoux herbs are used to make the liqueur that laces *papalines d'Avignon* (pink liqueur-laced chocolate balls). Almonds are turned into *gâteaux secs aux amandes* (snappy almond biscuits) around Nîmes, and black honey nougat everywhere. Countrywide, christening and wedding guests receive *dragées* – porcelain-smooth sugared almonds tinted pink for a girl, blue for a boy and white for a blushing bride.

Nice and Apt excel at *fruits confits* (crystallised or glazed fruits); see them made in Apt (p156), Pont du Loup and Nice. *Berlingots* are hard caramels originating in Carpentras, and *tarte Tropézienne* is a cream-filled sandwich cake from St-Tropez. A popular dessert in the Vaucluse is cantaloupe melon from Carpentras doused in Muscat de Beaumes de Venise, a sweet dessert wine made in a village nearby.

DON'T MISS...

TASTING IN SITU

★ **Camargue red rice & bull meat //** On a driving tour of the wild southeastern Camargue (p96)

★ **Banon cheese //** On a mountain cheese road trip (p174)

★ **Organic goat cheese //** At Ferme des Courmettes in Tourrettes-sur-Loup (p259)

★ **Duck in all its guises //** Over lunch at a duck farm in the Parc Naturel Régional du Verdon (p181)

★ **Olive oil, wine & citrus liqueurs //** From Domaine St-Joseph in Tourrettes-sur-Loup (p259)

★ **40 different farm-made jams & condiments //** At La Bastide des Minguet in Oppède-les-Poulivets (p162)

★ **Pastis //** In Marseille (p55)

BACKGROUND

FOOD GLOSSARY

· · · · · · ·

STARTERS

anchoïade on·sho·yad anchovy purée laced with garlic and olive oil

assiette de crudités a·syet de krew·dee·tay plate of raw vegetables with dressings

banon ba·no goat's-milk cheese dipped in *eau de vie* (brandy) and wrapped in chestnut leaves

bouillon boo·yon broth or stock

bourride boo·reed fish soup; usually eaten as a main course

brandade de morue bron·dad der mo·rew mix of crushed salted cod, olive oil and garlic

brebis brer·bee sheep's-milk dairy product

fromage de chèvre fro·mazh der shev·rer goat's-milk cheese (also called *brousse*)

pissala pee·sa·la Niçois paste mixed from puréed anchovies

pissaladière pee·sa·la·dyair anchovy, onion and black-olive 'pizza' from Nice

soupe au pistou soop o pees·too vegetable soup made with basil and garlic

soupe de poisson soop der pwa·son fish soup

tapenade ta·per·nad sharp, green- or black-olive-based dip

tomme arlésienne tom ar·lay·syen moulded goat's-milk cheese from Arles

MEAT, CHICKEN & POULTRY

agneau a·nyo lamb

alouettes sans tête a·loo·wet son tet nothing to do with 'headless larks'; rather a tomato beef stew

bœuf berf beef

bœuf haché berf ha·shay minced beef

canard ka·nar duck

chèvre shev·rer goat; also goat's-milk cheese

chevreau sher·vro kid (baby goat)

daube de bœuf à la Provençale dob der berf a la pro·von·sal beef stew with tomatoes

entrecôte on·trer·cot rib steak

épaule d'agneau e·pol da·nyo shoulder of lamb

estouffade de bœuf es·too·fad der berf Carmargais beef stew with tomatoes and olives

filet fee·lay tenderloin

gardianne de taureau gar·dyan der to·ro Camargais bull-meat stew

jambon zham·bon ham

lardoons lar·don pieces of chopped bacon

pieds de porc pyay der pork pig's trotters

pieds et paquets pyay ay pa·kay sheep's tripe; literally 'feet and packages'

poulet poo·lay chicken

saucisson d'Arles so·see·son darl sausage made from pork, beef, wine and spices

FISH & SEAFOOD

aïoli Provençale complet ay·o·lee pro·von·sal kom·play shellfish, vegetables, boiled egg and aïoli

anchois on·shwa anchovy

coquillage ko·kee·yazh shellfish

coquille St-Jacques ko·keey san zhak scallop

crevette grise krer·vet grees shrimp

crevette rose krer·vet ros prawn

estocaficada (in Niçois) es·to·ka·fee·ka·da stockfish (dried salt fish soaked in water for four to five days), stewed for two hours with onions, tomatoes and white wine, then combined with anchovies and black olives

fruits de mer frwee der mair seafood

gambas gom·ba king prawns

homard o·mar lobster

langouste lang·goost crayfish

langoustine lang·goos·teen small saltwater 'lobster'

oursin oor·san sea urchin

paella pa·ay·a rice dish with saffron, vegetables and shellfish

palourde pa·loord clam

rouget roo·zhay red mullet

tellines te·leen delicate pink nail-sized clams, best cooked with cream and garlic as a starter or mixed with spaghetti as a main

VEGETABLES, HERBS & SPICES

aïl ai garlic
artichaut ar·tee·sho artichoke
asperge a·spairzh asparagus
basilic ba·see·leek basil
blette de Nice blet der nees white beet
cèpe sep cep (boletus mushroom)
châtaigne sha·tayn·yer sweet chestnut
estragon es·tra·gon tarragon
fleur de courgette fler der koor·zhet courgette (zucchini) flower
légumes farcis lay·gewm far·see stuffed vegetables
mesclun mes·klun Niçois mix of lettuce
ratatouille ra·ta·too·yer casserole of aubergines, tomatoes, peppers and garlic
riz de Camargue ree der ka·marg Camargais rice
romarin ro·ma·run rosemary
salade Niçoise sa·lad nee·swaz green salad featuring tuna, egg and anchovies
thym tun thyme
tian tyan vegetable-and-rice gratin served in a dish called a *tian*
tourta de bléa toor·ta de blay·a Niçois white-beet-root and pine-kernel pie
truffe trewf black truffle

SAUCES

aïoli ay·o·lee garlicky sauce to accompany *bouillabaisse*
huile d'olive weel do·leev olive oil
pistou pees·too pesto (pounded mix of basil, hard cheese, olive oil and garlic)
Provençale pro·von·sal tomato, garlic, herb and olive-oil dressing or sauce
rouille roo·yer aïoli-based sauce spiced with chilli pepper; served with *bourride*
vinaigrette vun·ay·gret salad dressing made with oil, vinegar, mustard and garlic

BREAD & SWEETS

chichi freggi shee·shee fre·gee sugar-coated doughnuts from Marseille
fougasse foo·gas elongated Niçois bread stuffed with olives, chopped bacon or anchovies
fougassette foo·ga·set brioche perfumed with orange flower
gâteaux secs aux amandes ga·to sek o a·mond crisp almond biscuits
michettes mee·shet Niçois bread stuffed with cheese, olives, anchovies and onions
navettes na·vet canoe-shaped, orange-blossom-flavoured biscuits from Marseille
pain aux noix pun o nwa walnut bread
pain aux raisins pun o ray·zun sultana bread
pan-bagnat pun·ba·nya Niçois bread soaked in olive oil and filled with anchovies, olives and green peppers
panisse pa·nees Niçois potato-sized chunks of chickpea-flour patties
socca so·ka Niçois chickpea-flour and olive-oil pancake

ACCOMMODATION

FINDING ACCOMMODATION

Be it a quintessential French *auberge* (inn) with vine-clad facade and sun-bleached wooden shutters, a 19th-century château between vines or an urban-savvy designer space overlooking rooftops, accommodation in southern France is dreamy, delightful, abundant and often expensive.

Hotels have one to four stars. The cream of the crop languish in traditional properties such as Provençal *mas* (farmhouses), *monastères* (monasteries), *moulins à huile* (oil mills) and Riveria belle époque follies. Lakes, rose gardens and olive groves pepper the grounds of these vast estates, many of which fall under the exclusive umbrella organisations Relais & Châteaux (www.relaischateaux.fr) and Châteaux & Hôtels Collection (www.chateauxhotels.com). Reliable midrange choices are represented by Logis de France (www.logisdefrance.com).

Irrespective of price range, single rooms are rare (rather doubles are touted as faintly less expensive singles); doubles with bathtubs cost more than those with showers; and beds often sport neck-aching, hot-dog-shaped bolsters (regular pillows are usually hidden in a cupboard). Triples and quads, frequently available, have two double beds or a double and one/two singles – particularly ideal for families.

An increasingly modish way to sleep, eat and dream Provence is *à la chambre d'hôte* (B&B), the most stylish of which tag themselves as *maison d'hôte*. Many are on farms, wineries or a historic property and are highly sought-after. A feast of a homemade breakfast is included in the price, and many serve a delicious dinner around a shared table (known as *table d'hôte*). Some of the best are listed in this chapter; tourist offices also keep lists as does Gîtes de France (see opposite); or you can book online (opposite).

Tourist offices have lists of self-catering studios, apartments and villas to rent. The most sought-after are booked a year in advance. Many extra-charming *gîtes ruraux* (self-catering accommodation) – a century-old *mas* in a cherry-tree

WEB RESOURCES

Track atmospheric accommodation oozing soul with the following:

* **Avignon & Provence** (www.avignon-et-provence.com) Exceptional online accommodation guide: hotels, B&Bs, self-catering options

* **Fleurs de Soleil** (www.fleursdesoleil.fr) Quality label awarded to *chambres d'hôtes;* national guide online

* **Maisons d'Hôtes de Charme** (www.guidesdecharme.com) Hotel and B&B properties with bags of charm

* **Gîtes de France** (www.gites-de-france-paca.com) The reference for authentic self-catering accommodation

* **Gîtes Panda** (www.gites-panda.fr) The green arm of Gîtes de France; self-catering and B&B accommodation in national parks and nature reserves

orchard, converted farm stables surrounded by a menagerie of farmyard animals – are represented by **Gîtes de France** (www.gites-de-france-paca.com), an organisation that liaises between owners and renters. Amenities range from basic bathroom facilities and simple kitchenette (with oven, hot plates and fridge) to a bathroom, fully equipped kitchen with dishwasher, washing machine, TV, garden and pool. Linen can be rented. Gîtes Panda (above) are in regional and national parks.

PRICES & BOOKING

Budget hotels tend to charge the same rates year-round. Move into the midrange price bracket and there are frequently three sets of seasonally adjusted prices: low season (October/November to February/March), mid-season (March to May and September/October) and high season (June to September). Certain festivals like the Festival d'Avignon, Cannes film festival or Nîmes *férias* bump up prices beyond belief. Irrespective of season or price range, every hotel is obliged to charge a daily *taxe de séjour* (tourist tax) on each visitor in their jurisdiction; the daily tax (€0.20 to €1.50) is set by the local authoritiy and usually enforced Easter to September.

Out of season, it is quite possible to snag a room in a drop-dead gorgeous property on the spot – although many addresses close for at least two weeks for their *congé annuel* (annual closure) when no one's around. From Easter onwards, things hot up making advance booking essential. In July and August don't even contemplate the coast unless you have a reservation or are prepared to pay a fortune for the few rooms still available. The exception is rock-bottom budget accommodation, especially in Nice, which rarely gets booked up in advance – but is full by noon most days.

Tourist offices can invariably tell you where rooms are available; some run accommodation reservation services. Most midrange and top-end hotels only accept reservations accompanied by a credit-card number; many budget joints demand payment upon arrival.

Unless specified otherwise, room prices quoted in the chapter include private

PRICE GUIDE

The following is a guide to the pricing system used in this chapter. Unless otherwise stated, prices quoted are for a double room with private bathroom.

€	up to €80
€€	€80 to €175
€€€	€175 plus

ACCOMMODATION

bathroom. With the exception of prices for *chambre d'hôte* and *maison d'hôte* accommodation, rates don't include *petit dej* (breakfast), which costs anything from €7 to €30 per person.

MARSEILLE AREA

Urban Marseille has something for everyone, but better rooms are in short supply and need booking ahead – Marseille tourist office (p48) takes bookings.

Aix-en-Provence fills fast in summer and at weekends year-round. Its tourist office runs an accommodation **booking office** (☎ 04 42 16 11 84; resaix@aixenprovence tourism.com) and, November to March, takes bookings for hotels offering two nights' accommodation for the price of one.

MARSEILLE

☙ CASA HONORÉ €€€

Map p52; ☎ 04 96 11 01 62; www.casahonore.com; 123 rue Sainte, 7e; d incl breakfast from €150; ⊙ Sep-Jul; Ⓜ Vieux Port; 🐾 🛜 🖳

This *maison d'hôtes* is stylish. When the kids moved out, Madame transformed the family home – an old printing workshop – into a smart B&B with rich linens, designer lamps and scented candles. Four rooms open onto a foliage-filled interior courtyard with small swimming pool.

☙ HÔTEL BELLEVUE €€

Map p52; ☎ 04 96 17 05 40; 34 quai du Port, 2e; s €68-115, d €84-135; Ⓜ Vieux Port; 🐾

Inside this cream building cased in duck-egg blue shutters you'll find the best seats in the Vieux Port house, La Caravelle (p50), where breakfast is served. Otherwise, enjoy artsy rooms wrapped around a wrought-iron staircase and view art works in public spaces.

☙ HÔTEL EDMOND ROSTAND €€

Map p49; ☎ 04 91 37 74 95; www.hoteledmond rostand.com; 31 rue du Dragon, 6e; d €80-90; Ⓜ Estrangin-Préfecture; 🐾 🖳 ♿

Antique shops surround this good-value hotel in the elegant Quartier des Antiquaires, where art, design and antique boutiques reign. Its 16 rooms are stylish and contemporary: some overlook a tiny private garden, others rooftops and Notre Dame de Basilique. Public parking is available in the nearby Préfecture car park.

☙ HÔTEL HERMÈS €

Map p52; ☎ 04 96 11 63 63; www.hotelmarseille .com; 2 rue de la Bonneterie, 2e; s/d €50/77, nuptial ste €99; Ⓜ Vieux Port; Ⓟ 🐾 🛜

Nothing much to look at from the outside but the 28 rooms inside are a steal. The communal wood-decking rooftop terrace with tables and chairs is perfect for a sunset picnic or aperitif. Perched above it, up a metal stairway-to-heaven, you'll find the ship's-cabin-style nuptial suite with Notre Dame and port view: romance is second-nature here.

☙ HÔTEL LE CORBUSIER €€

Off Map p49; ☎ 04 91 16 78 00; www.hotelle corbusier.com; 280 bd Michelet, 8e; d €63-120; ⬚ 🐾

A treat for architecture aficionados, this 20-room hotel inside Le Corbusier's iconic concrete monolith (see p56) is

BOOK YOUR STAY ONLINE

For more accommodation reviews and recommendations by Lonely Planet authors, check out the online booking service at www.lonelyplanet.com/hotels. You'll find the true, insider low-down on the best places to stay. Reviews are thorough and independent. Best of all, you can book online.

an opportunity to experience the Swiss architect's legacy inside and out. Pick from a space-efficient cabin room or a spacious studio with decorative kitchen and sublime sea view.

❤ HÔTEL LE RICHELIEU €

Map p49; ☎ 04 91 31 01 92; www.hotelmarseille .com; www.lerichelieu-marseille.com; 52 corniche Président John F Kennedy, 7e; d/t €66/88; 🔀 🛜

This two-star hotel built into the rocks at Plage de Catalans just gets better and better: artists come here to lap up the breezy, beach-house vibe. Rooms are small but bold and modern; most open to balconies facing the sea and islands. Feel free to hang on the sundrenched breakfast terrace jutting over the water anytime of day.

❤ HÔTEL LUTETIA €

Map p52; ☎ 04 91 50 81 78; www.hotelmarseille .com, in French; 38 allées Léon Gambetta, 1er; d/tr €67/77; Ⓜ Réformés-Canabière; 🔀 🛜

Lutetia is a petite house with a perfectly kempt cream facade, oyster-grey shutters and a thimble-sized lift that whisks guests up to neat-as-a-pin rooms. Church bells ringing at the twin-steepled church up the street are a handy wake-up call.

❤ HÔTEL VERTIGO €

Map p49; ☎ 04 91 91 07 11; www.hotelvertigo.fr; 42 rue des Petites Maries, 1er; dm €23.90, d €55-65; Ⓜ St-Charles Gare SNCF; 🔀 🖥 🛜

One of Europe's new-generation boutique hostels, Vertigo kisses goodbye to dodgy bunk beds, itchy blankets and hospital-like decor and says a hip hello to vintage posters, designer chrome kitchen, retro bar and cool multilingual staff. Dorms max out at six beds and some even have a tiny terrace or balcony.

❤ NEW HÔTEL DE MARSEILLE €€€

Off Map p49; ☎ 04 91 31 53 15; www.new-hotel.com, in French; 71 bd Charles Livon, 7e; s/d €195/215; 🅿 🔀 🛜 🖥

Nestled between the Vieux Port and Plage des Catalans, this striking hotel fuses contemporary design with history. Reception sits inside the city's 19th-century Institut Pasteur, linked to the rest of the hotel – an unexciting four-storey, 100-room block – by a glass-topped gallery. Period brass railings outside are topped with a dash of fuschia pink and the herb garden is the last word in horticultural design.

❤ VILLA MONTICELLI €€

Off Map p49; ☎ 04 91 22 15 20; www.villamonticelli .com; 96 rue du Commandant Rolland, 8e; d €80-110; 🅿 🔀 🔀 🖥

Colette and Jean are passionate about their city and share their secrets and best addresses with guests. An amazing breakfast of homemade everything and panoramic views gets you started in the morning. Probably the best value of its kind.

CASSIS

❤ LE CLOS DES AROMES €€

☎ 04 42 01 71 84; www.le-clos-des-aromes.com; 10 rue Abbé P Mouton; d €85; 🔀 🛜

A short climb uphill from the portside madness, this garden hotel is charming. Bamboo shields guests from peeping Toms, plane trees shade the courtyard, cicadas sing, and dining at dusk is a peaceful affair. Its 14 rooms are typically patterned shades of yellow and blue.

SALON DE PROVENCE

❤ ABBAYE DE SAINTE CROIX €€€

☎ 04 90 56 24 55; www.relais-chateaux.com/sainte croix; Val de Cuech; d €150-380; ☺ Apr-Oct; 🅿 🔀 🖥 🛜 🖼

Akin to heaven on earth, this 12th-century abbey 2km east of Salon is one of Provence's great historic properties. Within its towering stone walls slumber 21 rooms to die for and a gourmet restaurant (menus €51 to €73) serving exalted contemporary cuisine.

AIX-EN-PROVENCE

♥ HÔTEL CARDINAL €

Map p70; ☎ 04 42 38 32 30; www.hotel-cardinal-aix .com; 24 rue Cardinale; s/d €60/70; reception ☯ 6am-11.30pm; ☁ ⚑

Empassioned collector Nathalie Bernard bought this hotel 20 years ago. Push open the old door, step onto patterned tiles and savour a canvas of floral drapes, fresh flower arrangements, marble fireplaces and sculpted cherubs. Nathalie's father painted the hallway art and an unknown was responsible for the fabulous 18th-century fresco on the stairwell. The annexe is a few doors down.

♥ LA PETITE MAISON DE CARLA €€

Map p70; ☎ 04 42 21 20 73, 06 74 18 60 98; maison-de-carla@wanadoo.fr; 7 rue du Puits Neuf; s/d/ste incl breakfast €70/90/145; ☁

Better known as Chez Carla or Chez Maria (Carla and Maria are sisters), this five-room B&B enlivens three floors of an 18th-century townhouse. Richly painted in earthy colours, it mixes Andalucian flamboyancy with muted Provence. There are flowers throughout and each room is different. Romantics love La Source and Manuela (the best in the house) comes with jacuzzi, open kitchen and roof terrace.

♥ L'ÉPICERIE €€

Map p70; ☎ 06 08 85 38 68; www.unechambreenville .eu; 12 rue du Cancel; s/d incl breakfast €80/100; ☁

This intimate B&B is the fabulous creation of Luc, a born-and-bred Pays d'Aix

lad who worked in theatre and cinema before nesting here. His breakfast room recreates a 1950s *épicerie* (grocery store), complete with straw-filled barrow and lacy whites hanging up to dry, and the flowery garden out back is perfect for evening dining (book in advance). But it is Luc's breakfasts – a feast that differs daily and is so copious you won't need lunch – that steal the show.

♥ LE MANOIR €

Map p70; ☎ 04 42 26 27 20; www.hotelmanoir.com; 8 rue d'Entrecasteaux; d €62-92, tr/q €85/102; ☯ Feb-Dec; ⓟ ⚑

A TV commercial for a car could be filmed here. Atmospherically set in a 14th-century cloister, the Manor sits in a quiet wedge of the old town. Its 40 rooms are 1970s, but breakfasting alfresco in the vaulted cloister and the free parking in the crunchy gravel courtyard easily compensate. A real family-friendly address.

AROUND AIX

♥ ARQUIER // ROQUEFAVOUR €

☎ 04 42 24 20 45; www.arquier-restaurant-hotel.com; 2980 rte du Petit-Moulin, Roquefavour; d/q €67/113; ⓟ

This roadside inn within prebreakfast strolling distance of the world's largest stone aqueduct is perfect for those who prioritise easy parking over town-centre location and like to dine well. Rooms are bedecked in Provençal colours and overlook pleasant greenery.

♥ DOMAINE DE LA BRILLANE // AIX-EN-PROVENCE €€

☎ 04 42 54 21 44, 06 80 93 55 63; www.labrillane .com; rte de Couteron, Aix-en-Provence; d incl breakfast €130-160

Stay in this brilliant spot surrounded by a sea of vineyards. Rupert tirelessly restored the château and worked with partner Mary to build the sterling reputation their estate has today. Five gorgeous *chambres d'hôtes* facing vines or Montagne Ste-Victoire complete the perfect Provence picture, guests also being privy to a behind-the-scenes look at real life on a winery (see p76). Follow the signpost 1km off the northbound D13 from Aix to St-Canadet.

THE CAMARGUE

Arles has reasonably priced accommodation, which only really fills during *férias* (bullfighting festival; p90). It is also one of the few places in the soggy wetland to have hotels open (and no mosquitoes) year-round; most places elsewhere function April to October or November.

If it's the stuff of cowboys you're after, low-rise 'ranch style' hotel accommodation lines the D570 heading into Stes-Maries de la Mer. Alternatively, the tourist office (p94) at Stes-Maries can help you find a self-catering *cabane de gardian* (traditional whitewashed cowboy cottage with thatched roof). For the ultimate bed amid nature, see p97.

ARLES

❦ HÔTEL ARLATAN €€

Map p87; ☎ 04 90 93 56 66; www.hotel-arlatan .fr; 26 rue du Sauvage; d €85-155; 🕑 Feb-Dec; 🄿 🏶 🖳 🛜 🕭

Run by the same family since the 1920s, this three-star hotel down an old-town alley has it all: heated pool in a pretty garden, courtyard with twisting vines, bags of original features. Take your pick from stone-flag, terracotta-tile or wood flooring, hefty beamed ceilings, rococo fireplaces and lots of chintzy floral fabrics.

❦ HÔTEL DE L'AMPHITHÉÂTRE €€

Map p87; ☎ 04 90 96 10 30; www.hotelamphi theatre.fr; 5-7 rue Diderot; s/d/tr/q €55/85/115/135; reception 🕑 7am-11pm; 🏶 🖳 🛜

Crimson, chocolate, terracotta and other rich earthy colours dress the 17th-century stone bones of this stylish hotel, which steals hearts with its narrow staircases, roaring fire and alfresco breakfasts in a courtyard. But the biggest heart-stealer is the romantic suite up top (€155), with dreamy lilac-walled terrace overlooking rooftops.

❦ HÔTEL DU MUSÉE €

Map p87; ☎ 04 90 93 88 88; www.hoteldumusee .com; 11 rue du Grand Prieuré; s/d/tr/q €50/58/70/90; 🕑 mid-Feb–mid-Jan; 🏶 🛜

In a fine 17th- to 18th-century building, this impeccable hotel has 28 comfortable rooms, a checkerboard-tiled breakfast room and a sugar-sweet patio garden brimming with pretty blossoms. Rooms with four beds are handy for families.

❦ LE BÉLVEDÈRE HÔTEL €€

Map p87; ☎ 04 90 91 45 94; www.hotellebelvedere -arles.fr; 5 place Voltaire; s/d €65/70-90; reception 🕑 8am-10pm; 🏶 🛜 🕭

This 17-room town hotel jostles at the top with the best of Arlésian pads. Its style mixes baroque and contemporary: from the red-glass chandelier in the lobby-lounge to the masculine red, chocolate brown, grey and beige colour-schemes, the Bélvèdere – meaning 'viewpoint' in French – is stylish.

❦ L'HÔTEL PARTICULIER €€€

Map p87; ☎ 04 90 52 51 40; www.hotel-particulier .com, in French; 4 rue de la Monnaie; d low/high from €209/229; 🕑 mid-Mar–mid-Nov & mid-Dec–mid-Jan; 🄿 🏶 🖳 🛜 🕭

A secret address in a backstreet few know, this exclusive boutique hotel with restaurant, spa and *hammam* (Turkish bath) oozes old-world charm. From the big black door with heavy door knocker to the old-fashioned lanterns lighting the street and the delightful garden and pool hidden out back, everything about the 18th-century *hôtel particulier* (private mansion) enchants.

STES-MARIES DE LA MER

❤ HÔTEL DE CACHAREL €€

☎ 04 90 97 95 45; www.hotel-cacharel.com; s/d/tr/q €116/124/135/156; Ⓟ Ⓧ 🖳

This isolated farmstead balances modern-day comforts with rural authenticity perfectly. Photographic portraits of the bull herder who created it in 1947 give the reception soul and B&W shots of *gardians* (cowboys), bullfights and other traditional festivals in the 1950s enliven the vintage dining room. Guests in the priciest rooms can watch the sun rise over the water.

❤ HÔTEL MÉDITERRANÉE €

☎ 04 90 97 82 09; www.mediterraneehotel.com, in French; 4 av Fréderic Mistral; d/tr €45-55/75; Ⓟ Ⓧ

A profusion of flowery blooms – overflowing from the windows sills, bijou breakfast garden and steps leading up to the front door – makes guests feel at home in this two-star hotel. Rooms are simple: the cheapest share a toilet, the most expensive have a tiny terrace. Find it seconds from the sea.

❤ LODGE SAINTE HÉLÈNE €€

☎ 04 90 97 83 29; www.lodge-saintehelene.com, in French; chemin des Petit Launes; d €130-173; Ⓟ Ⓧ

These pearly-white terraced cottages strung along a lake edge are prime real estate for bird watchers. As it's beautifully set away from the busy D570, the mood is exclusive, remote and so quiet you can practically hear flamingo wings flapping overhead.

❤ LE MAS DE PEINT €€€

☎ 04 90 97 20 62; www.masdepeint.com; Le Sambuc; d/tr from €205/305; ⌚ mid-Mar–mid-Nov & mid-Dec–mid-Jan; Ⓟ Ⓧ Ⓧ 🖳 ♿

Experience authentic farm life at this 17th-century barn and pigeon house, restored to become the Camargue's most upmarket *mas:* think chic, gentrified country quarters right out of the pages of design mag *Côte Sud.* Checked fabrics, antiques and stone-tiled floors dress its rooms; bathrooms are Victorian or mezzanine-modern; there are horses and bikes to ride, and a tasty restaurant to boot (p98).

AVIGNON AREA

Orange and Carpentras are the least expensive bases with ample budget accommodation; Avignon and upmarket St-Rémy de Provence offer rarified hotels and immaculate B&Bs. Reserve months ahead for the Festival d'Avignon or Nîmes' *férias*, when prices rise by as much as 25% and many places insist on multiple-day stays. Many hotels close for several weeks in winter.

AVIGNON

❤ HÔTEL DE LA MIRANDE €€€

Map p106; ☎ 04 90 14 20 20; www.la-mirande.fr; 4 place de l'Amirande; d €380-520, ste from €820; Ⓟ Ⓧ Ⓧ 🖳 Ⓡ

You'll feel like an 18th-century nobleman at this refined hotel based in a medieval cardinal's palace. Its 20 elegant rooms, most with views of the Palais des Papes, are lined with wood panelling and tapestries. Saunter down through the pretty interior courtyard for the afternoon pastry buffet (€12). There's also an innovative restaurant (*menus* €35 to €105). Parking €22 per night.

❤ HÔTEL DE L'HORLOGE €€

Map p106; ☎ 04 90 16 42 00; www.hotels-ocre-azur
.com; place de l'Horloge; d €85-165; 🗙 🛜
On Avignon's main square, the war-
renlike Horloge has 66 rooms with
stone-coloured walls, chocolate carpets
and natural fabrics. Superior rooms are
larger and come with tea-making facilities. There's no 'wow factor' – just plain,
good-value lodging in a fantastic location. Breakfast (€14) is an impressive
buffet banquet.

❤ HÔTEL DU PALAIS DES PAPES €€

Map p106; ☎ 04 90 86 04 13; www.hotel-avignon
.com; 3 place du Palais; d €72-123
It's not taking the palace's name in vain:
this might be an old-fashioned abode
with wrought-iron furniture, frescoed
ceilings and exposed stone walls, but the
pricier rooms do indeed sport views of
the Palais des Papes. There's also a wonderfully authentic, cavelike restaurant, Le
Lutrin (menus €25 to €40).

❤ LUMANI €€

Map p106; ☎ 04 90 82 94 11; www.avignon-lumani
.com; 37 rue du Rempart St-Lazare; d incl breakfast
€100-170; 🗙 🗙 🛜
This fabulous maison d'hôte run by Elisabeth, whose artworks are hung throughout the stunning house, and her husband
Jean, a saxophonist, is a fount of inspiration for artists. Lumani's stone walls
house five rooms (including two suites)
and a soundproofed music atelier overlooking a fountained garden. An adjacent
artists' workshop is available for rent.

NORTH OF AVIGNON

❤ CHÂTEAU DE MAZAN // MAZAN €€€

Off Map p125; ☎ 04 90 69 62 61; www.chateaude
mazan.fr; place Napoléon, Mazan; d €140-275, ste
€275-400; 🕑 Mar-Dec; 🅿 🗙 🖵 🖭 🕭

This magnificent castle 7km east of Carpentras belonged to the Marquis de Sade
in the 18th century. Today it houses 30
regal rooms and suites in an orchard of
colours. Gastronomic bliss is dished up
at the refined restaurant, l'Ingénue (menus from €40; closed Tuesday in summer
and Monday and Tuesday in winter).

❤ DOMAINE DE CABASSE // SÉGURET €€

☎ 04 90 46 91 12; www.cabasse.fr; rte de Sablet,
Séguret; d €135; 🕑 Apr-Oct; 🅿 🛜 🖭
Wine connoisseurs will appreciate this
wine-producing estate on the plains,
800m south of Séguret village. In addition to 12 sunlit rooms, a pool and
tennis courts, there are wines galore to
taste from the barrel-lined cellar; best
accompanied by taking up the option of
half-board, with meals prepared from
vegetables grown on the grounds.

❤ HOSTELLERIE DU VAL DE SAULT // SAULT €€

☎ 04 90 64 01 41; www.valdesault.com; rte de
St-Trinit, Sault; half-board per person €120-180;
🕑 Apr-Oct; 🅿 🖭 🕭
'Gourmet stays' is the elaborate but accurate description of the half-board options at this haven of peace, 2km north
of Sault along the D950 to Banon. Dine
on menus such as 'lavender flowers' and
'homage to truffles', then luxuriate in the
bubbling jacuzzi while looking out over
Mont Ventoux or swim in the heated
pool. Accommodation is in whisper-
quiet, wood-accented rooms and suites,
each with a private terrace.

❤ HOSTELLERIE LE BEFFROI // VAISON-LA-ROMAINE €€

☎ 04 90 36 04 71; www.le-beffroi.com; rue de
l'Évêché, Vaison-la-Romaine; d €90-144, tr €170;
🕑 closed late Jan–late Mar; 🅿 🖭 🕭

Within the Cité Médiévale's walls, this 1554-built *hostellerie* is housed over two buildings (the 'newer' one was built in 1690). A fairy-tale hideaway, its 22 rough-hewn stone-and-wood-beam rooms are romantically furnished, and the glass-paned breakfast room tumbles onto a rambling rose-and-herb garden with kids' swings. There are 11 hotly contested parking spaces out front, or a lock-up garage down the hill.

♥ HÔTEL BURRHUS // VAISON-LA-ROMAINE €

☎ 04 90 36 00 11; www.burrhus.com; 1 place de Montfort, Vaison-la-Romaine; d €53-85, apt €130; 🕑 closed mid-Nov–late Dec; ℗ 🛜

Right on Vaison's central square, Burrhus looks quaint and olde worlde from the outside, but inside its 38 rooms have stunning cutting-edge colours (including one vision in all white), funky streamlined furnishings, mosaic bathrooms and dramatic designer lighting. Parking costs €7.

♥ HÔTEL DU FIACRE // CARPENTRAS €€

Map p125; ☎ 04 90 63 03 15; www.hotel-du-fiacre .com; 153 rue Vigne, Carpentras; d €70-110; ℗ ✕

The genuine warmth of the welcome at this family-owned hotel makes you feel you're staying with favourite relatives. Set around a central walled stone courtyard in a beautifully restored 18th-century mansion, its rooms are furnished with floral quilts, canopied beds, antiques and original art. All have TV (including BBC).

♥ HÔTEL L'HERBIER D'ORANGE // ORANGE €

Map p116; ☎ 04 90 34 09 23; www.lherbierdorange .com; 8 place aux Herbes, Orange; s/d/tr from €37/42/55; ✕ 🛜

Budget-conscious travellers should head for L'Herbier. Its 19 rooms are clean and bright, with arctic-white walls and bedspreads in warm, cheerful tones of lavender, orange or chocolatey brown. The cheapest rooms come with sink only, but all have TV and telephone. It's a very friendly place, and the Roman theatre is conveniently just round the corner.

♥ LA MADELÈNE // MALAUCÈNE €€

☎ 04 90 62 19 33; rhonewineholidays@googlemail .com; ancien rte d'Entrechaux, Malaucène; d €130; ℗ 🛜 🛁

This delightful 12th-century Benedictine priory, sheltered from surrounding vineyards by stands of pine trees, exudes a monklike calm. The building has been restored with the utmost empathy, and the five airy bedrooms are havens of cool linen and carefully-chosen antiques. There are bikes to borrow, a *pétanque* pitch, and a swimming pool and gardens to lounge in. Find La Madelène 3km from Malaucène, on the way to Entrechaux. There is a two-night minimum stay.

♥ MAISON FELISA // ST-LAURENT DES ARBRES €€

☎ 04 66 39 99 84; www.maison-felisa.com; 6 rue des Barris, St-Laurent des Arbres; d incl breakfast €120-160; ℗ ✕ 🛌 🛁

In a medieval village 15km west of Châteauneuf du Pape (and handy if you're visiting the Pont du Gard and Nîmes), this tranquil *maison d'hôte* rejuvenates the weariest of travellers. Bed linen is ironed with jasmine-scented water, three rooms have jacuzzi, on-site spa treatments include Ayurvedic massages, and private cooking classes are available by reservation. Not a suitable accommodation option for children.

EAST OF AVIGNON

♥ AUBERGE LA FONTAINE // VENASQUE €€

☎ 04 90 66 02 96; www.auberge-lafontaine.com; place de la Fontaine, Venasque; d €125; ⚑ closed mid-Nov–mid-Dec; Ⓟ ⬔ ♿

This ivy-draped inn has four characterful apartments, each with their own kitchen, dining- and sitting-room, and staircases leading up the split level to a whitewashed bedroom. Wild asparagus, truffles, locally picked raspberries, and herb-fed rabbit feature at the six-tabled restaurant (menus from €35; open for dinner Thursday to Tuesday). The Auberge also runs regular intensive three-day cooking courses and occasional concerts.

♥ HÔTEL DU POÈTE // FONTAINE DE VAUCLUSE €€

☎ 04 90 20 34 05; www.hoteldupoete.com; Fontaine de Vaucluse; d €90-240; ⚑ Mar-Nov; ⬔ 🛜 🖵

On the right-hand riverbank as you enter the village, the Hôtel du Poète is based in a peach-tinged old mill. Its 24 lyrically categorised rooms like 'melody' and 'symphony' have creamy Provençal-style furnishings. Eat breakfast (€17) on the poolside terrace, or relax in the jacuzzi.

♥ HÔTEL PRATO-PLAGE // PERNES-LES-FONTAINES €€

☎ 04 90 61 37 75; www.pratoplage.com; rte de Carpentras, Pernes-les-Fontaines; d €144; Ⓟ 🛜 🖵

Despite its slightly unpromising location, 2km out of town, this hotel-restaurant is a pleasant surprise and a great family choice. An artificial lake and beach (with summer lifeguard) give it a resortlike atmosphere. Sunny rooms all have French windows, and the decent restaurant, with its terrace and Mont Ventoux views, serves strong regional dishes.

♥ LA MAISON SUR LA SORGUE // L'ISLE-SUR-LA-SORGUE €€€

☎ 04 90 20 74 86; www.lamaisonsurlasorgue.com; 6 rue Rose Goudard, L'Isle-sur-la-Sorgue; d incl breakfast €240-280; Ⓟ ⬔ ⬕ 🖵

A beautiful 17th-century private mansion underpins this luxurious chambre d'hôte, accessed via a glassed-in interior courtyard. Start your day with breakfast beneath a sycamore tree, and spend the evening snuggled up in the lounge. Ask hosts Marie-Claude and Frédéric to let you in on the mansion's intriguing history. Parking €10 by reservation.

♥ LA PRÉVÔTÉ // L'ISLE-SUR-LA-SORGUE €€

☎ 04 90 38 57 29; www.la-prevote.fr; 4bis rue Jean-Jacques Rousseau, L'Isle-sur-la-Sorgue; d incl breakfast €130-180; ⚑ closed late Feb–early Mar & mid-Nov–early Dec; ⬔ 🛜

Straddling a burbling waterway in L'Isle-sur-la-Sorgue's old town, this chambre d'hôte, pretty as a box of chocolates, has five dreamily painted rooms and a rooftop jacuzzi. It's an easy amble downstairs to one of the region's finest gastronomic restaurants (menus €26 to €68; closed Tuesday and Wednesday), where chef Jean-Marie Alloin concocts fare like foie gras ravioli and thyme and rosemary chocolate accompanied by pear sorbet.

LES ALPILLES

♥ FRAGRANCE // ST-RÉMY DE PROVENCE €

Off Map p132; ☎ 04 90 92 35 77; www.fragrance-saintremy.com; 2 rue Émile Daillan, St-Rémy de Provence; d incl breakfast €80-90; Ⓟ 🖵

A 200m stroll from the town centre, this sparkling chambre d'hôte filled with crisp white linens, unique artwork and fresh flowers is run by host Chantal Vallette, whose thoughtful touches, like heart-shaped soaps in the bathrooms, win guests' hearts. Take a dip in the inviting timber-decked pool and breakfast on homemade pastries and cakes.

❦ HÔTEL DE PROVENCE // TARASCON €

☎ 04 90 91 06 43; www.hotel-provence-tarascon .com; 7 bd Victor Hugo, Tarascon; d €64-84; ▨ ▯
Built into the town's ramparts, this delightful 18th-century nobleman's house has 11 individually decorated rooms: some have creamy colours and warm-toned antiques, while others go for a brighter palette and seminaive Provençal style. The best four have air-conditioning and open onto a plant-filled terrace.

❦ HÔTEL LES ATELIERS DE L'IMAGE // ST-RÉMY DE PROVENCE €€€

Map p132; ☎ 04 90 92 51 50; www.hotelphoto.com; 36 bd Victor Hugo, St-Rémy de Provence; d from €165, ste from €460; ▣ ▨ ▨ ▨ ▣ ▨
A darkroom allows photographers staying at this flash 'photography hotel' to develop prints; photography workshops enhance your skills; and regular photographic exhibitions provide inspiration. The hotel's grounds (including a hedge maze) also inspire, as do the glossy rooms (our favourite: No 28, with a drawbridge to a private tree house).

NÎMES

❦ HÔTEL DES TUILERIES €

Map p139; ☎ 04 66 21 31 15; www.hoteldestuileries .com; 22 rue Roussy; d €78; ▣ ▨ ▨
Taken over by English owners in 2008, this 11-roomed family-run hotel is slowly being spruced up. It's extremely well priced for such a central location, a short walk from the train station and Les Arènes. A creaky lift raises you to the simple but spic-and-span rooms, with balconies overlooking Nîmes' narrow streets.

❦ JARDINS SECRETS €€€

Off Map p139; ☎ 04 66 84 82 64; www.jardinssecrets .net; 3 rue Gaston Maruejols; d €195-320; ▣ ▨ ▨
Palm trees, clambering plants and a profusion of flourishing flowers grace the 'secret garden' at this fashionable *chambre d'hôte*, a five-minute stroll from Les Arènes. Inside, rooms glow with polished floorboards and rich colours, with luxurious touches like tassel-curtained bathtubs. Breakfast and parking are an additional €20 each.

THE LUBERON

Accommodation in the Luberon is of an extremely high calibre. Beautifully renovated farmhouses nestle in pastoral landscapes and sweet townhouses overlook village squares. Book well ahead in summer when they all fill up.

CAVAILLON

❦ HÔTEL TOPPIN €

☎ 04 90 71 30 42; 70 cours Léon Gambetta, Cavaillon; d €58-64, tr €62-77; ▣ ▨
This character-filled old hotel in Cavaillon's heart offers huge breakfasts of fruit, cereal and bread (€8) and free bike storage (€6 parking for cars). The pick are rooms 7 and 8 with private terraces. There's also a communal sun terrace.

GORDES & AROUND

❦ DOMAINE DES ANDÉOLS // ST-SATURNIN-LÈS-APT €€€

☎ 04 90 75 50 63; www.domainedesandeols.com; D2, 2km west of St-Saturnin-lès-Apt; ste €260-770; ▨ Apr-Nov; ▣ ▨ ▯ ▨
Alain Ducasse's ode to design sits in a velvet-green valley with views from the infinity pool to russet promontories. Individual houses are decorated down to the last cutting-edge detail. Or head to the restaurant (menus €39 to €59): on

summer nights candlelit tables cluster beneath stars.

♥ LE MAS DE LA BEAUME // GORDES €€

☎ 04 90 72 02 96; www.labeaume.com; at entrance Gordes village; d €120-145; P ⓐ

Behind a stone wall, this impeccable five-room *maison d'hôte* is the pride and joy of hosts Wendy and Miguel. The 'blue room' has views of Gordes' château and bell tower from the bed. Homegrown produce from the garden arrives on your plate at breakfast. *Table d'hôte* is €35.

♥ LE MAS REGALADE // LES IMBERTS €€

☎ 04 90 76 90 79; www.masregalade-luberon.com; D2, quartier de la Sénancole, near Gordes; d incl breakfast from €110; P ⓐ ⓔ

Conscientious owner, Stefane, has artfully decorated rooms with both modern touches and charming antiques. The artefacts spread poolside, too, where a vintage Citroën peeks out from hedgerows of lavender and rosemary. Located 3.5km from Gordes.

♥ LES PASSIFLORES // ROUSSILLON €

☎ 04 90 71 43 08; www.passiflores.fr; Hameau des Huguets, near Roussillon; d incl breakfast from €70; P ⓔ

The friendly owner welcomes you into this quiet *chambre d'hôte*, tucked into a back square in the tiny hamlet of Huguets. Tidy rooms have king-sized beds with floral quilts. The pool is a natural one, with plants in. *Table d'hôte* costs €23.

APT

♥ LE COUVENT €€

Map p157; ☎ 04 90 04 55 36; www.loucouvent.com, in French; 36 rue Louis Rousset, Apt; d incl breakfast €95-120; ⓔ

Hidden behind a high stone wall and flowering gardens in the town centre, this stunning *maison d'hôte* occupies a 17th-century convent and offers exceptional value: get one of just five sumptuous rooms with high-speed internet, and breakfast in a vaulted stone dining room.

RUSTREL & AROUND

♥ LA FORGE // RUSTREL €€

☎ 04 90 04 92 22; www.laforge.com.fr; Notre-Dame des Anges, Rustrel; d incl breakfast €86-199; P ⓐ ⓔ

Deep within the Colorado Provençal, bordered by forest, this 1840-built former iron foundry has been transformed into an incredible *maison d'hôte*. The exquisite structure shines through slightly over-the-top decor. Breakfast is served beneath a vine-trailed trellis. No credit cards.

LE PETIT LUBERON

♥ LA BOUQUIÈRE // BONNIEUX €€

☎ 04 90 75 87 17; www.labouquiere.com; 1km off of chemin des Gardioles, Bonnieux; d incl breakfast €90-120; P ⓔ

Down a meandering country lane through cherry orchards and vineyards, this remote *chambre d'hôte* has four airy rooms opening onto gardens filled with chirping birds, and at night a glittering sea of stars. Take in spectacular views from the shared kitchen gazebo.

TOP FIVE

ARTY SLEEPS
- ★ **La Maison du Frêne** (p395)
- ★ **La Colombe d'Or** (p395)
- ★ **Hôtel Windsor** (p391)
- ★ **Hôtel Normandy** (p392)
- ★ **Chambre de Séjour avec Vue** (p162)

☙ LE CLOS DU BUIS // BONNIEUX €€

☎ 04 90 75 88 48; www.leclosdubuis.fr; rue Victor Hugo, Bonnieux; d incl breakfast €84-112, cottages per week from €300; ⊙ mid-Feb–mid-Nov; Ⓟ ⊠ ⊚ ⊡

Smack-dab in the village, this stone townhouse spills out to a vast garden. The dining room serves up panoramic views along with *tables d'hôtes* (by reservation), and there's a self-catering kitchen. One of its rooms is wheelchair accessible.

LE GRAND LUBERON

☙ AUBERGE DE PRESBYTÈRE // SAIGNON €€

☎ 04 90 74 11 50; www.auberge-presbytere.com; place de la Fontaine, Saignon; d €85-145; ⊙ closed mid-Jan–mid-Feb

In the 11th and 12th centuries it was three presbyteries. Now it is a village inn with beautiful wood-beamed rooms and an enticing terrace restaurant (*menus* €26 to €35) overlooking the village fountain. Try to get a room overlooking the ruins and valley in the rear.

☙ LA MAGNANERIE // MÉNERBES €€

☎ 04 90 72 42 88; www.magnanerie.com; rte de Bonnieux, Lieu-dit le Roucas, Ménerbes; d €95; ⊙ mid-Mar–mid-Nov & mid-Dec–early Jan; Ⓟ ⊚ ⊡

At this welcoming *maison d'hôte* in the serene, misty hills enjoy one of six stylish rooms and homemade jams and cobblers at breakfast. Guests can barbecue meals in the summer kitchen. Find it 200m down a lane, signposted off the D103. Credit cards aren't accepted.

SOUTH OF THE LUBERON MOUNTAINS

☙ LE MAS DE FONCAUDETTE // LOURMARIN €€

☎ 04 90 08 42 51; www.foncaudette.com; signposted off the D27 btwn Lourmarin & Puyvert; d incl breakfast €110; Ⓟ ⊚ ⊡

Perfect colourful rooms, and some suites perfect for families, surround a fig-tree-shaded central courtyard. Friendly Aline runs this 16th-century *mas* and the pool and sweeping grounds enjoy views of the valley.

HAUTE-PROVENCE

Hotels and *chambres d'hôte* throughout Haute-Provence tend to be simple and relatively no-frills. Correspondingly, it is one of the least expensive regions in Provence. We've tried to pick the standouts for charm or gorgeous location.

VALLÉE DE LA DURANCE

☙ AUBERGE DE LA BANETTE // THOARD €

☎ 04 92 34 68 88; www.aubergelabannette.com; s/d incl breakfast from €48/53; Ⓟ

The friendly Wisner family runs this farmstead overlooking Thoard village. Rustic cabins sit beneath star-strewn skies, and their nightly meal is like a feast from the middle ages (*menu* for guests €20). In winter eat beside their gigantic fireplace. Villagers join you in the evening for homemade kir.

☙ BERGERIE DE BEAUDINE // FORCALQUIER €

☎ 04 92 75 01 52; http://perso.wanadoo.fr/bergerie labeaudine/; rte de Limans, Forcalquier; s/d incl breakfast from €49/59; Ⓟ ⊡

Escape to the 'burbs only 8km from the city centre on the D950 to Banon. Malou from Manosque keeps up a genial hideout complete with *boules* court, outdoor patios and romping puppies. Each room is a study in colour therapy.

☙ LE VIEIL AIGLUN // AIGLUN €€

☎ 04 92 34 67 00; www.vieil-aiglun.com; outside Aiglun; s/d incl breakfast from €65/85; Ⓟ ⊡

Retreat to a magical hilltop enclave in a painstakingly restored Celtic village. An old church, dating from 1555, still sits behind this one-of-a-kind gorgeous *chambre d'hôte*, where every detail is looked after. Each special room is named for the view it enjoys, and the owners couldn't be friendlier. Located 11km southwest of Digne-les-Bains.

♥ MAS SAINT-JOSEPH // CHÂTEAUNEUF-VAL-ST-DONAT €

☎ 04 92 62 47 54; www.lemassaintjoseph.com; D951 to Sisteron; d/q incl breakfast from €54/92; ☾ Apr-Oct; Ⓟ Ⓜ Ⓡ

Location, location, location: this converted farmhouse overlooks a sweeping valley, and is surrounded by layers of terraces and flower beds. Historic wood accents stand in beautiful contrast to serene whitewashed rooms with curving walls and splashes of bright colour in their linens. Amenities include jacuzzi and shared kitchen space.

PARC NATUREL RÉGIONAL DU VERDON

♥ GÎTE DE CHASTEUIL // GORGES DU VERDON €

Map p178; ☎ 04 92 83 72 45; www.gitedechasteuil .com; Hameau de Chasteuil, 12km west of Castellane; s/d/tr incl breakfast from €56/66/84; Ⓟ

This irresistible *chambre d'hôte* in an old schoolhouse in the 16th-century hamlet of Chasteuil has fantastic views to the mountains. Impeccable rooms with crisp linens are a perfect stop for walkers on the GR4, which passes right outside. Host Nancy hand-makes the soaps in the bathrooms.

♥ LA FERME ROSE // MOUSTIERS STE-MARIE €€

☎ 04 92 75 75 75; www.lafermerose.com; chemin de Quinson, Moustiers Ste-Marie; d €80-145; Ⓟ Ⓜ ☎

This fabulous converted farmhouse contains quirky collections including a Wurlitzer jukebox and a display case of coffee grinders. Its dozen boutique rooms draped with embroidered canopies are named for the colour dramatising each chic sleeping area.

♥ LE PETIT SÉGRIÈS // MOUSTIERS STE-MARIE €

☎ 04 92 74 68 83; www.gite-segries.fr; s/d incl breakfast from €50/60; Ⓟ

Friendly hosts Sylvie and Noël maintain six French-washed rooms and have lively *tables d'hôtes* (€21 including wine) at a massive chestnut table with farm-fresh lamb, rabbit and mountain honey. You can also get a picnic basket (€3.50 to €8). Guests and nonguests can rent bikes (€19 per half-day) or sign up for a bike tour (from €65 per half-day).

♥ NOUVEL HÔTEL RESTAURANT DU COMMERCE // CASTELLANE €€

☎ 04 92 83 61 00; www.hotel-fradet.com; place de l'Église, Castellane; s/d €75/95; ☾ Mar-Oct; Ⓟ Ⓜ ⌨ ☎

This exceptionally friendly spot was renovated in 2006 and opens to a large, private garden – and has free parking and internet. It is best known for its 'rustic-gastronomic' restaurant (*menus* €22 to €28), serving favourites so Provençal that Mistral himself would be proud.

PARC NATIONAL DU MERCANTOUR

VALLÉE DE L'UBAYE

♥ LES MÉANS // MÉOLANS-REVEL €€

☎ 04 92 81 03 91; www.les-means.com; D900 Gap-Barcelonette; d €75-110; Ⓟ

Flower-filled window boxes hang off this cosy stone house situated in the middle of mountains, rivers and lakes. The friendly owners, Elisabeth and Frédéric Millet, know the trails of the Ubaye Valley like the back of their hands.

VALLÉE DE LA VÉSUBIE

♥ LE BORÉON // LE BORÉON €

☎ 04 93 03 20 35; www.hotel-boreon.com, in French; d/tr €67/96, half-board per person €64; ⓟ
Magical mountain views unfold from the timber terrace of this secluded, quintessential Snow White chalet 8km north of St-Martin-Vésubie and just an hour north of Nice. Cosy up in one of its dozen rooms and watch the snowflakes fall outside while dining on Alpine specialities (*menu* from €22).

VALLÉE DE LA ROYA

♥ LE PRA REOUND // LA BRIGUE €

☎ 04 93 04 65 67; http://leprareound.ifrance.com; chemin St-Jean, La Brigue; s/d €30/38; ⓟ
Simple, tidy rooms are not the standout – the location in a tiny side-valley on the eastern edge of La Brigue is. Out in open fields of apples and raspberries this feels like a farmstay. Friendly proprietor Madame Molinaro will make breakfast (€5) or you can use the self-catering kitchen.

♥ LE PRIEURÉ // ST-DALMAS DE TENDE €

☎ 04 93 04 75 70; www.leprieure.org, in French; rue Jean Medecin, St-Dalmas de Tende; s/d €59/64; ⓟ ⓡ

TOP FIVE

CELESTIAL SEAVIEWS

★ **Les 3 Îles** (p399)

★ **Camping Les Romarins** (p392)

★ **Le Roquebrune & Les Deux Frères** (p393 & p393)

★ **Hôtel Le Richelieu** (p379)

★ **Hôtel Bor** (p401)

This rambling old priory was renovated in 2009. Ask for one of the rooms overlooking the river to watch crisp mountain water cascade over smooth, white rocks. The restaurant (*menus* €15 to €24) is one of the best in the valley.

NICE, MONACO & MENTON

NICE

♥ HI HÔTEL €€€

Map pp198-9; ☎ 04 97 07 26 26; www.hi-hotel.net; 3 av des Fleurs; d from €190; ⓟ ⊠ ⓤ ⓦ ⓡ
Designed by Philippe Starck protégé Matali Crasset, Hi has turned convention on its head: baths look like four-poster beds (White & White room), loos take pride of place on their elevated, glass-encased platforms (Strates rooms), and colours are loud or nonexistent. The state-of-the-art canteen serves strictly organic food.

♥ HÔTEL DU PETIT PALAIS €€

Map pp198-9; ☎ 04 93 62 19 11; www.petitpalaisnice.com, in French; 17 av Émile Bieckert; d with garden/seaview/seaview & terrace €130/150/180; ⓟ ⊠ ⓦ
This belle époque lemon-meringue-pie hotel in upmarket Cimiez is an attractive choice. Views of Vieux Nice and the Baie des Anges are stunning, and the decor is one of understated elegance throughout. Ground floor rooms have no view but their own little patio. Top picks are first floor rooms combining views and private terrace.

♥ HÔTEL SUISSE €€

Map pp198-9; ☎ 04 92 17 39 00; www.hotels-ocre-azur.com; 15 quai Rauba Capeu; d low/high season from €69/89
The wrought-iron balconies with teak tables and chairs strategically placed on

five floors overlooking the sweeping Baie des Anges are reason enough to stay at this attractive hotel on the prom. Rooms are spacious, the decor minimalist; ask for a room on the upper floors to avoid the worst of the traffic noise. Internet access is through modem cable.

☙ HÔTEL WILSON €

Map pp198-9; ☎ 04 93 85 47 79; www.hotel -wilson-nice.com; 39 rue de l'Hôtel des Postes; s/d with washbasin €35/40, with bathroom €50/55; ☞

'Sleep under a beautiful star' is the catchphrase of this charming hotel in a rambling town-centre building. Each of the 16 rooms has its own character and theme. Some have balconies; the cheapest share spotless bathrooms; but all have access to the delightfully eclectic dining room, where breakfast is served until a civilised noon. The hotel is on the 3rd floor – there's no lift.

☙ HÔTEL WINDSOR €€

Map pp198-9; ☎ 04 93 88 59 35; www.hotelwind sornice.com; 11 rue Dalpozzo; d with/without balcony €175/120; ℗ 🍴 ☞ 📺

This original boutique hotel has let artists' imaginations rip – be it with the graffiti mural by the pool, the weird-and-wonderful artists' rooms customised from ceiling to bedspread, the ignition count audio track in the lift, the lush exotic garden or the bold exhibitions in the hallway (popcorn garlands when we last visited).

☙ NICE GARDEN HOTEL €€

Map pp198-9; ☎ 04 93 87 35 62; www.nicegar denhotel.com; 11 rue du Congrès; d low/high season from €65/90; 🍴 ☞

Nestled in a bourgeois townhouse complete with fabulous walled garden, this is Nice's hidden gem. The work of the exquisite Marion, each room has its own

personality – some with original features such as mosaic floor, others with direct access to the beautiful garden. Incredibly, all this charm and serenity are just a couple of blocks from the Promenade des Anglais; a steal.

☙ NICE PEBBLES €€

Map pp198-9; ☎ 09 52 78 27 65; www.nicepebbles .com; 20 rue de l'Hôtel des Postes; apt per night low/high season from €65/140; ☞ 📺

Have you ever dreamt of feeling like a real Niçois? Coming back to your designer pad in Vieux Nice, opening a bottle of ice-cold rosé and cooking up a storm with the treats you bought at the market? All hail this holiday flat company set up by English couple Matt and Gayle. Their concept is simple: offering the quality of a four-star boutique hotel in holiday flats. The apartments (ranging from one to three bedrooms) are gorgeous and equipped to high standards (flatscreen TV, kitchen, linen bedding and, in some cases, wi-fi, swimming pool, balcony etc). Matt and Gayle also run Riviera Pebbles (www.rivierapebbles .com), with apartments in Cannes, Antibes and Monaco.

☙ ODYSSÉE €€

Off Map pp198-9; ☎ 06 03 64 88 98; www.odyssee -nice.com; 26 chemin du Piolet; d low/high season €95/110; ℗ 🍴 ☞ 📺

For those who like their own space, Odyssée is just the ticket. The two suites/apartments are totally independent from owners Jérôme and François's house, but have access to the drop-dead gorgeous roof terrace and swimming pool. Both apartments have a fridge, DVD player, MP3-player hi-fi and funky modern furnishings. One also has a kitchenette. Minimum stay is two nights. No credit cards.

❦ VILLA LA TOUR €€

Map pp198-9; ☎04 93 80 08 15; www.villa-la-tour
.com; 4 rue de la Tour; d standard/superior
€89/139; ⊠

Small but perfectly formed, Villa la Tour
is delightful, with warm, romantic Provençal rooms, a fabulous location at the
heart of the Vieux Nice and a diminu-
tive, flower-decked roof terrace with
views of the Colline du Château and the
surrounding roofs.

ARRIÈRE-PAYS NIÇOIS

❦ L'ALIVÚ // COARAZE €€

☎04 93 80 86 68; www.alivu.com; 816 rte des
Baisses, Coaraze; d incl breakfast €100; ℗ 🛜 🖵

Hidden among trees, L'Alivú was designed for long, lazy afternoons by the
pool: the plunging views from there are
inspirational indeed. Michèle and Christian are wonderful hosts too, ensuring
chilled rosé is always on standby and
dinner (€32) is available every night. The
only downside is the location, 2km down
a *very* windy lane. It's signposted from
the bridge south of the village.

❦ LA PARARE //
CHÂTEAUNEUF-VILLEVIEILLE €€

☎04 93 79 22 62; www.laparare.com; 67 calade
du Pastre, Châteauneuf Villevieille; d incl breakfast
low/high season €110/125; ℗ 🛜

Karin and Sydney are the widely travelled, multilingual couple behind this
fabulous *chambre d'hôte*, a stunningly
renovated 18th-century stone *bergerie*
(sheepfold) framed by terraced olive
groves. The spacious, stylish rooms,
each with their own fireplace, ooze romance. Breakfast is a lavish homemade
(bread, jams) affair with plenty of fresh
fruit and yoghurt. Karin and Sydney
also do *table d'hôte* (€35 to €50, including wine) twice a week, with local, seasonal products.

THE THREE CORNICHES

❦ CAMPING LES ROMARINS // ÈZE €

☎04 93 01 81 64; www.campingromarins.com;
Grande Corniche, Col d'Èze, Èze; 2 adults, tent & car
mid/high season from €23.60/26.10; 🕃mid-Jun–Sep

This lovely campground, at the western
end of the Col d'Èze, is as close as you'll
get to wild camping in this protected
neck of the woods. Pitch your tent on the
terraced hillside and wake up to incredible views of Cap Ferrat and the coast.

❦ DOMAINE PINS PAUL // ÈZE €€

☎04 93 41 22 66; www.domainepinspaul.fr; 4530
av des Diables Bleus, Grande Corniche, Èze; d incl
breakfast low/high season from €130/160; ℗ 🛜 🖵

Swimming in the panoramic pool of the
Domaine Pins Paul comes high on the
list of best swims ever: the views of the
sea and Èze village are out of this world.
Rooms in the grand Provençal *bastide*
(country house) are lovely too, and the
one hectare of pines, eucalyptus and fruit
trees are perfect for a stroll.

❦ HÔTEL NORMANDY //
CAP D'AIL €

☎04 93 78 77 77; www.hot-no.no; 6 allée des Or-
angers, Cap d'Ail; d with bathroom low/high season
from €55/89, without bathroom €39/64; 🛜

This delightful hotel in trendy Cap d'Ail
is run by a family of artists and it shows:
original modern pieces adorn the walls
everywhere and the spotless rooms ooze
charm with their simple, old-school
furniture (and sometimes fab sea views).
The bohemian, colourful dining room
and terrace are perfect places to meet
other travellers over breakfast or a drink.

❦ HÔTEL RIVIERA //
BEAULIEU-SUR-MER €

☎04 93 01 04 92; www.hotel-riviera.fr; 6 rue Paul
Doumer, Beaulieu-sur-Mer; d low/mid/high season
from €55/60/62; 🕃Jan-Oct; ⊠ 🛜

A breath of fresh air, this tasteful two-star hotel with Carrara marble staircase, Italian granite floors, wrought-iron balconies and a hibiscus-laden summer patio perfect for breakfasting is really hard to resist. Rooms are immaculate and comfortable, and the owners charming. Probably the best value on the coast.

🌱 LA BASTIDE AUX CAMÉLIAS // ÈZE €€

☎ 04 93 41 13 68; www.bastideauxcamelias.com; 23c rte de l'Adret, Èze; d incl breakfast low/high season from €110/130, ste €200/240; Ⓟ 🤶 🛋

Jacuzzi, *hammam*, olive-tree-framed pool, and sauna are among the lazy-weekend comforts to enjoy at this lovely *chambre d'hôte*. The four rooms are romantic and beautifully done, but the jewel in the crown is the suite that Fred and Sylviane renovated in the medieval village of Èze. Its rooftop terrace has plunging views of the Med and guests are just a five-minute drive from the Bastide, where they can use all the pampering facilities.

🌱 LE ROQUEBRUNE // CAP MARTIN €€

☎ 04 93 35 00 16; www.leroquebrune.com; 100 av Jean Jaurès, Cap Martin; d low/high season from €100/120; Ⓟ 🤶 🛜

Le Roquebrune could not be more superbly placed – slap bang on the Lower Corniche with plunging views of the sky-blue sea. The five rooms, each with their own stunning balcony/terrace, all have king-sized beds and lovely furnishings, and you can count on Patricia and Marine's heartfelt welcome to make you feel very much at home.

🌱 LES DEUX FRÈRES // ROQUEBRUNE €€

☎ 04 93 28 99 00; www.lesdeuxfreres.com; place des Deux Frères, Roquebrune; d €75-110; 🤶 🛜

This gorgeous boutique hotel on the village square is a gem. Rooms 1 and 2 steal the show with their heart-stopping views of the Med, but the other eight rooms hold their own, with exquisite themed decor (marine, African, Thousand and One Nights…) and incredibly good-value prices considering the location and standards.

MONACO

🌱 COLUMBUS MONACO €€€

Map p222; ☎ 92 05 90 00; www.columbushotels.com; 23 av des Papalins; d from €210; Ⓟ 🤶 🖥 🛜 🛋

Everything at this urban-chic, boutique hotel in Fontvieille is big: the names behind it (hugely successful Glaswegian hotelier Ken McCulloch, designer Amanda Rosa and British Formula One driver David Coulthard), the hotel itself (180 rooms), and the rooms with their king-sized beds, opulent furniture and enormous views of the hills.

🌱 HÔTEL MIRAMAR €€

Map p222; ☎ 93 30 86 48; www.hotel-miramar.mc; 1 av du Président JF Kennedy; d incl breakfast low/high season from €110/170; Ⓟ 🤶 🛜

This 1950s seaside hotel with rooftop terrace bar for those lazy breakfasts, lunches and evening drinks is a fabulous option right by the port. Except for the polka-dotted or stripy carpets, the decor is rather minimalist with plain walls and bedding. Seven of the 11 rooms have fabulous balconies overlooking the yachts.

🌱 NI HÔTEL €€

Map p222; ☎ 97 97 51 51; www.nihotel.com; 1bis rue Grimaldi; d from €150; 🤶 🛜

This uberhip and modern hotel is the new kid on the block in Monaco. Its distinctive design makes bold use of flashy primary colours (the shower walls, chairs and stairs are made of see-through coloured plastic). Everything else is a sobering black and white mix. The roof terrace is in a prime location for evening drinks.

MENTON

♥ LE PARIS-ROME €€
Off Map p231; ☎ 04 93 35 73 45; www.paris-rome .com; 79 av Porte-de-France; d low/high season from €82/98; **P 🔀 🛜**

By far the best place to stay in Menton, Le Paris-Rome sits right on the border with Italy, a 20-minute walk from the old town. The 20-odd rooms are all individually and tastefully decorated, with styles ranging from contemporary Zen to Louis XVI. Breakfast is served in the pretty dining room or the indoor patio.

CANNES AREA

Hotel prices in Cannes itself soar during the film festival, when you'll need to book months in advance. Search and book accommodation online with **Cannes Hôtel Booking** (www.cannes-hotel-reservation.fr), run by the tourist office. Check out **Riviera Pebbles** (www.rivierapebbles.com) for apartments in Cannes and Antibes.

CANNES

♥ HÔTEL 3.14 €€€
Map p242; ☎ 04 92 99 72 00; www.3-14hotel .com; 5 rue François Einesy; d/ste from €200/710; **P 🔀 🛜 🖼**

A barking fusion of kitsch, pop art and Zen (the hotel was designed according to feng shui rules), *trois-quatorze* is Cannes' most eccentric address: think four-star comforts and add a liberal sprinkling of glitter, gnomes, velvet, wicker and psychedelic colours. The rooftop pool with its exotic garden and jacuzzi overlooking the Carlton's cupolas is an absolute hit.

♥ HÔTEL ALNÉA €
Map p242; ☎ 04 93 68 77 77; www.hotel-alnea.com; 20 rue Jean de Riouffe; d small/large €70/80; 🔀 🛜

A breath of fresh air in a town of stars. You'll be won over by this wonderfully friendly place. Noémi and Cédric have put their heart and soul in their hotel, with bright, colourful rooms, original paintings, and numerous little details such as the afternoon coffee break, the self-service minibar and the bike or *boules* (to play *pétanque*) loans.

♥ HÔTEL MARTINEZ €€€
Off Map p242; ☎ 04 92 98 73 00; www.hotel-martinez .com; 73 bd de la Croisette; d low/mid/high season from €210/355/410; **P 🔀 🖥 🛜 🖼**

Arguably the loveliest luxury place to stay, this ultrasmart art deco–style hotel opened its doors in 1929, a year before Cannes' first official summer season. Luxurious and vast rooms feature wonderful art deco decor, from the furniture to the wallpaper. The top-floor Lancaster spa, heated pool and fabulous beach are just some of the perks to be enjoyed.

♥ HÔTEL MISTRAL €€
Map p242; ☎ 04 93 39 91 46; www.mistral-hotel.com; 13 rue des Belges; d small/large €87/107; 🔀 🛜

This small boutique hotel wins the *palme d'or* for best value in town: rooms are decked out in flattering red and plum tones, bathrooms feature lovely designer fittings, there are seaviews from the top floor and the hotel is a mere 50m from La Croisette.

♥ LA VILLA TOSCA €€
Map p242; ☎ 04 93 38 34 40; www.villa-tosca.com; 11 rue Hoche; d with/without balcony €129/109; 🔀 🛜

This elegant bourgeois townhouse is a great choice at the heart of Cannes' shopping area. Rue Hoche is semi-pedestrianised so you won't be bothered by the noise. Rooms, a palette of beige and brown, are comfortable and those with balcony are perfect for a spot of people watching. A 10% discount is available at Parking de la Gare.

ANTIBES

♨ HÔTEL LA JABOTTE €€

Off Map p249; ☎ 04 93 61 45 89; www.jabotte.com; 13 av Max Maurey; d incl breakfast low/mid/high season from €84/97/108; P ⊠ 🛜

A stone's throw from Plage de la Salis, La Jabotte has 10 lovely rooms, all carefully decorated by the talented Yves (find his paintings and ceramics for sale in the lobby), and a wonderful courtyard dotted with plants and fragrant trees. Breakfast features delicious homemade goodies such as jams, cakes and yoghurts. Parking is free but limited.

♨ VILLA VAL DES ROSES €€€

Off Map p249; ☎ 06 85 06 06 29; www.val-des-roses .com; 6 chemin des Lauriers; d incl breakfast low/high season from €140/250; P ⊠ 🖳 🛜 🏊

This beautiful 19th-century bourgeois villa with marble floors, laptop and jacuzzi bath in each room is a 20-minute stroll from the old town. But it's a mere moment from sandy Plage de la Salis, and its walled garden is an oasis of peace, best enjoyed in the morning whilst tucking into the grand breakfast buffet.

BIOT

♨ RESTAURANT DES ARCADES €€

☎ 04 93 65 01 04; 16 place des Arcades; d €70-100; ⊠

You'll find monumental fireplaces and stunning vintage furniture in this 13th-century building. Rooms on the upper floors are more modest in dimensions but balconies and original art make up for the lack of size and historical features:

TOP FIVE

DESIGN & QUIRK

- ★ **Hi Hôtel** (p390) and **Ni Hôtel** (p393)
- ★ **Hôtel 3.14** (opposite)
- ★ **Hôtel Burrhus** (p384)
- ★ **Domaine des Andéols** (p386)
- ★ The tree houses at **Château de Valmer** (p398), **Hôtel Les Ateliers de l'Image** (p386) and **Les Cabanes d'Orion** (p396)

Les Arcades was the party HQ of many 20th-century artists such as Léger and Vasarely, and many of their works adorn the walls.

VENCE

♨ LA MAISON DU FRÊNE €€

☎ 04 93 24 37 83; www.lamaisondufrene.com; 1 place du Frêne; d incl breakfast low/high season €140/180; 🕙 Feb-Dec; ⊠ 🖳 🛜

This arty guest house is quite astonishing. Yes, that Niki de Saint Phalle is an original. And yes, the César too. It's an essential sleepover for true art-lovers, if only to enjoy the superb rooms with their contemporary designer furniture and original works. Owners and avid art collectors Thierry and Guy are a mine of information on the local art scene too.

ST-PAUL DE VENCE

♨ LA COLOMBE D'OR €€€

☎ 04 93 32 80 02; www.la-colombe-dor.com, in French; place de Gaulle, St-Paul de Vence; d from €265; 🕙 mid-Dec–Oct; P ⊠ 🏊

Breakfasting under a Picasso or swimming in the shade of a giant Calder mobile are some of the unique pleasures awaiting at the Golden Dove. The 26 rooms are spacious and comfortable, and refreshingly un-sleek compared to many top-end establishments on the coast. It's all about the atmosphere, the staff (many of whom have been around for years), and the wonderful history.

☙ LES CABANES D'ORION €€€

☎ 06 75 45 18 64; www.orionbb.com; impasse des Peupliers, 2436 chemin du Malvan; d incl breakfast low/mid season from €650/750, min 3-night stay; P 🛜 🖭

Dragonflies flit above water lilies in the emerald-green swimming pool (filtered naturally), while guests slumber up top amid a chorus of frogs and cicadas in luxurious cedar-wood treehouses perched in the trees at this enchanting, ecofriendly B&B. In high season, the *cabanes* are only let on a weekly basis.

☙ VILLA ST MAXIME €€€

☎ 04 93 32 76 00; www.villa-st-maxime.com; 390 rte de la Colle; d incl breakfast low/high season from €170/185, with seaview from €200/240; P 🔀 🖳 🛜 🖭

You can imagine James Bond staying here. Run by an American couple, this *maison d'hôte* (upmarket *châmbre d'hôte*) is vast and full of architectural flair. Highlights include the show-stopping sliding glass roof, Champagne breakfast cooked up by a sabre-wielding John (he'll happily show you how), and the unbeatable views of hilltop St-Paul and the Med. Unusually, rates include evening drinks.

AROUND VENCE

☙ L'HOSTELLERIE DU CHÂTEAU // LE BAR-SUR-LOUP €€

☎ 04 93 42 41 10; www.lhostellerieduchateau.com; 6-8 place Francis Paulet; d from €130

It's hard to imagine that Bar-sur-Loup's majestic 15th-century castle lay in ruins for more than two centuries. Renovated between 2003 and 2005, it now hosts

six elegant and beautifully understated rooms. The palette is neutral, the furniture period-style and the rooms huge, and there are great views of the surrounding valleys.

☙ LE MAS DES CIGALES // TOURETTES-SUR-LOUP €€

☎ 04 93 59 25 73; www.lemasdescigales.com; 1673 rte des Quenières, Tourettes-sur-Loup; d incl breakfast low/high season €77/105; P 🔀 🛜 🖭

With its pretty Provençal *mas* (farmhouse), colourful garden, picture-perfect pool, sweeping views and amazing breakfast spread, it is likely you'll never want to leave this fabulous *chambre d'hôte*. Active types will love the tennis courts, and the *pétanque* pitch and bicycles, while those keen for a more relaxing afternoon will love the jacuzzi and view-commanding loungers. Truly blissful.

AROUND GRASSE

☙ LE MAS DU NAOC // CABRIS €€

☎ 04 93 60 63 13; www.lemasdunaoc.com; 580 chemin du Migranié, Cabris; d incl breakfast low/high season from €110/130; P 🔀 🛜 🖭

This renovated and vine-covered 18th-century pad in Cabris slumbers in the shade of century-old olive, jasmine, fig and orange trees – and fits the 'quintessentially Provençal' bill perfectly. Soft natural hues dress Sandra and Jérôme Maingret's four lovely rooms, and the coastal panorama from the pool is inspirational. No children under seven.

☙ LES ROSÉES // MOUGINS €€€

☎ 04 92 92 29 64; www.lesrosees.com; 238 chemin de Font Neuve, Mougins; d incl breakfast low/high season €250/310; P 🔀 🖳 🛜 🖭

Chic and authentic is its tagline, and it couldn't be more accurate. This stunning, 400-year-old stone manor house with four romantic suites, pool and century-old olive trees is a gem. The Serguey suite with its glass fireplace (watch the open fire from your lounge or bathtub) is simply divine. Breakfast is a copious organic affair.

MASSIF DE L'ESTÉREL

The efficient **Centrale de Réservation Estérel Côte d'Azur** (Map p267; ☎ 04 94 19 10 60; www.esterel-cotedazur.com; 72 rue Waldeck Rousseau) can help with bookings in the area.

❦ HÔTEL CYRNOS // ST-RAPHAËL €
Off Map p267; ☎ 04 94 95 17 13; www.hotel-cyrnos .com; 840 bd Alphonse Juin, St-Raphaël; d low/high season €35/48; P 🛜

Hiding at the back of a lush garden, this beautiful 1883 *maison de maître* (mansion) is a delightful address in the Santa Lucia neighbourhood. Rooms are simple but fresh, with traditional terracotta floors, tall ceilings, massive windows and great views on the first floor. Breakfast in the garden is another highlight.

❦ L'HIRONDELLE BLANCHE // ST-RAPHAËL €€
Off Map p267; ☎ 04 94 11 84 03; www.hirondelle -blanche.fr; bd de Général de Gaulle, St-Raphaël; d low/high season from €59/99; P 🈺 🛜

A short stroll from Port Santa Lucia, the White Sparrow has six elegantly decorated rooms in a lovely 19th-century villa. Breakfast is served until a very civilised 11.30am and can be anything from a quick *café-croissant* (€4.90) to the whole sweet-and-savoury shebang (eggs, cheese, ham as well as *viennoiseries*, €13).

FRÉJUS

❦ L'ARÉNA €€
Map p271; ☎ 04 94 17 09 40; www.arena-hotel.com; 145 rue du Général de Gaulle, Fréjus; d low/high season from €85/120; P 🈺 🛜 🅿

A hop and a skip from Fréjus' sights, L'Aréna is the perfect place to relax after a day touring Roman ruins: its pool and garden are simply glorious. The 39 rooms are comfortable and elegant in warm Provençal prints. Those in the Jasmine annexe are more spacious but there is no lift. Parking is €12.

ST-TROPEZ TO TOULON

Maison d'Hôtes du Var (www.mhvprovence .com) features a collection of stylish B&Bs in family homes, farms and castles throughout the Var region.

St-Tropez is no shoestring destination, but there are plenty of multistar campgrounds to the southeast along Plage de Pampelonne; the tourist office has a list.

ST-TROPEZ

❦ HÔTEL LA MÉDITERRANÉE €
Map p280; ☎ 04 94 97 00 44; www.hotelmediterranee .org; 21 bd Louis Blanc; s/d from €50/90; 🈺 🛜

Each of the 16 rooms at The Mediterranean are dressed in a simple but romantic decor and guests can opt for half-board, meaning a dinner of meaty Lyonnais fare in the quaint *bouchon* (Lyonnais bistro) with star-topped garden.

❦ HÔTEL LA MISTRALÉE €€
Map p280; ☎ 04 98 12 91 12; www.hotel-mistralee .com; 1 ave du Général Leclerc; d low/mid-/high season from €190/330/460; 🈺 🛜 🅿

The flamboyant former home of hairdresser-to-the-stars, Alexandre (famously sans surname), this totally over-the-top 1960s-decorated hotel includes, for example, fabric presented to Alexandre by the king of Morocco. The restaurant, tucked at the back of the luxurious garden by the mosaic-lined pool, feels like a Thousand-and-One-Nights palace at night.

❧ HÔTEL LOU CAGNARD €€

Map p280; ☎ 04 94 97 04 24; www.hotel-lou-cagnard
.com; 18 av du Paul Roussel; d low season €54-90, high
season d €67-130; ☺ Jan-Oct; 🅿 ❌ 🛜

This pretty Provençal house with lavender shutters has its very own jasmine-
scented garden, strung with fairy lights
between trees at night, *and* is decently
priced. Rooms – nothing fancy – are
light, bright and beautifully clean.
Lounge against lime-green cushions on
the candy-striped swing seat in the garden and congratulate yourself on what
brilliant value this hotel is. The cheapest
rooms have private washbasin and
standup-bathtub but share a toilet.

❧ LA MAISON BLANCHE €€€

Map p280; ☎ 04 94 97 52 66; www.hotellamaison
blanche.com; place des Lices; d low/mid-/high season
from €180/220/260; 🅿 ❌ 🖵 🛜

Design is everything at this elegant
town house with nine boutique rooms,
a beautiful interior courtyard-turned-
summer-garden and evening Champagne bar that creates an oasis of peace
between the hotel and hubbub of St-
Tropez's buzzing market-clad square.
Fresh white flowers, wood and natural
hues predominate at the White House
and room No 7 is the celebrity pick.

❧ PASTIS HÔTEL €€€

Map p280; ☎ 04 98 12 56 50; www.pastis-st-tropez
.com; 61 av du Général Leclerc; d low season
€250-300, high season d €400-600; ☺ Jan-Nov;
🅿 ❌ 🖵 🛜 🛋

Revel in a lazed pace at this chic town
house created by two London designers
who call Provence home after visiting for
30-something years. Its nine rooms fuse
soft natural hues with modern art: most
look down on the slate-grey pool backed
by centenary palms, and the best-in-house
venerates romance with fairy-tale gilded

mirror and intimate roof-covered terrace
that begs someone to fall on one knee.
Best up is the zinc bar, fireplace, piano
and Terry O'Neill original of Brigitte
Bardot.

THE PENINSULA

Options for seaside souls are quite divine
in this lesser-known corner of paradise,
with something outstanding to suit every
budget.

❧ CHÂTEAU DE VALMER // LA CROIX-VALMER €€€

☎ 04 94 55 15 15; www.chateauvalmer.com;
Gigaro, La Croix-Valmer; d low/mid-/high season
from €190/265/300, tree house €325/410/510;
🅿 ❌ 🖵 🛜 🛋

This fabulous 19th-century wine-
producer's mansion is for nature bods
with a penchant for luxury. Sleep above
vines in a *cabane perchée* (tree house),
stroll scented vegetable and herb gardens, and play hide-and-seek around
century-old palm and olive trees.

❧ FERME LADOUCEUR // RAMATUELLE €€

☎ 04 94 79 24 95; www.fermeladouceur.com;
quartier Les Roullière, Ramatuelle; d €110-120

Breakfast beneath a fig tree at this lovely
chambre d'hôte in a 19th-century *bastide*
with a rustic restaurant (*menu* including
wine €42) open to anyone who fancies an
evening taste of good old-fashioned farm
cuisine. Find it north of Ramatuelle,
signposted right off the northbound D61
to St-Tropez.

❧ HÔTEL BELLOVISTO // GASSIN €

☎ 04 94 56 17 30; www.bellovisto.eu; place des Bar-
rys, Gassin; d low/high season from €60/70; ❌

A large part of the charm of this hilltop
hotel in Gassin is the café-clad square
with panoramic view on which it resides.

The hotel itself is dead simple –
sage-green shutters, local bar on the
ground floor displaying trophies the
local *pétanque* club has won, and nine
rooms up top. Breakfasting on the terrace before the day-tripper crowds arrive
(or sipping an aperitif once they've gone)
is bliss.

☙ LES 3 ÎLES // GIGARO €€

☎ 04 94 49 03 73; www.3iles.com; rte du Gigaro, La
Croix-Valmer; d low/high season incl breakfast from
€160/190; ☽ mid-Mar–Oct; Ⓟ ⊠ ⊠

The views of the sea and those golden
Îles d'Hyères glistening on the horizon
will have you swooning. Beware: the
same seductive view awaits you in each
of the carefully thought-out eight rooms
and infinity pool. Tropezienne Catherine
and husband Jean-Paul, an ex-tennnis
player, are the creative energy behind
this faultless, oh-so-chic *maison d'hôtes*.

☙ LE REFUGE // GIGARO €

☎ 04 94 79 67 38, 06 17 95 65 38; plage de Gigaro,
Gigaro; d/tr/studio €89/84-140/97; ☽ Apr–Sep; Ⓟ

Around for 25 years already, this rustic
seaside house with wooden shutters is
set back off the sand at the end of a dead-
end lane between trees. Inside, 10 humble rooms and five studios with kitchenette provide simple sleeping, opening
onto private little tabled terraces. The
same people who run Le Refuge cook up
tasty grills at the same-named restaurant
at the start of the coastal path (p288).

HAUT-VAR

This is an idyllic area for lovers of peace,
solitude, lovely hilltop villages and top
dining. Hotel-restaurants Hôtel des
Deux Rocs (p295) in Seillans and Auberge du Parc in Correns (p291) cannot
be recommended enough – for eating
and sleeping.

☙ MAISON DE LA TREILLE // TOURTOUR €€

☎ 04 94 70 59 29; http://chambrestourtour.monsite
.orange.fr, in French; Rue Grande 22, Tourtour; d incl
breakfast €90

The hefty brass knocker piercing the
olive-green front door, the lush bush of
lavender outside and the covered breakfast terrace on the top floor immediately
catch the eye at this charming *maison
d'hôtes* in one of the Northern Var's most
beautiful hilltop villages.

☙ HOSTELLERIE DE L'ABBAYE DE LA CELLE // LA CELLE €€€

☎ 04 98 05 14 14; www.abbaye-celle.com; place du
Général de Gaulle, La Celle; d from €250; Ⓟ ⊠ ⊠

An address for gourmands, this four-star
hotel-restaurant oozes country chic with
alfresco dining to drool over. Of the 10
country-style rooms, the Cedar Tree is
for guests with a fondness for bathtubs
with legs. Top chef Alain Ducasse is the
creative energy behind the gastronomy.

MASSIF DES MAURES

There are a couple of simple village
hotels in chestnut capital Collobrières;
accommodation otherwise is predictably
limited in this forested massif.

☙ LA GRANDE MAISON DES CAMPAUX // BORMES-LES-MIMOSAS €€

☎ 04 94 49 55 40; www.lagrandemaisondescampaux
.com; 6987 rte du Dom, Bormes-les-Mimosas; d
€140-160, q €230; ☽ Mar-Nov; Ⓟ ⊠

This dreamy 17th-century country
house steals the B&B show. Languish-
ing in vineyards on the vast 128-hectare
Domaine des Campaux, five rooms
evoke a bygone era. Beams are sturdy
and age-old, a couple of bathtubs have
legs, floors are original stone flags or terracotta tiles and linens are crisp white.

Find it signposted off the N98 some 6km west of La Môle.

ÎLE DE PORQUEROLLES

Accommodation on this island paradise is pricey, limited and gets booked months in advance; hotels only accept guests on a half-board basis. The tourist office has details of self-catering apartments/villas and Porquerolles' three B&Bs. Or perhaps you want to sleep on a boat (p304)?

☙ AUBERGE DES GLYCINES €€

Map p301; ☎ 04 94 58 30 36; www.auberge-glycines .com; place d'Armes; d per person incl half-board low/mid-/high season from €99/119/149; ⊠
This inn overlooking the village square ranks as highly in the dining stakes as it does in the sleeping. Decor is traditional – note the cicada collection hanging on the wall in reception – and dining is *Porquerollaise*, in other words shoals of fish.

☙ LE MAS DU LANGOUSTIER €€€

Map p301; ☎ 04 94 58 30 09; www.langoustier.com; d per person incl half-board low/mid-/high season from €179/199/212; ⊠ ◪
The 'to die for' choice: guests have been known to drop in by helicopter at this exceptional hotel with a glamorous history going back to 1931, vineyards

---

TOP FIVE

WINE ESTATES & VILLAGE INNS

- ★ **Domaine de la Brillane** (p380)
- ★ **Domaine de Cabasse** (p383)
- ★ **Hôtel des Deux Rocs** (p295)
- ★ **Hôtel Bellovisto** (p398)
- ★ **Nouvel Hôtel Restaurant du Commerce** (p389)

---

and stunning views from its seaside perch. Everything, from its rooms to two restaurants (one for guests only), is impeccable.

☙ LES MÈDES €€

Map p301; ☎ 04 94 12 41 24; www.hotel-les-medes .fr; rue de la Douane; d incl breakfast low/mid-/high season from €93/99/129, 4-person apt per week €829/1276/1779; ⊠ ▢ 🛜
What a fabulous find. This hotel-residence mixes traditional hotel accommodation with self-catering studios and apartments for two to six guests. The icing on the cake is the terraced garden out back with fountain pool, sun loungers and bar seating beneath sails, great for whiling away starlit evenings.

☙ VILLA STE-ANNE €€

Map p301; ☎ 04 94 04 63 00; www.sainteanne.com; place d'Armes; d low/mid-/high season from €148/168/208; 🕙 Feb-Nov; ⊠
The main draw of this inn, tucked in a typical Porquerollais building with pretty apricot facade and cornflower-blue shutters on the main square, is its terracotta-tiled restaurant terrace overlooking the *pétanque* pitch. Borrow a set of *boules* should you fancy a spin.

ÎLE DE PORT-CROS

Accommodation on this exclusive national-park island is limited and requires booking months in advance.

☙ HOSTELLERIE PROVENÇALE €€

Map p305; ☎ 04 94 05 90 43; www.hostellerie -provencale.com; d per person incl half-board low/ high season €105/125; 🕙 Apr- Nov; ⊠
Run by the island's oldest and largest family since 1921, this bustling portside *hostellerie* sports five bright rooms facing the water; the best have a balcony. Daughter Stéphanie – the fourth genera-

tion to work here – tends the eye-catching cocktail bar on the waterfront. Look for canary-yellow sun umbrellas.

☙ LE MANOIR D'HÉLÈNE €€€

Map p305; ☎ 04 94 05 90 52; lemanoir.portcros@ wanadoo.fr; d per person incl half-board from €200; ☯ mid-Apr–Sep; ⊠ ⚙

An aloof 300m from Port-Cros' tiny port, this enchanting 23-room manor with white turreted facade is the exclusive option. Find it nestled in a sweet-smelling eucalyptus grove with outdoor pool, upmarket restaurant and an elegant air of island life of a few centuries back.

TOULON & AROUND

HYÈRES

The aged clutch of hotels in the Old Town just cannot keep up with the great-value hotels south near the beaches and Presqu'île de Giens, which are perfectly placed for day trips to the Îles des Hyères to boot.

☙ HÔTEL BOR €€

☎ 04 94 58 02 73; www.hotel-bor.com; 3 allée Émilie Gérard, Hyères Plage; d from €120; ☯ Apr–mid-Dec; ⴔ ⊠ ▯ ⚟ ⚙

This sleek boutique hotel on the sand is first-class and screams design. Palm trees and potted plants speckle its wood-decking terrace and sun loungers beg to be used on its minimalist pebble beach facing the waves. Rooms are in muted natural colours and the best have a terrace facing guess what.

☙ HÔTEL LE MÉDITERRANÉE €€

☎ 04 94 00 52 70; www.hotel-lemediterranee.com; 8 av de la Méditerranée, Hyères Plage; d/tr/q high season €84/98/113; ☯ mid-Jan–mid-Nov; ⴔ ⊠ ⚟

What a bargain this friendly 13-room hotel is abutting Hyères' horse-racing track (horses gallop around early each morning) – a one-minute walk to the pleasure-port restaurants and Plage d'Hyères. Bathrooms are modern, rooms are painted in typical Provençal colours and the best in the house has balcony with table for two. Breakfast alfresco then grab a bike and cycle to the beach, salt pans or an island (see p300).

TOWARDS MARSEILLE

☙ GOLF HÔTEL // BANDOL €

☎ 04 94 29 45 83; www.golfhotel.fr; 10 promenade de la Corniche, Bandol; d low/mid-/high season from €68/78/85; ☯ Jan–Nov; ⴔ ⚙

On the sand of Plage du Rénecros, this old-timer hotel, in business since 1910, has bags going for it. In the 1940s it served as the town casino, the same family has been here since the 1970s and it is a prime address for beachside sleeping and dining: its restaurant with terrace on the sand cooks up fresh fish, has tip-top presentation and ace desserts.

☙ LES QUATRE SAISONS // LE CASTELLET €€

☎ 04 94 25 24 90; www.lesquatresaisons.org; 370 montée des Oliviers, rte du Brûlat, Le Castellet; d incl breakfast €100-150; ⚟ ⚙

A few hair-pin bends downhill from the medieval hilltop village of Le Castellet, Patrice and Didier have decorated five exquisite rooms in the purest Provençal style. All rooms open onto a central swimming pool and Patrice's *table d'hôtes* (€40) is worth every cent. Don't miss his divine *vin d'orange amère* (bitter orange liquor).

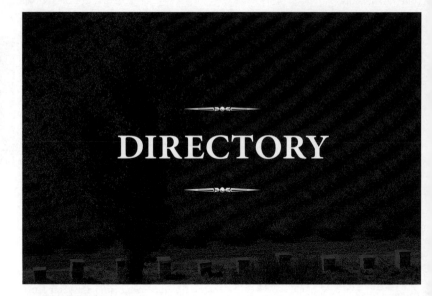

DIRECTORY

BUSINESS HOURS

A bakery is about all that is open Sunday morning when Provence sleeps. Shops open 9am or 9.30am to noon and again from between 1pm and 3pm to around 7pm Monday to Saturday. Many close for their *congé annuel* (annual holiday) for a month in winter, as do most hotels and restaurants.

In rural Provence many hotels, museums and *chambres d'hôtes* (B&Bs) only open *Pâques à la Toussaint* (Easter to All Saints' Day, 1 November). Unless listed otherwise in reviews in this book, restaurants generally take orders from noon or 12.30pm to 2.30pm or 3pm and again in the evening from 7pm to 9.30pm or 10pm up to six days a week. Many restaurants typically close on Sunday evening and all day Monday or Tuesday.

Opening hours for bars and clubs fluctuate wildly.

PRACTICALITIES

* France uses the metric system for weights and measures.

* Plugs have two round pins; and the electric current is 220V at 50Hz AC.

* Pick up regional news and chat with the Monte Carlo–based, English-language Riviera Radio (www.rivieraradio.mc).

* Radio stations Nice Music (102.3 FM) and Radio Azur (www.radioazur.com) are the sounds on the coast.

* Read regional news in French with *Nice Matin* (www.nicematin.fr) and *La Provence* (www.laprovence.com); and in English with the *Riviera Reporter* (www.riviera-reporter.com) and *Riviera Times* (www.rivieratimes.com).

* Switch on the box with private French TV stations TF1 and M6; or state-run France 2, France 3 and 5 (Arte after 7pm).

CUSTOMS

Goods brought in and exported within the EU incur no additional taxes, provided duty has been paid somewhere within the EU and the goods are for personal consumption. Duty-free shopping no longer exists within the EU; you have to be leaving Europe.

Coming from non-EU countries, duty-free adult allowances are: 200 cigarettes, 50 cigars, 1L of spirits, 2L of wine, 50ml of perfume, 250ml of eau de toilette and other goods up to the value of €175 (€90 for under 15yr). Anything over the limit must be declared and paid for; see www.douane.gouv.fr.

DANGERS & ANNOYANCES

BEACHES & RIVERS

Stinging jellyfish seem to be increasing in number with each and every summer; watch your step before diving in the sea. The most common are small and pale purple in colour. For tips on beach safety see p23.

Major rivers are connected to hydro-electric power stations operated by the national electricity company, Electricité de France (EDF). Water levels rise dramatically if the EDF opens a dam. White-water sports on the River Verdon of the Chaudanne Dam are forbidden when the water flow is less than 5 cu metres per second. For information on water levels and dam releases call ☎ 04 92 83 62 68.

Swimming is prohibited in lakes that are artificial and have unstable banks (ie Lac de Ste-Croix, southwest of the Gorges du Verdon; and Lac de Castillon and adjoining Lac de Chaudanne, northeast of the gorges). Sailing, windsurfing and canoeing are restricted to flagged areas.

EXTREME WEATHER

Thunderstorms in the mountains and on the hot southern plains can be sudden, violent and dangerous. Check weather reports before embarking on a long walk; even then, be prepared for a sudden change in the weather. Storms are common in August and September. Year-round the mistral can be really annoying (see also p15).

FOREST FIRES

Forest fires are common in July and August and spread incredibly quickly – 20m to 30m per minute. Between 1 July and the second Sunday in September, forest authorities close high-risk areas. Never walk in a closed zone. Tourist offices can tell you if a walking path is closed. To call the fire brigade dial ☎ 18.

Forests are crisscrossed with road tracks enabling fire crews to penetrate quickly. Signposted DFCI (Défense de la Forêt Contre l'Incendie; Forest Defence against Fire), they're closed to private vehicles but can be followed on foot.

Lighting a campfire is forbidden. Barbecues, even in private gardens, are forbidden in many areas in July and August.

POISONOUS MUSHROOMS

Wild-mushroom picking is a national pastime. Pick but don't eat until it has been positively identified as safe by a pharmacist. Most pharmacies in the region offer a mushroom-identification service.

THEFT

Theft – from backpacks, pockets, cars, trains, laundrettes – is a widespread problem, particularly along the Côte d'Azur. Keep an eagle eye on your bags,

DIRECTORY

especially at train and bus stations, on overnight train rides, in tourist offices and on beaches.

When swimming at the beach or taking a dip in the pool, have members of your party take turns sitting with packs and clothes. On the Prado beaches in Marseille, keeping your valuables in one of the free (staffed) lockers provided is a good idea.

Motorists in Marseille, Nice and other larger cities should keep their doors locked when stopped at traffic lights; it is not unheard of for aspiring bandits to open the door to your car, ask you what the time is and, at the same time, scan you and your car for valuables.

TRAFFIC

With the exception of Nice and Marseille, where heavy urban traffic, confusing one-way systems and madcap drivers can make driving beastly, motoring elsewhere is a pleasant affair – scenic, slow and stress free. If you have a fierce dislike of steep narrow mountain roads, vicious hairpin bends and signs warning of rocks falling, Haute-Provence and certain parts of the northern Var are probably not places for you.

DISCOUNTS

Many museums and monuments sell *billets jumelés* (combination tickets) covering admission to more than one sight and offering a considerable saving. Some cities have museum passes that cut sightseeing costs further. The **French Riviera Pass** (www.frenchrivierapass.com) gets you into all Nice's paying attractions plus a handful further afield.

People over 60 or 65 (depending on the museum) are entitled to discounts on public transport, museum admission fees

and so on. It's useful to have ID handy, though people are not always asked to show it. For details on train travel see p423.

FOOD & DRINK

For the full low-down on gastronomic Provence see p364.

In the restaurant reviews in this guide, we indicate the price of a main course and/or the price of a *menu* (two- or three-course meal at a set price); ordering à la carte is generally more expensive.

Budget restaurants (flagged with a lone euro symbol) serve simple, generally unadventurous meals for up to €20. Midrange places (flagged with two euro symbols), of which there are plenty, cook seasonal specialities accompanied by bags of atmosphere, with a meal costing €20 to €40 (less at lunchtime). More-formal service, creative cuisine, an unusual and stylish decor, and *menus* costing anything upwards of €40 are distinguishing features of top-end eating spots (flagged with three euro symbols).

Coffee, the usual way to end a meal, is served espresso-style – short, black and strong – unless you specify otherwise: *café crème* is an espresso with steamed milk or cream and *café au lait* is hot milk with a dash of coffee. Tea comes as an empty cup and a tea bag (no milk).

On 1 July 2009 the French government cut VAT in restaurants from 19.6% to 5.5% meaning, fingers crossed, a marginal drop in restaurant prices.

WHERE TO EAT & DRINK

Dining *à la provençal* can mean spending anything from lunch in a village bistro with no tablecloths to dining fine in a star-studded gastronomic temple. Irrespective of price, a *carte* (menu) is usually pinned up outside, allowing for a price and dish check.

The most authentic places to eat are invariably in tiny hamlets off the beaten track, touting just one *menu* with *vin compris* (wine included).

Some restaurants in larger towns and with illustrious addresses get crowded, so it's best to book. Few accept reservations for more than one seating, allowing ample time to linger over coffee and *digestif* (postdinner drink). Some don't accept credit cards.

Standard opening hours for eating places are listed in the Quick Reference (see inside front cover). Hours deviating from these are specified in individual reviews.

For tips on dining with children see p24.

FERMES AUBERGES & CHÂTEAUX

Feasting on homemade food on a *ferme auberge* (working farm) or a wine-producing estate (château or domaine) is a great way to dine. Typical Provençal cuisine and pace is guaranteed; portions appease the feistiest of appetites and dining is often around shared tables. A four-course *menu,* often with wine, costs €20 to €40.

Maisons des vins (wine houses) have lists of châteaux that serve food; **Gîtes de France** (www.gites-de-france-paca.com) has farm details.

CAFÉS

Cafés – the hub of village life – invariably double as bar and bistro, too. Most serve croissant-and-coffee breakfasts and lunchtime baguettes filled with cheese (around €4) or charcuterie (deli meat). In towns, cafés on grand boulevards or in chic spots, such as the Vieux Port in St-Tropez, charge more than a place

fronting a quiet side street. In fine café tradition, Aix-en-Provence's Les Deux Garçons (p69), the region's most famous café, hikes up its prices after 10pm.

QUICK EATS

Crêpe makers and ice cream and *beignet* (doughnut) stalls are common in seaside resorts, but in inland villages and towns people simply nip into a café for a sandwich, or a *salon de thé* (tea room) or pâtisserie for a slice of something sweet to munch sitting down or on the move.

VEGETARIANS & VEGANS

In a country where *viande* (meat) once meant 'food' too, it comes as no surprise that vegetarians and vegans are not catered for particularly well, if at all: vegetarian restaurants are nonexistent, as are vegetarian *menus*. That said, vegetables form the backbone of many typical Provençal dishes, meaning vegetarians won't starve (even if it does mean compiling a full meal from a selection of starters), while *produits biologiques* (organic products) are all the rage nowadays, even among carnivores.

Strict vegetarians and vegans should note that most cheeses in France are made with *lactosérum* (rennet), an enzyme derived from the stomach of a calf or young goat, and that some red wines are clarified with the albumin of egg whites. Vegetarian wine (clarified using a chemical substitute or not at all) is impossible to find in the region, but *le vin bio* (organic wine) – made from grapes grown without the aid of chemical fertilisers and pesticides and often bottled in recycled glass – is becoming increasingly popular.

See the Language chapter for useful phrases.

GAY & LESBIAN TRAVELLERS

There are large gay and lesbian communities in Aix-en-Provence, Nice, Cannes and Marseille, the latter being host to the colourful **Lesbian & Gay Pride march** (www.marseillepride.org, in French) in late June or early July.

The region's most active gay and lesbian groups are in Marseille. Lesbian group **Centre Évolutif Lilith** (CEL; ☎ 06 99 55 06 02; http://celmrs.free.fr, in French; 93 La Canebière) is particularly active. **Gay Provence** (☎ 04 91 84 08 96; www-gay-provence.org) and **Gay Map Marseille** (www.gaymapmarseille.com) have useful listings.

HEALTH

Excellent health care is readily available and for minor illnesses pharmacists give valuable advice and sell over-the-counter medications. The standard of dental care is usually good.

When you ring ☎ 15, the 24-hour dispatchers of the Service d'Aide Médicale d'Urgence (SAMU; Emergency Medical Aid Service) will take details of your problem and send out a private ambulance with a driver or, if necessary, a mobile intensive-care unit. For less serious problems SAMU can dispatch a doctor for a house call. If you prefer to be taken to a particular hospital, mention this to the ambulance crew, because the usual procedure is to take you to the nearest one. In emergency cases (for example, those requiring intensive-care units), billing will be taken care of later. Otherwise, you need to pay in cash at the time.

If your problem is not sufficiently serious to call SAMU but you still need to consult a doctor at night, call the 24-hour doctor service, operational in most towns in the region. Telephone numbers are listed under Essential Information in the relevant town sections, or see the Quick Reference (inside front cover).

Tap water is safe to drink, but the water spouting from fountains that tout a sign reading *eau non potable* (nondrinking water) isn't.

HOLIDAYS

FRENCH PUBLIC HOLIDAYS

Museums and shops (but not cinemas, restaurants or bakeries) and most business shut on the following *jours fériés* (public holidays). When one falls on a Thursday, many people make a *pont* (bridge, ie with the weekend), meaning they don't work the Friday either.

New Year's Day (Jour de l'An) 1 January
Easter Sunday & Monday (Pâques & lundi de Pâques) Late March/April
May Day (Fête du Travail) 1 May
Victoire 1945 8 May – celebrates the Allied victory in Europe that ended WWII
Ascension Thursday (L'Ascension) May – celebrated on the 40th day after Easter
Pentecost/Whit Sunday & Whit Monday (Pentecôte & lundi de Pentecôte) Mid-May to mid-June – celebrated on the seventh Sunday after Easter
Fête Nationale (Bastille Day/National Day) 14 July
Assumption Day (L'Assomption) 15 August
All Saints' Day (La Toussaint) 1 November
Remembrance Day (L'onze Novembre) 11 November – celebrates the WWI armistice
Christmas (Noël) 25 December

MONÉGASQUE PUBLIC HOLIDAYS

Monaco shares the same holidays with France *except* those on 8 May, 14 July and 11 November. Additional public holidays:

Feast of Ste-Dévote 27 January – patron saint of Monaco
Corpus Christi June – three weeks after Ascension

Fête Nationale (National Day) 19 November
Immaculate Conception 8 December

SCHOOL HOLIDAYS

Travelling to/from and around the region during French *vacances scolaires* (school holidays) is not recommended, especially in July and August when French families hit the coast for their annual summer holiday; Saturday is a horrendous day to travel in July and August.
Christmas-New Year Schools nationwide are closed 20 December to 4 January.
February-March The 'Feb' holidays last from about 7 February to 5 March; pupils in each of three zones are off for overlapping 15-day periods.
Easter The month-long spring break, which begins around Easter, also means pupils have overlapping 15-day holidays.
Summer The nationwide summer holiday lasts from the tail end of June until very early September.

INSURANCE

MEDICAL INSURANCE

If you're an EU citizen or from Switzerland, Iceland, Norway or Liechtenstein, the European Health Insurance Card (EHIC) covers you for emergency health care or in the case of accident while in the region. It will not cover you for non-emergencies or emergency repatriation. Every family member needs a separate card. In the UK, application forms are available from post offices or can be downloaded from the Department of Health website (www.dh.gov.uk).

Citizens of other countries should find out if there is a reciprocal arrangement for free medical care between their country and France. If you do need health insurance, strongly consider a policy that covers you for the worst possible scenario, such as an accident requiring an emergency flight home. Find out in advance if your insurance plan will make payments directly to providers or reimburse you later for overseas health expenditures. If you have to claim later, ensure you keep all documentation.

TRAVEL INSURANCE

A travel-insurance policy to cover theft, loss and medical problems is recommended. Some policies exclude dangerous activities such as scuba-diving, motorcycling and trekking up very high mountains – check what you're covered for.

Paying for your airline ticket with a credit card often provides limited travel-accident insurance. Ask your credit-card company what it's prepared to cover.

INTERNET ACCESS

Airports and some train stations in the region have wireless access, as do many hotels, cafés and public spaces in larger towns. More and more hotels provide free wi-fi access. But head into the hills or remote valleys of Haute-Provence and it is practically impossible to get online. Check sites such as www.wifinder.com or France-specific www.journaldunet.com/wifi for access points regionwide.

The same goes for internet cafés (marked on city maps in this book), where surfing costs around €4 per hour: easy to find in towns and cities, nonexistent in rural Provence.

ICON GUIDE

Only accommodation that provides an actual computer for guests to use to access the internet is flagged with a computer icon (▢) in this book; those that offer wi-fi, but no computer, are flagged with 🛜.

To access dial-up ISPs with your laptop, you'll need a telephone plug adaptor, available at supermarkets. On newer SNCF trains an 'office space' next to the luggage compartments between carriages is provided for passengers; it comes complete with desk and plug to hook your laptop into the electricity supply.

LEGAL MATTERS

French police have wide powers of search and seizure, and can ask you to prove your identity at any time. Foreigners must be able to prove their legal status in France (eg passport, visa, residency permit) without delay.

Verbally (and of course physically) abusing a police officer can carry a hefty fine, even imprisonment. You can refuse to sign a police statement, and you have the right to ask for a copy.

People who are arrested are considered innocent until proven guilty, but can be held in custody until trial. The website www.service-public.fr has information about legal rights.

French police are ultrastrict about security. Do not leave baggage unattended at airports or train stations: suspicious objects will be summarily blown up.

French law does not distinguish between 'hard' and 'soft' drugs. The penalty for any personal use of *stupéfiants* (including cannabis, amphetamines, ecstasy etc) can be a one-year jail sentence and a €3750 fine. Importing, possessing, selling or buying drugs can receive up to 10 years' prison and a fine of up to €500,000.

Being drunk (*ivresse*) in public is punishable by a €150 fine. It is illegal to drive with a blood-alcohol concentration (BAC) of over 0.05% (0.5g per litre of blood). The police conduct frequent random breathalyser tests.

Smoking is illegal in all public spaces, including restaurants, cafés and bars.

MAPS

CITY MAPS

Within the region you can find city maps at *maisons de la presse* (newsagencies), *papeteries* (stationery shops), tourist offices, travel bookshops and mainstream bookshops. Kümmerly & Frey, with its orange-jacketed *Blay-Foldex Plans-Guides* series, and Éditions Grafocarte, with its blue-jacketed *Plan Guide Bleu & Orange,* are the main city-map publishers. A city map typically costs around €7. The free street *plans* (maps) distributed by tourist offices range from the superb to the useless. The Marseille tourist office distributes a decent, free city map (note that its eastern point is at the top of the page where you'd normally find north).

DRIVING MAPS

Quality regional maps are widely available outside France. **Michelin** (http://boutique cartesetguides.michelin.fr, www.viamichelin.com) and **Institut Géographique National** (IGN; www.ign.fr, in French) both have online boutiques where you can purchase maps. Michelin's yellow-jacketed map *Provence and the Côte d'Azur No 245* covers the area included in this book at a scale of 1:200,000.

WALKING & CYCLING MAPS

The **Fédération Française de Randonnée Pédestre** (FFRP, French Walking Federation; www.ffrp.asso.fr, in French) publishes several French-language topoguides – map-equipped trail booklets (€14.40) – for the region: *Haute-Provence via the Gorges du Verdon, Mercantour Panorama, Vallée des Merveilles, Var à pied* (on foot), *Côte d'Azur* and so on. Its online boutique stocks the full collection. Local walking organisations also produce topoguides that supply details on trail conditions, flora, fauna, mountain shelters and so on; ask at tourist offices and bookshops.

IGN (www.ign.fr) publishes great topoguides and maps ideal for hiking, biking or walking. Best is its blue-jacketed series, *Carte de Randonnée* (Walking Map; 1:25,000), and even more detailed green-jacketed *Carte de Loisirs de Plein Air* (Outdoor Activity Map; 1:15,000), which maps trails and itineraries for popular walking areas like the Calanques around Marseille and Cassis.

Relevant maps are recommended in regional chapters throughout this book.

MONEY

The euro (€) is the only legal tender in France and Monaco.

One euro is divided into 100 cents, also called centimes in France. Coins come in one, two, five, 10, 20 and 50 cents and €1 and €2 denominations; the latter has a brass centre and silvery edges and the €1 has the reverse (silvery centre, brass edges). Euro banknotes, adorned with fictitious bridges (which bear a striking resemblance to the Pont du Gard) are issued in denominations of €5, €10, €20, €50, €100, €200 and the often-unwelcome €500.

Exchange rates are given in the Quick Reference (inside front cover). For information on costs see p8.

ATMS

ATMs – *distributeurs automatiques de billets* or *points d'argent* – invariably provide the easiest means of getting cash. Most spit out euro banknotes at a superior exchange rate through Visa or MasterCard, and there are plenty of ATMs in the region linked to the international Cirrus and Maestro networks. If you remember your PIN as a string of letters, translate it into numbers; French keypads don't show letters.

CREDIT & DEBIT CARDS

This is the cheapest way to pay for things and to get cash advances. Visa (Carte Bleue in France) is the most widely accepted, followed by MasterCard (Access or Eurocard). Amex cards are not very useful except at upmarket establishments, but they do allow you to get cash at certain ATMs and at Amex offices.

To report a lost or stolen credit card:
AmEx (☎ 01 47 77 72 00)
Diners Club (☎ 0810 314 159)
MasterCard (☎ 0 800 901 387)
Visa (Carte Bleue; ☎ 0800 901 179)

TIPPING

French law requires that restaurant, café and hotel bills include a service charge (usually 10% to 15%), so a tip is neither necessary nor expected, although most leave something (about 10%).

POST

Postal services are fast (next-day delivery for most domestic letters), reliable and expensive. Post offices are signposted **La Poste** (www.laposte.fr, in French). For a pretty postage stamp *(un timbre),* rather than the uninspiring blue sticker *(une vignette)* that comes out of post office coin-operated machines, go to a window marked *toutes opérations* (all services). Tobacconists and shops selling postcards sell stamps, too.

From France and Monaco, domestic letters up to 20g cost €0.55. For international post, a postcard or letter/package under 20g/2kg costs €0.65/12.30 to

Zone 1 (EU, Switzerland, Iceland, Norway) and €0.85/14 to Zone 2 (the rest of the world).

TELEPHONE

France and Monaco have separate telephone systems.

French telephone numbers have 10 digits and need no area code; those starting with the digits 06 are mobile-phone numbers. To call anywhere in Provence and the Côte d'Azur from Monaco and abroad, dial your country's international access code, followed by 33 (France's country code) and the 10-digit number, dropping the initial 0. To call abroad from Provence, dial ☎ 00 (France's international access code), followed by the country code, area code (dropping the initial 0 if necessary) and local number.

Telephone numbers in Monaco have eight digits and likewise need no area code. To call Monaco from France and abroad, dial the international access code, followed by 377 (Monaco's country code) and the eight-digit number. To call abroad (including France) from Monaco, dial 00, followed by the country code, area code (dropping the initial zero if necessary) and local number.

France uses GSM 900/1800, compatible with the rest of Europe and Australia but not with the North American GSM 1900 or the totally different system in Japan.

The three major providers of mobile phone access are **SFR** (www.sfr.com), **Bouygues** (www.bouyguestelecom.fr) and France Telecom's **Orange** (www.orange.fr). If you have a compatible phone, buy a 'prepay' phone kit, which gives you a SIM-card with a mobile-phone number and a set number of calls. Card packages are sold at phone shops and branches of Fnac in Avignon, Nice, Nîmes and Marseille; recharge cards are sold at *tabacs* (tobacconists).

Public telephones in France are card operated. Most have a button displaying two flags that you push for explanations in English. *Télécartes* (phonecards) cost €8 or €15 at post offices, *tabacs* and anywhere that you see a blue sticker reading *télécarte en vente ici*. There are two kinds of phonecards, *cartes à puce* (cards with a magnetic chip, which are inserted chip-first into public phones) and *cartes à code* (which you can use from public or private phones by dialling the free access number and then punching in the card's scratch-off code).

Your choice of card will depend on your needs. France Télécom offers different cards suited to national and international dialling. For help in English on all France Télécom's services, see www.francetelecom.com.

A whole bevy of other cards is available for cheap international calls and most can be used elsewhere in Europe. Compare advertised rates, or ask which one is best for the place you're calling.

USEFUL NUMBERS & CODES

International access code ☎ 00
France country code ☎ 33
Directory enquiries ☎ 12
International directory enquiries ☎ 118 700

TIME

French and Monégasque time is GMT/UTC plus one hour, except during daylight-saving time (from the last Sunday in March to the last Sunday in October), when it is GMT/UTC plus two hours. The UK and France are always one hour apart: when it's 6pm in London, it's 7pm in Nice. New York is six hours behind Nice.

France uses the 24-hour clock and writes time like this: 15h30 (ie 3.30pm). Time has no meaning for many people in Provence – locals often take a casual approach to appointments and such.

TOILETS

Public toilets, signposted *toilettes* or WC, are surprisingly few and far between, which means you can be left feeling really rather desperate. Towns that have public toilets generally tout them near the *mairie* (town hall) or in the port area. Many have coin-operated, self-flushing toilet booths – highly disconcerting should the automatic mechanism fail with you inside. These toilets can usually be found in car parks and public squares; they cost €0.20 to enter. Some places sport flushless, kerbside *urinoirs* (urinals) reeking with generations of urine.

Restaurants, cafés and bars are often woefully underequipped with such amenities, so start queuing ahead of time. Bashful males be warned: some toilets are almost unisex; the urinals and washbasins are in a common area through which all and sundry pass to get to the toilet stalls. Older establishments often have Turkish-style *toilettes à la turque*, a squat toilet with a high-pressure flushing mechanism that can soak your feet if you don't step back in time.

TOURIST INFORMATION

LOCAL TOURIST OFFICES

Every city and town and many villages have an *office de tourisme* (tourist office run by some unit of local government) or *syndicat d'initiative* (tourist office run by an organisation of local merchants). Both are excellent resources and can always provide a local map and accommodation information.

Regional tourist information is handled by five departmental offices with invaluable websites:

Alpes de Haute-Provence (www.alpes-haute -provence.com)
Alpes-Maritimes (www.guideriviera.com)
Bouches du Rhône (www.visitprovence.com)
Var (www.tourismevar.com)
Vaucluse (www.provenceguide.com)

For tourist information on the principality of Monaco, contact its national tourist office in Monte Carlo (see p221).

TOURIST OFFICES ABROAD

Abroad, several French tourist offices (www.franceguide.com) dole out information on France, including the **Maison de la France** (☎ 0207 399 35 45; http://uk.maison-de-la-france.com; 178 Piccadilly, London W1V 9AL) in the UK.

Monaco (www.visitmonaco.com) is likewise well-represented in the UK with its own **tourist office** (☎ 0207 491 42 64; dtc .london@gouv.mc; 7 Upper Grosvenor Street, Mayfair, London W1K 2LX)

TRAVELLERS WITH DISABILITIES

The region is gradually becoming more user-friendly for *handicapés* (people with disabilities), but kerb ramps remain rare, older public facilities and budget hotels lack lifts, and the cobblestone streets typical of hilltop villages are a nightmare to navigate in a *fauteuil rouant* (wheelchair).

But all is not lost. Many two- or three-star hotels are equipped with lifts. On the coast there are beaches with wheelchair

DIRECTORY

access – flagged *handiplages* on city maps – in Cannes, Marseille, Nice, Hyères, Ste-Maxime and Monaco.

Michelin's *Guide Rouge* indicates hotels with lifts and facilities for people with disabilities, and Gîtes de France (p405) provides a list of *gîtes ruraux* and *chambres d'hôtes* with wheelchair access.

International airports offer assistance to travellers with disabilities. TGV and regular trains are also accessible for passengers in wheelchairs; call the **SNCF Accessibilité Service** (☎ 08 90 64 06 50; www.accessibilite.sncf.com, in French) for information.

VISAS

For up-to-date information on visa requirements see www.diplomatie.gouv.fr.

EU nationals and citizens of Iceland, Norway and Switzerland need only a passport or national identity card in order to enter France and stay and/or work in the country. However, nationals of the 12 countries that joined the EU in 2004 and 2007 are subject to various limitations on living and working in France.

Citizens of Australia, Canada, Israel, Hong Kong, Japan, Malaysia, New Zealand, Singapore, the USA and many Latin American countries do not need visas to visit France as tourists for up to 90 days.

Other people wishing to come to France as tourists have to apply for a Schengen Visa, named after the agreements that abolished passport controls between 15 European countries: Austria, Belgium, Denmark, Finland, France, Germany, Greece, Iceland, Italy, Luxembourg, the Netherlands, Norway, Portugal, Spain and Sweden. It allows unlimited travel throughout the entire zone for a 90-day period. Application should be made to the consulate of the country

you are entering first, or that will be your main destination. Among other things, you will need travel and repatriation insurance and be able to show that you have sufficient funds to support yourself.

Tourist visas *cannot* be extended except in emergencies (such as medical problems). When your visa expires you'll need to leave and reapply from outside France.

WOMEN TRAVELLERS

Some French men have clearly given little thought to the concept of *harcèlement sexuel* (sexual harassment). Many still believe that staring suavely at a passing woman is paying her a compliment. Women need not walk around the region in fear, however. Suave stares are about as adventurous as most French men get, with women rarely being physically assaulted on the street or touched up in bars at night.

Unfortunately, it's not French men that women travellers have to concern themselves with. While women attract little unwanted attention in rural Provence, on the coast it's a different ball game. In the dizzying heat of high season, the Côte d'Azur is rampant with men and women of *all* nationalities out on the pull. Apply the usual 'women traveller' rules and the chances are you'll emerge from the circus unscathed. Remain conscious of your surroundings, avoid going to bars and clubs alone at night and be aware of potentially dangerous surrounds: deserted streets, lonely beaches, dark corners of large train stations, and night buses in certain districts of Marseille and Nice.

Topless sunbathing – ironically less and less the fashion on Côte d'Azur beaches where it is very much tops on these days – is not generally interpreted as deliberately provocative.

SOS Viol (www.sosviol.com, in French) staffs the national **rape-crisis hotline** (☎ 08 00 05 95 95), spearheaded in Marseille, Nice and other Provençal towns by **SOS Femmes** (www.sosfemmes.com), with contact details for local offices online.

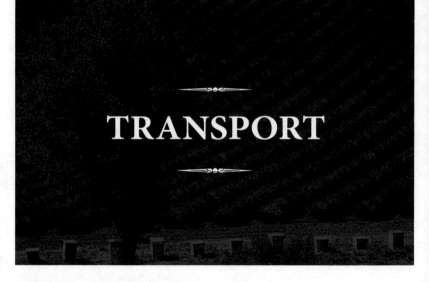

TRANSPORT

ARRIVAL & DEPARTURE

Thanks to European integration you'll usually cross quickly and easily between France and other EU countries without having to pass through customs or border checkpoints. If you're arriving from a non-EU country, you will need to show your passport (as well as your visa permit if you need one; see p412) and clear customs. If you're an EU citizen, you will need to show your identification card.

THINGS CHANGE...

The information in this chapter is particularly vulnerable to change. Check directly with the airline or a travel agent to make sure you understand how a fare (and ticket you may buy) works and be aware of the security requirements for international travel. Shop carefully. The details given in this chapter should be regarded as pointers and are not a substitute for your own careful, up-to-date research.

AIR

Fares to Provence fluctuate wildly: tickets are usually cheapest in early spring and late autumn, but shop around. International airport departure taxes are included in the price of your ticket.

Several 'no-frills' airlines (such as easyJet, Flybe, jet2.com and Ryanair) serve Avignon, Marseille, Nice, Nîmes and Toulon from European destinations. Some online ticket agencies will compare prices for you.

AIRPORTS

Provence has two major airports: Marseille-Provence and Nice-Côte d'Azur. Avignon-Caumont, Nîmes-Garons and Toulon-Hyères also serve some international destinations. Cannes and St-Tropez airports mainly serve private planes.

Avignon-Caumont (AVN; ☎ 04 90 81 51 51; www.avignon.aeroport.fr), 8km southeast of Avignon, has flights to/from Paris. From March, April and May to late September, there are regular weekly flights from the UK from Exeter and Southampton

(Flybe); and from Edinburgh and Leeds-Bradford (jet2.com).

Marseille-Provence (MRS; ☎ 04 42 14 14 14; www.marseille.aeroport.fr), located 25km northeast of Marseille, is one of the region's two major airports and has year-round flights to 45 destinations, including a number in the UK and Ireland. There are frequent flights to 20 French airports and two or three flights daily between Marseille and most other European cities. Marseille is also the hub for flights to and from North Africa, with regular flights to destinations in Algeria, Morocco and Tunisia.

Nice-Côte d'Azur (NCE; ☎ 08 20 42 33 33; www.nice.aeroport.fr), located 6km west of Nice, is France's second-largest airport, with year-round flights to 29 international and 30 French destinations, including many in UK and Ireland. There are flights two or three times daily between Nice and most other European cities, including a handful of interesting no-frills routes: easyJet offers year-round daily flights between Geneva, Berlin, Paris and Nice. From April to October, Swiss carrier Fly Baboo flies to Nice from Athens, Bucharest, Geneva, Naples, Valencia and Venice.

There are weekly flights to destinations in Algeria (Air Algérie); daily flights to Casablanca (Royal Air Maroc) and regular flights to Tunis and Monastir (Tunis Air and Air France).

Nîmes-Garons (FNI; www.nimes-aeroport .fr), 15km south of Nîmes, is served solely by low-fare operator Ryanair. The company has daily flights to London Luton and four flights weekly to Liverpool in the UK. It also has four flights weekly to Brussels.

Toulon-Hyères (TLN; www.toulon-hyeres .aeroport.fr), a small airport 25km east of Toulon, serves up to nine European cities depending on the season. There are daily flights to Paris year-round (Air France) and seasonal flights to the UK (Ryanair).

For details on travelling between airports and city centres, see the Transport sections in the relevant chapters.

TICKET SITES

Cheap Flights (www.cheapflights.co.uk)
ebookers.com (www.ebookers.com)
Expedia (www.expedia.com)
skyscanner (www.skyscanner.net)
STA Travel (www.statravel.com)
Travelocity (www.travelocity.com)

BICYCLE

European Bike Express (☎ 01430-422 111; www.bike-express.co.uk) transports cyclists and their bikes from the UK to places all over France. For travelling by train with your bicycle, see p417.

BUS

Eurolines (☎ 08 92 89 90 91; www.eurolines .com) is an association of companies forming Europe's largest international bus network. It links Provençal cities such as Nice, Marseille and Avignon with points all over western and central Europe, Scandinavia and Morocco. Most buses operate daily in summer and several times a week in winter; advance ticket purchases are necessary. Eurolines' website lists representatives in Europe. The **Eurolines Pass** (15-/30-day high-season pass €340/410, under 26 €260/310, cheaper mid-Sep–Jun) allows unlimited travel to 45 cities across Europe.

Linebús (Avignon ☎ 04 90 86 88 67; Nîmes ☎ 04 66 29 50 62; Barcelona ☎ 932 65 07 00, www .linebus.com, in Spanish) links Avignon (6½ hours, €45 one-way) and Nîmes (6¼

TRANSPORT

hours, €41 one-way) with Barcelona and other cities in Spain. Children aged four to 12 receive a 50% discount.

French transport policy favours its state-owned rail system: inter-regional bus services are an alien concept. When travelling to Provence from other regions of France, it's easiest to take the train.

CAR & MOTORCYCLE

High-speed trains operated by **Eurotunnel** (in the UK ☎ 0870-535 3535, in France ☎ 03 21 00 61 00; www.eurotunnel.com) shuttle between Folkestone via the Channel Tunnel to Coquelles, 5km southwest of Calais. Journey time is 35 minutes. Trains run 24 hours a day, every day of the year, with up to five departures an hour. A high-season return fare for a car and passengers costs around UK£200; for a motorcycle and rider, it's around UK£80; but there are numerous promotional fares. Advance reservations are mandatory. LPG and CNG tanks are not permitted, which eliminates many campers and caravans.

BRINGING YOUR OWN VEHICLE

If you bring your own vehicle to France you'll need registration papers, unlimited third-party liability insurance and a valid driving licence. In the UK, contact the **RAC** (☎ 08705 722 722; www.rac.co.uk) or the **AA** (☎ 0870 600 0371; www.theaa.com) for more advice. In other countries, contact your appropriate automobile association.

Vehicles entering France must display a sticker identifying their country of registration. A right-hand-drive vehicle brought from the UK or Ireland has to have deflectors fitted to the headlights to avoid dazzling oncoming traffic. A reflective breakdown triangle must be carried in your car.

DRIVING LICENCE & DOCUMENTATION

All drivers must carry a national ID card or passport; a valid driver's licence (*permis de conduire;* most foreign licences can be used in France for up to a year); papers of car ownership, known as a *carte grise* (grey card); and proof of third-party (liability) insurance. If you're stopped by the police and don't have one of these documents, you risk a hefty on-the-spot fine.

TRAIN

Thomas Cook's *European Rail Timetable,* updated monthly, has a complete listing of train schedules. It's available from Thomas Cook offices worldwide and online (www.thomascookpublishing.com) for around UK£14. A helpful resource is the info-packed website **The Man in Seat 61** (www.seat61.com), which lists train timetables and travel tips for France and beyond.

FROM THE REST OF FRANCE

France's efficient national rail network is run by the state-owned **Société Nationale des Chemins de Fer Français** (SNCF; www.sncf.fr, also www.raileurope.co.uk in the UK). SNCF's pride and joy is the **Train à Grande Vitesse** (TGV; www.tgv.com, also www.tgv-europe.com for overseas travellers) high-speed train service.

TGV Sud-Est links Paris with Dijon and Lyon, from where the TGV Rhône–Alpes continues southeast to Valence. Here, the TGV Méditerranée zips at 310km/h to Avignon, where the superfast track splits east to Marseille and west to Nîmes. Avignon and Aix-en-Provence have out-of-town TGV train stations, separate from the town-centre stations used by regional trains. Sample 1st-/2nd-class single TGV fares between Paris and Provence destinations: Avignon (€147/100, 3½ hours),

TRANSPORT

Marseille (€145/100, three hours), Nice (€170/120, six hours) and Orange (€145/100, 4½ hours).

SNCF also operates cheaper, slower rail services. Both *grande ligne* (main line) trains and those operated by **Transport Express Régional** (TER; www.ter-sncf .com) link smaller cities and towns with the TGV network. Many towns not on the SNCF network are linked with nearby railheads by buses.

With a Car

Under Motorail's AutoTrain scheme you can travel with your car on a train. Cars are loaded on the train one hour before departure and unloaded 30 minutes after arrival. Services from Calais to Nice run from late May to mid-September, stopping at Avignon and Fréjus (the rest of the year, your car can be transported as freight, but you have to organise separate transport for yourself). Information in the UK is available from Rail Europe (see p424). In France, ticketing is handled by SNCF.

With a Bicycle

Bicycles can be transported free of charge when packed down into a special 120cm x 90cm transit bag (available from bike shops). On some main-line trains, flagged with a bicycle symbol on timetables, you can put your bike in the luggage van without packing it down (but not during peak travel times). On night trains and certain TGV Sud-Est and TGV Méditerranée routes, bikes can only be transported in a four- to six-bicycle wagon, which must be reserved in advance (€10). See the multilingual SNCF brochure *Guide Train & Vélo* (free), available at train stations; or the website www.velo.sncf.com (in French).

The SNCF baggage service **Sernam** (☎ 3635, then say 'bagages' or dial ☎ 41) will transport your bicycle door-to-door in France for €49, with bicycles delivered within 48 hours excluding Saturdays, Sundays and public holidays.

FROM THE UK

The highly civilised **Eurostar** (France ☎ 08 92 35 35 39, www.voyages-sncf.com; UK ☎ 08705 186 186, www.eurostar.com) whisks you between London and Paris in just 2¼ hours. There are direct daily services from London St Pancras and Ashford (Kent) to Paris, Brussels, Lille, Parc Disneyland Paris and Calais-Fréthun. A direct seasonal service operates on Saturdays from early July to early September from London (six hours) and Ashford (five hours) to Avignon.

Eurostar fares vary enormously. A standard 2nd-class one-way ticket from London to Paris costs UK£179; from Paris, the standard fare to London is €245. You'll get better deals if you book nonflexible tickets, book a return journey, stay over a Saturday night, book 14 or seven days ahead, if you're under 25 or if you're a student. Student travel agencies may have youth fares not available directly from Eurostar. Eurail pass holders receive discounts. For information about train travel from northern France destinations to Provence and the Côte d'Azur, see opposite.

Travellers from the UK might consider changing trains in Lille rather than Paris, before heading south to Provence (which avoids schlepping across Paris city centre from Gare du Nord to Gare du Lyon).

FROM ITALY & SPAIN

Within the region, Nice is the major hub, sitting on the busy Barcelona–Rome train line. Day and overnight trains run in both directions. A single 1st-/2nd-class fare from Nice to Rome costs around €120/70 (plus from €30 for a couchette) for the 9½-hour journey. The 10-hour journey from Nice to Barcelona costs around €160/110 for a single 1st-/2nd-class fare. There are direct train services between Nice and Milan (€45/30, five hours).

SEA

Boats sail from Nice, Marseille and Toulon to/from Corsica (France), Sardinia (Italy) and North Africa. Rental cars cannot be taken on ferries.

FROM THE REST OF FRANCE
Ferries from Corsica to ports in Provence are operated by several lines:
Corsica Ferries (☎ 04 95 32 95 95; www.corsica ferries.com) Runs year-round from Nice and Toulon to Ajaccio, Bastia, Calvi and Île Rousse.
La Méridionale (☎ 08 10 20 13 20; www .lameridionale.fr) An SNCM subsidiary, this company has year-round sailings between Marseille and Ajaccio, Bastia and Propriano.
Société Nationale Maritime Corse-Méditerranée (SNCM; ☎ 08 25 88 80 88; www .sncm.fr) Services from Nice and Marseille to Ajaccio, Bastia, Île Rousse, Porto Vecchio and Propriano.

Daytime sailings from Nice to Corsica take around four hours; ferries from Marseille and Toulon (between 10 and 13 hours) are usually overnight.

In summer up to eight ferries depart daily (reservations are essential); in winter as few as eight depart a week and fares are much cheaper. In bad weather, boats can be cancelled at short notice (often on the day of departure).

High-season fares start at around €46 per adult one way for Nice to Bastia (discount and promotional specials are advertised in low season). An armchair seat/cabin berth starts from an additional €7/19. Transporting a small car costs upwards of €130 one way. Count on adding from around €23 one way for taxes.

FROM ITALY
SNCM (see left) runs up to four car ferries weekly from Marseille to Porto Torres on the Italian island of Sardinia (Sardaigne in French). Sailing time is 17 hours. In high season, a one-way passage including port taxes costs around €100/120 for an armchair seat/cabin berth. There are discounts for passengers aged under 25 and over 60. Transporting a car costs an extra €110.

Tickets and information are available from SNCM offices in Provence. In Sardinia, tickets are sold by SNCF agent **Paglietti Petertours** (☎ 079-51 44 77; Corso Vittorio Emanuele 19) in Porto Torres.

FROM NORTH AFRICA
Note that travel in Algeria is considered dangerous for foreign tourists due to ongoing political troubles and safety concerns.

Algérie Ferries (www.algerieferries.com) operates ferries between Marseille and Algiers, Bejaia, Annaba, Skikda and Oran (20 hours). A one-way/return fare on these routes costs €286/332 for a *fauteuil* (armchair seat) and €406/482 in a four-bunk cabin, plus port taxes of around €18 each way (tickets to/from Oran are around €30 more expensive).

SNCM (left) and Tunisian **CTN** (Compagnie Tunisienne de Navigation; ☎ 216-135 33 31; www.ctn.com.tn; 122 rue de Yougoslavie, Tunis) together operate several car ferries per week year-round between Marseille and Tunis (20 to 22 hours). A one-way *fauteuil* ticket costs €180 including port tax, with a cabin berth costing from an extra €24. If you're taking a vehicle (from €361), it's vital to book ahead.

FROM THE UK & IRELAND

There are no direct ferries to Provence, but you can sail year-round to northern France. Dover to Calais is the shortest crossing. Longer channel crossings include Dover to Boulogne and Dunkerque; Newhaven to Dieppe; Poole to Cherbourg and St-Malo; Portsmouth to Caen/Cherbourg/Le Havre/St-Malo; and Weymouth to St-Malo. There are also ferries from southern Ireland (Cork and Rosslare) to northern France. Fares vary crazily according to demand.

Brittany Ferries (www.brittany-ferries.co.uk); France (☎ 08 25 82 88 28); Ireland (☎ 021-437 8401); UK (☎ 0871 244 0744) Plymouth–Roscoff (eight hours), Poole–Cherbourg (4½ hours, high-speed crossing 2¼ hours), Portsmouth–Caen (six hours), Portsmouth–Cherbourg (three hours), Portsmouth–St-Malo (10¾ hours), Cork–Roscoff (14 hours).

Condor Ferries (www.condorferries.co.uk); France (☎ 08 25 135 135); UK (☎ 0845 609 1024) Portsmouth–Cherbourg (five hours), Weymouth/Poole–St-Malo with change of vessel in Guernsey or Jersey (eight hours/six hours).

Irish Ferries (www.irishferries.ie); France (☎ 01 70 72 03 26); Ireland (☎ 0818 300 400); UK (☎ 08717 300 400) Rosslare–Roscoff (18½ hours), Rosslare–Cherbourg (19½ hours).

LD Lines/Transmanche Ferries (www.transmancheferries.co.uk); France (☎ 08 25 30 43 04); UK (☎ 0844 576 8836) Dover–Boulogne (1½ hours), Newhaven–Dieppe (four hours), Portsmouth–Le Havre (5½ hours), Rosslare–Le Havre (20 hours).

Norfolk Line (UK ☎ 0844 847 5042, ☎ 0208 127 8303; www.norfolkline.com) Dover–Dunkerque (two hours) – foot passengers forbidden.

P&O Ferries (www.poferries.com); France (☎ 0825 120 156); UK (☎ 08716 645 645) Dover–Calais (1½ hours).

SeaFrance (www.seafrance.com); France (☎ 03 21 17 70 33); UK (☎ 0871 423 7119) Dover–Calais (2½ hours).

GETTING AROUND

BICYCLE

Provence – particularly the Luberon – is an eminently cyclable region, thanks to its extensive network of inland back roads with relatively light traffic. They're an ideal way to view Provence's celebrated lavender fields, vineyards and olive groves. On the coast there are also several excellent cycle paths; see p353 and individual chapters for information. Cycling in national parks in Provence is forbidden.

By law your bicycle must have two functioning brakes, a bell, a red reflector on the back and yellow reflectors on the pedals. After sunset and when visibility is poor, cyclists must turn on a white light in front and a red one in the rear. Cyclists must ride in single file when being overtaken by vehicles or other cyclists.

See p417 for information about transporting your bicycle by train.

A useful resource is the **Fédération Française de Cyclisme** (☎ 01 49 35 69 00; www.ffc.fr, in French).

Most towns have a bike-rental outlet, with hire costing around €18 per day.

BOAT

Provence is well connected by waterways, thanks to the Rhône. The most popular canal route to Provence is via the Canal du Midi, a 240km waterway that runs from Toulouse to the Bassin de Thau between Agde and Sète, from where you continue northeast to Aigues-Mortes in the Camargue. From Toulouse the Canal du Midi is connected with the Gardonne River leading west to the Atlantic Ocean at Bordeaux.

Barges such as the beautifully restored **Le Phénicien** (☎ 04 42 41 19 14; www.rhone

-croisiere.com) run tours along the Rhône. A six-night trip between Avignon and Aigues-Mortes aboard Le Phénicien including chef-prepared meals, drinks, daily excursions and use of bicycles costs from €2800 per person.

CANAL BOAT

The most relaxing way to see the Camargue is to cruise its canals and rivers in a houseboat. Boats usually accommodate two to 12 passengers and can be rented on a weekly basis. Anyone over 18 can pilot a river boat without a licence: learning the ropes takes about half an hour. The speed limit is 6km/h on canals and 10km/h on rivers.

The following companies rent out boats in Provence. Prices are for July and August; rates drop by around a third in the low season.

Le Boat (in France ☎ 04 68 94 42 80, in the UK ☎ 0844 463 3594; www.leboat.net) Rates around €1500/2300 per week for a four-/six-berth boat.
Rive de France (☎ 04 67 37 14 60; www.rive -de-france.tm.fr) Rates around €1435 to €2590 per week for a six-berth boat.

FERRY

A plethora of boats plies the waters from the coast to the offshore islands. Ferries also operate to/from St-Tropez and St-Raphaël, Port Grimaud and Ste-Maxime in the warmer months (generally April to October). See the relevant regional chapters for seasonal schedules and prices.

YACHT

One of Europe's largest *ports de plaisance* (pleasure ports) is located at Port Vauban, in Antibes.

CLIMATE CHANGE & TRAVEL

Climate change is a serious threat to the ecosystems that humans rely upon, and air travel is the fastest-growing contributor to the problem. Lonely Planet regards travel, overall, as a global benefit, but believes we all have a responsibility to limit our personal impact on global warming.

FLYING & CLIMATE CHANGE

Pretty much every form of motor travel generates CO_2 (the main cause of human-induced climate change) but planes are far and away the worst offenders, not just because of the sheer distances they allow us to travel, but because they release greenhouse gases high into the atmosphere. The statistics are frightening: two people taking a return flight between Europe and the US will contribute as much to climate change as an average household's gas and electricity consumption over a whole year.

CARBON OFFSET SCHEMES

Climatecare.org and other websites use 'carbon calculators' that allow jetsetters to offset the greenhouse gases they are responsible for with contributions to energy-saving projects and other climate-friendly initiatives in the developing world – including projects in India, Honduras, Kazakhstan and Uganda.

Lonely Planet, together with Rough Guides and other concerned partners in the travel industry, supports the carbon offset scheme run by climatecare.org. Lonely Planet offsets all of its staff and author travel.

For more information check out our website: lonelyplanet.com.

TRANSPORT

Yachts with or without a crew can be hired at most marinas along the coast, including the less-pompous sailing centres at Ste-Maxime and Le Lavandou. A complete list of yacht harbours can be found on the website www.guideriviera .com.

For up-to-date marina or harbour-master information, contact the **Fédération Française des Ports de Plaisance** (FFPP; ☎ 01 43 35 26 26; www.ffports-plaisance.com, in French).

BUS

Services and routes are extremely limited in rural areas. Bus services are more efficient between towns served by only a few (or no) trains.

Autocars (regional buses) are operated by a muddling host of different bus companies, which usually have an office at the *gare routière* (bus station) in the cities they serve. One company generally sells tickets for all the buses operating from the same station.

CAR & MOTORCYCLE

Your own wheels are vital for discovering the region's least-touched backwaters, which are impossible to uncover by public transport. Driving is easy on the Côte d'Azur, except in traffic-plagued July or August when it can take hours to move a few kilometres along the coast. For traffic reports in English, tune into 107.7MHz FM, which gives updates every 30 minutes in summer.

There are four types of intercity roads, which have alphanumeric designations:
Autoroutes (eg A8) Rapid-transit multilane highways, usually with *péages* (tolls)
Routes Nationales (N, RN) National highways
Routes Départementales (D) Local roads
Routes Communales (C, V) Minor rural roads

Autoroutes in southern France are managed by the **Autoroutes du Sud de la France** (www.asf.fr) and the **Société des Autoroutes Estérel Côte d'Azur-Provence-Alpes** (www.escota.com). The national **Association des Sociétés Françaises**

TRANSPORT

DISTANCE CHART (KM)

Note: Distances between destinations are approximate

	Marseille	Avignon	Cannes	Fréjus	Nice	Nîmes	Menton	Monaco	Orange	Toulon	Bordeaux	Calais	Lyon	Paris
Avignon	98													
Cannes	166	226												
Fréjus	127	180	35											
Nice	205	262	34	75										
Nîmes	123	50	250	228	279									
Menton	236	287	66	95	30	315								
Monaco	228	285	58	93	20	310	12							
Orange	115	29	243	220	274	56	304	302						
Toulon	65	160	120	92	143	185	180	170	177					
Bordeaux	648	573	775	740	804	532	836	834	584	717				
Calais	1071	982	1204	1200	1232	1011	1259	1255	955	1108	975			
Lyon	328	231	448	380	473	253	504	502	202	365	510	755		
Paris	781	692	911	911	941	720	966	965	615	872	686	289	462	
Toulouse	407	331	534	500	562	291	595	586	342	473	240	1067	536	699

d'Autoroutes (www.autoroutes.fr) has masses of traffic-related information online.

The websites www.viamichelin.com and www.mappy.fr plot itineraries between specified departure and arrival points.

FUEL & SPARE PARTS

Be warned that many service stations close on Saturday afternoon and Sunday. Some petrol pumps do stay open after hours, but you have to pay by credit card. *Essence* (petrol or gasoline), also known as *carburant* (fuel), is most expensive at the rest stops along the *autoroutes* and cheapest at supermarkets.

If your car is *en panne* (breaks down), you'll have to find a garage that handles your particular *marque* (make of car). Peugeot, Renault and Citroën garages are common, but if you have a non-French car you may have trouble finding someone to service it in the more remote areas.

HIRE

Prebooking your vehicle always works out cheaper. If you've left it too late, national French firms like ADA or National-Citer tend to be better value than international companies.

ADA (☎ 08 25 16 91 69; www.ada-sa.fr, in French)
Auto Europe (☎ 1 888 223 5555, from France ☎ 800 223 55555; www.autoeurope.com) US-based online hire company.
Avis (☎ 08 20 05 05 05; www.avis.com)
Budget (☎ 08 25 00 35 64; www.budget.com)
Easycar (in France ☎ 08 26 10 73 23, in the UK ☎ 08710 500 444; www.easycar.com)
Europcar (☎ 08 25 35 83 58; www.europcar.com)
Hertz (☎ 08 25 09 13 13; www.hertz.com)
Holiday Autos (☎ 0871 472 5229; www.holiday autos.co.uk) UK-based online hire company.
National-Citer (☎ 08 25 16 12 20; www.citer.fr, www.nationalcar.com)

Most rental companies require the driver to be at least 21 years old and have had a driving licence for over one year. Be sure that you understand what your liabilities are and what's included in the price (injury insurance, tax, collision damage waiver etc), and how many 'free' kilometres you'll get. *Kilométrage illimité* (unlimited mileage) means you can drive to your heart's content. You will probably be asked to leave a signed credit-card slip without a sum written on it as a *caution* (deposit). Make sure that it's destroyed when you return the car.

Note that rental cars with automatic transmission are rare in France. You will usually need to order one well in advance.

All rental cars registered in France have a distinctive number on the licence plate, making them instantly identifiable (including to thieves – never leave anything valuable in the car, even in the boot).

INSURANCE

Unlimited third-party liability insurance is mandatory for all automobiles. If you rent a car, this will be included in the package; however, collision damage waivers (CDW) vary greatly between rental companies. When comparing rates, the most important thing to check is the *franchise* (excess/deductible), which is around €800 for a small car. If you're in an accident where you are at fault, or the car is stolen or damaged by an unknown party, this is the amount you are liable to pay before the policy kicks in. Some US credit-card companies (such as Amex) have built-in CDW, although you may have to pay up, then reclaim the money when you get home.

PARKING

Provence's historic towns and cities, although wonderful to walk around, can be hellish to drive thanks to narrow streets, fiendish one-way systems and limited on-street parking. Many hotels have no private garages: guests drop off their bags, then either claim a temporary residents' parking permit from the hotel (if such a thing is available) and look for space in the street, or drive off to find a car park.

Large, often underground, car parks can be found in city centres – expect to pay about €2/15 per hour/day. A less stressful option is to park outside the centre and then walk.

ROAD RULES

A passenger car is permitted to carry a maximum of five people. French law requires *all* passengers to wear seat belts. Children weighing less than 10kg must travel in backward-facing child seats; children weighing up to 36kg must travel in child seats in the vehicle's rear seat.

North American drivers should remember that turning right on a red light is illegal in France.

Under the *priorité à droite* rule, any car entering an intersection (including a T-junction) from a road on your right has the right of way, unless the intersection is marked *vous n'avez pas la priorité* (you do not have right of way) or *cédez le passage* (give way). Thanks to this rather dangerous road rule, drivers may shoot out from intersections directly in front of you – so approach junctions with caution. *Priorité à droite* is suspended on priority roads, which are marked by an up-ended yellow square with a black square in the middle.

Mobile phones may only be used when accompanied by a hands-free kit or speakerphone. British drivers committing driving offences in France can receive on-the-spot fines and get penalty points added to their driving licence.

Riders of any type of two-wheeled vehicle with a motor (except motor-assisted bicycles) must wear a helmet. No special licence is required to ride a motorbike with an engine smaller than 50cc.

In forested areas, such as Haute-Provence, the Massif des Maures and the Massif de l'Estérel, unpaved tracks signposted DFCI (Défense de la Forêt Contre l'Incendie; Forest Defence against Fire) are for fire crews to gain quick entry in the event of a fire: they are strictly off limits to private vehicles.

TAXI

You can usually find taxi ranks at train and bus stations, or you can telephone for radio taxis. Fares are metered, with the minimum fare being €6; rates on top of this are roughly €1.60 per kilometre for one-way journeys.

TRAIN

The SNCF's regional rail network (Map p424) in Provence, served by **TER** (www.ter-sncf.com/paca), is comfortable and efficient. It comprises two routes: one that follows the coast (disappearing inland for the stretch between Hyères

---

SPEED LIMITS

* Built-up areas: 50km/h

* Undivided N and D highways: 90km/h (80km/h if it's raining)

* Dual carriageways (divided highways) or short sections of highway with a divider strip: 110km/h (100km/h if it's raining)

* *Autoroutes*: 130km/h (110km/h if it's raining, 60km/h in icy conditions)

TRANSPORT

and St-Raphaël), with an inland track from Cannes to Grasse; and another that traverses the interior, running from Marseille through Aix-en-Provence, Manosque and Sisteron before leaving the region northwards. A narrow-gauge railway links Nice with Digne-les-Bains in Haute-Provence (see p183).

Reservations are not mandatory on most regional trains. However, in summer it's advisable to buy your ticket for any straight-through trains well in advance. For information on transporting bicycles by train, see p417.

Two summertime regional passes are available to travellers of all ages, valid from July 1 to September 30.

Carte Bermuda (€5) One-day pass available weekends and public holidays giving unlimited 2nd-class travel between Marseille and Miramas on the Côte Bleue. Cannot be used on TGVs.

Carte Isabelle (€12) One-day pass allowing un-limited train travel along the coast between Fréjus and Ventimiglia, inland between Nice and Tende, and from Cannes to Grasse. Cannot be used on TGVs. Allows 1st-class travel at no additional cost.

For countrywide SNCF discounts and rail passes, see below.

CLASSES & COSTS

The following passes are sold at student travel agencies, major train stations within Europe and SNCF subsidiary **Rail Europe** (in Canada ☎ 1 800 361 7245, in the UK ☎ 0844 848 5848, in the USA ☎ 1 800 622 8600; www.raileurope.com, www.raileurope.co.uk).

SNCF Discount Fares & Passes

It's usually cheaper to buy tickets via the website www.voyages-sncf.com, which offers frequent internet-only reductions.

TRAIN ROUTES

To Paris; Lyons; Valence

To Gap; Briançon; Grenoble; Paris

ITALY

Orange
Sisteron
Château-Arnoux St-Auban
Digne-les-Bains
Thorame-Haute
Annot
Entrevaux
Puget-Théniers
Touët-sur-Var
Villars-sur-Var
Tende
Breil-sur-Roya
Avignon
L'Isle-sur-la-Sorgue
Barrème
St-André-les-Alpes
St-Martin du Var
Ventimiglia
Nîmes
Cavaillon
Manosque
PROVENCE & THE CÔTE D'AZUR
Colomars
Cagnes-sur-Mer
Menton
Monte Carlo
Tarascon
Grasse
Nice
Arles
Cannes
Miramas
Aix-en-Provence
Les Arcs-sur-Argens
Antibes
Pognac
Théoule-sur-Mer
L'Estague
St-Raphaël
Port de Bouc
MARSEILLE
Toulon
Hyères
Bandol

MEDITERRANEAN SEA

SNCF Regional Rail Network
Mountain Railway
TGV Méditerranée

TRANSPORT

STAMP IT!

It's important that you time-stamp your ticket in a *composteur* (a yellow post at the entrance to the train platform) just before boarding, or you risk a hefty fine.

Particularly good value are 'Prem's' – advance-purchase fares that can be bought from three months to two weeks before travel, and which can knock up to 50% off standard prices. These tickets cannot be exchanged or refunded.

Discounted fares and passes are available at all SNCF stations. Children aged under four travel free of charge; those aged four to 11 travel for half-price. Discounted fares (25% reduction) apply, subject to the terms and conditions of reservation, to travellers aged 12 to 25, seniors aged over 60, one to four adults travelling with a child aged four to 11, two people taking a return journey together, or anyone taking a return journey of at least 200km and spending a Saturday night away.

Guaranteed reductions of 25% to 50% are available with a **Carte 12-25** (€49), aimed at travellers aged 12 to 25; the **Carte Enfant Plus** (€70), for one to four adults travelling with a child aged four to 11; and a **Carte Sénior** (€56), for those aged over 60. A **Carte Escapades** (€85), for those aged 26 to 59, guarantees savings of 25% on a return journey of at least 200km including a Saturday night away.

The **France Railpass** (1st/2nd class US$293/250) entitles nonresidents of France to unlimited travel on SNCF trains for three days over a one-month period; you can also buy additional 1st-/2nd-class days of travel for US$45/37. The **France Saverpass** (1st/2nd class US$249/215) is similar but covers two

to five people travelling together; the **France Senior Pass** (1st class only US$268) covers those aged over 60; and the **France Youthpass** (1st/2nd class US$217/186) covers those aged under 26. Passes can be purchased from travel agencies, or online through agencies such as www.raileurope.com.

European Train Passes

If you're planning an extensive European journey, it may be worthwhile buying a **Eurail** (www.eurail.com) pass, available to non-European residents; or an **InterRail** (www.interrailnet.com) pass, available to European residents. All are valid on the national train network and allow unlimited travel for varying periods of time. See the website **The Man in Seat 61** (www.seat61 .com) for some sage advice on rail passes and whether they make economical sense for your planned itinerary.

Most train passes must be validated at a train station ticket window before you begin your first journey, in order to begin the period of validity.

LANGUAGE

Arming yourself with some French will broaden your travel experience, endear you to the locals and, in rural Haute-Provence (where English isn't widely spoken), ensure an easier ride around the region. On the coast, practically everyone you are likely to meet speaks basic English (and, in many cases, a rash of other European languages), but, again, a few words of French will go down well.

Standard French is taught and spoken in Provence. However, travellers accustomed to school-book French or the unaccented, standard French spoken in cities and larger towns will find the flamboyant French spoken in Provence's rural heart (and by most people in Marseille) somewhat bewildering. Here, words are caressed by the heavy southern accent and end with a flourish, vowels are sung, and the traditional rolling 'r' is turned into a mighty long trill. The word *douze* (the number 12), for example, becomes 'douz-eh' with an emphasised 'e', and *pain* (bread) becomes 'peng'. Once your ears become accustomed to

the local lilt, you'll soon start picking up the beat.

PRONUNCIATION

Most of the letters in the French alphabet are pronounced more or less the same as their English counterparts; a few that may cause confusion are listed below.

c	before **e** and **i**, as the 's' in 'sit'; before **a**, **o** and **u** it's pronounced as the 'k' in 'kick'
ç	always as the 's' in 'sit'
h	always silent (not pronounced)
j	as the 's' in 'leisure' (written 'zh' in the pronunciation guides)
r	pronounced from the back of the throat while constricting the muscles to restrict the flow of air
n, m	where a syllable ends in a single **n** or **m**, these letters are not pronounced, but the preceding vowel is given a nasal pronunciation
s	often not pronounced in plurals or at the end of words

PROVENÇAL

Despite the bilingual signs that visitors see when they enter most towns and villages, the region's mother tongue – Provençal – is scarcely heard on the street or in the home. Just a handful of older people in rural Provence (Prouvènço) keep alive the rich lyrics and poetic language of their ancestors.

Provençal (*prouvençau* in Provençal) is a dialect of the *langue d'oc* (Occitan), the traditional language of southern France. Its grammar is closer to Catalan (spoken in Spain) than to French. In the grand age of courtly love between the 12th and 14th centuries, Provençal was the literary language of France and northern Spain and was even used as far afield as Italy. Medieval troubadours and poets created melodies and elegant poems, and Provençal blossomed.

The 19th century witnessed a revival of Provençal after its rapid displacement by the *langue d'oïl*, the language of northern France that originated from the vernacular Latin spoken by the Gallo-Romans and that gave birth to modern French (*francés* in Provençal). The revival of Provençal was spearheaded by Frédéric Mistral (1830–1914), a poet from Vaucluse, whose works in Provençal won him the 1904 Nobel Prize for Literature.

BE POLITE

While the French, rightly or wrongly, have a reputation for assuming that everyone should speak French – until WWI it was the international language of culture and diplomacy – you'll find any attempt you make to communicate in French will be much appreciated.

What is often perceived as arrogance is often just a subtle objection to the assumption by many travellers that they should be able to speak English anywhere, in any situation, and be understood. You can easily avoid the problem by approaching people and addressing them in French. Even if the only phrase you learn is *Pardon, madame/monsieur, parlez-vous anglais?* (Excuse me, madam/sir, do you speak English?), you're sure to be more warmly received than if you stick to English.

An important distinction is made in French between *tu* and *vous,* which both mean 'you'; *tu* is only used when addressing people you know well, children or animals. If you're speaking to an adult who isn't a personal friend, you should use *vous* unless the person invites you to use *tu*. In general, younger people insist less on this distinction, and you will find that in many cases they use *tu* from the beginning of an acquaintance.

GRAMMAR

All nouns in French are either masculine or feminine and adjectives reflect the gender of the noun they modify. The feminine form of some nouns and adjectives is indicated by a silent e added to the masculine form, as in *ami* and *amie* (the masculine and feminine for 'friend'); other words undergo more complex changes.

In the following phrases both masculine and feminine forms have been indicated where necessary. The masculine and feminine forms are indicated by 'm' and 'f' respectively. The gender of a noun is often reflected by a preceding article, eg *le/un* (m) and *la/une* (f), meaning 'the/a'; or one of the possessive adjectives, eg *mon/ton/son* (m) and *ma/ta/sa* (f), meaning 'my/your/his, her'. French is unlike English in that the possessive adjective agrees in number and gender with the thing in question, eg 'his mother' and 'her mother' are both translated as *sa mère*.

ACCOMMODATION

I'm looking for a ...	*Je cherche ...*	zher shersh ...
camping ground	*un camping*	un kom·peeng
guest house	*une pension (de famille)*	ewn pon·syon (der fa·mee·yer)
hotel	*un hôtel*	un o·tel
youth hostel	*une auberge de jeunesse*	ewn o·berzh der zher·nes

Where can I find a cheap hotel?
Où est-ce qu'on peut — oo es kon per
trouver un hôtel pas cher? — troo·vay un o·tel pa shair
What is the address?
Quelle est l'adresse? — kel ay la·dres
Could you write the address, please?
Est-ce que vous pourriez écrire — es ker voo poo·ryay ay·kreer
l'adresse, s'il vous plaît? — la·dres seel voo play
Do you have any rooms available?
Est-ce que vous avez des — es ker voo·za·vay day
chambres libres? — shom·brer lee·brer
May I see the room?
Est-ce que je peux voir — es ker zher per vwa
la chambre? — la shom·brer
Where is the bathroom?
Où est la salle de bain? — oo ay la sal der bun
Where is the toilet?
Où sont les toilettes? — oo son lay twa·let

How much is it ...?	*Quel est le prix ...?*	kel ay ler pree ...
per night	*par nuit*	par nwee
per person	*par personne*	par per·son

I'm leaving today.
Je pars aujourd'hui. — zher par o·zhoor·dwee
We're leaving today.
On part aujourd'hui. — on par o·zhoor·dwee

MAKING A RESERVATION

Use these expressions in letters, faxes and emails:

To ...	*À l'attention de ...*
From ...	*De la part de ...*
Date	*Date*
I'd like to book ...	*Je voudrais réserver ...*
in the name of ...	*au nom de ...*
from ... to ...	*du ... au ...*
credit card (...)	*(...) carte de crédit*
number	*numéro de*
expiry date	*date d'expiration de la*
Please confirm availability and price.	*Veuillez confirmer la disponibilité et le prix.*

I'd like (a) ...	*Je voudrais ...*	zher voo·dray ...
single room	*une chambre à un lit*	ewn shom·brer a un lee
double-bed room	*une chambre avec un grand lit*	ewn shom·brer a·vek un gron lee
twin room (with two beds)	*une chambre avec des lits jumeaux*	ewn shom·brer a·vek day lee zhew·mo
room with a bathroom	*une chambre avec une salle de bain*	ewn shom·brer a·vek ewn sal der bun
to share a dorm	*coucher dans un dortoir*	koo·sher don zun dor·twa

CONVERSATION & ESSENTIALS

Hello.	*Bonjour.*	bon·zhoor
Goodbye.	*Au revoir.*	o rer·vwa
Yes.	*Oui.*	wee
No.	*Non.*	non
Please.	*S'il vous plaît.*	seel voo play
Thank you.	*Merci.*	mair·see
You're welcome.	*Je vous en prie.*	zher voo zon pree
	De rien. (inf)	der ree·en
Excuse me.	*Excusez-moi.*	ek·skew·zay·mwa
Sorry. (forgive me)	*Pardon.*	par·don

SIGNS

Entrée	Entrance
Fermé	Closed
Interdit	Prohibited
Ouvert	Open
(Commissariat de) Police	Police Station
Renseignements	Information
Sortie	Exit
Toilettes/WC	Toilets
Hommes	Men
Femmes	Women

What's your name?

Comment vous appelez-vous?	kom·mon voo za·pay·lay voo
Comment tu t'appelles? (inf)	kom·mon tew ta·pel

My name is …

Je m'appelle …	zher ma·pel …

Where are you from?

De quel pays êtes-vous?	der kel pay·ee et·voo
De quel pays es-tu? (inf)	der kel pay·ee ay·tew

I'm from …

Je viens de …	zher vyen der …

I like …

J'aime …	zhem …

I don't like …

Je n'aime pas …	zher nem pa …

Just a minute.

Une minute.	ewn mee·newt

DIRECTIONS

Where is …?

Où est …?	oo e …

Go straight ahead.

Continuez tout droit.	kon·teen·way too drwa

Turn left.

Tournez à gauche.	toor·nay a gosh

Turn right.

Tournez à droite.	toor·nay a drwat

at the corner

au coin	o kwun

at traffic lights

aux feux	o fer

beach	*la plage*	la plazh
bridge	*le pont*	ler pon
castle	*le château*	ler sha·to
cathedral	*la cathédrale*	la ka·tay·dral
church	*l'église*	lay·gleez
gallery	*la galerie*	la gal·ree
island	*l'île*	leel
lake	*le lac*	ler lak
main square	*la place centrale*	la plas son·tral
museum	*le musée*	ler mew·zay
old city	*la vieille ville*	la vyay veel
ruins	*les ruines*	lay rween
sea	*la mer*	la mair
square	*la place*	la plas
tourist office	*l'office de tourisme*	lo·fees der too·rees·mer

behind	*derrière*	dair·ryair
in front of	*devant*	der·von
far (from)	*loin (de)*	lwun (der)
near (to)	*près (de)*	pray (der)
opposite	*en face de*	on fas der

EATING OUT

I'd like …, please.

Je voudrais …, s'il vous plaît.	zher voo·dray … seel voo play

That was delicious!

C'était délicieux!	say·tay day·lee·syer

Please bring the bill.

Apportez-moi l'addition, s'il vous plaît.	a·por·tay·mwa la·dee·syon seel voo play

I'm vegetarian.

Je suis végétarien(ne). (m/f)	zher swee vay·zhay·ta·ryun/ryen

I'm allergic to …	*Je suis allergique …*	zher swee za·lair·zheek …
dairy produce	*aux produits laitiers*	o pro·dwee o lay·tyay
eggs	*aux œufs*	o zer
nuts	*aux noix*	o nwa
seafood	*aux fruits de mer*	o frwee der mair

LANGUAGE

HEALTH

antiseptic	*l'antiseptique*	lon·tee·sep·teek
condoms	*des préservatifs*	day pray·zair·va·teef
contraceptive	*le contraceptif*	ler kon·tra·sep·teef
diarrhoea	*la diarrhée*	la dee·ya·ray
medicine	*le médicament*	ler may·dee·ka·mon
nausea	*la nausée*	la no·zay
sunblock cream	*la crème solaire*	la krem so·lair
tampons	*des tampons*	day tom·pon
	hygiéniques	ee·zhen·eek

I'm ill.
  Je suis malade.   zher swee ma·lad
It hurts here.
  J'ai une douleur ici.   zhay ewn doo·ler ee·see

I'm allergic	*Je suis*	zher swee
to ...	*allergique ...*	za·lair·zheek ...
antibiotics	*aux antibiotiques*	o zon·tee·byo·teek
bees	*aux abeilles*	o za·bay·yer
penicillin	*à la*	a la
	pénicilline	pay·nee·see·leen

I'm ...	*Je suis ...*	zher swee ...
asthmatic	*asthmatique*	as·ma·teek
diabetic	*diabétique*	dee·a·bay·teek
epileptic	*épileptique*	ay·pee·lep·teek

LANGUAGE DIFFICULTIES

Do you speak English?
  Parlez-vous anglais?   par·lay·voo ong·glay
Does anyone here speak English?
  Y a-t-il quelqu'un qui   ee a·teel kel·kung kee
  parle anglais?   parl ong·glay
What does ... mean?
  Que veut dire ...?   ker ver deer ...
I don't understand.
  Je ne comprends pas.   zher ner kom·pron pa
Could you write it down, please?
  Est-ce que vous pourriez   es ker voo poo·ryay
  l'écrire, s'il vous plaît?   lay·kreer seel voo play
Can you show me (on the map)?
  Pouvez-vous m'indiquer   poo·vay·voo mun·dee·kay
  (sur la carte)?   (sewr la kart)

Help!	*Au secours!*	o skoor
Call ...!	*Appelez ...!*	a·play ...
a doctor	*un médecin*	un mayd·sun
the police	*la police*	la po·lees

There's been an accident!
  Il y a eu un accident!   eel ee a ew un ak·see·don
I'm lost.
  Je me suis égaré(e). (m/f)   zhe me swee·zay·ga·ray
Leave me alone!
  Fichez-moi la paix!   fee·shay·mwa la pay

NUMBERS

0	*zéro*	zay·ro
1	*un*	un
2	*deux*	der
3	*trois*	trwa
4	*quatre*	ka·trer
5	*cinq*	sungk
6	*six*	sees
7	*sept*	set
8	*huit*	weet
9	*neuf*	nerf
10	*dix*	dees
11	*onze*	onz
12	*douze*	dooz
13	*treize*	trez
14	*quatorze*	ka·torz
15	*quinze*	kunz
16	*seize*	sez
17	*dix-sept*	dee·set
18	*dix-huit*	dee·zweet
19	*dix-neuf*	deez·nerf
20	*vingt*	vung
21	*vingt et un*	vung tay un
22	*vingt-deux*	vung·der
30	*trente*	tront
40	*quarante*	ka·ront
50	*cinquante*	sung·kont
60	*soixante*	swa·sont
70	*soixante-dix*	swa·son·dees
80	*quatre-vingts*	ka·trer·vung
90	*quatre-vingt-dix*	ka·trer·vung·dees
100	*cent*	son
1000	*mille*	meel

PAPERWORK

name	*nom*	nom
nationality	*nationalité*	na·syo·na·lee·tay
date/place	*date/place*	dat/plas
of birth	*de naissance*	der nay·sons
sex/gender	*sexe*	seks
passport	*passeport*	pas·por
visa	*visa*	vee·za

QUESTION WORDS

Who?	*Qui?*	kee
What?	*Quoi?*	kwa
What is it?	*Qu'est-ce que c'est?*	kes ker say
When?	*Quand?*	kon
Where?	*Où?*	oo
Which?	*Quel(le)?* (m/f)	kel
Why?	*Pourquoi?*	poor·kwa
How?	*Comment?*	kom·mon
How much?	*Combien?*	kom·byun

SHOPPING & SERVICES

I'd like to buy …
  Je voudrais acheter …   zher voo·dray zash·tay …
I'm looking for …
  Je cherche …   zhe shersh …

more	*plus*	plews
less	*moins*	mwun
smaller	*plus petit*	plew per·tee
bigger	*plus grand*	plew gron

Can I pay by …?	*Est-ce que je peux*	es ker zher per
	payer avec …?	pay·yay a·vek …
credit card	*ma carte de*	ma kart der
	crédit	kray·dee
travellers	*des chèques de*	day shek der
cheques	*voyage*	vwa·yazh

How much is it?
  C'est combien?   say kom·byun
I don't like it.
  Cela ne me plaît pas.   ser·la ner mer play pa
May I look at it?
  Est-ce que je peux le/la   es·ker zher per ler/la
  voir? (m/f)   vwar

I'm just looking.
  Je regarde.   zher rer·gard
It's not expensive.
  Ce n'est pas cher.   ser nay pa shair
It's too expensive.
  C'est trop cher.   say tro shair
I'll take it.
  Je le/la prends. (m/f)   zher ler/la pron

a bank	*une banque*	ewn bonk
the (…)	*l'ambassade*	lam·ba·sahd
embassy	*(de …)*	(der …)
the hospital	*l'hôpital*	lo·pee·tal
the market	*le marché*	ler mar·shay
the police	*la police*	la po·lees
the post office	*le bureau de poste*	ler bew·ro der post
a public phone	*une cabine*	ewn ka·been
	téléphonique	tay·lay·fo·neek
a public toilet	*les toilettes*	lay twa·let

TIME & DATES

What time is it?
  Quelle heure est-il?   kel er ay til
It's (eight) o'clock.
  Il est (huit) heures.   il ay (weet) er
It's half past (…)
  Il est (…) heures et demie.   il ay (…) er ay der·mee
It's quarter to (…)
  Il est (…) heures moins   il ay (…) er mwun
  le quart.   ler kar
in the morning
  du matin   dew ma·tun
in the afternoon
  de l'après-midi   der la·pray·mee·dee
in the evening
  du soir   dew swar

today	*aujourd'hui*	o·zhoor·dwee
tomorrow	*demain*	der·mun
yesterday	*hier*	yair

Monday	*lundi*	lun·dee
Tuesday	*mardi*	mar·dee
Wednesday	*mercredi*	mair·krer·dee
Thursday	*jeudi*	zher·dee
Friday	*vendredi*	von·drer·dee
Saturday	*samedi*	sam·dee
Sunday	*dimanche*	dee·monsh

LANGUAGE

January	janvier	zhon·vyay
February	février	fayv·ryay
March	mars	mars
April	avril	a·vreel
May	mai	may
June	juin	zhwun
July	juillet	zhwee·yay
August	août	oot
September	septembre	sep·tom·brer
October	octobre	ok·to·brer
November	novembre	no·vom·brer
December	décembre	day·som·brer

ROAD SIGNS

Cédez la Priorité	Give Way
Danger	Danger
Défense de Stationner	No Parking
Entrée	Entrance
Interdiction de Doubler	No Overtaking
Péage	Toll
Ralentissez	Slow Down
Sens Interdit	No Entry
Sens Unique	One Way
Sortie	Exit

TRANSPORT

PUBLIC TRANSPORT

What time does	À quelle heure	a kel er
… leave/arrive?	part/arrive …?	par/a·reev …
boat	le bateau	ler ba·to
bus	le bus	ler bews
plane	l'avion	la·vyon
train	le train	ler trun

I want to go to …

| Je voudrais aller à … | zher voo·dray a·lay a … |

I'd like a …	Je voudrais	zher voo·dray
ticket.	un billet …	un bee·yay …
one-way	simple	sum·pler
return	aller-retour	a·lay·rer·toor
1st class	de première classe	der prem·yair klas
2nd class	de deuxième classe	der der·zyem klas

The train has been delayed.

| Le train est en retard. | ler trun ay ton rer·tar |

the first	le premier (m)	ler prer·myay
	la première (f)	la prer·myair
the last	le dernier (m)	ler dair·nyay
	la dernière (f)	la dair·nyair
platform	le numéro	ler new·may·ro
number	de quai	der kay
ticket office	le guichet	ler gee·shay
timetable	l'horaire	lo·rair
train station	la gare	la gar

PRIVATE TRANSPORT

I'd like to hire	Je voudrais	zher voo·dray
a/an…	louer …	loo·way …
4WD	un quatre-quatre	un kat·kat
bicycle	un vélo	un vay·lo
car	une voiture	ewn vwa·tewr
motorbike	une moto	ewn mo·to

petrol/gas	essence	ay·sons
diesel	diesel	dyay·zel

Is this the road to …?

| C'est la route pour …? | say la root poor … |

Where's a service station?

Où est-ce qu'il y a une	oo es keel ee a ewn
station-service?	sta·syon·ser·vees

Please fill it up.

| Le plein, s'il vous plaît. | ler plun seel voo play |

I'd like … litres.

| Je voudrais … litres. | zher voo·dray … lee·trer |

(How long) Can I park here?

(Combien de temps) Est-ce	(kom·byun der ton) es
que je peux stationner ici?	ker zher per sta·syo·nay ee·see

I've run out of petrol.

| Je suis en panne d'essence. | zher swee zon pan day·sons |

I need a mechanic.

J'ai besoin d'un	zhay ber·zwun dun
mécanicien.	me·ka·nee·syun

The car/motorbike has broken down (at …).

La voiture/moto est	la vwa·tewr/mo·to ay
tombée en panne (à …).	tom·bay on pan (a …)

I had an accident.

| J'ai eu un accident. | zhay ew un ak·see·don |

I have a flat tyre.

  Mon pneu est à plat.   mom pner ay ta pla

The car/motorbike won't start.

  La voiture/moto ne veut   la vwa·tewr/mo·to ner ver

  pas démarrer.   pa day·ma·ray

TRAVEL WITH CHILDREN

Is there a/an ...?

  Y a-t-il ...?   ee a·teel ...

I need ...

  J'ai besoin de ...   zhay ber·zwun der ...

Do you mind if I breastfeed here?

  Je peux allaiter mon   zher per a·lay·tay mon

  bébé ici?   bay·bay ee·see

Are children allowed?

  Les enfants sont permis?   lay zon·fon son pair·mee

a baby change room	*un endroit pour changer le bébé*	un on·drwa poor shon·zhay ler bay·bay
a car baby seat	*un siège-enfant*	un syezh·on·fon
a child-minding service	*une garderie*	ewn gar·dree
a children's menu	*un menu pour enfant*	un mer·new poor on·fon
disposable nappies/diapers	*couches-culottes*	koosh·kew·lot
an (English-speaking) babysitter	*une babysitter (qui parle anglais)*	ewn ba·bee·see·ter (kee parl ong·glay)
formula	*lait maternisé*	lay ma·ter·nee·zay
a highchair	*une chaise haute*	ewn shayz ot
a potty	*un pot de bébé*	un po der bay·bay
a pusher/stroller	*une poussette*	ewn poo·set

Also available from Lonely Planet:
French Phrasebook

GLOSSARY

Word gender is indicated as (m) masculine or (f) feminine; (pl) indicates plural.

abbaye (f) – abbey

AOC – Appellation d'Origine Contrôlée; wines and olive oils that have met stringent government regulations governing where, how and under what conditions the grapes or olives are grown and the wines and olive oils are fermented and bottled

arrondissement (m) – one of several districts into which large cities, such as Marseille, are split

atelier (m) – artisan's workshop

auberge (f) – inn

autoroute (f) – motorway or highway

baie (f) – bay

bastide (f) – country house

billetterie (f) – ticket office or counter

borie (f) – primitive beehive-shaped dwelling, built from dry limestone around 3500 BC

boulangerie (f) – bread shop or bakery

calanque (f) – rocky inlet

carnet (m) – a book of five or 10 bus, tram or metro tickets sold at a reduced rate

cave (f) – wine or cheese cellar

centre (de) hospitalier (m) – hospital

chambre d'hôte (f) – B&B accommodation, usually in a private home

charcuterie (f) – pork butcher's shop and delicatessen; also cold meat

château (m) – castle or stately home

chèvre (m) – goat; also goat's-milk cheese

col (m) – mountain pass

conseil général (m) – general council

corniche (f) – coastal or cliff road

corrida (f) – bullfight

cour (f) – courtyard

course Camarguaise (f) – Camargue-style bullfight

dégustation (f) – the fine art of tasting wine, cheese, olive oil or seafood

département (m) – administrative area (department)

DFCI – Défense de la Forêt Contre l'Incendie; fire road (public access forbidden)

digue (f) – dike
domaine (m) – a wine-producing estate

église (f) – church
épicerie (f) – grocery shop
étang (m) – lagoon, pond or lake

faïence (f) – earthenware
féria (f) – bullfighting festival
ferme auberge (f) – family-run inn attached to a farm or château; farmhouse restaurant
fête (f) – party or festival
formule (f) – fixed main course plus starter or dessert
fromagerie (f) – cheese shop

galets (m) – large smooth stones covering Châteauneuf du Pape vineyards
gardian (m) – Camargue horseman
gare (f) – train station
gare maritime (m) – ferry terminal
gare routière (m) – bus station
garrigue (f) – ground cover of aromatic scrub; see also *maquis*
gitan (m) – Roma, gypsy
golfe (m) – gulf
grotte (f) – cave

halles (f pl) – covered market; central food market
hôtel de ville (m) – town hall
hôtel particulier (m) – private mansion

jardin (botanique) (m) – (botanic) garden

mairie (f) – town hall
manade (f) – bull farm
maquis (m) – aromatic Provençal scrub; name given to the French Resistance movement; see also *garrigue*
marché (m) – market
mas (m) – Provençal farmhouse

menu (m) – meal at a fixed price with two or more courses
mistral (m) – incessant north wind
monastère (m) – monastery
Monégasque – native of Monaco
moulin à huile (m) – oil mill
musée (m) – museum

navette (f) – shuttle bus, train or boat

office du tourisme, office de tourisme (m) – tourist office (run by a unit of local government)
ONF – Office National des Forêts; National Forests Office

parc national (m) – national park
parc naturel régional (m) – regional nature park
pétanque (f) – a Provençal game, similar to lawn bowls
pic (m) – mountain peak
place (f) – square
plage (f) – beach
plan (m) – city map
plat du jour (m) – dish of the day
pont (m) – bridge
porte (f) – gate or door; old-town entrance
préfecture (f) – main town of a *département*
presqu'île (f) – peninsula
prieuré (m) – priory

quai (m) – quay or railway platform
quartier (m) – quarter or district

rade (f) – gulf or harbour
région (m) – administrative region
rond-point (m) – roundabout

salin (m) – salt marsh
santon (m) – traditional Provençal figurine
savon (f) – soap

savonnerie (f) – soap factory
sentier (m) – trail, footpath
sentier littoral (m) – coastal path
SNCF – Société Nationale des Chemins de Fer Français; state-owned railway company
SNCM – Société Nationale Maritime Corse-Méditerranée; state-owned ferry company linking Corsica and mainland France
stade (m) – stadium

tabac (m) – tobacconist (also sells newspapers, bus tickets etc)
taureau (m) – bull
TGV – Train à Grande Vitesse; high-speed train
théâtre antique (m) – Roman theatre

vendange (f) – grape harvest
vieille ville (f) – old town
vieux port (m) – old port
vigneron (m) – winegrower
VTT (m) – *vélo tout terrain;* mountain bike

BEHIND THE SCENES

THIS BOOK

This is the 6th edition of *Provence & the Côte d'Azur*. Nicola Williams and Catherine Le Nevez wrote the previous edition. This guidebook was commissioned in Lonely Planet's London office, and produced by the following:

Commissioning Editors Paula Hardy, Caroline Sieg

Coordinating Editor Laura Crawford

Coordinating Cartographer Anita Banh

Coordinating Layout Designer Jim Hsu

Managing Editor Annelies Mertens

Managing Cartographer Herman So

Managing Layout Designer Sally Darmody

Assisting Editors Daniel Corbett, Paul Harding, Victoria Harrison, Martine Power, Helen Yeates

Assisting Cartographers Ross Butler, Damien Demaj, Xavier Di Toro, Alex Leung, Ross Macaw

Cover Research Marika Mercer, lonelyplanetimages.com

Internal Image Research Aude Vauconsant, lonelyplanetimages.com

Language Content Robyn Loughnane

Project Managers Rachel Imeson, Glenn van der Knijff

Thanks to Mark Adams, Imogen Bannister, Lucy Birchley, Yvonne Bischofberger, Jessica Boland, Piotr Czajkowski, Melanie Dankel,

THE LONELY PLANET STORY

Fresh from an epic journey across Europe, Asia and Australia in 1972, Tony and Maureen Wheeler sat at their kitchen table stapling together notes. The first Lonely Planet guidebook, *Across Asia on the Cheap,* was born.

Travellers snapped up the guides. Inspired by their success, the Wheelers began publishing books to Southeast Asia, India and beyond. Demand was prodigious, and the Wheelers expanded the business rapidly to keep up. Over the years, Lonely Planet extended its coverage to every country and into the virtual world via lonelyplanet.com and the Thorn Tree message board.

As Lonely Planet became a globally loved brand, Tony and Maureen received several offers for the company. But it wasn't until 2007 that they found a partner whom they trusted to remain true to the company's principles of travelling widely, treading lightly and giving sustainably. In October of that year, BBC Worldwide acquired a 75% share in the company, pledging to uphold Lonely Planet's commitment to independent travel, trustworthy advice and editorial independence.

Today, Lonely Planet has offices in Melbourne, London and Oakland, with over 500 staff members and 300 authors. Tony and Maureen are still actively involved with Lonely Planet. They're travelling more often than ever, and they're devoting their spare time to charitable projects. And the company is still driven by the philosophy of *Across Asia on the Cheap*: 'All you've got to do is decide to go and the hardest part is over. So go!'

Janine Eberle, Owen Eszeki, Joshua Geoghegan, Mark Germanchis, Michelle Glynn, Imogen Hall, Aomi Hongo, Lauren Hunt, Laura Jane, Nic Lehman, John Mazzocchi, Lucy Monie, Wayne Murphy, Darren O'Connell, Trent Paton, Malisa Plesa, Julie Sheridan, Lyahna Spencer, John Taufa

THANKS

NICOLA WILLIAMS

As ever a flurry of enthusiasts eased my travels, not least Pascal Périer at the Maison des Vins du Bandol; Delphine Moreau from the Conseil Interprofessionnel des Vins de Provence, at the Maison des Vins Côtes de Provence in Les Arcs-sur-Argens; Caroline and Jean-Pierre at paradise *maison d'hôte* Les 3 Îles, near Plage de Gigaro; gardener Yves, who was sweet enough to hump my Twingo out a ditch; Provence garden-guru Louisa Jones; and Ciara Browne, who shared insider Stes-Marie de la Mer addresses. *Merci bien* to interviewees Christian Etienne (chef, Avignon), Bernard Meyssard (Meyssard melons, Cheval Blanc), Nicole Bérenguier (Moulin de Callas, Callas), Fabien Tamboloni (forest technician, La Garde Freinet), Michel Vivet (Domaine Valette, Les Arcs) and Jacques Maurel (Galimard, Grasse). On Twitter @Tripalong says *merci beaucoup* to @benjilanyado, @Frenchlandscapes, @FrenchBloggery, @TooMuchPastis, @TravelTweet and @WineTravel. Finally, salutations of respect to ace girl-team Alexis, Fran, Emilie, Caroline and Paula for sheer hard work, skill and dedication; and to Matthias, Niko, Mischa and Christa for tolerating the extreme hours with such grace.

ALEXIS AVERBUCK

Many thanks, as always, to Alexandra Stamopoulou for her invaluable tips, and to Véronique Powell and Alain Bloch for their insight into the Luberon. Thanks also to Alexandra Miliotis and to Sven Satzky in Cavaillon, Martine Di Cicco in Apt and Audric Jaubert in Moustiers Ste-Marie (who went beyond the call of duty to help me repair a broken car window). Special thanks are also due to Caroline Sieg for her leadership and editorial acumen and to Nicola Williams for pulling the book together with cool aplomb.

SEND US YOUR FEEDBACK

We love to hear from travellers – your comments keep us on our toes and help make our books better. Our well-travelled team reads every word on what you loved or loathed about this book. Although we cannot reply individually to postal submissions, we always guarantee that your feedback goes straight to the appropriate authors, in time for the next edition. Each person who sends us information is thanked in the next edition – and the most useful submissions are rewarded with a free book.

To send us your updates – and find out about Lonely Planet events, newsletters and travel news – visit our award-winning website: **lonelyplanet.com/contact**.

Note: We may edit, reproduce and incorporate your comments in Lonely Planet products such as guidebooks, websites and digital products, so let us know if you don't want your comments reproduced or your name acknowledged. For a copy of our privacy policy visit lonelyplanet.com/privacy.

EMILIE FILOU

I'd like to thank all the friends and family who came along during my research trip (Mum and Patrick in Cannes; Dad and Laurence in Nice and the Corniches; Cynthia in Nice) and accommodated the hectic schedule and vagaries of the weather with such good grace. Thanks also to André, Marie-Jo and Raph Cornet for the fun dinners and great company in Opio and Monaco, and to Jean-Marie, Laurent and Mélanie at Hôtel Wilson in Nice for making me feel at home. Finally thanks to Adolfo back home for putting up so stoically with the long absences.

FRAN PARNELL

Immense thanks to tourist office staff across the region, especially in Avignon and St-Rémy; Marielle, yet again (!); the angels at Hôtel Malaga and Carrosserie Apothéloz, Carpentras; Nicola Williams for composure, practical help and encouragement after the computer meltdown; Caroline Sieg for all her organisation and hard work; Glenn van der Knijff's deadline juggling; Flanny for absolutely invaluable technical assistance (plus the Losource deskspace); and Mum and Dad for a knockout time in Avignon/Villeneuve – xx.

OUR READERS

Many thanks to the travellers who used the last edition and wrote to us with helpful hints, useful advice and interesting anecdotes:
Philip Atkins, Scott Bartsch, Susan Bonas, Jack Bullard, Andrea Buso, Roberta Carlini, Nick Dillen, Tim Fowkes, Jennifer Gráf, John Henderson, Calvin Hilton, Ray Holton, Alain Horowitz, Susan Howe, Iain Mcintyre, Samantha Osborn, Bob Parsons, Andrea Potzler, Michael Rodin, Elin Sætersdal, Katie Shallow, Niels J Skjødt, Adrienne Smith, Peter Swedberg, Donald Thomson, Philip Thonemann, Maude Vanhaelen, Nuno Verdasca, Pieremilio Vizzini, Vic Walmsley, Malcolm Watson

ACKNOWLEDGMENTS

INDEX

INDEX

INDEX

INDEX

INDEX

MAP LEGEND

Note Not all symbols displayed below appear in this guide.

ROUTES

Tollway	Tunnel
Freeway	Pedestrian Mall
Primary Road	Steps
Secondary Road	Walking Track
Tertiary Road	Walking Path
Lane	Walking Tour
Unsealed Road	Walking Tour Detour
Under Construction	Pedestrian Overpass

TRANSPORT

Ferry Route & Terminal	Train Line & Station
Metro Line & Station	Underground Rail Line
Monorail & Stop	Tram Line & Stop
Bus Route & Stop	Cable Car, Funicular

AREA FEATURES

Airport	Land
Beach	Mall, Plaza
Building	Market
Campus	Park
Cemetery, Christian	Sportsground
Cemetery, Other	Urban

HYDROGRAPHY

River, Creek	
Canal	
Water	
Swamp	
Lake (Dry)	

BOUNDARIES

International	
State, Provincial	
Suburb	
City Wall	
Cliff	

SYMBOLS IN THE KEY

Essential Information
- Tourist Office
- Police Station

Exploring
- Beach
- Buddhist
- Castle, Fort
- Christian
- Diving, Snorkelling
- Garden
- Hindu
- Islamic
- Jewish
- Monument
- Museum, Gallery
- Place of Interest
- Snow Skiing
- Swimming Pool
- Ruin
- Tomb
- Winery, Vineyard
- Zoo, Bird Sanctuary

Gastronomic Highlights
- Eating
- Cafe

Nightlife
- Drinking
- Entertainment

Recommended Shops
- Shopping

Accommodation
- Sleeping
- Camping

Transport
- Airport, Airfield
- Cycling, Bicycle Path
- Border Crossing
- Bus Station
- Ferry
- General Transport
- Train Station
- Taxi Rank

Parking
- Parking

OTHER MAP SYMBOLS

Information
- Bank, ATM
- Embassy, Consulate
- Hospital, Medical
- Internet Facilities
- Post Office
- Telephone

Geographic
- Cave
- Lighthouse
- Lookout
- Mountain, Volcano
- National Park
- Picnic Area

LONELY PLANET OFFICES

AUSTRALIA
Head Office
Locked Bag 1, Footscray, Victoria 3011
☎ 03 8379 8000, fax 03 8379 8111
talk2us@lonelyplanet.com.au

USA
150 Linden St, Oakland, CA 94607
☎ 510 250 6400, toll free 800 275 8555
fax 510 893 8572
info@lonelyplanet.com

UK
2nd fl, 186 City Road, London EC1V 2NT
☎ 020 7106 2100, fax 020 7106 2101
go@lonelyplanet.co.uk

Published by Lonely Planet Publications Pty Ltd
ABN 36 005 607 983
© Lonely Planet 2010
© photographers as indicated 2010
Cover photograph Lavender landscape near Apt, Pierre Jacques/Getty Images. **Internal title-page photograph** Lavender rows on the Plateau de Valensole, Jean-Bernard Carillet/Lonely Planet Images. Many of the images in this guide are available for licensing from Lonely Planet Images: lonelyplanetimages.com.

Mixed Sources
Product group from well-managed forests and other controlled sources
www.fsc.org Cert no. SGS-COC-005002
© 1996 Forest Stewardship Council
FSC